FOUR CENTURIES OF SHAKESPEARIAN CRITICISM

Edited, with an Introduction, by
J. Frank Kermode

 DISCUS BOOKS/PUBLISHED BY AVON

Acknowledgments

The Editor has made every effort to trace the ownership of all copyrighted material. In the event of any question arising as to the use of any selection, the Editor, while expressing regret for any error he may have made, will be pleased to make the necessary corrections in future editions of this book. Thanks are due to the following authors, copyright holders, publishers, representatives, and publications for permission to use the selections noted below.

George Allen & Unwin Ltd. for "Ideal Development and Chronological Series" from *Ariosto, Shakespeare and Corneille* by Benedetto Croce; and for "Hamlet" from *Fifty Poems* by Boris Pasternak, translated by Mrs. Lydia Slater.

Edward Arnold (Publishers) Ltd. for a selection from *The Cease of Majesty* (1961) by M. M. Reese.

Barnes & Noble, Inc. for a selection from *Form and Meaning in Drama* by H. D. E. Kitto, and for "Hamlet" from *Fifty Poems* by Boris Pasternak, translated by Mrs. Lydia Slater.

The Bodley Head Ltd. for an extract from *Ulysses* by James Joyce.

Cambridge University Press for "History and Histrionics in *Cymbeline*" by J. P. Brockbank, from *Shakespeare Survey XI* (1958); for "Shakespeare and the Elizabethan Romans" by T. J. B. Spencer, from *Shakespeare Survey X* (1957); and "Shakespeare's Reading" by F. P. Wilson from *Shakespeare Survey III* (1950).

Chatto & Windus Ltd. for an extract from *The Structure of Complex Words* (1951) by William Empson; and for an extract from *Explorations* (1947) by L. C. Knights.

Columbia University Press for an extract from *Shakespeare's Audience* by Alfred Harbage, Columbia University Press, 1941.

Constable & Company Ltd. for "The Absense of Religion in Shakespeare" from *Interpretations of Poetry and Religion* by George Santayana.

Faber & Faber Ltd. for an extract from "Brothers and Others" from *The Dyer's Hand* by W. H. Auden.

Victor Gollancz, Ltd. for an extract from *Hamlet and Oedipus* by Ernest Jones.

Harcourt, Brace & World, Inc. for "Lear, Tolstoy and the Fool" from *Shooting an Elephant and Other Essays* by George Orwell, copyright, 1945, 1946, 1950, by Sonia Brownell Orwell. Reprinted by permission of Harcourt, Brace & World, Inc.

AVON BOOKS

A division of
The Hearst Corporation
959 Eighth Avenue
New York, New York 10019

Copyright © 1965 by Avon Book Division,
The Hearst Corporation.
ISBN: 0-380-00058-X

First Avon Printing, September, 1965.
Third Printing. (Discus Edition)

DISCUS TRADEMARK REG. U.S. PAT. OFF. AND
FOREIGN COUNTRIES, REGISTERED TRADEMARK—
MARCA REGISTRADA, HECHO EN CHICAGO, U.S.A.

Printed in the U.S.A.

Holt, Rinehart and Winston, Inc. for "Ideal Development and Chronological Series" from *Ariosto, Shakespeare and Corneille* by Benedetto Croce. Translated by Douglas Ainslie. Copyright 1920 by Holt, Rinehart and Winston, Inc. Copyright 1948 by Douglas Ainslie. Reprinted by permission of Holt, Rinehart and Winston, Inc.

Longmans, Green & Co. Limited for an extract from *Character and Motive in Shakespeare* (1949) by J. I. M. Stewart.

Macmillan & Co. Ltd., St. Martin's Press, Inc., The Macmillan Company of Canada, Ltd. for an extract from *Shakespearean Tragedy* (1905) by A. C. Bradley.

Methuen & Co. Ltd. for an extract from *Form and Meaning in Drama* (1959) by H. D. F. Kitto; and for extracts from *The Wheel of Fire* (1930) by G. Wilson Knight.

New Directions for an extract from *The Structure of Complex Words* by William Empson. All rights reserved. Reprinted by permission of the publishers, New Directions.

New Statesman for "Olivier's Moor" by Ronald Bryden (May 1, 1964).

New York University Press for an excerpt from *Explorations* by L. C. Knights. Copyright 1947 by George W. Stewart, Publishers, Inc. Reprinted by permission of New York University Press.

W. W. Norton & Company, Inc. for an extract from "The Psycho-Analytic Solution." Reprinted from *Hamlet and Oedipus* by Ernest Jones. By permission of W. W. Norton & Company, Inc. Copyright 1949 by Ernest Jones.

Princeton University Press for excerpts reprinted from *Shakespeare's Festive Comedies* by C. L. Barber, Copyright 1959 by Princeton University Press; reprinted by permission of Princeton University Press; and for excerpts reprinted from *The King's Two Bodies* by Ernest H. Kantorowicz, Copyright 1957 by Princeton University Press; London: Oxford University Press; reprinted by permission of Princeton University Press.

Random House, Inc. for an excerpt from *Ulysses*, by James Joyce. Copyright 1914, 1918 and renewed 1942, 1946 by Nora Joseph Joyce. Reprinted by permission of Random House, Inc.; and for an excerpt from "Brothers and Others" © Copyright 1962 by W. H. Auden. Reprinted from *The Dyer's Hand*, by W. H. Auden, by permission of Random House, Inc.

Routledge & Kegan Paul Ltd. for an extract from *The Story of the Night* (1962) by John Holloway.

Charles Scribner's Sons for "The Absence of Religion in Shakespeare." Reprinted with the permission of Charles Scribner's Sons from *Interpretations of Poetry and Religion* by George Santayana.

Martin Secker & Warburg Limited for "Lear, Tolstoy and the Fool" from *Collected Essays* by George Orwell.

The Shakespeare Association of America, Inc. for an extract from "Form and Formality in *Romeo and Juliet*" by Harry Levin, *Shakespeare Quarterly XI*, 1960.

Staples Press for an extract from *Shakespeare and the Popular Dramatic Tradition* (1944) by S. L. Bethell.

Alan Swallow Publisher for an extract reprinted from *Tradition and Poetic Structure* by J. V. Cunningham, by permission of the publisher, Alan Swallow. Copyright 1960 by J. V. Cunningham.

Frederick Ungar Publishing Co., Inc. for an extract from *Shakespeare Studies* by E. E. Stoll.

Peter Ure, The British Council and Longmans, Green & Co. Ltd. for "Troilus and Cressida" from Shakespeare's Problem Plays, 1961, 1964.

Curtis Brown Ltd. for an extract from *The Fool* by Enid Welsford (Faber & Faber, 1932).

Mrs. J. M. Wilson for "Shakespeare's Reading" by F. P. Wilson from *Shakespeare Survey III*.

CONTENTS

FOUR
CENTURIES OF
SHAKESPEARIAN
CRITICISM

INTRODUCTION

i

The bulk of Shakespearian commentary is notorious and yet, when one surveys it, a perpetually fresh astonishment. Only the Bible has attracted a greater quantity and diversity of explanation and criticism, or licensed so many curious fancies; and one of the first things to understand about Shakespeare's role in the intellectual life of the past two centuries is that his works did in fact become a kind of secular bible, requiring, like all holy books as they grow older, a constant effort of re-interpretation in respect of the text, the historical conditions under which they were produced, and their peculiar relevance to the age of the interpreter.

This book is largely concerned with the third of these aspects. Even after this reduction the available material is vast. Shakespeare's contemporaries were not much given to publishing their views on authors, especially dramatists; but a few scattered remarks survive, the earliest from the fifteen-nineties; so there is a continuous critical tradition which is already almost four hundred years old. And although there is naturally more criticism in English than in other languages, much has also been written—some of it very important—in German, French, Russian, Italian.

To choose from this vast library examples which fairly represent its scope, and can please the general reader who could not hope to range over the whole of it, is an undertaking that presents special problems. Should the editor try to represent as many varieties as possible, from sane to crazy, from Francis Meres to Jan Kott, from the grand generalisation to the minute scholarly perception? If he decides to represent 'mainstream' criticism, should he, in his own time, when the current has not set, try to pick the eccentric eddy which may produce the mainstream of the

13

future? Should he divide his space mathematically between past and present, giving the twentieth century its due sixth of the space? It might be judicious to do so; nothing is more certain than that even good criticism dies. It goes out of date, or perishes from neglect, being lost in the crowd (and the crowd is now so great that one might say of Shakespeare critics what is said of scientists, that 90 per cent of all who ever lived are now alive). It is lost simply by the action of time, or because it is not well enough written. Or it survives, either by some accident of history, or because authority endorses its insights, or because the critic himself seems interesting in himself. On the whole it dies, or survives, for reasons not very interesting to us. Yet in the nature of the case the work of our contemporaries speaks more directly to our needs and preoccupations than any other criticism; a minor twentieth-century writer can interest us more than a very good critic of a century back. And that is why the present collection includes an unfair proportion of modern work.

A word now about the other principles followed in this book. It is divided into four sections. In the first ('General Criticism') I have tried to represent the central (largely encomiastic) critical tradition, to give the texts which are famous on their own account or because they represent the view of a particular period. This is the 'mainstream'. It would be unthinkable on any account to leave out Ben Jonson or Dr. Johnson or Coleridge. There is, naturally, still a need to choose. Some major nineteenth-century figures I have left out because I could not persuade myself that their historical interest was sufficient to outweigh their extraordinary remoteness from our taste; Dowden is an example, though his book satisfied a generation, and happens to be the first book on Shakespeare I ever read. Continental criticism is another problem. Obviously the great European critics must be represented. One could not leave out Voltaire, who was the man for Shakespearian idolaters to beat in the eighteenth century. It was to A. W. Schlegel that Coleridge, founder of modern Shakespeare criticism, owed some of his basic philosophico-critical ideas, and even some of his Shakespearian insights. Taine, for good or ill, profoundly influenced the English and American methods of literary history. They must be in. But what of all the others

—Victor Hugo's enormous, rhapsodic book, Alfred de Vigny, Stendhal, the great tribe of German nineteenth-century commentators, Brandes? I have left them out. The French almost always saw Shakespeare in terms of a domestic quarrel; it is a vital episode in French literary history, but not in the criticism of Shakespeare. The Germans share with their English contemporaries a tendency to live under the shadow of later criticism which grew in part from a reaction against them.

So much for omissions from the first part. What is included should give a careful reader a just impression of the history and topics of Shakespeare criticism from the fifteen-nineties to the nineteen-fifties. I have accordingly, in this part, arranged the material chronologically. Certain topics —discussed later in this Introduction—recur frequently, but the tone and the method of admiration vary; Shakespeare is not at all times valued for the same reasons. The chronological arrangement offers a large view of both repetitions and novelties.

In the remaining three sections (on the Comedies, Histories and Tragedies) I have gone about it otherwise. Each section opens with an introduction to the group of plays concerned, but the order, though still chronological, is that of the plays, not of the critics. There was nothing to be gained, and much to be lost, from the alternative arrangement. The poems I have reluctantly left out, except for an extract from an essay by J. V. Cunningham, which may well stand for the best that has been accomplished in their interpretation. This omission gave me more space to deploy critical opinion of the dramatic works, which are after all the basis of Shakespeare's power and reputation.

ii

Shakespeare's contemporaries did not practise dramatic criticism in the modern sense, nor did they have the habit of recording their literary opinions. The first certain allusion to Shakespeare, in Greene's *Groatsworth of Wit* (1592), was hostile; on his deathbed the older man showed resentment at the intrusion of Shakespeare into the play-writing world. But Chettle, his friend, at once undid the harm; and despite a few genial sneers from Jonson, contemporary allusion is remarkably favorable. Francis Meres in 1598, rather tiresomely ranging the English against the Greek, Latin and Italian poets, made Shakespeare our Ovid in poetry and, in drama, our Plautus and our Seneca combined. His remarks have been most valued for the evidence they give of the existence of certain plays and sonnets in 1598 (and for the interesting puzzle as to the identity of *Love's Labour's Won*); but it remains true that five years after the establishment of the Lord Chamberlain's Men (later the King's Men)—the company in which Shakespeare was a 'sharer' and principal dramatist—his was the name first to hand in such a comparison. Harvey's jotting tells us that Shakespeare's public included the young and also the wise; and about the same time Weever was admiring both the poems and the early plays, including *Romeo and Juliet, Richard III* and *Julius Caesar*. And he was admired; we cannot be sure that Jonson had him in mind when he wrote the character of Virgil in *Poetaster* (1601) but the evidence of his obituary tributes suggests that he might not have opposed its application to Shakespeare.

> His learning labours not the schoole-like glosse,
> That most consists in *ecchoing* wordes, and termes,
> And soonest wins a man an empty name:
> Nor any long, or far-fetcht circumstance,
> Wrapt in the curious generalties of artes.
> But a direct, and *analyticke* summe
> Of all the worth and first effects of artes.
> And for his *poesie*, 'tis so ramm'd with life,
> That it shall gather strength of life, with being,
> And live hereafter, more admir'd, then now.

It is in Jonson and in Francis Beaumont that we find the origins of two related topics which were to dominate the criticism of Shakespeare for several generations after his death. Beaumont, writing before that event, admires Shakespeare for his lack of learning, and for his *natural* power (he works not by art, but 'by the dimme light of Nature'— the figure derives from theology, where the light of Nature is contrasted with that of Grace). Jonson, in his famous encomium, professed to prefer Shakespeare's Nature to the Art of the ancients, though he knew too much about the efforts required of a great writer to exclude 'Art' altogether from the process. The remark of Heminges and Condell—that there was 'scarce . . . a blot in his papers', must have reinforced the opinion that Shakespeare was a 'natural', rather than an 'artist', and Leonard Digges, who probably knew Shakespeare well, and provides valuable testimony to the popularity of certain plays, carried this view to the point of caricature by arguing that Shakespeare's 'Works' were not really Works at all, they came so easily; and by the demonstrably false claim that Shakespeare had no contact with literature in any other language than English. The young Milton also invoked the comparison between Nature and Art; and we may see in the preface written by the publisher Benson to the 1640 edition of the Sonnets a palpable blurb which, in falsely declaring that these were plain and perspicuous poems, seems to allude to what was already an established view of Shakespeare's simplicity.

We may well ask how such an opinion came to attach itself to the author of the late verse, and of *The Phoenix and the Turtle*. Nevertheless, it had great vitality and is still a live issue, as the extracts from Dryden and the eighteenth-century critics, and from Maginn in the nineteenth and F. P. Wilson in the twentieth centuries will show; even the enormous labours of T. W. Baldwin, notably in his *Shakespeare's Small Latine and Lesse Greeke* (1944, University of Illinois Press, 2 vols.), have not entirely laid it to rest. And just as the post-Restoration period felt free to patronise and in adaptations to 'improve' Shakespeare, so modern producers pervert him, especially in the comedies, to supply point and sense they presumably feel to be lacking in his text.

The argument for 'nature' could, of course, be used against Shakespeare. In due course he encountered a critic of legalistic and pedantic mind, a critic obsessed by the 'rules' of neo-classic drama as practised in France. Rymer's remarkable study of *Othello*—a violent and somewhat perverse attack—prompted him to what is probably the closest critical analysis of the language and action of a play in the whole period between Shakespeare's own day and the twentieth century. For the encomiasts were, for the most part, content with the encomium. Their methods are well represented by Dryden, who has been called 'the father of Shakespeare criticism'. Writing at a time when Shakespeare's reputation was still determined by comparisons with Jonson and Beaumont and Fletcher, he established a vocabulary of praise; but when he wanted to write a full analysis of a play of the period chose Jonson's *Epicoene* and not a work of Shakespeare. As to the question of Shakespeare's learning, so closely related to that of his 'art', Dryden argued that 'those who accuse him to have wanted learning give him the better commendation'.

It became partly a question of how to praise Shakespeare best: by granting him scholarship (which would make him in part derivative) or by crediting him with a semidivine ignorance. Upon one's answer to this problem depended one's attitude to what Nichol Smith, a great authority on eighteenth-century Shakespeare criticism, laid down as its four main topics: Shakespeare's neglect of the rules, the extent of his learning, the condition of his text, and his treatment of character. Of these the third does not concern us. The first two, as we have seen, are an invitation to discuss Shakespeare's 'art', if any; the third brought up questions of his carelessness, the rudeness of his age and the ignorance of his printers; the fourth touched off encomia of his 'nature', or, among the increasingly rare dissentients, complaints as to his literary decorum (as when Shaftesbury ridiculed Desdemona, or Dr. Johnson complained of Bertram's being 'dismissed to happiness' in *All's Well that Ends Well*).

The argument about Shakespeare's learning is a recurrent topic in the following pages. It was partly in response to a fashion, set by Upton and Zachary Gray, for representing Shakespeare as learned, that Farmer wrote his classic essay, which earned from Johnson high, though as it happens inaccurate, praise: 'Dr. Farmer, you have done that which was never done before; that is, you have completely finished a controversy beyond all further doubt.' Farmer, rephrasing a theme of Dryden's already taken up by Dennis, expressed amazement that 'any *real* friends of our immortal POET should be still willing to force him into a situation which is not tenable: treat him as a learned man'. And he justly claims to have 'removed a deal of *learned Rubbish*' from Shakespearian commentary; he was able, for instance, to show that Shakespeare read Plutarch not in Greek but in the Elizabethan translation which North had made from

Amyot's French translation, itself derived from a Latin version of the Greek.

On the matter of the rules, Voltaire was through a large proportion of the century Shakespeare's main detractor; he is here represented by a very small specimen of his Shakespearian criticism, just as the spirited defense of Mrs. Montagu here stands for the many replies to him. Voltaire's role became that of *advocatus diaboli,* and was certainly in part instrumental in the secular canonisation of Shakespeare; for the period of his activity coincided with that in which Shakespearian 'idolatry' most rapidly developed. Pope in 1725 had argued that 'To judge therefore of Shakespeare by Aristotle's rules, is like trying a man by the Laws of one Country, who acted under those of another.' But the authoritative English answer to the 'rules' criticism was given by Johnson in the fine passage which empirically examines Shakespeare's 'irregularity' in this respect (p. 77). Whether the product of 'design', or merely of 'happy accident', Johnson concludes, 'such violations of rules merely positive become the comprehensive genius of Shakespeare, and such censures are suitable to the minute and slender criticism of Voltaire.' This did not entirely end the argument; but it combined with an increasing scepticism about the origin of the Unities in Aristotle (who indeed can be said only to support the unity of action, the one Johnson allowed) and with the development of a notion very important for the Romantic movement: Nature transcended the rules anyway, and Shakespeare, now firmly established as the poet of Nature, had no business with them. 'There is always', as Johnson had said, 'an appeal open from criticism to nature.' This was the best answer also to charges that Shakespeare indiscriminately mingled comedy and tragedy, and failed to give characters their proper social insignia; thus to the criticism of Francis Gentleman, that Cassio should not have got drunk, and that Bianca was a 'despicable non-essential', Maurice Morgann replied that 'Indecorums respect the propriety of exhibiting certain actions; not their truth or falsehood when *exhibited*. Shakespeare stands to us in the place of *truth* and *nature*.'

The name of Maurice Morgann stands high on the list of those who created the custom of extolling Shakespeare's truth to nature in the representation of human character.

It had been a theme of earlier criticism, and was nobly sounded by Johnson in the greatest of all general essays on Shakespeare: see the passage on p. 78, beginning 'Characters thus ample and general . . .' This, it is true, is part of Johnson's praise of Shakespeare's 'adherence to general nature', his admiration for the poet's power to make men act and speak with probability. Upon this power depends Shakespeare's ability to satisfy Johnson's requirement that he instruct by pleasing; Johnson censures him for being readier to please than to instruct, but commends his fidelity to human nature as in a high degree useful and edifying. Morgann, on the other hand, has no reservations: 'Shakespeare is, in truth, an author whose mimic creation agrees in general so perfectly with that of nature, that it is not only wonderful in the great, but opens another scene of amazement to the discoveries of the microscope.' Accordingly, he thought no examination of the minutiæ, the truly distinguishing features of a Falstaff, could be excessive; and in his essay (certainly the most minute examination of a Shakespeare play since Rymer took *Othello* to pieces) he set new and extravagant standards for the analysis of character in all its integrity and individuality. Morgann's essay he himself called 'a novelty'; there had been studies devoted to character before, such as William Richardson's *Philosophical Analyses and Illustration of some of Shakespeare's remarkable Characters* (1774 and 1789); and Thomas Whately's *Remarks on Some of the Characters of Shakespeare* (pub. 1785). But Morgann was a man of very powerful *mind*, and this always tells in criticism. Dr. Johnson genially derided him: 'Why Sir, we shall have the man come forth again; and as he has proved Falstaff to be no coward, he may prove Iago to be a very good character.' He was for a time neglected. But after Morgann it was easier to treat Shakespeare's art, in the rendering of character, as equal to his natural abilities. The time was at hand when one could speak of a great poet as 'a power like one of nature's', and alter the whole relation of nature to art.

But although the eighteenth-century critics seem to us limited by the preoccupations of their period, it seems clear that their arguments about nature, the rules and Shakespeare's learning enabled them to found methods and traditions which, with altered emphasis, would persist in use beyond their period. Indeed, Mr. R. W. Babcock, in his authoritative book, *The Genesis of Shakespeare Idolatry* (1931), has a coda to illustrate the fact that the great critics of the next age—Coleridge, Lamb, Hazlitt—overstated the newness of the new nineteenth-century criticism, and in very many respects accurately reflected preoccupations already evident in their predecessors.

iii

Coleridge, who has long and very properly been regarded as the chief source of modern Shakespeare criticism, somewhat ungratefully rejected his eighteenth-century predecessors. 'His critics, among us, during the whole of the last century, have neither understood nor appreciated him.' Yet whether speaking of Shakespeare as the 'Poet of Nature', or arguing that his judgment was equal or superior to his genius, or rejecting the Porter scene in *Macbeth* as an indecorous interpolation, he is developing eighteenth-century ideas; and when he speaks of the characters as '*genera* intensely individualized', or denies the premises of neo-classical criticism, he is echoing Dr. Johnson, though he often opposed and belittled him.

Nevertheless, there can be no doubt that Coleridge brought to Shakespeare criticism a critical talent of extraordinary distinction and a new and vital body of thought. His study of German transcendentalist philosophy on his return from Germany at the turn of the century equipped him with, or perhaps confirmed him in, the philosophical concepts and vocabulary which he adapted to criticism, by a process unsatisfactorily described in the *Biographia Literaria*. He could accordingly bring to the study of 'myriad-minded Shakespeare' a doctrine of the creative imagination, and a theory of organic form, from which a new, adventurous and creative criticism might develop. He also studied, and probably over-rated, the German Shakespeare criticism of the preceding half-century. Lessing had used Voltaire as a whipping-boy, and proclaimed the superiority of Shakespeare to all neo-classic imitators of the ancients; explaining that the unities of time and place were tied to the ancient chorus. This was hardly new, though his proclamation of a special German quality in Shakespeare was. This became the constant claim of German critics (*unser Shakespeare*) and Coleridge evidently accepted it. Though he may have learnt something from *Wilhelm Meister* and from Herder, A. W. Schlegel was his chief creditor.

The relations between Schlegel and Coleridge are still matters of scholarly dispute. The difficulty, as elsewhere in Coleridge, is to distinguish between those places in which Coleridge, finding expressions appropriate to his own developing thought, hastily employed them, and those where he is directly indebted to Schlegel, as in the Ninth Lecture of his series of 1811-12, when he had admittedly just been reading Schlegel's lectures, published in 1808 and 1811. After this, his borrowings were very frequent, as we see in Raysor's edition of Coleridge's *Shakespearean Criticism*, 2 vols., (1930). These matters of priority are of small importance at present. The fact remains that Schlegel had developed an antithesis not only between classic and romantic, but between mechanical and organic form, the first 'pre-determined and external', the second 'innate, shaping itself from within according to its natural development' (Raysor I, xxxvii). Such a doctrine had been implicit or explicit in other German aesthetics known to Coleridge, and it was extremely congenial to his criticism, as it has been to most criticism and poetry since. It liberates authors as well as critics from the 'rules', and makes their task one of creating or understanding unique shapes. Shakespeare, always at odds with the rules, and as a universal genius a power creating new and organised creatures in the manner of nature, lent himself to these new critical methods. Herder said *King Lear* was like the universe because it has 'one interpenetrating, all-animating soul'; Goethe compared *Hamlet* to a tree: 'it is a trunk with boughs, leaves, buds, blossoms and fruit. Are they not all one, and there by means of each other?' And although Coleridge stayed closer to the eighteenth-century topics than he thought, this organic approach to Shakespeare is central to his thinking, and to ours.

The other English Romantic critics are smaller men. Lamb was touched by Coleridgean power, but for all his knowledge of the period and its drama, made too much of his inability to tolerate the tragedies on the stage. Hazlitt, a much more powerful and independent mind, wrote better, in one sense, than either Coleridge or Lamb, bringing to the plays his own passionate, radical and disputatious nature, and understanding the quality of some of the plays Coleridge disliked or neglected: *Measure for Measure*, and *All's Well that Ends Well*, for example. De Quincey's paper 'On the Knocking at the Gate in *Macbeth*' is justly a classic, and a predecessor of much free imaginative interpretation; later (1838) he wrote an excellent article on Shakespeare for the *Encyclopædia Britannica*. Keats was soaked in Shakespeare, as his poems and his copy of the plays, with its markings, demonstrate; and the two *obiter dicta* here extracted from his letters have quite disproportionate importance in the history of the subject, the first of them being a development, ultimately, of the 'natural' argument, yet one of the truly profound and seminal observations.

The task of the Romantic critics, and especially of Coleridge, was resumed by Carlyle, who emphasised the role of poetry as the superior of science in the service of truth, and gave a strong impetus to the study and cultivation of its symbolic powers. These were later in the century to dominate poetry and criticism. The poet being a 'Hero-soul' sent by Nature, Shakespeare, in Carlyle's lectures of 1840, becomes the characteristic representative of this class of symbolic seer. For this critic Shakespeare is, as a great poet must be, a great intellect, a perceiver of world-harmony not at all inferior in mental power to the greatest of scientists, though his intellectual power is in a sense unconscious, and the servant of his imagination. So in the exactly contemporary essay of Emerson, the mind of Shakespeare is called our mental horizon; in a sense he made us, and our world, what they are. If encomium could hardly go further than the eighteenth century had taken it, it remains true that these transcendentalist and symbolic ways of expressing it opened up many new ways of praising and understanding Shakespeare. Melville's impressive but tentative attempt to characterise Shakespeare's genius in the course of his argument for the affinity between Hawthorne's 'power of blackness' and Shakespeare's, also points forward, and

serves to explain how *Moby Dick* should at this point have
absorbed so much of Shakespeare into its wonderfully
original symbolic purposes.

The English-speaking world, and the Germans, had successfully conspired to find a way of speaking of Shakespeare
in terms of a high modern notion of the creative imagination. The French, until lately themselves absorbed in a
painful struggle for release from 'the rules', as yet stood
somewhat aside. The passage in which Taine considers
Shakespeare's style, though it finely characterises one element in that style, will show that he was still concerned with
what he saw as a lack of moderation, of *mesure,* in this
very un-French writer. I have included Santayana's beautifully composed essay as some further sign that critics of the
Latin tradition may qualify for characteristic reasons the
greatness of Shakespeare; and Croce's words stand, not
only I think for an illustration of how a mind strongly
possessed by its own aesthetic presumptions might approach
the subject, but also for a learned Italian scepticism on
some issues too easily obscured by rhetoric. It must be
allowed that on the whole the Latin world has not fully
shared our enthusiasm.

Yet, as I have said, our ways of expressing this enthusiasm change with the times. Coleridge was unfair to his
eighteenth-century predecessors; we find it difficult to love
ours of the nineteenth century. We do not speak their
language, and we do not use their texts. Yet they were many
and gifted. One omission from this anthology which cost
me more thought than most was that of R. G. Moulton
(*Shakespeare as a Dramatic Artist,* 1885). Moulton is very
strong but lengthy; to include him would have meant making an extract so long as to unbalance the book. Ralli's
pedestrian and replaceable history of Shakespeare criticism
has about 1150 pages, and Carlyle is discussed on p. 257.
Only after 500 more pages does he reach the twentieth
century. I have preferred to use my space on the formative
period, believing that the full and true effect of Coleridge's
changes was not felt until the present century. Thus we pass
over certain great Germans, and an army of Englishmen,
including Dowden, Swinburne, Spedding and Arthur Sy-
mons. But I include an example of Pater, as testimony to the

effort of the Paterians and aestheticists; it was an important preliminary to some kinds of modern criticism.

iv

At the gates of the century stands the still gigantic figure of Bradley. Bradley was a Hegelian, but there is no reason why this should trouble the reader; he had less philosophic power than Coleridge, but a much greater control over his material, and his generalisations are based upon a knowledge comprehensive, minute, and always available for the treatment of any issue. For a long time after 1930 or so he was more often disparaged than read; people could give you a distorted version of his defects more readily than a general account of his achievement. This is still true in some degree; yet I have noticed that students who are good enough to be unaffected by common prejudice continue to find his mind impressive and his observations relevant. Bradley himself has some eighteenth-century characteristics, for example his insistence on the generic quality of Shakespeare's individual characters, and his development of the concept of the ruling passion, a notion which he blends with the Aristotelian *hamartia* to produce his theory of the 'tragic flaw'. His psychological method has often been traced back to Morgann. But he has a systematised Coleridgean power, by which he perceives in Shakespeare a veneration for social and psychological order which is related to a concept of universal moral order; and he has a deep sense of the unique stature of Shakespeare among the world's great men. His defects are famous; he almost ignores the plays as theatrical pieces, echoing, for example, Lamb on *Lear*; and he allows his interest in psychology to overbear the poetry of the plays, occasionally (but for the most part in the appendices) considering the characters in isolation from the text, as if they were living people of whom it might be necessary to infer the darker portions of their biography.

These failings, and especially the last, have been somewhat exaggerated; but because the reaction against him was founded upon them, they are the first things to come to mind when Bradley is mentioned. At the risk of over-simplification, and of explaining the direction of too much modern criticism in terms of this reaction, one could say that the theatrical revision of Bradleyism was led by Harley Granville Barker, the psychological revision by E. E. Stoll, and the interpretative and poetic revisions by G. Wilson Knight and L. C. Knights.

Granville Barker was a distinguished playwright and producer, associated with Shaw in the great days of the Court Theatre early in the century. His aim was not to controvert other critics, but to get Shakespeare sensibly back to the stage; and his *Prefaces* embody the craft of Shakespeare's production as he learnt it by experience and study. His impact on theatrical presentations of Shakespeare was very great, though as a literary critic he seems to me to have been over-rated. Stoll wrote many books, informed by increasingly wide reading in world literature, and repeatedly expressed his opposition to Bradley and others like him. He insisted that one should not, given the conventions of Elizabethan theatre and story, look for consistency of characterisation or general realism; that there will in the nature of the case be improbabilities that seem gross if one looks at them thus, and that Shakespeare's psychology was bounded anyway by Elizabethan notions of this subject. In the tradition of Stoll there were many who studied Elizabethan psychology and stage conventions. The most doctrinaire of these was L. L. Schücking, the most useful M. C. Bradbrook, in *Themes and Conventions of Elizabethan Tragedy;* a little later came two books used in this collection, S. L. Bethell, *Shakespeare and the Popular Dramatic Tradition* (1944), and J. I. M. Stewart's *Character and Motive in Shakespeare* (1949). There are many others.

The quest for a plausible view of the Shakespearian theatre ancient and modern, and for an historically grounded approach to his characterisation, indicates the great increase in quantity and quality of historical scholarship in the modern period. Sooner or later this makes its impact on criticism; its importance is such that I have tried to represent it, obviously not very fully, in my choice of texts. Some of this work is simply good expository writing; an example is the work of M. M. Reese, who seeks only to convey what has for some time been received doctrine. Some represents original research; Alfred Harbage's book on the Elizabethan audience, which gave a new dimension to an old subject,

Post-Bradleyan criticism: theatrical (Gr-Barker)
psychol. (Stoll?)
interp. (G. Wilson Kn.)

INTRODUCTION

must here represent much scholarship on Shakespeare's theatre and his times—a whole library including fundamental historical work such as that of E. K. Chambers, G. E. Bentley, and Harbage himself, as well as the detective work of Leslie Hotson and (moving from the pole of fact to the pole of inference) enquiries into the beliefs, conventions and presumptions of Shakespeare's age. Other instances of fruitful scholarship are Miss Welsford's essay, which is only a part of an authoritative study of the long traditions of fools and folly. Such books are so useful as to be, in time, incorporated into the critical tradition, and employed without specific reference; another such, which proved intractable in the hands of the anthologist, is W. C. Curry's *Philosophical Patterns in Macbeth* (1937). A few specimens must stand for this quantity and variety of historical criticism; C. L. Barber's work on the relation of the comedies to popular festivals for all the searches into origins, and T. J. B. Spencer on the Elizabethan attitude to Roman history for a huge library of investigations into Elizabethan reading habits and intellectual assumptions. Work of this kind involves or is inseparable from critical appraisal, and occasionally, as in William Empson's investigations of the 'complex words' of Shakespeare's vocabulary, this union is very close.

There remains my third category of post-Bradleyan criticism: the modern phase of interpretative criticism. L. C. Knights, whose criticism has grown more conventional, less exclusively concerned with the texture of the verse, made a considerable impact in England with his pamphlet; the *Scrutiny* variety of Shakespeare criticism has other exponents also, the best known being Derek Traversi, who has written four full-length books and some shorter pieces of elaborate analysis. Historically speaking, however, the appearance of G. Wilson Knight's *The Wheel of Fire* has proved a more decisive event, and 1930 the decisive year; from it there also appeared Caroline Spurgeon's investigation of Shakespeare's imagery, and William Empson's remarkable *Seven Types of Ambiguity*, though this deals with Shakespeare only incidentally. Wilson Knight's principles of interpretation, in their purest form, are a post-Symbolist extension of the Coleridgean organic approach. They require a 'spatial' view of the work under discussion, a detection of secret patterns, figures in the carpet. The term spatial is probably unfortunate, since what is really involved is the holding of the entire work in the mind as a single image or 'extended metaphor', not, as Knight well understands, a neglect of the play in its temporal and progressive aspect. Knight is no enemy of Bradley, but his mind is more occult, less timid perhaps in the face of the inherently improbable, above all less ordinarily ethical in cast. It is a mind in the tradition of Nietzsche, extraordinary, unconventional, given to vast historical generalisation. It is also a product of the Symbolist tradition, and so, like so many modern critical approaches, holiest in its attitude to works of literature, and also anti-intentionalist; the work has its own organic constitution and laws, expressed in the multiple inter-relations of symbol, image, event and character, and controlled by no discoverable cause outside itself. Thus Knight has written, even in *The Wheel of Fire* and *The Imperial Theme*, criticism which one can find largely unacceptable (his essay on *Hamlet*, for instance) and criticism which is extraordinarily revealing, like the pieces on *Othello* and *Coriolanus*. He is a great champion of *Timon*, and his essay on that play is here in part reproduced. The influence of Knight has not been wholly good, and has encouraged much absurd allegorisation; but the benefits to more academic criticism can be judged by a reading of R. B. Heilman's books on *Lear* and *Othello (This Great Stage* [1948] and *Magic in the Web* [1956] omitted here solely because of the difficulty of making an extract of manageable length which would convey their quality).

I believe that the past thirty years have seen much Shakespeare criticism that is illuminating, and some that is of a high order. I have chosen, over the whole range of Shakespeare's work, examples of it which seem useful to the general reader and to the student. It is too early to guess what parts of this great body of criticism will, in the long run, seem worth reading for its own sake, so my criteria for more recent work are necessarily not the same as for the earlier. And yet, if the quantity is great (and well over a thousand books and articles a year are recorded in the bibliographies) the quality is also high enough to present an anthologist with a difficult embarrassment of choice. Critics and their admirers will surely forgive me for the omission of some fine and admired pieces. In scholarship it is evident that we have made great gains, and will make more; in criticism the liberation made possible by Coleridge and consolidated by the last generation of critics has created opportunities which, especially if combined with the researches of the scholar, may provide us with the great synthetic modern books on Shakespeare which are the only lack we may with any urgency complain of. Meanwhile every undergraduate who puts down his thoughts on a play by Shakespeare may feel himself a part of a tradition not only close on four hundred years old, but dignified by the activity of fine minds, not least in his own time.

A brief list of relevant books:

Augustus Ralli, *A History of Shakespearean Criticism.* 2 vols., Oxford, 1932.

D. Nichol Smith, *Eighteenth Century Essays on Shakespeare.* Glasgow, 1903.

——————————, *Shakespeare in the Eighteenth Century.* Oxford, 1928.

R. W. Babcock, *The Genesis of Shakespeare Idolatry, 1766-1799.* Chapel Hill, University of North Carolina Press, 1931.

T. M. Raysor, *Coleridge's Shakespearean Criticism.* 2 vols., Cambridge, Mass., 1930; reprint, revised and abbreviated, J. M. Dent, London, 1960.

Kenneth Muir, 'Fifty Years of Shakespearian Criticism, 1900-1950.' *Shakespeare Survey* 4 (1951), 1-25.

Annual bibliographies of Shakespeare studies are published in *Studies of Philology, Shakespeare Survey, Shakespeare Quarterly, The Year's Work in English Studies,* and the *Annual Bibliography.*

GENERAL CRITICISM

FRANCIS MERES

Francis Meres (1565-1647). A Cambridge man who lived in London in the 1590s. Palladis Tamia: Wits Treasury of 1598 contains 'a comparative discourse of our English Poets with the Greek, Latin and Italian poets', and here Shakespeare is mentioned.

SHAKESPEARE AND THE ANCIENTS*

. . . the sweete wittie soule of *Ouid* liues in mellifluous & hony-tongued *Shakespeare*, witnes his *Venus* and *Adonis,* his *Lucrece,* his sugred Sonnets among his priuate friends, &c.

As *Plautus* and *Seneca* are accounted the best for Comedy and Tragedy among the Latines: so *Shakespeare* among the English is the most excellent in both kinds for the stage; for Comedy, witnes his *Gentlemen of Verona,* his *Errors,* his *Loue labors lost,* his *Loue labours wonne,* his *Midsummers night dreame,* & his *Merchant of Venice*: for Tragedy his *Richard the 2. Richard the 3. Henry the 4. King Iohn, Titus Andronicus* and his *Romeo* and *Iuliet.*

As *Epius Stolo* said, that the Muses would speake with *Plautus* tongue, if they would speak Latin: so I say that the Muses would speak with *Shakespeares* fine filed phrase, if they would speake English . . .

* From *Palladis Tamia: Wits Treasury,* 1598.

GABRIEL HARVEY

Gabriel Harvey (1545?-1631). Argumentative Cambridge don, critical theorist and friend of Spenser.

SHAKESPEARE'S PUBLIC*

The younger sort takes much delight in Shakespeares Venus, & Adonis: but his Lucrece, & his tragedie of Hamlet, Prince of Denmarke, haue it in them, to please the wiser sort. Or such poets: or better: or none.

FRANCIS BEAUMONT

Francis Beaumont (1585?-1616). Collaborator with John Fletcher in about a dozen plays, including The Maid's Tragedy *(1610-11).*

SHAKESPEARE AND THE LIGHT OF NATURE†

          . . . heere I would let slippe
(If I had any in mee) schollershippe,
And from all Learninge keepe these lines as cleere

* From a marginal note in a copy of Speght's *Chaucer*. Harvey bought this in 1598, the year of its publication; but the date of the annotation cannot be precisely determined. One remark—'The Earle of Essex much commendes Albions England'—suggests that the note was written before the execution of Essex on Feb. 25, 1601. Whether the *Hamlet* mentioned was substantially the same as that which had its first authorised publication in 1604-5 is a large problem.

† From a verse-letter to Ben Jonson, of about 1615.

as Shakespeares best are, which our heires shall heare
Preachers apte to their auditors to showe
how farr sometimes a mortall man may goe
by the dimme light of Nature . . .

BEN JONSON

*Ben Jonson (1573-1637). The most eminent of Shake-
speare's playwright contemporaries. The son of a brick-
layer, he became a man of much learning, and his plays
are original exercises in the classic tradition as then
understood. He is known to have mocked Shakespeare's
indifference to this tradition, but these, the greatest of
contemporary tributes, are evidence that he felt his rival's
power. Among his best plays are* Volpone *(1605) and*
The Alchemist *(1610). He was also a prolific poet, and
his notes on criticism and literary theory* (Timber, or Discoveries, *published posthumously in 1641) include our
second passage. It is based upon a Latin text, in Jonson's
way. If there is anything in a recent suggestion that these
notes were used for lectures at Gresham College, we
have before us part of the earliest lecture on Shakespeare.*

To the memory of my beloued
The Avthor
Mr. William Shakespeare:
And
what he hath left vs.*

To draw no enuy (*Shakespeare*) on thy name,
  Am I thus ample to thy Booke, and Fame:
While I confess thy writings to be such,
  As neither *Man,* nor *Muse,* can praise too much.
'Tis true, and all mens suffrage. But these wayes
  Were not the paths I meant vnto thy praise:

* These verses were first printed in the First Folio of 1623.

For seeliest Ignorance on these may light,
    Which, when it sounds at best, but eccho's right;
Or blinde Affection, which doth ne're aduance
    The truth, but gropes, and vrgeth all by chance;
Or crafty Malice, might pretend this praise,
    And thinke to ruine, where it seem'd to raise.
These are, as some infamous Baud, or Whore,
    Should praise a Matron. What could hurt her more?
But thou art proofe against them, and indeed
    Aboue th'ill fortune of them, or the need.
I, therefore will begin. Soule of the Age!
    The applause! delight! the wonder of our Stage!
My *Shakespeare*, rise; I will not lodge thee by
    Chaucer, or *Spenser*, or bid *Beaumont* lye
A little further, to make thee a roome:
    Thou art a Moniment, without a tombe,
And art aliue still, while thy Booke doth liue,
    And we haue wits to read, and praise to giue.
That I not mixe thee so, my braine excuses;
    I meane with great, but disproportion'd *Muses:*
For, if I thought my iudgement were of yeeres,
    I should commit thee surely with thy peeres,
And tell, how farre thou didst our *Lily* out-shine,
    Or sporting *Kid*, or *Marlowes* mighty line.
And though thou hadst small *Latine*, and less *Greeke*,
    From thence to honour thee, I would not seeke
For names; but call forth thund'ring *Æschilus*,
    Euripides, and *Sophocles* to us,
Paccuuius, Accius, him of *Cordoua* dead,
    To life againe, to heare thy Buskin tread,
And shake a Stage: Or, when thy Sockes were on,
    Leaue thee alone, for the comparison
Of all, that insolent *Greece*, or haughtie *Rome*
    Sent forth, or since did from their ashes come.
Triumph, my *Britaine*, thou hast one to showe,
    To whom all scenes of *Europe* homage owe.
He was not of an age, but for all time!
    And all the *Muses* still were in their prime,
When like *Apollo* he came forth to warme
    Our eares, or like a *Mercury* to charme!
Nature her selfe was proud of his designes,
    And ioy'd to weare the dressing of his lines!

Which were so richly spun, and wouen so fit,
  As, sincè, she will vouchsafe no other Wit.
The merry *Greeke,* tart *Aristophanes,*
  Neat *Terence,* witty *Plautus,* now not please;
But antiquated, and deserted lye
  As they were not of Natures family.
Yet must I not giue Nature all: Thy Art,
  My gentle Shakespeare, must enioy a part.
For though the *Poets* matter, Nature be,
  His Art doth giue the fashion. And, that he,
Who casts to write a liuing line, must sweat,
  (Such as thine are) and strike the second heat
Vpon the Muses anuile: turne the same,
  (And himselfe with it) that he thinkes to frame;
Or for the lawrell, he may gaine a scorne,
  For a good *Poet's* made, as well as borne.
And such wert thou. Looke how the fathers face
  Liues in his issue, euen so, the race
Of *Shakespeares* minde, and manners brightly shines
  In his well torned, and true-filed lines:
In each of which, he seems to shake a Lance,
  As brandish't at the eyes of Ignorance.
Sweet Swan of *Auon!* what a sight it were
  To see thee in our waters yet appeare,
And make those flights vpon the bankes of *Thames,*
  That so did take *Eliza* and our *Iames!*
But stay, I see thee in the *Hemisphere*
  Aduanc'd, and made a Constellation there!
Shine forth, thou Starre of *Poets,* and with rage,
  Or influence, chide, or cheere the drooping Stage;
Which, since thy flight from hence, hath mourn'd like night,
  And despaires day, but for thy Volumes light.

THIS SIDE IDOLATRY*

I *remember,* the Players have often mentioned it as an
honour to *Shakespeare,* that in his writing, (whatsoever he
penn'd) hee never blotted out iine. My answer hath beene,
would he had blotted a thousand. Which they thought a
malevolent speech. I had not told posterity this, but for their

* From Jonson's critical notebook *Timber, or Discoveries.*

ignorance, who choose that circumstance to commend their friend by, wherein he most faulted. And to justifie mine own candor, (for I lov'd the man, and doe honour his memory (on this side Idolatry) as much as any.) Hee was (indeed) honest, and of an open, and free nature: had an excellent *Phantsie;* brave notions, and gentle expressions: wherein hee flow'd with that facility, that sometime it was necessary he should be stop'd: *Sufflaminandus erat:* as *Augustus* said of *Haterius.* His wit was in his owne power; would the rule of it had beene so too. Many times hee fell into those things, could not escape laughter: As when hee said in the person of *Cæsar,* one speaking to him: *Cæsar thou dost me wrong.* He replyed: *Cæsar did never wrong, but with just cause* and such like: which were ridiculous. But hee redeemed his vices with his vertues. There was ever more in him to be praysed, then to be pardoned.

JOHN HEMINGES and HENRY CONDELL

John Heminge (or Heminges) (d. 1630). See under Condell.

Henry Condell (d. 1627). Actor and friend of Shakespeare, who was with John Heminges responsible for the preparation of, and the Preface to, the First Folio of 1623.

TO THE GREAT VARIETY OF READERS*

It had bene a thing, we confesse, worthie to haue been wished, that the Author himselfe had liu'd to haue set forth, and ouerseen his owne writings; But since it hath bin ordain'd otherwise, and he by death departed from that right, we pray you do not envie his Friends, the office of their care, and paine, to haue collected & publish'd them; and so to haue publish'd them, as where (before) you were abus'd with diuerse stolne, and surreptitious copies, maimed,

* The editorial preface to the First Folio.

and deformed by the frauds and stealthes of iniurious im-
postors that expos'd them: euen those, are now offer'd to
your view cur'd, and perfect of their limbes; and all the
rest, absolute in their numbers, as he conceiued them. Who,
as he was a happie imitator of Nature, was a most gentle
expresser of it. His mind and hand went together: And
what he thought, he vttered with that easinesse, that wee
haue scarce receiued from him a blot in his papers. But it
is not our prouince, who onely gather his works, and giue
them you, to praise him. It is yours that reade him. And
there we hope, to your diuers capacities, you will finde
enough, both to draw, and hold you: for his wit can no
more lie hid, then it could be lost. Reade him, therefore;
and againe, and againe: And if then you doe not like him,
surely you are in some manifest danger, not to vnderstand
him. And so we leaue you to other of his Friends, whom if
you need, can bee your guides: if you neede them not, you
can leade your selues, and others. And such Readers we
wish him.

LEONARD DIGGES

*Leonard Digges (1588-1635). Acquaintance of Shake-
speare's, translator of Claudian's Rape of Proserpine.*

TO THE MEMORIE
OF THE DECEASED AUTHOR MAISTER
W. SHAKESPEARE.*

Shake-speare, at length thy pious fellowes giue
The world thy Workes: thy Workes, by which, out-liue
Thy Tombe, thy name must: when that stone is rent,
And Time dissolues thy Stratford Moniment,
Here we aliue shall view thee still. This Booke,

* From the prefatory matter of the First Folio.

When Brasse and Marble fade, shall make thee looke
Fresh to all Ages: when Posteritie
Shall loath what's new, thinke all is prodegie
That is not *Shake-speares;* eu'ry Line, each Verse,
Here shall reuiue, redeeme thee from thy Herse.
Nor Fire, nor cankring Age, as *Naso* said,
Of his, thy wit-fraught Booke shall once inuade.
Nor shall I e're beleeue, or thinke thee dead
(Though mist) untill our bankrout Stage be sped
(Impossible) with some new strain t' out-do
Passions of *Iuliet,* and her *Romeo;*
Or till I heare a Scene more nobly take,
Then when thy half-Sword parlying *Romans* spake,
Till these, till any of thy Volumes rest
Shall with more fire, more feeling be exprest,
Be sure, our *Shake-speare,* thou canst neuer dye,
But crown'd with Lawrell, liue eternally.

A POET BORN, NOT MADE*

Poets are borne not made, when I would prove
This truth, the glad rememberance I must love
Of never dying *Shakespeare,* who alone,
Is argument enough to make that one.
First, that he was a Poet none would doubt,
That heard th'applause of what he sees set out
Imprinted; where thou hast (I will not say)
Reader his Workes (for to contrive a Play
To him twas none) the patterne of all wit,
Art without Art unparaleld as yet.
Next Nature onely helpt him, for looke thorow
This whole Booke, thou shalt find he doth not borrow,
One phrase from Greekes, nor Latines imitate,
Nor once from vulgar Languages Translate,
Nor Plagiari-like from others gleane,
Nor begs he from each witty friend a Scene
To peece his Acts with, all that he doth write,
Is pure his owne, plot, language exquisite,
But oh! what praise more powerfull can we give

* From the 1640 edition of Shakespeare's *Poems.*

The dead, than that by him the Kings men live,
His Players, which should they but have shar'd the Fate,
All else expir'd within the short Termes date;
How could the Globe have prospered, since through want
Of change, the Plaies and Poems had growne scant.
But happy Verse thou shalt be sung and heard,
When hungry quills shall be such honour bard.
Then vanish upstart Writers to each Stage,
You needy Poetasters of this Age,
Where *Shakespeare* liv'd or spake, Vermine forbeare,
Least with your froth you spot them, come not neere;
But if you needs must write, if poverty
So pinch, that otherwise you starve and die,
On Gods name may the Bull or Cockpit have
Your lame blancke Verse, to keepe you from the grave:
Or let new Fortunes younger brethren see,
What they can picke from your leane industry.
I doe not wonder when you offer at
Blacke-Friers, that you suffer: tis the fate
Of richer veines, prime judgments that have far'd
The worse, with this deceased man compar'd.
So have I seene, when Cesar would appeare,
And on the Stage at halfe-sword parley were,
Brutus and *Cassius:* oh how the Audience,
Were ravish'd, with what wonder they went thence,
When some new day they would not brooke a line,
Of tedious (though well laboured) *Catiline;*
Sejanus too was irkesome, they priz'de more
Honest *Iago,* or the jealous Moore.
And though the Fox and subtill Alchimist,
Long intermitted could not quite be mist,
Though these have sham'd all the Ancients, and might raise,
Their Authors merit with a crowne of Bayes.
Yet these sometimes, even at a friend's desire
Acted, have scarce defraid the Seacoale fire
And doore-keepers: when let but *Falstaffe* come,
Hall, Poines, the rest you scarce shall have a roome
All is so pester'd: let but *Beatrice*
And *Benedicke* be seene, loe in a trice
The Cockpit Galleries, Boxes, all are full
To neare *Maluoglio* that crosse garter'd Gull.

Briefe, there is nothing in his wit fraught Booke,
Whose sound we would not heare, on whose worth looke
Like old coynd gold, whose lines in every page,
Shall pass true currant to succeeding age.
But why doe I dead *Shakespeares* praise recite,
Some second *Shakespeare* must of *Shakespeare* write;
For me tis needlesse, since an host of men,
Will pay to clap his praise, to free my Pen.

JOHN MILTON

*John Milton (1608-1674). Milton's interest in Shakespeare
has often been a subject of comment; it is especially
notable in* Comus *(1634), which is much affected by*
The Tempest.

ON SHAKESPEAR, 1630.*

What needs my *Shakespear* for his honour'd Bones,
The labour of an age in piled Stones,
Or that his hallow'd reliques should be hid
Under a Star-ypointing *Pyramid?*
Dear son of memory, great heir of Fame,
What need'st thou such weak witness of thy name?
Thou in our wonder and astonishment
Hast built thy self a live-long Monument.
For whilst toth' shame of slow-endeavouring art,
Thy easie numbers flow, and that each heart
Hath from the leaves of thy unvalu'd Book,
Those Delphick lines with deep impression took,
Then thou our fancy of it self bereaving,
Dost make us Marble with too much conceaving;
And so Sepulcher'd in such pomp dost lie,
That Kings for such a Tomb would wish to die.

* A compliment included in the Second Folio (1632).

THOMAS FULLER

*Thomas Fuller (1608-1661). His Worthies of England,
which appeared posthumously, occupied him over many
years.*

SHAKESPEARE AND JONSON*

He was an eminent instance of the truth of that Rule,
Poeta non fit, sed nascitur, one is not *made*, but *born* a
Poet. Indeed his Learning was very little, so that as *Cornish
diamonds* are not polished by any Lapidary, but are pointed
and smoothed even as they are taken out of the Earth,
so *nature* it self was all the *art* which was used upon him.

Many were the *wit-combates* betwixt him and *Ben Jonson*, which two I behold like a *Spanish great Gallion* and
an *English-man of War*; Master *Jonson* (like the former)
was built far higher in Learning; *Solid*, but *Slow* in his
performances. *Shake-spear*, with the *English-man of War*,
lesser in *bulk*, but lighter in *sailing*, could turn with all
tides, tack about and take advantage of all winds, by the
quickness of his Wit and Invention.

MARGARET CAVENDISH

*Margaret Cavendish, Duchess of Newcastle (1624-1674).
Poet and writer, wife of one of Charles I's generals.*

* From *Worthies, Warwickshire*, 1662.

A LETTER ON SHAKESPEARE*

Madam,

I Wonder how that Person you mention in your Letter, could either have the Conscience, or Confidence to Dispraise *Shakespear's* Playes, as to say they were made up onely with Clowns, Fools, Watchmen, and the like; . . .

Shakespear did not want Wit, to Express to the Life all Sorts of Persons, of what Quality, Profession, Degree, Breeding, or Birth soever; nor did he want Wit to Express the Divers, and Different Humours, or Natures, or Several Passions in Mankind; and so Well he hath Express'd in his Playes all Sorts of Persons, as one would think he had been Transformed into every one of those Persons he hath Described; and as sometimes one would think he was really himself the Clown or Jester he Feigns, so one would think, he was also the King, and Privy Counsellor; also as one would think he were Really the Coward he Feigns, so one would think he were the most Valiant, and Experienced Souldier; Who would not think he had been such a man as his Sir *John Falstaff*? and who would not think he had been *Harry* the Fifth? & certainly *Julius Cæsar, Augustus Cæsar,* and *Antonius,* did never Really Act their parts Better, if so Well, as he hath Described them, and I believe that *Antonius* and *Brutus* did not Speak Better to the People, than he hath Feign'd them; nay, one would think that he had been Metamorphosed from a Man to a Woman, for who could Describe *Cleopatra* Better than he hath done, and many other Females of his own Creating, as *Nan Page,* Mrs. *Page,* Mrs. *Ford,* the Doctors Maid, *Bettrice,* Mrs. *Quickly, Doll Tearsheet,* and others, too many to Relate? and in his Tragick Vein, he Presents Passions so Naturally, and Misfortunes so Probably, as he Peirces the Souls of his Readers with such a true Sense and Feeling thereof, that it Forces Tears through their Eyes, and almost Perswades them, they are Really Actors, or at least Present at those Tragedies. Who would not Swear he had been a Noble Lover, that could Woo so well? and there is not any person he hath Described in his Book, but nis Readers

* From her *Letters,* 1664.

might think they were Well acquainted with them; indeed *Shakespear* had a Clear Judgment, a Quick Wit, a Spreading Fancy, a Subtil Observation, a Deep Apprehension, and a most Eloquent Elocution; truly, he was a Natural Orator, as well as a Natural Poet, and he was not an Orator to Speak Well only on some Subjects, as Lawyers, who can make Eloquent Orations at the Bar, and Plead Subtilly and Wittily in Law-Cases, or Divines, that can Preach Eloquent Sermons, or Dispute Subtilly and Wittily in Theology, but take them from that, and put them to other Subjects, and they will be to seek; but *Shakespear*'s Wit and Eloquence was General, for, and upon all Subjects, he rather wanted Subjects for his Wit and Eloquence to Work on, for which he was Forced to take some of his Plots out of History, where he only took the Bare Designs, the Wit and Language being all his Own; and so much he had above others, that those, who Writ after him, were Forced to Borrow of him, or rather to Steal from him.

JOHN DRYDEN

John Dryden (1631-1700). Called 'the father of Shakespeare criticism', Dryden looked back to 'the giant age before the Flood' and found reasons for preferring Shakespeare to his contemporaries and successors.

SHAKESPEARE AND NATURE*

To begin, then, with Shakespeare. He was the man who of all modern, and perhaps ancient poets, had the largest and most comprehensive soul. All the images of Nature were still present to him, and he drew them, not laboriously, but luckily; when he describes any thing, you more than see it, you feel it too. Those who accuse him to have wanted learning, give him the greater commendation: he

* From the *Essay of Dramatic Poesy* (1668).

was naturally learn'd; he needed not the spectacles of books to read Nature; he looked inwards, and found her there. I cannot say he is every where alike; were he so, I should do him injury to compare him with the greatest of mankind. He is many times flat, insipid; his comic wit degenerating into clenches, his serious swelling into bombast. But he is always great, when some great occasion is presented to him; no man can say he ever had a fit subject for his wit, and did not then raise himself as high above the rest of poets,

Quantum lenta solent inter viburna cupressi.

The consideration of this made Mr. Hales of Eaton say, that there was no subject of which any poet ever writ, but he would produce it much better treated of in Shakespeare; and however others are now generally preferred before him, yet the age wherein he lived, which had contemporaries with him Fletcher and Jonson, never equalled them to him in their esteem: and in the last King's court, when Ben's reputation was at highest, Sir John Suckling, and with him the greater part of the courtiers, set our Shakespeare far above him.

SHAKESPEARE'S CHARACTERISATION*

To return once more to Shakespeare; no man ever drew so many characters, or generally distinguished 'em better from one another, excepting only Jonson. I will instance but in one, to show the copiousness of his intention; it is that of Caliban, or the monster, in the *Tempest*. He seems there to have created a person which was not in Nature, a boldness which, at first sight, would appear intolerable; for he makes him a species of himself, begotten by an incubus on a witch; but this, as I have elsewhere proved, is not wholly beyond the bounds of credibility, at least the vulgar still believe it. We have the separated notions of a spirit, and of a witch (and spirits, according to Plato, are vested with a subtle body; according to some of his followers, have different sexes); therefore, as from the distinct apprehen-

* From the *Preface to Troilus and Cressida* (1679).

sions of a horse, and of a man, imagination has formed a centaur; so, from those of an incubus and a sorceress, Shakespeare has produced his monster. Whether or no his generation can be defended, I leave to philosophy; but of this I am certain, that the poet has most judiciously furnished him with a person, a language, and a character, which will suit him, both by father's and mother's side: he has all the discontents and malice of a witch, and of a devil, besides a convenient proportion of the deadly sins; gluttony, sloth, and lust, are manifest; the dejectedness of a slave is likewise given him, and the ignorance of one bred up in a desert island. His person is monstrous, and he is the product of unnatural lust; and his language is as hobgoblin as his person; in all things he is distinguished from other mortals. The characters of Fletcher are poor and narrow, in comparison of Shakespeare's; I remember not one which is not borrowed from him; unless you will accept that strange mixture of a man in the *King and no King;* so that in this part Shakespeare is generally worth our imitation; and to imitate Fletcher is but to copy after him who was a copyer. . . .

If Shakespeare be allowed, as I think he must, to have made his characters distinct, it will easily be inferred that he understood the nature of the passions: because it has been proved already that confused passions make undistinguishable characters: yet I cannot deny that he has his failings; but they are not so much in the passions themselves, as in his manner of expression: he often obscures his meaning by his words, and sometimes makes it unintelligible. I will not say of so great a poet, that he distinguished not the blown puffy style from true sublimity; but I may venture to maintain, that the fury of his fancy often transported him beyond the bounds of judgment, either in coining of new words and phrases, or racking words which were in use, into the violence of a catachresis. It is not that I would explode the use of metaphors from passion, for Longinus thinks 'em necessary to raise it: but to use 'em at every word, to say nothing without a metaphor, a simile, an image, or description, is, I doubt, to smell a little too strongly of the buskin. I must be forced to give an example of expressing passion figuratively; but that I may do it with respect to Shakespeare, it shall not be taken from anything of his: 'tis an exclamation against Fortune, quoted in his *Hamlet* but written by some other poet—

> Out, out, thou strumpet, Fortune! all you gods,
> In general synod, take away her power;
> Break all the spokes and felleys from her wheel,
> And bowl the round nave down the hill of Heav'n,
> As low as to the fiends.

And immediately after, speaking of Hecuba, when Priam was killed before her eyes—

> The mobbled queen
> Threatning the flame, ran up and down
> With bisson rheum; a clout about that head
> Where late the diadem stood; and for a robe,
> About her lank and all o'er-teemed loins,
> A blanket in th' alarm of fear caught up.
> Who this had seen, with tongue in venom steep'd
> 'Gainst Fortune's state would treason have pronounced;
> But if the gods themselves did see her then,
> When she saw Pyrrhus make malicious sport
> In mincing with his sword her husband's limbs,
> The instant burst of clamour that she made
> (Unless things mortal move them not at all)
> Would have made milch the burning eyes of heaven,
> And passion in the gods.

What a pudder is here kept in raising the expression of trifling thoughts! Would not a man have thought that the poet had been bound prentice to a wheelwright, for his first rant? and had followed a ragman, for the clout and blanket in the second? Fortune is painted on a wheel, and therefore the writer, in a rage, will have poetical justice done upon every member of that engine: after this execution, he bowls the nave down-hill, from Heaven, to the fiends (an unreasonable long mark, a man would think); 'tis well there are no solid orbs to stop it in the way, or no element of fire to consume it: but when it came to the earth, it must be monstrous heavy, to break ground as low as the centre. His making milch the burning eyes of heaven

was a pretty tolerable flight too: and I think no man ever
drew milk out of eyes before him: yet, to make the wonder
greater, these eyes were burning. Such a sight indeed were
enough to have raised passion in the gods; but to excuse
the effects of it, he tells you, perhaps they did not see it.
Wise men would be glad to find a little sense couched
under all these pompous words; for bombast is commonly
the delight of that audience which loves Poetry, but understands it not: and as commonly has been the practice of
those writers, who, not being able to infuse a natural passion into the mind, have made it their business to ply the
ears, and to stun their judges by the noise. But Shakespeare
does not often thus; for the passions in his scene between
Brutus and Cassius are extremely natural, the thoughts are
such as arise from the matter, the expression of 'em not
viciously figurative. I cannot leave this subject, before I do
justice to that divine poet, by giving you one of his passionate descriptions: 'tis of Richard the Second when he
was deposed, and led in triumph through the streets of
London by Henry of Bullingbrook: the painting of it is so
lively, and the words so moving, that I have scarce read
anything comparable to it in any other language. Suppose
you have seen already the fortunate usurper passing through
the crowd, and followed by the shouts and acclamations of
the people; and now behold King Richard entering upon
the scene: consider the wretchedness of his condition, and
his carriage in it; and refrain from pity, if you can—

> As in a theatre, the eyes of men,
> After a well-graced actor leaves the stage,
> Are idly bent on him that enters next,
> Thinking his prattle to be tedious:
> Even so, or with much more contempt, men's eyes
> Did scowl on Richard: no man cried, God save him
> No joyful tongue gave him his welcome home,
> But dust was thrown upon his sacred head,
> Which with such gentle sorrow he shook off,
> His face still combating with tears and smiles
> (The badges of his grief and patience),
> That had not God (for some strong purpose) steel'd
> The hearts of men, they must perforce have melted,
> And barbarism itself have pitied him.

To speak justly of this whole matter: 'tis neither height of thought that is discommended, nor pathetic vehemence, nor any nobleness of expression in its proper place; but 'tis a false measure of all these, something which is like them, and is not them; 'tis the Bristol-stone, which appears like a diamond; 'tis an extravagant thought, instead of a sublime one; 'tis roaring madness, instead of vehemence; and a sound of words, instead of sense. If Shakespeare were stripped of all the bombasts in his passions, and dressed in the most vulgar words, we should find the beauties of his thoughts remaining; if his embroideries were burnt down, there would still be silver at the bottom of the melting-pot: but I fear (at least let me fear it for myself) that we, who ape his sounding words, have nothing of his thought, but are all outside; there is not so much as a dwarf within our giant's clothes. Therefore, let not Shakespeare suffer for our sakes; 'tis our fault, who succeed him in an age which is more refined, if we imitate him so ill, that we copy his failings only, and make a virtue of that in our writings which in his was an imperfection.

For what remains, the excellency of that poet was, as I have said, in the more manly passions; Fletcher's in the softer. Shakespeare writ better betwixt man and man; Fletcher, betwixt man and woman: consequently, the one described friendship better; the other love: yet Shakespeare taught Fletcher to write love: and Juliet and Desdemona are originals. 'Tis true, the scholar had the softer soul; but the master had the kinder. Friendship is both a virtue and a passion essentially; love is a passion only in its nature, and is not a virtue but by accident: good nature makes friendship; but effeminacy love. Shakespeare had an universal mind, which comprehended all characters and passions; Fletcher a more confined and limited: for though he treated love in perfection, yet honour, ambition, revenge, and generally all the stronger passions, he either touched not, or not masterly. To conclude all, he was a limb of Shakespeare.

I had intended to have proceeded to the last property of manners, which is, that they must be constant, and the characters maintained the same from the beginning to the end; and from thence to have proceeded to the thoughts and expressions suitable to a tragedy: but I will first see how this will relish with the age. It is, I confess, but cursorily written; yet the judgment, which is given here, is generally founded upon experience: but because many men are shocked at the name of rules, as if they were a kind of magisterial prescription upon poets, I will conclude with the words of Rapin, in his *Reflections* on Aristotle's work *of Poetry:* 'If the rules be well considered, we shall find them to be made only to reduce Nature into method, to trace her step by step, and not to suffer the least mark of her to escape us: 'tis only by these, that probability in fiction is maintained, which is the soul of poetry. They are founded upon good sense, and sound reason, rather than on authority; for though Aristotle and Horace are produced, yet no man must argue, that what they write is true, because they writ it; but 'tis evident, by the ridiculous mistakes and gross absurdities which have been made by those poets who have taken their fancy only for their guide, that if this fancy be not regulated, it is a mere caprice, and utterly incapable to produce a reasonable and judicious poem.'

NICHOLAS ROWE

Nicholas Rowe (1674-1718). Himself a considerable drama tist with an interest in Jacobean plays, Rowe produced, for his edition of 1709 (the first edition of Shakespeare), an Account *of the author's life, which remained the basis of biographical knowledge for a century. The critical topics proposed in this* Account *(e.g., Shakespeare's truth to nature, his faults, his learning) were taken up again and again.*

VIRTUES AND FAULTS OF SHAKESPEARE*

As I have not propos'd to my self to enter into a large and compleat criticism upon *Shakespear*'s Works, so I sup-

* From *Some Account of the Life of Mr. William Shakespear* (1709).

pose it will neither be expected that I should take notice of the severe remarks that have been formerly made upon him by Mr. *Rhymer*. I must confess, I can't very well see what could be the reason of his animadverting with so much sharpness, upon the faults of a man excellent on most occasions, and whom all the world ever was and will be inclin'd to have an esteem and veneration for. If it was to shew his own knowledge in the Art of Poetry, besides that there is a vanity in making that only his design, I question if there be not many imperfections as well in those schemes and precepts he has given for the direction of others, as well as in that sample of Tragedy which he has written to shew the excellency of his own *Genius*. If he had a pique against the man, and wrote on purpose to ruin a reputation so well establish'd, he has had the mortification to fail altogether in his attempt, and to see the world at least as fond of *Shakespear* as of his Critique. But I won't believe a gentleman, and a good-natur'd man, capable of the last intention. Whatever may have been his meaning, finding fault is certainly the easiest task of knowledge, and commonly those men of good judgment, who are likewise of good and gentle dispositions, abandon this ungrateful province to the tyranny of pedants. If one would enter into the beauties of *Shakespear*, there is a much larger, as well as a more delightful field; but as I won't prescribe to the tastes of other people, so I will only take the liberty, with all due submission to the judgments of others, to observe some of those things I have been pleas'd with in looking him over.

His Plays are properly to be distinguish'd only into Comedies and Tragedies. Those which are called Histories, and even some of his Comedies, are really Tragedies, with a run or mixture of Comedy amongst 'em. That way of Trage-comedy was the common mistake of that age, and is indeed become so agreeable to the *English* taste, that tho' the severer Critiques among us cannot bear it, yet the generality of our audiences seem to be better pleas'd with it than with an exact Tragedy. *The Merry Wives of* Windsor, *The Comedy of Errors,* and *The Taming of the Shrew,* are all pure Comedy; the rest, however they are call'd, have something of both kinds. 'Tis not very easy to determine which way of writing he was most excellent in. There is certainly a great deal of entertainment in his comical humours; and tho' they did not then strike at all ranks of people, as the Satyr of the present age has taken the liberty to do, yet there is a pleasing and a well-distinguish'd variety in those characters which he thought fit to meddle with. *Falstaff* is allow'd by every body to be a master-piece; the Character is always well-sustain'd, tho' drawn out into the length of three Plays; and even the account of his death, given by his old landlady Mrs. *Quickly*, in the first act of *Henry* V., tho' it be extremely natural, is yet as diverting as any part of his life. If there be any fault in the draught he has made of this lewd old fellow, it is, that tho' he has made him a thief, lying, cowardly, vain-glorious, and in short every way vicious, yet he has given him so much wit as to make him almost too agreeable; and I don't know whether some people have not, in remembrance of the diversion he had formerly afforded 'em, been sorry to see his friend *Hal* use him so scurvily, when he comes to the crown in the end of the second part of *Henry* the Fourth. Amongst other extravagances, in *The Merry Wives of* Windsor, he has made him a Deer-stealer, that he might at the same time remember his *Warwickshire* prosecutor, under the name of Justice *Shallow*; he has given him very near the same coat of arms which *Dugdale*, in his Antiquities of that county, describes for a family there, and makes the *Welsh* parson descant very pleasantly upon 'em. That whole play is admirable; the humours are various and well oppos'd; the main design, which is to cure *Ford* of his unreasonable jealousie, is extremely well conducted. *Falstaff*'s *Billet-Doux*, and Master *Slender*'s

Ah! Sweet *Ann Page*!

are very good expressions of love in their way. In *Twelfth-Night* there is something singularly ridiculous and pleasant in the fantastical steward *Malvolio*. The parasite and the vain-glorious in *Parolles*, in *All's Well that ends Well*, is as good as any thing of that kind in *Plautus* or *Terence*. *Petruchio*, in *The Taming of the Shrew*, is an uncommon piece of humour. The conversation of *Benedick* and *Beatrice*, in *Much Ado about Nothing*, and of *Rosalind* in *As you like it*, have much wit and sprightliness all along. His clowns, without which character there was hardly any play writ in that time, are all very entertaining: And, I believe, *Thersites* in *Troilus* and *Cressida,* and *Apemantus* in *Timon,* will be allow'd to be master-pieces of ill nature and satyrical snarling. To these I might add that incomparable character of *Shylock* the *Jew* in *The Merchant of* Venice; but tho' we have seen that play receiv'd and acted as a Comedy, and the part of the *Jew* perform'd by an excellent Comedian, yet I cannot but think it was design'd tragically by the Author. There appears in it such a deadly spirit of revenge, such a savage fierceness and fellness, and such a bloody designation of cruelty and mischief, as cannot agree either with the stile of characters of Comedy. The Play it self, take it all together, seems to me to be one of the most finish'd of any of *Shakespear*'s. The tale indeed, in that part relating to the caskets, and the extravagant and unusual kind of bond given by *Antonio,* is a little too much remov'd from the rules of probability: But taking the fact for granted, we must allow it to be very beautifully written. There is something in the friendship of *Antonio* to *Bassanio* very great, generous, and tender. The whole fourth act, supposing, as I said, the fact to be probable, is extremely fine. But there are two passages that deserve a particular notice. The first is, what *Portia* says in praise of mercy, and the other on the power of musick. The melancholy of *Jaques,* in *As you like it,* is as singular and odd as it is diverting. And if what *Horace* says,

Difficile est proprie communia dicere,

'twill be a hard task for any one to go beyond him in the description of the several degrees and ages of man's life, tho' the thought be old, and common enough.

——All the World's a Stage,
And all the men and women meerly Players;
They have their Exits and their Entrances,
And one man in his time plays many Parts,
His Acts being seven Ages. At first the Infant
Mewling and puking in the nurse's arms:
And then, the whining School-boy with his satchel,
And shining morning-face, creeping like snail
Unwillingly to school. And then the Lover

Sighing like furnace, with a woful ballad
Made to his Mistress' eye-brow. Then a Soldier
Full of strange oaths, and bearded like the Pard,
Jealous in honour, sudden and quick in quarrel,
Seeking the bubble Reputation
Ev'n in the cannon's mouth. And then the Justice
In fair round belly, with good capon lin'd,
With eyes severe, and beard of formal cut,
Full of wise saws and modern instances;
And so he plays his part. The sixth Age shifts
Into the lean and slipper'd Pantaloon,
With spectacles on nose, and pouch on side;
His youthful hose, well sav'd, a world too wide
For his shrunk shank; and his big manly voice
Turning again tow'rd childish treble, pipes
And whistles in his found: Last Scene of all,
That ends this strange eventful History,
Is second childishness and meer oblivion,
Sans teeth, sans eyes, sans taste, sans ev'ry thing.

His Images are indeed ev'ry where so lively, that the
thing he would represent stands full before you, and you
possess ev'ry part of it. I will venture to point out one
more, which is, I think, as strong and as uncommon as any
thing I ever saw; 'tis an image of Patience. Speaking of a
maid in love, he says,

——She never told her love,
But let concealment, like a worm i'th' bud,
Feed on her damask cheek: She pin'd in thought,
And sate like *Patience* on a monument,
Smiling at *Grief*.

What an Image is here given! and what a task would it have
been for the greatest masters of *Greece* and *Rome* to have
express'd the passions design'd by this sketch of Statuary!
The stile of his Comedy is, in general, natural to the characters, and easie in it self; and the wit most commonly
sprightly and pleasing, except in those places where he runs
into dogrel rhymes, as in *The Comedy of Errors,* and a passage or two in some other plays. As for his jingling sometimes, and playing upon words, it was the common vice of

the age he liv'd in: And if we find it in the Pulpit, made use of as an ornament to the Sermons of some of the gravest Divines of those times; perhaps it may not be thought too light for the Stage.

But certainly the greatness of this Author's genius do's no where so much appear, as where he gives his imagination an entire loose, and raises his fancy to a flight above mankind and the limits of the visible world. Such are his attempts in *The Tempest, Midsummer Night's Dream, Macbeth,* and *Hamlet.* Of these, *The Tempest,* however it comes to be plac'd the first by the former publishers of his works, can never have been the first written by him: It seems to me as perfect in its kind, as almost any thing we have of his. One may observe, that the Unities are kept here, with an exactness uncommon to the liberties of his writing; tho' that was what, I suppose, he valu'd himself least upon, since his excellencies were all of another kind. I am very sensible that he do's, in this play, depart too much from that likeness to truth which ought to be observ'd in these sort of writings; yet he do's it so very finely, that one is easily drawn in to have more faith for his sake, than reason does well allow of. His Magick has something in it very solemn and very poetical: And that extravagant character of *Caliban* is mighty well sustain'd, shews a wonderful invention in the Author, who could strike out such a particular wild image, and is certainly one of the finest and most uncommon Grotesques that was ever seen. The observation, which I have been inform'd[1] three very great men concurr'd in making upon this part, was extremely just: *That* Shakespear *had not only found out a new Character in his* Caliban, *but had also devis'd and adapted a new manner of Language for that Character.* Among the particular beauties of this piece, I think one may be allow'd to point out the tale of *Prospero* in the first Act; his speech to *Ferdinand* in the fourth, upon the breaking up the masque of *Juno* and *Ceres*; and that in the fifth, when he dissolves his charms, and resolves to break his magick rod. This Play has been alter'd by Sir *William D'Avenant* and Mr. *Dryden*; and tho' I won't arraign the judgment of those two great men, yet I think I may be allow'd to say, that there are some things left out by them, that might, and even ought to have been kept in. Mr.

[1] Ld. Falkland, *Ld. C. J.* Vaughan, *and Mr.* Selden.

Dryden was an admirer of our Author, and, indeed, he owed him a great deal, as those who have read them both may very easily observe. And, I think, in justice to 'em both, I should not on this occasion omit what Mr. *Dryden* has said of him.

> *Shakespear*, who, taught by none, did first impart
> To *Fletcher* Wit, to lab'ring *Johnson* Art:
> He, monarch-like, gave those his subjects Law,
> And is that Nature which they paint and draw.
> *Fletcher* reach'd that which on his heights did grow,
> Whilst *Johnson* crept and gather'd all below:
> This did his Love, and this his Mirth digest,
> One imitates him most, the other best.
> If they have since out-writ all other men,
> 'Tis with the drops which fell from *Shakespear*'s pen.
> The[1] Storm which vanish'd on the neighb'ring shoar,
> Was taught by *Shakespear*'s Tempest first to roar.
> That innocence and beauty which did smile
> In *Fletcher*, grew on this *Enchanted Isle*.
> But *Shakespear*'s Magick could not copied be,
> Within that Circle none durst walk but he.
> I must confess 'twas bold, nor would you now
> That liberty to vulgar Wits allow,
> Which works by Magick supernatural things:
> But *Shakespear*'s Pow'r is Sacred as a King's.
>
> Prologue to *The Tempest*,
> as it is alter'd by Mr. *Dryden*.

It is the same magick that raises the Fairies in *Midsummer Night's Dream*, the Witches in *Macbeth*, and the Ghost in *Hamlet*, with thoughts and language so proper to the parts they sustain and so peculiar to the talent of this Writer. But of the two last of these Plays I shall have occasion to take notice, among the Tragedies of Mr. *Shakespear*. If one undertook to examine the greatest part of these by those rules which are establish'd by *Aristotle*, and taken from the model of the *Grecian* stage, it would be no very hard task to find a great many faults: But as *Shakespear* liv'd under a kind of mere light of nature, and had never been made acquainted with the regularity of

[1] Alluding to the Sea-Voyage of *Fletcher*.

those written precepts, so it would be hard to judge him by a law he knew nothing of. We are to consider him as a man that liv'd in a state of almost universal licence and ignorance: There was no establish'd judge, but every one took the liberty to write according to the dictates of his own fancy. When one considers that there is not one play before him of a reputation good enough to entitle it to an appearance on the present Stage, it cannot but be a matter of great wonder that he should advance dramatick Poetry so far as he did. The Fable is what is generally plac'd the first, among those that are reckon'd the constituent parts of a Tragick or Heroick Poem; not, perhaps, as it is the most difficult or beautiful, but as it is the first properly to be thought of in the contrivance and course of the whole; and with the Fable ought to be consider'd the fit Disposition, Order, and Conduct of its several parts. As it is not in this province of the *Drama* that the strength and mastery of *Shakespear* lay, so I shall not undertake the tedious and ill-natur'd trouble to point out the several faults he was guilty of in it. His Tales were seldom invented, but rather taken either from true History, or Novels and Romances: And he commonly made use of 'em in that order, with those incidents, and that extent of time in which he found 'em in the Authors from whence he borrow'd them. So *The Winter's Tale*, which is taken from an old book, call'd *The Delectable History of* Dorastus *and* Faunia, contains the space of sixteen or seventeen years, and the Scene is sometimes laid in *Bohemia*, and sometimes in *Sicily*, according to the original order of the Story. Almost all his historical Plays comprehend a great length of time, and very different and distinct places: And in his *Antony* and *Cleopatra*, the Scene travels over the greatest part of the *Roman* empire. But in recompence for his carelessness in this point, when he comes to another part of the *Drama, The Manners of his Characters, in acting or speaking what is proper for them, and fit to be shown by the Poet,* he may be generally justify'd, and in very many places greatly commended. For those Plays which he has taken from the *English* or *Roman* history, let any man compare 'em, and he will find the character as exact in the Poet as the Historian. He seems indeed so far from proposing to himself any one action for a Subject, that the Title very often tells you, 'tis *The Life of*

King John, *King* Richard, &c. What can be more agreeable to the idea our historians give of *Henry* the Sixth, than the picture *Shakespear* has drawn of him! His manners are every where exactly the same with the story; one finds him still describ'd with simplicity, passive sanctity, want of courage, weakness of mind, and easie submission to the governance of an imperious Wife, or prevailing Faction: Tho' at the same time the Poet do's justice to his good qualities, and moves the pity of his audience for him, by showing him pious, disinterested, a contemner of the things of this world, and wholly resign'd to the severest dispensations of God's providence. There is a short Scene in the second part of *Henry* VI., which I cannot but think admirable in its kind. Cardinal *Beaufort,* who had murder'd the Duke of *Gloucester,* is shewn in the last agonies on his death-bed, with the good King praying over him. There is so much terror in one, so much tenderness and moving piety in the other, as must touch any one who is capable either of fear or pity. In his *Henry* VIII. that Prince is drawn with that greatness of mind, and all those good qualities which are attributed to him in any account of his reign. If his faults are not shewn in an equal degree, and the shades in this picture do not bear a just proportion to the lights, it is not that the Artist wanted either colours or skill in the disposition of 'em; but the truth, I believe, might be, that he forbore doing it out of regard to Queen *Elizabeth,* since it could have been no very great respect to the memory of his Mistress, to have expos'd some certain parts of her father's life upon the stage. He has dealt much more freely with the Minister of that great King, and certainly nothing was ever more justly written, than the character of Cardinal *Wolsey.* He has shewn him tyrannical, cruel, and insolent in his prosperity; and yet, by a wonderful address, he makes his fall and ruin the subject of general compassion. The whole man, with his vices and virtues, is finely and exactly describ'd in the second Scene of the fourth Act. The distresses likewise of Queen *Katherine,* in this Play, are very movingly touch'd; and tho' the art of the Poet has skreen'd King *Henry* from any gross imputation of injustice, yet one is inclin'd to wish, the Queen had met with a fortune more worthy of her birth and virtue. Nor are the Manners, proper to the persons represented, less justly observ'd in those characters taken from the *Roman* History; and of this, the fierceness and impatience of *Coriolanus*, his courage and disdain of the common people, the virtue and philosophical temper of Brutus, and the irregular greatness of mind in *M. Antony*, are beautiful proofs. For the two last especially, you find 'em exactly as they are describ'd by *Plutarch*, from whom certainly *Shakespear* copy'd 'em. He has indeed follow'd his original pretty close, and taken in several little incidents that might have been spar'd in a Play. But, as I hinted before, his design seems most commonly rather to describe those great men in the several fortunes and accidents of their lives, than to take any single great action, and form his work simply upon that. However, there are some of his pieces, where the Fable is founded upon one action only. Such are more especially, *Romeo* and *Juliet, Hamlet,* and *Othello.* The design in *Romeo* and *Juliet* is plainly the punishment of their two families, for the unreasonable feuds and animosities that had been so long kept up between 'em, and occasion'd the effusion of so much blood. In the management of this story, he has shewn something wonderfully tender and passionate in the love-part, and very pitiful in the distress. *Hamlet* is founded on much the same Tale with the *Electra* of *Sophocles.* In each of 'em a young Prince is engag'd to revenge the death of his father, their mothers are equally guilty, are both concern'd in the murder of their husbands, and are afterwards married to the murderers. There is in the first part of the *Greek* Tragedy, something very moving in the grief of *Electra*; but as Mr. *D'Acier* has observ'd, there is something very unnatural and shocking in the Manners he has given that Princess and *Orestes* in the latter part. *Orestes* embrues his hands in the blood of his own mother; and that barbarous action is perform'd, tho' not immediately upon the stage, yet so near, that the audience hear *Clytemnestra* crying out to *Ægysthus* for help, and to her son for mercy: While *Electra,* her daughter, and a Princess, both of them characters that ought to have appear'd with more decency, stands upon the stage and encourages her brother in the parricide. What horror does this not raise! *Clytemnestra* was a wicked woman, and had deserv'd to die; nay, in the truth of the story, she was kill'd by her own son; but to represent an action of this kind on the stage, is certainly an offence against those rules of manners proper to the persons, that ought to be observ'd there. On the contrary, let us only look a little on the conduct of *Shakespear*. *Hamlet* is represented with the same piety towards his father, and resolution to revenge his death, as *Orestes*; he has the same abhorrence for his mother's guilt, which, to provoke him the more, is heighten'd by incest: But 'tis with wonderful art and justness of judgment, that the Poet restrains him from doing violence to his mother. To prevent any thing of that kind, he makes his father's Ghost forbid that part of his vengeance.

> But howsoever thou pursu'st this Act,
> Taint not thy mind; nor let thy soul contrive
> Against thy mother ought; leave her to Heav'n,
> And to those thorns that in her bosom lodge,
> To prick and sting her.

This is to distinguish rightly between *Horror* and *Terror*. The latter is a proper passion of Tragedy, but the former ought always to be carefully avoided. And certainly no dramatick Writer ever succeeded better in raising *Terror* in the minds of an audience than *Shakespear* has done. The whole Tragedy of *Macbeth,* but more especially the scene where the King is murder'd, in the second Act, as well as this Play, is a noble proof of that manly spirit with which he writ; and both shew how powerful he was, in giving the strongest motions to our souls that they are capable of. I cannot leave *Hamlet* without taking notice of the advantage with which we have seen this Master-piece of *Shakespear* distinguish it self upon the stage, by Mr. *Betterton*'s fine performance of that part: A man who, tho' he had no other good qualities, as he has a great many, must have made his way into the esteem of all men of letters, by this only excellency. No man is better acquainted with *Shakespear*'s manner of expression, and indeed he has study'd him so well, and is so much a master of him, that whatever part of his he performs, he does it as if it had been written on purpose for him, and that the Author had exactly conceiv'd it as he plays it. I must own a particular obligation to him, for the most considerable part of the passages relating to this life, which I have here transmitted to the publick; his veneration for the memory of *Shakespear* having engaged him to make a journey into *Warwickshire*, on purpose to gather up what remains he could of a name for which he had so great a value. Since I had at first resolv'd not to enter into any critical controversie, I won't pretend to enquire into the justness of Mr. *Rhymer*'s Remarks on *Othello*; he has certainly pointed out some faults very judiciously; and indeed they are such as most people will agree, with him, to be faults: But I wish he would likewise have observ'd some of the beauties too; as I think it became an exact and equal Critique to do. It seems strange that he should allow nothing good in the whole: If the Fable and Incidents are not to his taste, yet the Thoughts are almost every where very noble, and the Diction manly and proper. These last, indeed, are parts of *Shakespear*'s praise, which it would be very hard to dispute with him. His Sentiments and Images of things are great and natural; and his Expression (tho' perhaps in some instances a little irregular) just, and rais'd in proportion to his subject and occasion. It would be even endless to mention the particular instances that might be given of this kind: But his Book is in the possession of the publick, and 'twill be hard to dip into any part of it, without finding what I have said of him made good.

JOHN DENNIS

John Dennis (1657-1734). Learned theatrical critic and inveterate enemy of Pope.

THE GENIUS OF SHAKESPEARE*

Sir,

I here send you the Tragedy of *Coriolanus*, which I have alter'd from the Original of *Shakespear*, and with it a short

* Extracted from the first of a series of letters to an un-named correspondent; they were published in 1712 as *An Essay on the Genius and Writings of Shakespear*.

Account of the Genius and Writings of that Author, both which you desired me to send to you the last time I had the good Fortune to see you. But I send them both upon this condition, that you will with your usual Sincerity tell me your Sentiments both of the Poem and of the Criticism.

Shakespear was one of the greatest Genius's that the World e'er saw for the Tragick Stage. Tho' he lay under greater Disadvantages than any of his Successors, yet had he greater and more genuine Beauties than the best and greatest of them. And what makes the brightest Glory of his Character, those Beauties were entirely his own, and owing to the Force of his own Nature; whereas his Faults were owing to his Education, and to the Age that he liv'd in. One may say of him as they did of *Homer,* that he had none to imitate, and is himself inimitable. His Imaginations were often as just, as they were bold and strong. He had a natural Discretion which never cou'd have been taught him, and his Judgment was strong and penetrating. He seems to have wanted nothing but Time and Leisure for Thought, to have found out those Rules of which he appears so ignorant. His Characters are always drawn justly, exactly, graphically, except where he fail'd by not knowing History or the Poetical Art. He has for the most part more fairly distinguish'd them than any of his Successors have done, who have falsified them, or confounded them, by making Love the predominant Quality in all. He had so fine a Talent for touching the Passions, and they are so lively in him, and so truly in Nature, that they often touch us more without their due Preparations, than those of other Tragick Poets, who have all the Beauty of Design and all the Advantage of Incidents. His Master-Passion was Terror, which he has often mov'd so powerfully and so wonderfully, that we may justly conclude, that if he had had the Advantage of Art and Learning, he wou'd have surpass'd the very best and strongest of the Ancients. His Paintings are often so beautiful and so lively, so graceful and so powerful, especially where he uses them in order to move Terror, that there is nothing perhaps more accomplish'd in our *English* Poetry. His Sentiments for the most part in his best Tragedies, are noble, generous, easie, and natural, and adapted to the Persons who use them. His Expression is in many

Places good and pure after a hundred Years; simple tho'
elevated, graceful tho' bold, and easie tho' strong. He seems
to have been the very Original of our *English* Tragical
Harmony; that is the Harmony of Blank Verse, diversifyed
often by Dissyllable and Trissyllable Terminations. For
that Diversity distinguishes it from Heroick Harmony, and,
bringing it nearer to common Use, makes it more proper
to gain Attention, and more fit for Action and Dialogue.
Such Verse we make when we are writing Prose; we make
such Verse in common Conversation.

If *Shakespear* had these great Qualities by Nature, what
would he not have been, if he had join'd to so happy a
Genius Learning and the Poetical Art? For want of the
latter, our Author has sometimes made gross Mistakes in
the Characters which he has drawn from History, against
the Equality and Conveniency of Manners of his Dramat-
ical Persons. Witness *Menenius* in the following Tragedy,
whom he has made an errant Buffoon, which is a great
Absurdity. For he might as well have imagin'd a grave
majestick *Jack-Pudding*, as a Buffoon in a *Roman* Senator.
Aufidius the General of the *Volscians* is shewn a base
and a profligate Villain. He has offended against the Equality of the Manners even in his Hero himself. For *Coriolanus*
who in the first part of the Tragedy is shewn so open, so
frank, so violent, and so magnanimous, is represented in
the latter part by *Aufidius,* which is contradicted by no
one, a flattering, fawning, cringing, insinuating Traytor.

For want of this Poetical Art, *Shakespear* has introduced things into his Tragedies, which are against the
Dignity of that noble Poem, as the Rabble in *Julius Cæsar,*
and that in *Coriolanus;* tho' that in *Coriolanus* offends
not only against the Dignity of Tragedy, but against the Truth
of History likewise, and the Customs of Ancient *Rome,*
and the Majesty of the *Roman* People, as we shall have
occasion to shew anon.

For want of this Art, he has made his Incidents less
moving, less surprizing, and less wonderful. He has been
so far from seeking those fine Occasions to move with
which an Action furnish'd according to Art would have
furnish'd him, that he seems rather to have industriously
avoided them. He makes *Coriolanus,* upon his Sentence
of Banishment, take his leave of his Wife and his Mother

out of sight of the Audience, and so has purposely as it were avoided a great occasion to move.

If we are willing to allow that *Shakespear*, by sticking to the bare Events of History, has mov'd more than any of his Successors, yet his just Admirers must confess, that if he had had the Poetical Art, he would have mov'd ten times more. For 'tis impossible that by a bare Historical Play he could move so much as he would have done by a Fable.

We find that a Romance entertains the generality of Mankind with more Satisfaction than History, if they read only to be entertain'd; but if they read History thro' Pride or Ambition, they bring their Passions along with them, and that alters the case. Nothing is more plain than that even in an Historical Relation some Parts of it, and some Events, please more than others. And therefore a Man of Judgment, who sees why they do so, may in forming a Fable, and disposing an Action, please more than an Historian can do. For the just Fiction of a Fable moves us more than an Historical Relation can do, for the two following Reasons: First, by reason of the Communication and mutual Dependence of its Parts. For if Passion springs from Motion, then the Obstruction of that Motion or a counter Motion must obstruct and check the Passion: And therefore an Historian and a Writer of Historical Plays, passing from Events of one nature to Events of another nature without a due Preparation, must of necessity stifle and confound one Passion by another. The second Reason why the Fiction of a Fable pleases us more than an Historical Relation can do, is, because in an Historical Relation we seldom are acquainted with the true Causes of Events, whereas in a feign'd Action which is duly constituted, that is, which has a just beginning, those Causes always appear. For 'tis observable, that, both in a Poetical Fiction and an Historical Relation, those Events are the most entertaining, the most surprizing, and the most wonderful, in which Providence most plainly appears. And 'tis for this Reason that the Author of a just Fable must please more than the Writer of an Historical Relation. The Good must never fail to prosper, and the Bad must be always punish'd: Otherwise the Incidents, and particularly the Catastrophe which is the grand Incident, are liable to be imputed rather to Chance, than to Almighty Conduct and to Sovereign Justice. The want of this impartial Distribution of Justice makes the *Coriolanus* of *Shakespear* to be without Moral. . . .

Thus have we endeavour'd to shew that, for want of the Poetical Art, *Shakespear* lay under very great Disadvantages. At the same time we must own to his Honour, that he has often perform'd Wonders without it.

ALEXANDER POPE

Alexander Pope (1688-1744). Pope's edition of Shakespeare appeared in 1725; he found the Aristotelian rules of drama inapplicable to Shakespeare, and made some accepted emendations, but made much too free with the text, relegating passages of which he disapproved to the margin.

EXCELLENCIES AND DEFECTS OF SHAKESPEARE*

It is not my design to enter into a Criticism upon this Author; tho' to do it effectually and not superficially would be the best occasion that any just Writer could take, to form the judgment and taste of our nation. For of all *English* Poets *Shakespear* must be confessed to be the fairest and fullest subject for Criticism, and to afford the most numerous as well as most conspicuous instances, both of Beauties and Faults of all sorts. But this far exceeds the bounds of a Preface, the business of which is only to give an account of the fate of his Works, and the disadvantages under which they have been transmitted to us. We shall hereby extenuate many faults which are his, and clear him from the imputation of many which are not: A design, which, tho' it can be no guide to future Criticks to do him justice in one way, will at least be sufficient to prevent their doing him an injustice in the other.

* From the Preface to his Edition of Shakespeare (1725).

I cannot however but mention some of his principal and characteristic Excellencies, for which (notwithstanding his defects) he is justly and universally elevated above all other Dramatic Writers. Not that this is the proper place of praising him, but because I would not omit any occasion of doing it.

If ever any Author deserved the name of an *Original,* it was *Shakespear. Homer* himself drew not his art so immediately from the fountains of Nature; it proceeded thro' *Ægyptian* strainers and channels, and came to him not without some tincture of the learning, or some cast of the models, of those before him. The Poetry of *Shakespear* was Inspiration indeed: he is not so much an Imitator, as an Instrument, of Nature; and 'tis not so just to say that he speaks from her, as that she speaks thro' him.

His *Characters* are so much Nature her self, that 'tis a sort of injury to call them by so distant a name as Copies of her. Those of other Poets have a constant resemblance, which shews that they receiv'd them from one another, and were but multiplyers of the same image: each picture, like a mock-rainbow, is but the reflexion of a reflexion. But every single character in *Shakespear* is as much an Individual as those in Life itself; it is as impossible to find any two alike; and such as from their relation or affinity in any respect appear most to be Twins, will upon comparison be found remarkably distinct. To this life and variety of Character, we must add the wonderful Preservation of it; which is such throughout his plays, that had all the Speeches been printed without the very names of the Persons, I believe one might have apply'd them with certainty to every speaker.

The *Power* over our *Passions* was never possess'd in a more eminent degree, or display'd in so different instances. Yet all along, there is seen no labour, no pains to raise them; no preparation to guide our guess to the effect, or be perceiv'd to lead toward it: But the heart swells, and the tears burst out, just at the proper places: We are surpriz'd, the moment we weep; and yet upon reflection find the passion so just, that we shou'd be surpriz'd if we had not wept, and wept at that very moment.

How astonishing is it again, that the passions directly opposite to these, Laughter and Spleen, are no less at his command! that he is not more a master of the *Great,* than of the *Ridiculous* in human nature; of our noblest tendernesses, than of our vainest foibles; of our strongest emotions, than of our idlest sensations!

Nor does he only excel in the Passions: In the coolness of Reflection and Reasoning he is full as admirable. His *Sentiments* are not only in general the most pertinent and judicious upon every subject; but by a talent very peculiar, something between Penetration and Felicity, he hits upon that particular point on which the bent of each argument turns, or the force of each motive depends. This is perfectly amazing, from a man of no education or experience in those great and publick scenes of life which are usually the subject of his thoughts: So that he seems to have known the world by Intuition, to have look'd thro' humane nature at one glance, and to be the only Author that gives ground for a very new opinion, That the Philosopher, and even the Man of the world, may be *Born,* as well as the Poet.

It must be own'd that with all these great excellencies he has almost as great defects; and that as he has certainly written better, so he has perhaps written worse, than any other. But I think I can in some measure account for these defects, from several causes and accidents; without which it is hard to imagine that so large and so enlighten'd a mind could ever have been susceptible of them. That all these Contingencies should unite to his disadvantage seems to me almost as singularly unlucky, as that so many various (nay contrary) Talents should meet in one man, was happy and extraordinary.

It must be allowed that Stage-Poetry of all other is more particularly levell'd to please the *Populace,* and its success more immediately depending upon the *Common Suffrage.* One cannot therefore wonder, if *Shakespear,* having at his first appearance no other aim in his writings than to procure a subsistance, directed his endeavours solely to hit the taste and humour that then prevailed. The Audience was generally composed of the meaner sort of people; and therefore the Images of Life were to be drawn from those of their own rank: accordingly we find that not our Author's only but almost all the old Comedies have their Scene among *Tradesmen* and *Mechanicks*: And even their Historical Plays strictly follow the common *Old Stories* or *Vulgar Traditions* of that kind of people. In Tragedy, nothing was so sure to *Surprize* and cause *Admiration,* as the most strange, unexpected, and consequently most unnatural, Events and Incidents; the most exaggerated Thoughts; the most verbose and bombast Expression; the most pompous Rhymes, and thundering Versification. In Comedy, nothing was so sure to *please,* as mean buffoonry, vile ribaldry, and unmannerly jests of fools and clowns. Yet even in these our Author's Wit buoys up, and is borne above his subject: his Genius in those low parts is like some Prince of a Romance in the disguise of a Shepherd or Peasant; a certain Greatness and Spirit now and then break out, which manifest his higher extraction and qualities.

It may be added, that not only the common Audience had no notion of the rules of writing, but few even of the better sort piqu'd themselves upon any great degree of knowledge or nicety that way, till *Ben Johnson* getting possession of the Stage brought critical learning into vogue: And that this was not done without difficulty, may appear from those frequent lessons (and indeed almost Declamations) which he was forced to prefix to his first plays, and put into the mouth of his Actors, the *Grex, Chorus,* &c. to remove the prejudices, and inform the judgment of his hearers. Till then, our Authors had no thoughts of writing on the model of the Ancients: their Tragedies were only Histories in Dialogue; and their Comedies follow'd the thread of any Novel as they found it, no less implictly than if it had been true History.

To judge therefore of *Shakespear* by *Aristotle*'s rules, is like trying a man by the Laws of one Country, who acted under those of another. He writ to the *People*; and writ at first without patronage from the better sort, and therefore without aims of pleasing them: without assistance or advice from the Learned, as without the advantage of education or acquaintance among them: without that knowledge of the best models, the Ancients, to inspire him with an emulation of them; in a word, without any views of Reputation, and of what Poets are pleas'd to call Immortality: Some or all of which have encourag'd the vanity, or animated the ambition, of other writers.

Yet it must be observ'd, that when his performances had merited the protection of his Prince, and when the encouragement of the Court had succeeded to that of the Town, the works of his riper years are manifestly raised above those of his former. The Dates of his plays sufficiently evidence that his productions improved, in proportion to the respect he had for his auditors. And I make no doubt this observation will be found true in every instance, were but Editions extant from which we might learn the exact time when every piece was composed, and whether writ for the Town or the Court.

Another Cause (and no less strong than the former) may be deduced from our Author's being a *Player*, and forming himself first upon the judgments of that body of men whereof he was a member. They have ever had a Standard to themselves, upon other principles than those of *Aristotle*. As they live by the Majority, they know no rule but that of pleasing the present humour, and complying with the wit in fashion; a consideration which brings all their judgment to a short point. Players are just such judges of what is *right*, as Taylors are of what is *graceful*. And in this view it will be but fair to allow, that most of our Author's faults are less to be ascribed to his wrong judgment as a Poet, than to his right judgment as a Player.

By these men it was thought a praise to *Shakespear*, that he scarce ever *blotted a line*. This they industriously propagated, as appears from what we are told by *Ben Johnson* in his *Discoveries*, and from the preface of *Heminges* and *Condell* to the first folio Edition. But in reality (however it has prevailed) there never was a more groundless report, or to the contrary of which there are more undeniable evidences: As, the Comedy of the *Merry Wives* of *Windsor*, which he entirely new writ; the *History* of Henry *the 6th*, which was first published under the Title of the *Contention of* York *and* Lancaster; and that of Henry *the 5th*, extreamly improved; that of *Hamlet* enlarged to almost as much again as at first, and many others. I believe the common opinion of his want of Learning proceeded from no better ground. This too might be thought a Praise by some; and to this his Errors have as injudiciously been ascribed by others. For 'tis certain, were it true, it would concern but a small part of them; the most are such as are not properly Defects, but Superfœtations: and arise not from want of learning or reading, but from want of thinking or judging: or rather (to be more just to our Author) from a compliance to those wants in others. As to a wrong choice of the subject, a wrong conduct of the incidents, false thoughts, forc'd expressions, &c. if these are not to be ascrib'd to the foresaid accidental reasons, they must be charg'd upon the Poet himself, and there is no help for it. But I think the two Disadvantages which I have mentioned (to be obliged to please the lowest of the people, and to keep the worst of company), if the consideration be extended as far as it reasonably may, will appear sufficient to mis-lead and depress the greatest Genius upon earth. Nay the more modesty with which such a one is endued, the more he is in danger of submitting and conforming to others, against his own better judgment.

But as to his *Want of Learning*, it may be necessary to say something more: There is certainly a vast difference between *Learning* and *Languages*. How far he was ignorant of the latter, ı cannot determine; but 'tis plain he had much Reading at least, if they will not call it Learning. Nor is it any great matter, if a man has Knowledge, whether he has it from one language or from another. Nothing is more evident than that he had a taste of natural Philosophy, Mechanicks, ancient and modern History, Poetical learning, and Mythology: We find him very knowing in the customs, rites, and manners of Antiquity. In *Coriolanus* and *Julius Cæsar,* not only the Spirit, but Manners, of the *Romans* are exactly drawn; and still a nicer distinction is shewn, between the manners of the *Romans* in the time of the former and of the latter. His reading in the ancient Historians is no less conspicuous, in many references to particular passages: and the speeches copy'd from *Plutarch* in *Coriolanus* may, I think, as well be made an instance of his learning, as those copy'd from *Cicero* in *Catiline,* of *Ben Johnson*'s. The manners of other nations in general, the *Egyptians, Venetians, French,* &c., are drawn with equal propriety. Whatever object of nature, or branch of science, he either speaks of or describes, it is always with competent, if not extensive knowledge: his descriptions are still exact; all his metaphors appropriated, and remarkably drawn from the true nature and inherent qualities of each subject. When he treats of Ethic or Politic, we may constantly observe a wonderful justness of distinction, as well as extent of comprehension. No one is more a master of the Poetical story, or has more frequent allusions to the various parts of it: Mr. *Waller* (who has been celebrated for this last particular) has not shown more learning this way than *Shakespear.* We have Translations from *Ovid* published in his name, among those Poems which pass for his, and for some of which we have undoubted authority (being published by himself, and dedicated to his noble Patron the Earl of *Southampton*). He appears also to have been conversant in *Plautus,* from whom he has taken the plot of one of his plays: he follows the *Greek* Authors, and particularly *Dares Phrygius,* in another (altho' I will not pretend to say in what language he read them). The modern *Italian* writers of Novels he was manifestly acquainted with; and we may conclude him to be no less conversant with the Ancients of his own country, from the use he has made of *Chaucer* in *Troilus* and *Cressida,* and in the *Two Noble Kinsmen,* if that Play be his, as there goes a Tradition it was (and indeed it has little resemblance of *Fletcher,* and more of our Author than some of those which have been received as genuine).

I am inclined to think, this opinion proceeded originally from the zeal of the Partizans of our Author and *Ben Johnson*; as they endeavoured to exalt the one at the expence of the other. It is ever the nature of Parties to be in extremes; and nothing is so probable, as that because *Ben Johnson* had much the more learning, it was said on the one hand that *Shakespear* had none at all; and because *Shakespear* had much the most wit and fancy, it was retorted on the other, that *Johnson* wanted both. Because *Shakespear* borrowed nothing, it was said that *Ben Johnson* borrowed every thing. Because *Johnson* did not write extempore, he was reproached with being a year about every piece; and because *Shakespear* wrote with ease and rapidity, they cryed, he never once made a blot. Nay the spirit of opposition ran so high, that whatever those of the one side objected to the other, was taken at the rebound, and turned into Praises; as injudiciously as their antagonists before had made them Objections.

Poets are always afraid of Envy; but sure they have as much reason to be afraid of Admiration. They are the *Scylla* and *Charybdis* of Authors; those who escape one, often fall by the other. *Pessimum genus inimicorum Lau-*

dantes, says *Tacitus*: and *Virgil* desires to wear a charm against those who praise a Poet without rule or reason.

——Si ultra placitum laudarit, baccare frontem
Cingito, ne Vati noceat——.

But however this contention might be carried on by the Partizans on either side, I cannot help thinking these two great Poets were good friends, and lived on amicable terms and in offices of society with each other. It is an acknowledged fact, that *Ben Johnson* was introduced upon the Stage, and his first works encouraged, by *Shakespear.* And after his death, that Author writes *To the memory of his beloved Mr.* William Shakespear, which shows as if the friendship had continued thro' life. I cannot for my own part find any thing *Invidious* or *Sparing* in those verses, but wonder Mr. *Dryden* was of that opinion. He exalts him not only above all his Contemporaries, but above *Chaucer* and *Spenser,* whom he will not allow to be great enough to be rank'd with him; and challenges the names of *Sophocles, Euripides,* and *Æschylus,* nay all *Greece* and *Rome* at once, to equal him: And (which is very particular) expressly vindicates him from the imputation of wanting *Art,* not enduring that all his excellencies shou'd be attributed to *Nature.* It is remarkable too, that the praise he gives him in his *Discoveries* seems to proceed from a *personal kindness*; he tells us that he lov'd the man, as well as honoured his memory; celebrates the honesty, openness, and frankness of his temper; and only distinguishes, as he reasonably ought, between the real merit of the Author, and the silly and derogatory applauses of the Players. *Ben Johnson* might indeed be sparing in his Commendations (tho' certainly he is not so in this instance) partly from his own nature, and partly from judgment. For men of judgment think they do any man more service in praising him justly, than lavishly. I say, I would fain believe they were Friends, tho' the violence and ill-breeding of their Followers and Flatterers were enough to give rise to the contrary report. I would hope that it may be with *Parties,* both in Wit and State, as with those Monsters described by the Poets; and that their *Heads* at least may have something humane, tho' their *Bodies* and *Tails* are wild beasts and serpents.

As I believe that what I have mentioned gave rise to the opinion of *Shakespear*'s want of learning; so what has continued it down to us may have been the many blunders and illiteracies of the first Publishers of his works. In these Editions their ignorance shines almost in every page; nothing is more common than *Actus tertia, Exit Omnes, Enter three Witches solus*. Their *French* is as bad as their *Latin*, both in construction and spelling: Their very *Welsh* is false, Nothing is more likely than that those palpable blunders of *Hector*'s quoting *Aristotle*, with others of that gross kind, sprung from the same root: It not being at all credible that these could be the errors of any man who had the least tincture of a School, or the least conversation with such as had. *Ben Johnson* (whom they will not think partial to him) allows him at least to have had *some Latin*; which is utterly inconsistent with mistakes like these. Nay the constant blunders in proper names of persons and places, are such as must have proceeded from a man who had not so much as read any history, in any language: so could not be *Shakespear*'s.

FOR GAIN, NOT GLORY*

Shakespear, (whom you and ev'ry Play-house bill
Style the divine, the matchless, what you will)
For gain, not glory, wing'd his roving flight
And grew Immortal in his own despight.

VOLTAIRE

François Marie Arouet de Voltaire (1694-1778). His attacks on Shakespeare continued, though not without interludes of praise, from 1733 to 1776, during which time he received many indignant answers from English critics. His main objection was to Shakespeare's 'natural' or 'barbaric'

* *Epistle to Augustus* (1737) 11.69-72.

*ignorance of the rules and of decorum and his grossness
and laziness in stealing other people's plots. Mrs. Montagu's answer was characteristic, and more vigorous than
most; the usual defence was based on Voltaire's mistranslations, his slips in describing the plays, his ignorance of
Shakespeare's period, and his alleged immorality as man
and writer. Coleridge dismissed his criticism as 'vulgar
abuse'.*

SHAKESPEARE'S MONSTROUS FARCES*

The *English* as well as the *Spaniards* were possess'd of
Theatres, at a Time when the French had no more than
moving, itinerant Stages. *Shakespear,* who was consider'd
as the *Corneille* of the first mention'd Nation, was pretty
near Contemporary with *Lopez de Vega,* and he created, as
it were, the *English* Theatre. *Shakespear* boasted a strong,
fruitful Genius: He was natural and sublime, but had not
so much as a single Spark of good Taste, or knew one Rule
of the Drama. I will now hazard a random, but, at the same
Time, true Reflection, which is, that the great Merit of this
Dramatic Poet has been the Ruin of the *English* Stage.
There are such beautiful, such noble, such dreadful Scenes
in this Writer's monstrous Farces, to which the Name of
Tragedy is given, that they have always been exhibited with
great Success. Time, which only gives Reputation to Writers, at last makes their very Faults venerable. Most of the
whimsical, gigantic Images of this Poet, have, thro' Length
of Time (it being an hundred and fifty Years since they
were first drawn) acquir'd a Right of passing for sublime.
Most of the modern dramatic Writers have copied him;
but the Touches and Descriptions which are applauded in
Shakespear, are hiss'd at in these Writers; and you'll easily
believe that the Veneration in which this Author is held,
increases in Proportion to the Contempt which is shown to
the Moderns. Dramatic Writers don't consider that they
should not imitate him; and the ill Success of *Shakespear's*
Imitators, produces no other Effect, than to make him be
consider'd as inimitable. You remember that in the Tragedy
of OTHELLO *Moor of* Venice, (a most tender Piece) a Man

* From *Letters Concerning the English Nation.*

strangles his Wife on the Stage; and that the poor Woman, whilst she is strangling, cries aloud, that she dies very unjustly. You know that in HAMLET *Prince of* Denmark, two Grave-Diggers made a Grave, and are all the Time drinking, singing Ballads, and making humourous Reflexions, (natural indeed enough to Persons of their Profession) on the several Skulls they throw up with their Spades; but a Circumstance which will surprize you is, that this ridiculous Incident has been imitated. In the Reign of King *Charles* the Second, which was that of Politeness, and the Golden Age of the Liberal Arts; *Otway*, in his VENICE PRESERV'D, introduces *Antonio* the Senator, and *Naki* his Curtezan, in the Midst of the Horrors of the Marquis of *Bedemar's* Conspiracy. *Antonio*, the superannuated Senator plays, in his Mistress's Presence, all the apish Tricks of a lewd, impotent Debauchee who is quite frantic and out of his Senses. He mimicks a Bull and a Dog; and bites his Mistress's Leg, who kicks and whips him. However, the Players have struck these Buffooneries (which indeed were calculated merely for the Dregs of the People) out of *Otway's* Tragedy; but they have still left in *Shakespear's* JULIUS CÆSAR, the Jokes of the *Roman* Shoemakers and Coblers, who are introduc'd in the same Scene with *Brutus* and *Cassius*. . . .

SAMUEL JOHNSON

Samuel Johnson (1709-1784). Johnson published Proposals for a new edition of Shakespeare in 1745, but the publication of Warburton's edition in 1747 delayed the project, and he began work in 1756. Further interrupted by journalism, the editing was resumed in 1763, and the work, with the Preface, appeared in 1765.

SHAKESPEARE*

That praises are without reason lavished on the dead, and that the honours due only to excellence are paid to antiquity,

* From the Preface to his Edition of Shakespeare (1765).

is a complaint likely to be always continued by those, who, being able to add nothing to truth, hope for eminence from the heresies of paradox; or those, who, being forced by disappointment upon consolatory expedients, are willing to hope from posterity what the present age refuses, and flatter themselves that the regard which is yet denied by envy, will be at last bestowed by time.

Antiquity, like every other quality that attracts the notice of mankind, has undoubtedly votaries that reverence it, not from reason, but from prejudice. Some seem to admire indiscriminately whatever has been long preserved, without considering that time has sometimes co-operated with chance; all perhaps are more willing to honour past than present excellence; and the mind contemplates genius through the shades of age, as the eye surveys the sun through artificial opacity. The great contention of criticism is to find the faults of the moderns, and the beauties of the ancients. While an author is yet living, we estimate his powers by his worst performance; and when he is dead, we rate them by his best.

To works, however, of which the excellence is not absolute and definite, but gradual and comparative; to works not raised upon principles demonstrative and scientifick, but appealing wholly to observation and experience, no other test can be applied than length of duration and continuance of esteem. What mankind have long possessed they have often examined and compared, and if they persist to value the possession, it is because frequent comparisons have confirmed opinion in its favour. As among the works of nature no man can properly call a river deep, or a mountain high, without the knowledge of many mountains, and many rivers; so in the production of genius, nothing can be stiled excellent till it has been compared with other works of the same kind. Demonstration immediately displays its power, and has nothing to hope or fear from the flux of years; but works tentative and experimental must be estimated by their proportion to the general and collective ability of man, as it is discovered in a long succession of endeavours. Of the first building that was raised, it might be with certainty determined that it was round or square; but whether it was spacious or lofty must have been referred to time. The Pythagorean scale of numbers was at once discovered to be perfect; but the poems of Homer we yet know not to transcend the common limits of human intelligence, but by remarking that nation after nation, and century after century, has been able to do little more than transpose his incidents, new name his characters, and paraphrase his sentiments.

The reverence due to writings that have long subsisted arises therefore not from any credulous confidence in the superior wisdom of past ages, or gloomy persuasion of the degeneracy of mankind, but is the consequence of acknowledged and indubitable positions, that what has been longest known has been most considered, and what is most considered is best understood.

The poet, of whose works I have undertaken the revision, may now begin to assume the dignity of an ancient, and claim the privilege of an established fame and prescriptive veneration. He has long outlived his century, the term commonly fixed as the test of literary merit. Whatever advantages he might once derive from personal allusions, local customs, or temporary opinions, have for many years been lost; and every topick of merriment or motive of sorrow, which the modes of artificial life afforded him, now only obscure the scenes which they once illuminated. The effects of favour and competition are at an end; the tradition of his friendships and his enmities has perished; his works support no opinion with arguments, nor supply any faction with invectives; they can neither indulge vanity, nor gratify malignity; but are read without any other reason than the desire of pleasure, and are therefore praised only as pleasure is obtained; yet, thus unassisted by interest or passion, they have past through variations of taste and changes of manners, and, as they devolved from one generation to another, have received new honours at every transmission.

But because human judgment, though it be gradually gaining upon certainty, never becomes infallible; and approbation, though long continued, may yet be only the approbation of prejudice or fashion; it is proper to inquire, by what peculiarities of excellence Shakespeare has gained and kept the favour of his countrymen.

Nothing can please many, and please long, but just representations of general nature. Particular manners can be known to few, and therefore few only can judge how nearly they are copied. The irregular combinations of fanciful invention may delight awhile, by that novelty of which the common satiety of life sends us all in quest; but the pleasures of sudden wonder are soon exhausted, and the mind can only repose on the stability of truth.

Shakespeare is above all writers, at least above all modern writers, the poet of nature; the poet that holds up to his readers a faithful mirror of manners and of life. His characters are not modified by the customs of particular places, unpractised by the rest of the world; by the peculiarities of studies or professions, which can operate but upon small numbers; or by the accidents of transient fashions or temporary opinions: they are the genuine progeny of common humanity, such as the world will always supply, and observation will always find. His persons act and speak by the influence of those general passions and principles by which all minds are agitated, and the whole system of life is continued in motion. In the writings of other poets a character is too often an individual; in those of Shakespeare it is commonly a species. — _Speech_

It is from this wide extension of design that so much instruction is derived. It is this which fills the plays of Shakespeare with practical axioms and domestick wisdom. It was said of Euripides, that every verse was a precept; and it may be said of Shakespeare, that from his works may be collected a system of civil and œconomical prudence. Yet his real power is not shewn in the splendor of particular passages, but by the progress of his fable, and the tenor of his dialogue; and he that tries to recommend him by select quotations, will succeed like the pedant in Hierocles, who, when he offered his house to sale, carried a brick in his pocket as a specimen.

It will not easily be imagined how much Shakespeare excels in accommodating his sentiments to real life, but by comparing him with other authors. It was observed of the ancient schools of declamation, that the more diligently they were frequented, the more was the student disqualified for the world, because he found nothing there which he should ever meet in any other place. The same remark may be applied to every stage but that of Shakespeare. The theatre, when it is under any other direction, is peopled by such characters as were never seen, conversing in a language which was never heard, upon topicks which will never arise in the commerce of mankind. But the dialogue of this author is often so evidently determined by the incident which produces it, and is pursued with so much ease and simplicity, that it seems scarcely to claim the merit of fiction, but to have been gleaned by diligent selection out of common conversation, and common occurrences.

Upon every other stage the universal agent is love, by whose power all good and evil is distributed, and every action quickened or retarded. To bring a lover, a lady, and a rival into the fable; to entangle them in contradictory obligations, perplex them with oppositions of interest, and harrass them with violence of desires inconsistent with each other; to make them meet in rapture, and part in agony; to fill their mouths with hyperbolical joy and outrageous sorrow; to distress them as nothing human ever was distressed; to deliver them as nothing human ever was delivered, is the business of a modern dramatist. For this, probability is violated, life is misrepresented, and language is depraved. But love is only one of many passions, and as it has no great influence upon the sum of life, it has little operation in the dramas of a poet who caught his ideas from the living world, and exhibited only what he saw before him. He knew that any other passion, as it was regular or exorbitant, was a cause of happiness or calamity.

Characters thus ample and general were not easily discriminated and preserved, yet perhaps no poet ever kept his personages more distinct from each other. I will not say with Pope, that every speech may be assigned to the proper speaker, because many speeches there are which have nothing characteristical; but, perhaps, though some may be equally adapted to every person, it will be difficult to find any that can be properly transferred from the present possessor to another claimant. The choice is right, when there is reason for choice.

Other dramatists can only gain attention by hyperbolical or aggravated characters, by fabulous and unexampled excellence or depravity, as the writers of barbarous romances invigorated the reader by a giant and a dwarf; and he that should form his expectation of human affairs from the play, or from the tale, would be equally deceived. Shakespeare has no heroes; his scenes are occupied only by men, who act and speak as the reader thinks that he should himself have spoken or acted on the same occasion: even where the agency is super-natural, the dialogue is level with life. Other writers disguise the most natural passions and most frequent incidents; so that he who contemplates them in the book will not know them in the world: Shakespeare approximates the remote, and familiarizes the wonderful; the event which he represents will not happen, but if it were possible, its effects would probably be such as he has assigned; and it may be said that he has not only shewn human nature as it acts in real exigences, but as it would be found in trials to which it cannot be exposed.

This therefore is the praise of Shakespeare, that his drama is the mirror of life; that he who has mazed his imagination, in following the phantoms which other writers raise up before him, may here be cured of his delirious ecstasies, by reading human sentiments in human language; by scenes from which a hermit may estimate the transactions of the world, and a confessor predict the progress of the passions.

His adherence to general nature has exposed him to the censure of criticks, who form their judgments upon narrower principles. Dennis and Rhymer think his Romans not sufficiently Roman; and Voltaire censures his kings as not completely royal. Dennis is offended that Menenius, a senator of Rome, should play the buffoon; and Voltaire perhaps thinks decency violated when the Danish usurper is represented as a drunkard. But Shakespeare always makes nature predominate over accident; and if he preserves the essential character, is not very careful of distinctions superinduced and adventitious. His story requires Romans or kings, but he thinks only on men. He knew that Rome, like every other city, had men of all dispositions; and wanting a buffoon, he went into the senate-house for that which the senate-house would certainly have afforded him. He was inclined to shew an usurper and a murderer not only odious, but despicable; he therefore added drunkenness to his other qualities, knowing that kings love wine like other men, and that wine exerts its natural power upon kings. These are the petty cavils of petty minds; a poet overlooks the casual distinction of country and condition, as a painter, satisfied with the figure, neglects the drapery.

The censure which he has incurred by mixing comick

and tragick scenes, as it extends to all his works, deserves more consideration. Let the fact be first stated, and then examined.

Shakespeare's plays are not in the rigorous and critical sense either tragedies or comedies, but compositions of a distinct kind; exhibiting the real state of sublunary nature, which partakes of good and evil, joy and sorrow, mingled with endless variety of proportion and innumerable modes of combination; and expressing the course of the world, in which the loss of one is the gain of another; in which, at the same time, the reveller is hasting to his wine, and the mourner burying his friend; in which the malignity of one is sometimes defeated by the frolick of another; and many mischiefs and many benefits are done and hindered without design.

Out of this chaos of mingled purposes and casualties, the ancient poets, according to the laws which custom had prescribed, selected some the crimes of men, and some their absurdities; some the momentous vicissitudes of life, and some the lighter occurrences; some the terrors of distress, and some the gaieties of prosperity. Thus rose the two modes of imitation, known by the names of *tragedy* and *comedy*, compositions intended to promote different ends by contrary means, and considered as so little allied, that I do not recollect among the Greeks or Romans a single writer who attempted both.

Shakespeare has united the powers of exciting laughter and sorrow not only in one mind, but in one composition. Almost all his plays are divided between serious and ludicrous characters, and, in the successive evolutions of the design, sometimes produce seriousness and sorrow, and sometimes levity and laughter.

That this is a practice contrary to the rules of criticism will be readily allowed; but there is always an appeal open from criticism to nature. The end of writing is to instruct; the end of poetry is to instruct by pleasing. That the mingled drama may convey all the instruction of tragedy or comedy cannot be denied, because it includes both in its alternations of exhibition, and approaches nearer than either to the appearance of life, by shewing how great machinations and slender designs may promote or obviate one another, and the high and the low co-operate in the general system by unavoidable concatenation.

It is objected that by this change of scenes the passions are interrupted in their progression, and that the principal event, being not advanced by a due gradation of preparatory incidents, wants at last the power to move, which constitutes the perfection of dramatick poetry. This reasoning is so specious, that it is received as true even by those who in daily experience feel it to be false. The interchanges of mingled scenes seldom fail to produce the intended vicissitudes of passion. Fiction cannot move so much, but that the attention may be easily transferred; and though it must be allowed that pleasing melancholy be sometimes interrupted by unwelcome levity, yet let it be considered likewise, that melancholy is often not pleasing, and that the disturbance of one man may be the relief of another; that different auditors have different habitudes; and that, upon the whole, all pleasure consists in variety.

The players, who in their edition divided our author's works into comedies, histories, and tragedies, seem not to have distinguished the three kinds, by any very exact or definite ideas.

An action which ended happily to the principal persons, however serious or distressful through its intermediate incidents, in their opinion constituted a comedy. This idea of a comedy continued long amongst us, and plays were written, which, by changing the catastrophe, were tragedies to-day, and comedies to-morrow.

Tragedy was not in those times a poem of more general dignity or elevation than comedy; it required only a calamitous conclusion, with which the common criticism of that age was satisfied, whatever lighter pleasure it afforded in its progress.

History was a series of actions, with no other than chronological succession, independent on each other, and without any tendency to introduce and regulate the conclusion. It is not always very nicely distinguished from tragedy. There is not much nearer approach to unity of action in the tragedy of *Antony and Cleopatra,* than in the history of *Richard the Second.* But a history might be continued through many plays; as it had no plan, it had no limits.

Through all these denominations of the drama, Shakespeare's mode of composition is the same; an interchange of seriousness and merriment, by which the mind is softened at one time, and exhilarated at another. But whatever be his purpose, whether to gladden or depress, or to conduct the story, without vehemence or emotion, through tracts of easy and familiar dialogue, he never fails to attain his purpose; as he commands us, we laugh or mourn, or sit silent with quiet expectation, in tranquillity without indifference.

When Shakespeare's plan is understood, most of the criticisms of Rhymer and Voltaire vanish away. The play of *Hamlet* is opened, without impropriety, by two centinels; Iago bellows at Brabantio's window, without injury to the scheme of the play, though in terms which a modern audience would not easily endure; the character of Polonius is seasonable and useful, and the Grave-diggers themselves may be heard with applause.

Shakespeare engaged in dramatick poetry with the world open before him; the rules of the ancients were yet known to few; the publick judgment was unformed; he had no example of such fame as might force him upon imitation, nor criticks of such authority as might restrain his extravagance: he therefore indulged his natural disposition, and his disposition, as Rhymer has remarked, led him to comedy. In tragedy he often writes with great appearance of toil and study, what is written at last with little felicity; but in his comick scenes, he seems to produce without labour, what no labour can improve. In tragedy he is always struggling after some occasion to be comick, but in comedy he seems to repose, or to luxuriate, as in a mode of thinking congenial to his nature. In his tragick scenes there is always something wanting, but his comedy often surpasses expectation or desire. His comedy pleases by the thoughts and the language, and his tragedy for the greater part by incident and action. His tragedy seems to be skill, his comedy to be instinct.

The force of his comick scenes has suffered little diminution from the changes made by a century and a half, in manners or in words. As his personages act upon principles arising from genuine passion, very little modified by particular forms, their pleasures and vexations are communicable to all times and to all places; they are natural, and therefore durable; the adventitious peculiarities of personal habits are only superficial dies, bright and pleasing for a little while, yet soon fading to a dim tinct, without any remains of former lustre; but the discriminations of true passion are the colours of nature; they pervade the whole mass, and can only perish with the body that exhibits them. The accidental compositions of heterogeneous modes are dissolved by the chance which combined them; but the uniform simplicity of primitive qualities neither admits increase, nor suffers decay. The sand heaped by one flood is scattered by another, but the rock always continues in its place. The stream of time, which is continually washing the dissoluble fabricks of other poets, passes without injury by the adamant of Shakespeare.

If there be, what I believe there is, in every nation, a stile which never becomes obsolete, a certain mode of phraseology so consonant and congenial to the analogy and principles of its respective language, as to remain settled and unaltered; this stile is probably to be sought in the common intercourse of life, among those who speak only to be understood, without ambition of elegance. The polite are always catching modish innovations, and the learned depart from established forms of speech, in hope of finding or making better; those who wish for distinction forsake the vulgar, when the vulgar is right; but there is a conversation above grossness and below refinement, where propriety resides, and where this poet seems to have gathered his comick dialogue. He is therefore more agreeable to the ears of the present age than any other author equally remote, and among his other excellencies deserves to be studied as one of the original masters of our language.

These observations are to be considered not as unexceptionably constant, but as containing general and predominant truth. Shakespeare's familiar dialogue is affirmed to be smooth and clear, yet not wholly without ruggedness or difficulty; as a country may be eminently fruitful, though it has spots unfit for cultivation: his characters are praised as natural, though their sentiments are sometimes forced, and their actions improbable; as the earth upon the whole is spherical, though its surface is varied with protuberances and cavities.

Shakespeare with his excellencies has likewise faults, and faults sufficient to obscure and overwhelm any other merit.

faults

I shall shew them in the proportion in which they appear to me, without envious malignity or superstitious veneration. No question can be more innocently discussed than a dead poet's pretensions to renown; and little regard is due to that bigotry which sets candour higher than truth.

His first defect is that to which may be imputed most of the evil in books or in men. He sacrifices virtue to convenience, and is so much more careful to please than to instruct, that he seems to write without any moral purpose. From his writings indeed a system of social duty may be selected, for he that thinks reasonably must think morally; but his precepts and axioms drop casually from him; he makes no just distribution of good or evil, nor is always careful to shew in the virtuous a disapprobation of the wicked; he carries his persons indifferently through right and wrong, and at the close dismisses them without further care, and leaves their examples to operate by chance. This fault the barbarity of his age cannot extenuate; for it is always a writer's duty to make the world better, and justice is a virtue independent on time or place.

The plots are often so loosely formed, that a very slight consideration may improve them, and so carelessly pursued, that he seems not always fully to comprehend his own design. He omits opportunities of instructing or delighting, which the train of his story seems to force upon him, and apparently rejects those exhibitions which would be more affecting, for the sake of those which are more easy.

It may be observed that in many of his plays the latter part is evidently neglected. When he found himself near the end of his work, and in view of his reward, he shortened the labour to snatch the profit. He therefore remits his efforts where he should most vigorously exert them, and his catastrophe is improbably produced or imperfectly represented.

He had no regard to distinction of time or place, but gives to one age or nation, without scruple, the customs, institutions, and opinions of another, at the expence not only of likelihood, but of possibility. These faults Pope has endeavoured, with more zeal than judgment, to transfer to his imagined interpolators. We need not wonder to find Hector quoting Aristotle, when we see the loves of Theseus and Hippolyta combined with the Gothick mythology of fairies.

see earlier: praises him for being general

Shakespeare, indeed, was not the only violator of chronology, for in the same age Sidney, who wanted not the advantages of learning, has, in his *Arcadia*, confounded the pastoral with the feudal times, the days of innocence, quiet, and security, with those of turbulence, violence, and adventure.

In his comick scenes he is seldom very successful, when he engages his characters in reciprocations of smartness and contests of sarcasm; their jests are commonly gross, and their pleasantry licentious; neither his gentlemen nor his ladies have much delicacy, nor are sufficiently distinguished from his clowns by any appearance of refined manners. Whether he represented the real conversation of his time is not easy to determine; the reign of Elizabeth is commonly supposed to have been a time of stateliness, formality, and reserve, yet perhaps the relaxations of that severity were not very elegant. There must, however, have been always some modes of gaiety preferable to others, and a writer ought to chuse the best.

In tragedy his performance seems constantly to be worse, as his labour is more. The effusions of passion, which exigence forces out, are for the most part striking and energetick; but whenever he solicits his invention, or strains his faculties, the offspring of his throes is tumour, meanness, tediousness, and obscurity.

In narration he affects a disproportionate pomp of diction and a wearisome train of circumlocution, and tells the incident imperfectly in many words, which might have been more plainly delivered in few. Narration in dramatick poetry is naturally tedious, as it is unanimated and inactive, and obstructs the progress of the action; it should therefore always be rapid, and enlivened by frequent interruption. Shakespeare found it an encumbrance, and instead of lightening it by brevity, endeavoured to recommend it by dignity and splendour.

His declamations or set speeches are commonly cold and weak, for his power was the power of nature; when he endeavoured, like other tragick writers, to catch opportunities of amplification, and instead of inquiring what the occasion demanded, to shew how much his stores of knowledge could supply, he seldom escapes without the pity or resentment of his reader.

(intense: seing it as means of characterization)

again external view

It is incident to him to be now and then entangled with an unwieldy sentiment, which he cannot well express, and will not reject; he struggles with it a while, and if it continues stubborn, comprises it in words such as occur, and leaves it to be disentangled and evolved by those who have more leisure to bestow upon it.

Not that always where the language is intricate the thought is subtle, or the image always great where the line is bulky; the equality of words to things is very often neglected, and trivial sentiments and vulgar ideas disappoint the attention, to which they are recommended by sonorous epithets and swelling figures.

But the admirers of this great poet have most reason to complain when he approaches nearest to his highest excellence, and seems fully resolved to sink them in dejection, and mollify them with tender emotions by the fall of greatness, the danger of innocence, or the crosses of love. What he does best, he soon ceases to do. He is not long soft and pathetick without some idle conceit, or contemptible equivocation. He no sooner begins to move, than he counteracts himself; and terror and pity, as they are rising in the mind, are checked and blasted by sudden frigidity.

A quibble is to Shakespeare what luminous vapours are to the traveller: he follows it at all adventures; it is sure to lead him out of his way, and sure to engulf him in the mire. It has some malignant power over his mind, and its fascinations are irresistible. Whatever be the dignity or profundity of his disquisition, whether he be enlarging knowledge or exalting affection, whether he be amusing attention with incidents, or enchaining it in suspense, let but a quibble spring up before him, and he leaves his work unfinished. A quibble is the golden apple for which he will always turn aside from his career, or stoop from his elevation. A quibble, poor and barren as it is, gave him such delight, that he was content to purchase it by the sacrifice of reason, propriety, and truth. A quibble was to him the fatal Cleopatra for which he lost the world, and was content to lose it.

It will be thought strange, that, in enumerating the defects of this writer, I have not yet mentioned his neglect of the unities; his violation of those laws which have been instituted and established by the joint authority of poets and of criticks.

For his other deviations from the art of writing, I resign him to critical justice, without making any other demand in his favour, than that which must be indulged to all human excellence; that his virtues be rated with his failings: but, from the censure which this irregularity may bring upon him, I shall, with due reverence to that learning which I must oppose, adventure to try how I can defend him.

His histories, being neither tragedies nor comedies, are not subject to any of their laws; nothing more is necessary to all the praise which they expect, than that the changes of action be so prepared as to be understood, that the incidents be various and affecting, and the characters consistent, natural, and distinct. No other unity is intended, and therefore none is to be sought.

In his other works he has well enough preserved the unity of action. He has not, indeed, an intrigue regularly perplexed and regularly unravelled; he does not endeavour to hide his design only to discover it, for this is seldom the order of real events, and Shakespeare is the poet of nature: but his plan has commonly what Aristotle requires, a beginning, a middle, and an end; one event is concatenated with another, and the conclusion follows by easy consequence. There are perhaps some incidents that might be spared, as in other poets there is much talk that only fills up time upon the stage; but the general system makes gradual advances, and the end of the play is the end of expectation.

To the unities of time and place he has shewn no regard; and perhaps a nearer view of the principles on which they stand will diminish their value, and withdraw from them the veneration which, from the time of Corneille, they have very generally received, by discovering that they have given more trouble to the poet, than pleasure to the auditor.

The necessity of observing the unities of time and place arises from the supposed necessity of making the drama credible. The criticks hold it impossible that an action of months or years can be possibly believed to pass in three hours; or that the spectator can suppose himself to sit in the theatre, while ambassadors go and return between distant kings, while armies are levied and towns besieged, while an exile wanders and returns, or till he whom they saw courting his mistress, shall lament the untimely fall of his son. The mind revolts from evident falsehood, and fiction loses its force when it departs from the resemblance of reality.

From the narrow limitation of time necessarily arises the contraction of place. The spectator, who knows that he saw the first act at Alexandria, cannot suppose that he sees the next at Rome, at a distance to which not the dragons of Medea could, in so short a time, have transported him; he knows with certainty that he has not changed his place; and he knows that place cannot change itself; that what was a house cannot become a plain; that what was Thebes can never be Persepolis.

Such is the triumphant language with which a critick exults over the misery of an irregular poet, and exults commonly without resistance or reply. It is time therefore to tell him, by the authority of Shakespeare, that he assumes, as an unquestionable principle, a position, which, while his breath is forming it into words, his understanding pronounces to be false. It is false that any representation is mistaken for reality; that any dramatick fable in its materiality was ever credible, or, for a single moment, was ever credited.

The objection arising from the impossibility of passing the first hour at Alexandria, and the next at Rome, supposes that when the play opens the spectator really imagines himself at Alexandria, and believes that his walk to the theatre has been a voyage to Egypt, and that he lives in the days of Antony and Cleopatra. Surely he that imagines this may imagine more. He that can take the stage at one time for the palace of the Ptolemies, may take it in half an hour for the promontory of Actium. Delusion, if delusion be admitted, has no certain limitation; if the spectator can be once persuaded that his old acquaintance are Alexander and Cæsar, that a room illuminated with candles is the plain of Pharsalia, or the bank of Granicus, he is in a state of elevation above the reach of reason, or of truth, and from the heights of empyrean poetry may despise the circumscriptions of terrestrial nature. There is no reason why a mind thus wandering in ecstasy should count the clock, or why an hour should not be a century in that calenture of the brains that can make the stage a field.

The truth is that the spectators are always in their senses, and know, from the first act to the last, that the stage is only a stage, and that the players are only players. They come to hear a certain number of lines recited with just gesture and elegant modulation. The lines relate to some action, and an action must be in some place; but the different actions that complete a story may be in places very remote from each other; and where is the absurdity of allowing that space to represent first Athens, and then Sicily, which was always known to be neither Sicily nor Athens, but a modern theatre.

By supposition, as place is introduced, time may be extended; the time required by the fable elapses for the most part between the acts; for, of so much of the action as is represented, the real and poetical duration is the same. If, in the first act, preparations for war against Mithridates are represented to be made in Rome, the event of the war may, without absurdity, be represented, in the catastrophe, as happening in Pontus; we know that there is neither war, nor preparation for war; we know that we are neither in Rome nor Pontus; that neither Mithridates nor Lucullus are before us. That drama exhibits successive imitations of successive actions, and why may not the second imitation represent an action that happened years after the first; if it be so connected with it, that nothing but time can be supposed to intervene. Time is, of all modes of existence, most obsequious to the imagination; a lapse of years is as easily conceived as a passage of hours. In contemplation we easily contract the time of real actions, and therefore willingly permit it to be contracted when we only see their imitation.

It will be asked how the drama moves, if it is not credited. It is credited with all the credit due to a drama. It is credited, whenever it moves, as a just picture of a real original; as representing to the auditor what he would himself feel, if he were to do or suffer what is there feigned to be suffered or to be done. The reflection that strikes the heart is not that the evils before us are real evils, but that they are evils to which we ourselves may be exposed. If there be any fallacy, it is not that we fancy the players, but that we fancy ourselves unhappy for a moment; but we rather lament the possibility than suppose the presence of misery, as a mother weeps over her babe, when she remembers that death may take it from her. The delight of tragedy proceeds from our consciousness of fiction; if we thought murders and treasons real, they would please no more.

Imitations produce pain or pleasure, not because they are mistaken for realities, but because they bring realities to mind. When the imagination is recreated by a painted landscape, the trees are not supposed capable to give us shade, or the fountains coolness; but we consider how we should be pleased with such fountains playing beside us, and such woods waving over us. We are agitated in reading the history of *Henry the Fifth,* yet no man takes his book for the field of Agincourt. A dramatick exhibition is a book recited with concomitants that increase or diminish its effect. Familiar comedy is often more powerful in the theatre, than on the page; imperial tragedy is always less. The humour of Petruchio may be heightened by grimace; but what voice or what gesture can hope to add dignity or force to the soliloquy of Cato?

A play read affects the mind like a play acted. It is therefore evident that the action is not supposed to be real; and it follows that between the acts a longer or shorter time may be allowed to pass, and that no more account of space or duration is to be taken by the auditor of a drama, than by the reader of a narrative, before whom may pass in an hour the life of a hero, or the revolutions of an empire.

Whether Shakespeare knew the unities, and rejected them by design, or deviated from them by happy ignorance, it is, I think, impossible to decide, and useless to enquire. We may reasonably suppose that, when he rose to notice, he did not want the counsels and admonitions of scholars and critiks, and that he at last deliberately persisted in a practice, which he might have begun by chance. As nothing is essential to the fable but unity of action, and as the unities of time and place arise evidently from false assumptions, and, by circumscribing the extent of the drama, lessen its variety, I cannot think it much to be lamented that they were not known by him, or not observed: nor, if such another poet could arise, should I very vehemently reproach him, that his first act passed at Venice, and his next in Cyprus. Such violations of rules merely positive become the comprehensive genius of Shakespeare, and such cen-

sures are suitable to the minute and slender criticism of
Voltaire:

> Non usque adeo permiscuit imis
> Longus summa dies, ut non, si voce Metelli
> Serventur leges, malint a Cæsare tolli.

Yet when I speak thus slightly of dramatick rules, I cannot but recollect how much wit and learning may be produced against me; before such authorities I am afraid to
stand, not that I think the present question one of those that
are to be decided by mere authority, but because it is to be
suspected that these precepts have not been so easily
received but for better reasons than I have yet been able to
find. The result of my enquiries, in which it would be
ludicrous to boast of impartiality, is that the unities of time
and place are not essential to a just drama, that though they
may sometimes conduce to pleasure, they are always to be
sacrificed to the nobler beauties of variety and instruction;
and that a play, written with nice observation of critical
rules, is to be contemplated as an elaborate curiosity, as the
product of superfluous and ostentatious art, by which is
shewn, rather what is possible, than what is necessary.

He that, without diminution of any other excellence, shall
preserve all the unities unbroken, deserves the like applause
with the architect who shall display all the orders of architecture in a citadel, without any deduction from its strength;
but the principal beauty of a citadel is to exclude the
enemy; and the greatest graces of a play are to copy nature,
and instruct life.

Perhaps what I have here not dogmatically but deliberately written, may recall the principles of the drama to a
new examination. I am almost frighted at my own temerity;
and when I estimate the fame and the strength of those that
maintain the contrary opinion, am ready to sink down in
reverential silence; as Æneas withdrew from the defence of
Troy, when he saw Neptune shaking the wall, and Juno
heading the besiegers.

Those whom my arguments cannot persuade to give their
approbation to the judgment of Shakespeare, will easily,
if they consider the condition of his life, make some allowance for his ignorance.

Every man's performance, to be rightly estimated, must be compared with the state of the age in which he lived, and with his own particular opportunities; and though to a reader a book be not worse or better for the circumstances of the author, yet as there is always a silent reference of human works to human abilities, and as the enquiry, how far man may extend his designs, or how high he may rate his native force, is of far greater dignity than in what rank we shall place any particular performance, curiosity is always busy to discover the instruments, as well as to survey the workmanship, to know how much is to be ascribed to original powers, and how much to casual and adventitious help. The palaces of Peru or Mexico were certainly mean and incommodious habitations, if compared to the houses of European monarchs; yet who could forbear to view them with astonishment, who remembered that they were built without the use of iron?

The English nation, in the time of Shakespeare, was yet struggling to emerge from barbarity. The philology of Italy had been transplanted hither in the reign of Henry the Eighth; and the learned languages had been successfully cultivated by Lilly, Linacre, and More; by Pole, Cheke, and Gardiner; and afterwards by Smith, Clerk, Haddon, and Ascham. Greek was now taught to boys in the principal schools; and those who united elegance with learning, read, with great diligence, the Italian and Spanish poets. But literature was yet confined to professed scholars, or to men and women of high rank. The publick was gross and dark; and to be able to read and write, was an accomplishment still valued for its rarity.

Nations, like individuals, have their infancy. A people newly awakened to literary curiosity, being yet unacquainted with the true state of things, knows not how to judge of that which is proposed as its resemblance. Whatever is remote from common appearances is always welcome to vulgar, as to childish credulity; and of a country unenlightened by learning, the whole people is the vulgar. The study of those who then aspired to plebeian learning was then laid out upon adventures, giants, dragons, and enchantments. *The Death of Arthur* was the favourite volume.

The mind which has feasted on the luxurious wonders

of fiction, has no taste of the insipidity of truth. A play which imitated only the common occurrences of the world, would, upon the admirers of *Palmerin* and *Guy of Warwick*, have made little impression; he that wrote for such an audience was under the necessity of looking round for strange events and fabulous transactions, and that incredibility, by which maturer knowledge is offended, was the chief recommendation of writings, to unskilful curiosity.

Our author's plots are generally borrowed from novels; and it is reasonable to suppose that he chose the most popular, such as were read by many, and related by more; for his audience could not have followed him through the intricacies of the drama, had they not held the thread of the story in their hands.

The stories which we now find only in remoter authors, were in his time accessible and familiar. The fable of *As you like it,* which is supposed to be copied from Chaucer's *Gamelyn,* was a little pamphlet of those times; and old Mr. Cibber remembered the tale of *Hamlet* in plain English prose, which the cricks have now to seek in *Saxo Grammaticus.*

His English histories he took from English chronicles and English ballads; and as the ancient writers were made known to his countrymen by versions, they supplied him with new subjects; he dilated some of Plutarch's lives into plays, when they had been translated by North.

His plots, whether historical or fabulous, are always crowded with incidents, by which the attention of a rude people was more easily caught than by sentiment or argumentation; and such is the power of the marvellous, even over those who despise it, that every man finds his mind more strongly seized by the tragedies of Shakespeare than of any other writer; others please us by particular speeches, but he always makes us anxious for the event, and has perhaps excelled all but Homer in securing the first purpose of a writer, by exciting restless and unquenchable curiosity, and compelling him that reads his work to read it through.

The shows and bustle with which his plays abound have the same original. As knowledge advances, pleasure passes from the eye to the ear, but returns, as it declines, from the ear to the eye. Those to whom our author's labours were exhibited had more skill in pomps or processions than in poetical language, and perhaps wanted some visible and discriminated events, as comments on the dialogue. He knew how he should most please; and whether his practice is more agreeable to nature, or whether his example has prejudiced the nation, we still find that on our stage something must be done as well as said, and inactive declamation is very coldly heard, however musical or elegant, passionate or sublime.

Voltaire expresses his wonder, that our author's extravagancies are endured by a nation which has seen the tragedy of *Cato*. Let him be answered, that Addison speaks the language of poets, and Shakespeare, of men. We find in *Cato* innumerable beauties which enamour us of its author, but we see nothing that acquaints us with human sentiments or human actions; we place it with the fairest and the noblest progeny which judgment propagates by conjunction with learning; but *Othello* is the vigorous and vivacious offspring of observation impregnated by genius. *Cato* affords a splendid exhibition of artificial and fictitious manners, and delivers just and noble sentiments, in diction easy, elevated, and harmonious, but its hopes and fears communicate no vibration to the heart; the composition refers us only to the writer; we pronounce the name of *Cato*, but we think on *Addison*.

The work of a correct and regular writer is a garden accurately formed and diligently planted, varied with shades, and scented with flowers; the composition of Shakespeare is a forest, in which oaks extend their branches, and pines tower in the air, interspersed sometimes with weeds and brambles, and sometimes giving shelter to myrtles and to roses; filling the eye with awful pomp, and gratifying the mind with endless diversity. Other poets display cabinets of precious rarities, minutely finished, wrought into shape, and polished into brightness. Shakespeare opens a mine which contains gold and diamonds in unexhaustible plenty, though clouded by incrustations, debased by impurities, and mingled with a mass of meaner minerals.

It has been much disputed, whether Shakespeare owed his excellence to his own native force, or whether he had the common helps of scholastick education, the precepts of critical science, and the examples of ancient authors.

There has always prevailed a tradition, that Shakespeare

wanted learning, that he had no regular education, nor much skill in the dead languages. Jonson, his friend, affirms that *he had small Latin, and less Greek;* who, besides that he had no imaginable temptation to falsehood, wrote at a time when the character and acquisitions of Shakespeare were known to multitudes. His evidence ought therefore to decide the controversy, unless some testimony of equal force could be opposed.

Some have imagined that they have discovered deep learning in many imitations of old writers; but the examples which I have known urged, were drawn from books translated in his time; or were such easy coincidences of thought, as will happen to all who consider the same subjects; or such remarks on life or axioms of morality as float in conversation, and are transmitted through the world in proverbial sentences.

I have found it remarked that, in this important sentence, *Go before, I'll follow,* we read a translation of, *I prae, sequar.* I have been told that when Caliban, after a pleasing dream, says, *I cry'd to sleep again,* the author imitates Anacreon, who had, like every other man, the same wish on the same occasion.

There are a few passages which may pass for imitations, but so few, that the exception only confirms the rule; he obtained them from accidental quotations, or by oral communication, and as he used what he had, would have used more if he had obtained it.

The *Comedy of Errors* is confessedly taken from the *Menæchmi* of Plautus; from the only play of Plautus which was then in English. What can be more probable, than that he who copied that, would have copied more, but that those which were not translated were inaccessible?

Whether he knew the modern languages is uncertain. That his plays have some French scenes proves but little; he might easily procure them to be written, and probably, even though he had known the language in the common degree, he could not have written it without assistance. In the story of *Romeo and Juliet* he is observed to have followed the English translation, where it deviates from the Italian; but this on the other part proves nothing against his knowledge of the original. He was to copy, not what he knew himself, but what was known to his audience.

It is most likely that he had learned Latin sufficiently to make him acquainted with construction, but that he never advanced to an easy perusal of the Roman authors. Concerning his skill in modern languages, I can find no sufficient ground of determination; but as no imitations of French or Italian authors have been discovered, though the Italian poetry was then in high esteem, I am inclined to believe that he read little more than English, and chose for his fables only such tales as he found translated.

That much knowledge is scattered over his works is very justly observed by Pope, but it is often such knowledge as books did not supply. He that will understand Shakespeare, must not be content to study him in the closet, he must look for his meaning sometimes among the sports of the field, and sometimes among the manufactures of the shop.

There is however proof enough that he was a very diligent reader, nor was our language then so indigent of books, but that he might very liberally indulge his curiosity without excursion into foreign literature. Many of the Roman authors were translated, and some of the Greek; the Reformation had filled the kingdom with theological learning; most of the topicks of human disquisition had found English writers; and poetry had been cultivated, not only with diligence, but success. This was a stock of knowledge sufficient for a mind so capable of appropriating and improving it.

But the greater part of his excellence was the product of his own genius. He found the English stage in a state of the utmost rudeness; no essays either in tragedy or comedy had appeared, from which it could be discovered to what degree of delight either one or other might be carried. Neither character nor dialogue were yet understood. Shakespeare may be truly said to have introduced them both amongst us, and in some of his happier scenes to have carried them both to the utmost height.

By what gradations of improvement he proceeded, is not easily known; for the chronology of his works is yet unsettled. Rowe is of opinion that *perhaps we are not to look for his beginning, like those of other writers, in his least perfect works; art had so little, and nature so large a share in what he did, that for ought I know,* says he, *the performances of his youth, as they were the most vigor-*

ous, were the best. But the power of nature is only the power of using to any certain purpose the materials which diligence procures, or opportunity supplies. Nature gives no man knowledge, and when images are collected by study and experience, can only assist in combining or applying them. Shakespeare, however favoured by nature, could impart only what he had learned; and as he must increase his ideas, like other mortals, by gradual acquisition, he, like them, grew wiser as he grew older, could display life better, as he knew it more, and instruct with more efficacy, as he was himself more amply instructed.

There is a vigilance of observation and accuracy of distinction which books and precepts cannot confer; from this almost all original and native excellence proceeds. Shakespeare must have looked upon mankind with perspicacity, in the highest degree curious and attentive. Other writers borrow their characters from preceding writers, and diversify them only by the accidental appendages of present manners; the dress is a little varied, but the body is the same. Our author had both matter and form to provide; for, except the characters of Chaucer, to whom I think he is not much indebted, there were no writers in English, and perhaps not many in other modern languages, which shewed life in its native colours.

The contest about the original benevolence or malignity of man had not yet commenced. Speculation had not yet attempted to analyse the mind, to trace the passions to their sources, to unfold the seminal principles of vice and virtue, or sound the depths of the heart for the motives of action. All those enquiries, which from that time that human nature became the fashionable study have been made sometimes with nice discernment, but often with idle subtilty, were yet unattempted. The tales with which the infancy of learning was satisfied, exhibited only the superficial appearances of action, related the events, but omitted the causes, and were formed for such as delighted in wonders rather than in truth. Mankind was not then to be studied in the closet; he that would know the world, was under the necessity of gleaning his own remarks, by mingling as he could in its business and amusements.

Boyle congratulated himself upon his high birth, because it favoured his curiosity, by facilitating his access. Shake-

speare had no such advantage; he came to London a needy
adventurer, and lived for a time by very mean employments. Many works of genius and learning have been performed in states of life that appear very little favourable to
thought or to enquiry; so many, that he who considers them
is inclined to think that he sees enterprize and perseverance
predominating over all external agency, and bidding help
and hindrance vanish before them. The genius of Shakespeare was not to be depressed by the weight of poverty,
nor limited by the narrow conversation to which men in
want are inevitably condemned; the incumbrances of his
fortune were shaken from his mind, *as dew-drops from a
lion's mane.*

Though he had so many difficulties to encounter, and so
little assistance to surmount them, he has been able to obtain
an exact knowledge of many modes of life, and many casts
of native dispositions; to vary them with great multiplicity;
to mark them by nice distinctions; and to shew them in full
view by proper combinations. In this part of his performances he had none to imitate, but has himself been imitated
by all succeeding writers; and it may be doubted, whether
from all his successors more maxims of theoretical knowledge, or more rules of practical prudence, can be collected,
than he alone has given to his country.

Nor was his attention confined to the actions of men;
he was an exact surveyor of the inanimate world; his
descriptions have always some peculiarities, gathered by
contemplating things as they really exist. It may be observed
that the oldest poets of many nations preserve their reputation, and that the following generations of wit, after a
short celebrity, sink into oblivion. The first, whoever they
be, must take their sentiments and descriptions immediately
from knowledge; the resemblance is therefore just, their
descriptions are verified by every eye, and their sentiments
acknowledged by every breast. Those whom their fame invites to the same studies, copy partly them, and partly
nature, till the books of one age gain such authority, as to
stand in the place of nature to another, and imitation, always deviating a little, becomes at last capricious and
casual. Shakespeare, whether life or nature be his subject,
shews plainly that he has seen with his own eyes; he gives
the image which he receives, not weakened or distorted by

the intervention of any other mind; the ignorant feel his representations to be just, and the learned see that they are complete.

Perhaps it would not be easy to find any author, except Homer, who invented so much as Shakespeare, who so much advanced the studies which he cultivated, or effused so much novelty upon his age or country. The form, the characters, the language, and the shows of the English drama are his. *He seems*, says Dennis, *to have been the very original of our English tragical harmony, that is, the harmony of blank verse, diversified often by dissyllable and trissyllable terminations. For the diversity distinguishes it from heroick harmony, and by bringing it nearer to common use makes it more proper to gain attention, and more fit for action and dialogue. Such verse we make when we are writing prose; we make such verse in common conversation.*

I know not whether this praise is rigorously just. The dissyllable termination, which the critick rightly appropriates to the drama, is to be found, though, I think, not in *Gorboduc*, which is confessedly before our author, yet in *Hieronymo*, of which the date is not certain, but which there is reason to believe at least as old as his earliest plays. This however is certain, that he is the first who taught either tragedy or comedy to please, there being no theatrical piece of any older writer, of which the name is known, except to antiquaries and collectors of books, which are sought because they are scarce, and would not have been scarce, had they been much esteemed.

To him we must ascribe the praise, unless Spenser may divide it with him, of having first discovered to how much smoothness and harmony the English language could be softened. He has speeches, perhaps sometimes scenes, which have all the delicacy of Rowe, without his effeminacy. He endeavours indeed commonly to strike by the force and vigour of his dialogue, but he never executes his purpose better, than when he tries to sooth by softness.

Yet it must be at last confessed that as we owe every thing to him, he owes something to us; that, if much of his praise is paid by perception and judgment, much is likewise given by custom and veneration. We fix our eyes upon his graces, and turn them from his deformities, and endure in him what we should in another loath or despise. If we endured without praising, respect for the father of our drama might excuse us; but I have seen, in the book of some modern critick, a collection of anomalies which shew that he has corrupted language by every mode of depravation, but which his admirer has accumulated as a monument of honour.

He has scenes of undoubted and perpetual excellence, but perhaps not one play, which, if it were now exhibited as the work of a contemporary writer, would be heard to the conclusion. I am indeed far from thinking that his works were wrought to his own ideas of perfection; when they were such as would satisfy the audience, they satisfied the writer. It is seldom that authors, though more studious of fame than Shakespeare, rise much above the standard of their own age; to add a little to what is best will always be sufficient for present praise, and those who find themselves exalted into fame, are willing to credit their encomiasts, and to spare the labour of contending with themselves. . . .

RICHARD FARMER

Richard Farmer (1735-1797). His An Essay on the Learning of Shakespeare *was Farmer's only book, but it gave the topic a new dimension and remains a classic of Shakespearian scholarship.*

SHAKESPEARE'S LEARNING*

"Shakespeare," says a Brother of the *Craft*, "is a vast garden of criticism": and certainly no one can be favoured with more weeders *gratis*.

But how often, my dear Sir, are weeds and flowers torn up indiscriminately?—the ravaged spot is re-planted in a

* From *An Essay on the Learning of Shakespeare* (1767).

moment, and a profusion of critical thorns thrown over it for security.

"A prudent man, therefore, would not venture his fingers amongst them."

Be, however, in little pain for your friend, who regards himself sufficiently to be cautious:—yet he asserts with confidence, that no improvement can be expected, whilst the natural soil is mistaken for a hot-bed, and the Natives of the banks of *Avon* are scientifically choked with the culture of exoticks.

Thus much for metaphor; it is contrary to the *Statute* to fly out so early: but who can tell, whether it may not be demonstrated by some critick or other, that a deviation from the rule is peculiarly happy in an Essay on Shakespeare!

You have long known my opinion concerning the literary acquisitions of our immortal Dramatist; and remember how I congratulated myself on my coincidence with the last and best of his Editors. I told you, however, that his *small Latin and less Greek* would still be litigated, and you see very assuredly that I was not mistaken. The trumpet hath been sounded against "the darling project of representing Shakespeare as one of the illiterate vulgar"; and indeed to so good purpose, that I would by all means recommend the performer to the army of the *braying Faction,* recorded by Cervantes. The testimony of his contemporaries is again disputed; constant tradition is opposed by flimsy arguments; and nothing is heard but confusion and nonsense. One could scarcely imagine this a topick very likely to inflame the passions: it is asserted by Dryden, that "those who accuse him to have wanted learning, give him the greatest commendation"; yet an attack upon an article of faith hath been usually received with more temper and complacence, than the unfortunate opinion which I am about to defend.

But let us previously lament, with every lover of Shakespeare, that the Question was not fully discussed by Mr. Johnson himself: what he sees intuitively, others must arrive at by a series of proofs; and I have not time to *teach* with precision: be contented therefore with a few cursory observations, as they may happen to arise from the Chaos of Papers you have so often laughed at, "a stock sufficient to set up an *Editor in form.*" I am convinced of the strength of my cause, and superior to any little advantage from sophistical arrangements.

General positions without proofs will probably have no great weight on either side, yet it may not seem fair to suppress them: take them therefore as their authors occur to me, and we will afterward proceed to particulars.

The testimony of Ben. stands foremost; and some have held it sufficient to decide the controversy: in the warmest Panegyrick that ever was written, he apologizes for what *he* supposed the only defect in his "beloved friend,—

——Soul of the age!
Th' applause! delight! the wonder of our stage!—

whose memory he honoured almost to idolatry": and conscious of the worth of ancient literature, like any other man on the same occasion, he rather carries his acquirements *above* than *below* the truth. "Jealousy!" cries Mr. Upton; "People will allow others any qualities, but those upon which they highly value *themselves*." Yes, where there *is* a competition, and the competitor formidable: but, I think, this Critick himself hath scarcely set in opposition the learning of Shakespeare and Jonson. When a superiority is universally granted, it by no means appears a man's literary interest to depress the reputation of his Antagonist.

In truth the received opinion of the pride and malignity of Jonson, at least in the earlier part of life, is absolutely groundless: at this time scarce a play or a poem appeared without Ben's encomium, from the original Shakespeare to the translator of Du Bartas.

But Jonson is by no means our only authority. Drayton, the countryman and acquaintance of Shakespeare, determines his excellence to the *naturall Braine* only. Digges, a wit of the town before our Poet left the stage, is very strong to the purpose,

——Nature only helpt him, for looke thorow
This whole book, thou shalt find he doth not borow
One phrase from Greekes, nor Latines imitate,
Nor once from vulgar languages translate.

Suckling opposes his *easier strain* to the *sweat of learned*

Jonson. Denham assures us that all he had was from *old Mother-wit. His native wood-notes wild,* every one remembers to be celebrated by Milton. Dryden observes prettily enough, that "he wanted not the spectacles of books to read Nature." He came out of her hand, as some one else expresses it, like Pallas out of Jove's head, at full growth and mature.

The ever memorable Hales of Eton (who, notwithstanding his Epithet, is, I fear, almost forgotten) had too great a knowledge both of Shakespeare and the Ancients to allow much acquaintance between them: and urged very justly on the part of Genius in opposition to Pedantry, That "if he had not *read* the Classicks, he had likewise not *stolen* from them; and if any Topick was produced from a Poet of antiquity, he would undertake to shew somewhat on the same subject, at least as well written by Shakespeare."

Fuller, a diligent and equal searcher after truth and quibbles, declares positively that "his learning was very little,—*Nature* was all the *Art* used upon him, as *he himself,* if alive, would confess." And may we not say he did confess it, when he apologized for his *untutored lines* to his noble patron the Earl of Southampton?—this list of witnesses might be easily enlarged; but I flatter myself, I shall stand in no need of such evidence.

One of the first and most vehement assertors of the learning of Shakespeare was the Editor of his Poems, the well-known Mr. Gildon; and his steps were most punctually taken by a subsequent labourer in the same department, Dr. Sewel.

Mr. Pope supposed "little ground for the common opinion of his want of learning": once indeed he made a proper distinction between *learning* and *languages,* as I would be understood to do in my Title-page; but unfortunately he forgot it in the course of his disquisition, and endeavoured to persuade himself that Shakespeare's acquaintance with the Ancients might be actually proved by the same medium as Jonson's.

Mr. Theobald is "very unwilling to allow him so poor a scholar as many have laboured to represent him"; and yet is "cautious of declaring too positively on the other side of the question."

Dr. Warburton hath exposed the weakness of some arguments from *suspected* imitations; and yet offers others, which, I doubt not, he could as easily have refuted.

Mr. Upton wonders "with what kind of reasoning any one could be so far imposed upon, as to imagine that Shakespeare had no learning"; and lashes with much zeal and satisfaction "the pride and pertness of dunces, who, under such a name, would gladly shelter their own idleness and ignorance."

He, like the learned Knight, at every anomaly in grammar or metre,

> Hath hard words ready to shew why,
> And tell what *Rule* he did it by.

How would the old Bard have been astonished to have found that he had very skilfully given the *trochaic dimeter brachycatalectic*, COMMONLY called the *ithyphallic* measure, to the Witches in *Macbeth!* and that now and then a halting Verse afforded a most beautiful instance of the *Pes proceleusmaticus!*

"But," continues Mr. Upton, "it was a learned age; Roger Ascham assures us that Queen Elizabeth read more Greek every day, than some *Dignitaries* of the Church did Latin in a whole week." This appears very probable; and a pleasant proof it is of the general learning of the times, and of Shakespeare in particular. I wonder he did not corroborate it with an extract from her injunctions to her Clergy, that "such as were but *mean Readers* should peruse over before, once or twice, the Chapters and Homilies, to the intent they might read to the better understanding of the people."

Dr. Grey declares that Shakespeare's knowledge in the Greek and Latin tongues cannot *reasonably* be called in question. Dr. Dodd supposes it *proved*, that he was not such a novice in learning and antiquity as *some people* would pretend. And to close the whole, for I suspect you to be tired of quotation, Mr. Whalley, the ingenious Editor of Jonson, hath written a piece expressly on this side the question: perhaps from a very excusable partiality, he was willing to draw Shakespeare from the field of Nature to classick ground, where alone, he knew, his Author could possibly cope with him.

These criticks, and many others their coadjutors, have supposed themselves able to trace Shakespeare in the writings of the Ancients; and have sometimes persuaded us of their own learning, whatever became of their Author's. Plagiarisms have been discovered in every natural description and every moral sentiment. Indeed by the kind assistance of the various *Excerpta, Sententiæ,* and *Flores,* this business may be effected with very little expense of time or sagacity; as Addison hath demonstrated in his Comment on *Chevy-chase,* and Wagstaff on *Tom Thumb*; and I myself will engage to give you quotations from the elder *English* writers (for, to own the truth, I was once idle enough to collect such) which shall carry with them at least an equal degree of similarity. But there can be no occasion of wasting any future time in this department: the world is now in possession of the *Marks of Imitation.*

"Shakespeare, however, hath frequent allusions to the *facts* and *fables* of antiquity." Granted:—and, as Mat. Prior says, to save the effusion of more Christian ink, I will endeavour to shew how they came to his acquaintance. . . .

ELIZABETH MONTAGU

Elizabeth Montagu (1720-1800). Leader of the "blue-stockings', a learned lady famous as a hostess, letter-writer, and essayist.

MRS. ELIZABETH MONTAGU AGAINST VOLTAIRE*

Shakefpear's felicity has been rendered compleat in this age. His genius produced works that time could not deftroy: but fome of the lighter characters were become illegible; thefe have been reftored by critics whofe learning and penetration traced back the veftiges of fuperannuated

* From *An Essay on the Writings and Genius of Shakespeare* (London 1769).

opinions and cuftoms. They are now no longer in danger of being effaced, and the teftimonies of thefe learned commentators to his merit, will guard our author's great monument of human wit from the prefumptuous invafions of our rafh critics, and the fquibs of our witlings; fo that the bays will flourifh unwithered and inviolate round his tomb; and his very fpirit feems to come forth and to animate his characters, as often as Mr. Garrick, who acts with the fame infpiration with which he wrote, affumes them on the ftage.

After our poet had received fuch important fervices from the united efforts of talents and learning in his behalf, fome apology feems neceffary for this work. Let it be remembered that the moft fuperb and lafting monument that ever was confecrated to beauty, was that to which every lover carried a tribute. I dare hope to do him honour only by augmenting the heap of volumes given by his admirers to his memory; I will own I was incited to this undertaking by great admiration of his genius, and ftill greater indignation at the treatment he had received from a French wit, who feems to think he has made prodigious conceffions to our prejudices in favour of the works of our countryman in allowing them the credit of a few fplendid paffages, while he fpeaks of every entire piece as a monftrous and ill-conftructed farce.—Ridiculoufly has our poet, and ridiculoufly has our tafte been reprefented, by a writer of univerfal fame; and through the medium of an almoft univerfal language. Superficial criticifms hit the level of fhallow minds, to whom a bon mot will ever appear reafon, and an epigrammatic turn argument; fo that many of our countrymen have haftily adopted this lively writer's opinion of the extravagance and total want of defign in Shakefpear's dramas. With the more learned, deep, and fober critics he lies under one confiderable difadvantage. For copying nature as he found it in the bufy walks of human life, he drew from an original, with which the literati are feldom well acquainted. They perceive his portraits are not of the Grecian or of the Roman fchool: after finding them unlike to the celebrated forms preferved in learned mufeums they do not deign to enquire whether they refemble the living perfons they were intended to reprefent.

Among thefse connoiffeurs, whofe acquaintance with the characters of men is formed in the library, not in the ftreet, the camp, or village, whatever is unpolifhed and uncouth paffes for fantaftic and abfurd, though, in fact, it is faithful reprefentation of a really exifting character.

But it muft be acknowledged, that, when this objection is obviated there will yet remain another caufe of cenfure; for though our author, from want of delicacy or from a defire to pleafe the popular tafte, thought he had done well when he faithfully copied nature, or reprefented cuftoms, it will appear to politer times the error of an untutored mind; which the example of judicious artifts, and the admonitions of delicate connoiffeurs had not taught, that only graceful nature and decent cuftoms give proper fubjects for imitation. It may be faid in mitigation of his fault that the vulgar here had not, as at Athens, been ufed to behold,

> Gorgeous tragedy
> In fcepter'd pall come fweeping by,
> Prefenting Thebes or Pelops' line,
> Or the tale of Troy divine.

Homer's works alone were fufficient to teach the Greek poets how to write, and their audience how to judge. The fongs fung by our bards at feafts and merry-makings were of a very coarfe kind: as the people were totally illiterate, and only the better fort could read even their mother tongue, their tafte was formed on thefe compofitions. As yet our ftage had exhibited only thofe palpable allegories by which rude unlettered moralifts inftruct and pleafe the grofs and ignorant multitude. Nothing can more plainly evince the opinion the poets of thofe times had of the ignorance of the people, than the condefcenfion fhewn to it by the learned Earl of Dorfet in his tragedy of Gorboduc; in which the moral of each act is reprefented on the ftage in dumb fhew. It is ftrange that Mr. de Voltaire who affects an impartial and philofophic fpirit, fhould not rather fpeak with admiration than contempt of an author, who by the force of genius rofe fo much above the age and circumftances in which he was born, and who, even when he deviates moſt from rules, *can riſe to faults true critics dare not mend*. In delineating characters he muſt be allowed far to furpaſs all dramatic writers, and even Homer himſelf; he gives an air of reality to every thing, and, in fpite of many and great faults, effects, better than any one has done, the chief purpoſes of the theatrical reprefentation. It avails little to prove that the means by which he effects them are not thoſe preſcribed in any art of poetry. While we feel the power and energy of his predominant genius, fhall we not be apt to treat the cold formal precepts of the critic, with the fame peeviſh contempt that the good lady in the Guardian, fmarting in the anguiſh of a burn, does her fon's pedantic intruſion of Mr. Lock's doctrine, to prove that there is no heat in fire. Nature and fentiment will pronounce our Shakefpear a mighty genius; judgment and tafte will confeſs that as a writer he is far from being faultlefs.

A. W. SCHLEGEL

A. W. Schlegel (1765-1845). Poet, critic, orientalist and translator of Shakespeare and Calderón. His lectures on art and literature were given in Vienna in 1808.

Our Shakespeare*

The admiration with which Shakespeare regarded Spenser, and the care with which he imitated him in his lyrical and idyllic poems, are circumstances of themselves sufficient to make us study, with the liveliest interest, the poem of the Fairy Queen. It is in these minor pieces of Shakespeare that we are first introduced to a personal knowledge of the great poet and his feelings. When he wrote sonnets, it seems as if he had considered himself as more a poet than when he wrote plays; he was the

* From the *History of Literature*.

manager of a theatre, and he viewed the drama as his business; on it he exerted all his intellect and power, but when he had feelings intense and secret to express, he had recourse to a form of writing with which his habits had rendered him less familiar. It is strange but delightful to scrutinize, in his short effusions, the character of Shakespeare. In them we see that he who stood like a magician above the world, penetrating with one glance into all the depths, and mysteries, and perplexities of human character, and having power to call up into open day the darkest workings of the human passions—that this great being was not deprived of any portion of his human sympathies, by the elevation to which he was raised, but preserved, amidst all his stern functions, a heart overflowing with tenderness, purity, and love. His feelings are intense, profound, acute almost to selfishness, but he expresses them so briefly and modestly, as to form a strange contrast with most of those poets who write concerning themselves. For the right understanding of his dramatic works, these lyrics are of the greatest importance. They shew us, that in his dramas he very seldom speaks according to his own feelings, or his own thoughts, but according to his knowledge. The world lay clear and distinct before his eyes, but between him and it there was a deep gulf fixed. He gives us a portrait of what he saw, without flattery or ornament—having the charm of unrivalled accuracy and truth. Were understanding, acuteness, and profoundness of thought (in so far as these are necessary for the characterizing of human life), to be considered as the first qualities of a poet, there is none worthy to be compared with Shakespeare. Other poets have endeavoured to transport us, at least for a few moments, into another and an ideal condition of mankind. But Shakespeare is the master of reality; he sets before us, with a truth that is often painful, man in his degraded state, in this corruption which penetrates and contaminates all his being, all that he does and suffers, all the thoughts and aspirations of his fallen spirit. In this respect he may not unfrequently be said to be a satirical poet; and well indeed may the picture which he presents of human debasement, and the enigma of our being, be calculated to produce an effect far more deep and abiding than the whole body of splenetic and passionate revilers, whom we commonly call by the name of satiric poets. In the midst of all the bitterness of Shakespeare, we perceive continually glimpses of thoughts and recollections more pure than satirists partake in; meditation on the original height and elevation of man, —the peculiar tenderness and noble-minded sentiment of a poet; the dark world of his representation is illuminated with the most beautiful rays of patriotic inspiration, serene philanthropy, and glowing love.

But even the youthful glow of love appears in his Romeo as the mere inspiration of death, and is mingled with the same sceptical and melancholy views of life which, in Hamlet, give to all our being an appearance of more than natural discord and perplexity, and which, in Lear, carry sorrow and passion into the utmost misery of madness. This poet, who externally seems to be most calm and temperate, clear and lively,—with whom intellect seems everywhere to preponderate; who, as we at first imagine, regards and represents every thing almost with coldness,—is found, if we examine into the internal feelings of his spirit, to be of all others the most deeply sorrowful and tragic.

Shakespeare regarded the drama as entirely a thing for the people, and at first treated it throughout as such. He took the popular comedy as he found it, and whatever enlargements and improvements he introduced into the stage, were all calculated and conceived, according to the peculiar spirit of his predecessors, and of the audience in London. Even in the earliest of his tragic attempts, he takes possession of the whole superstitions of the vulgar, and mingles in his poetry, not only the gigantic greatness of their rude traditions, but also the fearful, the horrible, and the revolting. All these, again, are blended with such representations and views of human debasement as passed—or still pass— with common spectators for wit, but were connected in the depths of his reflective and penetrating spirit, with the very different feelings of bitter contempt or sorrowful sympathy. He was not, in knowledge, far less in art, such as since the time of Milton, it has been usual to represent him. But I believe that the inmost feelings of his heart, the depths of his peculiar, concentrated, and solitary spirit, could be agitated only by the mournful voice of nature. The feeling by which he seems to have been most connected with ordinary men is that of nationality. He has represented the heroic and glorious period of English history, during the conquests in France, in a series of dramatic pieces, which possess all the simplicity and liveliness of the ancient chronicles, but approach, in their ruling spirit of patriotism and glory, to the most dignified and effectual productions of the epic muse.

In the works of Shakespeare a whole world is unfolded. He who has once comprehended this, and been penetrated with its spirit, will not easily allow the effect to be diminished by the form, or listen to the cavils of those who are incapable of understanding the import of what they would criticise. The form of Shakespeare's writings will rather appear to him good and excellent, because in it his spirit is expressed and clothed, as it were, in a convenient garment. The poetry of Shakespeare is near of kin to the spirit of the Germans, and he is more felt and beloved by them than any other foreign, I had almost said, than any vernacular, poet. Even in England, the understanding of Shakespeare is rendered considerably more difficult, in consequence of the resemblance which many very inferior writers bear to him in those points, which come most immediately before the eye. In Germany, we admire Shakespeare, and are free from this disadvantage; but we should beware of adopting, either the form or the sentiment of this great poet's writings, as the exclusive model of our own. They are indeed, in themselves, most highly poetical, but they are far from being the only poetical ones, and the dramatic art may attain perfection in many other ways besides the Shakespearian. . . .

S. T. COLERIDGE

S. T. Coleridge (1772-1834). Coleridge's Shakespeare criticism consists for the most part of the notes on individual plays, the reports on lectures made by J. P. Collier and others, and the material in Biographia Literaria. *The authoritative edition is that of T. M. Raysor. The place of Coleridge in the history of Shakespeare criticism is discussed in the Introduction.*

The Genius of Shakespeare*

The subject of the present lecture is no less than a question submitted to your understandings, emancipated from national prejudice: Are the plays of *Shakespeare* works of rude uncultivated genius, in which the splendor of the parts compensates, if aught can compensate, for the barbarous shapelessness and irregularity of the whole? To which not only the French critics, but even his own English admirers, say yes. Or is the form equally admirable with the matter, the judgement of the great poet not less deserving of our wonder than his genius? Or to repeat the question in other words, is Shakespeare a great dramatic poet on account only of these beauties and excellencies which he possesses in common with the ancients,—but with diminished claims to our love and honor to the full extent of his difference from them? Or are these very differences additional proofs of poetic wisdom, at once results and symbols of living power as contrasted with lifeless mechanism, of free and rival originality as contradistinguished from servile imitation, or more accurately, from a blind copying of effects instead of a true imitation of the essential principles? Imagine not I am about to oppose genius to rules. No! the comparative value of these rules is the very cause to be tried. The spirit of poetry, like all other living powers, must of necessity circumscribe itself by rules, were it only to unite power with beauty. It must embody in order to reveal itself; but a living body is of necessity an organized one,—and what is organization, but the connection of parts to a whole, so that each part is at once end and means! This is no discovery of criticism; it is a necessity of the human mind—and all nations have felt and obeyed it, in the invention of metre and measured sounds as the vehicle and involucrum of poetry, itself a fellow-growth from the same life, even as the bark is to the tree.

No work of true genius dare want its appropriate form; neither indeed is there any danger of this. As it must not, so

* From lecture notes.

neither can it, be lawless! For it is even this that constitutes it genius—the power of acting creatively under laws of its own origination. How then comes it that not only single Zoili, but whole nations have combined in unhesitating condemnation of our great dramatist, as a sort of African nature, fertile in beautiful monsters, as a wild heath where islands of fertility look greener from the surrounding waste, where the loveliest plants now shine out among unsightly weeds and now are choked by their parasitic growth, so intertwined that we cannot disentangle the weed without snapping the flower. In this statement I have had no reference to the vulgar abuse of Voltaire, save as far as his charges are coincident with the decisions of his commentators and (so they tell you) his almost idolatrous admirers. The true ground of the mistake, as has been well remarked by a continental critic,[1] lies in the confounding mechanical regularity with organic form. The form is mechanic when on any given material we impress a pre-determined form, not necessarily arising out of the properties of the material, as when to a mass of wet clay we give whatever shape we wish it to retain when hardened. The organic form, on the other hand, is innate; it shapes as it develops itself from within, and the fullness of its development is one and the same with the perfection of its outward form. Such is the life, such the form. Nature, the prime genial artist, inexhaustible in diverse powers, is equally inexhaustible in forms. Each exterior is the physiognomy of the being within, its true image reflected and thrown out from the concave mirror. And even such is the appropriate excellence of her chosen poet, of our own Shakespeare, himself a nature humanized, a genial understanding directing self-consciously a power and an implicit wisdom deeper than consciousness.

The Characteristics of Shakespeare.

1. Expectation in preference to surprize. "God said, let there be *light,* and there was *light,*"—not there *was* light. As the feeling with which we startle at a shooting star, compared with that of watching the sunrise at the pre-established moment, such and so low is surprize compared with expectation.

[1] Schlegel.

2. Signal adherence to the great law of nature that opposites tend to attract and temper each other. Passion in Shakespeare displays, libertinism involves, morality. The exception is characteristic of the individual, independent of the intrinsic value, as the farewell precepts of the parent, having some end beyond even the parental relation. Thus the Countess's beautiful precepts to Bertram, by elevating her character, elevate that of Helena, her favourite, and soften down the point in her which Shakespeare does not mean us not to see, but to see and forgive, and at length to justify. So Polonius, who is the personified *memory* of wisdom no longer actually possessed.

So again folly, dullness itself, the vehicles of wisdom. As all the deities of Homer were in armour, even Venus, etc., so all in Shakespeare strong. No difficulty in being a fool to imitate a fool; but to be, remain, and speak like a wise man, and yet so as to give a vivid representation of a fool, *hic labor, hoc opus*. Dogberry, etc.

3. Independence of the interest on the plot. The plot interests us on account of the characters, not *vice versâ*; it is the canvas only. Justification of the same stratagem in Benedict and Beatrice—same vanity, etc. Take away from *Much Ado About Nothing* all that which is not indispensable to the plot, either as having little to do with it, or at best, like Dogberry and his comrades, forced into the service when any other less ingeniously absurd watchmen and night-constables would have answered; take away Benedict, Beatrice, Dogberry, and the reaction of the former on the character of Hero, and what will remain? In other writers the main agent of the plot is always the prominent character. In Shakespeare so or not so, as the character is in itself calculated or not calculated to form the plot. So Don John, the mainspring of the plot, is merely shown and withdrawn.

4. Independence of the interest on *the story* as the groundwork of the plot. Hence Shakespeare did not take the trouble of inventing stories. It was enough for him to select from those that had been invented or recorded such as had one or other, or both, of two recommendations, namely, suitableness to his purposes, and second, their being already parts of popular tradition—names we had often heard of, and of their fortunes, and we should like

to see the *man* himself. It is the man himself that Shakespeare for the first time makes us acquainted with. *Lear* (omit the first scene, yet all remains). So Shylock.

5. The interfusion of the lyrical, of that which in its very essence is poetical, not only with the dramatic, as in the plays of Metastasio, where at the end of the scene comes the aria, as the exit speech of the character. Now songs in Shakespeare are introduced as *songs,* and just as songs are in real life, beautifully as they are often made characteristic of the person who has called for them, as Desdemona and the Count (Duke) in *As You Like It;* they are introduced not only with the dramatic, but as a part of the dramatic. The whole *Midsummer's Night's Dream* is one continued specimen of the lyrical dramatized. But take also the beginning of the third act of the first part of *Henry IV.*; represent the speech of Hotspur,—

> Marry, and I'm glad on't with all my heart:
> I had rather be a kitten and cry mew—

and then the transition to the lyrical speech of Mortimer—

> I understand thy looks: that pretty Welsh
> Which thou pour'st down from these swelling heavens
> I am too perfect in.

6. Closely connected with this is that Shakespeare's characters are like those in life, to be *inferred* by the reader, not *told to him.* Of this excellence I know no other instance; and it has one mark of real life—that Shakespeare's characters have been as generally misunderstood and from precisely the same causes as real persons. If you take what his friends say, you may be deceived— still more so, if his enemies; and the character himself sees himself thro' the medium of his character, not exactly as it is. But the clown or the fool will suggest a shrewd hint; and take all together, and the impression is right, and all the spectators have it. And it may be given as soon as the true Idea is given, and then all the speeches receive the light and attest by reflecting it. . . .

Even the very diction evidencing a mind that, proceeding from some one great conception, finds its only difficulty

the conceptual center of play

in arranging and disciplining the crowd of thoughts which from that matrix rush in to enlist themselves. No looking outward by wit or book-memory.

Character. Others so characteristic (*i.e.*, psychologic portraiture) as to be characterless, *quoad* the poet. How wonderfully is Shakespeare the living balance!

Meditation as contrasted with observation. Passion as contrasted with general truths. Contrast with the French drama, with Seneca. The lyric as contrasted with the dramatic—even with the ancients.

The heterogeneous united as in nature. Mistake of those who suppose a pressure or passion always acting—it is that by which the individual is distinguished from others, not what makes a separate kind of him.

The regular high road of human affections. It is not the poet's business to analyse and criticize the affections and faiths of men, but to assure himself, that such and such are affections and faiths grounded in human nature, not in mere accident of ignorance or disease. This is most important. He is the morning star of philosophy—the guide and pioneer.

In other writers, as Johnson, perpetual artifice to draw us away from ourselves. Shakespeare—oh, read him by this criterion only and then ask your own heart—ask your common sense even—to conceive the possibility of this man being a wild genius, etc., etc. What, are we to have miracles in sport? Or does God choose idiots to convey divine truths by?

I would try Shakespeare compared with any other writer by this criterion. Make out your amplest catalogue of all the human faculties—as reason or the moral law, the will, the *feeling* of the coincidence of the two (a feeling *sui generis,* and *demonstratio demonstrationum*) called the conscience, the understanding or prudence, wit, fancy, imagination, judgement—and then of the objects on which these can be employed, as the beauties of nature, the terrors or seeming caprices of nature, the realities and the capabilities, *i.e.,* the actual and the ideal of the human mind, conceived as individual or as social being, as in innocence or in guilt, in a play-paradise or a war-field of temptation—and then compare with him under each of these heads. I abhor beauties and selections in general, and even here if the effect of the poetry were considered; but as proof positive of unrivalled excellence I should like to see it.

The wonderful balance between the progressive action, and the immediate interest of the dialogue.

SHAKESPEARE'S ACHIEVEMENT*

Assuredly the Englishman who without reverence, who without a proud and affectionate reverence, can utter the name of Shakespeare, stands disqualified for the office. He wants one at least of the very senses, the language of which he is to employ, and will discourse at best but as a blind man, while the whole harmonious creation of light and shade with all its subtle interchange of deepening and dissolving colors rises in silence to the silent fiat of the uprising Apollo. However inferior in ability to some who have followed me, I am proud that I was the first in time who publicly demonstrated to the full extent of the position, that the supposed irregularity and extravagances of Shakespeare were the mere dreams of a pedantry that arraigned the eagle because it had not the dimensions of the swan. . . . It has been and it still remains my object to prove that in all points from the most important to the most minute, the judgement of Shakespeare is commensurate with his genius—nay, that his genius reveals itself in his judgement, as in its most exalted form. . . .

WILLIAM HAZLITT

William Hazlitt (1778-1830). Radical journalist and critic, friend of Keats and, before their political apostasy, of the Lake Poets; author of Characters of Shakespeare's Plays *(1817),* Lectures on the English Poets *(1818),* Lectures on the Comic Writers *(1819),* Dramatic Literature

* From lecture notes of 1817.

of the Age of Elizabeth *(1821)*, The Spirit of the Age *(1825) and many other books. The selections here repre-sent him as a Shakespearian controversialist and dramat-ic critic. In the latter capacity he reported Kean's per-formance over several years. After some initial resistance to the violence of the interpretation, Hazlitt came to re-gard it as 'the finest piece of acting in the world', but when Kean moderated his passion he praised the new version highly. His answer to Gifford was, incidentally, greatly admired by Keats.*

THE PLASTIC IMAGINATION*

The striking peculiarity of Shakespeare's mind was its generic quality, its power of communication with all other minds—so that it contained a universe of thought and feeling within itself, and had no one peculiar bias or exclu-sive excellence more than another. He was just like any other man, but that he was like all other men. He was the least of an egotist that it was possible to be. He was nothing in himself, but he was all that others were, or that they could become. He not only had in himself the germs of every faculty and feeling, but he could follow them by anticipation, intuitively, into all their conceivable ramifica-tions, through every change of fortune or conflict of passion, or turn of thought. He had 'a mind reflecting ages past' and present:—all the people that ever lived are there. There was no respect of persons with him. His genius shone equally on the evil and on the good, on the wise and the foolish, the monarch and the beggar. 'All corners of the earth, kings, queens, and states, maids, matrons, nay, the secrets of the grave,' are hardly hid from his searching glance. He was like the genius of humanity, changing places with all of us at pleasure, and playing with our purposes as with his own. He turned the globe round for his amuse-ment, and surveyed the generations of men, and the individ-uals as they passed, with their different concerns, passions, follies, vices, virtues, actions, and motives—as well those that they knew, as those which they did not know, or ac-

* From *Lectures on the English Poets*, 'On Shakespeare and Milton', 1818.

knowledge to themselves. The dreams of childhood, the ravings of despair, were the toys of his fancy. Airy beings waited at his call, and came at his bidding. Harmless fairies 'nodded to him, and did him curtesies:' and the night-hag bestrode the blast at the command of 'his so potent art.' The world of spirits lay open to him, like the world of real men and women: and there is the same truth in his delineations of the one as of the other; for if the preternatural characters he describes could be supposed to exist, they would speak, and feel, and act, as he makes them. He had only to think of any thing in order to become that thing, with all the circumstances belonging to it. When he conceived of a character, whether real or imaginary, he not only entered into all its thoughts and feelings, but seemed instantly, and as if by touching a secret spring, to be surrounded with all the same objects, 'subject to the same skyey influences,' the same local, outward, and unforeseen accidents which would occur in reality. Thus the character of Caliban not only stands before us with a language and manners of its own, but the scenery and situation of the enchanted island he inhabits, the traditions of the place, its strange noises, its hidden recesses, 'his frequent haunts and ancient neighbourhood,' are given with a miraculous truth of nature, and with all the familiarity of an old recollection. The whole 'coheres semblably together' in time, place, and circumstance. In reading this author, you do not merely learn what his characters say,—you see their persons. By something expressed or understood, you are at no loss to decipher their peculiar physiognomy, the meaning of a look, the grouping, the bye-play, as we might see it on the stage. A word, an epithet, paints a whole scene, or throws us back whole years in the history of the person represented. So (as it has been ingeniously remarked) when Prospero describes himself as left alone in the boat with his daughter, the epithet which he applies to her, 'Me and thy *crying* self,' flings the imagination instantly back from the grown woman to the helpless condition of infancy, and places the first and most trying scene of his misfortunes before us, with all that he must have suffered in the interval. How well the silent anguish of Macduff is conveyed to the reader, by the friendly expostulation of Malcolm:—'What! man, ne'er pull your hat upon your brows.' Again, Hamlet, in the scene with Rosencrantz and Guildenstern, somewhat abruptly concludes his fine soliloquy on life by saying, 'Man delights not me, nor woman neither, though by your smiling you seem to say so.' Which is explained by their answer—'My lord, we had no such stuff in our thoughts. But we smiled to think, if you delight not in man, what lenten entertainment the players shall receive from you, whom we met on the way:'—as if while Hamlet was making this speech, his two old schoolfellows from Wittenberg had been really standing by, and he had seen them smiling by stealth, at the idea of the players crossing their minds. It is not 'a combination and a form' of words, a set speech or two, a preconcerted theory of a character, that will do this: but all the persons concerned must have been present in the poet's imagination, as at a kind of rehearsal; and whatever would have passed through their minds on the occasion, and have been observed by others, passed through his, and is made known to the reader.—I may add in passing, that Shakespeare always gives the best directions for the costume and carriage of his heroes. Thus to take one example, Ophelia gives the following account of Hamlet; and as Ophelia had seen Hamlet, I should think her word ought to be taken against that of any modern authority.

> *Ophelia.* My lord, as I was reading in my closet,
> Prince Hamlet, with his doublet all unbrac'd,
> No hat upon his head, his stockings loose,
> Ungartred, and down-gyved to his ancle,
> Pale as his shirt, his knees knocking each other,
> And with a look so piteous,
> As if he had been sent from hell
> To speak of horrors, thus he comes before me.
>   *Polonius.* Mad for thy love!
>   *Oph.* My lord, I do not know,
> But truly I do fear it.
>   *Pol.* What said he?
>   *Oph.* He took me by the wrist, and held me hard;
> Then goes he to the length of all his arm;
> And, with his other hand thus o'er his brow,
> He falls to such perusal of my face,
> As he would draw it: long staid he so;
> At last, a little shaking of my arm,

And thrice his head thus waving up and down,
He rais'd a sigh so piteous and profound,
As it did seem to shatter all his bulk,
And end his being. That done, he lets me go,
And with his head over his shoulder turn'd,
He seem'd to find his way without his eyes;
For out of doors he went without their help,
And to the last bended their light on me.

Act II. Scene i.

How after this airy, fantastic idea of irregular grace and
bewildered melancholy any one can play Hamlet, as we
have seen it played, with strut, and stare, and antic right-
angled sharp-pointed gestures, it is difficult to say, unless it
be that Hamlet is not bound, by the prompter's cue, to study
the part of Ophelia. The account of Ophelia's death begins
thus:

There is a willow hanging o'er a brook,
That shows its hoary leaves in the glassy stream.—

Now this is an instance of the same unconscious power of
mind which is as true to nature as itself. The leaves of the
willow are, in fact, white underneath, and it is this part of
them which would appear 'hoary' in the reflection in the
brook. The same sort of intuitive power, the same faculty
of bringing every object in nature, whether present or
absent, before the mind's eye, is observable in the speech of
Cleopatra, when conjecturing what were the employments
of Antony in his absence:—'He's speaking now, or mur-
muring, where's my serpent of old Nile?' How fine to make
Cleopatra have this consciousness of her own character, and
to make her feel that it is this for which Antony is in love
with her! She says, after the battle of Actium, when Antony has resolved to risk another fight, 'It is my birth-day;
I had thought to have held it poor: but since my lord is
Antony again, I will be Cleopatra.' What other poet would
have thought of such a casual resource of the imagination,
or would have dared to avail himself of it? The thing happens in the play as it might have happened in fact.—That
which, perhaps, more than any thing else distinguishes the
dramatic productions of Shakespeare from all others, is

this wonderful truth and individuality of conception. Each of his characters is as much itself, and as absolutely independent of the rest, as well as of the author, as if they were living persons, not fictions of the mind. The poet may be said, for the time, to identify himself with the character he wishes to represent, and to pass from one to another, like the same soul successively animating different bodies. By an art like that of the ventriloquist, he throws his imagination out of himself, and makes every word appear to proceed from the mouth of the person in whose name it is given. His plays alone are properly expressions of the passions, not descriptions of them. His characters are real beings of flesh and blood; they speak like men, not like authors. One might suppose that he had stood by at the time, and overheard what passed. As in our dreams we hold conversations with ourselves, make remarks, or communicate intelligence, and have no idea of the answer which we shall receive, and which we ourselves make, till we hear it: so the dialogues in Shakespeare are carried on without any consciousness of what is to follow, without any appearance of preparation or premeditation. The gusts of passion come and go like sounds of music borne on the wind. Nothing is made out by formal inference and analogy, by climax and antithesis: all comes, or seems to come, immediately from nature. Each object and circumstance exists in his mind, as it would have existed in reality: each several train of thought and feeling goes on of itself, without confusion or effort. In the world of his imagination, everything has a life, a place, and being of its own!

Chaucer's characters are sufficiently distinct from one another, but they are too little varied in themselves, too much like identical propositions. They are consistent, but uniform; we get no new idea of them from first to last; they are not placed in different lights, nor are their subordinate *traits* brought out in new situations; they are like portraits or physiognomical studies, with the distinguishing features marked with inconceivable truth and precision, but that preserve the same unaltered air and attitude. Shakespeare's are historical figures, equally true and correct, but put into action, where every nerve and muscle is displayed in the struggle with others, with all the effect of collision and contrast, with every variety of light and shade. Chaucer's characters are narrative, Shakespeare's dramatic, Milton's epic. That is, Chaucer told only as much of his story as he pleased, as was required for a particular purpose. He answered for his characters himself. In Shakespeare they are introduced upon the stage, are liable to be asked all sorts of questions, and are forced to answer for themselves. In Chaucer we perceive a fixed essence of character. In Shakespeare there is a continual composition and decomposition of its elements, a fermentation of every particle in the whole mass, by its alternate affinity or antipathy to other principles which are brought in contact with it. Till the experiment is tried, we do not know the result, the turn which the character will take in its new circumstances. Milton took only a few simple principles of character, and raised them to the utmost conceivable grandeur, and refined them from every base alloy. His imagination, 'nigh sphered in Heaven,' claimed kindred only with what he saw from that height, and could raise to the same elevation with itself. He sat retired and kept his state alone, 'playing with wisdom;' while Shakespeare mingled with the crowd, and played the host, 'to make society the sweeter welcome.'

The passion in Shakespeare is of the same nature as his delineation of character. It is not some one habitual feeling or sentiment preying upon itself, growing out of itself, and moulding everything to itself; it is passion modified by passion, by all the other feelings to which the individual is liable, and to which others are liable with him; subject to all the fluctuations of caprice and accident; calling into play all the resources of the understanding and all the energies of the will; irritated by obstacles or yielding to them; rising from small beginnings to its utmost height; now drunk with hope, now stung to madness, now sunk in despair, now blown to air with a breath, now raging like a torrent. The human soul is made the sport of fortune, the prey of adversity: it is stretched on the wheel of destiny, in restless ecstasy. The passions are in a state of projection. Years are melted down to moments, and every instant teems with fate. We know the results, we see the process. Thus after Iago has been boasting to himself of the effect of his poisonous suggestions on the mind of Othello, 'which, with a little act upon the blood, will work like mines of sulphur,' he adds:—

> Look where he comes! not poppy, nor mandragora
> Nor all the drowsy syrups of the East,
> Shall ever medicine thee to that sweet sleep
> Which thou ow'dst yesterday.

And he enters at this moment, like the crested serpent, crowned with his wrongs and raging for revenge! The whole depends upon the turn of a thought. A word, a look, blows the spark of jealousy into a flame; and the explosion is immediate and terrible as a volcano. The dialogues in *Lear,* in *Macbeth,* that between Brutus and Cassius, and nearly all those in Shakespeare, where the interest is wrought up to its highest pitch, afford examples of this dramatic fluctuation of passion. The interest in Chaucer is quite different; it is like the course of a river, strong, and full, and increasing. In Shakespeare, on the contrary, it is like the sea, agitated this way and that, and loud-lashed by furious storms; while in the still pauses of the blast we distinguish only the cries of despair, or the silence of death! Milton, on the other hand, takes the imaginative part of passion—that which remains after the event, which the mind reposes on when all is over, which looks upon circumstances from the remotest elevation of thought and fancy, and abstracts them from the world of action to that of contemplation. The objects of dramatic poetry affect us by sympathy, by their nearness to ourselves, as they take us by surprise, or force us upon action, 'while rage with rage doth sympathise': the objects of epic poetry affect us through the medium of the imagination, by magnitude and distance, by their permanence and universality. The one fills us with terror and pity, the other with admiration and delight. There are certain objects that strike the imagination, and inspire awe in the very idea of them, independently of any dramatic interest, that is, of any connection with the vicissitudes of human life. For instance, we cannot think of the pyramids of Egypt, of a Gothic ruin, or an old Roman encampment, without a certain emotion, a sense of power and sublimity coming over the mind. The heavenly bodies that hang over our heads wherever we go, and 'in their untroubled element shall shine when we are laid in dust, and all our cares forgotten,' affect us in the same way. Thus Satan's address to the Sun has an epic, not a dramatic interest; for though the second person in the dialogue makes no answer and feels no concern, yet the eye of that vast luminary is upon him, like the eye of heaven, and seems conscious of what he says, like an universal presence. Dramatic poetry and epic in their perfection, indeed, approximate to and strengthen one another. Dramatic poetry borrows aid from the dignity of persons and things, as the heroic does from human passion, but in theory they are distinct. When Richard II. calls for the looking-glass to contemplate his faded majesty in it, and bursts into that affecting exclamation: 'Oh that I were a mockery-king of snow, to melt away before the sun of Bolingbroke!' we have here the utmost force of human passion, combined with the ideas of regal splendour and fallen power. When Milton says of Satan:

> ——His form had not yet lost
> All her original brightness, nor appear'd
> Less than archangel ruin'd, and th' excess
> Of glory obscur'd;

the mixture of beauty, of grandeur, and pathos, from the sense of irreparable loss, of never-ending, unavailing regret, is perfect.

The great fault of a modern school of poetry is, that it is an experiment to reduce poetry to a mere effusion of natural sensibility; or what is worse, to divest it both of imaginary splendour and human passion, to surround the meanest objects with the morbid feelings and devouring egotism of the writers' own minds. Milton and Shakespeare did not so understand poetry. They gave a more liberal interpretation both to nature and art. They did not do all they could to get rid of the one and the other, to fill up the dreary void with the Moods of their own Minds. They owe their power over the human mind to their having had a deeper sense than others of what was grand in the objects of nature, or affecting in the events of human life. But to the men I speak of there is nothing interesting, nothing heroical, but themselves. To them the fall of gods or of great men is the same. They do not enter into the feeling. They cannot understand the terms. They are even debarred from the last poor, paltry consolation of an unmanly triumph over fallen greatness; for their minds reject, with a convulsive effort and intolerable loathing, the very idea that there ever was, or was thought to be, anything superior to themselves. All that has ever excited the attention or admiration of the world, they look upon with the most perfect indifference; and they are surprised to find that the world repays their indifference with scorn. 'With what measure they mete, it has been meted to them again.'—

Shakespeare's imagination is of the same plastic kind as his conception of character or passion. 'It glances from heaven to earth, from earth to heaven.' Its movement is rapid and devious. It unites the most opposite extremes; or, as Puck says, in boasting of his own feats, 'puts a girdle round about the earth in forty minutes.' He seems always hurrying from his subject, even while describing it; but the stroke, like the lightning's, is sure as it is sudden. He takes the widest possible range, but from that very range he has his choice of the greatest variety and aptitude of materials. He brings together images the most alike, but placed at the greatest distance from each other; that is, found in circumstances of the greatest dissimilitude. From the remoteness of his combinations, and the celerity with which they are effected, they coalesce the more indissolubly together. The more the thoughts are strangers to each other, and the longer they have been kept asunder, the more intimate does their union seem to become. Their felicity is equal to their force. Their likeness is made more dazzling by their novelty. They startle, and take the fancy prisoner in the same instant. I will mention one or two which are very striking, and not much known, out of *Troilus and Cressida*. Æneas says to Agamemnon:

> I ask that I may waken reverence,
> And on the cheek be ready with a blush
> Modest as morning, when she coldly eyes
> The youthful Phœbus.

Ulysses urging Achilles to shew himself in the field, says—

> No man is the lord of any thing,
> Till he communicate his parts to others:
> Nor doth he of himself know them for aught,
> Till he behold them formed in the applause,
> Where they're extended! which, like an arch
>   reverberates
> The voice again, or like a gate of steel
> Fronting the sun, receives and renders back
> Its figure and its heat.

Patroclus gives the indolent warrior the same advice:

> Rouse yourself; and the weak wanton Cupid
> Shall from your neck unloose his amorous fold,
> And like a dew-drop from the lion's mane
> Be shook to air.

Shakespeare's language and versification are like the rest of him. He has a magic power over words: they come winged at his bidding; and seem to know their places. They are struck out at a heat, on the spur of the occasion, and have all the truth and vividness which arise from an actual impression of the objects. His epithets and single phrases are like sparkles, thrown off from an imagination, fired by the whirling rapidity of its own motion. His language is hieroglyphical. It translates thoughts into visible images. It abounds in sudden transitions and elliptical expressions. This is the source of his mixed metaphors, which are only abbreviated forms of speech. These, however, give no pain from long custom. They have, in fact, become idioms in the language. They are the building, and not the scaffolding to thought. We take the meaning and effect of a well-known passage entire, and no more stop to scan and spell out the particular words and phrases than the syllables of which they are composed. In trying to recollect any other author, one sometimes stumbles, in case of failure, on a word as good. In Shakespeare, any other word but the true one, is sure to be wrong. If anybody, for instance, could not recollect the words of the following description,

> ——Light thickens,
> And the crow makes wing to the rooky wood

he would be greatly at a loss to substitute others for them equally expressive of the feeling. These remarks, however, are strictly applicable only to the impassioned parts of Shakespeare's language, which flowed from the warmth and originality of his imagination, and were his own. The language used for prose conversation and ordinary business is sometimes technical, and involved in the affectation of the time. Compare, for example, Othello's apology to the Senate, relating 'his whole course of love,' with some of the preceding parts relating to his appointment, and the official dispatches from Cyprus. In this respect, 'the business of the state does him offence.'—His versification is no less powerful, sweet, and varied. It has every occasional excellence, of sullen intricacy, crabbed and perplexed, or of the smoothest and loftiest expansion—from the ease and familiarity of measured conversation to the lyrical sounds

> ——Of ditties highly penned,
> Sung by a fair queen in a summer's bower,
> With ravishing division to her lute.

It is the only blank verse in the language, except Milton's, that for itself is readable. It is not stately and uniformly swelling like his, but varied and broken by the inequalities of the ground it has to pass over in its uncertain course,

> And so by many winding nooks it strays,
> With willing sport to the wild ocean.

It remains to speak of the faults of Shakespeare. They are not so many or so great as they have been represented; what there are, are chiefly owing to the following causes:— The universality of his genius was, perhaps, a disadvantage to his single works; the variety of his resources sometimes diverting him from applying them to the most effectual purposes. He might be said to combine the powers of Æschylus and Aristophanes, of Dante and Rabelais, in his own mind. If he had been only half what he was, he would perhaps have appeared greater. The natural ease and indifference of his temper made him sometimes less scrupulous than he might have been. He is relaxed and careless in critical places; he is in earnest throughout only in *Timon, Macbeth,* and *Lear.* Again, he had no models of acknowledged excellence constantly in view to stimulate his efforts, and, by all that appears, no love of fame. He wrote for the 'great vulgar and the small' in his time, not for posterity. If Queen Elizabeth and the maids of honour laughed heartily at his worst jokes, and the catcalls in the gallery were silent at his best passages, he went home satisfied, and slept the next night well. He did not trouble himself about Voltaire's criticisms. He was willing to take advantage of the ignorance of the age in many things, and if his plays pleased others, not to quarrel with them himself. His very facility of production would make him set less value on his own excellences, and not care to distinguish nicely between what he did well or ill. His blunders in chronology and geography do not amount to above half a dozen, and they are offences against chronology and geography, not against poetry. As to the unities, he was right in setting them at defiance. He was fonder of puns than became so great a man. His barbarisms were those of his age. His genius was his own. He had no objection to float down with the stream of common taste and opinion: he rose above it by his own buoyancy, and an impulse which he could not keep under, in spite of himself, or others, and 'his delights did show most dolphin-like.'

SHAKESPEARE—A POLITICAL ISSUE*

. . . It would appear by your own account that Shakespeare had a discreet leaning to the arbitrary side of the question, and, had he lived in our time, would probably have been a writer in the Courier, or a contributor to the Quarterly Review!† It is difficult to know which to admire most in this, the weakness or the cunning. I have said that Shakespeare has described both sides of the question, and you ask me very wisely, 'Did he confine himself to one?' No, I say

---

* From the *Letter to William Gifford* (1819).
† In this sentence Hazlitt is paraphrasing Gifford's attack on his argument, which makes capital out of the apparent admission by the liberal Hazlitt of an authoritarian tendency in Shakespeare.

that he did not: but I suspect that he had a leaning to one side, and has given it more quarter than it deserved. My words are: '*Coriolanus* is a storehouse of political commonplaces. The arguments for and against aristocracy and democracy, on the privileges of the few and the claims of the many, on liberty and slavery, power and the abuse of it, peace and war, are here very ably handled, with the spirit of a poet and the acuteness of a philosopher. Shakespeare himself seems to have had a leaning to the arbitrary side of the question, perhaps from some feeling of contempt for his own origin, and to have spared no occasion of baiting the rabble. *What he says of them is very true: what he says of their betters is also very true, though he dwells less upon it.*'

I then proceed to account for this by shewing how it is that 'the cause of the people is but little calculated for a subject for poetry; or that the language of poetry naturally falls in with the language of power.' I affirm, Sir, that poetry, that the imagination, generally speaking, delights in power, in strong excitement, as well as in truth, in good, in right, whereas pure reason and the moral sense approve only of the true and good. I proceed to shew that this general love or tendency to immediate excitement or theatrical effect, no matter how produced, gives a bias to the imagination often inconsistent with the greatest good, that in poetry it triumphs over principle, and bribes the passions to make a sacrifice of common humanity. You say that it does not, that there is no such original sin in poetry, that it makes no such sacrifice or unworthy compromise between poetical effect and the still small voice of reason. And how do you prove that there is no such principle giving a bias to the imagination, and a false colouring to poetry? Why by asking in reply to the instances where this principle operates, and where no other can, with much modesty and simplicity— 'But are these the only topics that afford delight in poetry, &c.' No; but these objects do afford delight in poetry, and they afford it in proportion to their strong and often tragical effect, and not in proportion to the good produced, or their desirableness in a moral point of view. 'Do we read with more pleasure of the ravages of a beast of prey, than of the shepherd's pipe upon the mountain?' No; but we do read with pleasure of the ravages of a beast of prey, and we do so on the principle I have stated, namely, from the sense of power abstracted from the sense of good; and it is the same principle that makes us read with admiration and reconciles us in fact to the triumphant progress of the conquerors and mighty hunters of mankind, who come to stop the shepherd's pipe upon the mountains, and sweep away his listening flock. Do you mean to deny that there is anything imposing to the imagination in power, in grandeur, in outward shew, in the accumulation of individual wealth and luxury, at the expense of equal justice and the common weal? Do you deny that there is anything in 'the pride, pomp, and circumstance of glorious war, that makes ambition virtue,' in the eyes of admiring multitudes? Is this a new theory of the Pleasures of the Imagination, which says that the pleasures of the imagination do not take rise solely in the calculations of the understanding? Is it a paradox of my making, that 'one murder makes a villain, millions a hero!' Or is it not true that here, as in other cases, the enormity of the evil overpowers and makes a convert of the imagination by its very magnitude? You contradict my reasoning, because you know nothing of the question, and you think that no one has a right to understand what you do not. My offence against purity in the passage alluded to, 'which contains the concentrated venom of my malignity,' is, that I have admitted that there are tyrants and slaves abroad in the world; and you would hush the matter up, and pretend that there is no such thing, in order that there may be nothing else. Farther, I have explained the cause, the subtle sophistry of the human mind, that tolerates and pampers the evil, in order to guard against its approaches; you would conceal the cause in order to prevent the cure, and to leave the proud flesh about the heart to harden and ossify into one impenetrable mass of selfishness and hypocrisy, that we may not 'sympathise in the distresses of suffering virtue' in any case, in which they come in competition with the factitious wants and 'imputed weaknesses of the great.' You ask 'are we gratified by the cruelties of Domitian or Nero?' No, not we—they were too petty and cowardly to strike the imagination at a distance; but the Roman Senate tolerated them, addressed their perpetrators, exalted them into Gods, the Fathers of their people; they had pimps and scribblers of all sorts in their pay, their Senecas, &c. till a turbulent rabble thinking that there were no injuries to society greater than the endurance of unlimited and wanton oppression, put an end to the farce, and abated the nuisance as well as they could. Had you and I lived in those times, we should have been what we are now, I 'a sour mal-content,' and you 'a sweet courtier.' Your reasoning is ill put together; it wants sincerity, it wants ingenuity. To prove that I am wrong in saying that the love of power and heartless submission to it extend beyond the tragic stage to real life, to prove that there has been nothing heard but the shepherd's pipe upon the mountain, and that the still sad music of humanity has never filled up the pauses to the thoughtful ear, you bring in illustration the cruelties of Domitian and Nero, whom you suppose to have been without flatterers, train-bearers, or executioners, and 'the crimes of revolutionary France of a still blacker die,' (a sentence which alone would have entitled you to a post of honour and secrecy under Sejanus,) which you suppose to have been without aiders or abettors. You speak of the horrors of Robespierre's reign; (there you tread on velvet;) do you mean that these atrocities excited nothing but horror in revolutionary France, in undelivered France, in Paris, the centre and focus of anarchy and crime; or that the enthusiasm and madness with which they were acted and applauded, was owing to nothing but a long-deferred desire for truth and justice, and the collected vengeance of the human race? You do not mean this, for you never mean anything that has even an approximation to unfashionable truth in it. You add, 'We cannot recollect, however, that these crimes were heard of with much satisfaction in this country.' Then you have forgotten the years 1793 and 94, you have forgotten the addresses against republicans and levellers, you have forgotten Mr. Burke and his 80,000 incorrigible Jacobins.—'Nor had we the misfortune to know any individual, (though we will not take upon us to deny that Mr. Hazlitt may have been of that description,)' (I will take upon me to deny that) 'who cried havoc, and enjoyed the atrocities of Robespierre and Carnot.' Then at that time, Sir, you had not the good fortune to know Mr. Southey.[1]

To return, you find fault with my toleration of those

---

[1] It was a phrase, (I have understood,) common in this gentleman's mouth, that Robespierre, by destroying the lives of thousands, saved the lives of millions. Or, as Mr. Wordsworth has lately expressed the same thought with a different application, 'Carnage is the daughter of humanity.'

pleasant persons, Lucio, Pompey, and Master Froth, in
Measure for Measure, and with my use of the word 'natural
morality.' And yet, 'the word is a good word, being whereby
a man may be accommodated.' If Pompey was a common
bawd, you, Sir, are a court pimp. That is artificial morality.
'Go to, a feather turns the scale of your avoir-du-pois.' I
have also, it seems, erred in using the term *moral* in a way
not familiar to you, as opposed to *physical*; and in that sense
have applied it to the description of the mole on Imogen's
neck, 'cinque-spotted, like the crimson drops i' th' bottom
of a cowslip.' I have stated that there is more than a physical—there is a moral beauty in this image, and I think so
still, though you may not comprehend how. . . .

JOHN KEATS

*John Keats (1795-1821). Keats's special devotion to Shake-
speare is expressed directly only in the sonnet on* King
Lear *and scattered passages of his letters.*

NEGATIVE CAPABILITY*

. . . at once it struck me, what quality went to form a
Man of Achievement especially in Literature & which
Shakespeare possessed so enormously—I mean *Negative
Capability*, that is when a man is capable of being in
uncertainties, Mysteries, doubts, without any irritable reaching after fact & reason—Coleridge, for instance, would let
go by a fine isolated verisimilitude caught from the Pene-
tralium of mystery, from being incapable of remaining content with half knowledge . . .

SHAKESPEARE'S LIFE OF ALLEGORY†

A Man's life of any worth is a continual allegory—and
very few eyes can see the Mystery of his life—a life like

* From letter to George and Tom Keats, December, 1817.
† From letter to George and Georgiana Keats, 13 March, 1819.

the scriptures, figurative—which such people can no more make out than they can the hebrew Bible. Lord Byron cuts a figure—but he is not figurative—Shakespeare led a life of Allegory; his works are the comments on it . . .

THOMAS CARLYLE

Thomas Carlyle (1795-1881). Author of Sartor Resartus *(1835),* On Heroes, Hero-Worship and the Heroic in History *(1841),* Past and Present *(1843), historian of the French Revolution and biographer of Frederick the Great; the principal English champion of Goethe, whose* Wilhelm Meister *he translated (1824).*

SHAKESPEARE AS HERO*

In some sense it may be said that this glorious Elizabethan Era with its Shakspeare, as the outcome and flowerage of all which had preceded it, is itself attributable to the Catholicism of the Middle Ages. The Christian Faith, which was the theme of Dante's Song, had produced this Practical Life which Shakspeare was to sing. For Religion then, as it now and always is, was the soul of Practice; the primary vital fact in men's life. And remark here, as rather curious, that Middle-Age Catholicism was abolished, so far as Acts of Parliament could abolish it, before Shakspeare, the noblest product of it, made his appearance. He did make his appearance nevertheless. Nature at her own time, with Catholicism or what else might be necessary, sent him forth; taking small thoughts of Acts of Parliament. King-Henrys, Queen-Elizabeths go their way; and Nature too goes hers. Acts of Parliament, on the whole, are small, notwithstanding the noise they make. What Act of Parliament, debate at St. Stephen's, on the hustings or elsewhere, was it that brought this Shakspeare

* From 'The Hero as Poet' in *Lectures on Heroes, etc.,* 1841.

into being? No dining at Freemasons' Tavern, opening subscription-lists, selling of shares, and infinite other jangling and true or false endeavouring! This Elizabethan Era, and all its nobleness and blessedness, came without proclamation, preparation of ours. Priceless Shakspeare was the free gift of Nature; given altogether silently;—received altogether silently, as if it had been a thing of little account. And yet, very literally, it is a priceless thing. One should look at that side of matters too.

Of this Shakspeare of ours, perhaps the opinion one sometimes hears a little idolatrously expressed is, in fact, the right one; I think the best judgment not of this country only, but of Europe at large, is slowly pointing to the conclusion, That Shakspeare is the chief of all Poets hitherto; the greatest intellect who, in our recorded world, has left record of himself in the way of Literature. On the whole, I know not such a power of vision, such a faculty of thought, if we take all the characters of it, in any other man. Such a calmness of depth; placid joyous strength; all things imaged in that great soul of his so true and clear, as in a tranquil unfathomable sea! It has been said, that in the constructing of Shakspeare's Dramas there is, apart from all other 'faculties' as they are called, an understanding manifested, equal to that in Bacon's *Novum Organum*. That is true; and it is not a truth that strikes every one. It would become more apparent if we tried, any of us for himself, how, out of Shakspeare's dramatic materials, *we* could fashion such a result! The built house seems all so fit,—everyway as it should be, as if it came there by its own law and the nature of things,—we forget the rude disorderly quarry it was shaped from. The very perfection of the house, as if Nature herself had made it, hides the builder's merit. Perfect, more perfect than any other man, we may call Shakspeare in this: he discerns, knows as by instinct, what condition he works under, what his materials are, what his own force and its relation to them is. It is not a transitory glance of insight that will suffice; it is deliberate illumination of the whole matter; it is a calmly *seeing* eye; a great intellect, in short. How a man, of some wide thing that he has witnessed, will construct a narrative, what kind of picture and delineation he will give of it,—is the best measure you could get of what intellect is in the man. Which circumstance is vital and shall stand prominent; which unessential, fit to be suppressed; where is the true *beginning*, the true sequence and ending? To find out this, you task the whole force of insight that is in the man. He must *understand* the thing; according to the depth of his understanding, will the fitness of his answer be. You will try him so. Does like join itself to like; does the spirit of method stir in that confusion, so that its embroilment becomes order? Can the man say, *Fiat lux*, Let there be light; and out of chaos make a world? Precisely as there is *light* in himself, will he accomplish this.

Or indeed we may say again, it is in what I called Portrait-painting, delineating of men and things, especially of men, that Shakspeare is great. All the greatness of the man comes out decisively here. It is unexampled, I think, that calm creative perspicacity of Shakspeare. The thing he looks at reveals not this or that face of it, but its inmost heart, and generic secret: it dissolves itself as in light before him, so that he discerns the perfect structure of it. Creative, we said: poetic creation, what is this too but *seeing* the thing sufficiently? The *word* that will describe the thing, follows of itself from such clear intense sight of the thing. And is not Shakspeare's *morality*, his valour, candour, tolerance, truthfulness; his whole victorious strength and greatness, which can triumph over such obstructions, visible there too? Great as the world! No *twisted*, poor convex-concave mirror, reflecting all objects with its own convexities and concavities; a perfectly *level* mirror;—that is to say withal, if we will understand it, a man justly related to all things and men, a good man. It is truly a lordly spectacle how this great soul takes-in all kinds of men and objects, a Falstaff, an Othello, a Juliet, a Coriolanus; sets them all forth to us in their round completeness; loving, just, the equal brother of all. *Novum Organum*, and all the intellect you will find in Bacon, is of a secondary order; earthly, material, poor in comparison with this. Among modern men, one finds, in strictness, almost nothing of the same rank. Goethe alone, since the days of Shakspeare, reminds me of it. Of him too you say that he *saw* the object; you may say what he himself says of Shakspeare: 'His characters are like watches with dial-plates of transparent crystal; they show you the hour like others, and the inward mechanism also is all visible.'

The seeing eye! It is this that discloses the inner harmony of things; what Nature meant, what musical idea Nature has wrapped-up in these often rough embodiments. Something she did mean. To the seeing eye that something were discernible. Are they base, miserable things? You can laugh over them, you can weep over them; you can in some way or other genially relate yourself to them; —you can, at lowest, hold your peace about them, turn away your own and others' face from them, till the hour come for practically exterminating and extinguishing them! At bottom, it is the Poet's first gift, as it is all men's, that he have intellect enough. He will be a Poet if he have: a Poet in word; or failing that, perhaps still better, a Poet in act. Whether he write at all; and if so, whether in prose or in verse, will depend on accidents: who knows on what extremely trivial accidents,—perhaps on his having had a singing-master, on his being taught to sing in his boyhood! But the faculty which enables him to discern the inner heart of things, and the harmony that dwells there (for whatsoever exists has a harmony in the heart of it, or it would not hold together and exist), is not the result of habits or accidents, but the gift of Nature herself; the primary outfit for a Heroic Man in what sort soever. To the Poet, as to every other, we say first of all, *See*. If you cannot do that, it is of no use to keep stringing rhymes together, jingling sensibilities against each other, and *name* yourself a Poet; there is no hope for you. If you can, there is, in prose or verse, in action or speculation, all manner of hope. The crabbed old Schoolmaster used to ask, when they brought him a new pupil, 'But are ye sure he's *not a dunce*?' Why, really one might ask the same thing, in regard to every man proposed for whatsoever function; and consider it as the one inquiry needful: Are ye sure he's not a dunce? There is, in this world, no other entirely fatal person.

For, in fact, I say the degree of vision that dwells in a man is a correct measure of the man. If called to define Shakspeare's faculty, I should say superiority of Intellect, and think I had included all under that. What indeed are faculties? We talk of faculties as if they were distinct, things separable; as if a man had intellect, imagination, fancy, etc., as he has hands, feet, and arms. That is a capital error. Then again, we hear of a man's 'intellectual nature,' and of his 'moral nature,' as if these again were divisible, and existed apart. Necessities of language do perhaps prescribe such forms of utterance; we must speak, I am aware, in that way, if we are to speak at all. But words ought not to harden into things for us. It seems to me, our apprehension of this matter is, for the most part, radically falsified thereby. We ought to know withal, and to keep for ever in mind, that these divisions are at bottom but *names*; that man's spiritual nature, the vital Force which dwells in him, is essentially one and indivisible; that what we call imagination, fancy, understanding, and so forth, are but different figures of the same Power of Insight, all indissolubly connected with each other, physiognomically related; that if we knew one of them, we might know all of them. Morality itself, what we call the moral quality of a man, what is this but another *side* of the one vital Force whereby he is and works? All that a man does is physiognomical of him. You may see how a man would fight, by the way in which he sings; his courage, or want of courage, is visible in the word he utters, in the opinion he has formed, no less than in the stroke he strikes. He is *one*; and preaches the same Self abroad in all these ways.

Without hands a man might have feet, and could still walk: but, consider it,—without morality, intellect were impossible for him; a thoroughly immoral *man* could not know anything at all! To know a thing, what we can call knowing, a man must first *love* the thing, sympathise with it: that is, be *virtuously* related to it. If he have not the justice to put down his own selfishness at every turn, the courage to stand by the dangerous-true at every turn, how shall he know? His virtues, all of them, will lie recorded in his knowledge. Nature, with her truth, remains to the bad, to the selfish and the pusillanimous for ever a sealed book: what such can know of Nature is mean, superficial, small; for the uses of the day merely.—But does not the very Fox know something of Nature? Exactly so: it knows where the geese lodge! The human Reynard, very frequent everywhere in the world, what more does he know but this and the like of this? Nay, it should be considered too, that if the Fox had not a certain vulpine *morality*, he could not even know where the geese were, or get at the geese! If he spent his time in splenetic atrabiliar reflections on his own misery, his ill usage by Nature, Fortune and other Foxes, and so forth; and had not courage, promptitude, practicality, and other suitable vulpine gifts and graces, he would catch no geese. We may say of the Fox too, that his morality and insight are of the same dimensions; different faces of the same internal unity of vulpine life!—These things are worth stating; for the contrary of them acts with manifold very baleful perversion, in this time: what limitations, modifications they require, your own candour will supply.

If I say therefore, that Shakspeare is the greatest of Intellects, I have said all concerning him. But there is more in Shakspeare's intellect than we have yet seen. It is what I call an unconscious intellect; there is more virtue in it than he himself is aware of. Novalis beautifully remarks of him, that those Dramas of his are Products of Nature too, deep as Nature herself. I find a great truth in this saying. Shakspeare's Art is not Artifice; the noblest worth of it is not there by plan or precontrivance. It grows-up from the deeps of Nature, through this noble sincere soul, who is a voice of Nature. The latest generations of men will find new meanings in Shakspeare, new elucidations of their own human being; 'new harmonies with the infinite structure of the Universe; concurrences with later ideas, affinities with the higher powers and senses of man.' This well deserves meditating. It is Nature's highest reward to a true simple great soul, that he get thus to be a *part of herself*. Such a man's works, whatsoever he with utmost conscious exertion and forethought shall accomplish, grow up withal *un*consciously, from the unknown deeps in him; —as the oak-tree grows from the Earth's bosom, as the mountains and waters shape themselves; with a symmetry grounded on Nature's own laws, conformable to all Truth whatsoever. How much in Shakspeare lies hid; his sorrows, his silent struggles known to himself; much that was not known at all, not speakable at all: like *roots,* like sap and forces working underground! Speech is great; but Silence is greater.

Withal the joyful tranquillity of this man is notable. I will not blame Dante for his misery: it is as battle without victory; but true battle,—the first, indispensable thing. Yet I call Shakspeare greater than Dante, in that he fought truly, and did conquer. Doubt it not, he had his own sorrows: those *Sonnets* of his will even testify expressly in what deep waters he had waded, and swum struggling for his life;—as what man like him ever failed to have to do? It seems to me a heedless notion, our common one, that he sat like a bird on the bough; and sang forth, free and offhand, never knowing the troubles of other men. Not so; with no man is it so. How could a man travel forward from rustic deer-poaching to such tragedy-writing, and not fall-in with sorrows by the way? Or, still better, how could a man delineate a Hamlet, a Coriolanus, a Macbeth, so many suffering heroic hearts, if his own heroic heart had never suffered?—And now, in contrast with all this, observe his mirthfulness, his genuine overflowing love of laughter! You would say, in no point does he *exaggerate* but only in laughter. Fiery objurgations, words that pierce and burn, are to be found in Shakspeare; yet he is always in measure here; never what Johnson would remark as a specially 'good hater.' But his laughter seems to pour from him in floods; he heaps all manner of ridiculous nicknames on the butt he is bantering, tumbles and tosses him in all sorts of horse-play; you would say, with his whole heart laughs. And then, if not always the finest, it is always a genial laughter. Not at mere weakness, at misery or poverty; never. No man who *can* laugh, what we call laughing, will laugh at these things. It is some poor character only *desiring* to laugh, and have the credit of wit, that does so. Laughter means sympathy; good laughter is not 'the crackling of thorns under the pot.' Even at stupidity and pretension this Shakspeare does not laugh otherwise than genially. Dogberry and Verges tickle our very hearts; and we dismiss them covered with explosions of laughter: but we like the poor fellows only the better for our laughing; and hope they will get on well there, and

continue Presidents of the City-watch. Such laughter, like
sunshine on the deep sea, is very beautiful to me.

RALPH WALDO EMERSON

*Ralph Waldo Emerson (1803-1882). Provided the American
Renaissance with a Romantic philosophy, and played, as
it were, the roles of Coleridge and Carlyle in America.*

SHAKESPEARE, OR, THE POET*

Some able and appreciating critics think no criticism on
Shakspeare valuable that does not rest purely on the
dramatic merit; that he is falsely judged as poet and philosopher. I think as highly as these critics of his dramatic
merit, but still think it secondary. He was a full man, who
liked to talk; a brain exhaling thoughts and images, which,
seeking vent, found the drama next at hand. Had he been
less, we should have had to consider how well he filled his
place, how good a dramatist he was,—and he is the best
in the world. But it turns out that what he has to say is of
that weight as to withdraw some attention from the vehicle;
and he is like some saint whose history is to be rendered
into all languages, into verse and prose, into songs and pictures, and cut up into proverbs; so that the occasion which
gave the saint's meaning the form of a conversation, or of
a prayer, or of a code of laws, is immaterial compared with
the universality of its application. So it fares with the wise
Shakspeare and his book of life. He wrote the airs for all
our modern music: he wrote the text of modern life; the
text of manners: he drew the man of England and Europe;
the father of the man in America; he drew the man, and
described the day, and what is done in it: he read the hearts
of men and women, their probity, and their second thought
and wiles; the wiles of innocence, and the transitions by

* From *Representative Men* (1841).

which virtues and vices slide into their contraries: he could divide the mother's part from the father's part in the face of the child, or draw the fine demarcations of freedom and of fate: he knew the laws of repression which make the police of nature: and all the sweets and all the terrors of human lot lay in his mind as truly but as softly as the land-scape lies on the eye. And the importance of this wisdom of life sinks the form, as of Drama or Epic, out of notice. 'Tis like making a question concerning the paper on which a king's message is written.

Shakspeare is as much out of the category of eminent authors, as he is out of the crowd. He is inconceivably wise; the others, conceivably. A good reader can, in a sort, nestle into Plato's brain and think from thence; but not into Shakspeare's. We are still out of doors. For executive faculty, for creation, Shakspeare is unique. No man can imagine it better. He was the farthest reach of subtlety compatible with an individual self,—the subtilest of authors, and only just within the possibility of authorship. With this wisdom of life is the equal endowment of imaginative and of lyric power. He clothed the creatures of his legend with form and sentiments as if they were people who had lived under his roof; and few real men have left such distinct characters as these fictions. And they spoke in language as sweet as it was fit. Yet his talents never seduced him into an ostentation, nor did he harp on one string. An omni-present humanity co-ordinates all his faculties. Give a man of talents a story to tell, and his partiality will presently appear. He has certain observations, opinions, topics, which have some accidental prominence, and which he disposes all to exhibit. He crams this part and starves that other part, consulting not the fitness of the thing, but his fitness and strength. But Shakspeare has no peculiarity, no im-portunate topic; but all is duly given; no veins, no curiosi-ties; no cow-painter, no bird-fancier, no mannerist is he: he has no discoverable egotism: the great he tells greatly; the small subordinately. He is wise without emphasis or assertion; he is strong, as nature is strong, who lifts the land into mountain slopes without effort and by the same rule as she floats a bubble in the air, and likes as well to do the one as the other. This makes that equality of power in farce, tragedy, narrative and love-songs; a merit so incessant that each reader is incredulous of the perception of other readers.

This power of expression, or of transferring the inmost truth of things into music and verse, makes him the type of the poet and has added a new problem to metaphysics. This is that which throws him into natural history, as a main production of the globe, and as announcing new eras and ameliorations. Things were mirrored in his poetry without loss or blur: he could paint the fine with precision, the great with compass, the tragic and the comic indifferently and without any distortion or favor. He carried his powerful execution into minute details, to a hair point; finishes an eyelash or a dimple as firmly as he draws a mountain; and yet these, like nature's, will bear the scrutiny of the solar microscope.

In short, he is the chief example to prove that more or less of production, more or fewer pictures, is a thing indifferent. He had the power to make one picture. Daguerre learned how to let one flower etch its image on his plate of iodine, and then proceeds at leisure to etch a million. There are always objects; but there was never representation. Here is perfect representation, at last; and now let the world of figures sit for their portraits. No recipe can be given for the making of a Shakspeare; but the possibility of the translation of things into song is demonstrated.

His lyric power lies in the genius of the piece. The sonnets, though their excellence is lost in the splendor of the dramas, are as inimitable as they; and it is not a merit of lines, but a total merit of the piece; like the tone of voice of some incomparable person, so is this a speech of poetic beings, and any clause as unproducible now as a whole poem.

Though the speeches in the plays, and single lines, have a beauty which tempts the ear to pause on them for their euphuism, yet the sentence is so loaded with meaning and so linked with its foregoers and followers, that the logician is satisfied. His means are as admirable as his ends; every subordinate invention, by which he helps himself to connect some irreconcilable opposites, is a poem too. He is not reduced to dismount and walk because his horses are running off with him in some distant direction: he always rides.

The finest poetry was first experience; but the thought has

suffered a transformation since it was an experience. Cultivated men often attain a good degree of skill in writing verses; but it is easy to read, through their poems, their personal history: any one acquainted with the parties can name every figure; this is Andrew and that is Rachel. The sense thus remains prosaic. It is a caterpillar with wings, and not yet a butterfly. In the poet's mind the fact has gone quite over into the new element of thought, and has lost all that is exuvial. This generosity abides with Shakspeare. We say, from the truth and closeness of his pictures, that he knows the lesson by heart. Yet there is not a trace of egotism.

One more royal trait properly belongs to the poet. I mean his cheerfulness, without which no man can be a poet,— for beauty is his aim. He loves virtue, not for its obligation but for its grace: he delights in the world, in man, in woman, for the lovely light that sparkles from them. Beauty, the spirit of joy and hilarity, he sheds over the universe. Epicurus relates that poetry hath such charms that a lover might forsake his mistress to partake of them. And the true bards have been noted for their firm and cheerful temper. Homer lies in sunshine; Chaucer is glad and erect; and Saadi says, "It was rumored abroad that I was penitent; but what had I to do with repentance?" Not less sovereign and cheerful,—much more sovereign and cheerful, is the tone of Shakspeare. His name suggests joy and emancipation to the heart of men. If he should appear in any company of human souls, who would not march in his troop? He touches nothing that does not borrow health and longevity from his festal style.

HERMAN MELVILLE

Herman Melville (1819–1891). Melville wrote this review shortly before he met Hawthorne in 1850; he was working on Moby Dick, *upon which the influence of Shakespeare, and especially* King Lear, *is very strong.*

HAWTHORNE AND SHAKESPEARE*

How profound, nay appalling, is the moral evolved by the "Earth's Holocaust"; where—beginning with the hollow follies and affectations of the world,—all vanities and empty theories and forms are, one after another, and by an admirably graduated, growing comprehensiveness, thrown into the allegorical fire, till, at length, nothing is left but the all-engendering heart of man; which remaining still unconsumed, the great conflagration is naught.

Of a piece with this, is the "Intelligence Office," a wondrous symbolizing of the secret workings in men's souls. There are other sketches still more charged with ponderous import.

"The Christmas Banquet," and "The Bosom Serpent," would be fine subjects for a curious and elaborate analysis, touching the conjectural parts of the mind that produced them. For spite of all the Indian-summer sunlight on the hither side of Hawthorne's soul, the other side—like the dark half of the physical sphere—is shrouded in a blackness, ten times black. But this darkness but gives more effect to the ever-moving dawn, that for ever advances through it, and circumnavigates his world. Whether Hawthorne has simply availed himself of this mystical blackness as a means to the wondrous effects he makes it to produce in his lights and shades; or whether there really lurks in him, perhaps unknown to himself, a touch of Puritanic gloom,— this, I cannot altogether tell. Certain it is, however, that this great power of blackness in him derives its force from its appeals to that Calvinistic sense of Innate Depravity and Original Sin, from whose visitations, in some shape or other, no deeply thinking mind is always and wholly free. For, in certain moods, no man can weigh this world without throwing in something, somehow like Original Sin, to strike the uneven balance. At all events, perhaps no writer has ever wielded this terrific thought with greater terror than this same harmless Hawthorne. Still more: this black conceit pervades him through and through. You may be

* From 'Hawthorne and his Mosses', a review of *Mosses from an Old Manse* in *The Literary World*, Aug. 17-24, 1850.

witched by his sunlight,—transported by the bright gildings in the skies he builds over you; but there is the blackness of darkness beyond; and even his bright gildings but fringe and play upon the edges of thunder-clouds. In one word, the world is mistaken in this Nathaniel Hawthorne. He himself must often have smiled at its absurd misconception of him. He is immeasurably deeper than the plummet of the mere critic. For it is not the brain that can test such a man; it is only the heart. You cannot come to know greatness by inspecting it; there is no glimpse to be caught of it, except by intuition; you need not ring it, you but touch it, and you find it is gold.

Now, it is that blackness in Hawthorne, of which I have spoken, that so fixes and fascinates me. It may be, nevertheless, that it is too largely developed in him. Perhaps he does not give us a ray of his light for every shade of his dark. But however this may be, this blackness it is that furnishes the infinite obscure of his back-ground,—that back-ground, against which Shakspeare plays his grandest conceits, the things that have made for Shakspeare his loftiest but most circumscribed renown, as the profoundest of thinkers. For by philosophers Shakspeare is not adored as the great man of tragedy and comedy.—"Off with his head; so much for Buckingham!" This sort of rant, interlined by another hand, brings down the house,—those mistaken souls, who dream of Shakspeare as a mere man of Richard-the-Third humps and Macbeth daggers. But it is those deep far-away things in him; those occasional flashings-forth of the intuitive Truth in him; those short, quick probings at the very axis of reality;—these are the things that make Shakspeare, Shakspeare. Through the mouths of the dark characters of Hamlet, Timon, Lear, and Iago, he craftily says, or sometimes insinuates the things which we feel to be so terrifically true, that it were all but madness for any good man, in his own proper character, to utter, or even hint of them. Tormented into desperation, Lear, the frantic king, tears off the mask, and speaks the same madness of vital truth. But, as I before said, it is the least part of genius that attracts admiration. And so, much of the blind, unbridled admiration that has been heaped upon Shakspeare, has been lavished upon the least part of him. And few of his endless commentators and critics seem to have remembered, or even perceived, that the immediate products of a great mind are not so great as that undeveloped and sometimes undevelopable yet dimly-discernible greatness, to which those immediate products are but the infallible indices. In Shakspeare's tomb lies infinitely more than Shakspeare ever wrote. And if I magnify Shakspeare, it is not so much for what he did do as for what he did not do, or refrained from doing. For in this world of lies, Truth is forced to fly like a scared white doe in the woodlands; and only by cunning glimpses will she reveal herself, as in Shakspeare and other masters of the great Art of Telling the Truth,—even though it be covertly and by snatches.

But if this view of the all-popular Shakspeare be seldom taken by his readers, and if very few who extol him have ever read him deeply, or perhaps, only have seen him on the tricky stage (which alone made, and is still making him his mere mob renown)—if few men have time, or patience, or palate, for the spiritual truth as it is in that great genius;— it is then no matter of surprise, that in a contemporaneous age, Nathaniel Hawthorne is a man as yet almost utterly mistaken among men. Here and there, in some quiet armchair in the noisy town, or some deep nook among the noiseless mountains, he may be appreciated for something of what he is. But unlike Shakspeare, who was forced to the contrary course by circumstances, Hawthorne (either from simple disinclination, or else from inaptitude) refrains from all the popularizing noise and show of broad farce and blood-besmeared tragedy; content with the still, rich utterance of a great intellect in repose, and which sends few thoughts into circulation, except they be arterialized at his large warm lungs, and expanded in his honest heart.

Nor need you fix upon that blackness in him, if it suit you not. Nor, indeed, will all readers discern it; for it is, mostly, insinuated to those who may best understand it, and account for it; it is not obtruded upon every one alike.

Some may start to read of Shakspeare and Hawthorne on the same page. They may say, that if an illustration were needed, a lesser light might have sufficed to elucidate this Hawthorne, this small man of yesterday. But I am not willingly one of those who, as touching Shakspeare at least, exemplify the maxim of Rochefoucauld, that "we exalt the

reputation of some, in order to depress that of others";—
who, to teach all noble-souled aspirants that there is no
hope for them, pronounce Shakspeare absolutely unap-
proachable. But Shakspeare has been approached. There
are minds that have gone as far as Shakspeare into the
universe. And hardly a mortal man, who, at some time or
other, has not felt as great thoughts in him as any you will
find in Hamlet. We must not inferentially malign mankind
for the sake of any one man, whoever he may be. This is
too cheap a purchase of contentment for conscious mediocrity to make. Besides, this absolute and unconditional
adoration of Shakspeare has grown to be a part of our
Anglo-Saxon superstitions. The Thirty-Nine Articles are
now Forty. Intolerance has come to exist in this matter.
You must believe in Shakspeare's unapproachability, or
quit the country. But what sort of a belief is this for an
American, a man who is bound to carry republican progres-
siveness into Literature as well as into Life? Believe me, my
friends, that men, not very much inferior to Shakspeare,
are this day being born on the banks of the Ohio. And the
day will come when you shall say, Who reads a book by an
Englishman that is a modern? The great mistake seems to
be, that even with those Americans who look forward to the
coming of a great literary genius among us, they somehow
fancy he will come in the costume of Queen Elizabeth's
day; be a writer of dramas founded upon old English
history or the tales of Boccaccio. Whereas, great geniuses
are parts of the times, they themselves are the times, and
possess a correspondent coloring. It is of a piece with the
Jews, who, while their Shiloh was meekly walking in their
streets, were still praying for his magnificent coming; looking for him in a chariot, who was already among them on
an ass. Nor must we forget that, in his own lifetime,
Shakspeare was not Shakspeare, but only Master William
Shakspeare of the shrewd, thriving business firm of Condell, Shakspeare & Co., proprietors of the Globe Theatre in
London; and by a courtly author, of the name of Chettle,
was looked at as an "upstart crow," beautified "with other
birds' feathers." For, mark it well, imitation is often the
first charge brought against real originality. Why this is
so, there is not space to set forth here. You must have
plenty of sea-room to tell the Truth in; especially when it

seems to have an aspect of newness, as America did in 1492, though it was then just as old, and perhaps older than Asia, only those sagacious philosophers, the common sailors, had never seen it before, swearing it was all water and moonshine there.

Now I do not say that Nathaniel of Salem is a greater than William of Avon, or as great. But the difference between the two men is by no means immeasurable. Not a very great deal more, and Nathaniel were verily William.

WILLIAM MAGINN

William Maginn (1793-1842). Poet, journalist, writer, wit.

SHAKESPEARE AND OVID*

Ovid, also, he must have known only in translation, for the following reasons:—

"Prospero, in *The Tempest*, begins the address to his attendant *spirits*—

" 'Ye elves of hills, of standing lakes, and groves!' "

This speech, Dr. Warburton rightly observes to be borrowed from Medea in Ovid: and "it proves," says Mr. Holt, "beyond contradiction, that Shakespeare was perfectly acquainted with the sentiments of the ancients on the subject of enchantments." The original lines are these:—

" 'Auræque, et venti, montesque, amnesque, lacusque,
Dîque omnes nemorum, dîque omnes noctis adeste.
[Quorum ope, cum volui, ripis mirantibus, amnes

---

* From *The Shakespeare Papers of the Late William Maginn, LL.D.* (New York, 1856). The essay on 'The Learning of Shakespeare', from which these papers are taken, is an important nineteenth-century answer to Farmer, and Maginn's point about Prospero's speech is now generally accepted.

In fontes rediere suos; concussaque sisto,
Stantia concutio cantu freta; nubila pello;
Nubilaque induco: ventos abigoque vocoque,
Vipereas rumpo verbis et carmine fauces:
Vivaque saxa, sua convulsaque robora terra.
Et silvas moveo, jubeoque tremiscere montes;
Et mugire solum, manesque exire sepulcris,
Te quoque, Luna, traho, quanvis Temesæa labores
Æra tuos minuant. Currus quoque carmine nostro
Pallet avi, pallet nostris Aurora venenis.']

Metam., vii. 197-209.

"It happens, however, that the translation by Arthur Golding is by no means literal, and Shakespeare has closely followed it:—

" 'Ye ayres and windes, ye elves of hills, of brookes and woods alone,
Of standing lakes, and of the night, approche ye everychone;
[Through helpe of whom (the crooked bankes much wondering at the thing)
I have compelled streames to run cleane backward to their spring.
By charmes I make the calme seas rough, and make the rough seas playne;
And cover all the skie with cloudes, and chase them thence againe.
By charmes I raise and lay the windes, and burst the viper's jaw;
And from the bowels of the earth both stones and trees do draw.
Whole woods and forests I remove—I make the mountains shake;
And even the earth itself to groane, and fearfully to quake.
I call up dead men from their graves; and thee, O lightsome moone,
I darken oft, though beaten brass abate thy peril soon:
Our sorcerie dims the morning fair, and darks the sun at noone,' &c.]

Fol. 81."

Dr. Farmer has not supplied those parts of the quotations which I have enclosed in brackets; but I have put them together, for further comparison. Mr. Holt, whose very title page[1] proves him to have been a very silly person, which character every succeeding page of his *Attempt* amply sustains, could scarcely have read the passages of Shakespeare and Ovid together, when he said that the former was proved to be perfectly acquainted with the sentiments of the ancients, so far as close following of the Latin poet in this speech of Prospero affords such proof. It shows, however, that Shakespeare was perfectly acquainted with the difference between the enchantments of the ancients, and those which were suitable to the character of his Prospero. Golding, indeed mistook his author, when he translated

"Montesque, amnesque, lacusque,
Dîque omnes nemorum, dîque omnes noctis adeste,"

by "ye *elves* of hills, of brooks, and woods *alone,* of standing lakes, and of the night;" for the deities invoked by Medea were any thing but what, in our language, attaches to the idea of *elves;* while the epithet *alone,* though perhaps defensible, is introduced without sufficient warrant into the translation, and does not convey the exact thought intended by Ovid's "*Dîque omnes nemorum.*" But what was unsuitable for Ovid, was perfectly suitable for Shakespeare; and, accordingly, he had no scruple of borrowing a few words of romantic appeal to the tiny deities of fairy superstition. The lines immediately following, "Ye ayres, and windes," &c., address the powers which, with printless foot, dance upon the sands; which, by moonshine, from the green, sour ringlets, not touched by the ewe, which make midnight mushrooms for pastime, which rejoice to hear the solemn curfew; and not one of these things is connected with the notions of aërial habitants of wood or stream in classical days. When Shakespeare returns to Ovid, he is very little indebted to Golding. We find, indeed, in the *Tempest,* that Prospero boasts of having "bedimmed the noontide sun," which resembles Golding's

[1] An Attempt to rescue that aunciente English Poet and Playwright, Maister Williaume Shakespeare, from the Errours faulsely charged upon him by certain new-fangled Wits. London, 1749. 8vo.—W. M.

"Our sorcerie *dims* the morning fair, and darks the *sun at noone*."

But the analogous passage in Ovid would have been, in its literal state, of no use to Prospero,—

> "Currus quoque carmine nostro
> Pallet *avi*."

With this obligation, however, the compliment due to Golding ceases. *Ope quorum*. "Through *help* of whom." *Golding*. "By whose *aid*." *Shakespeare*. *Vivaque saxa, sua convulsaque robora terra, et silvas moveo*. "And from the bowels of the earth, both stone and *trees* do *draw*." *Golding*. "Rifted Jove's stout *oak* (robora) with his own bolt; and by the spurs *plucked up* (sua convulsa terra), the pine and cedar." *Shakespeare*. *Manesque exire sepulcris*. "I call up dead men from their graves." *Golding*. "Graves, at my command, have waked their sleepers; oped, and let them forth." *Shakespeare*. Ovid has contributed to the invocation of Prospero, at least as much as Golding.

HIPPOLYTE TAINE

Hippolyte Taine (1828-1893). He believed the purpose of literary history to be that of determining the causes of literature in terms of race, milieu and moment; by examining poetry one could understand the true nature of a civilisation. His History of English Literature *(1863) applies these principles.*

SHAKESPEARE'S STYLE*

Let us then look for the man, and in his style. The style explains the work; whilst showing the principal features of the genius, it infers the rest. When we have once grasped

* From *History of English Literature* (1863).

the dominant faculty, we see the whole artist developed like a flower.

Shakspeare imagines with copiousness and excess; he spreads metaphors profusely over all he writes; every instant abstract ideas are changed into images; it is a series of paintings which is unfolded in his mind. He does not seek them, they come of themselves; they crowd within him, covering his arguments; they dim with their brightness the pure light of logic. He does not labour to explain or prove; picture on picture, image on image, he is for ever copying the strange and splendid visions which are engendered one within another, and are heaped up within him. Compare to our dull writers this passage, which I take at hazard from a tranquil dialogue:

'The single and peculiar life is bound,
    With all the strength and ardour of the mind,
    To keep itself from noyance; but much more
    That spirit upon whose weal depend and rest
    The lives of many. The cease of majesty
    Dies not alone; but, like a gulf, doth draw
    What's near it with it: it is a massy wheel,
    Fix'd on the summit of the highest mount,
    To whose huge spokes ten thousand lesser things
    Are mortised and adjoin'd; which, when it falls,
    Each small annexment, petty consequence,
    Attends the boisterous ruin. Never alone
    Did the king sigh, but with a general groan.'[1]

Here we have three successive images to express the same thought. It is a whole blossoming; a bough grows from the trunk, from that another, which is multiplied into numerous fresh branches. Instead of a smooth road, traced by a regular line of dry and well-fixed stakes, you enter a wood, crowded with interwoven trees and luxuriant bushes, which conceal you and close your path, which delight and dazzle your eyes by the magnificence of their verdure and the wealth of their bloom. You are astonished at first, modern mind that you are, business man, used to the clear dissertations of classical poetry; you become cross; you think the author is joking, and that through self-

[1] *Hamlet*, iii, 8.

esteem and bad taste he is misleading you and himself in
his garden thickets. By no means; if he speaks thus, it is
not from choice, but of necessity; metaphor is not his whim,
but the form of his thought. In the height of passion, he
imagines still. When Hamlet, in despair, remembers his
father's noble form, he sees the mythological pictures with
which the taste of the age filled the very streets:

> 'A station like the herald Mercury
> New-lighted on a heaven-kissing hill.' [1]

This charming vision, in the midst of a bloody invective,
proves that there lurks a painter underneath the poet. Involuntarily and out of season, he tears off the tragic mask
which covered his face; and the reader discovers, behind
the contracted features of this terrible mask, a graceful
and inspired smile of which he had not dreamed.

Such an imagination must needs be vehement. Every
metaphor is a convulsion. Whosoever involuntarily and
naturally transforms a dry idea into an image, has his brain
on fire: true metaphors are flaming apparitions, which are
like a picture in a flash of lightning. Never, I think, in
any nation of Europe, or in any age of history, has so
deep a passion been seen. Shakspeare's style is a compound
of furious expressions. No man has submitted words to
such a contortion. Mingled contrasts, raving exaggerations, apostrophes, exclamations, the whole fury of the
ode, inversion of ideas, accumulation of images, the horrible and the divine, jumbled into the same line; it seems
to my fancy as though he never writes a word without
shouting it. 'What have I done?' the queen asks Hamlet.
He answers:

> 'Such an act
> That blurs the grace and blush of modesty,
> Calls virtue hypocrite, takes off the rose
> From the fair forehead of an innocent love,
> And sets a blister there, makes marriage-vows
> As false as dicers' oaths: O, such a deed
> As from the body of contraction plucks
> The very soul, and sweet religion makes

[1] Act. iii. Sc. 4.

A rhapsody of words, heaven's face doth glow;
Yea, this solidity and compound mass,
With tristful visage, as against the doom,
Is thought-sick at the act.' [1]

It is the style of phrensy. Yet I have not given all. The metaphors are all exaggerated, the ideas all verge on the absurd. All is transformed and disfigured by the whirlwind of passion. The contagion of the crime, which he denounces, has marred his whole nature. He no longer sees anything in the world but corruption and lying. To vilify the virtuous were little; he vilifies virtue herself. Inanimate things are sucked into the whirl of grief. The sky's red tint at sunset, the pallid shade spread by night over the landscape, become the blush and the pallor of shame, and the wretched man who speaks and weeps sees the whole world totter with him in the dimness of despair.

Hamlet, it will be said, is half-mad; this explains his vehemence of expression. The truth is that Hamlet, here, is Shakspeare. Be the situation terrible or peaceful, whether he is engaged on an invective or a conversation, the style is excessive throughout. Shakspeare never sees things tranquilly. All the powers of his mind are concentrated in the present image or idea. He is buried and absorbed in it. With such a genius, we are on the brink of an abyss; the eddying water dashes in headlong, devouring whatever objects it meets, bringing them to light again, if at all, transformed and mutilated. We pause stupefied before these convulsive metaphors, which might have been written by a fevered hand in a night's delirium, which gather a pageful of ideas and pictures in half a sentence, which scorch the eyes they would enlighten. Words lose their sense; constructions are put out of joint; paradoxes of style, apparently false expressions, which a man might occasionally venture upon with diffidence in the transport of his rapture, become the ordinary language; he dazzles, he repels, he terrifies, he disgusts, he oppresses; his verses are a piercing and sublime song, pitched in too high a key, above the reach of our organs, which offends our ears, of which our mind alone can divine the justice and beauty.

Yet this is little; for that singular force of concentration

[1] *Ibid.*

is redoubled by the suddenness of the dash which it displays. In Shakspeare there is no preparation, no adaptation, no development, no care to make himself understood. Like a too fiery and powerful horse, he bounds, but cannot run. He bridges in a couple of words an enormous interval; is at the two poles in a single instant. The reader vainly looks for the intermediate track; confounded by these prodigious leaps, he wonders by what miracle the poet has entered upon a new idea the very moment when he quitted the last, seeing perhaps between the two images a long scale of transitions, which we pace painfully step by step, but which he has spanned in a stride. Shakspeare flies, we creep. Hence comes a style made up of conceits, bold images shattered in an instant by others still bolder, barely indicated ideas completed by others far removed, no visible connexion, but a visible incoherence; at every step we halt, the track failing; and there, far above us, lo, stands the poet, and we find that we have ventured in his footsteps, through a craggy land, full of precipices, which he threads, as if it were a straightforward road, but on which our greatest efforts barely carry us along.

What will you think, further, if we observe that these vehement expressions, so unexpected, instead of following one after the other, slowly and with effort, are hurled out by hundreds, with an impetuous ease and abundance, like the bubbling waves from a welling spring, which are heaped together, rise one above another, and find no place wide enough to spread themselves and fall? You may find in *Romeo and Juliet* a score of examples of this inexhaustible inspiration. The two lovers pile up an infinite mass of metaphors, impassioned exaggerations, clenches, contorted phrases, amorous extravagances. Their language is like the trill of nightingales. Shakspeare's wits, Mercutio, Beatrice, Rosalind, his clowns, buffoons, sparkle with far-fetched jokes, which rattle out like a musketry-fire. There is none of them but provides enough play of words to stock a whole theatre. Lear's curses, or Queen Margaret's, would suffice for all the madmen in an asylum, or all the oppressed of the earth. The sonnets are a delirium of ideas and images, turned out with an energy enough to make a man giddy. His first poem, *Venus and Adonis,* is the sensual ecstasy of a Correggio, insatiable and excited. This exuberant fecundity intensifies qualities already in excess, and multiplies a hundred-fold the luxuriance of metaphor, the incoherence of style, and the unbridled vehemence of expression.[1]

All that I have said may be compressed into a few words. Objects were taken into his mind organised and complete; they pass into ours disjointed, decomposed, fragmentarily. He thought in the lump, we think piecemeal; hence his style and our style—two languages not to be reconciled. We, for our part, writers and reasoners, can note precisely by a word each isolated fraction of an idea, and represent the due order of its parts by the due order of our expressions. We advance gradually; we affiliate, go down to the roots, try and treat our words as numbers, our sentences as equations; we employ but general terms, which every mind can understand, and regular constructions, into which any mind can enter; we attain justness and clearness, not life. Shakspeare lets justness and clearness look out for themselves, and attains life. From amidst his complex conception and his coloured semi-vision he grasps a fragment, a quivering fibre, and shows it; it is for you, from this fragment, to divine the rest. He, behind the word, has a whole picture, an attitude, a long argument abridged, a mass of swarming ideas; you know them, these abbreviative, condensive words: these are they which we launch out from the furnace of invention, in a fit of passion—words of slang or of fashion, which appeal to local memory or individual experience; [2] little concocted and incorrect phrases, which, by their irregularity, express the suddenness and the breaks of the inner sensation; trivial words, exaggerated figures.[3] There is a gesture beneath each, a quick contraction of the brows, a curl of laughing lips, a clown's trick, an unhinging of the whole machine. None of them mark ideas; each is the extremity and issue of a complete mimic action; none is the expression and definition of a partial and limited idea. This is why Shakspeare is strange and powerful, obscure and

[1] This is why, in the eyes of a writer of the seventeenth century, Shakspeare's style is the most obscure, pretentious, painful, barbarous, and absurd, that could be imagined.

[2] Shakspeare's vocabulary is the most copious of all. It comprises about 15,000 words; Milton's only 8000.

[3] See the conversation of Laertes and his sister, and of Laertes and Polonius, in *Hamlet*. The style is foreign to the situation; and we see here plainly the natural and necessary process of Shakspeare's thought.

original, beyond all the poets of his or any other age; the most immoderate of all violators of language, the most marvellous of all creators of souls, the farthest removed from regular logic and classical reason, the one most capable of exciting in us a world of forms, and of placing living beings before us.

GEORGE SANTAYANA

George Santayana (1863-1952). One of the great masters of philosophical prose, Santayana taught at Harvard but after 1912 lived in Europe. His books include The Sense of Beauty *(1896),* The Life of Reason *(1905-6),* The Realms of Being *(1927-40),* Interpretations of Poetry and Religion *(1900) and* Three Philosophical Poets *(1910).*

THE ABSENCE OF RELIGION IN SHAKESPEARE*

We are accustomed to think of the universality of Shakespeare as not the least of his glories. No other poet has given so many-sided an expression to human nature, or rendered so many passions and moods with such an appropriate variety of style, sentiment, and accent. If, therefore, we were asked to select one monument of human civilisation that should survive to some future age, or be transported to another planet to bear witness to the inhabitants there of what we have been upon earth, we should probably choose the works of Shakespeare. In them we recognise the truest portrait and best memorial of man. Yet the archæologists of that future age, or the cosmographers of that other part of the heavens, after conscientious study of our Shakespearian autobiography, would misconceive our life in one important respect. They would hardly understand that man had had a religion.

There are, indeed, numerous exclamations and invocations in Shakespeare which we, who have other means of

* From *Interpretations of Poetry and Religion.*

information, know to be evidences of current religious ideas. Shakespeare adopts these, as he adopts the rest of his vocabulary, from the society about him. But he seldom or never gives them their original value. When Iago says "'*sblood*," a commentator might add explanations which should involve the whole philosophy of Christian devotion; but this Christian sentiment is not in Iago's mind, nor in Shakespeare's, any more than the virtues of Heracles and his twelve labours are in the mind of every slave and pander that cries "*hercule*" in the pages of Plautus and Terence. Oaths are the fossils of piety. The geologist recognises in them the relics of a once active devotion, but they are now only counters and pebbles tossed about in the unconscious play of expression. The lighter and more constant their use, the less their meaning.

Only one degree more inward than this survival of a religious vocabulary in profane speech is the reference we often find in Shakespeare to religious institutions and traditions. There are monks, bishops, and cardinals; there is even mention of saints, although none is ever presented to us in person. The clergy, if they have any wisdom, have an earthly one. Friar Lawrence culls his herbs like a more benevolent Medea; and Cardinal Wolsey flings away ambition with a profoundly Pagan despair; his robe and his integrity to heaven are cold comfort to him. Juliet goes to shrift to arrange her love affairs, and Ophelia should go to a nunnery to forget hers. Even the chastity of Isabella has little in it that would have been out of place in Iphigenia. The metaphysical Hamlet himself sees a "true ghost," but so far reverts to the positivism that underlies Shakespeare's thinking as to speak soon after of that "undiscovered country from whose bourn no traveller returns."

There are only two or three short passages in the plays, and one sonnet, in which true religious feeling seems to break forth. The most beautiful of these passages is that in "Richard II," which commemorates the death of Mowbray, Duke of Norfolk:—

> *Many a time hath banished Norfolk fought*
> *For Jesu Christ in glorious Christian field,*
> *Streaming the ensign of the Christian cross*
> *Against black Pagans, Turks, and Saracens;*

> And, toiled with works of war, retired himself
> To Italy; and there, at Venice, gave
> His body to that pleasant country's earth,
> And his pure soul unto his captain Christ,
> Under whose colours he had fought so long.

This is tender and noble, and full of an indescribable chivalry and pathos, yet even here we find the spirit of war rather than that of religion, and a deeper sense of Italy than of heaven. More unmixed is the piety of Henry V after the battle of Agincourt:—

> O God, thy arm was here;
> And not to us, but to thy arm alone,
> Ascribe we all!—When, without stratagem,
> But in plain shock and even play of battle,
> Was ever known so great and little loss,
> On one part and on the other?—Take it, God,
> For it is none but thine. . . .
> Come, go we in procession to the village,
> And be it death proclaimed through our host,
> To boast of this, or take that praise from God,
> Which is his only. . . .
> Do we all holy rites;
> Let there be sung Non nobis ana Te Deum.

This passage is certainly a true expression of religious feeling, and just the kind that we might expect from a dramatist. Religion appears here as a manifestation of human nature and as an expression of human passion. The passion, however, is not due to Shakespeare's imagination, but is essentially historical: the poet has simply not rejected, as he usually does, the religious element in the situation he reproduces.[1]

[1] "And so aboute foure of the clocke in the afternoone, the Kynge when he saw no apparaunce of enemies, caused the retreite to be blowen, and gathering his army togither, gave thankes to almightie god for so happy a victory, causing his prelates and chapleines to sing this psalm, In exitu Israell de Egipto, and commandyng every man to kneele downe on the grounde at this verse; Non nobis, domine, non nobis, sed nomini tuo da gloriam. Which done, he caused Te Deum, with certain anthems, to be song, giving laud & praise to god, and not boasting of his owne force or any humaine power." HOLINSHED.

With this dramatic representation of piety we may couple another, of a more intimate kind, from the Sonnets:—

Poor soul, the centre of my sinful earth,
Fooled by these rebel powers that thee array,
Why dost thou pine within and suffer dearth,
Painting thy outward walls so costly gay?
Why so large cost, having so short a lease,
Dost thou upon thy fading mansion spend?
Shall worms, inheritors of this excess,
Eat up thy charge? Is this thy body's end?
Then, soul, live thou upon thy servant's loss,
And let that pine to aggravate thy store;
Buy terms divine by selling hours of dross,
Within be fed, without be rich no more:
Then shalt thou feed on death, that feeds on men,
And death once dead, there's no more dying then.

This sonnet contains more than a natural religious emotion inspired by a single event. It contains reflection, and expresses a feeling not merely dramatically proper but rationally just. A mind that habitually ran into such thoughts would be philosophically pious; it would be spiritual. The Sonnets, as a whole, are spiritual; their passion is transmuted into discipline. Their love, which, whatever its nominal object, is hardly anything but love of beauty and youth in general, is made to triumph over time by a metaphysical transformation of the object into something eternal. At first this is the beauty of the race renewing itself by generation, then it is the description of beauty in the poet's verse, and finally it is the immortal soul enriched by the contemplation of that beauty. This noble theme is the more impressively rendered by being contrasted with another, with a vulgar love that by its nature refuses to be so transformed and transmuted. "Two loves," cries the poet, in a line that gives us the essence of the whole, "Two loves I have,—of comfort, and despair."

In all this depth of experience, however, there is still wanting any religious image. The Sonnets are spiritual, but, with the doubtful exception of the one quoted above, they are not Christian. And, of course, a poet of Shakespeare's time could not have found any other mould than Christianity for his religion. In our day, with our wide and conscientious historical sympathies, it may be possible for us to find in other rites and doctrines than those of our ancestors an expression of some ultimate truth. But for Shakespeare, in the matter of religion, the choice lay between Christianity and nothing. He chose nothing; he chose to leave his heroes and himself in the presence of life and of death with no other philosophy than that which the profane world can suggest and understand.

This positivism, we need hardly say, was not due to any grossness or sluggishness in his imagination. Shakespeare could be idealistic when he dreamed, as he could be spiritual when he reflected. The spectacle of life did not pass before his eyes as a mere phantasmagoria. He seized upon its principles; he became wise. Nothing can exceed the ripeness of his seasoned judgment, or the occasional breadth, sadness, and terseness of his reflection. The author of "Hamlet" could not be without metaphysical aptitude; "Macbeth" could not have been written without a sort of sibylline inspiration, or the Sonnets without something of the Platonic mind. It is all the more remarkable, therefore, that we should have to search through all the works of Shakespeare to find half a dozen passages that have so much as a religious sound, and that even these passages, upon examination, should prove not to be the expression of any deep religious conception. If Shakespeare had been without metaphysical capacity, or without moral maturity, we could have explained his strange insensibility to religion; but as it is, we must marvel at his indifference and ask ourselves what can be the causes of it. For, even if we should not regard the absence of religion as an imperfection in his own thought, we must admit it to be an incompleteness in his portrayal of the thought of others. Positivism may be a virtue in a philosopher, but it is a vice in a dramatist, who has to render those human passions to which the religious imagination has always given a larger meaning and a richer depth.

Those greatest poets by whose side we are accustomed to put Shakespeare did not forego this advantage. They gave us man with his piety and the world with its gods. Homer is the chief repository of the Greek religion, and Dante the faithful interpreter of the Catholic. Nature would have been inconceivable to them without the supernatural, or man without the influence and companionship of the gods. These poets live in a cosmos. In their minds, as in the mind of their age, the fragments of experience have fallen together into a perfect picture, like the bits of glass in a kaleidoscope. Their universe is a total. Reason and imagination have mastered it completely and peopled it. No chaos remains beyond, or, if it does, it is thought of with an involuntary shudder that soon passes into a healthy indifference. They have a theory of human life; they see man in his relations, surrounded by a kindred universe in which he fills his allotted place. He knows the meaning and issue of his life, and does not voyage without a chart.

Shakespeare's world, on the contrary, is only the world of human society. The cosmos eludes him; he does not seem to feel the need of framing that idea. He depicts human life in all its richness and variety, but leaves that life without a setting, and consequently without a meaning. If we asked him to tell us what is the significance of the passion and beauty he had so vividly displayed, and what is the outcome of it all, he could hardly answer in any other words than those he puts into the mouth of Macbeth:—

> To-morrow, and to-morrow, and to-morrow,
> Creeps in this petty pace from day to day,
> To the last syllable of recorded time;
> And all our yesterdays have lighted fools
> The way to dusty death. Out, out, brief candle!
> Life's but a walking shadow, a poor player
> That struts and frets his hour upon the stage
> And then is heard no more: it is a tale
> Told by an idiot, full of sound and fury,
> Signifying nothing.

How differently would Homer or Dante have answered that question! Their tragedy would have been illumined by a sense of the divinity of life and beauty, or by a sense of the sanctity of suffering and death. Their faith had enveloped the world of experience in a world of imagination, in which the ideals of the reason, of the fancy, and of the heart had a natural expression. They had caught in the reality the hint of a lovelier fable,—a fable in which that reality was

completed and idealised, and made at once vaster in its
extent and more intelligible in its principle. They had, as
it were, dramatised the universe, and endowed it with the
tragic unities. In contrast with such a luminous philosophy
and so well-digested an experience, the silence of Shakespeare and his philosophical incoherence have something
in them that is still heathen; something that makes us
wonder whether the northern mind, even in him, did not
remain morose and barbarous at its inmost core.

But before we allow ourselves such hasty and general
inferences, we may well stop to consider whether there is
not some simpler answer to our question. An epic poet,
we might say, naturally deals with cosmic themes. He needs
supernatural machinery because he depicts the movement
of human affairs in their generality, as typified in the figures
of heroes whose function it is to embody or to overcome
elemental forces. Such a poet's world is fabulous, because
his inspiration is impersonal. But the dramatist renders the
concrete reality of life. He has no need of a superhuman
setting for his pictures. Such a setting would destroy the
vitality of his creations. His plots should involve only human actors and human motives: the *deus ex machina* has
always been regarded as an interloper on his stage. The
passions of man are his all-sufficient material; he should
weave his whole fabric out of them.

To admit the truth of all this would not, however, solve
our problem. The dramatist cannot be expected to put cos-
mogonies on the boards. Miracle-plays become dramatic
only when they become human. But the supernatural world,
which the playwright does not bring before the footlights,
may exist nevertheless in the minds of his characters and
of his audience. He may refer to it, appeal to it, and imply
it, in the actions and in the sentiments he attributes to his
heroes. And if the comparison of Shakespeare with Homer
or Dante on the score of religious inspiration is invalidated
by the fact that he is a dramatist while they are epic poets,
a comparison may yet be instituted between Shakespeare
and other dramatists, from which his singular insensibility
to religion will as readily appear.

Greek tragedy, as we know, is dominated by the idea of
fate. Even when the gods do not appear in person, or where
the service or neglect of them is not the moving cause of

the whole play,—as it is in the "Bacchæ" and the "Hippolytus" of Euripides,—still the deep conviction of the limits and conditions of human happiness underlies the fable. The will of man fulfils the decrees of Heaven. The hero manifests a higher force than his own, both in success and in failure. The fates guide the willing and drag the unwilling. There is no such fragmentary view of life as we have in our romantic drama, where accidents make the meaningless happiness or unhappiness of a supersensitive adventurer. Life is seen whole, although in miniature. Its boundaries and its principles are studied more than its incidents. The human, therefore, everywhere merges with the divine. Our mortality, being sharply defined and much insisted upon, draws the attention all the more to that eternity of Nature and of law in which it is embosomed. Nor is the fact of superhuman control left for our reflection to discover; it is emphatically asserted in those oracles on which so much of the action commonly turns.

When the Greek religion was eclipsed by the Christian, the ancient way of conceiving the ultra-human relations of human life became obsolete. It was no longer possible to speak with sincerity of the oracles and gods, of Nemesis and ὕβρις. Yet for a long time it was not possible to speak in any other terms. The new ideas were without definition, and literature was paralysed. But in the course of ages, when the imagination had had time and opportunity to develop a Christian art and a Christian philosophy, the dramatic poets were ready to deal with the new themes. Only their readiness in this respect surpassed their ability, at least their ability to please those who had any memory of the ancient perfection of the arts.

The miracle-plays were the beginning. Their crudity was extreme and their levity of the frankest; but they had still, like the Greek plays, a religious excuse and a religious background. They were not without dramatic power, but their offences against taste and their demands upon faith were too great for them to survive the Renaissance. Such plays as the "Polyeucte" of Corneille and the "Devocion de la Cruz" of Calderón, with other Spanish plays that might be mentioned, are examples of Christian dramas by poets of culture; but as a whole we must say that Christianity, while it succeeded in expressing itself in painting and in architecture, failed to express itself in any adequate drama. Where Christianity was strong, the drama either disappeared or became secular; and it has never again dealt with cosmic themes successfully, except in such hands as those of Goethe and Wagner, men who either neglected Christianity altogether or used it only as an incidental ornament, having, as they say, transcended it in their philosophy.

The fact is, that art and reflection have never been able to unite perfectly the two elements of a civilisation like ours, that draws its culture from one source and its religion from another. Modern taste has ever been, and still is, largely exotic, largely a revolution in favour of something ancient or foreign. The more cultivated a period has been, the more wholly it has reverted to antiquity for its inspiration. The existence of that completer world has haunted all minds struggling for self-expression, and interfered, perhaps, with the natural development of their genius. The old art which they could not disregard distracted them from the new ideal, and prevented them from embodying this ideal outwardly; while the same ideal, retaining their inward allegiance, made their revivals of ancient forms artificial and incomplete. The strange idea could thus gain admittance that art was not called to deal with everything; that its sphere was the world of polite conventions. The serious and the sacred things of life were to be left unexpressed and inarticulate; while the arts masqueraded in the forms of a Pagan antiquity, to which a triviality was at the same time attributed which in fact it had not possessed. This unfortunate separation of experience and its artistic expression betrayed itself in the inadequacy of what was beautiful and the barbarism of what was sincere.

When such are the usual conditions of artistic creation, we need not wonder that Shakespeare, a poet of the Renaissance, should have confined his representation of life to its secular aspects, and that his readers after him should rather have marvelled at the variety of the things of which he showed an understanding than have taken note of the one thing he overlooked. To omit religion was after all to omit what was not felt to be congenial to a poet's mind. The poet was to trace for us the passionate and romantic embroideries of life; he was to be artful and humane, and above all he was to be delightful. The beauty and charm of things had nothing any longer to do with those painful mysteries and contentions which made the temper of the pious so acrid and sad. In Shakespeare's time and country, to be religious already began to mean to be Puritanical; and in the divorce between the fulness of life on the one hand and the depth and unity of faith on the other, there could be no doubt to which side a man of imaginative instincts would attach himself. A world of passion and beauty without a meaning must seem to him more interesting and worthy than a world of empty principle and dogma, meagre, fanatical, and false. It was beyond the power of synthesis possessed by that age and nation to find a principle of all passion and a religion of all life.

This power of synthesis is indeed so difficult and rare that the attempt to gain it is sometimes condemned as too philosophical, and as tending to embarrass the critical eye and creative imagination with futile theories. We might say, for instance, that the absence of religion in Shakespeare was a sign of his good sense; that a healthy instinct kept his attention within the sublunary world; and that he was in that respect superior to Homer and to Dante. For, while they allowed their wisdom to clothe itself in fanciful forms, he gave us his in its immediate truth, so that he embodied what they signified. The supernatural machinery of their poems was, we might say, an accidental incumbrance, a traditional means of expression, which they only half understood, and which made their representation of life indirect and partly unreal. Shakespeare, on the other hand, had reached his poetical majority and independence. He rendered human experience no longer through symbols, but by direct imaginative representation. What I have treated as a limitation in him would, then, appear as the maturity of his strength.

There is always a class of minds in whom the spectacle of history produces a certain apathy of reason. They flatter themselves that they can escape defeat by not attempting the highest tasks. We need not here stop to discuss what value as truth a philosophical synthesis may hope to attain, nor have we to protest against the æsthetic preference for the sketch and the episode over a reasoned and unified rendering of life. Suffice it to say that the human race hitherto, whenever it has reached a phase of comparatively high development and freedom, has formed a conception of its place in Nature, no less than of the contents of its life; and that this conception has been the occasion of religious sentiments and practices; and further, that every art, whether literary or plastic, has drawn its favourite themes from this religious sphere. The poetic imagination has not commonly stopped short of the philosophical in representing a superhuman environment of man.

Shakespeare, however, is remarkable among the greater poets for being without a philosophy and without a religion. In his drama there is no fixed conception of any forces, natural or moral, dominating and transcending our mortal energies. Whether this characteristic be regarded as a merit or as a defect, its presence cannot be denied. Those who think it wise or possible to refrain from searching for general principles, and are satisfied with the successive empirical appearance of things, without any faith in their rational continuity or completeness, may well see in Shakespeare their natural prophet. For he, too, has been satisfied with the successive description of various passions and events. His world, like the earth before Columbus, extends in an indefinite plane which he is not tempted to explore.

Those of us, however, who believe in circumnavigation, and who think that both human reason and human imagination require a certain totality in our views, and who feel that the most important thing in life is the lesson of it, and its relation to its own ideal,—we can hardly find in Shakespeare all that the highest poet could give. Fulness is not necessarily wholeness, and the most profuse wealth of characterisation seems still inadequate as a picture of experience, if this picture is not somehow seen from above and reduced to a dramatic unity,—to that unity of meaning that can suffuse its endless details with something of dignity, simplicity, and peace. This is the imaginative power found in several poets we have mentioned,—the power that gives certain passages in Lucretius also their sublimity, as it gives sublimity to many passages in the Bible.

For what is required for theoretic wholeness is not this or that system but some system. Its value is not the value of truth, but that of victorious imagination. Unity of conception is an æsthetic merit no less than a logical demand. A fine sense of the dignity and pathos of life cannot be attained unless we conceive somehow its outcome and its relations. Without such a conception our emotions cannot be steadfast and enlightened. Without it the imagination cannot fulfil its essential function or achieve its supreme success. Shakespeare himself, had it not been for the time and place in which he lived, when religion and imagination blocked rather than helped each other, would perhaps have allowed more of a cosmic background to appear behind his crowded scenes. If the Christian in him was not the real man, at least the Pagan would have spoken frankly. The material forces of Nature, or their vague embodiment in some northern pantheon, would then have stood behind his heroes. The various movements of events would have appeared as incidents in a larger drama to which they had at least some symbolic relation. We should have been awed as well as saddened, and purified as well as pleased, by being made to feel the dependence of human accidents upon cosmic forces and their fated evolution. Then we should not have been able to say that Shakespeare was without a religion. For the effort of religion, says Goethe, is to adjust us to the inevitable; each religion in its way strives to bring about this consummation.

BENEDETTO CROCE

Benedetto Croce (1866-1952). One of the most influential of recent Italian thinkers, he persuaded a generation that the common scholarly attitudes to historical fact and literary quality were philosophically unsound, advocating a doctrine of art as intuitive language. This passage on Shakespeare is characteristic in its emphasis of the poetic personality of the author rather than in literary analysis.

SHAKESPEARE'S IDEAL DEVELOPMENT*

It is clear that in considering the principal motives of Shakespeare's poetry and arranging them in series of increasing complexity, we have not availed ourselves of any quantitative criterion or rule of measurement, but have considered only the philosophical concept of the spirit, which is perpetual growth upon itself, and of which every new act, since it includes its predecessors, is in this sense more rich than they. We declare in the same way, that prose is more complex than poetry, because it follows poetry, assumes and dominates, while making use of it, and that certain concepts and problems imply and presuppose certain others; we further declare that a particular equality in poetry presupposes other poetry of a more elementary quality, and that a pessimistic song of love or sorrow, presupposes a simple love-song.

Thus, in the succession of his works as we have considered them, which might be more closely defined and particularised, we have nothing less than the ideal development of Shakespeare's spirit, deduced from the very quality of the poetical works themselves, from the physiognomy of each and from their reciprocal relations, which cannot but appear in relations which are serial and evolutionary. The comedies of love and the romantic comedies have the vagueness of a dream, followed by the hard reality of the historical plays, and from these we pass to the great tragedies, which are dream and reality and more than dream and reality. The general line followed by the poet even offered the temptation to construct his development by means of the dialectic triad of thesis, antithesis and synthesis. But we do not recommend this course, or if followed, it should only be with the view of reaching and adopting a compendious and brilliant formula, without suppressing in any way the consciousness of complexity and variety of many effective passages, much less the positive value of individual expressions.

This development does not in any case coincide with the

* From *Ariosto, Shakespeare and Corneille,* translated by Douglas Ainslie.

chronological order, because the chronological order takes the works in the order in which they are apprehensible from without, that is to say, in the order in which they have been written, acted or printed, and arranges them in a series that is qualitatively irregular, or in other words, chronicles them. Now this arrangement must not be opposed to or placed on a level with the other, as though it were the real opposed to the ideal development, for the ideal is the only truly real development, while the chronological is fictitious or arbitrary, and thus unreal; that is to say, in clear terms, it does not represent development, but simply a series or succession. To make this point yet more clear, by means of an example taken from common experience, we have all known men, who in their youth have practised or tried to practise some form of activity (music, versification, painting, philosophy, etc.) which they have afterwards abandoned for other activities, more suitable, because in them susceptible of richer development. These men, later on, in their maturity, or when old age is approaching, revert to those earlier occupations, and take delight in composing verses or music, in painting or in philosophising, returning, as they say, to their old loves. Such returns are certainly never pure and simple returns: they are always coloured to some extent by what has occurred in the interval. But they really and substantially belong to the anterior moment; the differences that we observe in them some part of that particular consideration which we have disregarded in considering the development of Shakespeare, while recommending it as a theme for special study. As we find in works which represent a return to the period of youth, echoes of the mature period, so in youthful works we sometimes find anticipations and suggestions of the mature period. This is the case with Shakespeare, not only in certain situations and characters of the historical plays, but also in certain effects of the *Dream,* the *Merchant of Venice* and *Romeo and Juliet.*

As the result of our argument, we cannot pass from the ideal to the extrinsic or chronological order, and therefore it could only indicate caprice, were we to conclude from the fact that *Titus Andronicus* represents a literary Shakespeare or a theatrical imitator, that it must chronologically precede *Romeo and Juliet,* or even *Love's*

Labour's Lost. The same applies to the argument that because *Cymbeline,* the *Winter's Tale* and *Pericles* are composed of romantic material similar to that of *All's Well,* of *Much Ado* and of *Twelfth Night* (where we find innocent maidens falsely accused and afterwards triumphant, dead women, who turn out to be alive, women dressed as men, and the like), that they must all have been written at the same time. The same holds good of the historical plays: we cannot argue from the fact that these plays represent a more complex condition of the soul than the love comedies and the romantic plays, that the historical plays are all of them to be dated later than the two groups above-mentioned; or that for the same reasons, *Hamlet,* the first *Hamlet,* could not by any means have been composed by Shakespeare in his very earliest period, about 1592, as Swinburne asserts, swears and takes his solemn oath is the case: and who knows but he is right?

In like manner, we cannot pass from the chronological to the ideal order, and since the chronology, documentary or conjectural, places *Coriolanus* after *Hamlet,* and also after *Othello, Macbeth, Lear* and *Anthony and Cleopatra,* must not, therefore, insist upon finding in it profound thoughts, which it does not contain, or deny that it belongs to the period of the "historical plays" with which it has the closest connection. Again, although the chronology places *Cymbeline* and the *Winter's Tale,* as has been said, in the last years of Shakespeare's life, we must not insist upon finding profound meanings in those works, or talk, as some have done, of a superior ethic, a "theological ethic," to which Shakespeare is supposed at last to have attained, or dwell upon the gracious idyllic scenes to be found in them, weighing them down with non-existent mysteries, making out that the Imogens and Hermiones are beings of equal or greater poetic intensity than Cordelia, or Desdemona, or take Leontes for Othello, Jacques for Iago, whereas, in the eyes of those possessed of poetic sentiment, the former stand to the latter in the relation of little decorative studies compared to works by Raphael or Giorgione. Proof of this is to be found in the fact that the latter have become popular and live in the hearts and minds of all, while the former please us, we admire them, and pass on.

All that can be admitted, because comformable to logic and experience, is that the two orders in general—but quite in general, and therefore with several exceptions and disagreements—big and little—correspond to one another. Indeed, if we take the usual chronological order, as fixed by philologists and to be found in all Shakespearean manuals and at the head of the plays, with little variation, we see that the first comedies of love and the tragedy of Romeo and Juliet, including the romantic element, which is common to all of them, belong to the first period, between 1591 and 1592. We next find the historical plays, the comedies of love and the romantic dramas, closely associated; then begins the period of the great tragedies, *Julius Caesar* and *Anthony and Cleopatra;* then again,—after a return to anterior forms with *Coriolanus, Cymbeline* and the *Winter's Tale,*—we reach the *Tempest,* which seems to be the last, or among the last of Shakespeare's works.

Biographers have tried to explain the last period of Shakespeare's poetry in various ways, sometimes as the period of his *"becoming serene,"* sometimes as that of his *"poetical exhaustion"* sometimes as *"an attempt after new forms of art";* but with such utterances as these, we find ourselves among those conjectural constructions, which we have purposely avoided, if for no other reason than that so many people, who are good for nothing else, make them every day, and we do not wish to deprive them of their occupation.

The *biographical* character of that period can be interpreted, as we please, as one of repose, of gay facility, of weariness, of expectation and training for new works, and so on: but the *poetical* character of the works in question, is such as we have described and such as all see and feel that it is. It is too but a biographical conjecture, however plausible,—but certainly most graceful and pleasing—, which maintains that the magician Prospero, who breaks his wand, buries his book of enchantments, and dismisses his aerial spirit Ariel, ready to obey his every nod, symbolizes William Shakespeare himself, who henceforth renounces his art and takes leave of the imaginary world, which he had created for his own delight and in obedience to the law of his own development and where till then he had lived as sovereign.

E. E. STOLL

E. E. Stoll (1874-1959). Professor of English, University of Minnesota, Stoll wrote much Shakespeare criticism, including Shakespeare Studies *(1927),* Poets and Playwrights *(1930),* Art and Artifice in Shakespeare *(1933) and* Shakespeare and other Masters *(1940). His work was influential in disseminating a more historical approach to the plotting and characterisation of Shakespeare and to Elizabethan stage conventions. See the Introduction.*

SHAKESPEARE'S CHARACTERISATION*

The big and serious inconsistencies in Shakespeare, then, arise mainly . . . out of the improbable but striking old plot he employed, or out of the simplified treatment of such a plot and the contrasts which he sought deliberately, or out of inadvertence or hastiness in workmanship. But that does not mean that Shakespeare had not a wide and liberal view of the range and Protean changes of human nature—the widest. If he had no apparent knowledge of the dark and furtive flights and evasions of the human spirit which modern psychology has discovered and modern fiction disclosed, he knew enough not to keep her strictly fettered to a rôle. He was not troubled by—does not trouble us with— psychology, but in tone and opinion no other poet's creatures change colour so freely while remaining the same. His characters are not always serious or humorous, not always stately or simple, not even always fixed at the same point of view, and neither rules of *decorum* nor principles of logic

* Extracted from *Shakespeare Studies* (Frederick Ungar Publishing Co., Inc., New York, 1927).

are there to limit them. His characters are the sons of nature—'we are the sons of women, Justice Shallow,' said
Falstaff; while those of Corneille and Racine belong to
court or camp, if not rather indeed to the stage. The human
heart contains four chambers, not one; the human brain is
folded into a thousand wrinkles and convolutions; and
Shakespeare gives us something of the variety of life itself.
To him man is not a fiddle with one string, as he often is in
French tragedy or comedy, but a harp provided with many;
and he fingers and sweeps them all. What a gamut is run in
Hamlet alone—love and tenderness, grief and melancholy,
hate, scorn, rage, despair, humour and irony, scepticism
and awe. Faulconbridge—even Cloten—rises to a pitch of
dignity, when as an Englishman he faces the foreigner;
Shylock, when he defends his race; Coriolanus, the oaken-
garlanded hero, flushed with victory, must—as in life he
some time or other would—go wash. Lady Macbeth, at the
supreme moment when Macbeth comes before her, his
hands stained at her bidding with the blood of their guest
and King, speaks the language of barest commonplace but
tensest passion, 'My husband!' nothing more. Again contrast counts: he is her husband still, nay—through the
blood—as he had never been. Macduff breaks silence with a
Humph! when he hears of his wife and children's murder.
Lear, the great King, in the throes of heart-break, groans,
'Pray undo this button,' which is the humblest of prayers or
services. Queen Cleopatra, having already chosen death as
the better part, does not even forget her cunning, but
endeavours like a sharper to cheat Cæsar out of her jewels
and treasure. And though Schlegel (*in vieler Hinsicht kein
Mann*) was, for all his learning and insight, not the one to
appreciate how Emilia, speaking lightly and loosely of the
marriage tie, could yet to her mistress be staunchly true, it
is not among the least of Shakespeare's glories that the like
cannot be said of him. And though of late Professor
Schücking has found the aria on Queen Mab to be out of
keeping on the smutty lips of Mercutio, Shakespeare, Aristophanes, the poets of the Restoration—Titania herself—
well knew that the lyric gift and a faery fancy are not incompatible with a sort of gay and gleeful indecency, and
would have detected the fantastic vein running all through
him. But this liberty of his characters to unbend and disport

themselves, to step down from poetry to prose, and from seriousness to humour, or from the humdrum to rise to the heights, is nothing to their liberty to be both one and the other at the same moment. Human emotion is a complex, a multiple mixture, and in French tragedy the serious element is abstracted—extracted one might say—and alone presented. But Hamlet jeers and gibes when his heart is breaking; Mercutio dies scolding but jesting still; Othello smiles as he faces the bright swords and with words that would have blunted them defends himself in court; and Juliet, finding the poisoned cup in her dead lover's hand, speaks to him, when at the moment perchance of rejoining him, with a pitiful flicker of the gaiety that she had shown while they had been together: 'O churl!' she murmurs— 'bad boy!'—

> O churl! drunk all, and left no friendly drop
> To help me after.

Death is a word lovers are slow to learn, and even now she is speaking to Romeo, not of him. And Cleopatra on her deathbed is still the amorous, intriguing, wrangling Queen, jealous of Iras who may meet Antony first—for without kissing what would Heaven be?—but tickled at the thought of outwitting by her death great Cæsar, 'ass unpolicied!'

That is Shakespeare's vein and not another's. His mind was creative and accretive, we have seen, not critical; synthetic, not analytic; and it comprehended human passion in all its mysterious amplitude. No one ever depicted it so truly, even in its changes and phases, as it waxes or wanes, or starts and quivers like a living thing. Hamlet, Othello, Mercutio, Juliet, however different, are always indubitably before us. But it was the passion as a whole that he presented; he laid nothing bare. It was the result of the change that interested him, not the internal mechanism, not the cause or motive which produced it. His touch seldom failed him, though his reasoning sometimes did. He made few discoveries or disclosures; there is little in his characters that is surprising and at the same time (as we must instantly realize) indisputably true. What is surprising is generally not true, or, else, like Cleopatra's cheating (taken from the source), left unexplained; and he has no characters like Diana of the Crossways, Manon Lescaut, Monna Vanna, Carmen, Stendhal's Duchess of Sanseverina, Dostoevsky's Liza or Stavrogin, and some of the characters of Browning. The good man Ivan, after he slew the woman, was found unconcernedly playing with the children, by the village elders who had sat in judgment on him. In all Shakespeare, I think, there is nothing like that. We have seen above that he had little casuistry in him, and dealt not in deep moral incongruities or paradoxes, in contentions or entanglements, keeping to the plain high road of life, as Coleridge said. An artist may be much interested in such things as questions and problems, and yet keep to the high road himself; but to be a discoverer he must in imagination venture to leave it, shift his mental and moral latitude or longitude, and go boldly out into the bush. There people live their own lives, and hold by their own values, not only for themselves, but for others, as they do not, we have seen, in Shakespeare. But though he knew not their lives and opinions, he had heard and caught the accents of their voices, and had powers within him to reproduce them, as has done no one before him or since.

G. WILSON KNIGHT

G. Wilson Knight (1897-   ). Author of Myth and Miracle *(1929),* The Wheel of Fire *(1930),* The Imperial Theme *(1931),* The Shakespearean Tempest *(1932),* The Crown of Life *(1947),* The Mutual Flame *(1955) and many other books. His place in Shakespeare criticism is discussed in the Introduction.*

SHAKESPEARE INTERPRETATION*

To receive the whole Shakespearian vision into the intellectual consciousness demands a certain and very definite

* Extracted from *The Wheel of Fire.*

act of mind. One must be prepared to see the whole play in space as well as in time. It is natural in analysis to pursue the steps of the tale in sequence, noticing the logic that connects them, regarding those essentials that Aristotle noted: the beginning, middle, and end. But by giving supreme attention to this temporal nature of drama we omit what, in Shakespeare, is at least of equivalent importance. A Shakespearian tragedy is set spatially as well as temporally in the mind. By this I mean that there are throughout the play a set of correspondences which relate to each other independently of the time-sequence which is the story: such are the intuition-intelligence opposition active within and across *Troilus and Cressida,* the death-theme in *Hamlet,* the nightmare evil of *Macbeth.* This I have sometimes called the play's 'atmosphere'. In interpretation of *Othello* it has to take the form of an essential relation, abstracted from the story, existing between the Othello, Desdemona, and Iago conceptions. Generally, however, there is unity, not diversity. Perhaps it is what Aristotle meant by 'unity of idea'. Now if we are prepared to see the whole play laid out, so to speak, as an area, being simultaneously aware of these thickly-scattered correspondences in a single view of the whole, we possess the unique quality of the play in a new sense. 'Faults' begin to vanish into thin air. Immediately we begin to realize necessity where before we saw irrelevance and beauty dethroning ugliness. For the Shakespearian person is intimately fused with this atmospheric quality; he obeys a spatial as well as a temporal necessity. Gloucester's mock-suicide, Malcolm's detailed confession of crimes, Ulysses' long speech on order, are cases in point. But because we, in our own lives and those of our friends, see events most strongly as a time-sequence—thereby blurring our vision of other significances—we next, quite arbitrarily and unjustly, abstract from the Shakespearian drama that element which the intellect most easily assimilates; and, finding it not to correspond with our own life as we see it, begin to observe 'faults'. This, however, is apparent only after we try to rationalize our impressions; what I have called the 'spatial' approach is implicit in our imaginative pleasure to a greater or a less degree always. It is, probably, the ability to see larger and still larger areas of a great work spatially with a continual widening of vision that causes us to appreciate it more deeply, to own it with our minds more surely, on every reading; whereas at first, knowing it only as a story, much of it may have seemed sterile, and much of it irrelevant. A vivid analogy to this Shakespearian quality is provided by a fine modern play, *Journey's End*. Everything in the play gains tremendous significance from war. The story, which is slight, moves across a stationary background: if we forget that background for one instant parts of the dialogue fall limp; remember it, and the most ordinary remark is tense, poignant—often of shattering power. To study *Measure for Measure* or *Macbeth* without reference to their especial 'atmospheres' is rather like forgetting the war as we read or witness *Journey's End*; or the cherry orchard in Tchekhov's famous play. There is, however, a difference. In *Journey's End* the two elements, the dynamic and static, action and background, are each firmly actualized and separated except in so far as Stanhope, rather like Hamlet, bridges the two. In *The Cherry Orchard* there is the same division. But with Shakespeare a purely spiritual atmosphere interpenetrates the action, there is a fusing rather than a contrast; and where a direct personal symbol growing out of the dominating atmosphere is actualized, it may be a supernatural being, as the Ghost, symbol of the death-theme in *Hamlet,* or the Weird Sisters, symbols of the evil in *Macbeth*. . . .

That soul-life of the Shakespearian play is, indeed, a thing of divine worth. Its perennial fire is as mysterious, as near and yet as far, as that of the sun, and, like the sun, it burns on while generations pass. If interpretation attempts to split the original beam into different colours for inspection and analysis it does not claim, any more than will the scientist, that its spectroscope reveals the whole reality of its attention. It discovers something: exactly what it discovers, and whether that discovery be of ultimate value, cannot easily be demonstrated. But, though we know the sun better in the spring fields than in the laboratory, yet we might remember that the spectroscope discovered Helium first in the solar ray, which chemical was after sought and found on earth. So, too, the interpretation of poetic vision may have its use. And if it seems sometimes to bear little relevance to its original, if its mechanical joints creak and its philosophy lumbers clumsily in attempt to follow the swift arrow-flight of poetry, it is, at least, no less rational a pursuit than that of the mathematician who writes a rhythmic curve in the stiff symbols of an algebraic equation.

I shall now shortly formulate what I take to be the main principles of right Shakespearian interpretation:

(i) Before noticing the presence of faults we should first regard each play as a visionary unit bound to obey none but its own self-imposed laws. To do this we should attempt to preserve absolute truth to our own imaginative reaction, whithersoever it may lead us in the way of paradox and unreason. We should at all costs avoid selecting what is easy to understand and forgetting the superlogical.

(ii) We should thus be prepared to recognize what I have called the 'temporal' and the 'spatial' elements: that is, to relate any given incident or speech either to the time-sequence of story or the peculiar atmosphere, intellectual or imaginative, which binds the play. Being aware of this new element we should not look for perfect verisimilitude to life, but rather see each play as an expanded metaphor, by means of which the original vision has been projected into forms roughly correspondent with actuality, conforming thereto with greater or less exactitude according to the demands of its own nature. It will then usually appear that many difficult actions and events become coherent and, within the scope of their universe, natural.

(iii) We should analyse the use and meaning of direct poetic symbolism—that is, events whose significance can hardly be related to the normal processes of actual life. Also the minor symbolic imagery of Shakespeare, which is extremely consistent, should receive careful attention. Where certain images continually recur in the same associative connexion, we can, if we have reason to believe that this associative force is strong enough, be ready to see the presence of the associative value when the images occur alone. Nor should we neglect the symbolic value of aural effects such as the discharge of cannon in *Hamlet* and *Othello* or the sound of trumpets in *Measure for Measure* and *King Lear*.

(iv) The plays from *Julius Caesar* (about 1599) to *The Tempest* (about 1611) when properly understood fall into a significant sequence. This I have called 'the Shakespeare

Progress'. Therefore in detailed analysis of any one play it may sometimes be helpful to have regard to its place in the sequence, provided always that thought of this sequence be used to illuminate, and in no sense be allowed to distort, the view of the play under analysis. Particular notice should be given to what I have called the 'hate-theme', which is turbulent throughout most of these plays: an especial mode of cynicism toward love, disgust at the physical body, and dismay at the thought of death; a revulsion from human life caused by a clear sight of its limitations—more especially limitations imposed by time. . . .

These arguments I have pursued at some length, since my interpretation reaches certain conclusions which may seem somewhat revolutionary. Especially will this be apparent in my reading of the Final Plays as mystical representations of a mystic vision. A first sketch of this reading I have already published in *Myth and Miracle*. Since the publication of my essay, my attention has been drawn to Mr. Colin Still's remarkable book *Shakespeare's Mystery Play: A Study of The Tempest* (Cecil Palmer, 1921). Mr. Still's interpretation of *The Tempest* is very similar to mine. His conclusions were reached by a detailed comparison of the play in its totality with other creations of literature, myth, and ritual throughout the ages; mine are reached solely through seeing *The Tempest* as the conclusion to the Shakespeare Progress. *The Tempest* is thus exactly located as a work of mystic insight with reference to the cross-axes of universal and Shakespearian vision. It would seem, therefore, that my method of interpretation as outlined in this essay has already met with some degree of empirical proof.

In conclusion, I would emphasize that I here lay down certain principles and make certain objections for my immediate purpose only. I would not be thought to level complaint against the value of 'criticism' in general. My private and personal distinction between 'criticism' and 'interpretation' aims at no universal validity. It can hardly be absolute. No doubt I have narrowed the term 'criticism' unjustly. Much of the critical work of to-day is, according to my distinction, work of a high interpretative order. Nor do I suggest that true 'criticism' in the narrow sense I apply to it is of any lesser order than true interpretation: it may well be a higher pursuit, since it is, in a sense, the more creative and endures a greater burden of responsibility. The relative value of the two modes must vary in exact proportion to the greatness of the literature they analyse: that is why I believe the most profitable approach to Shakespeare to be interpretation rather than criticism.

L. C. KNIGHTS

L. C. Knights (1906-   ). King Edward VII Professor of English Literature at Cambridge. Knights was an editor of Scrutiny, *the journal which over the years 1932-1953 represented the literary and educational attitudes associated with F. R. Leavis of Downing College, Cambridge. The radical re-appraisal of the function of criticism, which the* Scrutiny *group intended, was given its most striking application to Shakespeare in Knights'* How Many Children Had Lady Macbeth?, *first published in 1932, and later, with some indication of a change of attitude, in* Explorations *(1947). Knights has also published* Some Shakespearian Themes *(1959) and* An Approach to Hamlet *(1960), works of a more conventional character.*

SHAKESPEARE'S DRAMATIC POEMS*

A Shakespeare play is a dramatic poem. It uses action, gesture, formal grouping and symbols, and it relies upon the general convention governing Elizabethan plays. But, we cannot too often remind ourselves, its end is to communicate a rich and controlled experience by means of words—words used in a way to which, without some training, we are no longer accustomed to respond. To stress in the conventional way character or plot or any of the other abstractions that can be made is to impoverish the total response. "It is in the total situation rather than in the wrigglings of in-

* Extracted from *Explorations.* (The essay originally appeared in 1933.)

dividual emotion that the tragedy lies."[1] "We should not look for perfect verisimilitude to life," says Mr. Wilson Knight, "but rather see each play as an expanded metaphor, by means of which the original vision has been projected into forms roughly correspondent with actuality, conforming thereto with greater or less exactitude according to the demands of its nature. . . . The persons, ultimately, are not human at all, but purely symbols of a poetic vision." [2]

It would be easy to demonstrate that this approach is essential even when dealing with plays like *Hamlet* or *Macbeth* which can be made to yield something very impressive in the way of "character." And it is the only approach which will enable us to say anything at all relevant about plays like *Measure for Measure* or *Troilus and Cressida* which have consistently baffled the critics. And apart from Shakespeare, what are we to say of *Tamburlaine, Edward II, The Revenger's Tragedy* or *The Changeling* if we do not treat them primarily as poems?

Read with attention, the plays themselves supply the clue of how they should be read. But those who prefer another kind of evidence have only to consider the contemporary factors that conditioned the making of an Elizabethan play, namely the native tradition of English drama descending from the morality plays, the construction of the playhouse and the conventions depending, in part, upon that construction, and the tastes and expectations of the audience. I have not space to deal with any of these in detail. Schücking has shown how large a part was played in the Elizabethan drama by "primitive technique," but the full force of the morality tradition remains to be investigated. It is, I think, impossible to appreciate *Troilus and Cressida* on the one hand, or the plays of Middleton (and even of Ben Jonson) on the other, without an understanding of the "morality" elements that they contain. As for the second factor, the physical peculiarities of the stage and Elizabethan dramatic conventions, I can only refer to Miss Bradbrook's *Elizabethan Stage Conditions*. We can make a hasty summary by saying that each of these factors determined that Elizabethan drama should be non-realistic, conditioned by conventions that helped to govern the total response obtained by

[1] M. C. Bradbrook, *Elizabethan Stage Conditions*, p. 102.
[2] G. Wilson Knight, *The Wheel of Fire*, p. 16.

means of the language of each play. A consideration of
Shakespeare's use of language demands a consideration of
the reading and listening habits of his audience. Contrary to
the accepted view that the majority of these were crude and
unlettered, caring only for fighting and foolery, bombast
and bawdry, but able to *stand* a great deal of poetry, I
think there is evidence (other than the plays themselves)
that very many of them had an educated interest in words,
a passionate concern for the possibilities of language and
the subtleties of poetry. At all events they were trained,
by pamphlets, by sermons and by common conversation to
listen or to read with an athleticism which we, in the era of
the *Daily Mail* and the Best Seller, have consciously to
acquire or do our best to acquire. And all of them shared
the speech idiom that is the basis of Shakespeare's poetry.

We are faced with this conclusion: the only profitable
approach to Shakespeare is a consideration of his plays as
dramatic poems, of his use of language to obtain a total
complex emotional response. Yet the bulk of Shakespeare
criticism is concerned with his characters, his heroines, his
love of Nature or his "philosophy"—with everything, in
short, except with the words on the page, which it is
the main business of the critic to examine. . . .

Since everyone who has written about Shakespeare probably imagines that he has "treated him primarily as a poet,"
some explanation is called for. How should we read Shakespeare?

We start with so many lines of verse on a printed page
which we read as we should read any other poem. We have
to elucidate the meaning (using Dr. Richards's fourfold
definition[1]) and to unravel ambiguities; we have to estimate
the kind and quality of the imagery and determine the precise degree of evocation of particular figures; we have to
allow full weight to each word, exploring its "tentacular
roots," and to determine how it controls and is controlled
by the rhythmic movement of the passage in which it occurs.
In short, we have to decide exactly why the lines "are so
and not otherwise."

As we read other factors come into play. The lines have
a cumulative effect. "Plot," aspects of "character," recur-

[1] *Practical Criticism*, pp. 181-183.

rent "themes" and "symbols"—all "precipitates from the memory"—help to determine our reaction at a given point. There is a constant reference backwards and forwards. But the work of detailed analysis continues to the last line of the last act. If the razor-edge of sensibility is blunted at any point we cannot claim to have read what Shakespeare wrote, however often our eyes may have travelled over the page. A play of Shakespeare's is a precise, particular experience, a poem—and precision and particularity are exactly what is lacking in the greater part of Shakespeare criticism, criticism that deals with *Hamlet* or *Othello* in terms of abstractions that have nothing to do with the unique arrangement of words that constitutes these plays.

Obviously what is wanted to reinforce the case against the traditional methods is a detailed examination of a particular play. Unfortunately anything approaching a complete analysis is precluded by the scope of the present essay. The remarks on one play, *Macbeth*, are, therefore, not offered as a final criticism of the play; they merely point to factors that criticism must take into account if it is to have any degree of relevance, and emphasize the kind of effect that is necessarily overlooked when we discuss a Shakespeare play in terms of characters "copied from life," or of "Shakespeare's knowledge of the human heart."

Even here there is a further reservation to be made. In all elucidation there is an element of crudity and distortion. "The true generalization," Mr. Eliot reminds us, "is not something superposed upon an accumulation of perceptions; the perceptions do not, in a really appreciative mind, accumulate as a mass, but form themselves as a structure; and criticism is the statement in language of this structure; it is a development of sensibility."[1] Of course, the only *full* statement in language of this structure is in the exact words of the poem concerned; but what the critic can do is to aid "the return to the work of art with improved perception and intensified, because more conscious, enjoyment." He can help others to "force the subject to expose itself," he cannot fully expose it in his own criticism. And in so far as he paraphrases or "explains the meaning" he must distort. The main difference between good and bad critics

[1] *The Sacred Wood* (Second Edition, 1928), p. 15, and *Selected Essays*, p. 205.

is that the good critic points to something that is actually contained in the work of art, whereas the bad critic points away from the work in question; he introduces extraneous elements into his appreciation—smudges the canvas with his own paint. . . .

ALFRED HARBAGE

Alfred Harbage (1901-   ). Professor of English Literature at Harvard; author of Shakespeare's Audience *(1941),* As They Liked It *(1947) and other works on Shakespeare and his contemporaries.*

THE QUALITY OF SHAKESPEARE'S AUDIENCE*

Contemporary comments upon the quality of the audience are abundant but extremely difficult to interpret. They provide us actually with a series of contradictions. The danger is that the critic or historian will make a selection of the consistent statements and build a case upon them, failing to realize that the statements he has rejected are equally consistent with each other and completely nullify his case. In the present section of my study I shall counterpoise the various contemporary comments. . . .

The quality of spectators is usually referred to in Elizabethan times as their "understanding." The understanding of the spectators is frequently attacked, but we are never certain what portion of them is intended and what criteria the spokesman is bringing to bear. The penny patrons are the most frequent objects of attack, but the entire audience is lumped as the ignorant multitude and blasted with the identical terms applied to "groundlings" if it suits the writer's purpose at the moment. Thus Gosson, in his more severe mood, classified all playgoers as "the worste sort of people" who, because of their ignorance, their fickleness, and their fury, are "not to bee admitted in place of iudge-

* Extracted from *Shakespeare's Audience.*

ment."[1] Puttenham is offended at the "naturall ignoraunce" of the people who love plays, but apparently because they are indifferent to such technical fine points of prosody as concern himself: they "haue at all times their eares so attentiue to the matter, and their eyes vpon the shewes of the stage that they take little heede of the cunning of the rime."[2] Webster, after *The White Devil* failed, brought his charge against a specific theatre and its clientele: the Red Bull was too open, too dark (and too empty), and "most of the people that come to that Playhouse, resemble those ignorant asses."[3] But the poets who consoled Fletcher for the failure of *The Faithful Shepherdess* were equally emphatic that the audience was "common," "rude," a "monster," and a "rout of nifles,"[4] although the theatre in this case was a private playhouse. Dekker at some time must have been maltreated by the pit; he lashes out at plebeians with a fury unexplainable on the grounds of their mere incapacity —at "the Stinkards speaking all things, yet no man vnderstanding any thing."[5] He cannot withhold insults even from the printed versions of civic entertainments, which must be written simply, else the heads of the multitude "would miserably runne a wooll-gathering."[6]

The charge that the groundlings lacked understanding was made only when they had disliked the spokesman's play or had liked that of his rival. It will be considered further in a moment. It must be viewed in relation to a similar charge, made as frequently and under the same circumstances, against the genteel section of the audience. Jonson is as loud as any against the "rude, and beastly claps"[7] of the multitude, but he is equally loud against

> base detractors, and illiterate apes,
> That fill vp roomes in faire and formall shapes.[8]

[1] *Playes Confuted in Fiue Actions* (1582), in Hazlitt, ed., *English Drama and Stage*, p. 183.
[2] *Arte of English Poesie* (1589), ed. Arber, English Reprints, No. XV.
[3] Address to the Reader.
[4] Commendatory verses by Beaumont, Field, Aston, and Jonson.
[5] *Strange Horse-Race* (1613), in Grosart, ed., *Non-Dramatic Works*, III, 340.
[6] *Magnificent Entertainment* (1604).
[7] Dedication, *Volpone* (1605-6), in Herford and Simpson, eds., *Ben Jonson*.
[8] Prologue, *Poetaster* (1601), in *ibid.*

He inveighs against "fastidious impertinents,"[1] the "better, and braver sort of your people! Plush and Velvet-outsides! that stick your house round like so many eminences—Of clothes, not understandings?"[2] The rank and file do not always come off worst at the hands of the satirists. The formula for a good play dictated by Beaumont's Grocer is at least preferable to that dictated by Day's Gentleman. The Grocer wants to see Englishmen of low degree perform romantic prodigies, while the Gentleman demands bawdry and venery "an ell deepe and a fathome broad":

> 2 [GENT.]. Well, Ile sit out the play . . . but see it be baudy, or by this light I and all my friends will hisse.

> PROL. You should not deale gentlemen-like with us els.[3]

The company of Gentlemen is just as peremptory as the Grocer's family, just as narrow in its demands and somewhat less amiable.

Sometimes the audience is condemned without distinction of class. Beaumont assures Fletcher that spectators in general are swayed only by externals:

> One company knowing they judgement lack,
> Ground their belief on the next man in black.
> Others, on him that makes signs, and is mute,
> Some like as he does in the fairest sute,
> He as his mistress doth, and she by chance.
> Nor wants there those, who as the Boy doth dance
> Between the Acts, will censure the whole Play;
> Some if the Wax-lights be not new that day;
> But multitudes there are whose judgment goes
> Headlong according to the Actors' cloathes.[4]

[1] Dedication, *New Inn* (1629), in *ibid*.
[2] Induction, *Magnetick Lady* (1632), in *ibid*.
[3] Day, Induction, *Isle of Gulls* (1606), in Bullen, ed., *Works*. Another of the gentlemen prefers lampoons upon citizens, while a third seems to have really noble tastes. That the upper classes were those chiefly delighting in "wantonness" in plays was asserted as early as 1580 in a courageous and interesting passage in *A Second and Third Blast of Retrait from Plaies and Theaters*, in Hazlitt, ed., *English Drama and Stage*, pp. 146-47.
[4] Commendatory verses to *The Faithful Shepherdess*.

Middleton includes "mirth" and "passion" among the things delighting an audience, but he too stresses superficialities:

> How is't possible to suffice
> So many ears, so many eyes?
> Some in wit, some in shows
> Take delight, and some in clothes:
> Some for mirth they chiefly come,
> Some for passion,—for both some;
> Some for lascivious meetings, that's their arrant;
> Some to detract, and ignorance their warrant.
> How is't possible to please
> Opinion toss'd in such wild seas?
> Yet I doubt not, if attention
> Seize you above, and apprehension
> You below, to take things quickly,
> We shall both make you sad and tickle ye.[1]

The concluding lines provide the formula into which attacks upon the audience ultimately crystallized: the genteel spectators were uncoöperative, the plebeian spectators unintelligent. The formula is applied in explicit terms by Ben Jonson: "The people generally are very acceptiue and apt to applaud any meritable worke, but there are two sorts of persons that most commonly are infectious to a whole auditory." These are, first, "the rude barbarous crue, a people that haue no braines, yet grounded iudgements, these will hisse any thing that mounts aboue their grounded capacities"; and, second, "a few Caprichious gallants . . . they haue taken such a habit of dislike in all things, that they will approue nothing."[2] The condemnation is less all-inclusive of the elevated than of the "grounded" spectators at the moment, but in another mood Jonson finds more hope in those that "canst but spell" than in a "hundred fastidious impertinents."[3] Here, then, is the difficulty. The two classes of unsatisfactory spectators can be expanded at the will of the displeased playwright, or his modern interpreter, until the entire audience is embraced, and we are left puzzled

[1] Prologue, *No Wit, No Help like a Woman's* (c.1613), in Bullen, ed., *Works.*

[2] *The Case Is Altered* (before 1609), Act II, Scene vii, in Herford and Simpson, eds., *Ben Jonson.*

[3] Dedication, *New Inn* (1629), in *ibid.*

about the identity of the "people generally" who were "very acceptiue and apt to applaud any meritable worke."

We are likely to go seeking, as the incentive to good writing, not the average but the exceptional member of the audience—the "judicious" spectator. This alluring person is mentioned by Shakespeare's amateur of the drama: he "must in your allowance o'erweigh a whole theatre of others."[1] We hear of him again from Jonson:

> if I proue the pleasure but of one,
> So he iudicious be; He shall b' alone
> A Theatre vnto me:[2]

For the one or, at most, the few attentive and understanding auditors, Jonson purports to write:

> For these, Ile prodigally spend my selfe,
> And speake away my spirit into ayre;
> For these, Ile melt my braine into inuention,
> Coine new conceits, and hang my richest words,
> As polisht jewels in their bounteous eares.[3]

But on Jonson's pinnacle of Parnassus there is not always a foothold even for this select company, and the playwright must seek his crown only in "his owne free merit."[4]

That the creative artist in Shakespeare's age, as in all ages, sought the approbation of the best judges and of himself goes without saying. The difficulty lies in identifying these judges and in defining the forces which guided the artist in the formulation of his high personal standards. Our confidence in the "judicious" spectator is shaken when we discover that he is distinctly a party man: he qualifies for his place of lonely eminence just so long as he approves of the particular playwright's work; otherwise he becomes only "the Over-curious Critick."[5] Although practically no dra-

---

[1] *Hamlet* (c.1601), Act III, Scene ii, l. 25, ed. Furness, *New Variorum Edition.*

[2] To the Reader, *Poetaster* (1601), in Herford and Simpson, eds., *Ben Jonson.*

[3] Induction, *Every Man out of His Humor* (1599), in *ibid.*

[4] To the Reader, *Poetaster* (1601), in *ibid.*

[5] Dekker, Prologue, *Wonder of a Kingdom* (1623), in Shepherd, ed., *Dramatic Works.*

matic criticism found its way into print, there seems to have been no absence of critical attitudes. Plays were discussed in taverns and elsewhere, particularly in the theatres themselves. Gainsford speaks ironically of the nonpaying spectator: "He shall laugh as hartily, obserue as iudiciously, and repeat as exactly for nothing" as if he had paid, "Yea, you shall finde him able (or forward) in short time to correct the Actors, or censure the Poet."[1] Of the critical discussion provoked by their offerings, the playwrights show a considerable, and increasing, awareness, and they do not seem especially pleased. When Beaumont observes that

> One company, knowing they judgement lack,
> Ground their belief on the next man in black;

he obviously considers the man in black an incompetent and a dangerous bellwether. Chapman is quite severe with those who

>   in aim
> At higher objects, scorn to compose plays,
> (Though we are sure they could, would they vouchsafe it!)[2]

Dekker and Middleton have no love for those auditors who think

> that each Scoene should be a booke,
> Compos'd to all perfection; each one comes
> And brings a play in's head with him: up he summes,
> What he would of a Roaring Girl haue writ;
> If that he findes not here, he mewes at it.[3]

Now unless we are to consider the "judicious" simply as the playwright's own little putative claque, we must suppose them to have been the spectators who applied standards and assumed the role of critics. How, then, are we to reconcile

[1] *The Rich Cabinet Furnished with Varietie of Descriptions* (1616), in Hazlitt, ed., *English Drama and Stage*, p. xi.
[2] Prologue, *All Fools* (1599-1604), in Parrott, ed., *Plays and Poems*. See also his foreword to *The Middle Temple and Lincoln's Inn Mask* (1613).
[3] Dekker, Prologue, *Roaring Girl* (1604-10), in Shepherd, ed., *Dramatic Works*.

the contemporary irritation with critics and love of the "judicious"? In general, the playwrights rail at faultfinders and praise "the other sort, that heare with loue, and iudge with fauour."[1] We must take our choice of which sort qualified as the "judicious."

Plays which were "caviare to the general," which were directed to princes and other better judges, are a further trial to our faith in the "judicious" spectator. Daniel's *Philotas* was written "for the better sort of men, seeing with what idle fictions, and grosse follies, the Stage at this day abused mens recreations."[2] Jonson's *Cynthia's Revels* was not for "eu'rie vulgar, and adult'rate braine."[3] *Catiline* was a "legitimate Poeme" in "Iig-giuen times,"[4] intended for scholars, not for those who "commend the two first Actes, with the people, because they are the worst."[5] These are meritorious plays, but they are not the masterpieces of the age or even of their several authors. In reading *Catiline*, we find our tastes coinciding with those of "the people." Yet these are about the best of the plays written avowedly for superior spectators. Such plays usually convey us into depressing purlieus. Consider a later effort by Jonson himself:

> A Worke not smelling of the Lampe, to night,
>   But fitted for your Maiesties disport,
>   And writ to the Meridian of your Court,
> Wee bring; and hope it may produce delight:
> The rather, being offered, as a Rite,
>   To Schollers, that can iudge, and faire report
>   The sense they heare, aboue the vulgar sort
> Of Nut-crackers, that onely come for sight.

The play thus recommended in its Prologue was only *The Staple of News*. I need not mention the academic plays or that whole body of courtly writing which I have elsewhere

---

[1] Epilogue, *Wily Beguiled* (1596-1606), ed. Greg, Malone Society Reprints.
[2] The Apology, *Tragedy of Philotas* (1604), in Grosart, ed., *Complete Works*.
[3] Prologue, *Cynthia's Revels* (1600-1601,) in Herford and Simpson, eds., *Ben Jonson*.
[4] Dedication, in *ibid*.
[5] To the Reader in Ordinarie, *Catiline, His Conspiracy* (1611), in *ibid*.

dubbed cavalier drama[1] and which scarcely achieved mediocrity.

The tendency to attribute the failure of plays to the deficiency of the audience, particularly the groundlings, must ultimately have amused the dramatic fraternity. After Hamlet speaks of the play which "pleased not the million; 'twas caviare to the general," although he and other better judges found it "excellent," a speech is recited proving that noble piece to have been an outrageous example of bombast. We should be placed on our guard against taking Hamlet's dramatic pronouncements as literally Shakespeare's, yet Hamlet's later remark that groundlings "for the most part are capable of nothing but inexplicable dumb-shows and noise" has often been quoted by those who blame upon groundlings everything distasteful in Elizabethan plays. It is true that Hamlet at this later moment is in a more serious mood, but even if no satirical note is being sounded here, we must remember that the speaker is the Prince of Denmark, generically disdainful of groundlings. Yet times were changing: "By the Lord, Horatio," says Hamlet, moved by the wit of that indubitable groundling, the First Grave-digger, "these three years I have taken note of it; the age is grown so picked that the toe of the peasant comes so near the heel of the courtier, he galls his kibe."[2] All things can be proved by quoting Hamlet. Nowhere has Shakespeare suggested *in propria persona* that he has any quarrel with groundlings. The ironic note is clear enough in Day's *Isle of Gulls*. Warned that if he uses "a high and eleuate stile" in his projected play, his "auditories low and humble vnderstandings should neuer crall ouer't," a conceited buffoon replies: "Tush, I could fashion the bodie of my discourse fit to the eares of my auditorie: for to cast Eloquence amongst a companie of Stinctards is all one as if a man

---

[1] *Cavalier Drama*, pp. 7-47.

[2] Act V, Scene i, 1. 132, ed. Furness, *New Variorum Edition*. It is doubtful if Shakespeare would have depended upon the patrons in the yard to distinguish between the playwright's opinion and that of his protagonist. Hamlet's speech sounds like the insult direct; and, after the opening of the private theatres, the groundlings must have been more valuable than ever to the Globe. We may note that the quarto of 1603 reads not "groundlings" but "the ignoraut"—probably a wise acting variant.

should scatter Pearls amongst the hoggish animals ecliped Swine."[1]

Out of the welter of comment upon the audience emerges one amusing fact. The most successful writers were the least critical of the spectators' powers of discrimination, and the less successful writers were less critical when they had scored a hit. Dekker can say, despite his low opinion of the mob:

> 'Tis not a gay sute, or Distorted Face,
> Can beate his Merit off, Which has won Grace
> In the full Theatre.[2]

Even Jonson relaxes. In *Epicoene,* he wrote a play for everyone.

> Truth sayes, of old, the art of making plaies
>   Was to content the people; & their praise
>   Was to the Poet money, wine, and bayes.
> But in this age, a sect of writers are,
>   That, onely, for particular likings care,
>   And will taste nothing that is populare.
> With such we mingle neither braines, nor brests:
>   Our wishes, like to those (make publique feasts)
>   Are not to please the cookes tastes, but the guests.[3]

Jonson himself, earlier and later, professed membership in that very "sect" he now condemns, but, like his original audience, we are grateful for his periods of apostacy.

Honest Thomas Heywood was no railer at audiences. The general tenor of his addresses is simply "We have found you gracious Auditors." He is proud that his *Ages* "haue at sundry times thronged three seuerall Theatres, with numerous and mighty Auditories."[4] As with "our prose Shakespeare," so with Shakespeare himself. He submits to judgment:

[1] Act III, Scene i.
[2] Prologue, *Wonder of a Kingdom* (1623), in Shepherd, ed., *Dramatic Works.*
[3] Prologue, in Herford and Simpson, eds., *Ben Jonson.*
[4] To the Reader, *The Iron Age* (published 1632), in Pearson, ed., *Dramatic Works.*

Like, or find fault; do as your pleasures are:
Now good or bad, 'tis but the chance of war.[1]

His spectators are "gentles all" and are addressed pleasantly, unassumingly, respectfully. His tone is composed; the
dramatist seems content. Invidious appraisals of the understanding of the auditors, or distinctions among them,
are left to Hamlet or to the supercilious young collaborator
John Fletcher.[2] In his sonnets Shakespeare lets fall a few
words of discontent. He has "sold cheap what is most dear."
Fortune has provided for him only "public means which
public manners breeds," and his nature "like the dyer's
hand" is stained by what it works in. Briefly, Shakespeare
had moments of disgust with his own profession—as who
has not? Similar sensations have overtaken professors in
the refined atmosphere of their seminars, but unlike poets
they do not tell all.

That Shakespeare could come to terms with his audience
while Jonson could not reflects a basic distinction between
the two men. Jonson was torn by his critical self-conscious-
ness. His difficulty lay not in his independence of his audience but in his subjection to his idea of it. He refined upon
his analysis of what it wanted and should have until his
purposes became confused. He tried to write for sectors
of the audience and found himself bobbing for green ap-
ples. The pronouncements of a critic like Jonson are tempting to later critics, but so far as they concern the audience
they are full of mare's-nests. Not only can Jonson be quoted
constantly against himself, but his words contain implications which might sometimes embarrass those who quote
them. When he speaks of audiences commending "writers, as
they do Fencers, or Wrastlers; who if they come in robus-
tiously, and put for it with a great deal of violence, are
receiu'd for the brauer fellowes," he has particular writers
in mind; and when he distinguishes between those who
"utter all they can, how euer unfitly; and those that use
election and a meane," we begin to discern Jonson on one
side of the line and Shakespeare—"would he had blotted
a thousand"—on the other.

[1] Prologue, *Troilus and Cressida* (1601-3).
[2] Prologue, *Henry VIII* (1613).

I deny not, but that these men, who alwaies seeke to doe
more than inough, may some time happen on some thing
that is good, and great; but very seldome: And when it
comes it doth not recompence the rest of their ill. It sticks
out perhaps, and is more eminent, because all is sordide,
and vile about it: as lights are more discern'd in a thick
darknesse, then a faint shadow. I speake not this, out of
a hope to doe good on any man, against his will; for I
know, if it were put to the question of theirs and mine,
the worse would finde more suffrages: because the most
favour common errors.[1]

Read in comparison with the famous passage on Shakespeare in *Timber or Discoveries,* the above leaves little
doubt of whom Jonson had chiefly in mind. The measure
of Jonson's generosity in finally conceding the greatness of
Shakespeare is the effort it must have cost him. He had
relapses and was never fully reconciled to the unchastened
success of his great rival, to the preference shown by audiences for "some mouldy tale like Pericles."[2] In com-
forting Fletcher for the failure of *The Faithful Shepherdess,*
Jonson had predicted that

fire
Or moths shall eat what all these fools admire.

An appended list of the plays destined for oblivion would
have contained a fair number of titles by Shakespeare. A
list prepared by "all these fools" in the audiences would
have been more generous—and more prophetic.

It is not to the prologues, dedications, and epistles that
we must look for a fair evaluation of the quality of Shakespeare's audience. The complaining authors air too many
grievances, and their composite indictment, naming as it
does both the high and the low, the critical and the un-
critical, is too all-inclusive. The only persons worthy of the
plays appear to have been the dedicatees, a small but superbly discriminating sect. We must look about for those
who, perversely, appeared to appreciate good things.

[1] To the Reader, *Alchemist* (1610), in Herford and Simpson, eds.,
Ben Jonson.
[2] Ode to Himself, *New Inn,* (1629), in *ibid.*

We catch curious glimpses of a phenomenon that seems to have bewildered the cultivated—of the mob responding favorably to things too fine for their coarse intellects. The gifted playwright

> Can draw with Adamantine Pen (euen creatures
> Forg'de out of th' Hammer, on tiptoe, to Reach vp,
> And (from Rare silence) clap their Brawny hands,
> T' Applaud, what their charmd soule scarce vnderstands.[1]

Appreciation from a quarter where appreciation presumably could not be partook of the nature of the marvelous. The term "charmed" is repeated in *The Actors Remonstrance or Complaint,* where we hear of former playwrights "charming like Orpheus the dull and brutish multitude, scarce a degree above stones and forrests, into admiration though not into understanding."[2] At Shakespeare's plays, so the printer tells us, even "dull and heavy-witted worldlings . . . haue found that witte there, that they neuer found in them selues, and haue parted better wittied then they came: feeling an edge of witte set vpon them, more then euer they dreamd they had braine to grinde it on."[3] This ability to rise to the plays seemed at least to one generous observer a thing natural and benign: Thomas Heywood considered it one of their virtues that they had made "the ignorant more apprehensive."[4] . . . .

S. L. BETHELL

S. L. Bethell (1908-1955). Author of Shakespeare and the Popular Dramatic Tradition *(1944),* The Winter's Tale: A Study *(1946) and many original essays.*

[1] Dekker, Prologue, *If It Be Not Good the Devil Is in It* (1610-12), in Shepherd, ed., *Dramatic Works.*

[2] In Hazlitt, ed., *English Drama and Stage,* p. 264.

[3] "A neuer writer, to an euer reader. Newes," *Troilus and Cressida* (1609, 2d issue).

[4] *Apology for Actors* (1612), Shakespeare Society Publications, No. III, pp. 52-53.

Conventionalism and Naturalism
in Shakespeare*

Attention directed to the physical conditions of the Elizabethan theatre has revealed a number of conventions in dramatic production which are plainly survivals of the long-continued popular tradition of conventional drama. In *Romeo and Juliet*, to choose a popular example,[1] we are presented in Act I, Scene iv, with a party of maskers on their way to the Capulets' feast. At the end of the scene, according to a contemporary stage direction, 'they march about the stage'; and in the next scene, after a brief passage of comedy, Capulet delivers his speech of welcome to the guests and maskers. The maskers have thus, without leaving the stage, translated themselves from a street to a hall in the Capulets' house, by this conventional 'marching about', accompanied presumably by a conventional disclosure of the much disputed 'inner stage'. Now the miracle plays were often presented on a 'multiple' stage, on which more than one locality was represented at the same time, and 'journeys' might be undertaken from one such locality to another: Our Lord might thus be shown journeying between the judgment halls of Herod and Pilate, which would be represented by structures on different parts of the stage. The maskers' 'marching about' would seem to be a survival of such conventional 'journeying'. The suggestion [2] that they walk round the back of the stage—'off' and 'on' again— seems a much less likely interpretation of the stage direction. *Richard III*, Act v, Scene iii, provides another and less disputable instance of the survival of multiple-stage technique. The stage represents Bosworth field on the eve of battle, with the tents of the rival generals pitched on opposite sides—stage distance bearing no more relation to real distance than on the multiple stage. The ghosts, when they enter (presumably by a trap-door, centre stage), are thus

* Extracted from *Shakespeare and the Popular Dramatic Tradition*.
[1] C. M. Haines: 'The Development of Shakespeare's Stagecraft', in *Shakespeare and the Theatre*, by Members of the Shakespeare Association (O.U.P., 1927), p. 43.
[2] Mentioned by Miss M. C. Bradbrook in *Elizabethan Stage Conditions* (C.U.P., 1932), pp. 38-39.

enabled to pronounce maledictions upon Richard and blessings upon Richmond, turning solemnly from one side of the
stage to the other. Miss Bradbrook suggests[1] that Richmond
may have occupied the inner stage, but the principle is the
same in either event.

Psychological naturalism as the basis of Shakespearean
criticism reached its limit in A. C. Bradley's *Shakespearean
Tragedy*.[2] But already the physical conditions of Shakespeare's theatre had been patiently investigated; and this
new knowledge, coupled with the historical and comparative study of Shakespeare and his predecessors and contemporaries, was to produce among daring spirits a violent
reaction against the psychological approach. Professor
Schücking's treatise, translated as *Character Problems in
Shakespeare's Plays*,[3] shows how far even the presentation
of character depends on stage convention rather than the
direct representation of life. Apart from this seminal idea,
however, the book is of doubtful value. Professor Schücking
cannot appreciate the depth and subtlety of Shakespeare's
verse, and though he claims Shakespeare as conventional
rather than naturalistic, his sympathies seem to be with
modern naturalism, so that he is also incapable of appreciating the dramatic subtleties made available by a
conventional tradition. He speaks disparagingly of Shakespeare's 'primitive' art-form, and seems to confuse primitive technique with naïveté of thought and feeling. Believing in Shakespeare's naïveté, he misses all his deeper
meaning, and endlessly multiplies conventions in order to
account for everything he cannot understand. Professor
Stoll, in his *Art and Artifice in Shakespeare*,[4] has pushed
the argument of Professor Schücking even farther, since
to him Shakespeare's every tragic hero is built upon a
contradiction impossible to psychology but rendered plausible by dramatic and poetic art: Shakespeare's object is
'emotional illusion'.[5] However far we may feel Professors
Schücking and Stoll to be from a profound and comprehensive view of Shakespeare, they have certainly revealed
a body of dramatic conventions unsuspected by an earlier

[1] *op. cit.*, p. 36.
[2] Macmillan, 1904; 2nd edition, 1905.
[3] Harrap, 1922.
[4] C.U.P., 1933.
[5] *op. cit.*, p. 49.

generation of critics. We are told that, on the Elizabethan stage, disguise was conventionally impenetrable, slander was conventionally believed, and characters conformed to type: the Avenger, the Machiavel, the Melancholy Man. The villain was conventionally—not cynically—aware of his own villainy, and the hero—without priggishness— of his own virtues. It is all useful knowledge, provided we remember that these are not rules but sweeping generalities, and certainly not true of every instance. We can be safe only in a close study of each individual text. The greatest contribution to Shakespearean criticism has not, in fact, come from the specialists, but from those general critics who have taught us to take his poetry seriously, and to realise that, in Shakespeare, poetry and drama are not separable ingredients, but that the drama is a poetic creation, existing in the poetry like a Thomist *universale in re*. The suggestions of Mr. T. S. Eliot [1] and Dr. F. R. Leavis [2] have been followed out by Miss Bradbrook [3] and Dr. L. C. Knights: [4] the time has gone by for anthologising Shakespeare's 'beauties', and the poetry has at last been accorded that fundamental position which it naturally holds. It is difficult to see how it can ever have been otherwise— how the poetry can ever have been treated as a decorative inessential. The immense superiority of *Antony and Cleopatra* over Dryden's *All for Love* is quite clearly a superiority in poetry. Indeed, strip the poetry from a play of Shakespeare, and what is left but a rather haphazard story about a set of vaguely outlined and incredibly 'stagey' characters? There is no originality of plot, little subtlety of psychological analysis, no immediately accessible propaganda. Miss Bradbrook, uniting two lines of approach, has found pattern and convention in the poetry itself; and Professor Wilson Knight, by his 'mystical' interpretation,[5] again reminds us that Shakespeare was closer to *Everyman* than to *A Doll's House*. I am not attempting anything like a survey of recent criticism. I have said nothing of 'verse

[1] They appeared first in *The Sacrea Wood* (Methuen, 1920) but *v. Selected Essays, 1917-1932* (Faber & Faber, 1932).

[2] *v. How to Teach Reading* (Minority Press, 1932).

[3] In *Elizabethan Stage Conditions*, and in *Themes and Conventions of Elizabethan Tragedy* (C.U.P., 1935).

[4] *How Many Children Had Lady Macbeth?* (Minority Press, 1933).

[5] *v.* especially *The Wheel of Fire* (O.U.P. 1930; reprinted 1937).

tests', or of the tendency to split up nearly every play among a number of collaborators, and to detect several layers of revision: under the influence of genuinely literary criticism the tide has turned against such misapplication of scientific method. My purpose has been to trace what I consider the most important developments in recent Shakespearean criticism, so as to show how my own work links with that of previous writers. Every approach to Shakespeare has something in it of value, but I am convinced of the fundamental importance of the words themselves—of the poetry—and of the great, though secondary, importance of a knowledge of Elizabethan stage conditions. My own particular approach, considered in these pages, can be undertaken only in the closest association with pure literary criticism and a consideration of Shakespeare's stagecraft.

I have stressed the element of convention in Shakespeare, since it is generally overlooked. But it is necessary also to insist that Shakespeare and his contemporaries worked to no thought-out conventional system; indeed, their conventions are successful just because they are traditional and unconscious. Moreover, being unconscious, they were by no means rigidly adhered to: the Elizabethan playwright varies his position on the scale between conventionalism and naturalism, even in the course of a single play. This rapidity of adjustment is a principal component in Shakespeare's remarkable subtlety. Lapses into naturalism are especially frequent in Shakespeare: they are probably a major cause of his continuous popularity on the stage, and provide colour for a psychological approach which would have failed much more signally with, for example, Chapman or Tourneur. A single flash of natural dialogue, breaking the boundaries of convention, will reveal an intuitive understanding of human nature, unshared by his contemporaries. Othello, filled with the conflicting emotions of love and loathing, visits Desdemona in her chamber, and behaves there as if entering a brothel, calling upon Emilia to perform her 'mystery' as door-keeper. After a tense, but mannered and theatrical, display of passion, he makes an effective exit, still acting his abominable fiction:

We have done our course; there's money for your pains:
I pray you, turn the key and keep our counsel.
                                            (*Oth*. IV. ii. 93)

When he has gone out, Emilia addresses her mistress:

How do you, madam? how do you, my good lady?
                                            (IV. ii. 96)

Desdemona's answer is surprising: ' 'Faith, half asleep.' (IV.
ii. 97). Within the conventional framework of Elizabethan
poetic drama, such a reply is unlikely, and on that account
the more arresting. We expect an outburst in keeping with
the tone set by Othello, but instead there has been a transition without warning to the plane of naturalism. Tragedy
queens seldom complain of fatigue, though there is actually nothing so exhausting as a scene of tense emotion.
This sudden revelation of ordinary womanhood in Desdemona engages the audience's sympathy when it is particularly needed, and also points a contrast between her sensible normality and the emotional exaggeration of Othello.

The Elizabethan popular drama made the best of both
worlds: its compromise between conventionalism and naturalism is effective because completely unselfconscious.
When Shakespeare writes of his art, he is either severely
practical as in Hamlet's advice to the players, or he spec-
ulates upon the nature of poetry, which

> . . . gives to airy nothing
> A local habitation and a name.
>   (*M.N.D.* V. i. 16)

We never hear from him of the rules of dramatic composition. There is neither the classical pride in obedience,
nor the romantic impatience of restraint. There is, indeed,
only the most oblique recognition that such matters are
under contemporary discussion: *The Tempest* seems to
glance aside somewhat whimsically at the neo-Aristotelians.
Controversy in dramatic criticism was remarkably one-
sided in Elizabethan times, and it came from the side
which, on the whole, did not produce memorable plays.
Gentlemen amateurs of the Inns of Court, for example,

had time to interest themselves in Continental Renaissance criticism, and in the Italian revivals and translations of Seneca and Plautus. *Gorboduc*, the first English tragedy, had resulted from this cultivated preoccupation with the Ancients. It would be absurd to minimise the importance of the Renaissance contribution to Elizabethan drama: it was the grafting of this revived classicism upon the sturdy indigenous stock of miracle plays and interludes, which produced the unique dramatic activity of late Elizabethan and Jacobean days. But the Elizabethan drama we still revere and revive remained a popular drama: its writers, willing enough to plunder Renaissance hoards, did not as a rule share the Renaissance attitudes. They certainly felt no obligation to imitate the Ancients, or indeed to do anything but write good plays; and they were too immersed in creation to have time for critical theory. Critical selfconsciousness, combined with loyalty to the classics, remained the prerogative of a handful of amateurs, especially those gathered about the Countess of Pembroke and her brother, Sir Philip Sidney, and of a relatively small group of professionals who looked to them for patronage. Ben Jonson was the only great figure to combine a measure of practical success with this concern for classical purity; and even Jonson, though his critical theory permitted him success in the field of intellectual comedy, failed in the attempt to write 'classical' tragedies which would compete with those of the popular theatre. *Gorboduc*, however historically important, has little intrinsic worth; and from *Gorboduc* to *Sejanus*, and on again to the *Catos* and *Irenes* of the eighteenth century, we have a sequence of tragedies, all classically correct and all intolerably dull—a melancholy tale of artistic, and usually of practical, failure. The popular drama had absorbed everything classical that it could translate into terms of the popular tradition, and had ignored the rest. The purists, on the other hand, persisted in their attempt to substitute by violence an alien mode for the unconsciously matured tradition of the popular theatre; but their fervour for a more than Aristotelian strictness never ousted the popular tradition as it did in France. Nevertheless we may say that, in Elizabethan times, there were two 'schools' of drama: the popular school, who had little conscious devotion to a common cause, and made no attempt at dramatic criticism; and the neo-classical school, who, if negligible in the theatre, were sufficiently energetic in propaganda for the 'rules'. . . .

Despite a revival of symbolism, and recent middle-brow flirtations with the 'morality', naturalism still dominates the 'serious' theatre. The popular theatre, however, has never abandoned the popular tradition: music-hall, pantomime, revue, and musical comedy, together with the average purely commercial Hollywood film, require of an audience the same basic attitudes to dramatic illusion as a medieval 'miracle' or a play of Shakespeare. This is not a veiled appeal for commercial entertainment: I do not suggest that *Rose Marie,* or its most recent equivalent, is as good as *As You Like It* and better than *A Doll's House.* I am not concerned with relative value at all—though if I were, I might hint at the superiority of the unsophisticated 'gangster' or 'Western' film to a good deal that passes for serious theatre. Modern popular entertainment, however, differs from the Elizabethan in being more calculatedly commercialised: it is also depraved in values, superficial in ideas, false in sentiment, and insensitive to the quality of words. This is due in particular to the neo-classical—later naturalistic—influence in criticism and the theatre, which gradually lured the best minds away from the popular tradition. In general it is a part of the cultural decline consequent upon the triumph of post-Renaissance attitudes. What is even more serious, materialism, middle-brow psychological drama, the craze for scene-painting, and the cinema's habitual use of natural settings, have all tended to undermine the creative naïveté of the popular audience. Men are, however, more readily corrupted in their desires than altered in their modes of apprehension; and the essential psychology of the popular audience seems perennially the same, except that the capacity to cope with verbal subtlety has largely disappeared under the welter of modern appeals to eye and ear.

What, then, is the essence of this popular dramatic tradition—of the perennial psychology of the popular audience? Miss Bradbrook has a hint of it:

The Elizabethans liked the villain-hero, the ambiguous character who excited paradoxical feelings, and with whom a limited identification was possible. Hence the absurdity of approaching Vindice as a 'fallen angel', or a 'blasted splendour'; a Miltonic Satan to whom a single mixed response is given. His two sides must be seen separately, as Marston's Antonio saw Julio's two natures, and loved him while he carved him up, or as Othello kissed Desdemona ere he killed her:

> O thou weed
> That art so lovely fair, and smell'st so sweet.

The two views are held simultaneously and yet quite separately in his mind with a terrifying clearness, and yet they are irreconcilable. It is this which makes their peculiar intensity; it deepens them both, like the juxtaposition of complementary colours. Hamlet has a rather similar feeling about his mother:

> Sense sure you have,
> Else could you not have motion.
> (III. iv. 71)

Dissociation is at its simplest and strongest in Spenser: the Bower of Bliss is described and demolished with equal gusto; the gusto, in fact, largely depends on this reconciliation of opposites.[1]

I cannot agree with Miss Bradbrook's individual judgments. Spenser would have been a greater poet had he reconciled the 'æsthetic' values of the Bower of Bliss with its allegorical significance: as it is, unconscious and conscious attitudes pull him different ways. Further, I cannot rest content with an interpretation of character which makes no attempt to unify apparently irreconcilable characteristics. Miss Bradbrook seems to be following Professor Stoll into a complete denial of the relevance of psychology to characterisation in drama and fiction. I shall take up this whole matter in due course.[2] Meanwhile, though I doubt its existence in the connections named by Miss Bradbrook, she has at least adumbrated a capacity of the Elizabethan audience,

[1] *Elizabethan Stage Conditions*, p. 93.
[2] *v.* Ch. IV. *inf.*, especially for Stoll, pp. 78-79.

which I regard as fundamentally important: the ability to keep simultaneously in mind two opposite aspects of a situation. The pleasure apparently aroused in the Elizabethan theatre by a concurrence of seeming incompatibles is obviously related to the vogue of 'conceited' writing, especially as practised by the so-called 'metaphysical' poets: it is worth remembering that the important works of Shakespeare were contemporary with the secular poetry of John Donne. The conscious delight in paradox evinced by the Elizabethans and Jacobeans is a conscious assertion of the Christian tradition, assailed by new Renaissance attitudes. Later, with the triumph of neo-classicism, metaphor and conceit were simplified to the deliberate parallelism of simile, whilst naturalism crystallises expression on the level of events—the 'reporting' level, which makes its first unmistakable appearance in the novels of Defoe. Christianity, however, is founded upon the tension of opposites. God and man, nature and supernature; its doctrines define an union without confusion, between the spiritual and material. Indeed, any profound reading of experience calls naturally for paradoxical statement. The Elizabethan audience was perhaps especially receptive to this quality of experience, since it was consciously stressed in those times; out the basic psychological tensions I am to consider are largely unconscious and common to the popular theatre in every age. This partly reflects the Christian origin of post-classical drama, but even more, I think, reveals a tension fundamental to the nature of experience itself.

Instances of this trait, less equivocal than Miss Bradbrook's, may be discovered even in the field of character-representation. Characters, without being themselves made up of incompatible qualities, may evoke distinct and separate responses from the audience. Thus Falstaff is (a) amusing, and (b) morally reprehensible: an Elizabethan audience would applaud his wit, but approve his final dismissal. Victorian critics, however, displayed bitter resentment, not only against Henry, but against Shakespeare himself, for refusing to sentimentalise. Where the Victorian critic laughs, he must love; but a popular audience is never under this necessity. In the miracle plays, humour was mainly provided by Herod and the fiends, characters held in abhorrence; similarly the Vice of the moralities was forerunner of the Shakespearean clown (Does this account for a certain malignity in Feste?); and the pantomime audience to-day still laughs at the discomfiture of a comic devil. Not only character, but every aspect of the Elizabethan drama, is shot through with this quality of dual awareness. The mixture of conventionalism and naturalism demands a dual mode of attention. Awareness of the play as play implies the dual awareness of play-world and real world: upon this depends the piquancy of a play-within-the-play, or of the situation in which a boy plays the part of a girl playing the part of a boy (Julia, Jessica, Rosalind, Viola, Imogen). And the Elizabethan apparently enjoyed a song, when it broke the continuity of the play, perhaps criticising the performer's voice ('A mellifluous voice' (*T.N.* ii. iii. 54)) before taking up the play again where he dropped it for the counter-attraction of music.

The modern cinema-goer has a similar adaptability. It is not unusual for characters in an apparently 'straight' film to break into song, although the circumstances, considered naturalistically, would practically forbid such behaviour. A pair of lovers steal away from the company, discover a convenient garden-seat and, after some preliminary conversation, break into a love duet, to the accompaniment of an unseen orchestra. Even those little conversant with the etiquette of high society must be aware that this is an unusual method of proposing marriage. As the film setting is naturalistic, the strain upon credulity is correspondingly great, but I have noticed few traces of my own uneasiness in other members of the audience. It is not stupidity, but absence of technical sophistication, which can so rapidly accept a situation as conventional. In this instance, story is accepted as story, and song as song, simultaneously yet without confusion; and none of the awkward questions are asked which would result from a monistic attitude to dramatic illusion. The co-presence of song and story is the commonest example of an audience's ability to sustain two aspects of a situation at once: in opera, it is called for continuously, and Shakespeare's comedies are nearer in this respect to modern musical comedy than to the plays, say, of Galsworthy or Barrie. In the average Hollywood film, conventionalism and naturalism are deeply interwoven. Setting and presentation are usually naturalistic, but characters conform to well-known types, stories follow a recognised pattern, and startlingly unrealistic incidents may be introduced; indeed, criticism is usually levelled at 'slapstick' in serious films, much as neoclassical criticism objects to the mixture of comedy and tragedy in Shakespeare. Even in the cinema there are quite complicated instances of an audience's ability to attend simultaneously to various aspects of a situation. In one of Mr. Harold Lloyd's comedies, a number of years ago, the comedian performed a series of hair-raising evolutions on the front and very near the top of a formidable skyscraper. The audience must have had several concurrent reactions: (*a*) they would admire the performance of a brilliant 'equilibrist'; (*b*) they would be amused at his (recognisedly feigned) clumsiness; and (*c*) they would be concerned for the hero's safety, in sympathy with the heroine watching anxiously from below. The same incident demands attention from three different points of view simultaneously: as equilibristic performance, as farce, and as romance. And the audience responds in this complex way without conscious effort. This is the core of my present thesis: that a popular audience, uncontaminated by abstract and tendentious dramatic theory, will attend to several diverse aspects of a situation, simultaneously yet without confusion. . . .

F. P. WILSON

F. P. Wilson (1889-1963). Merton Professor of English Literature at Oxford. One of the great Elizabethan and Jacobean scholars of his time, and author of Elizabethan and Jacobean Studies *(1945),* Marlowe and the Early Shakespeare *(1953) etc.*

SHAKESPEARE'S READING*

John Selden is reported to have said: "No man is the

* Reprinted from *Shakespeare Survey* 3 (1950). This completes the documentation here offered of the controversy on Shakespeare's learning; see the extracts from Dennis, Farmer, Johnson and Maginn.

wiser for his learning: it may administer matter to work in, or objects to work upon, but wit and wisdom are born with a man." For two and a half centuries we have been asking how far learning administered matter for Shakespeare's wit and wisdom to work in or objects for them to work upon. If a friend had put to Shakespeare the Second Outlaw's question "Have you the tongues?", would he have answered, with Valentine, "My youthful travail therein made me happy"?

Soon after his death two poets wrote about Shakespeare in terms that suggest that his learning, that is, his knowledge of Greek and Latin, was scanty. One of them said that he had "small Latin, and less Greek": the other praised him as Fancy's child, warbling "his native wood-notes wild". But Jonson and Milton are among the most learned scholar-poets this country has produced; and if we test Shakespeare, as perhaps they were testing him, by their own severe standards of scholarship, then indeed we must say he had not even the "edging or trimming of a scholar".

In the eighteenth century two extreme points of view were expressed. On the one hand, critics like John Upton and Zachary Gray, bent on making Shakespeare 'polite', found him learned in both the tongues and traced to classical originals many a passage of natural description and many a moral sentiment. On the other hand, Richard Farmer, a man deeply read in Elizabethan literature, traced to many a forgotten English book the learning which the dramatist was supposed to have taken direct from the classics and went so far as to state that he "remembered perhaps enough of his *school-boy* learning to put the *Hig, hag, hog*, into the mouth of Sir Hugh Evans; and might pick up in the Writers of the time, or the course of his conversation, a familiar phrase or two of French or Italian: but his *Studies* were most demonstratively confined to *Nature* and *his own Language*".

To-day, our estimate of Shakespeare's learning will not be pitched so high as Upton's, yet neither will it be pitched so low as Farmer's. We shall say he had "small Latin and *no* Greek"; but that his Latin, small indeed in comparison with Jonson's, was yet sufficient to make him not wholly dependent upon translation. We shall say with the actor Will Beeston that he "understood Latin pretty well" and mean by that much what Jonson meant by 'small Latin'. That he read Ovid as well as Golding's Ovid, some Seneca and Virgil as well as English Seneca and Virgil is, I think, proved. Nor is it in the least unlikely. He lived in an age that respected learning, an age that built its educational system upon the belief that in the classics alone, the sacred writings excepted, was to be found "the best that is known and thought in the world". Consequently some knowledge of Latin was possessed by all who had had a grammar-school education. To find a writer wholly ignorant of Latin we have to descend as low in the literary hierarchy as John Taylor, the Water Poet, who acknowledged that his 'scholarship' was but 'scullership' and that in Latin he proceeded only from 'possum' to 'posset'. So far as his attainments in learning go, Shakespeare may be likened to another popular dramatist. No university wit and schooled we do not know where, Thomas Dekker could yet read Latin with some facility. He could and did translate sentences from the Church Fathers from that popular and long-lived anthology *Flores Doctorum* assembled by a thirteenth-century Irishman, Thomas Hibernicus; and he could describe the terrors of hell in words borrowed from Sebastian Barradas's vast commentary on the four Gospels, a work which has not been translated into English, and (it seems safe to say) never will be. Shakespeare could have done as much, if he had cared.

On these matters there is general agreement. Few who have read through T. W. Baldwin's treatise on *William Shakspere's Small Latine & Lesse Greeke* will have the strength to deny that Shakespeare acquired the grammar-school training of his day in grammar, logic, and rhetoric; that he could and did read in the originals some Terence and Plautus, some Ovid and Virgil; that possessing a reading knowledge of Latin all those short-cuts to learning in florilegia and compendia were at his service if he cared to avail himself of them; and that he read Latin not in the spirit of a scholar but of a poet. But granted that Shakespeare could read Latin, is there any evidence that he had access to any modern tongue other than his own? Here, I think, there is no general agreement. The evidence that he read Italian depends solely upon the fact that no English versions are known of some of the tales from which he took his plots. For *Cymbeline* did he turn to the *Decameron*, for *Othello* to Cinthio, and for *Measure for Measure* to Cinthio's *novella* and play as well as to George Whetstone's rendering of Cinthio? That an Englishman who can read Latin can make out the sense of an Italian *novella* has been proved experimentally again and again, but that Shakespeare read at all easily and widely in Italian literature—in Petrarch, Ariosto, and Tasso as well as in the writers of *novelle*—has not, I think, been proved. And as doubtful is the extent of his reading in French literature.

Let me illustrate the difficulty of coming to a decision by examining Shakespeare's alleged debt to Boccaccio. We know that Chaucer took the story of patient Griselda not from the *Decameron* but from Petrarch's Latin version of the last tale in the *Decameron*; and we argue that he did not know the *Decameron*, or at any rate possess a manuscript of it, because if he had he would most surely have made use of it. The evidence that Shakespeare had read the *Decameron* rests upon the resemblance between the wager-plot in *Cymbeline* and Boccaccio's tale of the four Italian merchants. If he knew the *Decameron*, it might be argued, it is odd that he did not give more evidence of it. But are we so certain that he knew even this one tale of Boccaccio's? That it could not have been his sole source has been proved. The stage-direction to the wager-scene in *Cymbeline* is sufficient to show this: "*Enter Philario, Iachimo, a Frenchman, a Dutchman, and a Spaniard.*" When Posthumus Leonatus joins them, representatives of five nations are upon the stage. To characterize the qualities of different nations was a common rhetorical device. Thomas Wilson recommends it in his *Art of Rhetoric* under 'Descriptio', and gives as an example: "The Englishman for feeding and changing of apparel: the Dutchman for drinking: the Frenchman for pride and inconstance: the Spaniard for nimbleness of body, and much disdain: the Italian for great wit and policy: the Scots for boldness: and the Boeme for stubbornness." Shakespeare followed example in more than one passing reference in his plays, and in *Cymbeline* itself the 'wit and policy' of the Italian (in the bad senses of those words) is referred to by Imogen and Iachimo. In *Henry V* Shakespeare passed from rhetoric to drama when he created representatives of the four peoples of these islands, with

the Welshman Fluellen so greatly outshining the rest. A
Jacobean audience, then, identifying upon the stage (as
perhaps they could from the appearance and costume of
the actors) an Italian (Iachimo), a Frenchman, a Dutchman and a Spaniard, might well expect some sharp satirical
observations on national character. They were given nothing
of the kind. The Italian and the Frenchman are necessary
to the action, but the Dutchman and the Spaniard are mutes
and hang loose upon the play as unnecessary encumbrances.

What has happened? It is not often that an examination
of Shakespeare's sources convicts him of taking over re-
calcitrant material which he does not bend to his dramatic
intention. Some critics, it is true, have argued that *Hamlet*
provides an example. Those who find that Bradley's *Hamlet*
is better than Shakespeare's "in the sense that . . . it hangs
together with a more irresistible logic", or those who believe that *Hamlet* is "full of some stuff that the writer could
not drag to light, contemplate, or manipulate into art" will
speak of Shakespeare's failure, or partial failure, to modify
or transmute the old traditional story which he knew from
the lost play of *Hamlet* and other sources;[1] and some see
in Hamlet's comments over the body of Polonius incongruous relics of that Amleth who dismembered the body of
the courtier he had slain and threw it to the pigs. That
Shakespeare in *Hamlet* found his materials intractable and
failed to impose upon them the subtle meanings of a new
design will not be universally agreed; but here in *Cymbeline*, in these fossil characters of the Dutchman and the
Spaniard, are clear vestiges of some unassimilated source.
That source could not have been Boccaccio, for there the
company is all Italian. There was, however, another treatment of this widely popular wager-theme, translated into
English from the Dutch early in the sixteenth century and
popular enough to go through at least three editions by
1560; and there sure enough, in *Frederick of Jennen*,[2] the
company is said to come from 'divers countries', Spain,
France, Florence and Genoa. *Frederick of Jennen* is a

[1] Cf. A. J. A. Waldock, *Hamlet* (1931), p. 49; T. S. Eliot, *The Sacred
Wood* (1920), p. 91.
[2] Apparently an error for *Jenuen*, Genoa. The tale has been edited by
J. Raith, *Aus Schrifttum und Sprache der Angelsachsen*, Band 4
(1936).

crude thing to put beside the choice Italian of Boccaccio, but in this detail and in a few others it is closer to *Cymbeline;* and editors have no longer the right to say that Shakespeare's sole source in this play was Boccaccio.[1]

Did Shakespeare then turn both to Boccaccio and to *Frederick of Jennen* or some similar analogue? Or was there some one work, now lost, in which he could have found all that he borrowed? It is here that conjecture raises its head, and with it rises the ghost of a lost play. I confess to feeling some impatience with those critics who, at a loss for a Shakespearian source, invent a hypothetical play. As Hamlet found, it is so difficult to test the honesty of a ghost. Belief upon belief is false heraldry, and false scholarship too. Yet I am not sure I am right to be impatient. That many printed books of that age have been lost I do not believe, but that many plays have been lost is certain. So serious are the losses that the historian of Elizabethan drama—especially of our drama in the sixteenth century, before the habit of reading plays had become popular—must often feel himself to be in the position of a man fitting together a jigsaw, most of the pieces of which are missing. Some sort of picture emerges, but is it the true picture? For example, how much of our dramatic history would need to be rewritten if those "two prose Books" were to turn up which were acted at the Bel Savage Inn in London before 1579? They were acted some years before Lyly turned dramatist, yet Stephen Gosson could not have chosen apter words if he had been describing the prose comedies of Lyly, "where you shall find never a word without wit, never a line without pith, never a letter placed in vain".[2] If by some happy chance the account-books of Shakespeare's company were to come to light, how many titles of lost plays might they reveal? We may argue that our losses are not so severe as for the companies which Philip Henslowe financed, because the Chamberlain-King's company was more stable and its plays worthier the reading. Yet we have lost much, and many a play which Shakespeare saw upon the stage, and perhaps acted in, has gone beyond recovery.

[1] Cf. H. R. D. Andrews, *Shakespeare's Books* (1904), p. 63, and especially W. F. Thrall, '*Cymbeline*, Boccaccio, and the Wager Story in England', *Studies in Philology* (1931), pp. 639-51.
[2] *The School of Abuse*, ed. Arber, p. 40.

What honey did he extract from that hive of activity, the Elizabethan stage, especially in his early years when he was finding himself? Here is a part of his reading and seeing and hearing where we cannot follow him, or can follow only imperfectly. Yet if I am told that his imagination may have taken impetus from some quite inferior play on a theme which he was contemplating, a play so inferior to his own as *The True Chronicle History of King Leir,* I cannot think that I am being told anything that is improbable.

But when all has been said of Shakespeare's knowledge and use of the tongues, the fact remains that what he read he read for the most part in English. Dryden said that "he needed not the spectacles of books to read Nature; he looked inwards and found her there". We shall do well to remember the context in which these words are placed. Dryden, himself a scholar-poet, was answering those critics who accused Shakespeare of wanting learning, that is, a knowledge of the classics, and was praising Shakespeare on the ground that they were not necessary to him. He is not saying that Shakespeare was indifferent to the world of books. I find it impossible to believe in a Shakespeare who was not at some time in his life an avid reader. Did he never put his head into the shop of his fellow-townsman Richard Field except to sell him *Venus and Adonis* or maybe to correct the proofs of that poem and *Lucrece*? As he walked through Paul's Churchyard, did he avert his eyes from the advertisements of new books plastered on every post? To read some critics we might suppose so. It has been pointed out that while a whole library of Jonson's books has survived with his name and motto inscribed upon them, of Shakespeare's books there survive only a few more or less doubtful specimens. What does this prove? That Shakespeare was a modest man, perhaps, who did not write his name in books. Or that he read not for scholarship and erudition but to keep himself level with life. He too was *tanquam explorator*,* though not in the same books and not in the same way.

Certainly he was no plodding reader. If Shakespeare is to be identified with any character in *Love's Labour's Lost* it is with Berowne, and Berowne says:

* Jonson's motto.

> Small have continual plodders ever won,
> Save base authority from others' books.

But the King of Navarre's answer will do for Shakespeare and Berowne: "How well he's read, to reason against reading!" One supposes him to have been a rapid reader who could tear the heart out of a book as quickly as any man. It is to be observed how little use he made in his plays of some of the books that he looked at. We catch him dipping into that spirited piece of anti-Catholic propaganda, Samuel Harsnett's *Declaration of egregious Popish Impostures,* and coming up with the names of Edgar's fiends—Flibbertigibbet and the rest—and a few phrases. He remembers from Sir William Segar's *Book of Honour and Arms* the first and second causes for a trial of arms and builds them into the character of Don Armado. When *The Tempest* was kindling in his mind, he remembered from Richard Eden's *History of Travel* the great devil of the Patagonian giants, and made him Setebos, the god of Caliban's dam; remembered also, so Malone suggested, some names for his characters, Alonso, Gonzalo, Ferdinand, and others.

These were books to be tasted, and we know such books were among Shakespeare's books (when we know it at all) only from the 'orts' and fragments that he used. But there are "some few to be chewed and digested". So a contemporary of Shakespeare's with whom he is sometimes confused. There was the Bible, and North's Plutarch, and Hall and Holinshed. The evidence suggests that when a theme took possession of his mind, especially a theme with a long tradition behind it, he read widely—not laboriously, but with a darting intelligence, which quickened his invention. When the theme of Macbeth took possession of him, he read Holinshed on Macbeth, but turned back also, twenty folio pages earlier, to the reign of King Duff, and there read the story of Donwald in whom the King had a 'special trust', of the King's visit to Donwald's castle, of how Donwald "though he abhorred the act greatly in heart, yet through instigation of his wife" contrived the King's death, of his pangs of conscience, his dreadful end, and the monstrous sights observed in nature after this monstrous deed, horses eating their own flesh, the sun continually covered with clouds, "a sparhawk also strangled by an owl". Three pages later he read how a brave husbandman and his two sons defended a walled lane against the Danes with such bravery that they turned defeat into victory, stored it away in his retentive memory, and with careful husbandry made use of it in *Cymbeline*. If we may believe Wilfrid Perrett, who published in 1904 the best account that we have of the story of King Lear from Geoffrey of Monmouth to Shakespeare, Shakespeare consulted not only Holinshed on Lear, and Spenser, and the old play, but also *The Mirror for Magistrates* and Camden's *Remains* and even the original version in Geoffrey of Monmouth's Latin. And we have to add that at some moment of time, as he was meditating on these materials, they coalesced with Sidney's story in the *Arcadia* of the Paphlagonian unkind king.

Are these the speculations of scholars creating Shakespeare in their own image? They sound very like it. Yet recent critics make even more startling claims for one of his plays. Not indeed for all. Shakespeare knew when to stop, even if his critics do not. North's Plutarch was sufficient for his Roman plays, Lodge's *Rosalynde* for *As You Like It,* Hall and Holinshed for *Richard III*. But the historical background for *Richard II*, they tell us, did not come merely from Hall and Holinshed. The play depends also for incident and interpretation of character upon Froissart, two versions of a French chronicle on the death of Richard, a metrical history also in French, an anonymous play *Thomas of Woodstock*, and Daniel's *Civil Wars*. It sounds incredible, so incredible that J. Dover Wilson falls back upon the hypothesis of a lost play written by an historical scholar which would have given Shakespeare just those episodes and hints which he could have found in the English books. But another able writer on the sources of *Richard II*, M. W. Black, observes with courageous logic that copies of the French works could have been borrowed in London from John Stow and John Dee—Holinshed tells us that—and argues that for a rapid reader, gifted in the art of skipping, the preparatory reading was not so formidable after all. And if Shakespeare prepared himself more thoroughly for this play than for any other play in the canon, he did so, says Black, "because he was enthralled with the story and because he was laying the foundation for a great cycle of history plays."[1]

So far, I have spoken almost exclusively of those works which gave him hints for plot and character. But what of the reflection in his plays of the political and moral beliefs of his time? What of that concern with order and disorder in the state, in society and in the mind of man, which Shakespeare shared with all thinking contemporaries and which is present in his plays more constantly and more powerfully than in those of any other dramatist? Was he, like Corin in *As You Like It*, a 'natural philosopher'? Did he absorb the culture of his age merely from the circumambient air? True it is that he was one who observed men and manners in court and city, town and country, church and tavern, and no man who writes on Shakespeare's reading should forget that the "ample sovereignty of eye and ear" gave him more than books can. Yet when we remember that he was profoundly concerned with the problem of good and evil, that most of the books published in his England were concerned with religion and morality, can we resist the conclusion that he was a reader of some of these? But which? The Bible, of course, which he knew as few men know it to-day, which he knew as intimately and naturally as if it had come to him by instinct. But which other books? When we ask this question of his contemporaries we can usually give a certain answer. We can track Jonson and Chapman, Marston and Webster everywhere in the snow of the moralists. Long before Charles Crawford provided the evidence John Addington Symonds guessed that Webster kept a commonplace-book. The contents of this commonplace-book he wove laboriously, though often skilfully, into the texture of his dialogue, and the verbal resemblances are so close that we cannot be in doubt.[2] But when Shakespeare is giving new

---

[1] *Joseph Quincey Adams: Memorial Studies* (1948), pp. 199-216.

[2] To cite an example which escaped F. L. Lucas's notice, the Cardinal's speech (*The Duchess of Malfi*, v, v.):

> "When I look into the Fishponds, in my Garden,
> Methinks I see a thing, arm'd with a Rake
> That seems to strike at me"

was suggested, as A. H. Bullen pointed out (*Gentleman's Magazine*, 1906, p. 78), by Julius Capitolinus, *Life of the Emperor Pertinax*. See also L. Lavater, *Of Ghosts*, ed. J. Dover Wilson and May Yardley (1929), p. 61.

life to some old commonplace we can never be sure in whose snow we are to track him. It is the rarest thing to find him borrowing from a book that is not his immediate source in words so close that they will convince a sceptic. When I have mentioned the opening of Prospero's speech, "Ye elves of hills, brooks, standing lakes, and groves", which comes from Golding's Ovid, and Gonzalo's description of an imaginary commonwealth, which comes from Montaigne's essay on 'Cannibals' as translated by Florio, I have mentioned two strikingly exceptional examples. How remarkable it is that the question whether Shakespeare owed much or anything to Montaigne or to Florio's translation is still unsettled. Some say that he owed much; others hold that the parallels which have been adduced could have come to Shakespeare from other writers, or are the commonplaces of all time, or are opinions which seem to us singular but were then widespread. The great Montaigne scholar, Pierre Villey, came to the conclusion that if Montaigne had never written his essays, nothing warrants us in supposing that except for one brief passage in *The Tempest* a single word would have been changed in the plays of Shakespeare.[1] Does this mean he was no reader? Or rather that his commonplace-book was his memory and he the very Midas of poets, transmuting all he touched?

Let me take as an example one thought and one image. And let the thought be Hamlet's "there is nothing either good or bad, but thinking makes it so". Had he been reading William Baldwin's *Treatise of Moral Philosophy* (1567) where it is attributed to Plato: "Nothing unto a man is miserable, [but] if he so think it: for all Fortune is good to him, that constantly with patience suffereth it"?[2] Or Jerome Cardan's *De Consolatione*: "A man is nothing but his mind: if the mind be discontented, the man is all disquiet though all the rest be well, and if the mind be contented though all the rest misdo it foreseeth little"?[3] Or had Shakespeare in mind Spenser's "It is the mind that maketh good or ill"?

[1] *Revue d'Histoire littéraire de la France* (1917), pp. 357-93.
[2] Cited by T. W. Baldwin, *William Shakespere's Small Latine & Lesse Greeke*, II, 353. But the passage had already appeared in Sir Thomas Elyot's *Of the Knowledge which Maketh a Wise Man* (1533), sig. M 3ᵛ.
[3] Translated by T. Bedingfield (1573); cited by Hardin Craig, "Hamlet's Book", *Huntington Library Bulletin*, VI (1934), 29.

Or, to come yet closer to *Hamlet* in wording and in date, had he been reading that anthology of *sententiae* published by Nicholas Ling in 1597, *Politeuphuia, Wit's Commonwealth*: "There is nothing grievous if the thought make it not"?[1]

And let the image be that one which came to his mind more than once when he was writing of the chaos and anarchy which follow violation of 'degree'. It is in the famous speech on 'degree' in *Troilus and Cressida*, in a scene in *Sir Thomas More*, in *Coriolanus*, in this speech of Albany's when his eyes are at last opened to the cruelty of Goneril and Regan to their king and father:

> If that the heavens do not their visible spirits
> Send quickly down to tame these vile offences,
> It will come,
> Humanity must perforce prey on itself,
> Like monsters of the deep.

Go back a hundred years and more to the morality-play *Everyman*, and we find these words put into the mouth of God:

> For and I leave the people thus alone
> In their life and wicked tempests,
> Verily they will become much worse than beasts;
> For now one would by envy another up eat.

Go back nearly a hundred years again to *The Pride of Life*, where a bishop complains that men have ceased to fear God, truth has gone to ground, the rich are ruthless, and men

> farit as fiscis in a pol
> The gret eteit the smal.

But this proverbial image is much older than *The Pride of Life*. We can trace it back to the Fathers. But as John Poynet does this for us in a book which Shakespeare could have read, let me quote his words. In this passage from *A Short Treatise of Politic Power* (1556) Poynet is writing

[1] P. 59 *b*. Where Ling took it from, I do not know.

about the necessity of order and degree in the state and of what disasters follow when these are not observed:

> The Ethnics . . . saw that without politic power and authority, mankind could not be preserved, nor the world continued. The rich would oppress the poor, and the poor seek the destruction of the rich, to have that he had: the mighty would destroy the weak, and as *Theodoretus* saith, the great fish eat up the small, and the weak seek revenge on the mighty: and so one seeking the other's destruction, all at length should be undone and come to destruction.

Shall we then say that this thought and this image were suggested by any one of the passages I have quoted? I would rather say they were suggested by none, yet were suggested by all. Somehow, like all thinking men in his day, he acquainted himself with that vast body of reflection upon the nature of man and man's place in society and in the universe which his age inherited in great part from the ancient and medieval worlds. And when the moment came, thought and image rose from the pool of his memory to receive its appropriate language and rhythm. We who are cut off for the most part from that great tradition in which Shakespeare was bred can realize only with difficulty how many thoughts and even images came to his audience with the pleasure not so much of discovery as of recognition, proverbial maxims and moral sentiments, not newer than the familiar stories which he took over for his plots. And yet, for his earliest audiences too, there was discovery, even when there was recognition; for what was old had become new. Always there was the power of "dressing old words new"; always the power of bodying forth dramatic theme and idea in characters at once particular and general; always the power of bringing whatever concerns the needs, high and low, of the natural man into the order of a great design.

THE COMEDIES AND THE PHOENIX AND THE TURTLE

WILLIAM HAZLITT

ON SHAKESPEARE'S COMEDY*

Dr. Johnson thought Shakspeare's comedies better than
his tragedies, and gives as a reason, that he was more at
home in the one than in the other. That comedies should
be written in a more easy and careless vein than tragedies,
is but natural. This is only saying that a comedy is not so
serious a thing as a tragedy. But that he shewed a greater
mastery in the one than the other, I cannot allow, nor is
it generally felt. The labour which the Doctor thought it
cost Shakspeare to write his tragedies, only shewed the
labour which it cost the critic in reading them, that is, his
general indisposition to sympathise heartily and spontane-
ously with works of high-wrought passion or imagination.
There is not in any part of this author's writings the slightest trace of his having ever been 'smit with the love of
sacred song,' except some passages in Pope. His habitually
morbid temperament and saturnine turn of thought required
that the string should rather be relaxed than tightened, that
the weight upon the mind should rather be taken off than
have any thing added to it. There was a sluggish moroseness
about his moral constitution that refused to be roused to
any keen agony of thought, and that was not very safely
to be trifled with in lighter matters, though this last was
allowed to pass off as the most pardonable offence against
the gravity of his pretensions. It is in fact the established
rule at present, in these cases, to speak highly of the Doctor's authority, and to dissent from almost every one of his
critical decisions. For my own part, I so far consider this
preference given to the comic genius of the poet as erro-
neous and unfounded, that I should say that he is the only
tragic poet in the world in the highest sense, as being on a
par with, and the same as Nature, in her greatest heights
and depths of action and suffering. There is but one who
durst walk within that mighty circle, treading the utmost
bound of nature and passion, shewing us the dread abyss
of woe in all its ghastly shapes and colours, and laying open
all the faculties of the human soul to act, to think, and suf-

* From *Lectures on the English Comic Writers* (1819).

fer, in direst extremities; whereas I think, on the other hand, that in comedy, though his talents there too were as wonderful as they were delightful, yet that there were some before him, others on a level with him, and many close behind him. I cannot help thinking, for instance, that Moliere was as great, or a greater comic genius than Shakspeare, though assuredly I do not think that Racine was as great, or a greater tragic genius. I think that both Rabelais and Cervantes, the one in the power of ludicrous description, the other in the invention and perfect keeping of comic character, excelled Shakspeare; that is, they would have been greater men, if they had had equal power with him over the stronger passions. For my own reading, I like Vanbrugh's City Wives' Confederacy as well, or ('not to speak it profanely') better than the Merry Wives of Windsor, and Congreve's Way of the World as well as the Comedy of Errors or Love's Labour Lost. But I cannot say that I know of any tragedies in the world that make even a tolerable approach to Hamlet, or Lear, or Othello, or some others, either in the sum total of their effect, or in their complete distinctness from every thing else, by which they take not only unquestioned, but undivided possession of the mind, and form a class, a world by themselves, mingling with all our thoughts like a second being. Other tragedies tell far more or less, are good, bad, or indifferent, as they have more or less excellence of a kind common to them with others: but these stand alone by themselves; they have nothing common-place in them; they are a new power in the imagination, they tell for their whole amount, they measure from the ground. There is not only nothing so good (in my judgment) as Hamlet, or Lear, or Othello, or Macbeth, but there is nothing like Hamlet, or Lear, or Othello, or Macbeth. There is nothing, I believe, in the majestic Corneille, equal to the stern pride of Coriolanus, or which gives such an idea of the crumbling in pieces of the Roman grandeur, 'like an unsubstantial pageant faded,' as the Antony and Cleopatra. But to match the best serious comedies, such as Moliere's Misanthrope and his Tartuffe, we must go to Shakspeare's tragic characters, the Timon of Athens or honest Iago, when we shall more than succeed. He put his strength into his tragedies, and played with comedy. He was greatest in what was greatest; and his *forte* was not trifling, according to the opinion here combated, even though he might do that as well as any body else, unless he could do it better than any body else.—I would not be understood to say that there are not scenes or whole characters in Shakspeare equal in wit and drollery to any thing upon record. Falstaff alone is an instance which, if I would, I could not get over. 'He is the leviathan of all the creatures of the author's comic genius, and tumbles about his unwieldy bulk in an ocean of wit and humour.' But in general it will be found (if I am not mistaken) that even in the very best of these, the spirit of humanity and the fancy of the poet greatly prevail over the mere wit and satire, and that we sympathise with his characters oftener than we laugh at them. His ridicule wants the sting of ill-nature. He had hardly such a thing as spleen in his composition. Falstaff himself is so great a joke, rather from his being so huge a mass of enjoyment than of absurdity. His re-appearance in the Merry Wives of Windsor is not 'a consummation devoutly to be wished,' for we do not take pleasure in the repeated triumphs over him.—Mercutio's quips and banter upon his friends shew amazing gaiety, frankness, and volubility of tongue, but we think no more of them when the poet takes the words out of his mouth, and gives the description of Queen Mab. Touchstone, again, is a shrewd biting fellow, a lively mischievous wag: but still what are his gibing sentences and chopped logic to the fine moralising vein of the fantastical Jacques, stretched beneath 'the shade of melancholy boughs?' Nothing. That is, Shakspeare was a greater poet than wit: his imagination was the leading and master-quality of his mind, which was always ready to soar into its native element: the ludicrous was only secondary and subordinate. In the comedies of gallantry and intrigue, with what freshness and delight we come to the serious and romantic parts! What a relief they are to the mind, after those of mere ribaldry or mirth! Those in Twelfth Night, for instance, and Much Ado about Nothing, where Olivia and Hero are concerned, throw even Malvolio and Sir Toby, and Benedick and Beatrice, into the shade. They 'give a very echo to the seat where love is throned.' What he has said of music might be said of his own poetry—

> 'Oh! it came o'er the ear like the sweet south
> Breathing upon a bank of violets,
> Stealing and giving odour.'

How poor, in general, what a falling-off, these parts seem in mere comic authors; how ashamed we are of them; and how fast we hurry the blank verse over, that we may get upon safe ground again, and recover our good opinion of the author! A striking and lamentable instance of this may be found (by any one who chooses) in the high-flown speeches in Sir Richard Steele's *Conscious Lovers.*—As good an example as any of this informing and redeeming power in our author's genius might be taken from the comic scenes in both parts of *Henry* IV. Nothing can go much lower in intellect or morals than many of the characters. Here are knaves and fools in abundance, of the meanest order, and stripped stark-naked. But genius, like charity, 'covers a multitude of sins:' we pity as much as we despise them; in spite of our disgust we like them, because they like themselves, and because we are made to sympathise with them; and the ligament, fine as it is, which links them to humanity, is never broken. Who would quarrel with Wart and Feeble, or Mouldy or Bull-calf, or even with Pistol, Nym, or Bardolph? None but a hypocrite. The severe censurers of the morals of imaginary characters can generally find a hole for their own vices to creep out at; and yet do not perceive how it is that the imperfect and even deformed characters in Shakspeare's plays, as done to the life, by forming a part of our personal consciousness, claim our personal forgiveness, and suspend or evade our moral judgment, by bribing our self-love to side with them. Not to do so, is not morality, but affectation, stupidity, or ill-nature. I have more sympathy with one of Shakspeare's pick-purses, Gadshill or Peto, than I can possibly have with any member of the Society for the Suppression of Vice, and would by no means assist to deliver the one into the hands of the other. Those who cannot be persuaded to draw a veil over the foibles of ideal characters, may be suspected of wearing a mask over their own! Again, in point of understanding and attainments, Shallow sinks low enough; and yet his cousin Silence is a foil to him; he is the shadow of

a shade, glimmers on the very verge of downright imbecility,
and totters on the brink of nothing. 'He has been merry
twice or once ere now,' and is hardly persuaded to break
his silence in a song. Shallow has 'heard the chimes at midnight,' and roared out glees and catches at taverns and inns
of court, when he was young. So, at least, he tells his cousin
Silence, and Falstaff encourages the loftiness of his pretensions. Shallow would be thought a great man among his
dependents and followers; Silence is nobody—not even in
his own opinion: yet he sits in the orchard, and eats his
carraways and pippins among the rest. Shakspeare takes
up the meanest subjects with the same tenderness that we
do an insect's wing, and would not kill a fly. To give a more
particular instance of what I mean, I will take the inimitable
and affecting, though most absurd and ludicrous dialogue,
between Shallow and Silence, on the death of old Double.

'*Shallow.* Come on, come on, come on; give me your
hand, Sir; give me your hand, Sir; an early stirrer, by the
rood. And how doth my good cousin Silence?

Silence. Good morrow, good cousin Shallow.

Shallow. And how doth my cousin, your bedfellow? and
your fairest daughter, and mine, my god-daughter Ellen?

Silence. Alas, a black ouzel, cousin Shallow.

Shallow. By yea and nay, Sir; I dare say, my cousin William is become a good scholar: he is at Oxford still, is he
not?

Silence. Indeed, Sir, to my cost.

Shallow. He must then to the Inns of Court shortly. I was
once of Clement's-Inn; where, I think, they will talk of mad
Shallow yet.

Silence. You were called lusty Shallow then, cousin.

Shallow. I was called any thing, and I would have done
any thing indeed, and roundly too. There was I, and little
John Doit of Staffordshire, and black George Bare, and
Francis Pickbone, and Will Squele a Cotswold man, you had
not four such swinge-bucklers in all the Inns of Court again;
and, I may say to you, we knew where the bona-robas were,
and had the best of them all at commandment. Then was
Jack Falstaff (now Sir John, a boy,) and page to Thomas
Mowbray, Duke of Norfolk.

Silence. This Sir John, cousin, that comes hither anon about soldiers?

Shallow. The same Sir John, the very same: I saw him break Schoggan's head at the court-gate, when he was a crack, not thus high; and the very same day did I fight with one Sampson Stockfish, a fruiterer, behind Gray's-Inn. O, the mad days that I have spent! and to see how many of mine old acquaintance are dead!

Silence. We shall all follow, cousin.

Shallow. Certain, 'tis certain, very sure, very sure: death (as the Psalmist saith) is certain to all, all shall die.—How a good yoke of bullocks at Stamford fair?

Silence. Truly, cousin, I was not there.

Shallow. Death is certain. Is old Double of your town living yet?

Silence. Dead, Sir.

Shallow. Dead! see, see! he drew a good bow: and dead? he shot a fine shoot. John of Gaunt loved him well, and betted much money on his head. Dead! he would have clapped i'th' clout at twelve score; and carried you a forehand shaft a fourteen and fourteen and a half, that it would have done a man's heart good to see.—How a score of ewes now?

Silence. Thereafter as they be: a score of good ewes may be worth ten pounds.

Shallow. And is old Double dead?'

There is not any thing more characteristic than this in all Shakspeare. A finer sermon on mortality was never preached. We see the frail condition of human life, and the weakness of the human understanding in Shallow's reflections on it; who, while the past is sliding from beneath his feet, still clings to the present. The meanest circumstances are shewn through an atmosphere of abstraction that dignifies them: their very insignificance makes them more affecting, for they instantly put a check on our aspiring thoughts, and remind us that, seen through that dim perspective, the difference between the great and little, the wise and foolish, is not much. 'One touch of nature makes the whole world kin:' and old Double, though his exploits had been greater, could but have had his day. There is a pathetic *naiveté* mixed up with Shallow's common-place reflections and impertinent digressions. The reader laughs (as well he may) in reading the passage, but he lays down the book to think. The wit, however diverting, is social and humane. But this is not the distinguishing characteristic of wit, which is generally provoked by folly, and spends its venom upon vice.

The fault, then, of Shakspeare's comic Muse is, in my opinion, that it is too good-natured and magnanimous. It mounts above its quarry. It is 'apprehensive, quick, forgetive, full of nimble, fiery, and delectable shapes:' but it does not take the highest pleasure in making human nature look as mean, as ridiculous, and contemptible as possible. It is in this respect, chiefly, that it differs from the comedy of a later, and (what is called) a more refined period. Genteel comedy is the comedy of fashionable life, and of artificial character and manners. The most pungent ridicule, is that which is directed to mortify vanity, and to expose affectation; but vanity and affectation, in their most exorbitant and studied excesses, are the ruling principles of society, only in a highly advanced state of civilisation and manners. Man can hardly be said to be a truly contemptible animal, till, from the facilities of general intercourse, and the progress of example and opinion, he becomes the ape of the extravagances of other men. The keenest edge of satire is required to distinguish between the true and false pretensions to taste and elegance; its lash is laid on with the utmost severity, to drive before it the common herd of knaves and fools, not to lacerate and terrify the single stragglers. In a word, it is when folly is epidemic, and vice worn as a mark of distinction, that all the malice of wit and humour is called out and justified to detect the imposture, and prevent the contagion from spreading. The fools in Wycherley and Congreve are of their own, or one another's making, and deserve to be well scourged into common sense and decency: the fools in Shakspeare are of his own or nature's making; and it would be unfair to probe to the quick, or hold up to unqualified derision, the faults which are involuntary and incorrigible, or those which you yourself encourage and exaggerate, from the pleasure you take in witnessing them. Our later comic writers represent a state of manners, in which to be a man of wit and pleasure about town was become the fashion, and in which the swarms of egregious pretenders in both kinds openly kept one another in countenance, and were become a public nuisance. Shakspeare, living in a state of greater rudeness and simplicity, chiefly gave certain characters which were a kind of *grotesques,* or solitary excrescences growing up out of their native soil without affectation, and which he undertook kindly to pamper for the public entertainment. For instance, Sir Andrew Aguecheek is evidently a creature of the poet's own fancy. The author lends occasion to his absurdity to shew itself as much as he pleases, devises antics for him which would not enter into his own head, makes him 'go to church in a galliard, and return home in a coranto;' adds fuel to his folly, or throws cold water on his courage; makes his puny extravagances venture out or slink into corners without asking his leave; encourages them into indiscreet luxuriance, or checks them in the bud, just as it suits him for the jest's sake. The gratification of the fancy, 'and furnishing matter for innocent mirth,' are, therefore, the chief object of this and other characters like it, rather than reforming the moral sense, or indulging our personal spleen. But Tattle and Sparkish, who are fops cast not in the mould of fancy, but of fashion, who have a tribe of forerunners and followers, who catch certain diseases of the mind on purpose to communicate the infection, and are screened in their preposterous eccentricities by their own conceit and by the world's opinion, are entitled to no quarter, and receive none. They think themselves objects of envy and admiration, and on that account are doubly objects of our contempt and ridicule.— We find that the scenes of Shakspeare's comedies are mostly laid in the country, or are transferable there at pleasure. The genteel comedy exists only in towns, and crowds of borrowed characters, who copy others as the satirist copies them, and who are only seen to be despised. 'All beyond Hyde Park is a desart to it:' while there the pastoral and poetic comedy begins to vegetate and flourish, unpruned, idle, and fantastic. It is hard to 'lay waste a country gentleman' in a state of nature, whose humours may have run a little wild or to seed, or to lay violent hands on a young booby 'squire, whose absurdities have not yet arrived at years of discretion: but my Lord Foppington, who is 'the prince of coxcombs,' and 'proud of being at the head of so prevailing a party,' deserves his fate. I am not for going so far as to pronounce Shakspeare's 'manners damnable, because he had not seen the court;' but I think that comedy does not find its richest harvest till individual infirmities have passed into general manners, and it is the example of courts, chiefly, that stamps folly with credit and currency, or glosses over vice with meretricious lustre. I conceive, therefore, that the golden period of our comedy was just after the age of Charles II. when the town first became tainted with the affectation of the manners and conversation of fashionable life, and before the distinction between rusticity and elegance, art and nature, was lost (as it afterwards was) in a general diffusion of knowledge, and the reciprocal advantages of civil intercourse. It is to be remarked, that the union of the three gradations of artificial elegance and courtly accomplishments in one class, of the affectation of them in another, and of absolute rusticity in a third, forms the highest point of perfection of the comedies of this period, as we may see in Vanbrugh's Lord Foppington, Sir Tunbelly Clumsy, and Miss Hoyden; Lady Townly, Count Basset, and John Moody; in Congreve's Millamant, Lady Wishfort, Witwoud, Sir Wilful Witwoud, and the rest.

In another point of view, or with respect to that part of comedy which relates to gallantry and intrigue, the difference between Shakspeare's comic heroines and those of a later period may be referred to the same distinction between natural and artificial life, between the world of fancy and the world of fashion. The refinements of romantic passion arise out of the imagination brooding over 'airy nothing,' or over a favourite object, where 'love's golden shaft hath killed the flock of all affections else:' whereas the refinements of this passion in genteel comedy, or in every-day life, may be said to arise out of repeated observation and experience, diverting and frittering away the first impressions of things by a multiplicity of objects, and producing, not enthusiasm, but fastidiousness or giddy dissipation. For the one a comparatively rude age and strong feelings are best fitted; for 'there the mind must minister to itself:'

to the other, the progress of society and a knowledge of the world are essential; for here the effect does not depend on leaving the mind concentred in itself, but on the wear and tear of the heart, amidst the complex and rapid movements of the artificial machinery of society, and on the arbitrary subjection of the natural course of the affections to every the slightest fluctuation of fashion, caprice, or opinion. Thus Olivia, in Twelfth Night, has but one admirer of equal rank with herself, and but one love, to whom she innocently plights her hand and heart; or if she had a thousand lovers, she would be the sole object of their adoration and burning vows, without a rival. The heroine of romance and poetry sits secluded in the bowers of fancy, sole queen and arbitress of all hearts; and as the character is one of imagination, 'of solitude and melancholy musing born,' so it may be best drawn from the imagination. Millamant, in the Way of the World, on the contrary, who is the fine lady or heroine of comedy, has so many lovers, that she surfeits on admiration, till it becomes indifferent to her; so many rivals, that she is forced to put on a thousand airs of languid affectation to mortify and vex them more; so many offers, that she at last gives her hand to the man of her heart, rather to escape the persecution of their addresses, and out of levity and disdain, than from any serious choice of her own. This is a comic character; its essence consists in making light of things from familiarity and use, and as it is formed by habit and outward circumstances, so it requires actual observation, and an acquaintance with the modes of artificial life, to describe it with the utmost possible grace and precision. Congreve, who had every other opportunity, was but a young man when he wrote this character; and that makes the miracle the greater.

I do not, in short, consider comedy as exactly an affair of the heart or the imagination; and it is for this reason only that I think Shakspeare's comedies deficient. I do not, however, wish to give a preference of any comedies over his; but I do perceive a difference between his comedies and some others that are, notwithstanding, excellent in their way, and I have endeavoured to point out in what this difference consists, as well as I could. Finally, I will not say that he had not as great a natural genius for comedy as any one; but I may venture to say, that he had not the same arti-

ficial models and regulated mass of fashionable absurdity
or elegance to work upon. . . .

C. L. BARBER

*C. L. Barber (1913-   ). Professor of English Literature
and Chairman of the Department at the University of
Indiana; author of* Shakespeare's Festive Comedy *(1959).*

THE SATURNALIAN PATTERN*

Messenger. Your honour's players, hearing your amend-
    ment,
  Are come to play a pleasant comedy . . .
Beggar. . . . Is not a comonty a Christmas gambold or a
    tumbling trick?
Lady. No, my good lord; it is more pleasing stuff.
Beggar. What, household stuff?
Lady. It is a kind of history.
Beggar. Well, we'll see it. Come, madam wife, sit by my
    side and let the world slip. We shall ne'er be younger.
          —Induction to *The Taming of the Shrew*

Much comedy is festive—all comedy, if the word festive
is pressed far enough. But much of Shakespeare's comedy is
festive in a quite special way which distinguishes it from
the art of most of his contemporaries and successors. The
part of his work which I shall be dealing with in this book,
the merry comedy written up to the period of *Hamlet* and
the problem plays, is of course enormously rich and wide
in range; each new play, each new scene, does something
fresh, explores new possibilities. But the whole body of this
happy comic art is distinguished by the use it makes of
forms for experience which can be termed saturnalian.
Once Shakespeare finds his own distinctive style, he is more

* From *Shakespeare's Festive Comedy.*

Aristophanic than any other great English comic dramatist, despite the fact that the accepted educated models and theories when he started to write were Terentian and Plautine. The Old Comedy cast of his work results from his participation in native saturnalian traditions of the popular theater and the popular holidays. Not that he "wanted art" —including Terentian art. But he used the resources of a sophisticated theater to express, in his idyllic comedies and in his clowns' ironic misrule, the experience of moving to humorous understanding through saturnalian release. "Festive" is usually an adjective for an atmosphere, and the word describes the atmosphere of Shakespeare's comedy from *Love's Labour's Lost* and *A Midsummer Night's Dream* through *Henry IV* and *Twelfth Night*. But in exploring this work, "festive" can also be a term for structure. I shall be trying to describe structure to get at the way this comedy organizes experience. The saturnalian pattern appears in many variations, all of which involve inversion, statement and counterstatement, and a basic movement which can be summarized in the formula, through release to clarification.

So much of the action in this comedy is random when looked at as intrigue, so many of the persons are neutral when regarded as character, so much of the wit is inapplicable when assessed as satire, that critics too often have fallen back on mere exclamations about poetry and mood. The criticism of the nineteenth century and after was particularly helpless, concerned as it was chiefly with character and story and moral quality. Recent criticism, concerned in a variety of ways with structure, has had much more to say. No figure in the carpet is the carpet. There is in the pointing out of patterns something that is opposed to life and art, an ungraciousness which artists in particular feel and resent. Readers feel it too, even critics: for every new moment, every new line or touch, is a triumph of opportunism, something snatched in from life beyond expectation and made design beyond design. And yet the fact remains that it is as we see the design that we see design outdone and brought alive.

> O body swayed to music, O brightening glance,
> How can we know the dancer from the dance?

To get at the form and meaning of the plays, which is my first and last interest, I have been led into an exploration of the way the social form of Elizabethan holidays contributed to the dramatic form of festive comedy. To relate this drama to holiday has proved to be the most effective way to describe its character. And this historical interplay between social and artistic form has an interest of its own: we can see here, with more clarity of outline and detail than is usually possible, how art develops underlying configurations in the social life of a culture. The saturnalian pattern came to Shakespeare from many sources, both in social and artistic tradition. It appeared in the theatrical institution of clowning: the clown or Vice, when Shakespeare started to write, was a recognized anarchist who made aberration obvious by carrying release to absurd extremes. The cult of fools and folly, half social and half literary, embodied a similar polarization of experience. One could formulate the saturnalian pattern effectively by referring first to these traditions: Shakespeare's first completely masterful comic scenes were written for the clowns. But the festival occasion provides the clearest paradigm. It can illuminate not only those comedies where Shakespeare drew largely and directly on holiday motifs, like *Love's Labour's Lost*, *A Midsummer Night's Dream*, and *Twelfth Night*, but also plays where there is relatively little direct use of holiday, notably *As You Like It* and *Henry IV*.

We can get hold of the spirit of Elizabethan holidays because they had form. "Merry England" was merry chiefly by virtue of its community observances of periodic sports and feast days. Mirth took form in morris-dances, sword-dances, wassailings, mock ceremonies of summer kings and queens and of lords of misrule, mummings, disguisings, masques—and a bewildering variety of sports, games, shows, and pageants improvised on traditional models. Such pastimes were a regular part of the celebration of a marriage, of the village wassail or wake, of Candlemas, Shrove Tuesday, Hocktide, May Day, Whitsuntide, Midsummer Eve, Harvest-home, Halloween, and the twelve days of the Christmas season ending with Twelfth Night. Custom prescribed, more or less definitely, some ways of making merry at each occasion. The seasonal feasts were not, as now, rare curiosities to be observed by folklorists in remote villages, but landmarks framing the cycle of the year, observed with varying degrees of sophistication by most elements in the society. Shakespeare's casual references to the holidays always assume that his audience is entirely familiar with them. . . .

MAY GAMES AND METAMORPHOSES ON A MIDSUMMER NIGHT*

If Shakespeare had called *A Midsummer Night's Dream* by a title that referred to pageantry and May games, the aspects of it with which I shall be chiefly concerned would be more often discussed. To honor a noble wedding, Shakespeare gathered up in a play the sort of pageantry which was usually presented piece-meal at aristocratic entertainments, in park and court as well as in hall. And the May game, everybody's pastime, gave the pattern for his whole action, which moves "from the town to the grove" and back again, bringing in summer to the bridal. These things were familiar and did not need to be stressed by a title.

Shakespeare's young men and maids, like those Stubbes described in May games, "run gadding over night to the woods, . . . where they spend the whole night in pleasant pastimes—" and in the fierce vexation which often goes with the pastimes of falling in and out of love and threatening to fight about it. "And no marvel," Stubbes exclaimed about such headlong business, "for there is a great Lord present among them, as superintendent and Lord over their pastimes and sports, namely, Satan, prince of hell." In making Oberon, prince of fairies, into the May king, Shakespeare urbanely plays with the notion of a supernatural power at work in holiday: he presents the common May game presided over by an aristocratic garden god. Titania is a Summer Lady who "waxeth wounder proud":

> I am a spirit of no common rate,
> The summer still doth tend upon my state . . .
> (III.i.157-158)

And Puck, as jester, promotes the "night-rule" version of

* From *Shakespeare's Festive Comedy*.

misrule over which Oberon is superintendent and lord in the "haunted grove." The lovers originally meet

> in the wood, a league without the town,
> Where I did meet thee once with Helena
> To do observance to a morn of May.
>   (I.i.165-167)

Next morning, when Theseus and Hippolyta find the lovers sleeping, it is after their own early "observation is performed"—presumably some May-game observance, of a suitably aristocratic kind, for Theseus jumps to the conclusion that

> No doubt they rose up early to observe
> The rite of May; and, hearing our intent,
> Came here in grace of our solemnity.
>   (IV.i.135-137)

These lines need not mean that the play's action happens on May Day. Shakespeare does not make himself accountable for exact chronological inferences; the moon that will be new according to Hippolyta will shine according to Bottom's almanac. And in any case, people went Maying at various times, "Against May, Whit-sunday, and other time" is the way Stubbes puts it. This Maying can be thought of as happening on a midsummer night, even on Midsummer Eve itself, so that its accidents are complicated by the delusions of a magic time. (May Week at Cambridge University still comes in June.) The point of the allusions is not the date, but the *kind* of holiday occasion.[1] The Maying is completed when Oberon and Titania with their trains come into the great chamber to bring the blessings of fertility. They are at once common and special, a May king and queen making their good luck visit to the manor house,

[1] A great deal of misunderstanding has come from the assumption of commentators that a Maying must necessarily come on May Day, May 1. The confusion that results is apparent throughout Furness' discussion of the title and date in his preface to the *Variorum* edition. He begins by quoting Dr. Johnson downright "I know not why Shakespeare calls this play 'A *Midsummer* Night's Dream' when he so carefully informs us that it happened on the night preceding *May* day" (p. v.).

and a pair of country gods, half-English and half-Ovid, come to bring their powers in tribute to great lords and ladies.

The play's relationship to pageantry is most prominent in the scene where the fairies are introduced by our seeing their quarrel. This encounter is the sort of thing that Elizabeth and the wedding party might have happened on while walking about in the park during the long summer dusk. The fairy couple accuse each other of the usual weakness of pageant personages—a compelling love for royal personages:

> Why art thou here,
> Come from the farthest steep of India,
> But that, forsooth, the bouncing Amazon,
> Your buskin'd mistress and your warrior love,
> To Theseus must be wedded, and you come
> To give their bed joy and prosperity?
>
> (II.i.68-73)

Oberon describes an earlier entertainment, very likely one in which the family of the real-life bride or groom had been concerned:

> My gentle Puck, come hither. Thou rememb'rest
> Since once I sat upon a promontory
> And heard a mermaid, on a dolphin's back . . .
> That very time I saw (but thou couldst not)
> Flying between the cold moon and the earth
> Cupid, all arm'd. A certain aim he took
> At a fair Vestal, throned by the West,
> And loos'd his love-shaft smartly from his bow,
> As it should pierce a hundred thousand hearts.
> But I might see young Cupid's fiery shaft
> Quench'd in the chaste beams of the wat'ry moon,
> And the imperial vot'ress passed on,
> In maiden meditation, fancy-free.
>
> (II.i.147-164)

At the entertainment at Elvetham in 1591, Elizabeth was throned by the west side of a garden lake to listen to music from the water; the fairy queen came with a round of dancers and spoke of herself as wife of Auberon. These and other similarities make it quite possible, but not necessary, that Shakespeare was referring to the Elvetham occasion.[1] There has been speculation, from Warburton on down, aimed at identifying the mermaid and discovering in Cupid's fiery shaft a particular bid for Elizabeth's affections; Leicester's Kenilworth entertainment in 1575 was usually taken as the occasion alluded to, despite the twenty years that had gone by when Shakespeare wrote.[2] No one, however, has cogently demonstrated any reference to court intrigue —which is to be expected in view of the fact that the play, after its original performance, was on the public stage. The same need for discretion probably accounts for the lack of internal evidence as to the particular marriage the comedy originally celebrated.[3] But what is not in doubt, and what matters for our purpose here, is the *kind* of occasion Oberon's speech refers to, the kind of occasion Shakespeare's scene is shaped by. The speech describes, in retrospect, just such a joyous overflow of pleasure into music and make-believe as is happening in Shakespeare's own play. The fact that what Shakespeare handled with supreme skill was just what was most commonplace no doubt contributes to our inability to connect what he produced with particular historical circumstances.

As we have seen, it was commonplace to imitate Ovid. Ovidian fancies pervade *A Midsummer Night's Dream,* and especially the scene of the fairy quarrel: the description of the way Cupid "loos'd his love shaft" at Elizabeth parallels the *Metamorphoses'* account of the god's shooting "his best arrow, with the golden head" at Apollo; Helena, later in the scene, exclaims that "The story shall be chang'd:/ Apollo flies; and Daphne holds the chase"—and proceeds to invert animal images from Ovid.[4] The game was not so much to lift things gracefully from Ovid as it was to make up fresh things in Ovid's manner, as Shakespeare here, by playful mythopoesis, explains the bad weather by his fairies' quarrel and makes up a metamorphosis of the little West-

[1] See E. K. Chambers, *Shakespearean Gleanings* (Oxford, 1944), pp. 63-64; and Venezky, *Pageantry,* pp. 140ff.

[2] The conjectures are summarized in *Variorum,* pp. 75-91.

[3] Chambers, *Gleanings,* pp. 61-67.

[4] Ovid, *Metamorphoses,* with an English translation by Frank Justus Miller (New York, 1916), pp. 34 and 36-37, Bk. I, ll. 465-474 and 505-506.

ern flower to motivate the play's follies and place Elizabeth superbly above them.[1] The pervasive Ovidian influence accounts for Theseus' putting fables and fairies in the same breath when he says, punning on ancient and antic,

> I never may believe
> These antique fables nor these fairy toys.
> (V.i.2-3)

The humor of the play relates superstition, magic and passionate delusion as "fancy's images." The actual title emphasizes a sceptical attitude by calling the comedy a "dream." It seems unlikely that the title's characterization of the dream, "a midsummer night's dream," implies association with the specific customs of Midsummer Eve, the shortest night of the year, except as "midsummer night" would carry suggestions of a magic time. The observance of Midsummer Eve in England centered on building bonfires or "bonefires," of which there is nothing in Shakespeare's moonlight play. It was a time when maids might find out who their true love would be by dreams or divinations. There were customs of decking houses with greenery and hanging lights, which just possibly might connect with the fairies' torches at the comedy's end. And when people gathered fern seed at midnight, sometimes they spoke of spirits whizzing invisibly past. If one ranges through the eclectic pages of *The Golden Bough*, guided by the index for Midsummer Eve, one finds other customs suggestive of Shakespeare's play, involving moonlight, seeing the moon in water, gathering dew, and so on, but in Sweden, Bavaria, or still more remote places, rather than England.[2] One can assume that parallel English customs have been lost, or one can assume

---

[1] There is a similar compliment to the Queen by Nashe in *Summer's Last Will and Testament*. Nashe also elaborates meteorology into make-believe: Summer blames the drying up of the Thames and earlier flooding of it on the pageant figure, Sol (McKerrow, *Nashe*, III, 250, ll. 541-565).

[2] A good summary of English Midsummer Eve customs is in *Brand's Antiquities*, ed. Ellis, pp. 298-337, which gives simply and briefly examples of almost all the English customs included in Frazer's far more complete survey (see *The Golden Bough*, Vol. XII, *Bibliography and General Index*, London, 1915, pp. 370-371). Ellis cites (p. 319) a song from Penzance which describes what is in many respects a Maying, held on Midsummer Eve with a Midsummer bonfire for

that Shakespeare's imagination found its way to similarities with folk cult, starting from the custom of Maying and the general feeling that spirits may be abroad in the long dusks and short nights of midsummer. Olivia in *Twelfth Night* speaks of "midsummer madness" (III.iv.61). In the absence of evidence, there is no way to settle just how much comes from tradition. But what *is* clear is that Shakespeare was not *simply* writing out folklore which he heard in his youth, as Romantic critics liked to assume. On the contrary, his fairies are produced by a complex fusion of pageantry and popular game, as well as popular fancy. Moreover, as we shall see, they are not serious in the menacing way in which the people's fairies were serious. Instead they are serious in a very different way, as embodiments of the May-game experience of eros in men and women and trees and flowers, while any superstitious tendency to believe in their literal reality is mocked. The whole night's action is presented as a release of shaping fantasy which brings clarification about the tricks of strong imagination. We watch a dream; but we are awake, thanks to pervasive humor about the tendency to take fantasy literally, whether in love, in superstition, or in Bottom's mechanical dramatics. As in *Love's Labour's Lost* the folly of wit becomes the generalized comic subject in the course of an astonishing release of witty invention, so here in the course of a more inclusive release of imagination, the folly of fantasy becomes the general subject, echoed back and forth between the strains of the play's imitative counterpoint.

the men and maids to dance around (such a local combination of the customs is to be expected):

> Bright Luna spreads its light around,
>   The gallants for to cheer,
> As they lay sporting on the ground,
>   At the fair June bonfire.

> All on the pleasant dewy mead,
>   They shared each other's charms,
> Till Phoebus' beams began to spread,
>   And coming day alarms.

Although reported as "sung for a long series of years at Penzance and the neighbourhood," the piece obviously was written after Shakespeare's period. But the customs it describes in its rather crude way are interesting in relation to *A Midsummer Night's Dream*, particularly the moonlight and dew, and the sun's beams coming to end it all.

W. H. AUDEN

W. H. Auden, (1907-   ). One of the most distinguished living poets and lately Professor of Poetry at Oxford, he has written a good deal of very speculative criticism, his most notable collection being The Dyer's Hand *(1963).*

LOVE AND USURY IN THE MERCHANT OF VENICE*

The Merchant of Venice is, among other things, as much a 'problem' play as one by Ibsen or Shaw. The question of the immorality or morality of usury was a sixteenth-century issue on which both the theologians and the secular authorities were divided. Though the majority of medieval theologians had condemned usury, there had been, from the beginning, divergence of opinion as to the correct inter-pretation of Deuteronomy xxiii. 19–20:

'Thou shalt not lend upon usury to thy brother; usury of money, usury of victuals, usury of any thing that is lent upon usury: Unto a stranger thou mayest lend upon usury' and Leviticus xxv. 35–7 which proscribe the taking of usury, not only from a fellow Jew, but also from the stranger living in their midst and under their protection.

Some Christian theologians had interpreted this to mean that, since the Christians had replaced the Jews as God's Chosen, they were entitled to exact usury from non-Chris-tians.[1]

'Who is your brother? He is your sharer in nature, co-heir in grace, every people, which, first, is in the faith, then under the Roman Law. Who, then, is the stranger?

---

* Extracted from 'Brothers and Others' in *Selected Essays.*
[1] N.B. For the quotations which follow, I am indebted to Benjamin Nelson's fascinating book *The Idea of Usury*, Princeton University Press.

the foes of God's people. From him, demand usury whom you rightly desire to harm, against whom weapons are lawfully carried. Upon him usury is legally imposed. Where there is the right of war, there also is the right of usury.' (ST. AMBROSE)

Several centuries later, St. Bernard of Siena, in a statement of which the sanctity seems as doubtful as the logic, takes St. Ambrose's argument even further.

'Temporal goods are given to men for the worship of the true God and the Lord of the Universe. When, therefore, the worship of God does not exist, as in the case of God's enemies, usury is lawfully exacted, because this is not done for the sake of gain, but for the sake of the Faith; and the motive is brotherly love, namely, that God's enemies may be weakened and so return to Him; and further because the goods they have do not belong to them, since they are rebels against the true faith; they shall therefore devolve upon the Christians.'

The majority, however, starting from the Gospel, command that we are to treat all men, even our enemies, as brothers, held that the Deuteronomic permission was no longer valid, so that under no circumstances was usury permissible. Thus, St. Thomas Aquinas, who was also, no doubt, influenced by Aristotle's condemnation of usury, says:

'The Jews were forbidden to take usury from their brethren, i.e., from other Jews. By this we are given to understand that to take usury from any man is simply evil, because we ought to treat every man as our neighbor and brother, especially in the state of the Gospel whereto we are called. They were permitted, however, to take usury from foreigners, not as though it were lawful, but in order to avoid a greater evil, lest to wit, through avarice to which they were prone, according to Isaiah, lvi. 7 they should take usury from Jews, who were worshippers of God.'

On the Jewish side, talmudic scholars had some interesting interpretations. Rashi held that the Jewish debtor is forbidden to pay interest to a fellow Jew, but he may pay interest to a Gentile. Maimonides, who was anxious to prevent Jews from being tempted into idolatry by associating with Gentiles, held that a Jew might borrow at usury from a Gentile, but should not make loans to one, on the ground that debtors are generally anxious to avoid their creditors, but creditors are obliged to seek the company of debtors.

Had Shakespeare wished to show Shylock the usurer in the most unfavourable light possible, he could have placed him in a medieval agricultural society, where men become debtors through misfortunes, like a bad harvest or sickness for which they are not responsible, but he places him in a mercantile society, where the role played by money is a very different one.

When Antonio says:

> *I neither lend nor borrow*
> *By taking or giving of excess*

he does not mean that, if he goes into partnership with another merchant contributing, say, a thousand ducats to their venture, and their venture makes a profit, he only asks for a thousand ducats back. He is a merchant and the Aristotelian argument that money is barren and cannot breed money, which he advances to Shylock, is invalid in his own case.

This change in the role of money had already been recognized by both Catholic and Protestant theologians. Calvin, for example, had come to the conclusion that the Deuteronomic injunction had been designed to meet a particular political situation which no longer existed.

'The law of Moses is political and does not obligate us beyond what equity and the reason of humanity suggest. There is a difference in the political union, for the situation in which God placed the Jews and many circumstances permitted them to trade conveniently among themselves without usuries. Our union is entirely different. Therefore I do not feel that usuries are forbidden to us simply, except in so far as they are opposed to equity and charity.'

The condemnation of usury by Western Christendom cannot be understood except in relation to the severity of its legal attitude, inherited from Roman Law, towards the defaulting debtor. The pound of flesh story has a basis in historical fact for, according to the Law of the Twelve Tables, a defaulting debtor could be torn to pieces alive. In many medieval contracts the borrower agreed, in the case of default, to pay double the amount of the loan as a forfeit, and imprisonment for debt continued into the nineteenth century. It was possible to consider interest on a loan immoral because the defaulting debtor was regarded as a criminal, that is to say, an exception to the human norm, so that lending was thought of as normally entailing no risk. One motive which led the theologians of the sixteenth century to modify the traditional theories about usury and to regard it as a necessary social evil rather than as a mortal sin was their fear of social revolution and the teachings of the Anabaptists and other radical utopians. These, starting from the same premise of Universal Brotherhood which had been the traditional ground for condemning usury, drew the conclusion that private property was unchristian, that Christians should share all their goods in common, so that the relation of creditor to debtor would be abolished. Thus, Luther, who at first had accused Catholic theologians of being lax towards the sin of usury, by 1524, was giving this advice to Prince Frederick of Saxony:

'It is highly necessary that the taking of interest should be regulated everywhere, but to abolish it entirely would not be right either, for it can be made just. I do not advise your Grace, however, to support people in their refusal to pay interest or to prevent them from paying it, for it is not a burden laid upon people by a Prince in his law, but it is a common plague that all have taken upon themselves. We must put up with it, therefore, and hold debtors to it and not let them spare themselves and seek a remedy of their own, but put them on a level with everybody else, as love requires.'

Shylock is a Jew living in a predominantly Christian society, just as Othello is a Negro living in a predominantly white society. But, unlike Othello, Shylock rejects the Christian community as firmly as it rejects him. Shylock and Antonio are at one in refusing to acknowledge a common brotherhood.

> *I will buy with you, sell with you, talk with you, walk*
> *with you, and so following, but I will not eat with you,*
> *drink with you nor pray with you.*   (SHYLOCK)

> *I am as like*
> *To spit on thee again, to spurn thee, too.*

> *If thou wilt lend this money, lend it not*
> *As to thy friends . . .*
> *But lend it rather to thine enemy,*
> *Who if he break, thou mayst with better face*
> *Exact the penalty.*   (ANTONIO)

In addition, unlike Othello, whose profession of arms is socially honourable, Shylock is a professional usurer who, like a prostitute, has a social function but is an outcast from the community. But, in the play, he acts unprofessionally; he refuses to charge Antonio interest and insists upon making their legal relation that of debtor and creditor, a relation acknowledged as legal by all societies. Several critics have pointed to analogies between the trial scene and the medieval *Processus Belial* in which Our Lady defends man against the prosecuting Devil who claims the legal right to man's soul. The Roman doctrine of the Atonement presupposes that the debtor deserves no mercy—Christ may substitute Himself for man, but the debt has to be paid by death on the cross. The Devil is defeated, not because he has no right to demand a penalty, but because he does not know that the penalty has been already suffered. But the differences between Shylock and Belial are as important as their similarities. The comic Devil of the mystery play can appeal to logic, to the letter of the law, but he cannot appeal to the heart or to the imagination, and Shakespeare allows Shylock to do both. In his 'Hath not a Jew eyes . . .' speech in Act III, scene i, he is permitted to appeal to the sense of human brotherhood, and in the trial scene, he is allowed to argue, with a sly appeal to the fear a merchant class has of radical social revolution:

> *You have among you many a purchased slave*
> *Which, like your asses and your dogs and mules,*
> *You use in abject and in slavish parts,*

which points out that those who preach mercy and brotherhood as universal obligations limit them in practice and are prepared to treat certain classes of human beings as things.

Furthermore, while Belial is malevolent without any cause except love of malevolence for its own sake, Shylock is presented as a particular individual living in a particular kind of society at a particular time in history. Usury, like prostitution, may corrupt the character, but those who borrow upon usury, like those who visit brothels, have their share of responsibility for this corruption and aggravate their guilt by showing contempt for those whose services they make use of.

It is, surely, in order to emphasize this point that, in the trial scene, Shakespeare introduces an element which is not found in *Pecorone* or other versions of the pound-of-flesh-story. After Portia has trapped Shylock through his own insistence upon the letter of the law of Contract, she produces another law by which any alien who conspires against the life of a Venetian citizen forfeits his goods and places his life at the Doge's mercy. Even in the rush of a stage performance, the audience cannot help reflecting that a man as interested in legal subtleties as Shylock, would, surely, have been aware of the existence of this law and that, if by any chance he had overlooked it, the Doge surely would very soon have drawn his attention to it. Shakespeare, it seems to me, was willing to introduce what is an absurd implausibility for the sake of an effect which he could not secure without it: at the last moment when, through his conduct, Shylock has destroyed any sympathy we may have felt for him earlier, we are reminded that, irrespective of his personal character, his status is one of inferiority. A Jew is not regarded, even in law, as a brother.

If the wicked Shylock cannot enter the fairy-story world of Belmont, neither can the noble Antonio, though his friend, Bassanio, can. In the fairy-story world, the symbol of final peace and concord is marriage, so that, if the story is concerned with the adventures of two friends of the same sex, male or female, it must end with a double wedding. Had he wished, Shakespeare could have followed the *Pecorone* story in which it is Ansaldo, not Gratiano, who marries the equivalent of Nerissa. Instead, he portrays Antonio as a melancholic who is incapable of loving a woman. He deliberately avoids the classical formula of the Perfect Friends by making the relationship unequal. When Salanio says of Antonio's feelings for Bassanio

I think he only loves the world for him

we believe it, but no one would say that Bassanio's affections are equally exclusive. Bassanio, high-spirited, elegant, pleasure-loving, belongs to the same world as Gratiano and Lorenzo; Antonio does not. When he says:

> I hold the world but as the world, Gratiano,
> A stage, where everyman must play a part,
> And mine a sad one

Gratiano may accuse him of putting on an act, but we believe him, just as it does not seem merely the expression of a noble spirit of self-sacrifice when he tells Bassanio:

> I am a tainted wether of the flock,
> Meetest for death; the weakest kind of fruit
> Drops earliest to the ground, and so let me.

It is well known that love and understanding breed love and understanding.

> The more people on high who comprehend each other,
> the more there are to love well, and the more
> love is there, and like a mirror, one giveth
> back to the other.
>
> (Purgatorio, xv)

So, with the rise of a mercantile economy in which money breeds money, it became an amusing paradox for poets to use the ignoble activity of usury as a metaphor for love, the most noble of human activities. Thus, in his Sonnets, Shakespeare uses usury as an image for the married love which begets children.

> Profitless usurer, why dost thou use
> So great a sum of sums, yet canst not live?
> For having traffic with thyself alone
> Thou of thyself thy sweet self dost deceive.
>
> (Sonnet IV)

> That use is not forbidden usury
> Which happies those that pay the willing loan,
> That's for thyself, to breed another thee,
> Or ten times happier, be it ten for one.
>
> (VI)

And, even more relevant, perhaps, to Antonio are the lines

But since she pricked thee out for women's pleasure
Mine be thy love, and thy love's use their treasure.
(XX)

There is no reason to suppose that Shakespeare had read Dante, but he must have been familiar with the association of usury with sodomy of which Dante speaks in the Eleventh Canto of the Inferno.

'It behoves man to gain his bread and to prosper. And because the usurer takes another way, he contemns Nature in herself and her followers, placing elsewhere his hope. . . . And hence the smallest round seals with its mark Sodom and the Cahors. . . .'

It can, therefore, hardly be an accident that Shylock the usurer has as his antagonist a man whose emotional life, though his conduct may be chaste, is concentrated upon a member of his own sex.

In any case, the fact that Bassanio's feelings are so much less intense makes Antonio's seem an example of that inordinate affection which theologians have always condemned as a form of idolatry, a putting of the creature before the creator. In the sixteenth century, suretyship, like usury, was a controversial issue. The worldly-wise condemned the standing surety for another on worldly grounds.

'Beware of standing suretyship for thy best friends; he that payeth another man's debts seeketh his own decay: neither borrow money of a neighbour or a friend, but of a stranger.' (LORD BURGHLEY)

'Suffer not thyself to be wounded for other men's faults, or scourged for other men's offences, which is the surety for another: for thereby, millions of men have been beggared and destroyed . . . from suretyship as from a manslayer or enchanter, bless thyself.' (SIR WALTER RALEIGH)

And clerics like Luther condemned it on theological grounds.

'Of his life and property a man is not certain for a single moment, any more than he is certain of the man for whom he becomes surety. Therefore the man who becomes surety acts unchristian like and deserves what he gets, because he pledges and promises what is not his and not in his power, but in the hands of God alone. . . . These sureties act as though their life and property were their own and were in their power as long as they wished to have it; and this is nothing but the fruit of unbelief. . . . If there were no more of this becoming surety, many a man would have to keep down and be satisfied with a moderate living, who now aspires night and day after high places, relying on borrowing and standing surety.'

The last sentence of this passage applies very well to Bassanio. In *Pecorone,* the Lady of Belmonte is a kind of witch and Gianetto gets into financial difficulties because he is the victim of magic, a fate which is never regarded as the victim's fault. But Bassanio had often borrowed money from Antonio before he ever considered wooing Portia and was in debt, not through magic or unforeseeable misfortune, but through his own extravagances,

> *'Tis not unknown to you, Antonio,*
> *How much I have disabled my estate*
> *By something showing a more swelling port*
> *Than my faint means would grant continuance*

and we feel that Antonio's continual generosity has encouraged Bassanio in his spendthrift habits. Bassanio seems to be one of those people whose attitude towards money is that of a child; it will somehow always appear by magic when really needed. Though Bassanio is aware of Shylock's malevolence, he makes no serious effort to dissuade Antonio from signing the bond because, thanks to the ever-open purse of his friend, he cannot believe that bankruptcy is a real possibility in life.

Shylock is a miser and Antonio is openhanded with his money; nevertheless, as a merchant, Antonio is equally a member of an acquisitive society. He is trading with Tripoli, the Indies, Mexico, England, and when Salanio imagines himself in Antonio's place, he describes a possible shipwreck thus:

> *. . . the rocks*
> *Scatter all her spices on the stream,*
> *Enrobe the roaring waters with my silks.*

The commodities, that is to say, in which the Venetian merchant deals are not necessities but luxury goods, the consumption of which is governed not by physical need but by psychological values like social prestige, so that there can be no question of a Just Price. Then, as regards his own expenditure, Antonio is, like Shylock, a sober merchant who practises economic abstinence. Both of them avoid the carnal music of this world. Shylock's attitude towards the Masquers

> *Lock up my doors and when you hear the drum*
> *And the vile squeaking of the wry-necked fife*
> *Clamber not you up the casement then,*
> *Let not the sound of shallow foppery enter*
> *My sober house*

finds an echo in Antonio's words a scene later:

> *Fie, fie, Gratiano. Where are all the rest?*
> *Tis nine o'clock: our friends all stay for you.*
> *No masque to-night—the wind is come about.*

Neither of them is capable of enjoying the carefree happiness for which Belmont stands. In a production of the play, a stage director is faced with the awkward problem of what to do with Antonio in the last act. Shylock, the villain, has been vanquished and will trouble Arcadia no more, but, now that Bassanio is getting married, Antonio, the real hero of the play, has no further dramatic function. According to the Arden edition, when Alan McKinnon produced the play at the Garrick theatre in 1905, he had Antonio and Bassanio hold the stage at the final curtain, but I cannot picture Portia, who is certainly no Victorian doormat of a wife, allowing her bridegroom to let her enter the house by herself. If Antonio is not to fade away into a nonentity, then the married couples must enter the lighted house and leave Antonio standing alone on the darkened stage, outside the Eden from which, not by the choice of others, but by his own nature, he is excluded.

Without the Venice scenes, Belmont would be an Arcadia without any relation to actual times and places, and where, therefore, money and sexual love have no reality

of their own, but are symbolic signs for a community in a
state of grace. But Belmont is related to Venice, though their
existences are not really compatible with each other. This
incompatibility is brought out in a fascinating way by the
difference between Belmont time and Venice time. Though
we are not told exactly how long the period is before Shylock's loan must be repaid, we know that it is more than
a month. Yet Bassanio goes off to Belmont immediately,
submits immediately on arrival to the test of the caskets,
and has just triumphantly passed it when Antonio's letter
arrives to inform him that Shylock is about to take him to
court and claim his pound of flesh. Belmont, in fact, is like
one of those enchanted palaces where time stands still. But
because we are made aware of Venice, the real city, where
time is real, Belmont becomes a real society to be judged
by the same standards we apply to any other kind of society.
Because of Shylock and Antonio, Portia's inherited fortune
becomes real money which must have been made in this
world, as all fortunes are made, by toil, anxiety, the enduring and inflicting of suffering. Portia we can admire because,
having seen her leave her Earthly Paradise to do a good
deed in this world (one notices, incidentally, that in this
world she appears in disguise), we know that she is aware
of her wealth as a moral responsibility, but the other inhabitants of Belmont, Bassanio, Gratiano, Lorenzo and Jessica,
for all their beauty and charm, appear as frivolous members
of a leisured class, whose carefree life is parasitic upon the
labours of others, including usurers. When we learn that
Jessica has spent fourscore ducats of her father's money
in an evening and bought a monkey with her mother's ring,
we cannot take this as a comic punishment for Shylock's
sin of avarice; her behaviour seems rather an example of
the opposite sin of conspicuous waste. Then, with the example in our minds of self-sacrificing love as displayed by
Antonio, while we can enjoy the verbal felicity of the love
duet between Lorenzo and Jessica, we cannot help noticing
that the pairs of lovers they recall, Troilus and Cressida,
Aeneas and Dido, Jason and Medea, are none of them
examples of self-sacrifice or fidelity. Recalling that the in-
scription on the leaden casket ran, 'Who chooseth me, must
give and hazard all he hath,' it occurs to us that we have

seen two characters do this. Shylock, however unintention-
ally, did, in fact, hazard all for the sake of destroying the
enemy he hated, and Antonio, however unthinkingly he
signed the bond, hazarded all to secure the happiness of the
friend he loved. Yet it is precisely these two who cannot
enter Belmont. Belmont would like to believe that men and
women are either good or bad by nature, but Shylock and
Antonio remind us that this is an illusion: in the real world,
no hatred is totally without justification, no love totally
innocent.

As a society, Venice is more efficient and successful than
Henry IV's England. Its citizens are better off, more secure
and nicer mannered. Politically speaking, therefore, one
may say that a mercantile society represents an advance
upon a feudal society, as a feudal society represents an advance upon a tribal society. But every step forward brings
with it its own dangers and evils, for the more advanced
a social organization, the greater the moral demands it
makes upon its members and the greater the degree of guilt
which they incur if they fail to meet these demands. The
members of a society with a primitive self-sufficient economy can think of those outside it as others, not brothers,
with a good conscience, because they can get along by themselves. But, first, money and, then, machinery have created
a world in which, irrespective of our cultural traditions and
our religious or political convictions, we are all mutually
dependent. This demands that we accept all other human
beings on earth as brothers, not only in law, but also in our
hearts. Our temptation, of course, is to do just the opposite,
not to return to tribal loyalties—that is impossible—but,
each of us, to regard everybody else on earth not even as
an enemy, but as a faceless algebraical cipher.

> They laid the coins before the council.
> Kay, the king's steward, wise in economics, said:
> 'Good; these cover the years and the miles
> and talk one style's dialects to London and Omsk.
> Traffic can hold now and treasure be held,
> streams are bridged and mountains of ridged space
> tunnelled; gold dances deftly over frontiers.

THEOPHILE GAUTIER

Théophile Gautier (1811-1872). Author of the influential book of poems Emaux et Camées *(1852) and* Mademoiselle de Maupin *(1835), a novel with great historical importance for the later 'aesthetic' movement.*

Sex in As You Like It*

The rehearsal went off much better than I had ventured to hope. Theodore especially was splendid, and I also was considered to have played in a superior fashion. That was not due, however, to my possessing the qualities which one needs in order to be a good actor, and it would be a great mistake to suppose that I am capable of playing other parts equally well; but by singular fortune, the words I had to speak were so well suited to my situation that they seemed to be of my own invention rather than learned from a book. Had my memory played me false in certain places I should assuredly not have hesitated a moment to fill the gap with improvised words. Orlando was as much myself as I was Orlando, and a more remarkable coincidence would be impossible.

In the wrestling scene, when Theodore took the chain from his neck and presented it to me, as is laid down in the part, he gave me a look so softly languorous, so full of promises, and he uttered with such grace and nobleness the words, "Fair sir, wear this in memory of me,—of a maiden who would fain give you more had she more to give," that I was fairly upset, and I could scarce return: "What passion ties my tongue and binds it with fetters? I cannot speak to her, yet doth she desire to entertain me. O wretched Orlando!"

In the third act, Rosalind, dressed in male attire and bear-

* From *Mademoiselle de Maupin.*

ing the name of Ganymede, reappears with her cousin, who has changed her name to Aliena. The impression I then received was painful. I had already grown so accustomed to the woman's dress which permitted my desire to harbour some hope and kept up a perfidious but seductive error! We quickly accustom ourselves to look upon our wishes as realised, upon the faith of the most fleeting appearances, and I became quite gloomy when Theodore reappeared in his man's dress,—gloomier than I had been before; for joy but brings out grief more strongly, the sun but deepens the horror of darkness, and the brightness of white is intended but to enhance the full sadness of black. His coat was most gallant and coquettish, elegantly and fancifully cut, and richly adorned with frillings and ribbons, somewhat in the fashion of the "moulds of form" of the Court of Louis XIII; a high-crowned felt hat, with long curly feather, shaded his beautiful locks, and a damascened sword cocked up his travelling-cloak.

Yet he was dressed in a way that made one feel there was a female filling to these masculine garments; the greater width of the hips, the greater fulness of the bosom, something of wavy that stuffs never show on a man's form, left but slight doubts as to the sex of the wearer.

He had a semi-deliberate, semi-timid look most amusing to behold; with infinite art he had managed to give himself an air of being as ill at ease in a dress he daily wore, as he had of being quite at his ease in an attire unfamiliar to him.

I recovered somewhat my peace of mind, and again I persuaded myself that he was in very deed a woman. I became collected enough to proceed properly with my part.

Do you know the play? Perhaps not. For the past fortnight I have been doing nothing but read and spout it, and I know it all by heart, so I cannot conceive that everybody else is not as fully cognizant of the knot and the plot as I am myself. I am rather given to making the mistake of fancying, when I am drunk, that the whole world is drunk and lurching against the walls, and if I knew Hebrew you may be sure I should tell my servant in Hebrew to bring me my dressing-gown and my slippers, and I should be much surprised if he did not understand me. You shall read the play if you like; meanwhile I shall assume that you have read it and I shall refer to those parts only which bear upon the situation in which I find myself.

Rosalind, walking in the forest with her cousin, is greatly surprised to find that the bushes bear, instead of blackberries and brambleberries, madrigals in her praise, strange fruits, which are not, happily, in the habit of growing there, for it is much preferable, when one is athirst, to come upon good berries than poor sonnets. Celia, who has already met Orlando, tells her, after much pressing, that the author of the verses is none other than the youth who vanquished Charles, the duke's wrestler.

Orlando himself soon appears, and Rosalind opens the conversation by inquiring the time of day. This is certainly an extremely simple opening; there cannot well be anything more commonplace. But do not fear; out of that commonplace, every-day phrase will forthwith spring up a crop of unexpected concetti, full of quaint flowers and comparisons, as from the most fertile and well-enriched soil.

After a few lines of sparkling dialogue, in which every word, as it strikes the sentence, sends flying right and left a shower of mad sparks, as a hammer strikes them from a red-hot iron bar, Rosalind asks Orlando if perchance he knows the man who hangs odes upon hawthorns and elegies on brambles, and who seems to have the quotidian of love upon him,—a disorder for which he possesses a certain cure. Orlando owns to her that he is himself the love-shak'd swain, and that since he, Ganymede, boasts of having more than one infallible recipe for the cure of the malady, he will do him the favour of giving him one. "You in love?" replies Rosalind; "there is none of the true lover's marks upon you: a lean cheek, which you have not; a blue eye and sunken, which you have not; your hose should be un-garter'd, your sleeve unbutton'd, but on the contrary the ribbon on your shoe is most gracefully tied. If you are in love it is with your own self, and my remedies are of no use to you."

It was with real feeling that I replied in the words of my part, which I here set down textually,—

"Fair youth, I would I could make thee believe I love."

That utterly unexpected, utterly strange reply, for which

no preparation is made, and which a poet's foresight seemed to have written expressly for me, impressed me deeply as I spoke it to Theodore, whose divine lips still pouted slightly with the ironic expression in the words he had just uttered, whilst his eyes smiled with inexpressible sweetness, and a bright beam of kindness lighted all the upper part of his young and lovely face.

"Me believe it! You may as soon make her that you love believe it; which, I warrant, she is apter to do than to confess she does; that is one of the points in the which women still give the lie to their consciences. But, in good sooth, are you he that hangs the verses on the trees, wherein Rosalind is so admired? And do you really need a remedy for your lunacy?"

When she has fully assured herself that it is indeed Orlando, and none else, who has rimed these admirable many-footed verses, fair Rosalind consents to impart her recipe to him. It consists in this: she pretended to be the fair of of the love-sick swain, who was set to court her as if she were really his mistress, and in order to disgust him with his love, she indulged in the most fantastic caprices—now weeping, now laughing; now welcoming, now repulsing him; she scratched him, spat in his face; was never two minutes the same,—coquettish, flighty, prudish, languorous; she was all in turns and, besides, all that boredom, vapours, and blue devils can suggest in the way of disjointed fancies to an empty-headed coquette; all this the poor devil had to bear with or had to perform. A will o' the wisp, a monkey, and an attorney rolled into one could not have invented more tricks. This miraculous treatment had not failed to produce its effect; the patient had been driven from his mad humour of love to a living humour of madness; which was, to forswear the full stream of this world, and to live in a nook merely monastic,—a most satisfactory result, which, besides, might reasonably be expected.

Orlando, it will readily be believed, cares little to recover his health by such means, but Rosalind insists, and is resolved to undertake the cure. And she spoke these words, "I would cure you if you would but call me Rosalind, and come every day to my cote and woo me," with so marked and plain a meaning, and casting on me a glance so strange, that I could not avoid giving it a wider import than the words themselves contain, or refrain from understanding it as an indirect invitation to declare my real feelings. And when Orlando replies, "With all my heart, good youth," she said, still more significantly and as if annoyed at not being understood, "Nay, you must call me Rosalind."

I may have been mistaken and have fancied I saw what was not there, but it seemed to me that Theodore had perceived my love, although I never breathed a word of it to him, and that under the veil of these borrowed expressions, under the stage mask, with these hermaphrodite speeches, he alluded to his real sex and to the situation we were in. It is out of the question that so clever a woman as she is, who has so great a knowledge of the world, should have failed to discern, from the very outset, what was going on in my heart. If my lips were closed, my eyes and my emotions spoke plainly enough, and the veil of ardent friendship I had thrown over my love was not so impenetrable but that an attentive and interested observer could easily see through it. The most innocent girl, with the least knowledge of the world, would not have been stopped a minute by it. . . .

Rosette played her part with a mournful, caressing grace, and spoke in a pained and resigned tone that went to the heart; and when Rosalind said to her, "I would love you, if I could," the tears nearly welled from her eyes, and she found it difficult to restrain them, for Phebe's story is hers, as Orlando's is mine, saving this difference, that all ends happily for Orlando, while Phebe, deceived in her love, is reduced to wed Silvius, instead of the lovely ideal she sought to embrace. Such is life; one man's happiness is another man's curse. It is lucky for me that Theodore is a woman and very unfortunate for Rosette that he is not a man, for she is now stranded amid the love impossibilities by which I was but recently beset.

At the end of the play Rosalind exchanges the doublet of Ganymede the page for the garments proper to her sex, and makes herself known to the duke as his daughter, to Orlando as his mistress, and the god Hymen arrives with his saffron liveries and his legitimising torches. Three weddings take place: Orlando weds Rosalind; Phebe, Silvius; and Touchstone the clown, Audrey the simple wench. Then the epilogue speaks its farewell and the curtain falls.

The whole thing interested and enthralled us greatly. It was in some sort a play within a play, a drama invisible and unknown to the other spectators, which we were playing for ourselves alone, and which, with its symbolical expressions, summed up our whole life and expressed our most secret desires. But for Rosalind's curious remedy, I should be worse than ever, without even the hope of a distant cure, and I should continue to wander sadly in the oblique paths of the dark forest. . . .

PETER URE

Peter Ure (1919-   ). Joseph Cowan Professor of English Literature at the University of Newcastle upon Tyne. Author of three books on Yeats: Towards a Mythology *(1946),* Yeats the Playwright *(1963), and* W. B. Yeats *(1964); editor of* Richard II *in the new Arden series (1956), with* Two Noble Kinsmen *forthcoming.*

TROILUS AND CRESSIDA*

Sir Walter Greg called *Troilus and Cressida* 'a play of puzzles'. Its classification was long disputed, though we may call it at best a 'problem tragedy'. Its diction is often obscure; its love-poetry is passionate and intellectually tough in Donne's manner. It differs from Shakespeare's earlier plays by its special stress on staged debates between characters, and by the absence of a single major character on whom our imagination may fasten (instead, there is an exceptionally large number of important speaking parts). Ideas and attitudes are kept in constant movement throughout it; there are many speeches which openly acknowledge their allegiance to rhetorical disciplines and at the same time transcend them with a richness of figure and feeling that seems very personal to Shakespeare, and here encom-

* Extracted from *Shakespeare: The Problem Plays.*

passes an element of bitter bawdry which for some readers colours the whole play. Peter Alexander's theory that it was specially written for an Inns of Court audience has been generally approved. A crowd of young barristers and their guests would probably have enjoyed more than the popular audience at the Globe would the obliquity of the play, its occasional legal jokes, and its angry, metaphysical and highbrow temper.

Although Shakespeare took his title from the love-story, the war-story is just as important. The two themes of love and war, which are handled with such plangent nobility in Othello's dedication of himself and all his romantic history to his 'fair warrior' and which for so long had been a literary archetype, here suffer their traditional equilibrium to become a 'torture', in the words of John Crowe Ransom's poem:

> At length I saw these lovers fully were come
> Into their torture of equilibrium.

The themes, as Theodore Spencer said, are 'interwoven in a deliberate and elaborate pattern'; Thersites's crude summary of them 'Lechery, lechery; still wars and lechery; nothing else holds fashion' is not the last word about them or about the experience of Troilus and Cressida, and although the play is difficult to classify, its writing and planning give no impression that Shakespeare was half-hearted or inattentive.

It is a mistake to exaggerate the sardonic nature of Shakespeare's treatment of the war-story by comparing it directly with the *Iliad*. The Homeric tale had long been modified by the medieval bias in favour of the Trojans and by the habit of thinking of the Greeks as grossly unchivalric. Many European countries traced their ancestry back to the Trojans (Holinshed, Shakespeare's great source-book for English history, was misinforming his readers in Shakespeare's own time that the name 'Britain' derived from Aeneas's grandson Brutus). There was a large body of pseudo-historical writing about the war, which was regarded as having as much or greater authority than Homer. Shakespeare's principal source was Caxton's ever-popular *Recuyell* (or 'collection') *of the Historyes of Troye*, 1475), a work which ultimately derives from a twelfth-century French composition that claims to know more history than Homer. From the same ultimate source came Lydgate's *Troy Book*, which many believe was also used by Shakespeare. Shakespeare probably did not read the *Iliad* in Greek, but when his play was written (*c.* 1602) some instalments (Books i, ii, and vii to ix) of the first English translation by George Chapman had appeared, and it is more than likely that Shakespeare did not neglect Chapman's defiantly epoch-making enterprise. He would have found in it, for example, the character of Thersites, who is unknown to Caxton or Lydgate.

Although it has been doubted, it is also very probable that he knew the two great preceding treatments of the love-story, Chaucer's *Troilus and Criseyde* and Robert Henryson's *Testament of Cresseid*. The latter would have been available to him in editions of Chaucer which print Henryson's fine poem as a sequel. It takes a much more mordant view than Chaucer did, and by Shakespeare's time this had become traditional: Cressida is the prototype of the fickle wanton, Pandarus of the vile go-between, and Troilus of the faithful, cheated lover. Shakespeare shows himself very conscious of their eponymous roles, as in Pandarus's declaration:

> If ever you prove false one to another, since I have taken such pains to bring you together, let all pitiful goers-between be call'd to the world's end after my name—call them all Pandars; let all constant men be Troiluses, all false women Cressidas, and all brokers between Pandars. Say 'Amen'.

Thus, while Shakespeare's treatment of Troilus remains relatively the same as Chaucer's, he is much less kindly to the other two, although it is true that Pandarus is a comic bustler, who is certainly not scourged from our sympathy after the manner of Jonsonian satire; whose final disappointment, therefore, is not a matter for self-righteous pleasure, but saddens us a little. Chaucer was writing within the tradition of courtly love, which had now been supplanted by that of Christian marriage. As is common within that latter tradition, Shakespeare tends to gloss over the man's share in the mutual breach of prescribed sexual ethics, while making it plain that the lovers consummated their betrothal pledge without benefit of priest.[1]

The sardonic nature of Shakespeare's rendering of both these ancient, famous stories, as well as his practice of interweaving them, are clearly announced in the play's first few minutes. The 'armed' Prologue, in curiously mannered and almost Miltonic diction, sounds loud with brass and the rattle of armament:

> Now on Dardan plains
> The fresh and yet unbruised Greeks do pitch
> Their brave pavilions: Priam's six-gated city,
> Dardan, and Tymbria, Helias, Chetas, Troien,
> And Antenorides, with massy staples
> And corresponsive and fulfilling bolts,
> Sperr up the sons of Troy.
> Now expectation, tickling skittish spirits
> On one and other side, Troyan and Greek,
> Sets all on hazard.

This slightly self-deriding exercise in onomatopoeia is a splendidly discordant version of that other Prologue to famous victories in *Henry V*. It is followed by a scene which strikes sharply across it with another discord. The rousing fights for which the Prologue tickles expectation do not occur. Instead, there enters the sick-hearted Troilus, not arming but unarming:

> Call here my varlet; I'll unarm again:
> Why should I war without the walls of Troy
> That find such cruel battle here within?

This is one of those juxtapositions which Shakespeare made into a high art of dramatic contrast, especially in this play. Pandarus, who has been at work for some time as go-between, leaves in a huff because Troilus won't be patient (the lover woos the pandar, another ironic inversion), and by the end of the first scene the clangorous Prologue appears shrill and diminished. The second scene makes more of this. It introduces Cressida: a bold, witty, courtly person

[1] On the sources see especially Alice Walker's New Cambridge edition (1957), and K. Muir, *Shakespeare's Sources I* (1957), 78-96.

thoroughly able to manage Pandarus. Their conversation reveals that Cressida's consent is a foregone conclusion (and this throws an ironical jest back at Troilus's agonies and frustrations) and depicts the Trojan world as an urbane civilization which does not take itself too seriously.

When we turn in the next scene (I.iii) to war, politics, and the Greeks, we find a people, or, rather, a beleaguered army, which does take its situation much more gravely. This is the first of the two great debate-scenes. It is not too much to say that the Greek debate and what follows it, and the Trojan debate in II.ii, are the keys to the meaning and construction of the entire play. In the Greek debate we meet all at once the major Homeric personages except Achilles and Ajax, who are both present by implication: for all the debaters have Achilles's insubordination and Ajax's pride in mind. In the bristly and rather empty rhetoric of Agamemnon's exordium the tone of the armed Prologue recurs. Of Ulysses's two long speeches, the first (ll. 54-137), the famous speech on 'degree' (= 'rank', social order viewed as the mirror of cosmic order), exposes the principle by which an army and a campaign ought to be run; the second (ll. 141-84) gives a vivid account of how Achilles is causing chaos by disregarding what is due to rank. The Greeks have just exhausted this theme (but seem to have no plan for remedial action) when Aeneas arrives as herald to deliver Hector's challenge to single combat: a challenge of a purely chivalric-medieval kind in which the knights are to pledge the beauty and honour of their ladies. Greek and Trojan are here distinguished as blunt or ceremonious. At first Agamemnon simply cannot understand Aeneas's courtly rendering of 'Which of you is Agamemnon?':

> *Aen.*   How may
> A stranger to those most imperial looks
> Know them from eyes of other mortals?
> *Agam.* How?
> *Aen.* Ay;
> I ask, that I might waken reverence,
> And bid the cheek be ready with a blush
> Modest as Morning when she coldly eyes
> The youthful Phoebus.

Which is that god in office, guiding men?
Which is the high and mighty Agamemnon?
Agam. This Troyan scorns us, or the men of Troy
Are ceremonious courtiers.   (I. iii. 223-34)

Such a passage makes fun of the difference between the two sides, but does not espouse either. When the Greeks accept the challenge, they also accept Ulysses's plan for using it as a means of bringing Achilles back into the war: the boastful Ajax is to be treated as though he were the Greek's best man and elected challenger; if he loses, there's no great harm done, since the Greek army can spare him; but if he wins, then Achilles will feel that his reputation is in deadly danger and will, they hope, arm for battle again. Most of the rest of the Achilles-story in the play revolves round this simple scheme.

Because Ulysses unfolds the theme of 'degree' with the magnification proper to an orator addressing a council of war, amplifying it with the macrocosmic analogy, the speech has often been extrapolated as a statement of the Shakespearian or Elizabethan world-view. It may be so; but if we keep it in its dramatic context, we perceive that there is a sardonic contrast between Ulysses's insistence on rank and his subsequent plan to invert, for politico-military ends, the due precedence of Achilles over Ajax. By manipulating Ajax's conceit against Achilles's pride, putting the weak above the head of the strong, the Greeks hope to enforce proper order again. This is a politic game, the art of the possible, and it defines the 'degree' speech, with some irony, as the rhetoric of an ideal. Furthermore, the ingenious scheme is opportunist in character; Aeneas's quite unexpected challenge, not anything decided by a debate which seemed to be getting nowhere, gave Ulysses the idea for it. And, although it is elaborately maintained up to the fifth Act and looks almost like succeeding, nothing comes of it in the end. Achilles suddenly withdraws from the combat for a remarkably trivial and vague reason (V. i. 35ff), and when he does finally fight it is for a quite different cause: to revenge Patroclus's death on Hector. Thus the huge structure built on the Greek debate-scene is deliberately left roofless; Ulysses the master-politician and tireless orator has affairs jerked from his hands and is left darkling.

The issue before the Trojans in *their* debate-scene (II.ii) is not how to continue the war but whether to continue it. This is the strangest scene in the play and has caused much dispute. The debate is much more of a genuine debate than the Greek one; Shakespeare seems determined to keep our sympathies swaying back and forth between the appeal to reason (Hector's) and that to passion (Troilus's). Because he is uncertain of the future and thinks that the lives squandered in Helen's cause are worth more than she is, Hector advises peace. Troilus bursts out that Priam's honour, which depends upon keeping Helen, is not to be measured by Hector's fears and reasons, and when the priest Helenus rebukes him for this he merely taunts him for being a coward. There is something romantic and absolute about Troilus's youthful fervour here and elsewhere which is very attractive to a part of our minds. The debate then goes deeper. Troilus and Hector begin to discuss whether they ought to be motivated by the value of Helen in herself, or by the value they have put upon her in the past by committing themselves to fighting for her. Both seem to agree that in herself Helen is not worth much, and Hector wants the Trojans simply to remember this; it is madness to continue to value an object simply because it was once thought a prize worth having. Troilus replies with an analogy: a man chooses a wife, a matter in which both 'will' (= 'passion') and judgement are involved, and therefore a very delicate choice. But the choice once made is irrevocable, if the man is to 'stand firm by honour'. So the Trojans, thinking her valuable, stole Helen; now they are distasted with her. But if they are to avoid inconsistency, cowardice, and dishonour, they can no more give her up than a man can give up the wife whom he has grown to dislike. Cassandra now makes her first entrance, and, after her prophecy of doom, Hector asks Troilus whether the thought that Troy may be conquered makes any difference. Troilus faces up to this: the rightness of a course is not affected by whether it succeeds or not:

> Why, brother Hector,
> We may not think the justness of each act
> Such and no other than event doth form it.
> (II.ii. 118-20)

Paris seconds him, with different arguments. Troilus had argued that the original rape of Helen was a just act of revenge (for the Greeks' rape of Priam's sister, Hesione); Paris claims that, if the rape of Helen was a crime, the disgrace can be wiped off by 'honourable keeping her'. Hector's reply to all this, an appeal to the law of nature and of nations, is unanswerable on its own level. His argument is a very Elizabethan one and would perhaps have seemed wholly persuasive to an Elizabethan audience. It is all very well, he says, to talk about what we owe ourselves in honour, but the plain fact is that Helen is Menelaus's wife and the Trojans have no right to her:

> If Helen, then, be wife of Sparta's king—
> As it is known she is—these moral laws
> Of nature and of nations speak aloud
> To have her back return'd. Thus to persist
> In doing wrong extenuates not wrong,
> But makes it much more heavy.   (II. ii. 183-8)

Hector's next step, his sudden retraction, is the most puzzling incident in the play:

>   Hector's opinion
> Is this, in way of truth. Yet, ne'er the less,
> My spritely brethren, I propend to you
> In resolution to keep Helen still;
> For 'tis a cause that hath no mean dependence
> Upon our joint and several dignities.   (II. ii. 188-93)

Probably the 'explanation' for it is simply that otherwise the play would have had to stop. This is an explanation that supplies a motive which Hector himself could hardly have recognized, and is therefore unsatisfactory from the point of view of consistent characterization; but that is not the only criterion in a work of dramatic art.

The Trojan decision is fatal to them. For the rest of the play Hector relapses into the noble, doomed warrior of tradition. But Troilus remains consistent with the self which he had exposed in the debate, which therefore continues to reverberate during the rest of both the war-action and the love-action. His notion that honour resides in a man's not ratting on his own choice is carefully contrasted with the Achillean notion, which is deliberately aggravated by Ulysses for his politic purposes in his great speech on the subject (III.iii. 145-90), that honour is what is given to you by other people and is therefore ruled by time and chance. It was precisely this notion of honour as 'opinion', an outward thing measured by other men's judgements and the vulgar fancies of the fickle mob, which was passionately repudiated by Chapman and many other Elizabethan writers when they tried to discern what greatness really is. Ulysses, however, vividly states the facts of political life and not the austere longings of Elizabethan neo-Stoicism. Achilles's consequent alarm at the state of his reputation is at once a response to those facts, for which he cannot be blamed, and a designed contrast with Troilus's passionate commitment to the view that time and fortune modify original virtue.

This commitment is of a piece with his deception by Cressida and his total pledge to her. In a world which contains the Ulyssean facts (that women are fickle and that reputations fade), Shakespeare shows both the glorious and the self-destructive character of Troilus's absoluteness, his truth to himself. With his glory and his fault locked together in him, Troilus very closely resembles Othello, and is a tragic hero.

The scene (III.ii) in which the lovers finally come together is treated by Shakespeare as the birth of a legend, but is not to be taken simply as a satirical version of it. Troilus's feelings are too genuine for that. There is no doubt that Theodore Spencer is right as against O. J. Campbell when he says that Troilus's love is both sensual *and* idealistic. He has placed, to the accompaniment of some hard-breathing desire, an ideal valuation on the false Cressid, and to this he clings for ever. She can respond seriously for the time being, and continues to do so later on in the three continuous scenes (IV.ii-iv) which deal with their parting. Campbell's view that they are both depicted as a couple of sated sensualists is quite unacceptable and derives from his determination to make the whole play conform to the satirical mode. It is a much more subtle play than Thersites thinks. At the first news that Cressida must go to the Greek camp, Troilus is shocked into silence and simplicity; her grief contains no hint that she is merely behaving. But she knows little of herself, of the time-directed nature of her truth, as her indignation at Troilus's plea to her to be true reveals. Time is the enemy of all lovers, and both the constant and the fickle are here seen beneath that climbing shadow, which puts satire far from us as we contemplate them in these scenes.

This shadow is removed from Cressida when her unstable and fickle nature is revealed in IV.v. Passively she allows herself to be carried on the tide of events, somewhat in the manner of Chaucer's heroine. The two speeches by Ulysses in this scene, one about Cressida, the other about Troilus, make it plain that the Helen-situation, as examined in the Trojan debate, is being repeated in the relation of Troilus to Cressida. The object to which Troilus attaches such value is shown *by time* to be valueless. Once it was not so, just as once, for Troilus, Helen was a true prize and a just deed. But 'once' for Troilus is 'always', as the debate showed. This is the source of his agony in the last of the love-story scenes (V.ii) where Troilus watches Cressida's wanton invitation to Diomed. His speech is a complete confusion between the value he once put upon Cressida and what she now appears by 'ocular proof' to be. His commitment to what she was makes it impossible for him to accept what she is. This is Troilus's peculiarly personal fate, or punishment:

> This she? No; this is Diomed's Cressida.
> If beauty have a soul, this is not she;
> If souls guide vows, if vows be sanctimonies,
> If sanctimony be the gods' delight,
> If there be rule in unity itself,
> This was not she. O madness of discourse,
> That cause sets up with and against itself!
> Bifold authority! where reason can revolt
> Without perdition, and loss assume all reason
> Without revolt: this is, and is not, Cressid.
>
> (V. ii.135-44)

Although the speech ends with a cluster of the food-and-taste images frequent in this play, revealing Troilus's apprehension of grossness in the valued object, he can no more give up his love than he could accept Hector's argument that things are what they are, and that losses ought to be cut. During the rest of the play Troilus is mastered by his passionate consistency, vows revenge on Diomed, proclaims his love, and urges to the fight with reckless courage. The 'worthless' cause for which he fights is Cressida's now as well as Helen's.

Shakespeare does not suggest that we should withhold our admiration and pity for this; but in what remains of the war-story he does suggest, Ulysses-like, that Troilus is out of accord with the facts of the Trojan war and is likely to come to grief. The finale of the play strengthens the sardonic treatment of hopes and ideals which is the air that Thersites, Ulysses, and Diomed breathe, and which Troilus is none the worse for finding stifling. When Hector is slain by Achilles the incident is deliberately made a far seamier affair than it was in Shakespeare's source—the opportunist murder of an unarmed man by a troop of soldiers. In his last speech, knowing Troy must fall, Troilus breathes vengeance on Achilles; an audience may remember that Troilus is soon to die—at Achilles's hands.

The death of Hector is just sufficiently decisive to give the play an ending, but is in a minor key of melancholy. Shakespeare's sophisticated treatment of the whole story, in which elaborate schemes run to waste (those of Pandarus as well as Ulysses) and paths of motivation peter out in the jungle of accident, is sufficiently pointed by this conclusion in which nothing is concluded, except in the audience's foreknowledge. This wonderfully composed and highly-wrought work is thus sharply bent towards the satirical and the off-beat, and is darkened throughout with Thersites's savage, ineffectual commentary. But Shakespeare was not content to accept the tale of Troy only as a sardonic amusement, a way of cutting ancient heroes down to size. In the heart of all its accomplished inversions and achieved rhetoric, its diminishing commentary and its squalid opportunism, denied by them and yet given in our imaginations real power to deny them, lies what was in such a context the most difficult, because the most simple, artifact of all: the simply constant Troilus, who might well have borrowed Parolles's astounding line: 'Simply the thing I am shall make me live':

> Alas,
> I am as true as truth's simplicity
> And simpler than the infancy of truth.

WALTER PATER

Walter Pater (1839-1894). Author of Studies in the History of the Renaissance *(1873),* Marius the Epicurean *(1885),* Imaginary Portraits *(1887),* Appreciations *(1889). Among his works are essays on* Richard II *and* Measure for Measure, *valuable in themselves but also as examples of a literary approach and a prose style which were the models of a critical generation.*

MEASURE FOR MEASURE*

In *Measure for Measure,* as in some other of his plays, Shakespeare has remodelled an earlier and somewhat rough composition to "finer issues," suffering much to remain as it had come from the less skilful hand, and not raising the whole of his work to an equal degree of intensity. Hence perhaps some of that depth and weightiness which make this play so impressive, as with the true seal of experience, like a fragment of life itself, rough and disjointed indeed, but forced to yield in places its profounder meaning. In *Measure for Measure,* in contrast with the flawless execution of *Romeo and Juliet,* Shakespeare has spent his art in just enough modification of the scheme of the older play to make it exponent of this purpose, adapting its terrible essential incidents, so that Coleridge found it the only painful work among Shakespeare's dramas, and leaving for the reader of to-day more than the usual number of difficult expressions; but infusing a lavish colour and a profound

* From *Appreciations.*

significance into it, so that under his touch certain select portions of it rise far above the level of all but his own best poetry, and working out of it a morality so characteristic that the play might well pass for the central expression of his moral judgments. It remains a comedy, as indeed is congruous with the bland, half-humorous equity which informs the whole composition, sinking from the heights of sorrow and terror into the rough scheme of the earlier piece; yet it is hardly less full of what is really tragic in man's existence than if Claudio had indeed "stooped to death." Even the humorous concluding scenes have traits of special grace, retaining in less emphatic passages a stray line or word of power, as it seems, so that we watch to the end for the traces where the nobler hand has glanced along, leaving its vestiges, as if accidentally or wastefully, in the rising of the style.

The interest of *Measure for Measure*, therefore, is partly that of an old story told over again. We measure with curiosity that variety of resources which has enabled Shakespeare to refashion the original material with a higher motive; adding to the intricacy of the piece, yet so modifying its structure as to give the whole almost the unity of a single scene; lending, by the light of a philosophy which dwells much on what is complex and subtle in our nature, a true human propriety to its strange and unexpected turns of feeling and character, to incidents so difficult as the fall of Angelo, and the subsequent reconciliation of Isabella, so that she pleads successfully for his life. It was from Whetstone, a contemporary English writer, that Shakespeare derived the outline of Cinthio's "rare history" of *Promos and Cassandra*, one of that numerous class of Italian stories, like Boccaccio's *Tancred of Salerno*, in which the mere energy of southern passion has everything its own way, and which, though they may repel many a northern reader by a certain crudity in their colouring, seem to have been full of fascination for the Elizabethan age. This story, as it appears in Whetstone's endless comedy, is almost as rough as the roughest episode of actual criminal life. But the play seems never to have been acted, and some time after its publication Whetstone himself turned the thing into a tale, included in his *Heptameron of Civil Discourses*, where it still figures as a genuine piece, with touches of undesigned poetry, a quaint field-flower here and there of diction or sentiment, the whole strung up to an effective brevity, and with the fragrance of that admirable age of literature all about it. Here, then, there is something of the original Italian colour: in this narrative Shakespeare may well have caught the first glimpse of a composition with nobler proportions; and some artless sketch from his own hand, perhaps, putting together his first impressions, insinuated itself between Whetstone's work and the play as we actually read it. Out of these insignificant sources Shakespeare's play rises, full of solemn expression, and with a profoundly designed beauty, the new body of a higher, though sometimes remote and difficult poetry, escaping from the imperfect relics of the old story, yet not wholly transformed, and even as it stands but the preparation only, we might think, of a still more imposing design. For once we have in it a real example of that sort of writing which is sometimes described as *suggestive,* and which by the help of certain subtly calculated hints only, brings into distinct shape the reader's own half-developed imaginings. Often the quality is attributed to writing merely vague and unrealised, but in *Measure for Measure,* quite certainly, Shakespeare has directed the attention of sympathetic readers along certain channels of meditation beyond the immediate scope of his work.

Measure for Measure, therefore, by the quality of these higher designs, woven by his strange magic on a texture of poorer quality, is hardly less indicative than *Hamlet* even, of Shakespeare's reason, of his power of moral interpretation. It deals, not like *Hamlet* with the problems which beset one of exceptional temperament, but with mere human nature. It brings before us a group of persons, attractive, full of desire, vessels of the genial, seed-bearing powers of nature, a gaudy existence flowering out over the old court and city of Vienna, a spectacle of the fulness and pride of life which to some may seem to touch the verge of wantonness. Behind this group of people, behind their various action, Shakespeare inspires in us the sense of a strong tyranny of nature and circumstance. Then what shall there be on this side of it—on our side, the spectator's side, of this painted screen, with its puppets who are really glad or sorry all the time? what philosophy of life, what sort of equity?

Stimulated to read more carefully by Shakespeare's own profounder touches, the reader will note the vivid reality, the subtle interchange of light and shade, the strongly contrasted characters of this group of persons, passing across the stage so quickly. The slightest of them is at least not ill-natured: the meanest of them can put forth a plea for existence—*Truly, sir, I am a poor fellow that would live!* —they are never sure of themselves, even in the strong tower of a cold unimpressible nature: they are capable of many friendships and of a true dignity in danger, giving each other a sympathetic, if transitory, regret—one sorry that another "should be foolishly lost at a game of tick-tack." Words which seem to exhaust man's deepest sentiment concerning death and life are put on the lips of a gilded, witless youth; and the saintly Isabella feels fire creep along her, kindling her tongue to eloquence at the suggestion of shame. In places the shadow deepens: death intrudes itself on the scene, as among other things "a great disguiser," blanching the features of youth and spoiling its goodly hair, touching the fine Claudio even with its disgraceful associations. As in Orcagna's fresco at Pisa, it comes capriciously, giving many and long reprieves to Barnardine, who has been waiting for it nine years in prison, taking another thence by fever, another by mistake of judgment, embracing others in the midst of their music and song. The little mirror of existence, which reflects to each for a moment the stage on which he plays, is broken at last by a capricious accident; while all alike, in their yearning for untasted enjoyment, are really discounting their days, grasping so hastily and accepting so inexactly the precious pieces. The Duke's quaint but excellent moralising at the beginning of the third act does but express, like the chorus of a Greek play, the spirit of the passing incidents. To him in Shakespeare's play, to a few here and there in the actual world, this strange practical paradox of our life, so unwise in its eager haste, reveals itself in all its clearness.

The Duke disguised as a friar, with his curious moralising on life and death, and Isabella in her first mood of renunciation, a thing "ensky'd and sainted," come with the quiet of the cloister as a relief to this lust and pride of life: like some grey monastic picture hung on the wall of a gaudy room, their presence cools the heated air of the piece. For a moment we are within the placid conventual walls, whither they fancy at first that the Duke has come as a man crossed in love, with Friar Thomas and Friar Peter, calling each other by their homely, English names, or at the nunnery among the novices, with their little limited privileges, where

> "If you speak you must not show your face,
> Or if you show your face you must not speak."

Not less precious for this relief in the general structure of the piece, than for its own peculiar graces is the episode of Mariana, a creature wholly of Shakespeare's invention, told, by way of interlude, in subdued prose. The moated grange, with its dejected mistress, its long, listless, discontented days, where we hear only the voice of a boy broken off suddenly in the midst of one of the loveliest songs of Shakespeare, or of Shakespeare's school,[1] is the pleasantest of many glimpses we get here of pleasant places —the fields without the town, Angelo's gardenhouse, the consecrated fountain. Indirectly it has suggested two of the most perfect compositions among the poetry of our own generation. Again it is a picture within a picture, but with fainter lines and a greyer atmosphere: we have here the same passions, the same wrongs, the same continuance of affection, the same crying out upon death, as in the nearer and larger piece, though softened, and reduced to the mood of a more dreamy scene.

Of Angelo we may feel at first sight inclined to say only *guarda e passa!* or to ask whether he is indeed psychologically possible. In the old story, he figures as an embodiment of pure and unmodified evil, like "Hyliogabalus of Rome or Denis of Sicyll." But the embodiment of pure evil is no proper subject of art, and Shakespeare, in the spirit of a philosophy which dwells much on the complications of outward circumstance with men's inclinations, turns into a subtle study in casuistry this incident of the austere judge fallen suddenly into utmost corruption by a momentary contact with supreme purity. But the main interest in *Measure for Measure* is not, as in *Promos and Cassandra*, in the relation of Isabella and Angelo, but rather in the relation of Claudio and Isabella.

[1] Fletcher, in the *Bloody Brother*, gives the rest of it.

Greek tragedy in some of its noblest products has taken for its theme the love of a sister, a sentiment unimpassioned indeed, purifying by the very spectacle of its passionlessness, but capable of a fierce and almost animal strength if informed for a moment by pity and regret. At first Isabella comes upon the scene as a tranquillising influence in it. But Shakespeare, in the development of the action, brings quite different and unexpected qualities out of her. It is his characteristic poetry to expose this cold, chastened personality, respected even by the worldly Lucio as "something ensky'd and sainted, and almost an immortal spirit," to two sharp, shameful trials, and wring out of her a fiery, revealing eloquence. Thrown into the terrible dilemma of the piece, called upon to sacrifice that cloistral whiteness to sisterly affection, become in a moment the ground of strong contending passions, she develops a new character and shows herself suddenly of kindred with those strangely conceived women, like Webster's Vittoria, who unite to a seductive sweetness something of a dangerous and tigerlike changefulness of feeling. The swift, vindictive anger leaps, like a white flame, into this white spirit, and, stripped in a moment of all convention, she stands before us clear, detached, columnar, among the tender frailties of the piece. Cassandra, the original of Isabella in Whetstone's tale, with the purpose of the Roman Lucretia in her mind, yields gracefully enough to the conditions of her brother's safety; and to the lighter reader of Shakespeare there may seem something harshly conceived, or psychologically impossible even, in the suddenness of the change wrought in her, as Claudio welcomes for a moment the chance of life through her compliance with Angelo's will, and he may have a sense here of flagging skill, as in words less finely handled than in the preceding scene. The play, though still not without traces of nobler handiwork, sinks down, as we know, at last into almost homely comedy, and it might be supposed that just here the grander manner deserted it. But the skill with which Isabella plays upon Claudio's well-recognised sense of honour, and endeavours by means of that to insure him beforehand from the acceptance of life on baser terms, indicates no coming laxity of hand just in this place. It was rather that there rose in Shakespeare's conception, as there may for the reader, as there certainly would in any good acting of the part, something of that terror, the seeking for which is one of the notes of romanticism in Shakespeare and his circle. The stream of ardent natural affection, poured as sudden hatred upon the youth condemned to die, adds an additional note of expression to the horror of the prison where so much of the scene takes place. It is not here only that Shakespeare has conceived of such extreme anger and pity as putting a sort of genius into simple women, so that their "lips drop eloquence," and their intuitions interpret that which is often too hard or fine for manlier reason; and it is Isabella with her grand imaginative diction, and that poetry laid upon the "prone and speechless dialect" there is in mere youth itself, who gives utterance to the equity, the finer judgments of the piece on men and things.

From behind this group with its subtle lights and shades, its poetry, its impressive contrasts, Shakespeare, as I said, conveys to us a strong sense of the tyranny of nature and circumstance over human action. The most powerful expressions of this side of experience might be found here. The bloodless, impassible temperament does but wait for its opportunity, for the almost accidental coherence of time with place, and place with wishing, to annul its long and patient discipline, and become in a moment the very opposite of that which under ordinary conditions it seemed to be, even to itself. The mere resolute self-assertion of the blood brings to others special temptations, temptations which, as defects or overgrowths, lie in the very qualities which make them otherwise imposing or attractive; the very advantage of men's gifts of intellect or sentiment being dependent on a balance in their use so delicate that men hardly maintain it always. Something also must be conceded to influences merely physical, to the complexion of the heavens, the skyey influences, shifting as the stars shift; as something also to the mere caprice of men exercised over each other in the dispensations of social or political order, to the chance which makes the life or death of Claudio dependent on Angelo's will.

The many veins of thought which render the poetry of this play so weighty and impressive unite in the image of Claudio, a flowerlike young man, whom, prompted by a few hints from Shakespeare, the imagination easily clothes with all the bravery of youth, as he crosses the stage before us on his way to death, coming so hastily to the end of his pilgrimage. Set in the horrible blackness of the prison, with its various forms of unsightly death, this flower seems the braver. Fallen by "prompture of the blood," the victim of a suddenly revived law against the common fault of youth like his, he finds his life forfeited as if by the chance of a lottery. With that instinctive clinging to life, which breaks through the subtlest casuistries of monk or sage apologising for an early death, he welcomes for a moment the chance of life through his sister's shame, though he revolts hardly less from the notion of perpetual imprisonment so repulsive to the buoyant energy of youth. Familiarised, by the words alike of friends and the indifferent, to the thought of death, he becomes gentle and subdued indeed, yet more perhaps through pride than real resignation, and would go down to darkness at last hard and unblinded. Called upon suddenly to encounter his fate, looking with keen and resolute profile straight before him, he gives utterance to some of the central truths of human feeling, the sincere, concentrated expression of the recoiling flesh. Thoughts as profound and poetical as Hamlet's arise in him; and but for the accidental arrest of sentence he would descend into the dust, a mere gilded, idle flower of youth indeed, but with what are perhaps the most eloquent of all Shakespeare's words upon his lips.

As Shakespeare in *Measure for Measure* has refashioned, after a nobler pattern, materials already at hand, so that the relics of other men's poetry are incorporated into his perfect work, so traces of the old "morality," that early form of dramatic composition which had for its function the inculcating of some moral theme, survive in it also, and give it a peculiar ethical interest. This ethical interest, though it can escape no attentive reader, yet, in accordance with that artistic law which demands the predominance of form everywhere over the mere matter or subject handled, is not to be wholly separated from the special circumstances, necessities, embarrassments, of these particular dramatic persons. The old "moralities" exemplified most often some rough-and-ready lesson. Here the very intricacy and subtlety of the moral world itself, the difficulty of seizing the true relations of so complex a material, the difficulty of just judgment, of judgment that shall not be unjust, are the lessons conveyed. Even in Whetstone's old story this peculiar vein of moralising comes to the surface: even there, we notice the tendency to dwell on mixed motives, the contending issues of action, the presence of virtues and vices alike in unexpected places, on "the hard choice of two evils," on the "imprisoning" of men's "real intents." *Measure for Measure* is full of expressions drawn from a profound experience of these casuistries, and that ethical interest becomes predominant in it: it is no longer *Promos and Cassandra*, but *Measure for Measure*, its new name expressly suggesting the subject of *poetical justice*. The action of the play, like the action of life itself for the keener observer, develops in us the conception of this poetical justice, and the yearning to realise it, the true justice of which Angelo knows nothing, because it lies for the most part beyond the limits of any acknowledged law. The idea of justice involves the idea of rights. But at bottom rights are equivalent to that which really is, to facts; and the recognition of his rights therefore, the justice he requires of our hands, or our thoughts, is the recognition of that which the person, in his inmost nature, really is; and as sympathy alone can discover that which really is in matters of feeling and thought, true justice is in its essence a finer knowledge through love.

> " 'Tis very pregnant:
> The jewel that we find we stoop and take it,
> Because we see it; but what we do not see
> We tread upon, and never think of it."

It is for this finer justice, a justice based on a more delicate appreciation of the true conditions of men and things, a true respect of persons in our estimate of actions, that the people in *Measure for Measure* cry out as they pass before us; and as the poetry of this play is full of the peculiarities of Shakespeare's poetry, so in its ethics it is an epitome of Shakespeare's moral judgments. They are the moral judgments of an observer, of one who sits as a spectator, and knows how the threads in the design before him hold together under the surface: they are the judgments of the humourist also, who follows with a half-amused but always pitiful sympathy, the various ways of human disposition, and sees less distance than ordinary men between what are called respectively great and little things. It is not always that poetry can be the exponent of morality; but it is this aspect of morals which it represents most naturally, for this true justice is dependent on just those finer appreciations which poetry cultivates in us the power of making, those peculiar valuations of action and its effect which poetry actually requires.

J. P. BROCKBANK

J. P. Brockbank (1922-   ). Since 1963, Professor of English at the new University of York.

HISTORY AND HISTRIONICS IN CYMBELINE*

The sources of *Cymbeline* are sufficiently known. What now are we to do with them? Source-hunting offers its own satisfactions and it is an acceptable mode of conspicuous leisure, but it should be possible still to bring it to bear more closely on the problems of literary criticism.[1] Its bearing, however, may differ from play to play. It is salutary, for instance, to recognize that striking debt owed by *The Tempest* to travel literature.[2] When we find that Shakespeare's contemporaries allegorized the historical event we may more readily discount E. E. Stoll's scepticism about allegory in the play. I think, too, that the play sheds a backward light upon its sources, making us more alive to their dramatic and poetic potential.

Cymbeline is a different problem. It is not so self-evident a masterpiece. There is the common passage and there is the strain of rareness. The sources and analogues could be used to explain away whatever fails to make an imme-

* Reprinted from *Shakespeare Survey* 11.
[1] I have in mind Hardin Craig's observations in 'Motivation in Shakespeare's Choice of Materials', *Shakespeare Survey*, 4 (1951). For the *Cymbeline* sources see J. M. Nosworthy's Arden edition.
[2] The material of *The Tempest* is reprinted in Frank Kermode's Arden edition (1954).

diate, effacing impression. But they have too, I think, a
more positive value. They can show that many of the play's
uniquely impressive effects could have been won only out
of that specific area of convention that Shakespeare chose
to explore. Within this area we can distinguish something like
a dramatic genre, and as a label we might take Polonius'
infelicity 'historical-pastoral' or, in deference to received
opinion, 'historical romance'. Such labels are useful because
they tell us what sort of conventions to look out for,
although each play is apt to define its own area, make its
own map. My emphasis will be on the 'historical', for there
is, I think, a way of reading the sources which lends support to Wilson Knight's claim that *Cymbeline* is to be regarded "mainly as an historical play".[1] Criticism may fault
his quite remarkable 'interpretation' for trying to evoke
a maximum pregnancy from conventions that are insuffi-
ciently transmuted from their chronicle and theatrical analogues; but it cannot fault him for recognizing that the fictions of *Cymbeline,* while owing nothing to the factual
disciplines commonly called 'historical', seek nevertheless
to express certain truths about the processes which have
shaped the past of Britain. I shall argue that even the 'romantic significance'[2] of the play is worth mastering, and
that we can best master it by way of the chronicle sources.

To initiate the appropriate dialogue between the play and
its sources, we might say that *Cymbeline* is about a golden
world delivered from a brazen by the agency of a miraculous providence. That archaic formulation would not have
startled Shakespeare's contemporaries, and it might equally
preface a discussion of the play's alleged transcendent meaning or of its manifest indebtedness to convention. I mean
to use it first, however, as a clue to track Shakespeare's reading through the labyrinth of Holinshed.[3]

Holinshed's brief notice of the reign of Kymbeline reads

[1] G. Wilson Knight, *The Crown of Life,* 2nd ed. (1948), p. 129.
[2] Cf. F. R. Leavis, "Shakespeare . . . has taken over a romantic convention and has done little to give it anything other than a romantic
significance". *The Common Pursuit* (1952), p. 177.
[3] I have assumed that Shakespeare used the 1587 Holinshed, and have
ignored a few passages in lesser-known chronicles which might be
faintly nearer the play. My longer quotations are of material not
reprinted by Nosworthy or by W. G. Boswell-Stone in *Shakespeare's
Holinshed* (1896).

like an old tale, and Shakespeare clearly felt no obligation to treat it as fact. He distinguished firmly between the Tudor material, whose documentary force he retained in the earlier histories, and the Brutan, with which he took the fullest liberties in *Lear* and *Cymbeline*.

There is, however, no obvious reason why he should have turned his attention unhesitatingly to Kymbeline, and since the names of the characters are scattered over a wide span of pages in the second edition of Holinshed, we may be confident that he was widely read in the Brutan phase of the history, that he began at the beginning, and that he read it quite early, culling the name "Iago" in its course. We may indeed regard *Cymbeline* and *Henry VIII* as the last fruits of the Brutan and Tudor chronicles in Shakespeare's dramatic art. They might be presented as complemental plays —a fantastical history and an historical fantasy, but the exercise would be premature without some excursion into the reading behind *Cymbeline*.

The First Chapter of the *Second Booke of the Historie of England* did most, I think, to determine the form and tenor of the play. It tells of the descent and early life of Brute, and includes this passage.[1]

To this opinion Giouan Villani a Florentine in his vniuersall historie, speaking of Aeneas and his ofspring kings in Italie, seemeth to agree, where he saith: "Siluis (the sonne of Aeneas by his wife Lauinia) fell in loue with a neece of his mother Lauinia, and by hir had a sonne, of whom she died in trauell, and therefore was called Brutus, who after as he grew in some stature, and hunting in a forrest slue his father vnwares, and therevpon for feare of his grandfather Siluius Posthumus he fled the countrie, and with a retinue of such as followed him, passing through diuers seas, at length he arriued in the Ile of Britaine."

Concerning therefore our Brute, whether his father Iulius was sonne to Ascanius the sonne of Aeneas by his wife Creusa, or sonne to Posthumus called also Ascanius, and sonne to Aeneas by his wife Lauinia, we will not further stand. But this, we find, that when he came to the age of 15. yeeres, so that he was now able to ride abrode

[1] Holinshed (1587), Vol. 1, H. E. p. 7/B.

with his father into the forrests and chases, he fortuned (either by mishap, or by God's prouidence) to strike his father with an arrow, in shooting at a deere, of which wound he also died. His grandfather (whether the same was Posthumus, or his elder brother) hearing of this great misfortune that had chanced to his sonne Siluius, liued not long after, but died for verie greefe and sorow (as is supposed) which he conceiued thereof. And the yoong gentleman, immediatlie after he had slaine his father (in maner before alledged) was banished his countrie, and therevpon got him into Grecia, where trauelling the countrie, he lighted by chance among some of the Troian ofspring, and associating himselfe with them, grew by meanes of the linage (whereof he was descended) in proces of time into great reputation among them: chieflie by reason there were yet diuers of the Troian race, and that of great authoritie in that countrie.

There is little here that would be admitted as a 'source' by the criteria of Boswell-Stone, but Shakespeare may well have recognized an opportunity to deploy the conventions of romance in a play made from one or other of the Brutan legends. His story of the lost princes as it has finally reached us is an invention not owed to, but consonant with the strange adventures of Brute. And *Cymbeline* touches, in a different order and to changed effect, the motifs of mysterious descent, hunting, murder (a boy killing a prince), banishment, and chance (or providential) encounter with offspring of the same lineage. There is a kind of obligation here, and in his choice of the names of Posthumus and Innogen (the wife of Brute) Shakespeare seems to offer a playful salute of acknowledgement.

The second chapter offers another piece of ready-made theatrical apparatus. Brute and Innogen "arrive in Leogitia" and "aske counsell of an oracle where they shall inhabit". Brute kneels, "holding in his right hand a boll prepared for sacrifice full of wine, and the bloude of a white hinde", and after he has done his "praier and ceremonie . . . according to the pagane rite and custome", he falls asleep. The goddess Diana speaks Latin verses (which the chronicle translates) sending him to an isle "farre by-west beyond the Gallike land". "After he awaked out of sleepe", the chronicle goes on, "and had called his dreame to remembrance, he first doubted whether it were a verie dreame, or a true vision, the goddess hauing spoken to him with liuelie voice". Once again, the vision is not a source but an occasion. It may have licensed the vision of Posthumus—a stage theophany in a play which, like the myth, is concerned with the ancestral virtue and destiny of Britain. Shakespeare drew of course on his own experience of the theatre and perhaps on a memory of *The Rare Triumphs* for the specific form of the theophany, but whether by chance or design the verse form is oddly consonant with the chronicle.[1]

These early passages are important because they reveal most clearly the romantic, numinous aspect of Geoffrey's myth. But Geoffrey was also something of a tactical political moralist, and for him the high magical destiny of Britain was needlessly thwarted by emulation, "revenging" and "dividing". In the chapters between Brute and Kymbeline Shakespeare would have passed much material already exploited to serve a political moral by the authors of *Locrine, Leir, Gorboduc* and the pseudo-historical part of *Nobody and Somebody*—reigns which for the most part ask to be treated in the spirit of Richard Harvey's *Philadelphus,* as tracts for the times.[2]

The Third Booke opens with an account of Mulmucius Dunwallō, the law-giver, named in *Cymbeline* but evidently more fully celebrated in a lost play called after him.[3] Whether he took it from the old play or the chronicle, the name Cloten (given by Harrison to the father of Mulmucius[4]) may have had for Shakespeare a sly historical as well

---

[1] Cf. 'An Ile which with the ocean seas/inclosed is about,/Where giants dwelt sometime,/but now is desart ground'. Holinshed (1587), Vol 1, H. E., p. 9(A).

[2] Richard Harvey, *Philadelphus, or a defence of Brutes and the Brutan history* (1593). It argues that the Brutans did exist as they show the qualities (mostly bad) that Aristotle leads us to expect from human nature. Harvey took from the history the cautionary politics Geoffrey put into it.

[3] Other lost Brutan plays were the *Conquest of Brute (Brute Greenshield)* and *Uther Pendragon.* Had they survived we might have been better placed to recognize the conventions behind *Cymbeline.*

[4] Holinshed (1587), Vol. 1, Description, p. 117/A. Boswell-Stone cites a later page where "Cloten" and "Clotenus" are named. But Harrison has "Cloten" with a "Morgan" nearby. Shakespeare may have known Chapter 22 of the 'Description of Britaine'; it gives an abstract of the whole history.

as articulatory propriety. The brassy Cloten and his mother are hypostatized versions of the arbitrary spleen and malevolence that Geoffrey often found antecedent to the rule of law.

Of the fifty or so rulers between Mulmucius and Cassibelane, Holinshed briefly describes a quarter and catalogues the rest. Only one (Elidure) seems to have been touched by the playwrights, but Shakespeare ignored them and his interest was not quickened again until he reached the point where Geoffrey is confronted by Caesar, the old tale foiled by the modern history, fantasy by fact, romance by Rome. Shakespeare accepted the challenge to admit both, and I think J. M. Nosworthy mistaken in wishing he had done otherwise.[1] For had he done otherwise we might never have heard that "odd and distinctive music" which F. R. Leavis derives from *Cymbeline's* "interplay of contrasting themes and modes".

Kymbeline is named at the centre of a long section dealing with the Roman conquest and the tribute variously yielded and denied by the line from Cassibelane to Arviragus. Shakespeare's readiness to see the tribute as a momentous historical symbol is clear enough from the play, but before we begin to admire and analyse it is worth remarking that he was not alone in trying by supernatural stage machinery and symbolic verse to give something like apocalyptic scale to the tribute settlement. Jasper Fisher's academic play *The True Trojans,* probably later than *Cymbeline* but apparently independent, testifies equally to a contemporary interest in the conflict and reconciliation of the two "valorous races" represented by Cassibelane and Caesar.[2] But Shakespeare's treatment yields far more of the potential of Geoffrey's myth than Fisher's.

So far then, Shakespeare's reading offers a paradigm for an action which makes the reconciliation with Rome a high event in the magical movement of British history from the vision of Brute to the golden prospect of the vision of Cadwallader. But it is substance rather for a pageant or a masque than a play. To give it a richer content Shakespeare had to rely in the end on his own resources, but he had scope still to exercise his imagination on other elements

[1] Arden *Cymbeline* (1955) p. 1.
[2] The play is printed in Hazlitt's *Dodsley,* 4th ed. (1875), Vol. XII.

in the chronicle. In pursuit of that "odd and distinctive music" he chose to modulate from the Brutan into the Roman key and from the Roman into the Renaissance Italian. The exercise is exquisitely playful, but what prompted him to attempt it?

Holinshed does not often chime well with Boccaccio; Geoffrey's 'romance' was not the sort which delighted sophisticated Italy. And yet it happens, oddly, that the chronicle can supply a gloss to Iachimo's confession in the last act: the dullness of Britain and the subtlety of Italy are Harrison's themes in chap. xx of his *Description of Britaine*. "For that we dwell northward", he says, "we are commonly taken . . . to be men of great strength and little policie, much courage and small shift"; and after entertaining and dismissing several versions of the same criticism he finishes by giving it a sharp twist to Britain's advantage.[1]

> For if it be a vertue to deale vprightlie with singlenesse of mind, sincerelie and plainlie, without anie such suspicious fetches in all our dealings, as they commonlie practise in their affaires, then are our countrimen to be accompted wise and vertuous. But if it be a vice to colour craftinesse, subtile practises, doublenesse, and hollow behauiour, with a cloake of policie, amitie and wisedome: then are Comineus and his countrimen to be reputed vicious.

Harrison would have found Wilson Knight's emphasis on Posthumus as "the simple islander in danger of moral ruin" entirely congenial.[2] The conventional sentiment of the chronicle is concerned with the national character as well as the national destiny. Shakespeare may have seen in Boccaccio an opportunity to mediate the two.

There may have been a second little motive for calling *The Decameron* and *Frederick of Jennen* into the play. W. W. Lawrence compares Posthumus in Italy with "a young Englishman making the grand tour at the end of the sixteenth century", and the allegedly absurd anachronism

---

[1] Holinshed (1587), vol. I, Description, p. 115/A.
[2] *The Crown of Life* (1948), p. 147. Other points made there could be illustrated from the Description, Book ii, chap. 7.

might be lightly excused by a Chronicle passage used for one of Cymbeline's speeches.[1]

> it is reported, that Kymbeline being brought vp in Rome, & knighted in the court of Augustus, euer shewed himselfe a friend to the Romans, & chieflie was loth to breake with them, because the youth of the Britaine nation should not be depriued of the benefit to be trained and brought vp among the Romans, whereby they might learne both to behaue themselues like ciuill men, and to atteine to the knowledge of feats of warre.

Within the spacious perspectives of *Cymbeline* the integrity of Britain is at once nourished and jeopardized by the 'civilizing' impact of ancient Rome and modern Italy upon its heroic and innocent but vulnerable youth.

The play's preoccupation with natural and sophisticated man is, however, something far more searching than anything the sources can suggest to jaded modern eyes. But we can get an inkling of how it might have struck Shakespeare from John Speed's *History* of 1611. Kymbeline himself was not much more for Speed than a name on a coin, but the period of his reign was a theme for rhapsody; it was the time that Christ was born and Augustus ruled in Rome. "Then were the times that great Kings and Prophets desired to see, but saw them not, when the Wolfe and the Lambe, the Leopard and the Kid, the Calfe and the Lyon fed together."[2] In a later passage Speed celebrates the marvellous correspondences between Virgilian and Messianic prophecy: "hee vseth the very words of the *Prophets* in speaking of *a Maid,* and *a Child of a new progenie borne and sent downe from heaven,* by whom the brassy and iron-like world should cease, and a pure *golden age* succeed." Even had it been published earlier, there would be no reason to suppose that Shakespeare read the *History.* The point is that the sceptical historian was a theologian still and could see fit to display these high conventional sentiments at this moment of his account of Britain. Holinshed's (or Fabyan's) brevities

---

[1] W. W. Lawrence, *Shakespeare's Problem Comedies* (New York, 1931), p. 188. The Holinshed passage (vol. I, H.E., p. 33/A) is quoted by Boswell-Stone, cf. *Cymbeline,* III, i, 70.

[2] John Speed, *The History of Great Britaine* (1611), p. 174. See also p. 189.

noticing the birth of Christ and the rule of Augustus may
have stimulated in Shakespeare's imagination a comparable
range of thought; hence what Wilson Knight calls the
"theological impressionism" of *Cymbeline*.

The same part of Speed's *History* offers reflections on the
"Originals of Particular Nations", comparing them on the
one hand with "that first beginning of the universall pro-
semination of Mankind . . . simple and far from those arti-
ficiall fraudes, which some call *Wit* and *cunning*", and on
the other to "that first neglective condition" to which men
would revolve if "Lawes, discipline, and Customes" did not
restrain them.[1] It is a polarity retained but greatly complicated in the play where the episodes of Cloten and the
princes explore very nicely the possibilities of man exempt
from the rule of law.

That fussy phrase 'historical-pastoral' invites in this context a theological exegesis, but Shakespeare tactfully sub-
dues his material to honour the decorum of the theatre
rather than that of theological history. Finding that within
the span of Kymbeline's reign he could sustain the spell of
Brute's, he undertook to charm Boccaccio and Caesar into
the same "system of life".

It is one of the tasks of criticism to observe the poise of
the dialogue, to adapt Derek Traversi's phrase, "between
convention and analysis". But the poise registers, too, in
the handling of stage conventions; the calculated anachronisms of the play as history are matched by a calculated
naïvety in its theatrical technique: "the art that displays
art", as Granville Barker has it. It seems possible that this
springs from small beginnings in the chronicle too. An
analysis of the peculiar use made of disguise and garments
in *Cymbeline* might fairly open with Harrison's observation,
"Oh how much cost is bestowed now adaies vpon our bodies
and how little vpon our soules! how manie sutes of apparell
hath the one and how little furniture hath the other?"[2]
And it might pass to Holinshed's story of Hamo "apparelling
himselfe like a Britaine" to kill Guiderius and of Arviragus
who "caused himselfe to be adorned with the kings cote
armour"; and then to the Scottish chronicle where Haie
(Shakespeare's model for Belarius and his sons in the battle

---

[1] Speed, *History* (1611), p. 179.
[2] Holinshed (1587), vol. L. Description, p. 172/A.

scene) refused the rich robes that the king offered him and "was contented to go with the king in his old garments"[1] Shakespeare could keep one eye here on the chronicle and the other on the fashionable theatre.

In turning from the history to the histrionics in the play, however, we must distinguish between that kind of theatrical virtuosity whose effects are merely startling and arbitrary, and that which serves a responsible purpose. The themes which the chronicle offered are portentous and had Shakespeare engaged with them too profoundly he would have tested the resources of the language and the responsiveness of the audience too severely. He would also have lost touch with the mood of the *Brut,* as he certainly does in *Lear.* He abstains therefore from using his giant's strength and allows certain points to be carried by a conventional gesture. His handling of disguise, soliloquy, stage situations, properties and even characters, secures in turn an apt "suspension of disbelief" and an equally apt "suspension of belief". Cloten and the Queen, for example, may be said to represent a range of complemental vices (roughly speaking, the boorish and sophisticated) which menace the natural integrity of the British court. But this is true only of the conventional configuration; they are never allowed to touch the audience deeply or urgently threaten their composure. "The euils she hatch'd, were not effected", it is said of the Queen; and they are not effected because Shakespeare uses soliloquies and asides to make her guile transparent, and allows even her gulls to see right through her. *Cymbeline* indeed lets us into all the secrets, even into the secrets of the playmaker's craft. The 'inconsistency' of Cloten and the Queen is not analysed, for example, but simply exhibited; with a faint but distinct irony and a touch of burlesque their vices are made compatible with that minimal virtue of defiant patriotism they display before the Roman ambassador.[2] The tension (such as it is) is kept on the surface, while in that

---

[1] Holinshed (1587), vol. II H.S., p. 155/B. See also M. C. Bradbrook, 'Shakespeare and the Use of Disguise in Elizabethan Drama', *Essays in Criticism* (2, 1952), 159-68.

[2] I think Warren D. Smith, *Studies in Philology*, 49 (1952), p. 184-95 overstates his claim that Cloten is merely the "vulgar, ill-mannered villain" in this scene. Shakespeare writes perhaps with some memory of Holinshed's *Voadicea* (H.E., Bk. iv, Chap. II) as well as an eye on Jacobean courtly proprieties.

earlier instance of Queen Margaret in *Henry VI* it has to be dug out. If the characters were defined and explored analytically the discordant potential of the material would fracture the play. It is indeed a tribute to the decorum of the piece that Posthumus cannot for long be compared with Othello, nor Iachimo with Iago, the Queen with Lady Macbeth or Margaret, Cymbeline with Lear, nor yet Cloten with Edmund or Faulconbridge. The stresses are less between good and evil characters than between the ingenuous and the disingenuous—the lighter way of putting it is the apter.

The play offers yet more daring sophistications of stage conventions than those deployed in the plots of the disarmed (and disarming) villains. The iteration, for instance, of the phrase "his meanest garment" leading up to that grotesque mock-recognition scene. In a play which makes so much of deceptive appearances and false judgments, there is sly irony in making the innocent Imogen a false judge and in allowing Cloten's indignation to be vindicated after death. The prevailing transparency of artifice makes one suspect that the 'clotpole' stage head was deliberately displayed as a hollow property to give bizarre point to the lines introducing it, "an empty purse, There was no money in't", and it refines or civilizes the violent pagan force of the symbolic justice administered to "That harsh, noble, simple, nothing" Cloten.

In detail as in large design the mode is self-confessedly artificial. The postulates are openly declared: "Howsoere, 'tis strange, Or that the negligence may well be laugh'd at: Yet is it true, sir"; "do not play in Wench-like words with that Which is so serious"; "This was strange chance"; "By accident I had a feigned Letter of my Masters Then in my pocket"; "Shall's have a play of this? Thou scornful page, there lye thy part"; "Let him shew his skill in the construction". Other touches recall *A Midsummer Night's Dream* rather than *Love's Labour's Lost:* " 'Twas but a bolt of nothing, shot at nothing, Which the Braine makes of Fumes"; "What Fayeries haunt this ground?"; "mine's beyond, beyond". There are moments too of self-parody: when Cymbeline interrupts a more than usually mannered late-Shakespearian speech from Iachimo with "I stand on fire. Come to the matter"; and again (one suspects) when the gaoler's "fear no more Tauerne bils" might be Shake-speare's tongue-in-cheek backward glance at Imogen's ob-sequies. One needs to step lightly on these points; they are slender platforms for commentary. And much the same ap-plies to the play's imagery; the patterns and iterations traced by Wilson Knight, Traversi and Nosworthy are undoubted-ly there, but they are signs of opportunities lightly taken as occasion offers; they strike as sequences meant to be glimpsed rather than grasped.

All this does not mean that the entertainment is incon-sequential. However conventional the frame of *Cymbeline*, it is still meaningful and it sets the more evocative and searching passages in the order of a significant design. But no matter how sharply-cut the stones in the filigree, we are reminded that the skilled craftsman has the strength to crush the fabric at will. "The best in this kind are but shadows."

It remains true, however, that *Cymbeline* is not organized from "a deep centre" like *The Winter's Tale*.[1] We are haunted by intimations of a profound significance, but it is constantly clear that the apocalyptic destiny of Britain cannot be reconciled with the form of pastoral-romance on any but the terms which Shakespeare offers.

We may sum up by taking a last glance at Imogen. Her votaries from Swinburne onwards may be allowed their extravagances and let pass with an " 'Ods pittikins" if they will admit that perfection is not, after all, indivisible. Imo-gen's perfection is playfully extended to her cookery—"He cut our roots in characters". But she remains in some sense, still, the centre of the play. It is fitting that she should voice most memorably a version of the Virgil verse transmitted through the chronicle, "Et penitus toto diuisos orbe Britan-nos": "I'th'worlds Volume Our Britaine seemed as of it, but not in't: In a great Poole, a Swannes-nest."[2] She is a princess of Britain, yet theme for the praise of a Renaissance courtier; a pretty page for the Roman Lucius, yet aptly called a "heavenly angel". Her symbolic role is secured both by the dialogue (see the 2nd Lord's speech just before the bedchamber scene) and by the spectacle: "And be her Sense but as a Monument, Thus in a Chappell lying." When

[1] F. R. Leavis, *The Common Pursuit*, p. 174.
[2] Holinshed (1587), vol. L, Description, p. 2/A.

she lies 'dead' alongside the body of Cloten in the clothes of Posthumus, the spectacle is an evocative symbol of a triple sacrifice (though the word is too strong)—of an innocence that will revive, an animal barbarity which is properly exterminated and a duplicity (involving Posthumus) which has still to be purged.

Lucius is appropriately named after the first of the Christian kings of the British chronicle, and it happens that the political solution—the tribute allowed from sense of fitness and not won by force of arms—can endorse the ethical in a pageant finale announcing the Golden World with a touch of that "pagane rite and custome" which opens the *Brut*: "And let our crooked Smoakes climbe to their Nostrils From our blest Altars . . . And in the Temple of great Iupiter Our Peace wee'l ratifie."

My conclusion perhaps resembles too closely the "fierce abridgment" of the last act which "distinction should be rich in". But I would claim that substantially the same result could be reached through an inquiry into the theatrical analogues, from *The Rare Triumphs* through *Clyomon and Clamydes, James IV, Edward I, Common Conditions, The Wounds of Civil War, Tancred and Gismunda* and *The Dumb Knight* to the revived *Mucedorus,* the plays of Field and Beaumont and Fletcher to *The Second Maiden's Tragedy*. It might be shown, I think, that Shakespeare reconciled the conventions of primitive and sophisticated romantic drama to express similar reconciliations accomplished in the substance of the plot.

S. T. COLERIDGE

NOTES ON THE WINTER'S TALE AND OTHELLO*

Altho' on the whole exquisitely respondent to its title, and even in the fault I am about to mention, still a winter's tale, yet it seems a mere indolence of the great bard not to

* From lecture notes.

have in the oracle provided some ground for Hermione's seeming death and fifteen years concealment, voluntary concealment. This might have been easily affected by some obscure sentence of the oracle, as, e.g., "Nor shall he ever recover an heir if he have a wife before that recovery."

S.T.C.

Difference of style in the first scene between two chit-chatters (Camillo and Archidamus), and the rise of diction on the introduction of the kings and Hermione.

Admirable preparation in Polixenes' obstinate refusal to Leontes—

> There is no tongue that moves, no, none i' the world,
> So soon as yours could win me—

and yet his after-yielding to Hermione, which is at once perfectly natural from mere courtesy of sex and the exhaustion of the will by the former effort, and yet so well calculated to set in nascent action the jealousy of Leontes. And this, once excited, increased by Hermione—

> Yet, good deed, Leontes,
> I love thee not a jar o' the clock behind
> What lady she her lord—

accompanied (as a good actress ought to represent it) by an expression and recoil of apprehension that she had gone too far. The first working of this—

> At my request he would not.

This judiciously introduced or accompanied by a definition of *jealousy*, not of all so-called by persons imperfectly acquainted with the circumstances, but of what really is so; *i.e.*, [jealousy] as a *vice* of the mind, a culpable despicable tendency.

The natural effects and concomitants of this passion.

1. Excitability by the most inadequate causes, "Too hot, too hot." Eagerness to snatch at proofs.

2. Grossness of conception, and a disposition to degrade the object of it. Sensual fancies and images. . . .

3. Shame of his own feelings exhibited in moodiness and soliloquy.

4. And yet from the violence of the passion forced to *utter* itself, and, therefore, catching occasion to ease the mind by ambiguities, equivoques, talking to those who cannot and who are known not to be able to understand what is said—a soliloquy in the mask of dialogue. Hence confused, broken manner, fragmentary, in the dialogue with the little boy.

5. The dread of vulgar ridicule, as distinct from the high sense of honor—

> They're here with me already; whispering, rounding
> Sicilia is a so-forth, etc.—

and out of this, selfish vindictiveness. How distinguished from the feeling of high honor (as in Othello), a mistaken sense of duty.

Shakespeare in drawing the very worst kings always introduces some corrective of the indignation, lest it should extend too far, as Camillo's speech,

> I must be the poisoner
> Of good Polixenes: and my ground to do't
> Is the obedience to a master, one
> Who, in rebellion with himself, will have
> All that are his so too. To do this deed,
> Promotion follows. If I could find example
> Of thousands that had struck anointed kings
> And flourish'd after, I'ld not do't.

Shakespeare's exquisite tenderness, playful tenderness, sweetness and amiability of nature in all his scenes with children. Lady Macduff.

Othello's self-government opposed to Leontes:

> Hold your hands,
> Both you of my inclining and the rest:
> Were it my cue to fight, I should have known it
> Without a prompter. Where will you that I go
> To answer this your charge?

Entirely by the best moral feelings that Desdemona attached herself to Othello and Othello to Desdemona:

> She loved me for the dangers I had pass'd
> And I loved her that she did pity them;
> This only is the witchcraft I have used.
> Here comes the lady; let her witness it.

The direct opposite to Leontes' grossness in Othello's speech to the Duke's council:

> Let her have your voices.
> Vouch with me, heaven, I therefore beg it not
> To please the palate of my appetite;
> Nor to comply with heat—the young affects
> In me defunct—and proper satisfaction;
> But to be free and bounteous to her mind.

Othello's trusting nature, displayed in his speech to the duke:

> . . . So please your grace, my ancient
> A man he is of honesty and trust:
> To his conveyance I assign my wife—

contrasted with Leontes' behaviour to his true friend, Camillo.

And in Iago's soliloquy (II.i.280-306) note the dreadful habit of thinking of moral feelings and qualities only as prudential ends to means.

Othello's *belief* not jealousy; forced upon him by Iago, and such as any man would and must feel who had believed of Iago as Othello. His great mistake that *we* know Iago for a villain from the first moment.

Proofs of the contrary character in Othello.

But in considering the essence of the Shakespearian Othello, we must perseveringly place ourselves in his situation, and under his circumstances. Then we shall immediately feel the fundamental difference between the solemn agony of the noble Moor, and the wretched fishing jealousies of Leontes, and the morbid suspiciousness of Leonatus, who is, in other respects, a fine character. Othello had no life

but in Desdemona:—the belief that she, his angel, had
fallen from the heaven of her native innocence, wrought a
civil war in his heart. She is his counterpart; and, like him,
is almost sanctified in our eyes by her absolute unsuspicious-
ness, and holy entireness of love. As the curtain drops,
which do we pity the most?

J. V. CUNNINGHAM

*J. V. Cunningham (1911-   ). Poet and Professor of Eng-
lish at Brandeis University; author of* Woe *and* Wonder,
*a study of Shakespearian tragedy, which is incorporated
in* Tradition and Poetic Structure *(1960), the work containing the present essay.*

THE PHOENIX AND THE TURTLE

. . . We are concerned, however, only with the central part
of the poem, which states clearly, technically, and reitera-
tively the relationship of the lovers, and here there is no
uncertainty:

> Here the anthem doth commence:
> Love and constancy is dead,
> Phoenix and the turtle fled
> In a mutual flame from hence.
>
> So they lov'd as love in twain
> Had the essence but in one;
> Two distincts, division none:
> Number there in love was slain.
>
> Hearts remote, yet not asunder;
> Distance, and no space was seen
> 'Twixt this turtle and his queen;
> But in them it were a wonder.

> So between them love did shine
> That the turtle saw his right
> Flaming in the phoenix's sight:
> Either was the other's mine.
>
> Property was thus appalled,
> That the self was not the same;
> Single nature's double name
> Neither two nor one was called.
>
> Reason, in itself confounded,
> Saw division grow together,
> To themselves yet either neither,
> Simple were so well compounded;
>
> That it cried, 'How true a twain
> Seemeth this concordant one!
> Love hath reason, reason none,
> If what parts can so remain.'

Here is stated in exact, technical, scholastic language the relationship of the lovers. They are Love and Constancy, Beauty and Truth, Phoenix and Turtle. The nature of their love was such that love in each had the essence (the defining principle by which anything that is, is what it is) only in one. Obviously, then, the effect of their love was unitive. But in what way? in terms of what scheme of ideas is this union conceived? Let us examine the possibilities. It is not unlike, of course, the Neo-Platonic union, in which the soul, being reduced to the trace of the One which constitutes its resemblance to it, is absorbed, submerged, and lost in the presence of the One. There is no more distance, no doubleness, the two fuse in one.

But the language here is Latin and has passed, as had the doctrine of Plotinus, through the disputations of the Schoolmen: *essence, distincts, division, property, single nature's double name, simple, compounded.* Furthermore, the chief point of Shakespeare's poem is lost in the Plotinan formulation: for the central part of the poem consists wholly in the reiteration—line after line as if the poet would have you understand even to exhaustion—of the paradox that though identical the two are distinct; they are both truly one and truly two. Thus, for example, in the Plotinan union there is no interval between the two—*And no space was seen*—but the contrary element of the paradox—*distance*—is lacking.

The language and the ideas of the poem, then, are technical and scholastic. But is this the scholastic doctrine of love? Is the scheme of thought here of the same order as the material of the poem? The doctrine of Thomas Aquinas on this point is sufficiently representative of the scholastic position. Love, he tells us (he is quoting the Neo-Platonist, the Pseudo-Dionysius) is a unitive force. The manner of this union, the way in which the beloved can be said to be in the lover, can be comprehended by an analogy. For just as when someone understands something there is a certain notion of the thing in the man who understands, so when someone loves something there is a certain impress, so to speak, of what is loved in the feeling of the lover, and with reference to this one can say that what is loved is in the lover as what is understood is in him who understands (ST, 1. 37.1). But union in this sense by no means amounts to absolute identification; it is not possible to say according to this account that she is my essence.

Thomas in another place distinguishes a three-fold sense in which union is related to love. There is the union which is the cause of love, and this is a genuine and substantial union with respect to one's love of himself; it is a union based on similitude with respect to one's love of others. Secondly, there is that union which is essentially love itself, and which involves a certain conformation of feeling toward the object (see ST, 1-2, 28. 5). If this is the love of friendship, the nature of the relationship is similar to the substantial union spoken of above, for the lover loves the other as himself; if it is the love of desire, he loves the other as something that belongs to him. There is, finally, a third kind of union which is an effect of love, and that is that union of the parties involved which the lover seeks of the loved. This union is in accordance with the demands of love, for, as Aristotle says in the *Politics* (2. 4. 1262 b 11), "Aristophanes said that lovers desire from being two to become one," but since "the result of this would be to destroy either one of them or both," they seek a suitable and proper union, namely to live and speak together and to be joined in other ways of this nature (ST, 1-2. 28. 1 ad 2).

From this much it is clear how carefully Thomas distinguishes and how painstakingly he points out that the effect of union in love, together with those other related effects which he goes on to discuss—a mutual inherence of one in the other, an ecstatic going out of oneself, and a zealousness in appropriating the good which one loves (1-2. 28. 2-4)—only take place in a certain sense. The love of desire, it is true, does not rest with attaining any external or surface enjoyment of what it loves, but seeks to possess it absolutely, penetrating as if to the very heart of the beloved (1-2.28.2). But it is only *as if*. For human love admits of no real identification. Though we desire it, if it were attained, one or both would be destroyed.

In Shakespeare's poem, however, the lover is identified with the beloved; the beloved is his essence; they become one and yet neither is annihilated. The lovers are of course destroyed in that they have passed in a mutual flame from this life, but clearly they have only passed into the real life of Ideas from the unreal life of materiality.

It might be suspected . . . , that the relation implied here is that of the Beatific Vision, in which our love of God and God's love for us finds its ultimate fulfilment. If this were so it would certainly offer us what we are looking for. It would offer us a model or paradigm by means of which the relationship of the lovers in this poem is constructed and construed. But though the doctrine of the Beatific Vision be thorny and difficult to understand, nevertheless one thing is clear: even in that last eternal embrace, in which, no longer through a glass darkly, we see the essence of God face to face (ST, 1. 12. 1: "We shall see Him as He is." 1 Jn. 3. 2.), there is no absolute identification of essence. Thomas makes this clear in the following passage, which I translate paraphrastically in order to render it as easy as possible to the uninitiated (the italics are mine).

Since some form is required in any cognition by which the object can be cognised or seen, there is required for the cognition of separated substances nothing less than the separated substance itself which is conjoined to our intellect as the form, being both the object and the means of understanding. In fact, whether this apply or not to other separated substances, it behooves us to accept that mode of understanding as applying to the vision of God through His essence, because in no other way could we be conducted to the divine essence. *But this explanation is not to be taken in the sense that the divine essence is really the form of our intellect, or that there results an absolute unity from the fusion of the divine essence and our intellect,* as is the case with form and matter in natural, as distinguished from supernatural, things. Rather, there is a proportion of the divine essence to our intellect on the analogy of form to matter. For, whenever there are two things in the same receptacle, of which one is more perfect than the other, they maintain a proportionate relationship of the more perfect to the less perfect, like that of form to matter.

                                            3. 92. 1., c. sub fin.

But anything is forgiven a lover, the reader may exclaim at this point, even the grossest hyperbole. Perhaps this is so; our present business, however, is simply with interpreting a text. Now, if anything be clear in the history of the lyric, it is that *The Phoenix and Turtle,* whatever its merits, is not a gracious and charming trifle, and could not have been intended as such. One half of the poem consists of a grimly reiterated paradox, stated with the minimum of decoration and the maximum of technical exactitude. The inference is that the poet was trying to say something precisely, and this lays on us the obligation, if we wish to read the poem at all, of trying to find out precisely what he was saying.

The doctrine of the poem is not sanctioned by the scholastic doctrine of human love, nor indeed, so far as I know, by the facts of nature. It is not sanctioned by the doctrine of the Beatific Vision. Is there a source in the tradition from which is derived the structure of thought and the technical terms by which it is displayed? There is, in fact, only one model in the tradition for the notion that distinct persons may have only one essence, and that is the doctrine of the Trinity. Not, of course, the Incarnation, for the two Natures (or Essences) of Christ are distinct (ST, 3. 2). The relation of lover and beloved in Shakespeare's poem is that of the Persons of the Trinity, and the technical language employed is that of scholastic discussion on the subject. With this clue, all the difficulties of the expository part of the poem are resolved, and if it still remains difficult to understand, it is no more difficult than the Trinity.

The principal point of the doctrine of the Trinity in this connection is summed up in Hooker's *Laws of Ecclesiastical Polity*:

> The Persons of the Godhead, by reason of the unity of their substance, do as necessarily remain one within another, as they are of necessity to be distinguished one from another . . . And sith they all are but one God in number, one indivisible essence or substance, their distinction cannot possibly admit separation . . . Again, sith all things accordingly love their offspring as themselves are more or less contained in it, he which is thus the only-begotten, must needs be in this degree the only-beloved of the Father. He therefore which is in the Father by eternal derivation of being and life from him, must needs be in him through an eternal affection of love.
>   5. 56. 2-3

The Father and Son are distinct persons, yet one essence. Furthermore, as the learned Doctors tell us, the Son proceeds from the Father by way of the intellect in that he is the Father's understanding of Himself; and the Holy Ghost proceeds from both by way of the will in that He is the mutual love of both. But when anyone understands and loves himself, he is in himself not only through the identity of the subject, but also in the way in which what is understood is in the one who understands, and what is loved is in the lover. Thus the Holy Ghost, who proceeds from the reciprocal relation of the Father and Son, is a distinct person, but is at the same time the bond between Them, inasmuch as He is Love (ST, 1. 37. 1. c and ad 3):

> So they lov'd as love in twain
> Had the essence but in one . . .

In the next line—*Two distincts, division non*e—the terminology is obviously scholastic, and its context is the doctrine of the Trinity. "To avoid the Arian heresy," Thomas says, "we must avoid the terms *diversity* and *difference* so as not to take away the unity of essence; we can, however, use the term *distinction* . . . So also to avoid taking away the simplicity of the divine essence we must avoid the terms *separation* and *division*, which apply to parts of a whole . . ." (ST, 1. 31. 2.).

Number there in love was slain, for plurality is always the consequence of a division, as Thomas points out; but the division of a continuum from which springs number, which is a species of quantity, is found only in material things. But number in this sense cannot be applied to God. When numerical terms are used they signify only the things of which they are said, and so we may say one essence, signifying only the essence undivided, and many persons, signifying only those persons and the undividedness of each. (ST, 1. 30. 3). *Hearts remote, yet not asunder* repeats the central paradox. *Distance, and no space was seen*; the Son is co-eternal with the Father in order of time (1. 42. 2) and hence in order of space (1. 42. 1., and see 1. 81. ad 3.). *But in them* (and in God!) *it were a wonder*.

The next stanzas are based on the scholastic distinction of *proprium* and *alienum*: what is proper is what belongs to the one, but not to the other; what is alien is what belongs to the other, but not to the one. The terms are contraries, and exclude each other. But in the Trinity the relations which constitute the three Persons are their several Properties. Though property is the same as person, yet in the Father and the Son, as there is one essence in the two persons, so also there is one property in the two persons (ST, 1.40.1.), So also in the Phoenix and Turtle: love so shone between them (and Love is the relationship of the Father and the Son in the Holy Ghost—1.37.2) that the one saw what belonged to him ("his right": *suum proprium*) in the sight of the other; but the other's sight was the instrument by which the second saw reciprocally what belonged to him in the sight of the first. Each was the other's "mine": *meum*. No wonder *Property was thus appalled*: for *property* is the personification of *proprium*.

Single nature's double name: Each of the Persons of the Trinity has His proper name, yet they are all of one nature, one essence (1.13; 1.33.2; 1.34.1-2; 1.36.1; and especially 1.39.2-7), and the name *God* stands of itself for the common nature—hence, *Neither two nor one was called*.

Reason, in itself confounded,—for reason is the principle of distinction and its method is division—*Saw division grow together;* each of the two was distinct (*To themselves*), yet neither one of them was one or the other (*yet either neither*). And the last line of this stanza repeats again the same paradox, and again by one of the common scholastic dichotomies: *Simple were so well compounded.* Any separated substance is simple; thus the Phoenix and the Turtle are simples, but are so compounded as to form a simple. Hence, at the final recapitulation of the paradox, Reason confesses its inadequacy to deal with the mystery of love: *Love has reason, reason none / If what parts* can remain unparted (*can so remain*).

The relation of the Phoenix to the Turtle is now clear. It is conceived and expressed in terms of the scholastic doctrine of the Trinity, which forms in this sense the principle of order of the poem. The Phoenix and Turtle are distinct persons, yet one in love, on the analogy of the Father and the Son in the Holy Ghost. If the reader does not immediately understand this mystery, the point of the poem is that it is a mystery at which Reason is confounded and confesses that true Reason is above it and is Love.

THE HISTORY PLAYS

S. T. COLERIDGE

ON THE HISTORIES*

Fully to comprehend the nature of the Historic Drama, the difference should be understood between the epic and tragic muse. The latter recognizes and is grounded upon the free-will of man; the former is under the control of destiny, or, among Christians, an overruling Providence. In epic, the prominent character is ever under this influence, and

* From a report of a lecture given at Bristol late in 1813.

when, accidents are introduced, they are the result of causes over which our will has no power. An epic play begins and ends arbitrarily; its only law is, that it possess beginning, middle, and end. Homer ends with the death of Hector; the final fate of Troy is left untouched. Virgil ends with the marriage of Aeneas; the historical events are left imperfect.

In the tragic, the free-will of man is the first cause, and accidents are never introduced; if they are, it is considered a great fault. To cause the death of a hero by accident, such as slipping off a plank into the sea, would be beneath the tragic muse, as it would arise from no mental action.

Shakespeare, in blending the epic with the tragic, has given the impression of the drama to the history of his country. By this means he has bequeathed as a legacy the pure spirit of history. Not that his facts are implicitly to be relied on, or is he to be read, as the Duke of Marlborough read him, as an historian; but as distance is destroyed by a telescope, and by the force of imagination we see in the constellations, brought close to the eye, a multitude of worlds, so by the law of impressiveness, when we read his plays, we seem to live in the era he portrays.

One great object of his historic plays . . . was to make his countrymen more patriotic; to make Englishmen proud of being Englishmen. . . .

M. M. REESE

M. M. Reese (1910-   ). Author of Shakespeare *(1953) and* The Cease of Majesty *(1961).*

INTRODUCTION TO THE HISTORIES*

The period of English history stretching from Richard II to Richard III provided Shakespeare with the material he needed for his speculations about power and his illustra-

* Extracted from *The Cease of Majesty.*

tion of contemporary problems and dangers. Moreover, it was safe to write about the fifteenth century, as it would not have been safe to write about the Tudors. 'I might have been more pleasing to the Reader, if I had written the story of mine own times; having been permitted to draw water as near the well-head as any other,' Raleigh said in the preface to his *History of the World*. 'To this I answer, that who-so-ever in writing a modern History, shall follow truth too near the heels, it may happily strike out his teeth.'

Men had to be very careful what they said. All historical writing was understood to be to some extent allegorical, even when the subject was Persia, Rome or ancient Britain, and since the historian's avowed purpose was to instruct his own age, he could not be surprised if people sometimes made identifications that he would have preferred them to avoid. Raleigh took pains to protect himself from such identifications.

It is enough for me (being in that state I am) to write of the eldest times: wherein also why may it not be said, that in speaking of the past, I point at the present, and tax the vices of those that are yet living, in their persons that are long since dead; and have it laid to my charge? But this I cannot help, though innocent. And certainly if there be any, that finding themselves spotted like the Tigers of old time, shall find fault with me for painting them over anew; they shall therein accuse themselves justly, and me falsely.

The most alarming of these identifications was that between Richard II and the Queen herself. According to a reasonably authenticated anecdote, Elizabeth was examining a parcel of records brought to her by William Lambarde, her Keeper of the Tower, when she 'fell upon the reign of King Richard II, saying, "I am Richard II. Know ye not that?"' When Lambarde loyally demurred, she observed rather obscurely, 'He that will forget God will also forget his benefactors'; adding that 'this tragedy was played forty times in open streets and houses'. In essentials there was little resemblance between Richard and Elizabeth, for Elizabeth's mind was the servant of no man's and she did not waver in doing her duty as she conceived it. But her people, who could not always follow her tortuous policies, sometimes felt differently about her. In her feminine wiles and tergiversations she could be an exasperating woman, and there were times when she seemed to bring the country to the edge of disaster by sheer wanton irresolution. Superficially there were flaws in her character grave enough to disturb men who already had the fate of Richard heavily on their minds. Her more sober advisers were painfully conscious of their equivocal position, and they earnestly disclaimed any resemblance between themselves and the favourites of Richard II. In a letter written to the Queen in 1578 Sir Francis Knollys excused himself for giving advice that he knew would be unwelcome to her. He would not, he said, 'play the parts of King Richard the Second's men'. In almost the same words the first Lord Hunsdon declared that 'I was never one of Richard II's men'. Evidently it was a current phrase; and if her most loyal servants were aware of supposed similarities between Elizabeth and Richard, it can never have been far absent from their minds that she might suffer the same fate.

Richard's reign was therefore a dangerous theme for writers, and probably the more so after the acting of *Thomas of Woodstock* in the early nineties. Perhaps the anonymous author showed deliberate caution in stopping short with the death of Gloucester, for he had been frankly hostile to Richard and one wonders what he would have made of the abdication if he had reached it. The orthodox cannot have found *Woodstock* reassuring. Although Gloucester himself continued to profess his loyalty, his brothers closed the play by swearing to avenge his death; and if Gloucester's death cried for vengeance, did not Mary's too? Many of the charges brought against Richard might at this time have been brought against Elizabeth herself. In unfriendly eyes his sentimental pacifism might correspond to her thrifty reluctance to press the war against Spain, his dependence on favourites to her doting on the unstable Essex, his neglect of his senior counsellors to her hectoring way with the Commons.

At any rate, when Shakespeare's play was printed in 1597, and twice re-issued in the following year, it was printed without the deposition scene (IV i 154-318). This scene had almost certainly been acted in the original performances, for the version printed for the first time in 1608 was apparently based on some kind of memorisation, and it may be that the public acting of a king's deposition had so much alarmed the authorities that they had forbidden it to be printed. The reign of Richard had become a topic that wise men did well to avoid. In 1599 a sober and well-intentioned historian, Sir John Hayward, disregarded the omens and ran head-first into trouble by publishing a *History of Henry IV*, which he was further unwise enough to dedicate to Essex. Hayward's theme was the familiar one of the disasters following upon the treatment of Richard and the country's final redemption in the accession of Henry VII. In fact he went farther back than most historians in suggesting that the collapse of the fine hopes embodied in the seven goodly sons of Edward III may have originated in Edward's own part in the deposition of his father. But in detail he devoted most of his book—some 135 pages out of 150; so it is not altogether surprising that the authorities, already sensitive on this subject, misunderstood him—to reviewing the causes of Richard's fall. His conclusions were entirely respectable, for he decided that the people have no right to depose their sovereign, whatever the provocation, and that the heir should peaceably await the death of his predecessor without trying to force the event. The dedication to Essex was possibly cautionary, to remind him of the wickedness of rebellion, but the government decided otherwise and Hayward went to prison.

The last episode in the curiously linked story of Elizabeth and Richard is the most remarkable of all. In 1601, on the eve of the Essex rebellion, some members of his faction (two Percies among them) approached Shakespeare's company and asked them to give a special performance of *Richard II*: the idea apparently being that the spectacle of a royal deposition would incite the Londoners to fall in with Essex and his nebulous designs. The actors objected that the play was 'so old and so long out of use that they should have small or no company at it', but the conspirators guaranteed their losses by promising them forty shillings above their usual fee, and the performance was accordingly given. Augustine Phillips was later summoned before the Privy Council to make an explanation, and he appears to have satisfied the authorities that the players had no knowledge of the intended rising, for there is no record of their being punished in any way. Instead they were commanded to give a performance at court on the night before Essex died on the block; but we do not know the name of the play with which the Queen consoled herself.

Daniel was another playwright who found himself in trouble for having supposedly given support to Essex. His *Philotas* was thought to be seditious, and he published the play in order to vindicate himself and show that this was not his intention.[1] Greville cautiously adapted the sources he used for *Alaham*, so as to escape any suspicion that his Mahomet might be intended to represent Essex come to purify the state after the misgovernment of an old and feeble ruler. Another play he even thought it prudent to destroy altogether. It was about Antony and Cleopatra, whose irregular passions he condemned in 'forsaking empire to follow sensuality', and he destroyed the manuscript because the characters had 'some childish wantonness in them, apt enough to be construed, or strained to a personating of vices in the present Governors, and government'. He feared that some might judge the play 'in the practice of the world, seeing the like instances not poetically, but really fashioned in the Earl of Essex then falling'.

Such were the dangers besetting all who wrote on historical subjects,[2] and Shakespeare had always to expect the accusation that he was glancing at living persons. That, so far as we know, he escaped this suspicion is an unconscious

---

[1] This was in 1605, after both Essex and the Queen were dead; and Philotas was only a Macedonian general who was executed for conspiracy against Alexander the Great. After the misfortunes of Hayward, the publisher of a quarto of *2 Henry IV* in 1600 thought it prudent to delete references to Richard II and his abdication, as well as part of the Archbishop of York's speech in support of rebellion. Many years later the authorities were still touchy about the theme. The hymn-writer Nahum Tate produced a characteristic adaptation of *Richard II* just at the time when the fabrications of Titus Oates had again made deposition a dangerous topic. With 'exclusion' in the air, the government were in no mood for a production of *Richard II*. The hopeful Tate altered the setting and the names of the characters and re-christened the play as *The Sicilian Usurper*; but no one was deceived, and the second version, like the first, was suppressed.

[2] Cf. the instruction of the Master of the Revels of the *MS.* of *Sir Thomas More*: 'Leave out insurrection wholly, and the cause thereof, at your perils.'

tribute to an artistic tact that knew how to generalise upon immediate experience. None the less the theme of his histories is Elizabethan England, and modern historians have few better sources to preserve them from misunderstanding this anxiety-ridden age. Although his genius transcended his theme, to give his exploration of government a universal value, the histories have an inner consistency that distinguishes them from all his other work.

Serious political reflection occurs everywhere in his drama—even a knockabout farce like *The Taming of the Shrew* moralises upon the duty of obedience—and Shakespeare never ceases to remind men of their social obligations. In a sense, therefore, it is true that the histories by themselves do not contain the full scope and variety of his political thought; and since with the doubtful and uncharacteristic exception of *Henry VIII*, he wrote no further histories in the last dozen years of his professional career, it may also be argued that they do not present his final conclusions on the great questions of state upon which as a younger man he had brooded so earnestly. But the distinguishing quality of the English histories is that here, and here alone, political virtue is the only standard of reference. The characters exist in a single dimension and are judged solely by the dramatist's overriding conception of the welfare of society. Admittedly there are occasional relaxations of this austerity, but these exceptions to the prevailing mood are seemingly casual and quite astonishingly few. Sentimental misunderstandings about the rejection of Falstaff occur because his admirers (who perhaps would like him less if he lived next door) choose to ignore his real function in Shakespeare's story of England. His very existence, or the sort of existence he was allowed to develop, certainly raises questions to which the history plays give no direct answer. Shakespeare made the same mistake with Shylock, and did not make it with Malvolio. But the only pertinent question at the end of *Henry IV* is whether Falstaff would be a suitable companion for a king newly dedicated to 'mock the expectation of the world'. Nor has there ever been any doubt about the answer. As the embodiment of a certain political attitude he stands condemned. Within the limits of a history play he has no need of private emotions like shame or grief, and so he does not ask for pity.

Parolles, an infinitely lesser Falstaff, could say, when he was humiliated: 'Simply the thing I am Shall make me live.' Falstaff could not have said it, and that is the irreconcilable difference between them, and the difference, too, between the histories and all the other plays. The histories lie uniformly within a comprehensive vision which determines plot, argument and characterisation in sole reference to the safety of England and the political qualities that minister to it. Outside this, the characters have no individual life whatever—or if they do, it is a superfluity, an irrelevance or an artistic blunder. The private essences which many of them do in fact develop are an overflow of Shakespeare's creative energy, and an admission of his inability to write strictly to a formula. But he never loses sight of his main structural purpose, and from time to time he brings us up short, as with Falstaff, puts an end to indulgence and thrusts his characters back into the play. If for a moment they have seemed to feel and bleed, it was only an illusion.

Parolles, then, had that in him which would let him live; but Falstaff, politically discredited, could only die. Outside the histories, the characters have inner lives and they are free from the constant pressure of a particular judgment that lies so heavily on the kings and statesmen of the histories. In spite of the wealth of political reference elsewhere, only the histories may truly be described as political plays. *Coriolanus*, with its picture of class division and competing sectional interests, is in some ways the most elaborate as well as the subtlest of Shakespeare's political studies, but at its climax it is focused upon an individual's decision in an issue that has ceased to be political at all. There is the feeling, too, that all the decisions that Coriolanus makes in the play are for him the right ones; and we should not feel that about him if these things had happened in sixteenth-century England. Antony and Cleopatra throw away an empire, but they are not judged, as they surely would be if the play were political. In other plays—*Measure for Measure, Troilus and Cressida, The Winter's Tale, The Tempest* and all the great tragedies—political situations, with their attendant judgments, are implicit but do not develop, or just develop subordinately to something larger and more important. Shakespeare will often open a play with a political issue and then let it be absorbed in a much wider examination of human

behaviour.[1] In this less constricted atmosphere his characters enjoy a freedom and fullness of growth that remain
inaccessible in the histories. It means that they are admitted
to a complex of judgments and sympathies in which political
conduct is only incidental. Respect for the social order may
not always be the most sustaining of the virtues, nor rebellion the greatest of crimes.

This requires an important qualification of the political
sentiments to be found in the plays written after about 1600.
Once he had completed his historical cycle with *Henry V*,
Shakespeare never again wrote a play whose values were
exclusively political. He seems to have found this a liberation, and henceforth his political comment operates in a
much wider context. It is noticeably coloured by the scepticism that pervades his so-called tragic period, and on a narrow view he seems to have lost his optimism about society.
One after another, his heroes are politically disastrous, and
sin so darkens the world that power is only possessed to be
abused. The ugly spirit of Thersites dominates the scene.
'Lechery, lechery; still wars and lechery; nothing else holds
fashion.' Power seems inevitably to corrupt the possessor,
and the leaders of men are 'incontinent varlets' all. Nevertheless we should be wrong to forget the very different terms
of reference and suppose that all this invalidates the conclusions of the histories. The histories show clearly enough
what Shakespeare thought power and office could do to a
man, and in the tragedies and the 'bitter' comedies he chose
to examine their consequences in, apparently, a mood of
total disillusion. The abuse of power is often the comple-
ment, and sometimes the mainspring, of disorders much
more serious. But we have to see Shakespeare's values in the
right perspective. Politics are no longer the main issue, and
Macbeth, Lear, Hamlet, Othello, Troilus, Angelo, Leontes,
Prospero and others are political failures only because they
have other and more destructive defects. Shakespeare's apparent pessimism about the state is here only a minor aspect
of a much more comprehensive pessimism about mankind
generally. He is not condemning majesty. These later plays
simply show a series of situations in which, for various evident reasons, majesty is not able to operate: Angelo's lust,

---

[1] Notably *Measure for Measure*, which opens as though it were to be
a play about government but soon breaks off into other themes.

Othello's personal immaturity, Hamlet's paralysing scepticism, Lear's want of self-knowledge, and so on. It is important to remember that the social and personal values stated in the histories are not impugned. Shakespeare's later heroes demand to be judged by different standards, and the earlier standards stay intact. Dedication, discipline, kindness, love of country are still the cardinal political virtues, and Shakespeare nowhere suggests that where these are found, society will not be happy.

Wales: king (nature/body)
Flint Castle: Fool
Westminster: God (Christ)

ERNST H. KANTOROWICZ

Ernst H. Kantorowicz (1895-1963). His great work on Frederick II was published in 1927. After his flight to America he grew interested in the curious legal fiction of the 'King's Two Bodies' and wrote a remarkable book, which has affected knowledge of a wide range of legal and political history. Shakespeare's interest in the subject is marginal to Kantorowicz's book, but I include it as evidence that discoveries in apparently remote fields can sometimes be fruitfully applied to Shakespeare studies. The implications of the idea are much greater than Kantorowicz was concerned to suggest; the idea is present not only in the Histories, but also in some tragedies, for instance in Julius Caesar *and* King Lear, *and Kantorowicz's explanation of the concept of* aevum—*a kind of secular perpetuity in which the King's Dignity survived—is valuable to all students of Shakespeare.*

SHAKESPEARE: KING RICHARD II*

Twin-born with greatness, subject to the breath
Of every fool, whose sense no more can feel
But his own wringing. What infinite heart's ease
Must kings neglect that private men enjoy! . . .
What kind of god art thou, that suffer'st more
Of mortal griefs than do thy worshippers?

* Extracted from Chapter II of *The King's Two Bodies.*

King's two bodies: The role — as king, fool, or god vs. wretched humanity

[margin, right side:] "in contrast to One another — distinct from one another . . . political — no longer one with the immortal body / godhead + manhood show as being . . . Body natural is no longer one with the immortal body

Such are, in Shakespeare's play, the meditations of King Henry V on the godhead and manhood of a king.[1] The king is "twin-born" not only with greatness but also with human nature, hence "subject to the breath of every fool."

It was the humanly tragic aspect of royal "gemination" which Shakespeare outlined and not the legal capacities which English lawyers assembled in the fiction of the King's Two Bodies. However, the legal jargon of the "two Bodies" scarcely belonged to the arcana of the legal guild alone. That the king "is a Corporation in himself that liveth ever," was a commonplace found in a simple dictionary of legal terms such as Dr. John Cowell's *Interpreter* (1607);[2] and even at an earlier date the gist of the concept of kingship which Plowden's *Reports* reflected, had passed into the writings of Joseph Kitchin (1580)[3] and Richard Crompton (1594).[4] Moreover, related notions were carried into public when, in 1603, Francis Bacon suggested for the crowns of England and Scotland, united in James I, the name of "Great Britain" as an expression of the "perfect union of bodies, politic as well as natural." [5] That Plowden's *Reports* were widely known is certainly demonstrated by the phrase "The case is altered, quoth Plowden," which was used proverbially in England before and after 1600.[6] The suggestion that Shakespeare may have known a case (*Hales* v. *Petit*) reported by Plowden, does not seem far-fetched,[7] and it gains strength

---

[1] *King Henry V*, IV.i.254ff.

[2] Dr. John Cowell, *The Interpreter or Booke Containing the Signification of Words* (Cambridge, 1607), s.v. "King *(Rex),*" also s.v. "Prerogative," where Plowden is actually quoted. See, in general, Chrimes, "Dr. John Cowell," *EHR*, LXIV (1949), 483.

[3] Joseph Kitchin, *Le Court Leete et Court Baron* (London, 1580), fol.1ʳ⁻ᵛ, referring to the case of the Duchy of Lancaster.

[4] Richard Crompton, *L'Authoritie et Jurisdiction des Courts de la Maiestie de la Roygne* (London, 1594), fol. 134 ʳ⁻ᵛ, reproducing on the basis of Plowden the theory about the Two Bodies in connection with the Lancaster case.

[5] See Bacon's *Brief Discourse Touching the Happy Union of the Kingdoms of England and Scotland,* in J. Spedding, *Letters and Life of Francis Bacon* (London, 1861-74), III,90ff; see, for the print of 1603, S. T. Bindoff, "The Stuarts and their Style," *EHR*,LX (1945), 206,n.2, who (p. 207) quotes the passage.

[6] A. P. Rossiter, *Woodstock* (London, 1946), 238.

[7] About Shakespeare and Plowden, see C. H. Norman, "Shakespeare and the Law," *Times Literary Supplement,* June 30, 1950, p. 412, with the additional remarks by Sir Donald Somervell, *ibid.*, July 21, 1950, p. 453.

on the ground that the anonymous play *Thomas of Woodstock*, of which Shakespeare "had his head full of echoes" and in which he may even have acted,[1] ends in the pun: "for I have plodded in Plowden, and can find no law."[2] Besides, it would have been very strange if Shakespeare, who mastered the lingo of almost every human trade, had been ignorant of the constitutional and judicial talk which went on around him and which the jurists of his days applied so lavishly in court. Shakespeare's familiarity with legal cases of general interest cannot be doubted, and we have other evidence of his association with the students at the Inns and his knowledge of court procedure.[3]

Admittedly, it would make little difference whether or not Shakespeare was familiar with the subtleties of legal speech. The poet's vision of the twin nature of a king is not dependent on constitutional support, since such vision would arise very naturally from a purely human stratum. It therefore may appear futile even to pose the question whether Shakespeare applied any professional idiom to the jurists of his time, or try to determine the die of Shakespeare's coinage. It seems all very trivial and irrelevant, since the image of the twinned nature of a king, or even of man in general, was most genuinely Shakespeare's own and proper vision. Nevertheless, should the poet have chanced upon the legal definitions of kingship, as probably he could not have failed to do when conversing with his friends at the Inns, it will be easily imagined how apropos the simile of the King's Two Bodies would have seemed to him. It was anyhow the live essence of his art to reveal the numerous planes active in any human being, to play them off against each other, to confuse them, or to preserve their equilibrium, depending all upon the pattern of life he bore in mind and wished to create anew. How convenient then to find those ever contending planes,

---

[1] John Dover Wilson, in his edition of *Richard II* (see p. 313, n. 1), "Introduction," p. lxxiv; see pp. xlviii ff, for Shakespeare and *Woodstock* in general.

[2] *Woodstock*, V.vi.34f, ed. Rossiter, 169.

[3] See, in general George W. Keeton, *Shakespeare and His Legal Problems* (London, 1930); also Max Radin, "The Myth of Magna Carta," *Harvard Law Review*, LX (1947), 1086, who stresses very strongly Shakespeare's association "with the turbulent students at the Inns."

as it were, legalised by the jurists' royal "christology" and readily served to him!

The legal concept of the King's Two Bodies cannot, for other reasons, be separated from Shakespeare. For if that curious image, which from modern constitutional thought has vanished all but completely, still has a very real and human meaning today, this is largely due to Shakespeare. It is he who has eternalized that metaphor. He has made it not only the symbol, but indeed the very substance and essence of one of his greatest plays: *The Tragedy of King Richard II* is the tragedy of the King's Two Bodies.

Perhaps it is not superfluous to indicate that the Shakespearian Henry V, as he bemoans a king's twofold estate, immediately associates that image with King Richard II. King Henry's soliloquies precede directly that brief intermezzo in which he conjures the spirit of his father's predecessor and to the historic essence of which posterity probably owes that magnificent ex-voto known as the Wilton Diptych.[1]

> Not to-day, O Lord!
> O! not to-day, think not upon the fault
> My father made in encompassing the crown.
> I Richard's body have interr'd anew,
> And on it have bestow'd more contrite tears,
> Than from it issu'd forced drops of blood.
>
> (IV.i.312ff)

Musing over his own royal fate, over the king's two-natured being, Shakespeare's Henry V is disposed to recall Shakespeare's Richard II, who—at least in the poet's concept—appears as the prototype of that "kind of god that suffers more of mortal griefs than do his worshippers."

It appears relevant to the general subject of this study, and also otherwise worth our while, to inspect more closely the varieties of royal "duplications" which Shakespeare has unfolded in the three bewildering central scenes of *Richard*

[1] V. H. Galbraith, "A New Life of Richard II," *History*, XXVI (1942), 237ff; for the artistic problems and for a full bibliography, see Erwin Panofsky, *Early Netherlandish Painting* (Cambridge, Mass., 1953), 118 and 404f,n.5, and Francis Wormald, "The Wilton Diptych," *Warburg Journal*, XVII (1954), 191-203.

II.[1] The duplications, all one, and all simultaneously active, in Richard—"Thus play I in one person many people" (V.v.31)—are those potentially present in the King, the Fool, and the God. They dissolve, perforce, in the Mirror. Those three prototypes of "twin-birth" intersect and overlap and interfere with each other continuously. Yet, it may be felt that the "King" dominates in the scene on the Coast of Wales (III.ii), the "Fool" at Flint Castle (III.iii), and the "God" in the Westminster scene (IV.i), with Man's wretchedness as a perpetual companion and antithesis at every stage. Moreover, in each one of those three scenes we encounter the same cascading: from divine kingship to kingship's "Name," and from the name to the naked misery of man.

Gradually, and only step by step, does the tragedy proper of the King's Two Bodies develop in the scene on the Welsh coast. There is as yet no split in Richard when, on his return from Ireland, he kisses the soil of his kingdom and renders that famous, almost too often quoted, account of the loftiness of his royal estate. What he expounds is, in fact, the indelible character of the king's body politic, godlike or angel-like. The balm of consecration resists the power of the elements, the "rough rude sea," since

> The breath of worldly man cannot depose
> The deputy elected by the Lord.
>
> (III.ii.54ff)

Man's breath appears to Richard as something inconsistent

---

[1] The authoritative edition of *Richard II* is by John Dover Wilson, in the Cambridge *Works of Shakespeare* (Cambridge, 1939). Mr. Wilson's "Introduction," pp. vii-lxxvi, is a model of literary criticism and information. I confess my indebtedness to those pages on which I have drawn more frequently than the footnotes may suggest. In the same volume is a likewise most efficient discussion by Harold Child, "The Stage-History of *Richard II*," pp. lxxvii-xcii. The political aspects of the play are treated in a stimulating fashion by John Leslie Palmer, *Political Characters of Shakespeare* (London, 1945), 118ff, from whose study, too, I have profited more than my acknowledgments may show. See also Keeton, *op.cit.*, 163ff. With regard to the historical Richard II, the historian finds himself in a less fortunate position. The history of this king is in the midst of a thorough revaluation of both sources and general concepts, of which the numerous studies of Professor Galbraith and others bear witness. A first effort to sum up the analytic studies of the last decades has been made by Anthony Steel, *Richard II* (Cambridge, 1941).

with kingship. Carlisle, in the Westminster scene, will emphasize once more that God's Anointed cannot be judged "by inferior breath" (IV.i.128). It will be Richard who "with his own breath" releases at once kingship and subjects (IV.i.210), so that finally King Henry V, after the destruction of Richard's divine kingship, could rightly complain that the king is "subject to the breath of every fool."[1]

When the scene (III.ii) begins, Richard is, in the most exalted fashion, the "deputy elected by the Lord" and "God's substitute . . . anointed in his sight" (I.ii.37). Still is he the one that in former days gave "good ear" to the words of his crony, John Busshy, Speaker of the Commons in 1397, who, when addressing the king, "did not attribute to him titles of honour, due and accustomed, but invented unused termes and such strange names, as were rather agreeable to the divine maiestie of God, than to any earthly potentate."[2] He still appears the one said to have asserted that the "Laws are in the King's mouth, or sometimes in his breast,"[3] and to have demanded that "if he looked at any-

---

[1] See also *King John*, III.iii.147f:

> What earthly name to interrogatories
> Can task the free breath of a sacred king?

[2] This is reported only by Holinshed; see W. G. Boswell-Stone, *Shakespeare's Holinshed* (London, 1896), 130; Wilson, "Introduction," p. lii. *The Rotuli Parliamentorum* do not refer to the speech of John Busshy, in 1397. To judge, however, from the customary parliamentary sermons, the speaker in 1397 may easily have gone far in applying Biblical metaphors to the king; see, e.g., Chrimes, *Const.Ideas*, 165ff.

[3] "Dixit expresse, vultu austero et protervo, quod leges suae erant in ore suo, et aliquotiens in pectore suo: Et quod ipse solus posset mutare et condere leges regni sui." This was one of the most famous of Richard's so-called "tyrannies" with which he was charged in 1399; see E. C. Lodge and G. A. Thornton, *English Constitutional Documents 1307-1485* (Cambridge, 1935), 28f. Richard II, like the French king, merely referred to a well known maxim of Roman and Canon Laws. Cf. *C*.6,23,19,1, for the maxim *Omnia iura in scrinio* (*pectoris*) *principis*, often quoted by the glossators, e.g., *Glos.ord.*, on *D*.33,10,3, v. *usum imperatorem*, or on c.16, *C*.25,q.2, v. *In iuris*, and quoted also by Thomas Aquinas (Tolomeo of Lucca), *De regimine principum*, II,c.8, IV,c.1. The maxim became famous through Pope Boniface VIII; see c.1 VI 1,2, ed. Emil Friedberg, *Corpus iuris canonici* (Leipzig, 1879-81), II,937: "Licet Romanus Pontifex, qui iura omnia in scrinio pectoris sui censetur habere, constitutionem condendo posteriorem, priorem . . . revocare noscatur. . . ." (probably the place referred to by Richard if the correctness of the charges be granted). For the meaning of the

one, that person had to bend the knee."[1] He still is sure of himself, of his dignity, and even of the help of the celestial hosts, which are at his disposal.

> For every man that Bolingbroke hath press'd . . . ,
> God for his Richard hath in heavenly pay
> A glorious angel.

(III.ii.60)

This glorious image of kingship "By the Grace of God" does not last. It slowly fades, as the bad tidings trickle in. A curious change in Richard's attitude—as it were, a meta-morphosis from "Realism" to "Nominalism"—now takes place. The Universal called "Kingship" begins to disinte-grate; its transcendental "Reality," its objective truth and god-like existence, so brilliant shortly before, pales into a nothing, a *nomen*.[2] And the remaining half-reality resem-bles a state of amnesia or of sleep.

---

maxim (i.e., the legislator should have the relevant laws present to his mind), see F. Gillman, "Romanus pontifex iura omnia in scrinio pectoris sui censetur habere," *AKKR*, XCII (1912), 3ff, CVI (1926), 156ff (also CVIII [1928], 534; CIX [1929], 249f); also Gaines Post, "Two Notes," *Traditio*, IX (1953), 311, and "Two Laws," *Speculum*, XIX (1954), 425,n.35. See also Steinwenter, "Nomos," 256ff; *Erg.Bd.*, 85; Oldradus de Ponte, *Consilia*, LII,n.1 (Venice, 1571), fol. 19ʳ. The maxim occasionally was transferred also to the judge (Walter Ullman, *The Mediaeval Idea of Law as Represented by Lucas de Penna* [London, 1946], 107) and to the fisc (Gierke, *Gen.R.*, III,359, n.17) as well as to the council. For Richard's other claim (*mutare et condere leges*), the papal and imperial doctrines likewise were responsible; see Gregory VII's *Dictatus papae*, §VII, ed. Caspar (*MGH*, Epp.scl., II), 203; also Frederick II's *Liber aug.*, I,38, ed. Cervone, 85, with the gloss referring to *C.*1,17,2,18.

[1] For the genuflection, see *Eulogium Historiarum*, ed. Hayden (Rolls Series, 1863), III,378; see Steel, *Richard II*, 278. The annalist men-tions it in connection with "Festival Crownings" (which thus were continued during the reign of Richard) and gives an account of the king's uncanny deportment:

> In diebus solemnibus, in quibus utebatur de more regalibus, iussit sibi in camera parari thronum, in quo post prandium se ostentans sedere solebat usque ad vesperas, nulli loquens, sed singulos aspi-ciens. Et cum aliquem respiceret, cuiuscumque gradus fuerit, opor-tuit genuflectere.

[2] For the body politic as mere name, see, e.g., Pollock and Maitland, *History*, I,490,n.8: "le corporacion . . . n'est que un nosme, que ne poit my estre vieu, et n'est my substance." See also Gierke, *Gen.R.*, III,281, for corporate bodies as *nomina iuris, a nomen intellectuale*, and the connections with the philosophic Nominalism.

> I had forgot myself, am I not king?
> Awake thou coward majesty! thou sleepest,
> Is not the king's name twenty thousand names?
> *Arm, arm, my name!* A puny subject strikes
> At thy great glory.
>
> (III.ii.83ff)

This state of half-reality, of royal oblivion and slumber, adumbrates the royal "Fool" of Flint Castle. And similarly the divine prototype of gemination, the God-man, begins to announce its presence, as Richard alludes to Judas' treason:

> Snakes, in my heart-blood warm'd, that sting my heart!
> Three Judases, each one thrice worse than Judas!
>
> (III.ii.131)

It is as though it has dawned upon Richard that his vicariate of the God Christ might imply also a vicariate of the man Jesus, and that he, the royal "deputy elected by the Lord," might have to follow his divine Master also in his human humiliation and take the cross.

However, neither the twin-born Fool nor the twin-born God are dominant in that scene. Only their nearness is forecast, while to the fore there steps the body natural and mortal of the king:

> Let's talk of graves, of worms and epitaphs . . .
>
> (III.ii.145ff)

Not only does the king's manhood prevail over the godhead of the Crown, and mortality over immortality; but, worse than that, kingship itself seems to have changed its essence. Instead of being unaffected "by Nonage or Old Age and other natural Defects and Imbecilities," kingship itself comes to mean Death, and nothing but Death. And the long procession of tortured kings passing in review before Richard's eyes is proof of that change:

> For God's sake let us sit upon the ground,
> And tell sad stories of the death of kings—
> How some have been deposed, some slain in war,
> Some haunted by the ghosts they have deposed,
> Some poisoned by their wives, some sleeping killed;

All murdered—for within the hollow crown
That rounds the mortal temples of a king,
Keeps Death his court, and there the antic sits
Scoffing his state and grinning at his pomp,
Allowing him a breath, a little scene,
To monarchize, be feared, and kill with looks,
Infusing him with self and vain conceit,
As if the flesh which walls about our life,
Were brass impregnable: and humoured thus,
Comes at the last, and with a little pin
Bores through his castle wall, and farewell king!

                              (III.ii.155ff)

The king that "never dies" here has been replaced by the king that always dies and suffers death more cruelly than other mortals. Gone is the oneness of the body natural with the immortal body politic, "this double Body, to which no Body is equal". Gone also is the fiction of royal prerogatives of any kind, and all that remains is the feeble human nature of a king:

                    mock not flesh and blood
With solemn reverence, throw away respect,
Tradition, form, and ceremonious duty,
For you have but mistook me all this while:
I live with bread like you, feel want,
 Taste grief, need friends—subjected thus,
How can you say to me, I am a king?

                              (III.ii.171ff)

The fiction of the oneness of the double body breaks apart. Godhead and manhood of the King's Two Bodies, both clearly outlined with a few strokes, stand in contrast to each other. A first low is reached. The scene now shifts to Flint Castle.

The structure of the second great scene (III.iii) resembles the first. Richard's kingship, his body politic, has been hopelessly shaken, it is true; but still there remains, though hollowed out, the semblance of kingship. At least this might be saved. "Yet looks he like a king," states York at Flint Castle (III.iii.68); and in Richard's temper there dominates, at first, the consciousness of his royal dignity. He had made up his mind beforehand to appear a king at the Castle:

> A king, woe's slave, shall kingly woe obey.
> (III.iii.210)

He acts accordingly; he snorts at Northumberland who has omitted the vassal's and subject's customary genuflection before his liege lord and the deputy of God:

> We are amazed, and thus long have we stood
> To watch the fearful bending of thy knee,
> Because we thought ourself thy lawful king:
> And if we be, how dare thy joints forget
> To pay their awful duty to our presence?
> (III.iii.73ff)

The "cascades" then begin to fall as they did in the first scene. The celestial hosts are called upon once more, this time avenging angels and "armies of pestilence," which God is said to muster in his clouds—"on our behalf" (III.iii.85f). Again the "Name" of kingship plays its part:

> O, that I were as great
> As is my grief, or lesser than my *name*!
> (III.iii.136)

> Must (the king) lose
> The *name* of king? a God's *name*, let it go.
> (III.iii.145f)

From the shadowy name of kingship there leads, once more, the path to new disintegration. No longer does Richard impersonate the mystic body of his subjects and the nation. It is a lonely man's miserable and mortal nature that replaces the king as King:

> I'll give my jewels for a set of beads:
> My gorgeous palace for a hermitage:
> My gay apparel for an almsman's gown:
> My figured goblets for a dish of wood:
> My sceptre for a palmer's walking-staff:
> My subjects for a pair of carved saints,
> And my large kingdom for a little grave,
> A little little grave, an obscure grave.
> (III.iii.147ff)

The shiver of those anaphoric clauses is followed by a profusion of gruesome images of High-Gothic *macabresse*.
However, the second scene—different from the first—does
not end in those outbursts of self-pity which recall, not a
Dance of Death, but a dance around one's own grave. There
follows a state of even greater abjectness.

The new note, indicating a change for the worse, is struck
when Northumberland demands that the king come down
into the base court of the castle to meet Bolingbroke, and
when Richard, whose personal badge was the "Sun emerg-
ing from a cloud," retorts in a language of confusing brightness and terrifying puns:

> Down, down I come like glist'ring Phaethon:
> Wanting the manage of unruly jades. . . .
> In the base court? Base court, where kings grow
>   base,
> To come at traitors' calls, and do them grace.
> In the base court? Come down? Down court! down
>   king!
> For night-owls shriek where mounting larks should
>   sing.

(III.iii.178ff)

It has been noticed at different times how prominent a place
is held in *Richard II* by the symbolism of the Sun, and
occasionally a passage reads like the description of a Roman
Oriens Augusti coin (III.ii.36-53).[1] The Sun imagery, as

[1] For Richard's symbol of the "Rising Sun," see Paul Reyher, "Le
symbole du soleil dans la tragédie de Richard II," *Revue de l'en-
seignement des langues vivantes*, XL (1923), 254-260; for further
literature on the subject, see Wilson, "Introduction," p. xii, n.3, and,
for possible predecessors using that badge, John Gough Nichols,
"Observations on the Heraldic Devices on the Effigies of Richard
the Second and his Queen," *Archaeologia*, XXIX (1842), 47f. See,
for the "Sun of York" (*K. Richard III*, I.i.2), also Henry Green,
Shakespeare and the Emblem Writers (London, 1870), 223; and,
for the *Oriens Augusti* problem, see my study.—The "sunne arys-
ing out of the clouds" was actually the banner borne by the Black
Prince; Richard II had a sun shining carried by a white hart,
whereas his standard was sprinkled with ten suns "in splendor"
with a white hart lodged; see Lord Howard de Walden, *Banners,
Standards, and Badges from a Tudor Manuscript in the College of
Arms* (De Walden Library, 1904), figs. 4, 5, 71. I am greatly obliged
to Mr. Martin Davies, of the National Gallery in London, for having called this MS to my attention.

interwoven in Richard's answer, reflects the "splendour of the catastrophe" in a manner remindful of Breughel's *Icarus* and Lucifer's fall from the empyrean, reflecting also those "shreds of glow. . . . That round the limbs of fallen angels hover." On the other hand, the "traitors' calls" may be reminiscent of the "three Judases" in the foregoing scene. In general, however, biblical imagery is unimportant at Flint Castle: it is saved for the Westminster scene. At Flint, there is another vision which, along with foolish Phaethons and Icari, the poet now produces.

> I talk but idly, and you laugh at me,

remarks Richard (III.iii.171), growing self-conscious and embarrassed. The sudden awkwardness is noticed by Northumberland, too:

> Sorrow and grief of heart
> Makes him speak fondly like a frantic man.
> (III.iii.185)

Shakespeare, in that scene, conjures up the image of another human being, the Fool, who is two-in-one and whom the poet otherwise introduces so often as counter-type of lords and kings. Richard II plays now the rôles of both: fool of his royal self and fool of kingship. Therewith, he becomes somewhat less than merely "man" or (as on the Beach) "king body natural." However, only in that new rôle of Fool —a fool playing king, and a king playing fool—is Richard capable of greeting his victorious cousin and of playing to the end, with Bolingbroke in genuflection before him, the comedy of his brittle and dubious kingship. Again he escapes into "speaking fondly," that is, into puns:

> Fair cousin, you debase your princely knee,
> To make the base earth proud with kissing it. . . .
> Up, cousin, up—your heart is up, I know,
> Thus high *(touching his own head)* at least, although
>   your knee be low.
> (III.iii.190ff)

The jurists had claimed that the king's body politic is utterly void of "natural Defects and Imbecilities." Here, however, "Imbecility" seems to hold sway. And yet, the very bottom has not been reached. Each scene, progressively, designates a new low. "King body natural" in the first scene, and "Kingly Fool" in the second: with those two twin-born beings there is associated, in the half-sacramental abdication scene, the twin-born deity as an even lower estate. For the "Fool" marks the transition from "King" to "God," and nothing could be more miserable, it seems, than the God in the wretchedness of man.

As the third scene (IV.i) opens, there prevails again—now for the third time—the image of sacramental kingship. On the Beach of Wales, Richard himself had been the herald of the loftiness of kingship by right divine; at Flint Castle, he had made it his "program" to save at least the face of a king and to justify the "Name," although the title no longer fitted his condition; at Westminster, he is incapable of expounding his kingship himself. Another person will speak for him and interpret the image of God-established royalty; and very fittingly, a bishop. The Bishop of Carlisle now plays the *logothetes*; he constrains, once more, the *rex imago Dei* to appear:

> What subject can give sentence on his king?
> And who sits here that is not Richard's subject? . . .
> And shall the figure of God's majesty,
> His captain, steward, deputy-elect,
> Anointed, crowned, planted many years,
> Be judged by subject and inferior breath,
> And he himself not present? O, forfend it, God,
> That in a Christian climate souls refined
> Should show so heinous, black, obscene a deed!
>
> (IV.i.121ff)

Those are, in good mediaeval fashion, the features of the *vicarius Dei*. And it likewise agrees with mediaeval tradition that the Bishop of Carlisle views the present against the background of the Biblical past. True, he leaves it to Richard to draw the final conclusions and to make manifest the resemblance of the humbled king with the humbled Christ. Yet, it is the bishop who, as it were, prepares the Biblical climate by prophesying future horrors and foretelling England's Golgotha:

Disorder, horror, fear, and mutiny
Shall here inhabit, and this land be called
The field of Golgotha and dead men's skulls.

(IV.i.142ff)

The bishop, for his bold speech, was promptly arrested; but into the atmosphere prepared by him there enters King Richard.

When led into Westminster Hall, he strikes the same chords as the bishop, those of Biblicism. He points to the hostile assembly, to the lords surrounding Bolingbroke:

Did they not sometimes cry 'all hail' to me?
So Judas did to Christ: But He, in twelve,
Found truth in all, but one: I in twelve thousand,
        none.   (IV.i.169)

For the third time the name of Judas is cited to stigmatize the foes of Richard. Soon the name of Pilate will follow and make the implied parallel unequivocal. But before being delivered up to his judges and his cross, King Richard has to "un-king" himself.

The scene in which Richard "undoes his kingship" and releases his body politic into thin air, leaves the spectator breathless. It is a scene of sacramental solemnity, since the ecclesiastical ritual of undoing the effects of consecration is no less solemn or of less weight than the ritual which has built up the sacramental dignity. Not to mention the rigid punctilio which was observed at the ousting of a Knight of the Garter or the Golden Fleece,[1] there had been set a famous precedent by Pope Celestine V who, in the Castel

---

[1] The ecclesiastical *Forma degradationis* was, on the whole, faithfully observed; see the Pontifical of William Durandus (ca. 1293-95), III,c.7, §§21-24, ed. M. Andrieu, *Le pontifical romain au moyen-âge* (Studi e testi, LXXXVIII, Rome, 1940), III,607f and Appendix IV, pp. 680f. The person to be degraded has to appear in full pontificals; then the places of his chrismation are rubbed with some acid; finally "seriatim et sigillatim detrahit [episcopus] illi omnia insignia, sive sacra ornamenta, que in ordinum susceptione recepit, et demum exuit illum habitu clericali. . ." See also S. W. Findlay, *Canonical Norms Governing the Deposition and Degradation of Clerics* (Washington, 1941). For knights, see Otto Cartellieri, *Am Hofe der Herzöge von Burgund* (Basel, 1926), 62 (with notes on p. 272); also Du Cange, *Glossarium*, s.v. "Arma reversata."

Nuovo at Naples, had "undone" himself by stripping off from his body, with his own hands, the insignia of the dignity which he resigned—ring, tiara, and purple. But whereas Pope Celestine resigned his dignity to his electors, the College of Cardinals, Richard, the hereditary king, resigned his office to God—*Deo ius suum resignavit*.[1] The Shakespearian scene in which Richard "undoes himself with hierophantic solemnity," has attracted the attention of many a critic, and Walter Pater has called it very correctly an inverted rite, a rite of degradation and a long agonizing ceremony in which the order of coronation is reversed.[2] Since none is entitled to lay finger on the Anointed of God and royal bearer of a *character indelibilis*,[3] King Richard, when defrocking himself, appears as his own celebrant:

Am I both priest and clerk? well then, amen.
(IV.i.173)

[1] For Pope Celestine V, see F. Baethgen, *Der Engelpapst* (Leipzig, 1943), 175; for Richard, *Chronicle of Dieulacres Abbey*, ed. M. V. Clarke and V. H. Galbraith, "The Deposition of Richard II," *Bulletin of the John Rylands Library*, XIV (1930), 173, also 146.

[2] Walter Pater, *Appreciations* (London, 1944), 205f; Wilson, XV f; Palmer, *Political Characters*, 166.

[3] Cf. Chrimes, *Const. Ideas*, 7, n. 2, quoting *Annales Henrici Quarti*, ed. Riley (Rolls Series), 286: "Noluit renunciare spirituali honori *characteris sibi impressi* et inunctioni, quibus renunciare non potuit nec ab hiis cessare." The question as to whether or not the king, through his anointment, ever owned in a technical sense a *character indelibilis* is too complicated to be discussed here. In fact, the notion of the "sacramental character" was developed only at the time when the royal (imperial) consecrations were excluded from the number of the seven sacraments; cf. Ferdinand Brommer, *Die Lehre vom sakramentalen Charakter in der Scholastik bis Thomas von Aquino inklusive* (Forschungen zur christlichen Literatur- und Dogmengeschichte, VIII, 2), Paderborn, 1908. A different matter is the common opinion about the sacramental character of royal anointings and the inaccurate use of the term *sacramentum*; see, for the latter, e.g., P. E. Schramm, "Der König von Navarra (1035-1512)," *ZfRG*, germ. Abt., LXVIII (1951), 147, n. 72 (Pope Alexander IV referring to a royal consecration as *sacramentum*). See, in general, Eduard Eichmann, *Die Kaiserkrönung im Abendland* (Würzburg, 1942), I, 86ff, 90, 208, 279, II, 304; Philipp Oppenheim, "Die sakralen Momente in der deutschen Herrscherweihe bis zum Investiturstreit," *Ephemerides Liturgicae*, LVIII (1944), 42ff; and, for England, the well known utterances of Peter of Blois (*PL*, CCVII, 440D) and Grosseteste (*Ep.*, CXXIV, ed. Luard, 350). Actually, the lack of precision was great at all times.

Bit by bit he deprives his body politic of the symbols of its dignity and exposes his poor body natural to the eyes of the spectators:

> Now mark me how I will undo myself:
> I give this heavy weight from off my head,
> And this unwieldy sceptre from my hand,
> The pride of kingly sway from out my heart;
> With mine own tears I wash away my balm,
> With mine own hands I give away my crown,
> With mine own tongue deny my sacred state,
> With mine own breath release all duteous oaths:
> All pomp and majesty do I forswear. . . .
>
> (IV.i.203ff)

Self-deprived of all his former glories, Richard seems to fly back to his old trick of Flint Castle, to the rôle of Fool, as he renders to his "successor" some double-edged acclamations.[1] This time, however, the fool's cap is of no avail. Richard declines to "ravel out his weaved-up follies," which his cold-efficient foe Northumberland demands him to read aloud. Nor can he shield himself behind his "Name." This, too, is gone irrevocably:

> I have no name. . . .
> And know not now what name to call myself.
>
> (IV.i.254ff)

In a new flash of inventiveness, he tries to hide behind another screen. He creates a new split, a chink for his former glory through which to escape and thus to survive. Over against his lost outward kingship he sets an inner kingship, makes his true kingship to retire to inner man, to soul and mind and "regal thoughts":

> You may my glories and my state depose,
> But not my griefs, still am I king of those.
>
> (IV.i.192ff)

Invisible his kingship, and relegated to within: visible his flesh, and exposed to contempt and derision or to pity and

[1] IV.i.214ff.

mockery—there remains but one parallel to his miserable self: the derided Son of man. Not only Northumberland, so Richard exclaims, will be found "damned in the book of heaven," but others as well:

> Nay, all of you, that stand and look upon me,
> Whilst that my wretchedness doth bait myself,
> Though some of you, with Pilate, wash your hands,
> Showing an outward pity; yet you Pilates
> Have here delivered me to my sour cross,
> And water cannot wash away your sin.
>
> (IV.i.237)

It is not at random that Shakespeare introduces here, as antitype of Richard, the image of Christ before Pilate, mocked as King of the Jews and delivered to the cross. Shakespeare's sources, contemporary with the events, had transmitted that scene in a similar light.

> At this hour did he (Bolingbroke) remind me of Pilate, who caused our Lord Jesus Christ to be scourged at the stake and afterwards had him brought before the multitude of the Jews, saying, "Fair Sirs, behold your king!" who replied, "Let him be crucified!" Then Pilate washed his hands of it, saying, "I am innocent of the just blood." And so he delivered our Lord unto them. Much in the like manner did Duke Henry, when he gave up his rightful lord to the rabble of London, in order that, if they should put him to death, he might say, "I am innocent of this deed." [1]

[1] The passage is found in the *Chronique de la Traïson et Mort de Richard II*, ed. B. Williams, in: *English Historical Society*, 1846, and in Creton's French metrical *History of the Deposition of Richard II*, ed. J. Webb, in: *Royal Society of the Antiquaries* (London, 1819). A fifteenth-century English version, which has been rendered here, was edited by J. Webb, in *Archaeologia*, xx (1824), 179. See, on those sources, Wilson, "Introduction," lviii, cf. xvi f and 211. The crime of treason would naturally evoke the comparison with Judas. The comparison with Pilate was likewise quite common (see, e.g., Dante, *Purg.*, xx, 91), though his role was not always purely negative; see, e.g., O. Treitinger, *Die oströmische Kaiser- und Reichsidee nach ihrer Gestaltung im höfischen Zeremoniell* (Jena, 1938), 231, n. 104, for Pilate's inkpot in the ceremonial of the Byzantine emperor, who on Ash Wednesday symbolically "washed his hands."

The parallel of Bolingbroke-Richard and Pilate-Christ reflects a widespread feeling among the anti-Lancastrian
groups. Such feeling was revived, to some extent, in Tudor
times. But this is not important here; for Shakespeare, when
using the biblical comparison, integrates it into the entire
development of Richard's misery, of which the nadir has
yet not been reached. The Son of man, despite his humiliation and the mocking, remained the *deus absconditus,* remained the "concealed God" with regard to inner man,
just as Shakespeare's Richard would trust for a moment's
length in his concealed inner kingship. This inner kingship,
however, dissolved too. For of a sudden Richard realizes
that he, when facing his Lancastrian Pilate, is not at all
like Christ, but that he himself, Richard, has his place
among the Pilates and Judases, because he is no less a
traitor than the others, or is even worse than they are:
he is a traitor to his own immortal body politic and to kingship such as it had been to his day:

> Mine eyes are full of tears, I cannot see. . . .
> But they can see a sort of traitors here.
> Nay, if I turn mine eyes upon myself,
> I find myself a traitor with the rest:
> For I have given here my soul's consent
> T'undeck the pompous body of a king. . . .
> (IV.i.244)

That is, the king body natural becomes a traitor to the king
body politic, to the "pompous body of a king." It is as
though Richard's self-indictment of treason anticipated the
charge of 1649, the charge of high treason committed by
the *k*ing against the *K*ing.

This cleavage is not yet the climax of Richard's duplications, since the splitting of his personality will be continued
without mercy. Once more does there emerge that metaphor
of "Sun-kingship." It appears, however, in the reverse order,
when Richard breaks into that comparison of singular
imagination:

> O, that I were a mockery king of snow,
> Standing before the sun of Bolingbroke,
> To melt myself away in water-drops!
> (IV.i.260ff)

But it is not before that new Sun—symbol of divine majesty throughout the play—that Richard "melts himself away," and together with his self also the image of kingship in the early liturgical sense; it is before his own ordinary face that there dissolves both his bankrupt majesty and his nameless manhood.

The mirror scene is the climax of that tragedy of dual personality. The looking-glass has the effects of a magic mirror, and Richard himself is the wizard who, comparable to the trapped and cornered wizard in the fairy tales, is forced to set his magic art to work against himself. The physical face which the mirror reflects, no longer is one with Richard's inner experience, his outer appearance, no longer identical with inner man. "Was this the face?" The treble question and the answers to it reflect once more the three main facets of the double nature—King, God (Sun), and Fool:

> Was this the face
> That every day under his household roof
> Did keep ten thousand men?
>   Was this the face
> That, like the sun, did make beholders wink?
> Was this the face, that faced so many follies,
> And was at last outfaced by Bolingbroke?
>   (IV.i.281)

When finally, at the "brittle glory" of his face, Richard dashes the mirror to the ground, there shatters not only Richard's past and present, but every aspect of a superworld. His catoptromancy has ended. The features as reflected by the looking-glass betray that he is stripped of every possibility of a second or super-body—of the pompous body politic of king, of the God-likeness of the Lord's deputy elect, of the follies of the fool, and even of the most human griefs residing in inner man. The splintering mirror means, or is, the breaking apart of any possible duality. All those facets are reduced to one: to the banal face and insignificant *physis* of a miserable man, a *physis* now void of any metaphysis whatsoever. It is both less and more than Death. It is the *demise* of Richard, and the rise of a new body natural.

Could one call duality the "role-playing"

Bolingbroke:
> Go, some of you, convey him to the Tower.

Richard:
> O, good! convey? conveyors are you all,
> That rise thus nimbly by a great king's fall.

> (IV.i.316f)

Plowden:
> Demise is a word, signifying that there is a Separation of
> the two Bodies; and that the Body politic is conveyed
> over from the Body natural, now dead or removed from
> the Dignity royal, to another Body natural.[1]

The Tragedy of King Richard II has always been felt to
be a political play.[2] The deposition scene, though performed
scores of times after the first performance in 1595, was
not printed, or not allowed to be printed, until after the
death of Queen Elizabeth.[3] Historical plays in general attracted the English people, especially in the years following the destruction of the Armada; but *Richard II* attracted
more than the usual attention. Not to speak of other causes,
the conflict between Elizabeth and Essex appeared to Shakespeare's contemporaries in the light of the conflict between
Richard and Bolingbroke. It is well known that in 1601,
on the eve of his unsuccessful rebellion against the Queen,
the Earl of Essex ordered a special performance of *Richard
II* to be played in the Globe Theatre before his supporters
and the people of London. In the course of the state trial
against Essex that performance was discussed at some length
by the royal judges—among them the two greatest lawyers
of that age, Coke and Bacon—who could not fail to recognize the allusions to the present which the performance of
that play intended.[4] It is likewise well known that Elizabeth
looked upon that tragedy with most unfavorable feelings.
At the time of Essex' execution she complained that "this
tragedy had been played 40 times in open streets and
houses," and she carried her self-identification with the title

[1] Plowden, *Reports*, 233a.
[2] Palmer, *Political Characters*, 118f.
[3] Wilson, "Introduction," xvi ff, xlix; also Child *(ibid.)*, lxxvii ff; cf.
Keeton, *Legal Problems*, 163.
[4] Wilson, xxx ff; Keeton, 166, 168.

character so far as to exclaim: "I am Richard II, know ye not that?"[1]

Richard II remained a political play. It was suppressed under Charles II in the 1680's. The play illustrated perhaps too overtly the latest events of England's revolutionary history, the "Day of the Martyrdom of the Blessed King Charles I" as commemorated in those years in the Book of Common Prayer.[2] The Restoration avoided these and other recollections and had no liking for that tragedy which centered, not only on the concept of a Christ-like martyr king, but also on that most unpleasant idea of a violent separation of the King's Two Bodies.

It would not be surprising at all had Charles I himself thought of his tragic fate in terms of Shakespeare's *Richard II* and of the king's twin-born being. In some copies of the *Eikon Basilike* there is printed a lament, a long poem otherwise called *Majesty in Misery,* which is ascribed to Charles I and in which the unfortunate king, if really he was the poet, quite obviously alluded to the King's Two Bodies:

> With my own power my majesty they wound,
> In the King's name the king himself uncrowned.
> So does the dust destroy the diamond.[3]

[handwritten annotation: For Richard the role entertained is always finds a counterpart in the humanity — he slips out of it — or makes it clear that it is a role (after Wales scene) — so a duality exists. This duality is the split of body natural and body politic]

MAURICE MORGANN

Maurice Morgann (1726-1802). Morgann wrote his essay in a short time in 1774, and later revised and enlarged it for publication. It remained little known for nearly half a

---

[1] Wilson, xxxii.

[2] Wilson, xvii; Child, lxxix.

[3] According to Rosemary Freeman, *English Emblem Books* (London, 1948), 162, n.1, the poem was first printed in the *Eikon Basilike,* edition of 1648. Margaret Barnard Pickel, *Charles I as Patron of Poetry and Drama* (London, 1938), who prints the whole poem in Appendix C, seems to assume (p. 178) that it was first published in Bishop Burnet's *Memoirs of the Duke of Hamilton* (London, 1677), a work dedicated to Charles II. A few stanzas have been published also by F. M. G. Higham, *Charles I* (London, 1932), 276.

century, but is now regarded as the true ancestor of such criticism as Hazlitt's, and of the elaborate 'character analysis' which was a staple of Shakespeare criticism until the dethronement of Bradley in the 1930s.

SHAKESPEARE AND FALSTAFF*

Shakespeare is a name so interesting, that it is excusable to stop a moment, nay it would be indecent to pass him without the tribute of some admiration. He differs essentially from all other writers: Him we may profess rather to feel than to understand; and it is safer to say, on many occasions, that we are possessed by him, than that we possess him. And no wonder;—He scatters the seeds of things, the principles of character and action, with so cunning a hand, yet with so careless an air, and, master of our feelings, submits himself so little to our judgment, that every thing seems superior. We discern not his course, we see no connection of cause and effect, we are rapt in ignorant admiration, and claim no kindred with his abilities. All the incidents, all the parts, look like chance, whilst we feel and are sensible that the whole is design. His Characters not only act and speak in strict conformity to nature, but in strict relation to us; just so much is shewn as is requisite, just so much is impressed; he commands every passage to our heads and to our hearts, and moulds us as he pleases, and that with so much ease, that he never betrays his own exertions. We see these Characters act from the mingled motives of passion, reason, interest, habit, and complection, in all their proportions, when they are supposed to know it not themselves; and we are made to acknowledge that their actions and sentiments are, from those motives, the necessary result. He at once blends and distinguishes every thing;—every thing is complicated, every thing is plain. I restrain the further expressions of my admiration lest they should not seem applicable to man; but it is really astonishing that a mere human being, a part of humanity only, should so perfectly comprehend the whole; and that he should possess such exquisite art, that whilst every woman and every child shall feel the whole effect, his learned Edi-

* From *An Essay on the Dramatic Character of Falstaff* (1777).

tors and Commentators should yet so very frequently mistake or seem ignorant of the cause. A sceptre or a straw are in his hands of equal efficacy; he needs no selection; he converts every thing into excellence; nothing is too great, nothing is too base. Is a character efficient like *Richard*, it is every thing we can wish: Is it otherwise, like *Hamlet*, it is productive of equal admiration: Action produces one mode of excellence, and inaction another: The Chronicle, the Novel, or the Ballad; the king, or the beggar, the hero, the madman, the sot, or the fool; it is all one;—nothing is worse, nothing is better: The same genius pervades and is equally admirable in all. Or, is a character to be shewn in progressive change, and the events of years comprized within the hour;—with what a Magic hand does he prepare and scatter his spells! The Understanding must, in the first place, be subdued; and lo! how the rooted prejudices of the child spring up to confound the man! The Weird sisters rise, and order is extinguished. The laws of nature give way, and leave nothing in our minds but wildness and horror. No pause is allowed us for reflection: Horrid sentiment, furious guilt and compunction, air-drawn daggers, murders, ghosts, and inchantment, shake and *possess us wholly*. In the mean time the *process* is completed. *Macbeth* changes under our eye, *the milk of human kindness is converted to gall; he has supped full of horrors*, and his *May of life is fallen into the sear, the yellow leaf;* whilst we, the fools of amazement, are insensible to the shifting of place and the lapse of time, and, till the curtain drops, never once wake to the truth of things, or recognize the laws of existence.—On such an occasion, a fellow, like *Rymer*, waking from his trance, shall lift up his Constable's staff, and charge this great Magician, this daring *practicer of arts inhibited*, in the name of *Aristotle*, to surrender; whilst *Aristotle* himself, disowning his wretched Officer, would fall prostrate at his feet and acknowledge his supremacy.—O supreme of Dramatic excellence! (*might he say*) not to me be imputed the insolence of fools. The bards of *Greece* were confined within the narrow circle of the Chorus, and hence they found themselves constrained to practice, for the most part, the precision, and copy the details of nature. I followed them, and knew not that a larger circle might be drawn, and the Drama extended to the whole reach of human genius. Convinced, I see that a more compendious *nature* may be obtained; a nature of *effects* only, to which neither the relations of place, or continuity of time, are always essential. Nature, condescending to the faculties and apprehensions of man, has drawn through human life a regular chain of visible causes and effects: But Poetry delights in surprise, conceals her steps, seizes at once upon the heart, and obtains the Sublime of things without betraying the rounds of her ascent: True Poesy is *magic,* not *nature;* an effect from causes hidden or unknown. To the Magician I prescribed no laws; his law and his power are one; his power is his law. Him, who neither imitates, nor is within the reach of imitation, no precedent can or ought to bind, no limits to contain. If his end is obtained, who shall question his course? Means, whether apparent or hidden, are justified in Poesy by success; but then most perfect and most admirable when most concealed. But whither am I going! This copious and delightful topic has drawn me far beyond my design; I hasten back to my subject, and am guarded, for a time at least, against any further temptation to digress.

I was considering the dignity of *Falstaff* so far as it might seem connected with or productive of military merit, and I have assigned him *reputation* at least, if not *fame,* noble connection, birth, attendants, title, and an honourable pension; every one of them presumptive proofs of Military merit, and motives of action. What deduction is to be made on these articles, and why they are so much obscured may, perhaps, hereafter appear.

I have now gone through the examination of all the Persons of the Drama from whose mouths any thing can be drawn relative to the Courage of *Falstaff,* excepting the Prince and *Poins,* whose evidence I have begged leave to *reserve,* and excepting a very severe censure passed on him by Lord *John* of *Lancaster,* which I shall presently consider: But I must first observe that, setting aside the jests of the Prince and *Poins,* and this censure of *Lancaster,* there is not one expression uttered by any character in the Drama that can be construed into any impeachment of *Falstaff's* Courage;—an observation made before as respecting some of the Witnesses;—it is now extended to all: And though this silence be a negative proof only, it cannot, in my opinion, under the circumstances of the case, and whilst uncontradicted by facts, be too much relied on. If *Falstaff* had been intended for the character of a *Miles Gloriosus*, his behaviour ought and therefore would have been commented upon by others. *Shakespeare* seldom trusts to the apprehensions of his audience; his characters interpret for one another continually, and when we least suspect such artful and secret management: The conduct of *Shakespeare* in this respect is admirable, and I could point out a thousand passages which might put to shame the advocates of a formal Chorus, and prove that there is as little of necessity as grace in so mechanic a contrivance.[1] But I confine my censure of the Chorus to its supposed use of comment and interpretation only.

Falstaff is, indeed, so far from appearing to my eye in the light of a *Miles Gloriosus*, that, in the best of my taste and judgment, he does not discover, except in consequence of the robbery, the least *trait* of such a character. All his boasting speeches are humour, mere humour, and carefully spoken to persons who cannot misapprehend them, who cannot be imposed on: They contain indeed, for the most part, an unreasonable and imprudent ridicule of himself, the usual subject of his good humoured merriment; but in the company of ignorant people, such as the Justices, or his own followers, he is remarkably reserved, and does not hazard any thing, even in the way of humour, that may be subject to mistake: Indeed he no where seems to suspect that his character is open to censure on this side, or that he needs the arts of imposition.—"*Turk Gregory never did* "*such deeds in arms as I have done this day*" is spoken, whilst he breathes from action, to the Prince in a tone of jolly humour, and contains nothing but a light ridicule of his own inactivity: This is as far from real boasting as his saying before the battle, "*Wou'd it were bed-time, Hal,* "*and all were well,*" is from meanness or depression. This articulated wish is not the fearful outcry of a *Coward*, but the frank and honest breathing of a *generous fellow*, who does not expect to be seriously reproached with the character. Instead, indeed, of deserving the name of a vain glorious *Coward*, his modesty perhaps on his head, and whimsical

---

[1] Ænobarbus, in Anthony and Cleopatra, is in effect the Chorus of the Play; as Menenius Agrippa is of Coriolanus.

ridicule of himself, have been a principal source of the imputation.

But to come to the very serious reproach thrown upon him by that *cold blooded* boy, as he calls him, *Lancaster.*— *Lancaster* makes a solemn treaty of peace with the *Archbishop of York, Mowbray,* &c. upon the faith of which they disperse their troops; which is no sooner done than *Lancaster* arrests the Principals, and pursues the *scattered stray*: A transaction, by the bye, so singularly perfidious, that I wish *Shakespeare,* for his own credit, had not suffered it to pass under his pen without marking it with the blackest strokes of Infamy.—During this transaction, *Falstaff* arrives, joins in the pursuit, and takes Sir *John Coleville* prisoner. Upon being seen by *Lancaster* he is thus addressed:—

> "Now, Falstaff, where have you been all this while?
> "When every thing is over, then you come:
> "These tardy tricks of yours will, on my life,
> "One time or other break some gallows' back."

This may appear to many a very formidable passage. It is spoken, as we may say, in the hearing of the army, and by one intitled as it were by his station to decide on military conduct; and if no punishment immediately follows, the forbearance may be imputed to a regard for the Prince of Wales, whose favour the delinquent was known so unworthily to possess. But this reasoning will by no means apply to the real circumstances of the case. The effect of this passage will depend on the credit we shall be inclined to give to *Lancaster* for integrity and candour, and still more upon the facts which are the ground of this censure, and which are fairly offered by *Shakespeare* to our notice.

We will examine the evidence arising from both; and to this end we must in the first place a little unfold the character of this young Commander in chief;—from a review of which we may more clearly discern the general impulses and secret motives of his conduct: And this is a proceeding which I think the peculiar character of *Shakespeare*'s Drama will very well justify.

We are already well prepared what to think of this young

man:—We have just seen a very pretty manœuvre of his in a matter of the highest moment, and have therefore the less reason to be surprized if we find him practising a more petty fraud with suitable skill and address. He appears in truth to have been what *Falstaff* calls him, *a cold, reserved, sober-blooded boy*; a politician, as it should seem, by nature; bred up moreover in the school of *Bolingbroke* his father, and tutored to betray: With sufficient courage and ability perhaps, but with too much of the knave in his composition, and too little of enthusiasm, ever to be a great and superior character. That such a youth as this should, even from the propensities of character alone, take any plausible occasion to injure a frank unguarded man of wit and pleasure, will not appear unnatural. But he had other inducements. *Falstaff* had given very general scandal by his distinguished wit and noted poverty, insomuch that a little cruelty and injustice towards him was likely to pass, in the eye of the grave and prudent part of mankind, as a very creditable piece of fraud, and to be accounted to *Lancaster* for virtue and good service. But *Lancaster* had motives yet more prevailing; *Falstaff* was a Favourite, without the power which belongs to that character; and the tone of the Court was strongly against him, as the misleader and corrupter of the Prince; who was now at too great a distance to afford him immediate countenance and protection. A scratch then, between jest and earnest as it were, something that would not too much offend the prince, yet would leave behind a disgraceful scar upon *Falstaff*, was very suitable to the temper and situation of parties and affairs. With these observations in our thought, let us return to the passage: It is plainly intended for disgrace, but how artful, how cautious, how insidious is the manner! It may pass for sheer pleasantry and humour: *Lancaster* assumes the familiar phrase and *girding* tone of *Harry*; and the gallows, as he words it, appears to be in the most danger from an encounter with *Falstaff*.—With respect to the matter, 'tis a kind of *miching malicho*; it means mischief indeed, but there is not precision enough in it to intitle it to the appellation of a formal charge, or to give to *Falstaff* any certain and determined ground of defence. *Tardy tricks* may mean not Cowardice but neglect only, though the *manner* may seem to carry the imputation to both.—The reply of *Falstaff* is exactly suited to the qualities of the speech;—for *Falstaff* never wants ability, but conduct only. He answers the general effect of this speech by a feeling and serious complaint of injustice; he then goes on to apply his defence to the vindication both of his diligence and courage; but he deserts by degrees his serious tone, and taking the handle of pleasantry which *Lancaster* had held forth to him, he is prudently content, as being sensible of *Lancaster*'s high rank and station, to let the whole pass off in buffoonery and humour. But the question is, however, not concerning the adroitness and management of either party: Our business is, after putting the credit of *Lancaster* out of the question, to discover what there may be of truth and of fact either in the charge of the one, or the defence of the other. From this only, we shall be able to draw our inferences with fairness and with candour. The charge against *Falstaff* is already in the possession of the reader: The defence follows.—

Fals. "*I would be sorry, my lord, but it should be thus:* "*I never knew yet but that rebuke and check were the re-* "*ward of valour. Do you think me a swallow, an arrow, or a* "*bullet? Have I in my poor and old motion the expedition of* "*thought? I speeded hither within the very extremest inch* "*of possibility. I have foundered ninescore and odd posts* "(deserting by degrees his serious tone, for *one* of more ad- "dress and advantage), *and here, travel-tainted as I am,* "*have I in my pure and immaculate valour taken Sir John* "*Coleville of the dale, a most furious Knight and valorous* "*enemy.*"

Falstaff's answer then is that he used all possible expedition to join the army; the not doing of which, with an implication of Cowardice as the cause, is the utmost extent of the charge against him; and to take off this implication he refers to the evidence of a fact present and manifest,— the surrender of *Coleville*; in whose hearing he speaks, and to whom therefore he is supposed to appeal. Nothing then remains but that we should inquire if *Falstaff*'s answer was really founded in truth; "*I speeded hither,*" says he, "*within* "*the extremest inch of possibility*": If it be so, he is justified: But I am afraid, for we must not conceal any thing, that *Falstaff* was really detained too long by his debaucheries in London; at least, if we take the Chief Justice's words very strictly.

Ch. Just. *"How now, Sir John? What are you brawling
"here? Doth this become your* PLACE, *your* TIME, *your*
"BUSINESS? *You should have been well on your way to*
"*York."*

Here then seems to be a delay worthy perhaps of rebuke;
and if we could suppose *Lancaster* to mean nothing more
by *tardy tricks* than idleness and debauch, I should not possibly think myself much concerned to vindicate *Falstaff*
from the charge; but the words imply, to my apprehension,
a designed and deliberate avoidance of danger. Yet to the
contrary of this we are furnished with very full and complete evidence. *Falstaff*, the moment he quits London, discovers the utmost eagerness and impatience to join the
army; he gives up his gluttony, his mirth, and his ease. We
see him take up in his passage some recruits at *Shallow*'s
house; and tho' he has pecuniary views upon *Shallow*, no
inducement stops him; he takes no refreshment, he cannot
tarry dinner, he hurries off; *"I will not,"* says he to the
Justices, *"use many words with you. Fare ye well, Gentle-
"men both; I thank ye, I must a dozen miles to night."*—
He misuses, it is true, at this time the *King's Press dam-
nably;* but that does not concern me, at least not for the
present; it belongs to other parts of his character.—It appears then manifestly that *Shakespeare* meant to shew *Falstaff* as really using the utmost speed in his power; he arrives
almost literally *within the extremest inch of possibility*; and
if *Lancaster* had not accelerated the event by a stroke of
perfidy much more subject to the imputation of Cowardice
than the *Debauch* of *Falstaff*, he would have been time
enough to have shared in the danger of a fair and honest
decision. But great men have, it seems, a privilege; *"that in
"the* General's *but a choleric word, which in the* Soldier
"were *flat blasphemy."* Yet after all, *Falstaff* did really come
time enough, as it appears, to join in the villainous triumphs
of the day, to take prisoner *Coleville of the dale, a most
furious Knight and valorous enemy*.—Let us look to the
fact. If this incident should be found to contain any striking
proof of *Falstaff*'s Courage and Military fame, his defence
against *Lancaster* will be stronger than the reader has even
a right to demand. *Falstaff* encounters *Coleville* in the field,
and; having demanded his name, is ready to assail him; but
Coleville asks him if he is not Sir *John Falstaff;* thereby

implying a purpose of surrender. *Falstaff* will not so much as furnish him with a pretence, and answers only, that *he is as good a man.* "Do you yield Sir, or shall I swear for "you?"' "I think," says Coleville, "you are Sir John Falstaff, "and in that thought yield me." This fact, and the incidents with which it is accompanied, speak loudly; it seems to have been contrived by the author on purpose to take off a rebuke so authoritatively made by *Lancaster*. The fact is set before our eyes to confute the censure: *Lancaster* himself seems to give up his charge, tho' not his ill will; for upon *Falstaff*'s asking leave to pass through Glostershire, and artfully desiring that, upon *Lancaster*'s return to Court, *he might stand well in his report*, *Lancaster* seems in his answer to mingle malice and acquittal. *"Fare ye well, Fal-* "staff, I in my condition shall better speak of you than you "deserve." "I would," says *Falstaff*, who is left behind in the scene, "You had but the wit; 'twere better than your Duke-"dom." He continues on the stage some time chewing the cud of dishonour, which, with all his facility, he cannot well swallow. "Good faith," says he, accounting to himself as well as he could for the injurious conduct of *Lancaster*, "this "sober-blooded boy does not love me." This he might well believe. "A man," says he, "cannot make him laugh; there's "none of these demure boys come to any proof; but that's no "marvel, they drink no sack."—*Falstaff* then it seems knew no drinker of sack who was a Coward; at least the instance was not home and familiar to him.—"They all," says he, "fall into a kind of Male green sickness, and are generally "fools and Cowards." Anger has a privilege, and I think *Falstaff* has a right to turn the tables upon *Lancaster* if he can; but *Lancaster* was certainly no fool, and I think upon the whole no Coward; yet the Male green sickness which *Falstaff* talks of seems to have infected his manners and aspect, and taken from him all external indication of gallantry and courage. He behaves in the battle of Shrewsbury beyond the promise of his complexion and deportment: *"By* "heaven thou hast deceived me Lancaster," says Harry, "I "did not think thee Lord of such a spirit!" Nor was his father less surprized "at his holding Lord Percy at the point "with lustier maintenance than he did look for from such "an unripe warrior." But how well and unexpectedly soever he might have behaved upon that occasion, he does not seem to have been of a temper to trust fortune too much or too often with his safety; therefore it is that, in order to keep the event in his own hands, he loads the Die, in the present case, with villainy and deceit: The event however he piously ascribes, like a wise and prudent youth as he is, without paying that worship to himself which he so justly merits, to the special favour and interposition of Heaven.

> *"Strike up your drums, pursue the scattered stray.*
> *"Heaven, and not we, have safely fought to-day."*

But the profane *Falstaff,* on the contrary, less informed and less studious of supernatural things, imputes the whole of this conduct to thin potations, and the not drinking largely of good and excellent *sherris*; and so little doubt does he seem to entertain of the Cowardice and ill disposition of this youth, that he stands devising causes, and casting about for an hypothesis on which the whole may be physically explained and accounted for;—but I shall leave him and Doctor *Cadogan* to settle that point as they may.

The only serious charge against *Falstaff*'s Courage, we have now at large examined; it came from great authority, from the Commander in chief, and was meant as chastisement and rebuke; but it appears to have been founded in ill-will, in the particular character of *Lancaster,* and in the wantonness and insolence of power; and the author has placed near, and under our notice, full and ample proofs of its injustice.—And thus the deeper we look unto *Falstaff*'s character, the stronger is our conviction that he was not intended to be shewn as a Constitutional coward: Censure cannot lay sufficient hold on him,—and even malice turns away, and more than half pronounces his acquittal.

But as yet we have dealt principally in parole and circumstantial evidence, and have referred to *Fact* only incidentally. But *Facts* have a much more operative influence: They may be produced, not as arguments only, but Records; not to dispute alone, but to decide.—It is time then to behold *Falstaff* in actual service as a soldier, in danger, and in battle. We have already displayed one fact in his defence against the censure of *Lancaster*; a fact extremely unequivocal and decisive. But the reader knows I have others, and doubtless goes before me to the action at *Shrewsbury*. In the midst and in the heat of battle we see him come forwards;—what are his words? *"I have led my "Rag-o-muffians where they are peppered; there's not three "of my hundred and fifty left alive."* But to *whom* does he say this? To himself only; he speaks *in soliloquy*. There is no questioning the fact, *he had* led *them; they were peppered; there were not* three *left alive*. He was in luck, being in bulk equal to any two of them, to escape unhurt. Let the author answer for that, I have nothing to do with it: He was the Poetic maker of the whole *Corps,* and he might dispose of them as he pleased. Well might the Chief justice, as we now find, acknowledge *Falstaff*'s services in this day's battle; an acknowledgment which amply confirms the fact. A Modern officer, who had performed a feat of this kind, would expect, not only the praise of having done his duty, but the appellation of a hero. But poor *Falstaff* has too much wit to thrive: In spite of probability, in spite of inference, in spite of fact, he must be a Coward still. He happens unfortunately to have more Wit than Courage, and therefore we are maliciously determined that he shall have no Courage at all. But let us suppose that his modes of expression, even *in soliloquy*, will admit of some abatement; —how much shall we abate? Say that he brought off *fifty* instead of *three*; yet a Modern captain would be apt to look big after an action with two thirds of his men, as it were, in his belly. Surely *Shakespeare* never meant to exhibit this man as a Constitutional coward; if he did, his means were sadly destructive of his end. We see him, after he had expended his Rag-o-muffians, with sword and target in the midst of battle, in perfect possession of himself, and replete with humour and jocularity. He was, I presume, in some immediate personal danger, in danger also of a general defeat; too corpulent for flight; and to be led a prisoner was probably to be led to execution; yet we see him laughing and easy, offering a bottle of sack to the Prince instead of a pistol, punning, and telling him, *"there was that which "would sack a city."*—*"What, is it a time,"* says the Prince, *"to jest and dally now?"* No, a sober character would not jest on such an occasion, but a Coward could not; he would neither have the inclination, or the power. And what could support *Falstaff* in such a situation? Not principle; he is not suspected of the Point of honour; he seems indeed fairly to renounce it. *"Honour cannot set a leg or an arm; it has "no skill in surgery:—What is it? a word only; meer air. It "is insensible to the dead; and detraction will not let it live "with the living."* What then but a strong natural constitutional Courage, which nothing could extinguish or dismay? —In the following passages the true character of *Falstaff* as to Courage and Principle is finely touched, and the different colours at once nicely blended and distinguished. *"If "Percy be alive, I'll* pierce *him. If he do come in my way, "*so:*—If he do not, if I come in his willingly, let him make a "Carbonado of me. I like not such grinning honour as Sir "Walter hath; give me life; which if I can save,* so; *if not, "honour comes unlook'd for, and there's an end."* One cannot say which prevails most here, profligacy or courage; they are both tinged alike by the same humour, and mingled in one common mass; yet when we consider the superior force of *Percy,* as we must presently also that of *Douglas,* we shall be apt, I believe, in our secret heart, to forgive him. These passages are spoken in soliloquy and in battle: If every soliloquy made under similar circumstances were as audible as *Falstaff*'s, the imputation might perhaps be found too general for censure. These are among the passages that have impressed on the world an idea of Cowardice in *Falstaff;*—yet why? He is resolute to take his fate: If *Percy* do come in his way, *so;*—if not, he will not seek inevitable destruction; he is willing to save his life, but if that cannot be, why,—"honour comes unlook'd for, and there's an end." This surely is not the language of Cowardice: It contains neither the Bounce or Whine of the character; he derides, it is true, and seems to renounce that grinning idol of Military zealots, *Honour.* But *Falstaff* was a kind of Military free-thinker, and has accordingly incurred the obloquy of his condition. He stands upon the ground of natural Courage only and common sense, and has, it seems, too much wit for a hero.—But let me be well understood;—I do not justify *Falstaff* for renouncing the point of honour; it proceeded doubtless from a general relaxation of mind, and profligacy of temper. Honour is calculated to aid and strengthen natural courage, and lift it up to heroism; but natural courage, which can act as such without honour, is natural courage still; the very quality I wish to maintain to *Falstaff*. And if, without the aid of honour, he can act with firmness, his portion is only the more eminent and distinguished. In such a character, it is to his actions, not his sentiments, that we are to look for conviction. But it may be still further urged in behalf of *Falstaff*, that there may be false honour as well as false religion. It is true; yet even in that case candour obliges me to confess that the best men are most disposed to conform, and most likely to become the dupes of their own virtue. But it may however be more reasonably urged that there are particular tenets both in honour and religion, which it is the grossness of folly not to question. To seek out, to court assured destruction, without leaving a single benefit behind, may be well reckoned in the number: And this is precisely the very folly which *Falstaff* seems to abjure;—nor are we, perhaps, intitled to say more, in the way of censure, than that he had not virtue enough to become the dupe of honour, nor prudence enough to hold his tongue. I am willing however, if the reader pleases, to compound this matter, and acknowledge, on my part, that *Falstaff* was in all respects the *old soldier*; that he had put himself under the sober discipline of discretion, and renounced, in a great degree at least, what he might call the Vanities and Superstitions of honour; if the reader will, on his part, admit that this might well be, without his renouncing, at the same time, the natural firmness and resolution he was born to. . . .

J. I. M. STEWART

J. I. M. Stewart (1906-   ). Student of Christ Church, Oxford. Author of Character and Motive in Shakespeare *(1949),* Eight Modern Writers *(1963), and, under the name Michael Innes, of many novels and radio programmes, including some on Shakespeare.*

THE REJECTION OF FALSTAFF*

... The little tour we have just concluded should at least give us the main terms of the problem, a problem adumbrated by Nicholas Rowe in 1709 when he wrote of Falstaff:

> [Shakespeare] has given him so múch Wit as to make him almost too agreeable; and I don't know whether some People have not, in remembrance of the Diversion he had formerly afforded 'em, been sorry to see his Friend *Hal* use him so scurvily, when he comes to the Crown in the End of the Second Part of *Henry* the Fourth.

The "scurvy" treatment of Falstaff is quite in keeping with a certain insensibility in the Elizabethans which appears in many gulling scenes on the stage. But we are liable to feel it not consonant either with Shakespeare's humanity to a major creation, or with the sympathy and admiration which must surely be claimed from us for Hal, a character who is being "groomed" (as the studios say) for the field of Agincourt. We may now consider more at large certain efforts at a solution of the problem.

Can we find some light in which the rejection of Falstaff commends itself to our sympathies while operating wholly within the sphere of psychological realism? I must say in advance that I think the answer to be "No." All through the trilogy there are penetrations enough into a deeper Harry Monmouth, and the rejection can be analysed in terms of these. But, by and large, I think something profounder is operating here than Shakespeare's understanding of the son of Henry Bolingbroke. There are times in all drama when immemorial forces come into play, and with the end of Falstaff we touch once more what Professor Schücking is fond of calling the limits of Shakespearian realism.

In terms of essential drama Falstaff's rejection and death are very important—indeed they are the end of the whole business. Falstaff's corner of *Henry V* is extremely won-

* From *Character and Motive in Shakespeare*. The title here given is that of a famous essay by A. L. Bradley, mentioned in the text; the topic, as Mr. Stewart shows, is old.

derful; the rest is a slack-water play, stirred here and there by simple patriotic feeling. For comedy now Shakespeare had so little list that he fell back upon comic Scots, Irish and Welshmen—the resource, I think I may say, of a professional entertainer hard pressed indeed. Moreover, that the poet of *Romeo and Juliet* should have executed the wooing of Katharine—that *ne plus ultra* of all obtuseness—must fill us with dismay until we persuade ourselves (with a school of critics romantic, no doubt) that there here glints at us from behind the mask the master's most inscrutable smile. In a word, all this matter ends for Shakespeare with Falstaff and not with a foreign conquest; and there must be reason for this.

And first there is Bradley, whose acknowledgment of the uncomfortableness of the rejection is emphatic. If we have enjoyed the Falstaff scenes (and Shakespeare surely meant them to be enjoyed), we feel a good deal of pain and some resentment when Henry first turns upon his old companion with talk like a clergyman's and then sends back the Chief Justice to commit him to prison; nor are our regrets diminished when, in *Henry V*, it is powerfully suggested to us that Falstaff has, in fact, died of wounded affection. Why did Shakespeare end his drama with a scene which, though undoubtedly striking, leaves an impression so unpleasant?

What troubles us is not only the disappointment of Falstaff—it is the conduct of Henry. Shakespeare might surely have so arranged the matter that "the King could have communicated his decision, and Falstaff could have accepted it, in a private interview rich in humour and merely touched with pathos." Instead, we are given something both ungenerous and insincere—for with what colour can this strong and independent prince, whose wildness (or appearance of it) has by his own confession been matter of deliberate policy, speak either of Falstaff as the tutor and the feeder of his riots, or of Falstaff's inconsiderable followers as his misleaders? Part, surely, of the explanation of our discomfort must be this: that we have misread both the Prince's character and Shakespeare's attitude to character in general. We conventionalise Shakespeare by expecting him to mark his approval or disapproval of characters, and even by expecting him to divide them into simple sheep and goats; if he is impartial he disconcerts us; if he does *not* make sign of disapproval we neglect the possibility of his nevertheless disapproving—and so we blame him for indifference. And in this particular place:

> Our fault lies not in our resentment at Henry's conduct but in our surprise at it; . . . if we had read his character truly in the light that Shakespeare gave us, we should have been prepared for a display both of hardness and of policy at this point in his career.

Both as prince and as king Henry is deservedly a favourite, but a strong strain of policy has been evident in him from the first, as has an incapacity for any warmth of personal relations outside his own family. Thus his conduct in rejecting Falstaff proves on scrutiny to be in perfect keeping with his character on its unpleasant side, as well as on that finer side which leads him to dedicate himself to kingship.

But all this—Bradley continues—will not solve the problem. For we are left supposing that Shakespeare *intended* us to feel resentment against Henry, and this cannot be. It follows that he must have designed our sympathy with Falstaff to be so far weakened that we should accept the rejection and pass lightly over that disclosure of unpleasant traits in the King's character which the poet's artistry would not let him suppress. The conclusion of this part of the argument is clear:

> Thus our pain and resentment, if we feel them, are wrong, in the sense that they do not answer to the dramatist's intention. But it does not follow that they are wrong in a further sense. They may be right, because the dramatist has missed what he aimed at. And this, though the dramatist was Shakespeare, is what I would suggest. In the Falstaff scenes he overshot his mark. He created so extraordinary a being, and fixed him so firmly on his intellectual throne, that when he sought to dethrone him he could not. The moment comes when we are to look at Falstaff in a serious light, and the comic hero is to figure as a baffled schemer; but we cannot make the required change, either in our attitude or in our sympathies.

So in what, we are now asked, essentially consists Falstaff's indefeasible attractiveness? The bliss of freedom gained in humour is the essence of him. He denies that life is real or life is earnest, and delivers us from the oppression of such nightmares, and lifts us into an atmosphere of perfect freedom—as for example when he maintains untouched, in the face of imminent peril and even when he *feels* the fear of death, the very same power of dissolving it in persiflage that he shows when he sits at ease in his inn. Again, his lies are not designed to win serious conviction; there is nothing serious in any of them except the refusal to take anything seriously. And again, his cowardice and running away are presented as the characteristics rather of one who has risen superior to all serious motives than of one who is, in the ordinary sense, a coward.

But although the main source, then, of our sympathetic delight in Falstaff is his humorous superiority to everything serious, and the freedom of soul enjoyed in it, yet this, of course, is not the whole of his character. His godlike freedom has consequences and conditions; he cannot eat and drink for ever without money; and so he is driven to evil deeds—and these in themselves make an ugly picture. Now, *Henry IV* was to be in the main a historical play, and its chief hero Prince Henry. Falstaff at last *must* be disgraced, and must therefore appear no longer as the invincible humorist, but as an object of ridicule and even of aversion. Shakespeare's purpose being thus to work a gradual change in our feelings towards him, and to tinge the humorous atmosphere more and more deeply with seriousness, we see him carrying out this purpose in the Second Part. Here he separates the Prince from Falstaff as much as he can, and exhibits more and more of the knight's seamy side: the heartless destroyer of Mrs. Quickly, the ruffian seriously defying the Chief Justice, the pike preparing to snap up the poor old dace Shallow, the worn-out lecher. Yet all this fails of its effect, and could have succeeded only had Shakespeare resigned himself to clouding over or debasing the humour of Falstaff. This he was too much of an artist to do, and so he does not succeed in changing our sympathy into repulsion. Shakespeare, in fact, was caught up on the wind of his own genius, and carried so far that he could not

descend to earth at the selected spot. And yet the issue is
not finally to be regretted very much:

> To show that Falstaff's freedom of soul was in part
> illusory, and that the realities of life refused to be con-
> jured away by his humour—this was what we might ex-
> pect from Shakespeare's unfailing sanity, but it was surely
> no achievement beyond the power of lesser men. The
> achievement was Falstaff himself, and the conception of
> that freedom of soul, a freedom illusory only in part, and
> attainable only by a mind which had received from
> Shakespeare's own the inexplicable touch of infinity
> which he bestowed on Hamlet and Macbeth and Cleo-
> patra, but denied to Henry the Fifth.

There is so much of suggestion in Bradley's essay that
more than one critic has found in it a starting-point for
reflections of his own. Thus the germ of Professor Charlton's interpretation is essentially in the notion "that Falstaff's freedom of soul was in part illusory, and that the
realities of life refused to be conjured away by his humour"
—or in this and an earlier statement of Bradley's that, like
no other Shakespearian character, "Falstaff was degraded
by Shakespeare himself."

In *The Merry Wives of Windsor* Shakespeare, as it were,
reconventionalises Falstaff; turns him so decidedly into a
gull and a buffoon that the thing is like a rejection in itself,
or a manifesto of complete eventual disinterest in the character. Why does Shakespeare, even more cruelly than
Henry, thus trample Falstaff into extinction? Because,
Charlton says, Falstaff had let Shakespeare down. Falstaff
revealed himself as being not what Shakespeare sought: an
adequate comic hero, equipped for the true freedom of the
world of comedy. And this letting Shakespeare down seems
to have provoked a positive animus in the poet against his
creation. Not only did it produce the "ruthless exposure,
[the] almost malicious laceration" of the *Merry Wives*; it is
the reason why Falstaff was not gently dismissed on some
pre-coronation deathbed, but brutally in "a scene which has
aroused more repugnance than any other in Shakespeare,"
and as a result of actions in Henry which are "an offence

against humanity, and an offence which dramatically never becomes a skill."

What, then, according to this theory, is that true nature of a comic hero to which Falstaff fails to measure up? Since a comedy is a play which ends happily its hero, we are told, must be

> likely to overcome whatever impediments to his well-being may be presented by the episodes of the play; and these episodes . . . must be representative of the obstacles which, in experience at large, are presented to man in the dilemmas inherent in more or less normal encounters with the world as the world is.

The comic hero, in fact, "must be endowed with the temperament and the arts to triumph over the stresses of circumstance." Now, Falstaff is insatiably curious to provide situations which test or even strain his genius for overcoming them. Mastery of circumstance is his pride—and so superficially he is an incomparable comic hero. But on a deeper view his attitude or philosophy is inadequate to cope with life even within that scope of worldly wisdom which is the philosophy of comedy. In the scene which a mature comedy must contemplate there are forces which Falstaff's measuring-stick cannot measure, and

> the world in which Falstaff's successors in comedy would have to prove their genius for mastery, would necessarily have to be a larger and a richer world than Falstaff's.

Hence Falstaff's failure, and Shakespeare's ruthless writing of him off.

If there is anything in the argument I have earlier advanced—to wit, that the major creations of a dramatist represent so many possible blendings or equilibriums of the abundant raw materials of personality which are his in virtue of his artist's nature—we must regard Charlton's argument as of considerable interest. But whatever be the dynamics of dramatic creation it would surely be extravagant to suggest that the artist's various progeny represent so many tentative essays in self-improvement—the bad shots among which he will then be prompted to "trample into extinction." For the dramatist is quite plainly not seeking about for an exemplar; rather he is like a pagan constructing a pantheon in which there shall be variously reflected the many sides of his own nature; and his satisfaction is simply in creation and in abundance. Thus such a psychological theory as I have hinted at affords no reason to suppose that Shakespeare would be particularly prone to turn upon Falstaff and disown or destroy him. If, on the other hand, we eschew psychology and stick to aesthetics, and with Charlton view Shakespeare's problem simply as one within the theory of comedy, we may believe indeed that Shakespeare might lose interest in Falstaff, but not that he would harry him. And it is just our sense of a persecution that has to be explained. Bradley's is still, perhaps, the best explanation: our having this sense results from Shakespeare's tailing of his intention to manœuvre Falstaff into an unsympathetic light. But is there anything more to be said?

Obviously, one possibility remains. Shakespeare *succeeded* in manœuvring Falstaff into an unsympathetic light. If, with Bradley, we feel otherwise, we are being sentimental, un-Elizabethan, and disregardful of the fortunes of Falstaff as the drama develops. This is the contention of Professor Dover Wilson.

That Shakespeare himself rejected Falstaff is nonsense, Dover Wilson says; in the Epilogue to *Henry IV* he promised more of him, and if, instead, *Henry V* gave an account of his death this was simply the best way of dealing with the awkward fact that Will Kempe, who created the part, had left the Lord Chamberlain's men. Thus all that falls to be considered is the propriety and dramatic fitness of Henry's dismissing Falstaff in the way he does. In discussing Falstaff, therefore, Dover Wilson would hold within the bounds of the two parts of *Henry IV*; and his case is that we should mark at once their unity and—more adequately than Bradley—their presentation of a Falstaff who by no means remains the same person throughout. His status changes. As a result of ludicrous deception, and quite without any deserving, he becomes a person of altogether more consideration than he was at first. This rise in his fortunes—from something like "the prince's jester," "an allowed fool" or a "rascally old camp-follower," to one generally supposed the vanquisher of Hotspur—discovers him to be arrogant and overweening; and these traits if they are not obscured to us do in fact alienate our sympathies. Moreover Shakespeare's dramatic intention is perfectly clear if we do not, like Bradley who ignores the serial character of dramatic representation, construct our own portrait of Falstaff almost entirely from the first part of the play. If we really *follow* the play we shall find that though Falstaff's wit grows no less fascinating he comes to inspire less and less affection. And this is enough to render the rejection palatable—always supposing that we remember another relevant fact, to the exposition of which Dover Wilson devotes much space. The story of the Prodigal Prince and his Misleader is, at a certain important level, a Morality. It is the Morality of a Ruler who has to make choice between Vanity and Government; it is "a Tudor version of a time-honoured theme," in which "the forces of iniquity were allowed full play upon the stage, including a good deal of horse-play, provided they were brought to nought, or safely locked up in Hell, at the end." So must not Falstaff, then, be locked up in the Fleet? The fact is that

the Falstaff-Hal plot embodies a composite myth which had been centuries amaking, and was for the Elizabethans full of meaning that has largely disappeared since then. . . . They [the audience] knew, from the beginning, that the reign of this marvellous Lord of Misrule must have an end, that Falstaff must be rejected by the Prodigal Prince, when the time for reformation came. . . . Prince Hal and Falstaff, for us merely characters in a play, were for the Elizabethans that and a great deal more. They embodied in dramatic form a miscellaneous congeries of popular notions and associations, almost all since gone out of mind, in origin quasi-historical or legendary, pagan and Christian, ethical and political, theatrical, topographical and even gastronomic.

In other words, the Falstaff-Hal story subsumes divers traditional significances for the most part already embodied in drama, and the rejection scene is unexceptionable to an audience aware of and properly balancing these. Thus Falstaff partakes of the character not only of the *miles gloriosus* of Latin comedy, of the Devil of the Miracle Plays, of the Vice of the Moralities, of the traditional boon-companion of Henry, of the historical Oldcastle and Fastolfe; he partakes too of the character of Riot in the early Tudor interludes, and in one of these—*The Enterlude of Youth*—he is quite remarkably paralleled. This little play

> opens with a dialogue between Youth and Charity. The young man, heir to his father's land, gives insolent expression to his self-confidence, lustihood, and contempt for spiritual things. Whereupon Charity leaves him, and he is joined by Riot, that is to say wantonness, who presently introduces him to Pride and Lechery. The dialogue then becomes boisterous, and continues in that vein for some time, much no doubt to the enjoyment of the audience. Yet, in the end, Charity reappears with Humility; Youth repents; and the interlude terminates in the most seemly fashion imaginable. . . .
>
> Riot, like Falstaff, escapes from tight corners with a quick dexterity; like Falstaff, commits robbery on the highway; like Falstaff, jests immediately afterwards with his young friend on the subject of hanging; and like Falstaff, invites him to spend the stolen money at a tavern, where, he promises, "We will drink diuers wine" and "Thou shalt have a wench to kysse Whansoeuer thou wilte"; allurements which prefigure the Boar's Head and Mistress Doll Tearsheet.

Riot, then, "prefigures" Falstaff, and the Tudor attitude to Riot must be taken into account when we come to consider the discomfiture of the knight.

What Dover Wilson is really providing here, it might be maintained, is a sort of second line of defence. As a person, or character in a drama realistically conceived, Falstaff is gradually so developed that we are not disturbed at seeing him turned off by another character carefully developed in terms of the same sort of realistic drama. But if we *are* disturbed we are to recall that this representation has a sort of abstract or allegorical quality as well, and fortify ourselves by considering "what would have followed had the Prince chosen Vanity instead of Government, Falstaff and not the

Lord Chief Justice." Is this an illogical way of tackling the problem, arguing both for the psychological integrity of the drama and for an overriding myth which the characters must obey? It seems to me an explanation not much contrary to the logic of the theatre, where actions and situations have frequently more than one significance, and where these significances are often at an obscure interplay. Shakespeare's characters, I think, are nearly always real human beings before they are anything else; but undeniably they *are* at times something else: they take on the simpler rôles of archetypal drama; and then there will be "edges" (as the painters say) between generic character and psychological portraiture which the dramatist must cope with, using what finesse he can. It seems to me, therefore, that Dover Wilson gets furthest with the problem; and I am only concerned to wonder whether a further stone or two may yet be added to the edifice he has raised.

Two points would seem to be significant. If Shakespeare does indeed succeed in making the rejection palatable to persons adequately aware of traditional matters lying behind the play, it is yet in the theatre that he does so, for that the thing continues to *read* uncomfortably after all that Dover Wilson has to say I believe there will be few to deny. What does this mean? It means that although Shakespeare doubtless relied on certain contemporary attitudes to Riot and the like, he relied even more on something perennially generated in the consciousness or disposition of an audience in a theatre—whether they belong to Elizabethan times or to our own. And it is here that I would knit the debate on Falstaff to the theme of the present book. For what I have tried to urge is simply this: that in the interpretation of Shakespeare a study of the psychology of poetic drama (which leads us to understand his *medium*) is at least as important as a study of the contemporary climate of opinion (which gives simply *conditions* under which he worked).

The second point concerns the emphatic and wonderful account in *Henry V* of the death of Falstaff. It is all very well for Dover Wilson to point to the promise of more Falstaff made in the Epilogue to *2 Henry IV* and infer that the subsequent death was a matter of mere theatrical convenience. But surely the Epilogue to *Henry IV* is dramatically altogether less authoritative than the account of Falstaff's passing in the later play; and what Shakespeare there wrote appears to me (because it is so wonderful) much less like an expedient dictated by changes in personnel in his company than the issue of his reflections on the inner significance of what had happened at the close of the earlier drama. "The King has kild his heart," says Mistress Quickly as Falstaff lies dying. "The King hath run bad humors on the Knight," says Nym, and Pistol at once responds: "*Nym, thou hast spoke the right, his heart is fracted and corroborate.*" None of these worthies would cut much of a figure in a witness-box; nevertheless there is no mistaking the dramatic function of the three consenting voices. The truth of the matter is summed here; there follows the new king's dexterous, necessary but none too pleasant entrapping of Cambridge, Scroope and Gray; then comes the tremendous account of Falstaff's end—and after that we are set for Agincourt and the regeneration and triumph of England. It is of set purpose, then, that the rejection of Falstaff is so resounding, so like a killing. And the reverberation of that purpose sounds here in *Henry V.* What is it? There is an allegorical purpose, Dover Wilson says, and with this I agree. But I think, too, that among the "notions and associations . . . gone out of mind" embodied in this "composite myth which had been centuries amaking" there conceivably lies something deeper, something which belongs equally with drama and with magic.

When Shakespeare makes Falstaff die "ev'n just betweene Twelve and One, ev'n at the turning o' th' Tyde," he is touching a superstition, immemorial not only along the east coast of England from Northumberland to Kent but in many other parts of the world too—one shared by Dickens's Mr. Peggotty (who speaks of it expressly) and the Haidas on the Pacific coast of North America. But there is more of magic about Falstaff than this; and Dover Wilson, whom the editing of Shakespeare has schooled in a fine awareness of the reverberations of English words, is more than once well on the scent. "How doth the Martlemas, your Master?" Poins asks Bardolph. And Dover Wilson comments:

Martlemas, or the feast of St Martin, on 11 November, was in those days of scarce fodder the season at which most of the beasts had to be killed off and salted for the winter, and therefore the season for great banquets of fresh meat. Thus it had been for centuries, long before the coming of Christianity. In calling him a "Martlemas" Poins is at once likening Falstaff's enormous proportions to the prodigality of fresh-killed meat which the feast brought, and acclaiming his identity with Riot and Festivity in general.

Falstaff, in fact, is the "sweet beef," "the roasted Manning-tree ox with the pudding in his belly," who reigns supreme on the board of the Boar's Head in Eastcheap—"a London tavern . . . almost certainly even better known for good food than for good drink." There is thus from the first a symbolical side to his vast and genuine individuality; and again and again the imagery in which he is described likens him to a whole larder of "fat meat."

'Call in Ribs, call in Tallow' is Hal's cue for Falstaff's entry in the first great Boar's Head scene; and what summons to the choicest feast in comedy could be more apt? For there is the noblest of English dishes straightaway: Sir John as roast Sir Loin-of-Beef, gravy and all.

Is it not—I find myself asking—as if the "brawn," Sir John, "the sow that hath overwhelmed all her litter but one," were some vast creature singled out from the herd and dedicated to a high festival indeed? But such festivals commemorate more than the need to reduce stock against a winter season. They commemorate a whole mythology of the cycle of the year, and of sacrifices offered to secure a new fertility in the earth.

Now, anthropologists are always telling us of countries gone waste and barren under the rule of an old, impotent and guilty king, who must be ritually slain and supplanted by his son or another before the saving rains can come bringing purification and regeneration to the land. Is not Henry IV in precisely the situation of this king? Dover Wilson avers that it is so, without any thought of magical implication:

. . . his reign and all his actions are overhung with the

consciousness . . . of personal guilt . . . a fact that Shakespeare never misses an opportunity of underlining. . . . We see him first at the beginning of act 3 crushed beneath the disease that afflicts his body and the no less grievous diseases that make foul the body of his kingdom.

Perhaps, then, we glimpse here a further reason why the rejection of Falstaff is inevitable—not merely traditionally and moralistically inevitable but symbolically inevitable as well. And this may be why, when in the theatre, we do not really rebel against the rejection; why we find a fitness too in its being sudden and catastrophic. As long as we are in the grip of drama it is profoundly fit that Hal, turning king and clergyman at once, should run bad humours on the knight, should kill his heart. For the killing carries something of the ritual suggestion, the obscure *pathos*, of death in tragedy.

I suggest that Hal, by a displacement common enough in the evolution of ritual, kills Falstaff instead of killing the king, his father. In a sense Falstaff *is* his father; certainly is a "father-substitute" in the psychologist's word; and this makes the theory of a vicarious sacrifice the more colourable. All through the play there is a strong implicit parallelism between Henry Bolingbroke and his policies and Falstaff and *his* policies; and at one point in the play the two fathers actually, as it were, fuse (like Leonardo's two mothers in his paintings of the Virgin and St. Anne), and in the Boar's Head tavern King Falstaff sits on his throne while his son Prince Henry kneels before him. And Falstaff, in standing for the old king, symbolises all the accumulated sin of the reign, all the consequent sterility of the land. But the young king draws his knife at the altar—and the heart of that grey iniquity, that father ruffian, is as fracted and corroborate as Pistol avers. Falstaff's rejection and death are very sad, but Sir James Frazer would have classed them with the Periodic Expulsion of Evils in a Material Vehicle, and discerned beneath the skin of Shakespeare's audience true brothers of the people of Leti, Moa and Lakor.

If this addition of another buried significance to the composite myth of Hal and Falstaff should seem extravagant, or an injudicious striving after Morgann's "lightness of air," let it be remembered that drama, like religious ritual, plays upon atavic impulses of the mind. All true drama penetrates through representative fiction to the condition of myth. And Falstaff is in the end the dethroned and sacrificed king, the scapegoat as well as the sweet beef. For Falstaff, so Bacchic, so splendidly with the Maenads Doll and Mistress Quickly a creature of the wine-cart and the cymbal, so fit a sacrifice (as Hal early discerns) to lard the lean, the barren earth, is of the primitive and magical world upon which all art, even if with a profound unconsciousness, draws.

THE TRAGEDIES

CHARLES LAMB

Charles Lamb (1775-1834). Lamb was deeply interested in the Elizabethan and Jacobean drama, and helped to revive interest in it. His views on the unsuitability of the tragedies to theatrical performance persisted, and Bradley echoed him on Lear.

ON THE TRAGEDIES*

It may seem a paradox, but I cannot help being of opinion that the plays of Shakspeare are less calculated for performance on a stage, than those of almost any other dramatist whatever. Their distinguished excellence is a reason that they should be so. There is so much in them, which comes not under the province of acting, with which eye, and tone, and gesture, have nothing to do.

The glory of the scenic art is to personate passion, and the turns of passion; and the more coarse and palpable the passion is, the more hold upon the eyes and ears of the spectators the performer obviously possesses. For this reason, scolding scenes, scenes where two persons talk them-

* From 'On the Tragedies of Shakespeare', 1811.

selves into a fit of fury, and then in a surprising manner talk themselves out of it again, have always been the most popular upon our stage. And the reason is plain, because the spectators are here most palpably appealed to, they are the proper judges in this war of words, they are the legitimate ring that should be formed round such "intellectual prize-fighters." Talking is the direct object of the imitation here. But in all the best dramas, and in Shakspeare above all, how obvious it is, that the form of *speaking,* whether it be in soliloquy or dialogue, is only a medium, and often a highly artificial one, for putting the reader or spectator into possession of that knowledge of the inner structure and workings of mind in a character, which he could otherwise never have arrived at *in that form of composition* by any gift short of intuition. We do here as we do with novels written in the *epistolary form.* How many improprieties, perfect solecisms in letter-writing, do we put up with in Clarissa and other books, for the sake of the delight which that form upon the whole gives us.

But the practice of stage representation reduces every thing to a controversy of elocution. Every character, from the boisterous blasphemings of Bajazet to the shrinking timidity of womanhood, must play the orator. The love-dialogues of Romeo and Juliet, those silver-sweet sounds of lovers' tongues by night; the more intimate and sacred sweetness of nuptial colloquy between an Othello or a Posthumus with their married wives, all those delicacies which are so delightful in the reading, as when we read of those youthful dalliances in Paradise—

As beseem'd
Fair couple link'd in happy nuptial league,
Alone:

by the inherent fault of stage representation, how are these things sullied and turned from their very nature by being exposed to a large assembly; when such speeches as Imogen addresses to her lord, come drawling out of the mouth of a hired actress, whose courtship, though nominally addressed to the personated Posthumus, is manifestly aimed at the spectators, who are to judge of her endearments and her returns of love.

The character of Hamlet is perhaps that by which, since the days of Betterton, a succession of popular performers have had the greatest ambition to distinguish themselves. The length of the part may be one of their reasons. But for the character itself, we find it in a play, and therefore we judge it a fit subject of dramatic representation. The play itself abounds in maxims and reflexions beyond any other, and therefore we consider it as a proper vehicle for conveying moral instruction. But Hamlet himself—what does he suffer meanwhile by being dragged forth as a public schoolmaster, to give lectures to the crowd! Why, nine parts in ten of what Hamlet does, are transactions between himself and his moral sense, they are effusions of his solitary musings, which he retires to holes and corners and the most sequestered parts of the palace to pour forth; or rather, they are the silent meditations with which his bosom is bursting, reduced to *words* for the sake of the reader, who must else remain ignorant of what is passing there. These profound sorrows, these light-and-noise-abhorring ruminations, which the tongue scarce dares utter to deaf walls and chambers, how can they be represented by a gesticulating actor, who comes and mouths them out before an audience, making four hundred people his confidants at once? I say not that it is the fault of the actor so to do; he must pronounce them *ore rotundo,* he must accompany them with his eye, he must insinuate them into his auditory by some trick of eye, tone, or gesture, or he fails. *He must be thinking all the while of his appearance, because he knows that all the while the spectators are judging of it.* And this is the way to represent the shy, negligent, retiring Hamlet.

It is true that there is no other mode of conveying a vast quantity of thought and feeling to a great portion of the audience, who otherwise would never earn it for themselves by reading, and the intellectual acquisition gained this way may, for aught I know, be inestimable; but I am not arguing that Hamlet should not be acted, but how much Hamlet is made another thing by being acted. I have heard much of the wonders which Garrick performed in this part; but as I never saw him, I must have leave to doubt whether the representation of such a character came within the province of his art. Those who tell me of him, speak of his eye, of the magic of his eye, and of his commanding voice: physical properties, vastly desirable in an actor, and without which he can never insinuate meaning into an auditory,—but what have they to do with Hamlet? what have they to do with intellect? In fact, the things aimed at in theatrical representation, are to arrest the spectator's eye upon the form and the gesture, and so to gain a more favourable hearing to what is spoken: it is not what the character is, but how he looks; not what he says, but how he speaks it. I see no reason to think that if the play of Hamlet were written over again by some such writer as Banks or Lillo, retaining the process of the story, but totally omitting all the poetry of it, all the divine features of Shakspeare, his stupendous intellect; and only taking care to give us enough of passionate dialogue, which Banks or Lillo were never at a loss to furnish; I see not how the effect could be much different upon an audience, nor how the actor has it in his power to represent Shakspeare to us differently from his representation of Banks or Lillo. Hamlet would still be a youthful accomplished prince, and must be gracefully personated; he might be puzzled in his mind, wavering in his conduct, seemingly-cruel to Ophelia, he might see a ghost, and start at it, and address it kindly when he found it to be his father; all this in the poorest and most homely language of the servilest creeper after nature that ever consulted the palate of an audience; without troubling Shakspeare for the matter: and I see not but there would be room for all the power which an actor has, to display itself. All the passions and changes of passion might remain: for those are much less difficult to write or act than is thought, it is a trick easy to be attained, it is but rising or falling a note or two in the voice, a whisper with a significant foreboding look to announce its approach, and so contagious the counterfeit appearance of any emotion is, that let the words be what they will, the look and tone shall carry it off and make it pass for deep skill in the passions.

It is common for people to talk of Shakspeare's plays being *so natural;* that every body can understand him. They are natural indeed, they are grounded deep in nature, so deep that the depth of them lies out of the reach of most of us. You shall hear the same persons say that George Barnwell is very natural, and Othello is very natural, that they are both very deep; and to them they are the same kind of thing. At the one they sit and shed tears, because a good sort of young man is tempted by a naughty woman to commit *a trifling peccadillo,* the murder of an uncle or so, that is all, and so comes to an untimely end, which is so *moving;* and at the other, because a blackamoor in a fit of jealousy kills his innocent white wife: and the odds are that ninety-nine out of a hundred would willingly behold the same catastrophe happen to both the heroes, and have thought the rope more due to Othello than to Barnwell. For of the texture of Othello's mind, the inward construction marvellously laid open with all its strengths and weaknesses, its heroic confidences and its human misgivings, its agonies of hate springing from the depths of love, they see no more than the spectators at a cheaper rate, who pay their pennies a-piece to look through the man's telescope in Leicester-fields, see into the inward plot and topography of the moon. Some dim thing or other they see, they see an actor personating a passion, of grief, or anger, for instance, and they recognize it as a copy of the usual external effects of such passions; or at least as being true to *that symbol of the emotion which passes current at the theatre for it,* for it is often no more than that: but of the grounds of the passion, its correspondence to a great or heroic nature, which is the only worthy object of tragedy,—that common auditors know any thing of this, or can have any such notions dinned into them by the mere strength of an actor's lungs,—that apprehensions foreign to them should be thus infused into them by storm, I can neither believe, nor understand how it can be possible.

We talk of Shakspeare's admirable observation of life, when we should feel, that not from a petty inquisition into those cheap and every-day characters which surrounded him, as they surround us, but from his own mind, which was, to borrow a phrase of Ben Jonson's, the very "sphere of humanity," he fetched those images of virtue and of knowledge, of which every one of us recognizing a part, think we comprehend in our natures the whole; and oftentimes mistake the powers which he positively creates in us, for nothing more than indigenous faculties of our own minds, which only waited the application of corresponding virtues in him to return a full and clear echo of the same. . . .

I mean no disrespect to any actor, but the sort of pleasure

which Shakspeare's plays give in the acting seems to me
not at all to differ from that which the audience receive
from those of other writers; and, *they being in themselves
essentially so different from all others,* I must conclude that
there is something in the nature of acting which levels all
distinctions. And in fact, who does not speak indifferently
of the Gamester and of Macbeth as fine stage performances,
and praise the Mrs. Beverley in the same way as the Lady
Macbeth of Mrs. S.? Belvidera, and Calista, and Isabella,
and Euphrasia, are they less liked than Imogen, or than
Juliet, or than Desdemona? Are they not spoken of and remembered in the same way? Is not the female performer
as great (as they call it) in one as in the other? Did not Garrick shine, and was he not ambitious of shining in every
drawling tragedy that his wretched day produced,—the productions of the Hills and the Murphys and the Browns,—
and shall he have that honour to dwell in our minds for ever
as an inseparable concomitant with Shakspeare? A kindred
mind! O who can read that affecting sonnet of Shakspeare
which alludes to his profession as a player:—

> Oh for my sake do you with Fortune chide,
> The guilty goddess of my harmful deeds,
> That did not better for my life provide
> Than public means which public custom
>   [manners] breeds—
> Thence comes it that my name receives a brand;
> And almost thence my nature is subdued
> To what it works in, like the dyer's hand—

Or that other confession:—

> Alas! 'tis true, I have gone here and there,
> And made myself a motly to thy view,
> Gor'd mine own thoughts, sold cheap what
>   is most dear—

Who can read these instances of jealous self-watchfulness
in our sweet Shakspeare, and dream of any congeniality
between him and one that, by every tradition of him, appears to have been as mere a player as ever existed; to have
had his mind tainted with the lowest players' vices,—envy

and jealousy, and miserable cravings after applause; one who in the exercise of his profession was jealous even of the women-performers that stood in his way; a manager full of managerial tricks and stratagems and finesse: that any resemblance should be dreamed of between him and Shakspeare,—Shakspeare who, in the plenitude and consciousness of his own powers, could with that noble modesty, which we can neither imitate nor appreciate, express himself thus of his own sense of his own defects:—

> Wishing me like to one more rich in hope,
> Featur'd like him, like him with friends possest;
> Desiring *this man's art, and that man's scope.*

I am almost disposed to deny to Garrick the merit of being an admirer of Shakspeare. A true lover of his excellencies he certainly was not; for would any true lover of them have admitted into his matchless scenes such ribald trash as Tate and Cibber, and the rest of them, that

> With their darkness durst affront his light,

have foisted into the acting plays of Shakspeare? I believe it impossible that he could have had a proper reverence for Shakspeare, and have condescended to go through that interpolated scene in Richard the Third, in which Richard tries to break his wife's heart by telling her he loves another woman, and says, "if she survives this she is immortal." Yet I doubt not he delivered this vulgar stuff with as much anxiety of emphasis as any of the genuine parts; and for acting, it is as well calculated as any. But we have seen the part of Richard lately produce great fame to an actor by his manner of playing it, and it lets us into the secret of acting, and of popular judgments of Shakspeare derived from acting. Not one of the spectators who have witnessed Mr. C.'s exertions in that part, but has come away with a proper conviction that Richard is a very wicked man, and kills little children in their beds, with something like the pleasure which the giants and ogres in children's books are represented to have taken in that practice; moreover, that he is very close and shrewd and devilish cunning, for you could see that by his eye.

But is in fact this the impression we have in reading the Richard of Shakspeare? Do we feel any thing like disgust, as we do at that butcher-like representation of him that passes for him on the stage? A horror at his crimes blends with the effect which we feel, but how is it qualified, how is it carried off, by the rich intellect which he displays, his resources, his wit, his buoyant spirits, his vast knowledge and insight into characters, the poetry of his part,—not an atom of all which is made perceivable in Mr. C.'s way of acting it. Nothing but his crimes, his actions, is visible; they are prominent and staring; the murderer stands out, but where is the lofty genius, the man of vast capacity,—the profound, the witty, accomplished Richard?

The truth is, the Characters of Shakspeare are so much the objects of meditation rather than of interest or curiosity as to their actions, that while we are reading any of his great criminal characters,—Macbeth, Richard, even Iago,—we think not so much of the crimes which they commit, as of the ambition, the aspiring spirit, the intellectual activity, which prompts them to overleap those moral fences. Barnwell is a wretched murderer; there is a certain fitness between his neck and the rope; he is the legitimate heir to the gallows; nobody who thinks at all can think of any alleviating circumstances in his case to make him a fit object of mercy. Or to take an instance from the higher tragedy, what else but a mere assassin is Glenalvon! Do we think of any thing but of the crime which he commits, and the rack which he deserves? That is all which we really think about him. Whereas in corresponding characters in Shakspeare so little do the actions comparatively affect us, that while the impulses, the inner mind in all its perverted greatness, solely seems real and is exclusively attended to, the crime is comparatively nothing. But when we see these things represented, the acts which they do are comparatively every thing, their impulses nothing. The state of sublime emotion into which we are elevated by those images of night and horror which Macbeth is made to utter, that solemn prelude with which he entertains the time till the bell shall strike which is to call him to murder Duncan,—when we no longer read it in a book, when we have given up that vantage-ground of abstraction which reading possesses over seeing, and come to see a man in his bodily shape before our eyes actually preparing to commit a murder, if the acting be true and impressive, as I have witnessed it in Mr. K.'s performance of that part, the painful anxiety about the act, the natural longing to prevent it while it yet seems unperpetrated, the too close pressing semblance of reality, give a pain and an uneasiness which totally destroy all the delight which the words in the book convey, where the deed doing never presses upon us with the painful sense of presence: it rather seems to belong to history,—to something past and inevitable, if it has any thing to do with time at all. The sublime images, the poetry alone, is that which is present to our minds in the reading.

So to see Lear acted,—to see an old man tottering about the stage with a walking-stick, turned out of doors by his daughters in a rainy night, has nothing in it but what is painful and disgusting. We want to take him into shelter and relieve him. That is all the feeling which the acting of Lear ever produced in me. But the Lear of Shakspeare cannot be acted. The contemptible machinery by which they mimic the storm which he goes out in, is not more inadequate to represent the horrors of the real elements, than any actor can be to represent Lear: they might more easily propose to personate the Satan of Milton upon a stage, or one of Michael Angelo's terrible figures. The greatness of Lear is not in corporal dimension, but in intellectual: the explosions of his passion are terrible as a volcano: they are storms turning up and disclosing to the bottom that sea, his mind, with all its vast riches. It is his mind which is laid bare. This case of flesh and blood seems too insignificant to be thought on; even as he himself neglects it. On the stage we see nothing but corporal infirmities and weakness, the impotence of rage; while we read it, we see not Lear, but we are Lear,—we are in his mind, we are sustained by a grandeur which baffles the malice of daughters and storms; in the aberrations of his reason, we discover a mighty irregular power of reasoning, immethodized from the ordinary purposes of life, but exerting its powers, as the wind blows where it listeth, at will upon the corruptions and abuses of mankind. What have looks, or tones, to do with that sublime identification of his age with that of the *heavens themselves,* when in his reproaches to them for conniving at the injustice of his children, he reminds them that "they themselves are old." What gesture shall we appropriate to this? What has the voice or the eye to do with such things? But the play is beyond all art, as the tamperings with it shew: it is too hard and stony; it must have love-scenes, and a happy ending. It is not enough that Cordelia is a daughter, she must shine as a lover too. Tate has put his hook in the nostrils of this Leviathan, for Garrick and his followers, the showmen of the scene, to draw the mighty beast about more easily. A happy ending!—as if the living martyrdom that Lear had gone through,—the flaying of his feelings alive, did not make a fair dismissal from the stage of life the only decorous thing for him. If he is to live and be happy after, if he could sustain this world's burden after, why all this pudder and preparation,— why torment us with all this unnecessary sympathy? As if the childish pleasure of getting his gilt robes and sceptre again could tempt him to act over again his misused station,—as if at his years, and with his experience, any thing was left but to die.

Lear is essentially impossible to be represented on a stage. But how many dramatic personages are there in Shakspeare, which though more tractable and feasible (if I may so speak) than Lear, yet from some circumstance, some adjunct to their character, are improper to be shewn to our bodily eye. Othello for instance. Nothing can be more soothing, more flattering to the nobler parts of our natures, than to read of a young Venetian lady of highest extraction, through the force of love and from a sense of merit in him whom she loved, laying aside every consideration of kindred, and country, and colour, and wedding with a *coal-black Moor*—(for such he is represented, in the imperfect state of knowledge respecting foreign countries in those days, compared with our own, or in compliance with popular notions, though the Moors are now well enough known to be by many shades less unworthy of a white woman's fancy) —it is the perfect triumph of virtue over accidents, of the imagination over the senses. She sees Othello's colour in his mind. But upon the stage, when the imagination is no longer the ruling faculty, but we are left to our poor unassisted senses, I appeal to every one that has seen Othello played, whether he did not, on the contrary, sink Othello's mind in his colour; whether he did not find something extremely revolting in the courtship and wedded caresses of Othello and Desdemona; and whether the actual sight of the thing did not over-weigh all that beautiful compromise which we make in reading;—and the reason it should do so is obvious, because there is just so much reality presented to our senses as to give a perception of disagreement, with not enough of belief in the internal motives,—all that which is unseen,—to overpower and reconcile the first and obvious prejudices.[1] What we see upon a stage is body and bodily action; what we are conscious of in reading is almost exclusively the mind, and its movements: and this I think may sufficiently account for the very different sort of delight with which the same play so often affects us in the reading and the seeing. . . .

A. C. BRADLEY

A. C. Bradley (1851-1935). Professor of Literature at Liverpool and Glasgow, Professor of Poetry at Oxford. Author of Shakespearean Tragedy *(1904) and* Oxford Lectures on Poetry *(1909).*

CONSTRUCTION IN SHAKESPEARE'S TRAGEDIES*

Having discussed the substance of a Shakespearean tragedy, we should naturally go on to examine the form. And under this head many things might be included; for example,

[1] The error of supposing that because Othello's colour does not offend us in the reading, it should also not offend us in the seeing, is just such a fallacy as supposing that an Adam and Eve in a picture shall affect us just as they do in the poem. But in the poem we for a while have Paradisaical senses given us, which vanish when we see a man and his wife without clothes in the picture. The painters themselves feel this, as is apparent by the awkward shifts they have recourse to, to make them look not quite naked; by a sort of prophetic anachronism, antedating the invention of fig-leaves. So in the reading of the play, we see with Desdemona's eyes; in the seeing of it, we are forced to look with our own.

* From *Shakespearean Tragedy.*

Shakespeare's methods of characterisation, his language, his
versification, the construction of his plots. I intend, however,
to speak only of the last of these subjects, which has been
somewhat neglected; [1] and, as construction is a more or
less technical matter, I shall add some general remarks on
Shakespeare as an artist.

1

As a Shakespearean tragedy represents a conflict which
terminates in a catastrophe, any such tragedy may roughly
be divided into three parts. The first of these sets forth or
expounds the situation,[2] or state of affairs, out of which
the conflict arises; and it may, therefore, be called the Exposition. The second deals with the definite beginning, the
growth and the vicissitudes of the conflict. It forms accordingly the bulk of the play, comprising the Second, Third
and Fourth Acts, and usually a part of the First and a part
of the Fifth. The final section of the tragedy shows the
issue of the conflict in a catastrophe.[3]

The application of this scheme of division is naturally
more or less arbitrary. The first part glides into the second,
and the second into the third, and there may often be difficulty in drawing the lines between them. But it is still harder
to divide spring from summer, and summer from autumn;
and yet spring is spring, and summer summer.

---

[1] The famous critics of the Romantic Revival seem to have paid
very little attention to this subject. Mr. R. G. Moulton has written
an interesting book on *Shakespeare as a Dramatic Artist* (1885). In
parts of my analysis I am much indebted to Gustav Freytag's *Tech-
nik des Dramas,* a book which deserves to be much better known
than it appears to be to Englishmen interested in the drama. I may
add, for the benefit of classical scholars, that Freytag has a chapter
on Sophocles. The reader of his book will easily distinguish, if he
cares to, the places where I follow Freytag, those where I differ from
him, and those where I write in independence of him. I may add
that in speaking of construction I have thought it best to assume in
my hearers no previous knowledge of the subject; that I have not
attempted to discuss how much of what is said of Shakespeare would
apply also to other dramatists; and that I have illustrated from the
tragedies generally, not only from the chosen four.

[2] This word throughout the lecture bears the sense it has here, which,
of course, is not its usual dramatic sense.

[3] In the same way a comedy will consist of three parts, showing the
'situation,' the 'complication' or 'entanglement,' and the *dénouement*
or 'solution.'

The main business of the Exposition, which we will consider first, is to introduce us into a little world of persons; to show us their positions in life, their circumstances, their relations to one another, and perhaps something of their characters; and to leave us keenly interested in the question what will come out of this condition of things. We are left thus expectant, not merely because some of the persons interest us at once, but also because their situation in regard to one another points to difficulties in the future. This situation is not one of conflict,[1] but it threatens conflict. For example, we see first the hatred of the Montagues and Capulets; and then we see Romeo ready to fall violently in love; and then we hear talk of a marriage between Juliet and Paris; but the exposition is not complete, and the conflict has not definitely begun to arise, till, in the last scene of the First Act, Romeo the Montague sees Juliet the Capulet and becomes her slave.

The dramatist's chief difficulty in the exposition is obvious, and it is illustrated clearly enough in the plays of unpractised writers; for example, in *Remorse,* and even in *The Cenci.* He has to impart to the audience a quantity of information about matters of which they generally know nothing and never know all that is necessary for his purpose.[2] But the process of merely acquiring information is unpleasant, and the direct imparting of it is undramatic. Unless he uses a prologue, therefore, he must conceal from his auditors the fact that they are being informed, and must tell them what he wants them to know by means which are interesting on their own account. These means, with Shakespeare, are not only speeches but actions and events. From the very beginning of the play, though the conflict has not arisen, things are happening and being done which in some degree arrest, startle, and excite; and in a few scenes we have mastered the situation of affairs without perceiving

[1] It is possible, of course, to open the tragedy with the conflict already begun, but Shakespeare never does so.

[2] When the subject comes from English history, and especially when the play forms one of a series, some knowledge may be assumed. So in *Richard III.* Even in *Richard II.* not a little knowledge seems to be assumed, and this fact points to the existence of a popular play on the earlier part of Richard's reign. Such a play exists, though it is not clear that it is a genuine Elizabethan work. See the *Jahrbuch d. deutschen Sh.-gesellschaft* for 1899.

the dramatist's designs upon us. Not that this is always so with Shakespeare. In the opening scene of his early *Comedy of Errors,* and in the opening speech of *Richard III.,* we feel that the speakers are addressing us; and in the second scene of the *Tempest* (for Shakespeare grew at last rather negligent of technique) the purpose of Prospero's long explanation to Miranda is palpable. But in general Shakespeare's expositions are masterpieces.[1]

His usual plan in tragedy is to begin with a short scene, or part of a scene, either full of life and stir, or in some other way arresting. Then, having secured a hearing, he proceeds to conversations at a lower pitch, accompanied by little action but conveying much information. For example, *Romeo and Juliet* opens with a street-fight, *Julius Caesar* and *Coriolanus* with a crowd in commotion; and when this excitement has had its effect on the audience, there follow quiet speeches, in which the cause of the excitement, and so a great part of the situation, are disclosed. In *Hamlet* and *Macbeth* this scheme is employed with great boldness. In *Hamlet* the first appearance of the Ghost occurs at the fortieth line, and with such effect that Shakespeare can afford to introduce at once a conversation which explains part of the state of affairs at Elsinore; and the second appearance, having again increased the tension, is followed by a long scene, which contains no action but introduces almost all the *dramatis personae* and adds the information left wanting. The opening of *Macbeth* is even more remarkable, for there is probably no parallel to its first scene, where the senses and imagination are assaulted by a storm of thunder and supernatural alarm. This scene is only eleven lines long, but its influence is so great that the next can safely be occupied with a mere report of Macbeth's battles, —a narrative which would have won much less attention if it had opened the play.

When Shakespeare begins his exposition thus he generally at first makes people talk about the hero, but keeps the hero himself for some time out of sight, so that we await

[1] This is one of several reasons why many people enjoy reading him, who, on the whole, dislike reading plays. A main cause of this very general dislike is that the reader has not a lively enough imagination to carry him with pleasure through the exposition, though in the theatre, where his imagination is helped, he would experience little difficulty.

his entrance with curiosity, and sometimes with anxiety. On the other hand, if the play opens with a quiet conversation, this is usually brief, and then at once the hero enters and takes action of some decided kind. Nothing, for example, can be less like the beginning of *Macbeth* than that of *King Lear*. The tone is pitched so low that the conversation between Kent, Gloster, and Edmund is written in prose. But at the thirty-fourth line it is broken off by the entrance of Lear and his court, and without delay the King proceeds to his fatal division of the kingdom.

This tragedy illustrates another practice of Shakespeare's. *King Lear* has a secondary plot, that which concerns Gloster and his two sons. To make the beginning of this plot quite clear, and to mark it off from the main action, Shakespeare gives it a separate exposition. The great scene of the division of Britain and the rejection of Cordelia and Kent is followed by the second scene, in which Gloster and his two sons appear alone, and the beginning of Edmund's design is disclosed. In *Hamlet,* though the plot is single, there is a little group of characters possessing a certain independent interest,—Polonius, his son, and his daughter; and so the third scene is devoted wholly to them. And again, in *Othello,* since Roderigo is to occupy a peculiar position almost throughout the action, he is introduced at once, alone with Iago, and his position is explained before the other characters are allowed to appear.

But why should Iago open the play? Or, if this seems too presumptuous a question, let us put it in the form, What is the effect of his opening the play? Is it that we receive at the very outset a strong impression of the force which is to prove fatal to the hero's happiness, so that, when we see the hero himself, the shadow of fate already rests upon him. And an effect of this kind is to be noticed in other tragedies. We are made conscious at once of some power which is to influence the whole action to the hero's undoing. In *Macbeth* we see and hear the Witches, in *Hamlet* the Ghost. In the first scene of *Julius Caesar* and of *Coriolanus* those qualities of the crowd are vividly shown which render hopeless the enterprise of the one hero and wreck the ambition of the other. It is the same with the hatred between the rival houses in *Romeo and Juliet,* and with Antony's infatuated passion. We realise them at the

end of the first page, and are almost ready to regard the
hero as doomed. Often, again, at one or more points during the exposition this feeling is reinforced by some expression that has an ominous effect. The first words we hear
from Macbeth, 'So foul and fair a day I have not seen,'
echo, though he knows it not, the last words we heard from
the Witches, 'Fair is foul, and foul is fair.' Romeo, on his
way with his friends to the banquet, where he is to see
Juliet for the first time, tells Mercutio that he has had a
dream. What the dream was we never learn, for Mercutio
does not care to know, and breaks into his speech about
Queen Mab; but we can guess its nature from Romeo's last
speech in the scene:

> My mind misgives
> Some consequence yet hanging in the stars
> Shall bitterly begin his fearful date
> With this night's revels.

When Brabantio, forced to acquiesce in his daughter's stolen
marriage, turns, as he leaves the council-chamber, to Othello, with the warning,

> Look to her, Moor, if thou hast eyes to see;
> She has deceived her father, and may thee,

this warning, and no less Othello's answer, 'My life upon
her faith,' make our hearts sink. The whole of the coming
story seems to be prefigured in Antony's muttered words
(I. ii. 120):

> These strong Egyptian fetters I must break,
> Or lose myself in dotage;

and, again, in Hamlet's weary sigh, following so soon on
the passionate resolution stirred by the message of the
Ghost:

> The time is out of joint. Oh cursed spite,
> That ever I was born to set it right.

These words occur at a point (the end of the First Act)
which may be held to fall either within the exposition or

beyond it. I should take the former view, though such questions, as we saw at starting, can hardly be decided with certainty. The dimensions of this first section of a tragedy depend on a variety of causes, of which the chief seems to be the comparative simplicity or complexity of the situation from which the conflict arises. Where this is simple the exposition is short, as in *Julius Caesar* and *Macbeth*. Where it is complicated the exposition requires more space, as in *Romeo and Juliet, Hamlet,* and *King Lear*. Its completion is generally marked in the mind of the reader by a feeling that the action it contains is for the moment complete but has left a problem. The lovers have met, but their families are at deadly enmity; the hero seems at the height of success, but has admitted the thought of murdering his sovereign; the old king has divided his kingdom between two hypocritical daughters, and has rejected his true child; the hero has acknowledged a sacred duty of revenge, but is weary of life: and we ask, What will come of this? Sometimes, I may add, a certain time is supposed to elapse before the events which answer our question make their appearance and the conflict begins; in *King Lear*, for instance, about a fortnight; in *Hamlet* about two months.

2

We come now to the conflict itself. And here one or two preliminary remarks are necessary. In the first place, it must be remembered that our point of view in examining the construction of a play will not always coincide with that which we occupy in thinking of its whole dramatic effect. For example, that struggle in the hero's soul which sometimes accompanies the outward struggle is of the highest importance for the total effect of a tragedy; but it is not always necessary or desirable to consider it when the question is merely one of construction. And this is natural. The play is meant primarily for the theatre; and theatrically the outward conflict, with its influence on the fortunes of the hero, is the aspect which first catches, if it does not engross, attention. For the average playgoer of every period the main interest of *Hamlet* has probably lain in the vicissitudes of his long duel with the King; and the question, one may almost say, has been which will first kill the other.

And so, from the point of view of construction, the fact that Hamlet spares the King when he finds him praying, is, from its effect on the hero's fortunes, of great moment; but the cause of the fact, which lies within Hamlet's character, is not so.

In the second place we must be prepared to find that, as the plays vary so much, no single way of regarding the conflict will answer precisely to the construction of all; that it sometimes appears possible to look at the construction of a tragedy in two quite different ways, and that it is material to find the best of the two; and that thus, in any given instance, it is necessary first to define the opposing sides in the conflict. I will give one or two examples. In some tragedies, as we saw in our first lecture, the opposing forces can, for practical purposes, be identified with opposing persons or groups. So it is in *Romeo and Juliet* and *Macbeth*. But it is not always so. The love of Othello may be said to contend with another force, as the love of Romeo does; but Othello cannot be said to contend with Iago as Romeo contends with the representatives of the hatred of the houses, or as Macbeth contends with Malcolm and Macduff. Again, in *Macbeth* the hero, however much influenced by others, supplies the main driving power of the action; but in *King Lear* he does not. Possibly, therefore, the conflict, and with it the construction, may best be regarded from different points of view in these two plays, in spite of the fact that the hero is the central figure in each. But if we do not observe this we shall attempt to find the same scheme in both, and shall either be driven to some unnatural view or to a sceptical despair of perceiving any principle of construction at all.

With these warnings, I turn to the question whether we can trace any distinct method or methods by which Shakespeare represents the rise and development of the conflict.

(1) One at least is obvious, and indeed it is followed not merely during the conflict but from beginning to end of the play. There are, of course, in the action certain places where the tension in the minds of the audience becomes extreme. We shall consider these presently. But, in addition, there is, all through the tragedy, a constant alternation of rises and falls in this tension or in the emotional

pitch of the work, a regular sequence of more exciting and less exciting sections. Some kind of variation of pitch is to be found, of course, in all drama, for it rests on the elementary facts that relief must be given after emotional strain, and that contrast is required to bring out the full force of an effect. But a good drama of our own time shows nothing approaching to the *regularity* with which in the plays of Shakespeare and of his contemporaries the principle is applied. And the main cause of this difference lies simply in a change of theatrical arrangements. In Shakespeare's theatre, as there was no scenery, scene followed scene with scarcely any pause; and so the readiest, though not the only, way to vary the emotional pitch was to interpose a whole scene where the tension was low between scenes where it was high. In our theatres there is a great deal of scenery, which takes a long time to set and change; and therefore the number of scenes is small, and the variations of tension have to be provided within the scenes, and still more by the pauses between them. With Shakespeare there are, of course, in any long scene variations of tension, but the scenes are numerous and, compared with ours, usually short, and variety is given principally by their difference in pitch.

It may further be observed that, in a portion of the play which is relatively unexciting, the scenes of lower tension may be as long as those of higher; while in a portion of the play which is specially exciting the scenes of low tension are shorter, often much shorter, than the others. The reader may verify this statement by comparing the First or the Fourth Act in most of the tragedies with the Third; for, speaking very roughly, we may say that the First and Fourth are relatively quiet acts, the Third highly critical. A good example is the Third Act of *King Lear*, where the scenes of high tension (ii., iv., vi.) are respectively 95, 186 and 122 lines in length, while those of low tension (i., iii., v.) are respectively 55, 26 and 26 lines long. Scene vii., the last of the Act, is, I may add, a very exciting scene, though it follows scene vi., and therefore the tone of scene vi. is greatly lowered during its final thirty lines.

(2) If we turn now from the differences of tension to the sequence of events within the conflict, we shall find the principle of alternation at work again in another and a

quite independent way. Let us for the sake of brevity call the two sides in the conflict A and B. Now, usually, as we shall see presently, through a considerable part of the play, perhaps the first half, the cause of A is, on the whole, advancing; and through the remaining part it is retiring, while that of B advances in turn. But, underlying this broad movement, all through the conflict we shall find a regular alternation of smaller advances and retirals; first A seeming to win some ground, and then the counter-action of B being shown. And since we always more or less decidedly prefer A to B or B to A, the result of this oscillating movement is a constant alternation of hope and fear, or rather of a mixed state predominantly hopeful and a mixed state predominantly apprehensive. An example will make the point clear. In *Hamlet* the conflict begins with the hero's feigning to be insane from disappointment in love, and we are shown his immediate success in convincing Polonius. Let us call this an advance of A. The next scene shows the King's great uneasiness about Hamlet's melancholy, and his scepticism as to Polonius's explanation of its cause: advance of B. Hamlet completely baffles Rosencrantz and Guildenstern, who have been sent to discover his secret, and he arranges for the test of the play-scene: advance of A. But immediately before the play-scene his soliloquy on suicide fills us with misgiving; and his words to Ophelia, overheard, so convince the King that love is *not* the cause of his nephew's strange behaviour, that he determines to get rid of him by sending him to England: advance of B. The play-scene proves a complete success: decided advance of A. Directly after it Hamlet spares the King at prayer, and in an interview with his mother unwittingly kills Polonius, and so gives his enemy a perfect excuse for sending him away (to be executed): decided advance of B. I need not pursue the illustration further. This oscillating movement can be traced without difficulty in any of the tragedies, though less distinctly in one or two of the earliest.

(3) Though this movement continues right up to the catastrophe, its effect does not disguise that much broader effect to which I have already alluded, and which we have now to study. In all the tragedies, though more clearly in some than in others, one side is distinctly felt to be on the whole advancing up to a certain point in the conflict, and

then to be on the whole declining before the reaction of the other. There is therefore felt to be a critical point in the action, which proves also to be a turning point. It is critical sometimes in the sense that, until it is reached, the conflict is not, so to speak, clenched; one of the two sets of forces might subside, or a reconciliation might somehow be effected; while, as soon as it is reached, we feel this can no longer be. It is critical also because the advancing force has apparently asserted itself victoriously, gaining, if not all it could wish, still a very substantial advantage; whereas really it is on the point of turning downward towards its fall. This Crisis, as a rule, comes somewhere near the middle of the play; and where it is well marked it has the effect, as to construction, of dividing the play into five parts instead of three; these parts showing (1) a situation not yet one of conflict, (2) the rise and development of the conflict, in which A or B advances on the whole till it reaches (3) the Crisis, on which follows (4) the decline of A or B towards (5) the Catastrophe. And it will be seen that the fourth and fifth parts repeat, though with a reversal of direction as regards A or B, the movement of the second and third, working towards the catastrophe as the second and third worked towards the crisis.

In developing, illustrating and qualifying this statement, it will be best to begin with the tragedies in which the movement is most clear and simple. These are *Julius Caesar* and *Macbeth*. In the former the fortunes of the conspiracy rise with vicissitudes up to the crisis of the assassination (III. i.); they then sink with vicissitudes to the catastrophe, where Brutus and Cassius perish. In the latter, Macbeth, hurrying, in spite of much inward resistance, to the murder of Duncan, attains the crown, the upward movement being extraordinarily rapid, and the crisis arriving early: his cause then turns slowly downward, and soon hastens to ruin. In both these tragedies the simplicity of the constructional effect, it should be noticed, depends in part on the fact that the contending forces may quite naturally be identified with certain persons, and partly again on the fact that the defeat of one side is the victory of the other. Octavius and Antony, Malcolm and Macduff, are left standing over the bodies of their foes.

This is not so in *Romeo and Juliet* and *Hamlet,* because

here, although the hero perishes, the side opposed to him, being the more faulty or evil, cannot be allowed to triumph when he falls. Otherwise the type of construction is the same. The fortunes of Romeo and Juliet rise and culminate in their marriage (II. vi.), and then begin to decline before the opposition of their houses, which, aided by accidents, produces a catastrophe, but is thereupon converted into a remorseful reconciliation. Hamlet's cause reaches its zenith in the success of the play-scene (III. ii.). Thereafter the reaction makes way, and he perishes through the plot of the King and Laertes. But they are not allowed to survive their success.

The construction in the remaining Roman plays follows the same plan, but in both plays (as in *Richard II*. and *Richard III*.) it suffers from the intractable nature of the historical material, and is also influenced by other causes. In *Coriolanus* the hero reaches the topmost point of success when he is named consul (II. iii.), and the rest of the play shows his decline and fall; but in this decline he attains again for a time extraordinary power, and triumphs, in a sense, over his original adversary, though he succumbs to another. In *Antony and Cleopatra* the advance of the hero's cause depends on his freeing himself from the heroine, and he appears to have succeeded when he becomes reconciled to Octavius and marries Octavia (III. ii.); but he returns to Egypt and is gradually driven to his death which involves that of the heroine.

There remain two of the greatest of the tragedies, and in both of them a certain difficulty will be felt. *King Lear* alone among these plays has a distinct double action. Besides this, it is impossible, I think, from the point of view of construction, to regard the hero as the leading figure. If we attempt to do so, we must either find the crisis in the First Act (for after it Lear's course is downward), and this is absurd; or else we must say that the usual movement is present but its direction is reversed, the hero's cause first sinking to the lowest point (in the Storm-scenes) and then rising again. But this also will not do; for though his fortunes may be said to rise again for a time, they rise only to fall once more to a catastrophe. The truth is, that after the First Act, which is really filled by the exposition, Lear suffers but hardly initiates action at all; and the right way to look at the matter, *from the point of view of construction,* is to regard Goneril, Regan and Edmund as the leading characters. It is they who, in the conflict, initiate action. Their fortune mounts to the crisis, where the old King is driven out into the storm and loses his reason, and where Gloster is blinded and expelled from his home (III. vi. and vii.). Then the counter-action begins to gather force, and their cause to decline; and, although they win the battle, they are involved in the catastrophe which they bring on Cordelia and Lear. Thus we may still find in *King Lear* the usual scheme of an ascending and a descending movement of one side in the conflict.

The case of *Othello* is more peculiar. In its whole constructional effect *Othello* differs from the other tragedies, and the cause of this difference is not hard to find, and will be mentioned presently. But how, after it is found, are we to define the principle of the construction? On the one hand the usual method seems to show itself. Othello's fortune certainly advances in the early part of the play, and it may be considered to reach its topmost point in the exquisite joy of his reunion with Desdemona in Cyprus; while soon afterwards it begins to turn, and then falls to the catastrophe. But the topmost point thus comes very early (II. i.), and, moreover, is but faintly marked; indeed, it is scarcely felt as a crisis at all. And, what is still more significant, though reached by conflict, it is not reached by conflict with the force which afterwards destroys it. Iago, in the early scenes, is indeed shown to cherish a design against Othello, but it is not Iago against whom he has at first to assert himself, but Brabantio; and Iago does not even begin to poison his mind until the third scene of the Third Act.

Can we then, on the other hand, following the precedent of *King Lear,* and remembering the probable chronological juxtaposition of the two plays, regard Iago as the leading figure from the point of view of construction? This might at first seem the right view; for it is the case that *Othello* resembles *King Lear* in having a hero more acted upon than acting, or rather a hero driven to act by being acted upon. But then, if Iago is taken as the leading figure, the usual mode of construction is plainly abandoned, for there will nowhere be a crisis followed by a descending movement. Iago's cause advances, at first slowly and quietly, then rapidly, but it does nothing but advance until the catastrophe swallows his dupe and him together. And this way of regarding the action does positive violence, I think, to our natural impressions of the earlier part of the play.

I think, therefore, that the usual scheme is so far followed that the drama represents first the rise of the hero, and then his fall. But, however this question may be decided, one striking peculiarity remains, and is the cause of the unique effect of *Othello*. In the first half of the play the main conflict is merely incubating; then it bursts into life, and goes storming, without intermission or change of direction to its close. Now, in this peculiarity *Othello* is quite unlike the other tragedies; and in the consequent effect, which is that the second half of the drama is immeasurably more exciting than the first, it is approached only by *Antony and Cleopatra*. I shall therefore reserve it for separate consideration, though in proceeding to speak further of Shakespeare's treatment of the tragic conflict I shall have to mention some devices which are used in *Othello* as well as in the other tragedies.

3

Shakespeare's general plan, we have seen, is to show one set of forces advancing, in secret or open opposition to the other, to some decisive success, and then driven downward to defeat by the reaction it provokes. And the advantages of this plan, as seen in such a typical instance as *Julius Caesar*, are manifest. It conveys the movement of the conflict to the mind with great clearness and force. It helps to produce the impression that in his decline and fall the doer's act is returning on his own head. And, finally, as used by Shakespeare, it makes the first half of the play intensely interesting and dramatic. Action which effects a striking change in an existing situation is naturally watched with keen interest; and this we find in some of these tragedies. And the spectacle, which others exhibit, of a purpose forming itself and, in spite of outward obstacles and often of inward resistance, forcing its way onward to a happy consummation or a terrible deed, not only gives scope to that psychological subtlety in which Shakespeare is scarcely rivalled, but is also dramatic in the highest degree.

But when the crisis has been reached there come difficulties and dangers, which, if we put Shakespeare for the moment out of mind, are easily seen. An immediate and crushing counter-action would, no doubt, sustain the interest, but it would precipitate the catastrophe, and leave a feeling that there has been too long a preparation for a final effect so brief. What seems necessary is a momentary pause, followed by a counter-action which mounts at first slowly, and afterwards, as it gathers force, with quickening speed. And yet the result of this arrangement, it would seem, must be, for a time, a decided slackening of tension. Nor is this the only difficulty. The persons who represent the counter-action and now take the lead, are likely to be comparatively unfamiliar, and therefore unwelcome, to the audience; and, even if familiar, they are almost sure to be at first, if not permanently, less interesting than those who figured in the ascending movement, and on whom attention has been fixed. Possibly, too, their necessary prominence may crowd the hero into the back-ground. Hence the point of danger in this method of construction seems to lie in that section of the play which follows the crisis and has not yet approached the catastrophe. And this section will usually comprise the Fourth Act, together, in some cases, with a part of the Third and a part of the Fifth.

Shakespeare was so masterly a playwright, and had so wonderful a power of giving life to unpromising subjects, that to a large extent he was able to surmount this difficulty. But illustrations of it are easily to be found in his tragedies, and it is not always surmounted. In almost all of them we are conscious of that momentary pause in the action, though, as we shall see, it does not generally occur *immediately* after the crisis. Sometimes he allows himself to be driven to keep the hero off the stage for a long time while the counter-action is rising; Macbeth, Hamlet and Coriolanus during about 450 lines, Lear for nearly 500, Romeo for about 550 (it matters less here, because Juliet is quite as important as Romeo). How can a drama in which this happens compete, in its latter part, with *Othello*? And again, how can deliberations between Octavius, Antony and Lepidus, between Malcolm and Macduff, between the Capulets, between Laertes and the King, keep us at the pitch, I do not say of the crisis, but even of the action which led up to it? Good critics—writers who have criticised Shakespeare's dramas from within, instead of applying to them some standard ready-made by themselves or derived from dramas and a theatre of quite other kinds than his— have held that some of his greatest tragedies fall off in the Fourth Act, and that one or two never wholly recover themselves. And I believe most readers would find, if they examined their impressions, that to their minds *Julius Caesar, Hamlet, King Lear* and *Macbeth* have all a tendency to 'drag' in this section of the play, and that the first and perhaps also the last of these four fail even in the catastrophe to reach the height of the greatest scenes that have preceded the Fourth Act. I will not ask how far these impressions are justified. The difficulties in question will become clearer and will gain in interest if we look rather at the means which have been employed to meet them, and which certainly have in part, at least, overcome them.

(*a*) The first of these is always strikingly effective, sometimes marvellously so. The crisis in which the ascending force reaches its zenith is followed quickly, or even without the slightest pause, by a reverse or counter-blow not less emphatic and in some cases even more exciting. And the effect is to make us feel a sudden and tragic change in the direction of the movement, which, after ascending more or less gradually, now turns sharply downward. To the assassination of Caesar (III. i.) succeeds the scene in the Forum (III. ii.), where Antony carries the people away in a storm of sympathy with the dead man and of fury against the conspirators. We have hardly realised their victory before we are forced to anticipate their ultimate defeat and to take the liveliest interest in their chief antagonist. In *Hamlet* the thrilling success of the play-scene (III. ii.) is met and undone at once by the counter-stroke of Hamlet's failure to take vengeance (III. iii.) and his misfortune in killing Polonius (III. iv.). Coriolanus has no sooner gained the consulship than he is excited to frenzy by the tribunes and driven into exile. On the marriage of Romeo follows immediately the brawl which leads to Mercutio's death and the banishment of the hero (II. vi. and III. i.). In all of these instances excepting that of *Hamlet* the scene of the counter-stroke is at least as exciting as that of the crisis, perhaps more so. Most people, if asked to mention the scene that occupies the *centre* of the action in *Julius Caesar* and in *Coriolanus,* would mention the scenes of Antony's speech and Coriolanus' banishment. Thus that apparently necessary pause in the action does not, in any of these dramas, come directly after the crisis. It is deferred; and in several cases it is by various devices deferred for some little time; *e.g.* in *Romeo and Juliet* till the hero has left Verona, and Juliet is told that her marriage with Paris is to take place 'next Thursday morn' (end of Act III.); in *Macbeth* till the murder of Duncan has been followed by that of Banquo, and this by the banquet-scene. Hence the point where this pause occurs is very rarely reached before the end of the Third Act.

(*b*) Either at this point, or in the scene of the counter-stroke which precedes it, we sometimes find a peculiar effect. We are reminded of the state of affairs in which the conflict began. The opening of *Julius Caesar* warned us that, among a people so unstable and so easily led this way or that, the enterprise of Brutus is hopeless; the days of the Republic are done. In the scene of Antony's speech we see this same people again. At the beginning of *Antony and Cleopatra* the hero is about to leave Cleopatra for Rome. Where the play takes, as it were, a fresh start after the crisis, he leaves Octavia for Egypt. In *Hamlet,* when the counter-stroke succeeds to the crisis, the Ghost, who had appeared in the opening scenes, reappears. Macbeth's action in the first part of the tragedy followed on the prediction of the Witches who promised him the throne. When the action moves forward again after the banquet-scene the Witches appear once more, and make those fresh promises which again drive him forward. This repetition of a first effect produces a fateful feeling. It generally also stimulates expectation as to the new movement about to begin. In *Macbeth* the scene is, in addition, of the greatest consequence from the purely theatrical point of view.

(*c*) It has yet another function. It shows, in Macbeth's furious irritability and purposeless savagery, the internal reaction which accompanies the outward decline of his fortunes. And in other plays also the exhibition of such inner changes forms a means by which interest is sustained in this difficult section of a tragedy. There is no point in *Hamlet* where we feel more hopeless than that where the hero, having missed his chance, moralises over his irresolution and determines to cherish now only thoughts of blood, and then departs without an effort for England. One purpose, again, of the quarrel-scene between Brutus and Cassius (IV. iii.), as also of the appearance of Caesar's ghost just afterwards, is to indicate the inward changes. Otherwise the introduction of this famous and wonderful scene can hardly be defended on strictly dramatic grounds. No one would consent to part with it, and it is invaluable in sustaining interest during the progress of the reaction, but it is an episode, the removal of which would not affect the actual sequence of events (unless we may hold that, but for the emotion caused by the quarrel and reconciliation, Cassius would not have allowed Brutus to overcome his objection to the fatal policy of offering battle at Philippi).

(d) The quarrel-scene illustrates yet another favourite expedient. In this section of a tragedy Shakespeare often appeals to an emotion different from any of those excited in the first half of the play, and so provides novelty and generally also relief. As a rule this new emotion is pathetic; and the pathos is not terrible or lacerating, but, even if painful, is accompanied by the sense of beauty and by an outflow of admiration or affection, which come with an inexpressible sweetness after the tension of the crisis and the first counter-stroke. So it is with the reconciliation of Brutus and Cassius, and the arrival of the news of Portia's death. The most famous instance of this effect is the scene (IV. vii.) where Lear wakes up from sleep and finds Cordelia bending over him, perhaps the most tear-compelling passage in literature. Another is the short scene (IV. ii.) in which the talk of Lady Macduff and her little boy is interrupted by the entrance of the murderers, a passage of touching beauty and heroism. Another is the introduction of Ophelia in her madness twice in different parts of IV. v.), where the effect, though intensely pathetic, is beautiful and moving rather than harrowing; and this effect is repeated in a softer tone in the description of Ophelia's death (end of Act IV.). And in *Othello* the passage where pathos of *this* kind reaches its height is certainly that where Desdemona and Emilia converse, and the willow-song is sung, on the eve of the catastrophe (IV. iii.).

(e) Sometimes, again, in this section of a tragedy we find humorous or semi-humorous passages. On the whole such passages occur most frequently in the early or middle part of the play, which naturally grows more sombre as it nears the close; but their occasional introduction in the Fourth Act, and even later, affords variety and relief, and also heightens by contrast the tragic feelings. For example, there is a touch of comedy in the conversation of Lady Macduff with her little boy. Purely and delightfully humorous are the talk and behaviour of the servants in that admirable scene where Coriolanus comes disguised in mean apparel to the house of Aufidius (IV. v.); of a more mingled kind is the effect of the discussion between Menenius and the sentinels in v. ii.; and in the very middle of the supreme scene between the hero, Volumnia and Virgilia, little Marcus makes us burst out laughing (v. iii.). A little before the catastrophe in *Hamlet* comes the grave-digger passage, a passage ever welcome, but of a length which could hardly be defended on purely dramatic grounds; and still later, occupying some hundred and twenty lines of the very last scene, we have the chatter of Osric with Hamlet's mockery of it. But the acme of audacity is reached in *Antony and Cleopatra,* where, quite close to the end, the old countryman who brings the asps to Cleopatra discourses on the virtues and vices of the worm, and where his last words, 'Yes, forsooth: I wish you joy o' the worm,' are followed, without the intervention of a line, by the glorious speech,

> Give me my robe; put on my crown; I have
> Immortal longings in me. . . .

In some of the instances of pathos or humour just mentioned we have been brought to that part of the play which immediately precedes, or even contains, the catastrophe. And I will add at once three remarks which refer specially to this final section of a tragedy.

(*f*) In several plays Shakespeare makes here an appeal which in his own time was evidently powerful: he introduces scenes of battle. This is the case in *Richard III., Julius Caesar, King Lear, Macbeth* and *Antony and Cleopatra.* Richard, Brutus and Cassius, and Macbeth die on the battlefield. Even if his use of this expedient were not enough to show that battle-scenes were extremely popular in the Elizabethan theatre, we know it from other sources.

It is a curious comment on the futility of our spectacular effects that in our theatre these scenes, in which we strive after an 'illusion' of which the Elizabethans never dreamt, produce comparatively little excitement, and to many spectators are even somewhat distasteful.[1] And although some of them thrill the imagination of the reader, they rarely, I think, quite satisfy the *dramatic* sense. Perhaps this is partly because a battle is not the most favourable place for the exhibition of tragic character; and it is worth notice that Brutus, Cassius and Antony do not die fighting, but commit suicide after defeat. The actual battle, however, does make us feel the greatness of Antony, and still more does it help us to regard Richard and Macbeth in their day of doom as heroes, and to mingle sympathy and enthusiastic admiration with desire for their defeat.

(*g*) In some of the tragedies, again, an expedient is used, which Freytag has pointed out (though he sometimes finds it, I think, where it is not really employed). Shakespeare very rarely makes the least attempt to surprise by his catastrophes. They are felt to be inevitable, though the precise way in which they will be brought about is not, of course, foreseen. Occasionally, however, where we dread the catastrophe because we love the hero, a moment occurs, just before it, in which a gleam of false hope lights up the darkening scene; and, though we know it is false, it affects us. Far the most remarkable example is to be found in the final Act of *King Lear*. Here the victory of Edgar and the deaths of Edmund and the two sisters have almost made us forget the design on the lives of Lear and Cordelia. Even when we are reminded of it there is still room for hope that Edgar, who rushes away to the prison, will be in time to save them; and, however familiar we are with the play, the sudden entrance of Lear, with Cordelia dead in his arms, comes on us with a shock. Much slighter, but quite perceptible, is the effect of Antony's victory on land, and of the last outburst of pride and joy as he and Cleopatra meet (iv. viii.). The frank apology of Hamlet to Laertes, their reconciliation, and a delusive appearance of quiet and even confident firmness in the tone of the hero's conversation with Horatio, almost blind us to our better knowledge, and give to the catastrophe an added pain. Those in the

[1] The end of *Richard III.* is perhaps an exception.

audience who are ignorant of *Macbeth,* and who take more simply than most readers now can do the mysterious prophecies concerning Birnam Wood and the man not born of woman, feel, I imagine, just before the catastrophe, a false fear that the hero may yet escape.

(*h*) I will mention only one point more. In some cases Shakespeare spreads the catastrophe out, so to speak, over a considerable space, and thus shortens that difficult section which has to show the development of the counter-action. This is possible only where there is, besides the hero, some character who engages our interest in the highest degree, and with whose fate his own is bound up. Thus the murder of Desdemona is separated by some distance from the death of Othello. The most impressive scene in *Macbeth,* after that of Duncan's murder, is the sleep-walking scene; and it may truly, if not literally, be said to show the catastrophe of Lady Macbeth. Yet it is the opening scene of the Fifth Act, and a number of scenes in which Macbeth's fate is still approaching intervene before the close. Finally, in *Antony and Cleopatra* the heroine equals the hero in importance, and here the death of Antony actually occurs in the Fourth Act, and the whole of the Fifth is devoted to Cleopatra. . . .

HARRY LEVIN

Harry Levin (1912-   ). Professor of Comparative Literature at Harvard. Author of James Joyce *(1941) and many other works, including* The Question of Hamlet *(1959) and other essays on Shakespeare and his contemporaries.*

Form and Formality in Romeo and Juliet*

"Fain would I dwell on form—", says Juliet from her window to Romeo in the moonlit orchard below,

* Reprinted from *Shakespeare Quarterly,* XI (1960).

Fain would I dwell on form—fain, fain deny
What I have spoke; but farewell compliment!
                    (II. ii. 88-89)[1]

Romeo has just violated convention, dramatic and otherwise, by overhearing what Juliet intended to be a soliloquy.
Her cousin, Tybalt, had already committed a similar breach
of social and theatrical decorum in the scene at the Capulets' feast, where he had also recognized Romeo's voice to
be that of a Montague. There, when the lovers first met,
the dialogue of their meeting had been formalized into a
sonnet, acting out the conceit of his lips as pilgrims, her
hand as a shrine, and his kiss as a culminating piece of stage-
business, with an encore after an additional quatrain: "You
kiss by th' book" (I. v. 112). Neither had known the identity
of the other; and each, upon finding it out, responded with
an ominous exclamation coupling love and death (120,
140). The formality of their encounter was framed by the
ceremonious character of the scene, with its dancers, its
masquers, and—except for Tybalt's stifled outburst—its air
of old-fashioned hospitality. "We'll measure them a measure", Benvolio had proposed; but Romeo, unwilling to join
the dance, had resolved to be an onlooker and carry a torch
(I. iv. 10). That torch may have burned symbolically, but
not for Juliet; indeed, as we are inclined to forget with
Romeo, he attended the feast in order to see the dazzling but
soon eclipsed Rosaline. Rosaline's prior effect upon him is
all that we ever learn about her; yet it has been enough to
make Romeo, when he was presented to us, a virtual stereo-
type of the romantic lover. As such, he has protested a good
deal too much in his preliminary speeches, utilizing the conventional phrases and standardized images of Elizabethan
eroticism, bandying generalizations, paradoxes, and sestets
with Benvolio, and taking a quasi-religious vow which his
introduction to Juliet would ironically break (I. ii. 92-97).
Afterward this role has been reduced to absurdity by the
humorous man, Mercutio, in a mock-conjuration evoking
Venus and Cupid and the inevitable jingle of "love" and
"dove" (II. i. 10). The scene that follows is actually a continuation, marked in neither the Folios nor the Quartos,

[1] Line references are to the separate edition of G. L. Kittredge's text
  (Boston, 1940).

and linked with what has gone before by a somewhat eroded rhyme.

> 'Tis in vain
> To seek him here that means not to be found,

Benvolio concludes in the absence of Romeo (41, 42). Whereupon the latter, on the other side of the wall, chimes in:

> He jests at scars that never felt a wound.   (II. ii. 1)

Thus we stay behind, with Romeo, when the masquers depart. Juliet, appearing at the window, does not hear his descriptive invocation. Her first utterance is the very sigh that Mercutio burlesqued in the foregoing scene: "Ay, me!" (II. ii. 25). Then, believing herself to be alone and masked by the darkness, she speaks her mind in sincerity and simplicity. She calls into question not merely Romeo's name but—by implication—all names, forms, conventions, sophistications, and arbitrary dictates of society, as opposed to the appeal of instinct directly conveyed in the odor of a rose. When Romeo takes her at her word and answers, she is startled and even alarmed for his sake; but she does not revert to courtly language.

> I would not for the world they saw thee here,

she tells him, and her monosyllabic directness inspires the matching cadence of his response:

> And but thou love me, let them find me here.   (77, 79)

She pays incidental tribute to the proprieties with her passing suggestion that, had he not overheard her, she would have dwelt on form, pretended to be more distant, and played the not impossible part of the captious beloved. But farewell compliment! Romeo's love for Juliet will have an immediacy which cuts straight through the verbal embellishment that has obscured his infatuation with Rosaline. That shadowy creature, having served her Dulcinea-like purpose, may well be forgotten. On the other hand, Romeo has his more tangible foil in the person of the County Paris, who is cast in that ungrateful part which the Italians call *terzo incòmodo,* the inconvenient third party, the unwelcome member of an amorous triangle. As the official suitor of Juliet, his speeches are always formal, and often sound stilted or priggish by contrast with Romeo's. Long after Romeo has abandoned his sonneteering, Paris will pronounce a sestet at Juliet's tomb (V. iii. 11-16). During their only colloquy, which occurs in Friar Laurence's cell, Juliet takes on the sophisticated tone of Paris, denying his claims and disclaiming his compliments in brisk stichomythy. As soon as he leaves, she turns to the Friar, and again—as so often in intimate moments—her lines fall into monosyllables:

> O, shut the door! and when thou hast done so,
> Come weep with me—past hope, past cure, past help!
> (IV. i. 44-45)

Since the suit of Paris is the main subject of her conversations with her parents, she can hardly be sincere with them. Even before she met Romeo, her consent was hedged in prim phraseology:

> I'll look to like, if looking liking move.   (I. iii. 97)

And after her involvement she becomes adept in the stratagems of mental reservation, giving her mother equivocal rejoinders and rousing her father's anger by chopping logic (III. v. 69-205). Despite the intervention of the Nurse on her behalf, her one straightforward plea is disregarded. Significantly Lady Capulet, broaching the theme of Paris in stiffly appropriate couplets, has compared his face to a volume: [1]

> This precious book of love, this unbound lover,
> To beautify him only lacks a cover.
> The fish lives in the sea, and 'tis much pride
> The fair without the fair within to hide.   (I. iii. 87-90)

---

[1] On the long and rich history of this trope, see the sixteenth chapter of E. R. Curtius, *European Literature and the Latin Middle Ages,* tr. W. R. Trask (New York, 1953).

That bookish comparison, by emphasizing the letter at the expense of the spirit, helps to lend Paris an aspect of unreality; to the Nurse, more ingenuously, he is "a man of wax" (76). Later Juliet will echo Lady Capulet's metaphor, transferring it from Paris to Romeo:

> Was ever book containing such vile matter
> So fairly bound?   (III. ii. 83-84)

Here, on having learned that Romeo has just slain Tybalt, she is undergoing a crisis of doubt, a typically Shakespearian recognition of the difference between appearance and reality. The fair without may not cover a fair within, after all. Her unjustified accusations, leading up to her rhetorical question, form a sequence of oxymoronic epithets: "Beautiful tyrant, fiend angelical, . . . honorable villain!" (75-79) W. H. Auden, in a recent comment on these lines,[1] cannot believe they would come from a heroine who had been exclaiming shortly before: "Gallop apace, you fiery-footed steeds. . . !" Yet Shakespeare has been perfectly consistent in suiting changes of style to changes of mood. When Juliet feels at one with Romeo, her intonations are genuine; when she feels at odds with him, they should be unconvincing. The attraction of love is played off against the revulsion from books, and coupled with the closely related themes of youth and haste, in one of Romeo's long-drawn-out leavetakings:

> Love goes toward love as schoolboys from their books;
> But love from love, towards school with heavy looks.
>   (II. ii. 157-158)

The school for these young lovers will be tragic experience. When Romeo, assuming that Juliet is dead and contemplating his own death, recognizes the corpse of Paris, he will extend the image to cover them both:

> O give me thy hand,
> One writ with me in sour misfortune's book!
>   (V. iii. 82)

[1] In the paper-bound Laurel Shakespeare, ed. Francis Fergusson (New York, 1958), p. 26.

It was this recoil from bookishness, together with the farewell to compliment, that animated *Love's Labour's Lost,* where literary artifice was so ingeniously deployed against itself, and Berowne was taught—by an actual heroine named Rosaline—that the best books were women's eyes. Some of Shakespeare's other early comedies came even closer to adumbrating certain features of *Romeo and Juliet:* notably, *The Two Gentlemen of Verona,* with its locale, its window scene, its friar and rope, its betrothal and banishment, its emphasis upon the vagaries of love. Shakespeare's sonnets and erotic poems had won for him the reputation of an English Ovid. *Romeo and Juliet,* the most elaborate product of his so-called lyrical period, was his first successful experiment in tragedy.[1] Because of that very success, it is hard for us to realize the full extent of its novelty, though scholarship has lately been reminding us of how it must have struck contemporaries.[2] They would have been surprised, and possibly shocked, at seeing lovers taken so seriously. Legend, it had been heretofore taken for granted, was the proper matter for serious drama; romance was the stuff of the comic stage. Romantic tragedy—*"an excellent conceited Tragedie of Romeo and Juliet",* to cite the title-page of the First Quarto—was one of those contradictions in terms which Shakespeare seems to have delighted in resolving. His innovation might be described as transcending the usages of romantic comedy, which are therefore very much in evidence, particularly at the beginning. Subsequently, the leading characters acquire together a deeper dimension of feeling by expressly repudiating the artificial language they have talked and the superficial code they have lived by. Their formula might be that of the anti-Petrarchan sonnet:

> Foole said My muse to mee, looke in thy heart and write.[3]

[1] H. B. Charlton, in his British Academy lecture for 1939, *"Romeo and Juliet" as an Experimental Tragedy,* has considered the experiment in the light of Renaissance critical theory.

[2] Especially F. M. Dickey, *Not Wisely But Too Well: Shakespeare's Love Tragedies* (San Marino, 1957), pp. 63-88.

[3] Sir Philip Sidney, *Astrophel and Stella,* ed. Albert Feuillerat (Cambridge, 1922), p. 243.

An index of this development is the incidence of rhyme, heavily concentrated in the First Act, and its gradual replacement by a blank verse which is realistic or didactic with other speakers and unprecedentedly limpid and passionate with the lovers. "Love has no need of euphony", the eminent Russian translator of the play, Boris Pasternak, has commented. "Truth, not sound, dwells in its heart."[1]

Comedy set the pattern of courtship, as formally embodied in a dance. The other *genre* of Shakespeare's earlier stagecraft, history, set the pattern of conflict, as formally embodied in a duel. *Romeo and Juliet* might also be characterized as an anti-revenge play, in which hostile emotions are finally pacified by the interplay of kindlier ones. Romeo sums it up in his prophetic oxymorons:

> Here's much to do with hate, but more with love.
> Why then, O brawling love! O loving hate!
> O anything, of nothing first create!   (I. i. 162-164)

And Paris, true to type, waxes grandiose in lamenting Juliet:

> O love! O life! not life, but love in death!   (IV. v. 58)

Here, if we catch the echo from Hieronimo's lament in *The Spanish Tragedy*,

> O life! no life, but lively form of death,

we may well note that the use of antithesis, which is purely decorative with Kyd, is functional with Shakespeare. The contrarieties of his plot are reinforced on the plane of imagery by omnipresent reminders of light and darkness,[2] youth and age, and many other antitheses subsumed by the all-embracing one of Eros and Thanatos, the *leitmotif* of the *Liebestod*, the myth of the tryst in the tomb. This attraction of ultimate opposites—which is succinctly implicit in the Elizabethan ambiguity of the verb *to die*—is generalized when the Friar rhymes "womb" with "tomb", and particu-

---

[1] Boris Pasternak, "Translating Shakespeare," tr. Manya Harari, *The Twentieth Century*, CLXIV, 979 (September, 1958), p. 217.

[2] Caroline Spurgeon, *Shakespeare's Imagery and What It Tells Us* (New York, 1936), pp. 310-316.

larized when Romeo hails the latter place as "thou womb of death" (I. iii. 9, 10; V. iii. 45). Hence the "extremities" of the situation, as the Prologue to the Second Act announces, are tempered "with extreme sweet" (14). Those extremes begin to meet as soon as the initial prologue, in a sonnet disarmingly smooth, has set forth the feud between the two households, "Where civil blood makes civil hands unclean" (4). Elegant verse yields to vulgar prose, and to an immediate riot, as the servants precipitate a renewal—for the third time—of their masters' quarrel. The brawl of Act I is renewed again in the *contretemps* of Act III and completed by the swordplay of Act V. Between the street-scenes, with their clashing welter of citizens and officers, we shuttle through a series of interiors, in a flurry of domestic arrangements and family relationships. The house of the Capulets is the logical center of action, and Juliet's chamber its central sanctum. Consequently, the sphere of privacy encloses Acts II and IV, in contradistinction to the public issues raised by the alternating episodes. The temporal alternation of the play, in its accelerating continuity, is aptly recapitulated by the impatient rhythm of Capulet's speech:

> Day, night, late, early,
> At home, abroad, alone, in company,
> Waking or sleeping . . .   (III. v. 177-179)

The alignment of the *dramatis personae* is as symmetrical as the antagonism they personify. It is not without relevance that the names of the feuding families, like the Christian names of the hero and heroine, are metrically interchangeable (though "Juliet" is more frequently a trochee than an amphimacer). Tybalt the Capulet is pitted against Benvolio the Montague in the first street-fight, which brings out—with parallel stage-directions—the heads of both houses restrained by respective wives. Both the hero and heroine are paired with others, Rosaline and Paris, and admonished by elderly confidants, the Friar and the Nurse. Escalus, as Prince of Verona, occupies a superior and neutral position; yet, in the interchange of blood for blood, he loses "a brace of kinsman", Paris and Mercutio (V. iii. 295). Three times he must quell and sentence the rioters before he can pronounce the final sestet, restoring order to the city-state through the lovers' sacrifice. He effects the resolution by summoning the patriarchal enemies, from their opposite sides, to be reconciled. "Capulet, Montague," he sternly arraigns them, and the polysyllables are brought home by monosyllabics:

> See what a scourge is laid upon your hate
> That heaven finds means to kill your joys with love.
> (291-293)

The two-sided counterpoise of the dramatic structure is well matched by the dynamic symmetry of the antithetical style. One of its peculiarities, which surprisingly seems to have escaped the attention of commentators, is a habit of stressing a word by repeating it within a line, a figure which may be classified in rhetoric as a kind of *ploce*. I have cited a few examples incidentally; let me now underline the device by pointing out a few more. Thus Montague and Capulet are accused of forcing their parties

> To wield old partisans in hands as old,
> Cank'red with peace, to part your cank'red hate.
> (I. i. 101, 102)

This double instance, along with the wordplay on "cank'red," suggests the embattled atmosphere of partisanship through the halberds; and it is further emphasized in Benvolio's account of the fray:

> Came more and more, and fought on part and part.
> (122)

The key-words are not only doubled but affectionately intertwined, when Romeo confides to the Friar:

> As mine on hers, so hers is set on mine. (II. iii. 59)

Again, he conveys the idea of reciprocity by declaring that Juliet returns "grace for grace and love for love" (86). The Friar's warning hints at poetic justice:

> These violent delights have violent ends. (II. vi. 9)

Similarly Mercutio, challenged by Tybalt, turns "point to point", and the Nurse finds Juliet—in *antimetabole*—"Blubb'ring and weeping, weeping and blubbering" (III. ii. 165; iii. 87). Statistics would prove illusory, because some repetitions are simply idiomatic, grammatical, or—in the case of old Capulet or the Nurse—colloquial. But it is significant that the play contains well over a hundred such lines, the largest number being in the First Act and scarcely any left over for the Fifth.

The significance of this tendency toward reduplication, both stylistic and structural, can perhaps be best understood in the light of Bergson's well-known theory of the comic: the imposition of geometrical form upon the living data of formless consciousness. The stylization of love, the constant pairing and counterbalancing, the *quid pro quo* of Capulet and Montague, seem mechanical and unnatural. Nature has other proponents besides the lovers, especially Mercutio their fellow victim, who bequeaths his curse to both their houses. His is likewise an ironic end, since he has been as much a satirist of "the new form" and Tybalt's punctilio in duelling "by the book of arithmetic" as of "the numbers that Petrarch flowed in" and Romeo's affectations of gallantry (II. iv. 34, 38; III. i. 104). Mercutio's interpretation of dreams, running counter to Romeo's premonitions, is naturalistic, not to say Freudian; Queen Mab operates through fantasies of wish-fulfilment, bringing love to lovers, fees to lawyers, and tithe-pigs to parsons; the moral is that desires can be mischievous. In his repartee with Romeo, Mercutio looks forward to their fencing with Tybalt; furthermore he charges the air with bawdy suggestions that—in spite of the limitations of Shakespeare's theatre, its lack of actresses and absence of close-ups—love may have something to do with sex, if not with lust, with the physical complementarity of male and female.[1] He is abetted, in that respect, by the malapropistic garrulity of the Nurse, Angelica, who is naturally bound to Juliet through having been her wet-nurse, and who has lost the infant daughter that might have been Juliet's age. None the less, her crotchety hesita-

---

[1] Coleridge's persistent defense of Shakespeare against the charge of gross language does more credit to that critic's high-mindedness than to his discernment. The concentrated ribaldry of the gallants in the street (II. iv) is deliberately contrasted with the previous exchange between the lovers in the orchard.

tions are contrasted with Juliet's youthful ardors when the Nurse acts as go-between for Romeo. His counsellor, Friar Laurence, makes a measured entrance with his sententious couplets on the uses and abuses of natural properties, the medicinal and poisonous effects of plants:

> For this, being smelt, with that part cheers each part;
> Being tasted, slays all senses with the heart.
>
> (II. iii. 25, 26)

His watchword is "Wisely and slow", yet he contributes to the grief at the sepulcher by ignoring his own advice, "They stumble that run fast" (94).[1] When Romeo upbraids him monosyllabically,

> Thou canst not speak of that thou doest not feel,

it is the age-old dilemma that separates the generations: *Si jeunesse savait, si vieillesse pouvait* (III. iii. 64). Banished to Mantua, Romeo has illicit recourse to the Apothecary, whose shop—envisaged with Flemish precision—unhappily replaces the Friar's cell, and whose poison is the sinister counterpart of Laurence's potion.

Against this insistence upon polarity, at every level, the mutuality of the lovers stands out, the one organic relation amid an overplus of stylized expressions and attitudes. The naturalness of their diction is artfully gained, as we have noticed, through a running critique of artificiality. In drawing a curtain over the consummation of their love, Shakespeare heralds it with a prothalamium and follows it with an epithalamium. Juliet's "Gallop apace, you fiery-footed steeds", reversing the Ovidian *"lente currite, noctis equi"*, is spoken "alone" but in breathless anticipation of a companion (III. ii. 1). After having besought the day to end, the sequel to her solo is the duet in which she begs the night to continue. In the ensuing *débat* of the nightingale and the lark, a refinement upon the antiphonal song of the owl and the cuckoo in *Love's Labour's Lost*, Romeo more realistically discerns "the herald of the morn" (III. v. 6). When Juliet reluctantly agrees, "More light and light it

[1] This is the leading theme of the play, in the interpretation of Brents Stirling, *Unity in Shakespearian Tragedy: The Interplay of Themes and Characters* (New York, 1956), pp. 10-25.

grows", he completes the paradox with a doubly redupli-
cating line:

> More light and light—more dark and dark our woes!
> (35, 36)

The precariousness of their union, formulated arithmeti-
cally by the Friar as "two in one" (II. vi. 37), is brought
out by the terrible loneliness of Juliet's monologue upon
taking the potion:

> My dismal scene I needs must act alone.   (IV. iii. 19)

Her utter singleness, as an only child, is stressed by her
father and mourned by her mother:

> But one, poor one, one poor and loving child.   (v. 46)

Tragedy tends to isolate where comedy brings together, to
reveal the uniqueness of individuals rather than what they
have in common with others. Asking for Romeo's profession of love, Juliet anticipates: "I know thou wilt say 'Ay' "
(II. ii. 90). That monosyllable of glad assent was the first
she ever spoke, as we know from the Nurse's childish anecdote (I. iii. 48). Later, asking the Nurse whether Romeo
has been killed, Juliet pauses self-consciously over the pun
between "Ay" and "I" or "eye":

> Say thou but 'I,'
> And that bare vowel 'I' shall poison more
> Than the death-darting eye of cockatrice.
> I am not I, if there be such an 'I';
> Or those eyes shut that make thee answer 'I.'
> If he be slain, say 'I'; or if not, 'no.'
> Brief sounds determine of my weal or woe.
> (III. ii. 45-51)

Her identification with him is negated by death, conceived
as a shut or poisoning eye, which throws the pair back
upon their single selves. Each of them dies alone—or, at
all events, in the belief that the other lies dead, and without
the benefit of a recognition-scene. Juliet, of course, is still
alive; but she has already voiced her death-speech in the

potion scene. With the dagger, her last words, though richly symbolic, are brief and monosyllabic:

> This is thy sheath; there rest, and let me die.
>   (V. iii. 170)

The sense of vicissitude is re-enacted through various gestures of staging; Romeo and Juliet experience their exaltation "aloft" on the upper stage; his descent via the rope is, as she fears, toward the tomb (III. v. 56).[1] The antonymous adverbs *up* and *down* figure, with increasing prominence, among the brief sounds that determine Juliet's woe (e.g., V. ii. 209-210). The overriding pattern through which she and Romeo have been trying to break—call it Fortune, the stars, or what you will—ends by closing in and breaking them; their private world disappears, and we are left in the social ambiance again. Capulet's house has been bustling with preparations for a wedding, the happy ending of comedy. The news of Juliet's death is not yet tragic because it is premature; but it introduces a peripety which will become the starting point for *Hamlet*.

> All things that we ordained festival
> Turn from their office to black funeral—

the old man cries, and his litany of contraries is not less poignant because he has been so fond of playing the genial host:

> Our instruments to melancholy bells,
> Our wedding cheer to a sad burial feast;
> Our solemn hymns to sullen dirges change;
> Our bridal flowers serve for a buried corse;
> And all things change them to the contrary.
>   (IV. v. 84-90)

His lamentation, in which he is joined by his wife, the Nurse, and Paris, reasserts the formalities by means of what is virtually an operatic quartet. Thereupon the music becomes explicit, when they leave the stage to the Musi-

---

[1] One of the more recent and pertinent discussions of staging is that of Richard Hosley, "The Use of the Upper Stage in *Romeo and Juliet*", *Shakespeare Quarterly*, V, 4 (Autumn, 1954), 371-379.

cians, who have walked on with the County Paris. Normally these three might play during the *entr'acte,* but Shakespeare has woven them into the dialogue terminating the Fourth Act.[1] Though their art has the power of soothing the passions and thereby redressing grief, as the comic servant Peter reminds them with a quotation from Richard Edward's lyric *In Commendacion of Musicke,* he persists in his query: "Why 'silver sound'?" (131) Their answers are those of mere hirelings, who can indifferently change their tune from a merry dump to a doleful one, so long as they are paid with coin of the realm. Yet Peter's riddle touches a deeper chord of correspondence, the interconnection between discord and harmony, between impulse and discipline. "Consort", which can denote a concert or a companionship, can become the fighting word that motivates the unharmonious pricksong of the duellists (III. i. 48). The "sweet division" of the lark sounds harsh and out of tune to Juliet, since it proclaims that the lovers must be divided (v. 29). Why "silver sound"? Because Romeo, in the orchard, has sworn by the moon

That tips with silver all these fruit-tree tops. (II. i. 108)

Because Shakespeare, transporting sights and sounds into words, has made us imagine

How silver-sweet sound lovers' tongues by night,
Like softest music to attending ears! (167-168)

T. J. B. SPENCER

T. J. B. Spencer (1915-   ). Professor of English Literature at Birmingham University, and formerly of the

[1] Professor F. T. Bowers reminds me that inter-act music was probably not a regular feature of public performance when *Romeo and Juliet* was first performed. Some early evidence for it has been gathered by T. S. Graves in "The Act-Time in Elizabethan Theatres", *Studies in Philology,* XII, 3 (July, 1915), 120-124—notably contemporary sound cues, written into a copy of the Second Quarto and cited by Malone. But if—as seems likely—such practices were exceptional, then Shakespeare was innovating all the farther.

Queen's University, Belfast; Director of the Shakespeare Institute, Stratford-upon-Avon. Author of Fair Greece, Sad Relic *(1954) and editor of* Shakespeare's Plutarch *(1964).*

Shakespeare and the Elizabethan Romans*

Shakespeare has, at various times, received some very handsome compliments for his ancient Romans; for his picture of the Roman world, its institutions, and the causation of events; for his representation of the Roman people at three critical stages of their development: the turbulent republic with its conflict of the classes; the transition from an oligarchic to a monarchic government which was vainly delayed by the assassination of Julius Caesar; and the final stages by which the rule of the civilized world came to lie in the hands of Octavius Caesar. These are quite often praised as veracious or penetrating or plausible. Moreover, the compliments begin early, and they begin at a time when no high opinion was held of Shakespeare's learning. The name of Nahum Tate, for example, is not a revered one in the history of Shakespeare studies; yet in 1680 he wrote:

> I confess I cou'd never yet get a true account of his Learning, and am apt to think it more than Common Report allows him. I am sure he never touches on a Roman Story, but the Persons, the Passages, the Manners, the Circumstances, the Ceremonies, all are Roman.[1]

And Dryden, too, in conversation said "that there was something in this very tragedy of *Coriolanus,* as it was writ by Shakespeare, that is truly great and truly Roman".[2] And Pope (for all his comparison of Shakespeare to "an ancient majestick piece of *Gothick* Architecture") declared in his Preface that he found him

very knowing in the customs, rites, and manners of An-

---

* Reprinted from *Shakespeare Survey* X (1957).
[1] Letter before *The Loyal General, A Tragedy* (1680); *The Shakspere Allusion Book* . . . 1591 to 1700 (Oxford, 1932), II. 266.
[2] Reported by Dennis; see D. Nichol Smith, *Eighteenth Century Essays on Shakespeare* (Glasgow, 1903), p. 309.

tiquity. In *Coriolanus* and *Julius Caesar,* not only the Spirit, but Manners, of the *Romans* are exactly drawn; and still a nicer distinction is shewn, between the manners of the *Romans* in the time of the former and of the latter.[1]

The odd thing is that this veracity or authenticity was approved at a time when Shakespeare's educational background was suspect; when the word "learning" practically meant a knowledge of the Greek and Roman writers; when the usual description of Shakespeare was "wild"; when he was regarded as a member of what Thomas Rymer called "the gang of the strolling fraternity".

There were, of course, one or two exceptions; Rymer wrote, towards the end of the seventeenth century, in his most cutting way about *Julius Caesar*:

> *Caesar* and *Brutus* were above his conversation. To put them in Fools Coats, and make them Jack-puddens in the *Shakespear* dress, is a *Sacriledge.* . . . The Truth is, this authors head was full of villainous, unnatural images, and history has only furnish'd him with great names, thereby to recommend them to the World.[2]

There was, too, the problem of Shakespeare's undignified Roman mobs. It was obvious that Cleopatra's vision of a Rome where

> mechanic slaves
> With greasy aprons, rules, and hammers, shall
> Uplift us to the view

was derived from Shakespeare's own London. And Casca's description: "The rabblement hooted and clapped their chopped hands and threw up their sweaty night-caps . . ."— this was the English populace and not the Roman *plebs.* Dennis thought that the introduction of the mob by Shakespeare "offends not only against the Dignity of Tragedy, but against the Truth of History likewise, and the Customs of Ancient *Rome,* and the majesty of the *Roman* people".[3]

[1] D. Nichol Smith, *op. cit.* p. 26.
[2] *A Short View of Tragedy* (1963), p. 148.
[3] D. Nichol Smith, *op. cit.* p. 26.

But the opinions of Rymer and Dennis were eccentric; the worst they could say against Shakespeare's Romans was that they were not sufficiently dignified; and this counted for very little beside the usual opinion of better minds that Shakespeare got his Romans right.

More surprising, therefore, was Shakespeare's frequent neglect of details; and it was just at *this* time that the scholars and critics (if not the theatrical and reading publics) were becoming sensitive to Shakespeare's anachronisms, his aberrations from good sense and common knowledge about the ancients, and were carefully scrutinizing his text for mistakes. It was apparent that, when it came to details, Shakespeare's Romans often belonged to the time of Queen Elizabeth and King James. And the industrious commentators of the eighteenth century collected a formidable array of nonsense from his plays on classical antiquity: how clocks strike in ancient Rome; how Cleopatra has lace in her stays and plays at billiards; how Titus Lartius compares Coriolanus's *hm* to the sound of a battery; and so on. Above all, it could be observed that Shakespeare was occasionally careless or forgetful about ancient costume. Coriolanus stood in the Forum waving his hat. The very idea of a Roman candidate for the consulship standing waving his hat was enough to make a whole form of schoolboys break into irrepressible mirth. Pope softened the horror by emending *hat* to *cap*; and Coriolanus was permitted to wave his cap, not his hat, in the texts of Theobald, Hanmer, Warburton, and Dr Johnson, and perhaps even later. What seemed remarkable and what made the eighteenth-century editors so fussy about these anachronisms was Shakespeare's inconsistency in his historical reconstructions: his care and scrupulosity over preserving Roman manners, alongside occasional carelessness or indifference. The very reason they noticed the blunders was that they jarred against the pervading sense of authenticity everywhere else in the Roman plays.

I take it that Dryden and Pope were right; that Shakespeare knew what he was doing in writing Roman plays; that part of his intention was a serious effort at representing the Roman scene as genuinely as he could. He was not telling a fairy tale with Duke Theseus on St Valentine's Day, nor dramatizing a novelette about Kings of Sicilia and Bohemia, but producing a *mimesis* of the veritable history of the most important people (humanly speaking) who ever lived, the concern of every educated man in Europe and not merely something of local, national, patriotic interest; and he was conscious of all this while he was building up his dramatic situations and expositions of characters for the players to fulfil. It can, therefore, hardly fail to be relevant to our interpretations of the plays to explore the views of Roman history in Shakespeare's time. It is at least important to make sure that we do not unthinkingly take it for granted that they were the same as our own in the twentieth century to which we belong or the nineteenth century from which we derive. It is worth while tracing to what extent Shakespeare was in step with ideas about ancient Rome among his contemporaries and to what extent (and why) he diverged from them.

"Histories make men wise." Ancient, and in particular Roman, history was explored as the material of political lessons, because it was one of the few bodies of consistent and continuous historical material available. Modern national history (in spite of patriotism) could not be regarded as so central, nor were the writers so good; and the narratives in the scriptures were already overworked by the parson. Roman history was written and interpreted tendentiously in Europe in the sixteenth century, as has happened at other times. In writing his Roman plays Shakespeare was touching upon the gravest and most exciting as well as the most pedantic of Renaissance studies, of European scholarship. Although Shakespeare himself turned to Roman history after he had been occupied with English history for some years, nevertheless it was Roman history which usually had the primacy for the study of political morality. Yet in spite of the widespread interest in ancient culture among educated persons, the actual writing of the history of the Greeks and Romans was not very successful in England in the sixteenth century. There was no history of the Romans in Shakespeare's lifetime comparable (for example) to the *History of Great Britain* by John Speed or the *Generall Historie of the Turkes* by Richard Knolles. Sir Walter Raleigh did not get very far in his *History of the World* and dealt only with the earlier and duller centuries of Rome. Probably the reason for the scarcity of books of

Roman history and their undistinguished nature was that the sense of the supremacy of the ancients and of the impudence of endeavouring to provide a substitute for Livy and Tacitus, was too strong.[1] So explained William Fulbecke, who published a book called *An Historicall Collection of the Continuall Factions, Tumults, and Massacres of the Romans* in 1601 and dedicated it to Sackville, Lord Buckhurst (the primary author of *A Mirror for Magistrates*). "I do not despaire" (wrote Fulbecke) "to follow these Romanes, though I do not aspire to their exquisite and industrious perfection: for that were to climbe above the climates: but to imitate any man, is every mans talent." His book is a poor thing. And so is Richard Reynoldes' *Chronicle of all the Noble Emperours of the Romaines* (1571). And the translations of the Roman historians, apart from North's Plutarch, before the seventeenth century are not particularly distinguished. But for this very reason the books on Roman history are useful evidence for the normal attitude to the Romans and their story in Shakespeare's lifetime. For it is not so much what we can find in Plutarch, but what Shakespeare noticed in Plutarch that we need to know; not merely Plutarch's narrative, but the preconceptions with which his biographies could be read by a lively modern mind about the turn of the seventeenth century; for

> men may construe things after their fashion
> Clean from the purpose of the things themselves.

It is by no means certain that we, by the unaided light of reason and mid-twentieth-century assumptions, will always be able to notice the things to which Shakespeare was sensitive.

First then, the title of William Fulbecke's book is worth attention: *An Historicall Collection of the Continuall Factions, Tumults, and Massacres of the Romans and Italians during the space of one hundred and twentie yeares*

[1] Cf. A. Momigliano, *Contributo alla storia degli studi classici* (Rome, 1955), pp. 75-6: "To the best of my knowledge, the idea that one could write a history of Rome which should replace Livy and Tacitus was not yet born in the early seventeenth century. The first Camden Praelector of history in the University of Oxford had the statutory duty of commenting on Florus and other ancient historians (1622). . . . Both in Oxford and Cambridge Ancient History was taught in the form of a commentary on ancient historians."

next before the peaceable Empire of Augustus Caesar.
There is not much of the majesty of the Roman People
(which Dennis desiderated) in these continual factions,
tumults and massacres. In his preface Fulbecke writes:

> The use of this historie is threefold; first the revealing
> of the mischiefes of discord and civill discention. . . .
> Secondly the opening of the cause hereof, which is noth-
> ing else but ambition, for out of this seed groweth a
> whole harvest of evils. Thirdly the declaring of the
> remedie, which is by humble estimation of our selves, by
> living well, not by lurking well: by conversing in the light
> of the common weale with equals, not by complotting
> in darke conventicles against superiors.[1]

Equally tendentious is what we read on the title-page of the
translation of Appian as *An Auncient Historie and exquisite
Chronicle of the Romanes Warres, both Civile and Foren*
in 1578;

> In the which is declared:
> Their greedy desire to conquere others.
> Their mortall malice to destroy themselves.
> Their seeking of matters to make warre abroade.
> Their picking of quarels to fall out at home.
> All the degrees of Sedition, and all the effects of Ambition.
> A firme determination of Fate, thorowe all the changes of
> Fortune.
> And finally, an evident demonstration, That peoples rule
> must give place, and Princes power prevayle.

This kind of material (the ordinary stuff of Roman history
in the sixteenth century) does not lend itself to chatter about
the majesty of the Roman people. In fact, the kind of classical dignity which we associate perhaps with Addison's *Cato*
or Kemble's impersonation of Coriolanus is not to be taken
for granted in Shakespeare's time. The beginning of Virgil's
Aeneid, with its simple yet sonorous *arma virumque cano,*
might by us be taken as expressive of true Roman dignity.
Richard Stanyhurst, however, in his translation of Virgil in
1582 rendered it:

[1] Sig. A2.

Now manhood and garboyles I chaunt. . . .

"Garboyles", it will be remembered, was Antony's favourite word to describe the military and political exploits of Fulvia.

So much for Roman history as "garboyles". Secondly, besides the "garboyles" and encouraging them, there was a limitation in viewpoint due to the fact that the moral purpose of history in general, and of Roman history in particular, was directed towards *monarchs*. When Richard Reynoldes published his *Chronicle of all the Noble Emperours of the Romaines, from Julius Caesar orderly. . . . Setting forth the great power, and devine providence of almighty God, in preserving the godly Princes and common wealthes* in 1571, he gave the usual panegyric: "An historie is the glasse of Princes, the image most lively bothe of vertue and vice, the learned theatre or spectacle of all the worlde, the councell house of Princes, the trier of all truthes, a witnes of all tymes and ages . . ." and so forth. The really important and interesting and relevant political lessons were those connected with *princes*. It was this that turned the attention away from republican Rome to monarchical Rome: the Rome of the Twelve Caesars and their successors. Republican Rome was not nearly so useful for models of political morality, because in sixteenth-century Europe republics happened to be rather rare. (Venice, the important one, was peculiar, not to say unique, anyway.) Republics were scarce. But there were aspiring Roman Emperors all over the place.

Sometimes the political lesson was a very simple one. In dedicating his *Auncient Historie and exquisite Chronicle of the Romanes Warres* in 1578, the translator states:

How God plagueth them that conspire againste theyr Prince, this Historie declareth at the full. For all of them, the coniured against *Caius Caesar,* not one did escape violent death. The which this Author hathe a pleasure to declare, bycause he would affray all men from disloyaltie toward their Soveraigne.

We need not, perhaps, put too much emphasis upon this argument, because the book was being dedicated to the

Captain of the Queen's Majesty's Guard. But more sophisticated writers showed the same interest. Sir Walter Raleigh in his *History of the World* on occasions pointed the suitable political moral. But the problems that interested him and set him off on one of his discussions were those relevant to the political situation in the sixteenth and early seventeenth centuries. The story of Coriolanus, for example, does not interest him at all; he compresses Livy's fine narrative into nothingness, though he spares a few words for Coriolanus's mother and wife who prevailed upon him "with a pitiful tune of deprecation".[1] But the problem of the growth of tyranny fascinates him. He never got as far as Julius Caesar. He had to wind up his *History* at the beginning of the second century B.C. But he gets Caesar into his discussion. The problem of the difference between a benevolent monarchy and an odious tyranny, and the gradations by which the one may merge into the other—that was the real interest; and Imperial Rome was the true material for that.

So that, in spite of literary admiration for Cicero, the Romans in the imagination of the sixteenth century were Suetonian and Tacitan rather than Plutarchan. An occasional eccentric enthusiasm for one or both of the two Brutuses does not weigh against the fact that it was the busts of the Twelve Caesars that decorated almost every palace in Europe. And it required a considerable intellectual feat to substitute the Plutarchan vision of Rome (mostly republican) for the customary line of the Imperial Caesars. Montaigne and Shakespeare were capable of that feat. Not many others were. The Roman stuff that got into *A Mirror for Magistrates* naturally came from Suetonius and historians of the later Caesars. One of the educators of Europe in the sixteenth century was the Spaniard Antonio de Guevara. His *Dial of Princes* (which was a substitute for the still unprinted *Meditations* of the Emperor Marcus Aurelius) was translated by North with as much enthusiasm as Plutarch was. Guevara, whose platitudinous remarks on politics and morals—he was a worthy master for Polonius —gave him a European reputation, naturally turned to Imperial Rome to illustrate his maxims and observations on

[1] *The History of the World*, IV, vii, i; *Works* (Oxford, 1832) V, 531-2.

life. The Emperor Marcus Aurelius was his model of virtue (though he included love-letters from the Emperor to a variety of young women in Rome—which seems rather an incongruous thing to do for the over-virtuous author of the *Meditations*); and when Guevara wanted example of vices as well as virtue, to give more varied moral and political lessons, he again naturally turned to the Roman monarchs. His *Decada,* in fact, gives lives from Trajan onwards. Among them appears a blood-curdling life of a certain Emperior Bassianus, a name which we shall not remember from our reading of Gibbon, but one with which we are thoroughly familiar from *Titus Andronicus.* This account of Bassianus is a shocking thing, translated with considerable energy into English in 1577 by Edward Hellowes in *A Chronicle, conteyning the lives of tenne Emperours of Rome* and dedicated to the Queen. The life of Bassianus (whom we know by his nickname of Caracalla—but Renaissance writers had too much respect for Roman Emperors to use only their vulgar nicknames) is one of almost unparalleled cruelty: how he slew his brother in the arms of his mother; how he slew half the Vestal Virgins because (so he said) they were not virgins, and then slew the other half because (so he said) they were. I will not say that it is a positive relief to pass from the life of Bassianus by Guevara to Shakespeare's *Titus Andronicus* (and there to find, by the way, that Bassianus is the better of the two brothers). Still, we feel that we are in the same world. *Titus Andronicus* is Senecan, yes; and it belongs to what Mr Shandy would call "no year of our Lord"; and its *sources* probably belong to medieval legend. Yet, as made into the play we know, it is also a not untypical piece of Roman history, or would seem to be so to anyone who came fresh from reading Guevara. Not the most high and palmy state of Rome, certainly. But an authentic Rome, and a Rome from which the usual political lessons could be drawn. *Titus* was entered in the Stationers' Register in 1594 as "a Noble Roman Historye", and it was published the same year as a "Most Lamentable Romaine Tragedie", and by sixteenth-century standards the claim was justified. One could say almost without paradox that, in many respects, *Titus Andronicus* is a more typical Roman play, a more characteristic piece of Roman history, than the three great plays of Shakespeare which are generally grouped under that name. The Elizabethans had far less of a low opinion of the Low Empire than we have learned to have. In fact, many of the qualities of Romanity are in *Titus*. The garboils; the stoical or Senecal endurance; the many historical properties: senators and tribunes and patricians. It was obviously *intended* to be a faithful picture of Roman civilization. Indeed, the political institutions in *Titus* are a subject that has been rather neglected.[1] They are certainly peculiar, and cannot be placed at any known period in Roman history, as can those in *Coriolanus* or *Julius Caesar*; and they afford a strange contrast with the care and authenticity of those later plays. In *Titus Andronicus* Rome seems to be, at times, a free commonwealth, with the usual mixture of patrician and plebeian institutions. Titus is himself elected emperor of Rome on account of his merits, because the senate and people do not recognize an hereditary principle of succession. But Titus disclaims the honour in favour of the late Emperor's elder (and worser) son. Titus is a devoted adherent (not to say a maniacal one) of the hereditary monarchical principle in a commonwealth that only partly takes it into account, and he eventually acknowledges his mistake. He encourages, by his subservience, the despotic rule on which Saturninus embarks, passing to a world of Byzantine intrigue, in which the barbarians (Southern and Northern, Moors and Goths), both by personalities and armies, exert their baneful or beneficent influence. And finally, by popular acclaim, Lucius is elected emperor "to order well the state" (says the second Quarto). Now, all these elements of the political situation can be found in Roman history, but not combined in this way. The play does not assume a political situation known to Roman history; it is, rather, a summary of Roman politics. It is not so much that any particular set of political institutions is assumed in *Titus,* but rather that it includes *all* the political institutions that Rome ever had. The author seems anxious, not to get it all right, but to get it all in. It has been suggested that *Titus Andronicus* was the work of a fairly well-informed scholar. It seems to be a quintessence of impressions derived from an eager reading of Roman history rather than a real effort at verisimilitude.

[1] William Watkiss Lloyd in 1856 made some pertinent remarks. *Critical Essays on the Plays of Shakespeare* (1894), p. 352.

Still, I think that *Titus* would easily be recognized as typical Roman history by a sixteenth-century audience; the claim that it was a "noble Roman history" was a just one.

Bearing this in mind, one can see why Plutarch was no rival to Suetonius (and his imitators and followers) as a source of impressions of the Romans. Suetonius's rag-bag of gossip, scandal, piquant and spicy *personalia*, provided the material for a large proportion of the plays written on Roman themes, including a number of University plays. Indeed the estimate of the popularity of Plutarch in the sixteenth century seems to have been rather exaggerated— at least, the popularity of Plutarch's *Lives*. It was Plutarch's *Moralia* which were most admired, and most influential, those essays on such subjects as 'Tranquillity of Mind', and 'Whether Virtue can be Taught', and so forth, which constantly provided exercises for translation, including one by the Queen herself. These things came home to men's business and bosoms far more than the parallel lives of the Greeks and Romans, and were admired for much the same reason as Dr Johnson's *Ramblers* and Martin Tupper's *Proverbial Philosophy*: they perfectly hit the moral preoccupations of the time; and were the model for Montaigne, and thence for Bacon. It was really the eighteenth century that was the great age of Plutarch's *Lives*, when there were two complete new translations, many partial ones, and frequent convenient reprints. In Shakespeare's time the *Lives* were confined to large and cumbrous folios. We, when we want to study the relation between Shakespeare's Roman plays and Plutarch's lives, can turn to those handy selections prepared for the purpose by Skeat or Tucker Brooke or Carr. Or, if we are prompted by curiosity or conscience to set about reading the whole thing, we can turn to the manageable volumes of the Tudor Translations or to the handy little pocket volumes of the Temple Classics. But Shakespeare, when he read Plutarch, could not turn to a volume of selections illustrating Shakespeare's Roman plays. He had to take a very heavy folio in his hands. We have to read 1010 folio pages in the 1579 edition before we come to the death of Cleopatra. (It need not be suggested that Shakespeare read 1010 folio pages before *he* came to the death of Cleopatra.) It is certainly not a literary experience comparable with picking up a novelette like *Pandosto* or *Rosalynde,* or reading a little book about the Continual Factions, Tumults and Massacres of the Romans. It was rather a serious thing for a busy man of the theatre to do. It was probably the most serious experience that Shakespeare had of the bookish kind.

In Shakespeare's three principal Roman plays we see a steadily advancing independence of thought in the reconsideration of the Roman world. In *Julius Caesar,* it seems to me, he is almost precisely in step with sound Renaissance opinion on the subject. There has been a good deal of discussion of this play because of a supposed ambiguity in the author's attitude to the two principal characters. It has been suggested, on the one hand, that Brutus is intended to be a short-sighted political blunderer who foolishly or even wickedly struck down the foremost man in all the world; Dante and survivals of medieval opinion in the sixteenth century can be quoted here. We have, on the contrary, been told, on very high authority in Shakespeare studies, that Shakespeare followed the Renaissance admiration for Brutus and detestation for Caesar. It has also been suggested that Shakespeare left the exact degrees of guilt and merit in Caesar and Brutus deliberately ambiguous in the play, to give a sense of depth, to keep the audience guessing and so make the whole dramatic situation more telling. But all this, it seems to me, obscures the fact that the reassessment and reconsideration of such famous historical figures was a common literary activity in the Renaissance, not merely in poetry and drama (where licence is acceptable), but in plain prose, the writing of history. It seems hardly legitimate to talk about "tradition", to refer to "traditional" opinions about Caesar and Brutus, when in fact the characters of each of them had been the subject of constant discussion. In the nineteenth century you could weigh up the varying views of Caesar held by Mommsen or Froude or Anthony Trollope or Napoleon III of France, and read their entertaining books on the subject. It was not so very different in the sixteenth century. I am not suggesting that Shakespeare read the great works on the life and character of Julius Caesar by Hubert Goltz (1563) or by Stefano Schiappalaria (1578) where everything about him was collected and collated and assessed and criticized. But other people did. And Shakespeare, writing a play of the subject,

could hardly live in such intellectual isolation as to be un-
aware of the discussion. It would, I think, be quite wrong to
suggest by quotation from any one writer such as Montaigne that Caesar was generally agreed to be a detestable
character. On the contrary, the problem was acknowledged
to be a complicated and fascinating one; and the discussion
began early, and in ancient times. Men have often disputed
(wrote Seneca in his *De Beneficiis,* a work translated both
by Arthur Golding and by Thomas Lodge), whether Brutus
did right or wrong. "For mine owne part, although I
esteemed *Brutus* in all other things a wise and vertuous
man, yet meseemeth that in this he committed a great
errour"; and Seneca goes on to explain the error: Brutus

> imagined that such a Citie as this might repossesse her
> ancient honour, and former lustre, when vertue and the
> primitive Lawes were either abolished, or wholly ex-
> tinguished; Or that Iustice, Right, and Law, should be
> inviolably observed in such a place, where he had seene
> so many thousand men at shocke and battell, not to the
> intent to discerne whether they were to obay and serve,
> but to resolve under whom they ought to serve and obay.
> Oh how great oblivion possessed this man! how much
> forgot he both the nature of affaires, and the state of his
> Citie! to suppose that by the death of one man there
> should not some other start up after him, that would
> usurpe over the common-weale.[1]

Likewise William Fullbecke (writing in 1586, though his
book was not published until 1601), while seeing the
calamities Caesar was bringing upon the Roman state, could
not praise Brutus for permitting himself to participate in
political assassinations:

> M. Brutus, the chiefe actor in Caesars tragedie, was in
> counsel deepe, in wit profound, in plot politicke, and one
> that hated the principality whereof he devested Caesar.
> But did Brutus looke for peace by bloudshed? did he
> thinke to avoyd tyrannie by tumult? was there no way to
> wound Caesar, but by stabbing his own conscience? & no

---

[1] Lodge's translation in *The Workes of Lucius Annaeus Seneca, Both
Morall and Naturall* (1614), pp. 30-1; Of Benefits, II, XX.

way to make Caesar odious, but by incurring the same obloquie?[1]

Fulbecke summarized his position in the controversy: "Questionlesse the Romanes should not have nourished this lyon in their Citie, or being nourished, they should not have disgraced him."

In writing *Julius Caesar* and *Antony and Cleopatra* Shakespeare was keeping within a safe body of story. Those persons had been dignified by tragedies in many countries of Europe and many times before Shakespeare arose and drove all competitors from the field. But with *Coriolanus* it was different. There was apparently no previous play on the subject. It was more of a deliberate literary and artistic choice than either of the other two Roman plays. He must have discovered Coriolanus in Plutarch. As for Caesar and Cleopatra, he presumably went to Plutarch knowing that they were good subjects for plays. But no one had directed him to Coriolanus. The story was hardly well known and not particularly attractive. The story of the ingratitude he suffered, the revenge he purposed and renounced, was told by Livy, and, along with one or two other stories of Roman womenfolk (Lucretia, Virginia), it was turned into a *novella* in Painter's *Pallace of Pleasure*; there is a mention in *Titus Andronicus*. More than *Julius Caesar* or than *Antony and Cleopatra, Coriolanus* (perhaps by the rivalry or stimulation of Ben Jonson) shows a great deal of care to get things right, to preserve Roman manners and customs and allusions. We have, of course, the usual Roman officials, and political and religious customs familiarly referred to; and we have the Roman mythology and pantheon. But we are also given a good deal of Roman history worked into the background. Even the eighteenth-century editors who took a toothcomb through the play for mistaken references to English customs could find very little; and it requires considerable pedantry to check these. Moreover, in *Coriolanus* there is some effort to make literary allusions appropriate. The ladies know their Homer and the Tale of Troy. The personal names used are all authentically derived from somewhere in Plutarch; Shakespeare has turned the pages to find something suitable. He is taking great care. He is on

[1] *Op. cit.* sig. Z I^v.

his mettle. Dozens of poetasters could write plays on Julius Caesar or on Cleopatra. Dozens did. But to write *Coriolanus* was one of the great feats of the historical imagination in Renaissance Europe.

Setting aside poetical and theatrical considerations, and merely referring to the artist's ability to "create a world" (as the saying is), we may ask if there was anything in prose or verse, in Elizabethan or Jacobean literature, which bears the same marks of careful and thoughtful consideration of the ancient world, a deliberate effort of a critical intelligence to give a consistent picture of it, as there is in Shakespeare's plays. Of course, Ben Jonson's *Catiline* and *Sejanus* at once suggest themselves. The comparison between Shakespeare's and Ben Jonson's Roman plays is a chronic one, an inevitable one, and it is nearly always, I suppose, made to Jonson's disadvantage. At least it had its origin in their own time; for Leonard Digges tells us, in his verses before the 1640 *Poems,* that audiences were ravished by such scenes as the quarrel between Brutus and Cassius, when they would not brook a line of tedious (though well-laboured) *Catiline*. Of course, Ben Jonson's two plays are superior to any other Roman plays of the period outside Shakespeare (those of Lodge, Chapman, Massinger, Marston, or Webster, or the several interesting anonymous ones). But when Ben Jonson's are compared with Shakespeare's, as they cruelly must, their defect is a lack not so much of art as of sophistication. There is a certain naïvety about Ben Jonson's understanding of Roman history. Of course, in a way, there is more obvious learning about *Catiline* and *Sejanus* than about Shakespeare's Roman plays. There must have been a great deal of note-book work, a great deal of mosaic work. It is possible to sit in the British Museum with the texts of the classical writers which Jonson used around you and watch him making his play as you follow up his references (not all, I think, at first hand). But the defect of Jonson's *Sejanus* is lack of homogeneity of style and material. Jonson mixes the gossip of Suetonius with the gloomily penetrating and disillusioned comments on men and their motives by Tacitus. It is the old story; "who reads incessantly and to his reading brings not a spirit and judgment equal or superior" is liable to lose the advantages of his reading. After all, it doesn't require very much effort to *seem* learned. What is so difficult to acquire is the judgment in dealing with the material in which one is learned. This is not something that can in any way be tested by collecting misspellings of classical proper names in an author whose works have been unfairly printed from his foul papers and prompt-book copies. Shakespeare brought a judgment equal or superior to whatever ancient authors he read however he read them. Ben Jonson did not; his dogged and determined scholarship was not ripe enough; he had the books but not always the spirit with which to read them. There are occasions when we can legitimately place parts of their plays side by side. Consider the portents which accompanied the death of Julius Caesar, something which obviously interested Shakespeare very much. His description of them in *Hamlet* is unforgettable. His introduction of them in *Julius Caesar* is beautifully done. Some of the excitable Romans are prepared to believe any yarn about lions and supernatural fires and so forth. The amiable and unperturbed Cicero asks Casca:

> Why are you breathless? and why stare you so?

And he answers Casca's fustian about "a tempest dropping fire" with mild scepticism:

> Why, saw you any thing more wonderful?

His response to the contagious panic which Casca has acquired from

> a hundred ghastly women,
> Transformed with their fear; who swore they saw
> Men all in fire walk up and down the streets,

is to be quite unimpressed by anything that a lot of hysterical old women *swore they saw*; and he then leaves, with the remark that the weather is too bad for a walk that evening:

> Good night then, Casca: this disturbed sky
> Is not to walk in.

Compare this with the account of the portents that accompany the conspirators' oath and the blood-drinking in *Catiline*. (Jonson got little of it from the excellent Sallust but from an inferior source.) It is given no connexion with the varying emotions of the observers, there is no sceptical note: it merely seems to be there because "mine author hath it so". Indeed there is something medieval about it, and about Jonson's treatment of his characters in *Catiline*. He takes sides emphatically. He does what some critics would like Shakespeare to do in *Julius Caesar*; that is to tell us plainly which is the good man and which is the bad man. There is a sort of pre-Renaissance naïvety about Jonson's setting up Catiline as an example of unmitigated villainy and Cicero as an example of unmitigated virtue. It is comparable with what you find in Chaucer or in Lydgate about the slaying of the glorious and victorious Julius Caesar by that wicked Judas-like figure called Brutus Cassius with bodkins hid in his sleeve. There is a sense of unreality about it, a recurring feeling that Ben Jonson doesn't really know what he is talking about—the feeling of hollowness you get when Jonson starts praising Shakespeare by shouting

> Call forth thund'ring *Æschilus*,
> *Euripides,* and *Sophocles* to us,
> *Pacuvius, Accius,* him of *Cordova* dead,
> To life againe, to heare thy Buskin tread,
> And shake a Stage. . . .

Is this the writing of a well-informed person? We can stand for Seneca, of course. But it is hard to include the Greek tragedians, too little known and too little available to make the comparison intelligent; and as for Accius and Pacuvius, there could be few criticisms more pointless than to ask anybody to call forth their meagre fragments, those ghostly writers, mere names in biographical dictionaries. Perhaps it is only Ben Jonson's fun. I would like to think so. But I doubt it. I fear he wants to be impressive. Like a medieval poet, he has licence to mention the names of great authors without their books.

There may very well be, in Shakespeare's writings, a good many vestiges of the medieval world-picture. His mind may have been encumbered, or steadied, by several objects, orts, and relics of an earlier kind of intellectual culture. But it is scarcely perceptible in his Roman plays, which can be brought to the judgment bar of the Renaissance revivification of the ancient world, and will stand the comparison with the major achievements of Renaissance Humanism (as Ben Jonson's will not). We find there a writer who seems in the intellectual current of his times. Shakespeare had what might be described as the scholarship of the educated creative writer—the ability to go and find out the best that is known and thought in his day; to get it quickly (as a busy writer must, for Shakespeare wrote more than a million words in twenty years); to get it without much trouble and without constant access to good collections of books (as a busy man of the theatre must, one often on tour and keeping up two homes); and to deal with his sources of information with intelligence and discrimination. The favourite notions of learning get around in ways past tracing. Anyone who is writing a play or a book on any subject has by that very fact a peculiar alertness and sensitivity to information and attitudes about his subject. Shakespeare did not write in isolation. He had friends. It would be an improbable hypothesis that he worked cut off from the intellectual life of his times. Indeed, all investigations of the content of his plays prove the obvious: that he was peculiarly sensitive to the intellectual tendencies of his age, in all spheres of thought. His scholarship was of a better quality than Jonson's, because (one might guess) he was a better listener, not so self-assertive in the company of his betters, and was therefore more able, with that incomparable celerity of mind of his, to profit from any well-informed acquaintance.

Finally, in understanding the picture of the ancient world in these plays, the part played by Shakespeare himself in creating our notions of the ancient Romans should not be forgotten. It has become difficult to see the plays straight, to see the thing in itself as it really is, because we are all in the power of Shakespeare's imagination, a power which has been exercised for several generations and from which it is scarcely possible to extricate ourselves. It is well known, I believe, that Shakespeare practically created the fairies; he was responsible for having impressed them on the imagination, the dainty, delightful, beneficent beings which have become part of the popular mythology. To suggest that

Shakespeare also practically created the ancient Romans might be regarded as irresponsible. Still, the effect that Shakespeare has had on the way the Romans exist in our imaginations is something that might well be explored. We have had in England no great historian of Rome to impose his vision of the Roman world upon readers. Gibbon begins too late; and the English historians of Rome who wrote in the sixteenth, seventeenth and eighteenth centuries are mediocre and practically unread. We have had, on the one hand, no Mommsen; on the other, we have had no Racine, no Poussin, no David, no Napoleon. But since the early nineteenth century generations of schoolboys have been trained on *Julius Caesar* and *Coriolanus*. When English gradually penetrated into the schools as a reputable subject, it was in the sheep's clothing of Shakespeare's Roman plays that it entered the well-guarded fold; and so gave the *coup de grâce* to classical education in England. It can hardly be doubted that Shakespeare's *Julius Caesar* has had more effect than Caesar's own *Commentaries* in creating our impressions of his personality. Indeed, Shakespeare has had no serious rival on the subject of Ancient Rome. Neither *All for Love* nor *Cato* has stood the test of time and changing tastes. Neither the importation of *Ben Hur* from America nor the importation of *Quo Vadis* from Poland has affected Shakespeare's domination over the imagination. Besides, they belong to the wrong period. Novel writers have generally turned to the age of the Twelve Caesars, rather than to the Republic, for precisely the same reasons as did Shakespeare's contemporary playwrights; it is so much more lurid; there are so many more "garboyles". The spirit of Suetonius lives on. Shakespeare, perhaps, chose with a better instinct or with surer taste.

Hamlet in the Novel

HENRY FIELDING

Henry Fielding (1707-1754). Dramatist, Justice of the Peace, and, in Tom Jones *(1749) founder of the novel*

of plot. His other novels are Joseph Andrews *(1742)*
and Amelia *(1751); his total literary output includes sev-*
eral successful plays, the satire Jonathan Wild *(1743), a*
mass of journalism, and pamphlets on subjects of social
concern.

PARTRIDGE ON GARRICK'S HAMLET*

As soon as the play, which was "Hamlet, Prince of Denmark," began, Partridge was all attention, nor did he break
silence till the entrance of the ghost; upon which he asked
Jones, "What man that was in the strange dress; something,"
said he, "like what I have seen in a picture. Sure it is not
armour, is it?" Jones answered, "That is the ghost." To
which Partridge replied with a smile, "Persuade me to that,
sir, if you can. Though I can't say I ever actually saw a
ghost in my life, yet I am certain I should know one, if I
saw him, better than that comes to. No, no, sir, ghosts don't
appear in such dresses as that, neither." In this mistake,
which caused much laughter in the neighbourhood of Partridge, he was suffered to continue, till the scene between
the ghost and Hamlet, when Partridge gave that credit to
Mr. Garrick, which he had denied to Jones, and fell into
so violent a trembling, that his knees knocked against each
other. Jones asked him what was the matter, and whether
he was afraid of the warrior upon the stage? "Oh, la! sir,"
said he, "I perceive now it is what you told me. I am not
afraid of anything; for I know it is but a play. And if it
was really a ghost, it could do one no harm at such a distance, and in so much company; and yet if I was frightened, I am not the only person." "Why, who," cries Jones,
"dost thou take to be such a coward here besides thyself?"
"Nay, you may call me coward if you will; but if that little
man there upon the stage is not frightened, I never saw any
man frightened in my life. Aye, aye; go along with you!
Aye, to be sure! Who's fool then? Will you? Lud have
mercy upon such fool-hardiness!—Whatever happens, it is
good enough for you.——Follow you? I'd follow the devil
as soon. Nay, perhaps, it is the devil——for they say he can
put on what likeness he pleases.—Oh! here he is again.——
No farther! No, you have gone far enough already; farther

* From *The History of Tom Jones.*

than I'd have gone for all the king's dominions." Jones offered to speak, but Partridge cried "Hush, hush, dear sir; don't you hear him?" And during the whole speech of the ghost, he sat with his eyes fixed partly on the ghost, and partly on Hamlet, and with his mouth open; the same passions which succeeded each other in Hamlet, succeeding likewise in him.

When the scene was over, Jones said, "Why, Partridge, you exceed my expectations. You enjoy the play more than I conceived possible." "Nay, sir," answered Partridge, "if you are not afraid of the devil, I can't help it; but, to be sure, it is natural to be surprised at such things, though I know there is nothing in them: not that it was the ghost that surprised me, neither; for I should have known that to have been only a man in a strange dress: but when I saw the little man so frightened himself, it was that which took hold of me." "And dost thou imagine, then, Partridge," cries Jones, "that he was really frightened?" "Nay, sir," said Partridge, "did not you yourself observe afterwards, when he found it was his own father's spirit, and how he was murdered in the garden, how his fear forsook him by degrees, and he was struck dumb with sorrow, as it were, just as I should have been, had it been my own case?—But hush! Oh, la! what noise is that? There he is again.——Well, to be certain, though I know there is nothing at all in it, I am glad I am not down yonder, where those men are." Then, turning his eyes again upon Hamlet: "Aye, you may draw your sword; what signifies a sword against the power of the devil?"

During the second act, Partridge made very few remarks. He greatly admired the fineness of the dresses; nor could he help observing upon the king's countenance. "Well," said he, "how people may be deceived by faces! *Nulla fides fronti* is, I find, a true saying. Who would think, by looking in the king's face, that he had ever committed a murder?" He then enquired after the ghost; but Jones, who intended he should be surprised, gave him no other satisfaction, than, "that he might possibly see him again soon, and in a flash of fire."

Partridge sat in fearful expectation of this; and now, when the ghost made his next appearance, Partridge cried out, "There, sir, now; what say you now? is he frightened now or no? As much frightened as you think me, and, to be sure, nobody can help some fears, I would not be in so bad a condition as what's his name, squire Hamlet, is there, for all the world. Bless me! what's become of the spirit? As I am a living soul, I thought I saw him sink into the earth." "Indeed, you saw right," answered Jones. "Well, well," cries Partridge, "I know it is only a play; and besides, if there was anything in all this, Madam Miller would not laugh so: for as to you, sir, you would not be afraid, I believe, if the devil was here in person.—There, there— Aye, no wonder you are in such a passion; shake the vile wicked wretch to pieces. If she was my own mother, I should serve her so. To be sure, all duty to a mother is forfeited by such wicked doings.——Aye, go about your business; I hate the sight of you."

Our critic was now pretty silent till the play, which Hamlet introduces before the king. This he did not at first understand, till Jones explained it to him; but he no sooner entered into the spirit of it, than he began to bless himself that he had never committed murder. Then turning to Mrs. Miller, he asked her, "If she did not imagine the king looked as if he was touched; though he is," said he, "a good actor, and doth all he can to hide it. Well, I would not have so much to answer for, as that wicked man there hath, to sit upon a much higher chair than he sits upon.—No wonder he run away; for your sake I'll never trust an innocent face again."

The grave-digging scene next engaged the attention of Partridge, who expressed much surprise at the number of skulls thrown upon the stage. To which Jones answered, "That it was one of the most famous burial-places about town." "No wonder then," cries Partridge, "that the place is haunted. But I never saw in my life a worse grave-digger. I had a sexton, when I was clerk, that should have dug three graves while he is digging one. The fellow handles a spade as if it was the first time he had ever had one in his hand. Aye, aye, you may sing. You had rather sing than work, I believe."—Upon Hamlet's taking up the skull, he cried out, "Well, it is strange to see how fearless some men are: I never could bring myself to touch anything belonging to a dead man on any account.—He seemed frightened enough too at the ghost, I thought. *Nemo omnibus horis sapit.*"

Little more worth remembering occurred during the play; at the end of which Jones asked him, "Which of the players he had liked best?" To this he answered, with some appearance of indignation at the question, "The king, without doubt." "Indeed, Mr. Partridge," says Mrs. Miller, "you are not of the same opinion with the town; for they are all agreed, that Hamlet is acted by the best player who ever was on the stage." "He the best player!" cries Partridge, with a contemptuous sneer, "why, I could act as well as he myself. I am sure, if I had seen a ghost, I should have looked in the very same manner, and done just as he did. And then, to be sure, in that scene, as you called it, between him and his mother, where you told me he acted so fine, why, Lord help me, any man, that is, any good man, that had such a mother, would have done exactly the same. I know you are only joking with me; but indeed, madam, though I was never at a play in London, yet I have seen acting before in the country; and the king for my money; he speaks all his words distinctly, half as loud again as the other.— Anybody may see he is an actor." . . .

Thus ended the adventure at the playhouse; where Partridge had afforded great mirth; not only to Jones and Mrs. Miller, but to all who sat within hearing, who were more attentive to what he said, than to anything that passed on the stage.

He durst not go to bed all that night, for fear of the ghost; and for many nights after sweated two or three hours before he went to sleep, with the same apprehensions, and waked several times in great horrors, crying out, "Lord have mercy upon us! there it is."

JOHANN WOLFGANG VON GOETHE

Johann Wolfgang von Goethe (1749-1832). Wilhelm Meisters Lehrjahre (1795-6), in its treatment of Hamlet, strongly reflected the 'organicist' approach to Shakespeare, and also helped to establish the new role of that play as a mirror of the modern mind.

WILHELM MEISTER ON HAMLET*

Seeing the company so favourably disposed, Wilhelm now hoped he might farther have it in his power to converse with them on the poetic merit of the pieces which might come before them. "It is not enough," said he next day, when they were all again assembled, "for the actor merely to glance over a dramatic work, to judge of it by his first impression, and thus, without investigation, to declare his satisfaction or dissatisfaction with it. Such things may be allowed in a spectator, whose purpose it is rather to be entertained and moved than formally to criticise. But the actor, on the other hand, should be prepared to give a reason for his praise or censure: and how shall he do this, if he have not taught himself to penetrate the sense, the views and feelings of his author? A common error is, to form a judgment of a drama from a single part in it; and to look upon this part itself in an isolated point of view, not in its connection with the whole. I have noticed this, within a few days, so clearly in my own conduct, that I will give you the account as an example, if you please to hear me patiently.

"You all know Shakspeare's incomparable Hamlet: our public reading of it at the Castle yielded every one of us the greatest satisfaction. On that occasion, we proposed to act the piece; and I, not knowing what I undertook, engaged to play the Prince's part. This I conceived that I was studying, while I began to get by heart the strongest passages, the soliloquies, and those scenes in which force of soul, vehemence and elevation of feeling have the freest scope; where the agitated heart is allowed to display itself with touching expressiveness.

"I farther conceived that I was penetrating quite into the spirit of the character, while I endeavoured as it were to take upon myself the load of deep melancholy under which my prototype was labouring, and in this humour to pursue him through the strange labyrinths of his caprices and his singularities. Thus learning, thus practising, I doubted not but I should by and by become one person with my hero.

* From *Wilhelm Meister's Apprenticeship*, 1795-6, translated by Thomas Carlyle. (This is only a sample of the passages on *Hamlet*, which are many.)

"But the farther I advanced, the more difficult did it become for me to form any image of the whole, in its general bearings; till at last it seemed as if impossible. I next went through the entire piece, without interruption; but here too I found much that I could not away with. At one time the characters, at another time the manner of displaying them, seemed inconsistent; and I almost despaired of finding any general tint, in which I might present my whole part with all its shadings and variations. In such devious paths I toiled, and wandered long in vain; till at length a hope arose that I might reach my aim in quite a new way.

"I set about investigating every trace of Hamlet's character, as it had shown itself before his father's death: I endeavoured to distinguish what in it was independent of this mournful event; independent of the terrible events that followed; and what most probably the young man would have been, had no such thing occurred.

"Soft, and from a noble stem, this royal flower had sprung up under the immediate influences of majesty: the idea of moral rectitude with that of princely elevation, the feeling of the good and dignified with the consciousness of high birth, had in him been unfolded simultaneously. He was a prince, by birth a prince; and he wished to reign, only that good men might be good without obstruction. Pleasing in form, polished by nature, courteous from the heart, he was meant to be the pattern of youth and the joy of the world.

"Without any prominent passion, his love for Ophelia was a still presentiment of sweet wants. His zeal in knightly accomplishments was not entirely his own; it needed to be quickened and inflamed by praise bestowed on others for excelling in them. Pure in sentiment, he knew the honourable-minded, and could prize the rest which an upright spirit tastes on the bosom of a friend. To a certain degree, he had learned to discern and value the good and the beautiful in arts and sciences; the mean, the vulgar was offensive to him; and if hatred could take root in his tender soul, it was only so far as to make him properly despise the false and changeful insects of a court, and play with them in easy scorn. He was calm in his temper, artless in his conduct; neither pleased with idleness, nor too violently eager for employment. The routine of a university he seemed to continue when at court. He possessed more mirth of humour than of heart; he was a good companion, pliant, courteous, discreet, and able to forget and forgive an injury; yet never able to unite himself with those who overstept the limits of the right, the good, and the becoming.

"When we read the piece again, you shall judge whether I am yet on the proper track. I hope at least to bring forward passages that shall support my opinion in its main points."

This delineation was received with warm approval: the company imagined they foresaw that Hamlet's manner of proceeding might now be very satisfactorily explained; they applauded this method of penetrating into the spirit of a writer. Each of them proposed to himself to take up some piece, and study it on these principles, and so unfold the author's meaning. . . .

. . . "Conceive a prince such as I have painted him, and that his father suddenly dies. Ambition and the love of rule are not the passions that inspire him. As a king's son he would have been contented; but now he is first constrained to consider the difference which separates a sovereign from a subject. The crown was not hereditary; yet a longer possession of it by his father would have strengthened the pretensions of an only son, and secured his hopes of the succession. In place of this, he now beholds himself excluded by his uncle, in spite of specious promises, most probably forever. He is now poor in goods and favour, and a stranger in the scene which from youth he had looked upon as his inheritance. His temper here assumes its first mournful tinge. He feels that now he is not more, that he is less, than a private nobleman; he offers himself as the servant of every one; he is not courteous and condescending, he is needy and degraded.

"His past condition he remembers as a vanished dream. It is in vain that his uncle strives to cheer him, to present his situation in another point of view. The feeling of his nothingness will not leave him.

"The second stroke that came upon him wounded deeper, bowed still more. It was the marriage of his mother. The faithful tender son had yet a mother, when his father passed away. He hoped, in the company of his surviving noble-minded parent, to reverence the heroic form of the departed; but his mother too he loses, and it is something worse than death that robs him of her. The trustful image, which a good child loves to form of its parents, is gone. With the dead there is no help; on the living no hold. She also is a woman, and her name is Frailty, like that of all her sex.

"Now first does he feel himself completely bent and orphaned; and no happiness of life can repay what he has lost. Not reflective or sorrowful by nature, reflection and sorrow have become for him a heavy obligation. It is thus that we see him first enter on the scene. I do not think that I have mixed aught foreign with the piece, or overcharged a single feature of it."

Serlo looked at his sister, and said, "Did I give thee a false picture of our friend? He begins well; he has still many things to tell us, many to persuade us of." Wilhelm asseverated loudly, that he meant not to persuade, but to convince; he begged for another moment's patience.

"Figure to yourselves this youth," cried he, "this son of princes; conceive him vividly, bring his state before your eyes, and then observe him when he learns that his father's spirit walks; stand by him in the terrors of the night, when the venerable ghost itself appears before him. A horrid shudder passes over him; he speaks to the mysterious form; he sees it beckon him; he follows it, and hears. The fearful accusation of his uncle rings in his ears; the summons to revenge, and the piercing oft-repeated prayer, Remember me!

"And when the ghost has vanished, who is it that stands before us? A young hero panting for vengeance? A prince by birth, rejoicing to be called to punish the usurper of his crown? No! trouble and astonishment take hold of the solitary young man; he grows bitter against smiling villains, swears that he will not forget the spirit, and concludes with the significant ejaculation:

> The time is out of joint: O cursed spite,
> That ever I was born to set it right!

"In these words, I imagine, will be found the key to Hamlet's whole procedure. To me it is clear that Shakspeare meant, in the present case, to represent the effects of a great action laid upon a soul unfit for the performance of it. In this view the whole piece seems to me to be composed. There is an oak-tree planted in a costly jar, which should have borne only pleasant flowers in its bosom; the roots expand, the jar is shivered.

"A lovely, pure, noble and most moral nature, without the strength of nerve which forms a hero, sinks beneath a burden which it cannot bear and must not cast away. All duties are holy for him; the present is too hard. Impossibilities have been required of him; not in themselves impossibilities, but such for him. He winds, and turns, and torments himself; he advances and recoils; is ever put in mind, ever puts himself in mind; at last does all but lose his purpose from his thoughts; yet still without recovering his peace of mind."

JAMES JOYCE

James Joyce (1882-1941). The present extract gives only a hint of the formidable and brilliant Shakespearian exercise of Stephen Dedalus in the Scylla *and* Charybdis *episode of* Ulysses *(1922); and none of its deep relation to the rest of the novel.*

STEPHEN DEDALUS ON HAMLET*

. . . Mr Best turned an unoffending face to Stephen.

— Mallarmé, don't you know, he said, has written those wonderful prose poems Stephen MacKenna used to read to me in Paris. The one about *Hamlet*. He says: *il se promène, lisant au livre de lui-même,* don't you know, *reading the book of himself.* He describes *Hamlet* given in a French town, don't you know, a provincial town. They advertised it.

His free hand graciously wrote tiny signs in air.

HAMLET
ou
LE DISTRAIT
Pièce de Shakespeare

* From *Ulysses* (1922).

He repeated to John Eglinton's newgathered frown:

— *Pièce de Shakespeare,* don't you know. It's so French, the French point of view. *Hamlet ou.* . .

— The absentminded beggar, Stephen ended.

John Eglinton laughed.

— Yes, I suppose it would be, he said. Excellent people, no doubt, but distressingly shortsighted in some matters.

Sumptuous and stagnant exaggeration of murder.

— A deathsman of the soul Robert Greene called him, Stephen said. Not for nothing was he a butcher's son wielding the sledded poleaxe and spitting in his palm. Nine lives are taken off for his father's one, Our Father who art in purgatory. Khaki Hamlets don't hesitate to shoot. The bloodboltered shambles in act five is a forecast of the concentration camp sung by Mr Swinburne.

Cranly, I his mute orderly, following battles from afar.

> *Whelps and dams of murderous foes whom none*
> *But we had spared. . .*

Between the Saxon smile and yankee yawp. The devil and the deep sea.

— He will have it that *Hamlet* is a ghoststory, John Eglinton said for Mr Best's behoof. Like the fat boy in Pickwick he wants to make our flesh creep.

> *List! List! O list!*

My flesh hears him: creeping, hears.

> *If thou didst ever. . .*

— What is a ghost? Stephen said with tingling energy. One who has faded into impalpability through death, through absence, through change of manners. Elizabethan London lay as far from Stratford as corrupt Paris lies from virgin Dublin. Who is the ghost from *limbo patrum,* returning to the world that has forgotten him? Who is king Hamlet?

John Eglinton shifted his spare body, leaning back to judge.

Lifted.

— It is this hour of a day in mid June, Stephen said, begging with a swift glance their hearing. The flag is up on the playhouse by the bankside. The bear Sackerson growls in the pit near it, Paris garden. Canvasclimbers who sailed with Drake chew their sausages among the groundlings.

Local colour. Work in all you know. Make them accomplices.

— Shakespeare has left the huguenot's house in Silver street and walks by the swanmews along the riverbank. But he does not stay to feed the pen chivying her game of cygnets towards the rushes. The swan of Avon has other thoughts.

Composition of place. Ignatius Loyola, make haste to help me!

— The play begins. A player comes on under the shadow, made up in the castoff mail of a court buck, a wellset man with a bass voice. It is the ghost, the king, a king and no king, and the player is Shakespeare who has studied *Hamlet* all the years of his life which were not vanity in order to play the part of the spectre. He speaks the words to Burbage, the young player who stands before him beyond the rack of cerecloth, calling him by a name:

Hamlet I am thy father's spirit

bidding him list. To a son he speaks, the son of his soul, the prince, young Hamlet and to the son of his body, Hamnet Shakespeare, who has died in Stratford that his namesake may live for ever.

Is it possible that that player Shakespeare, a ghost by absence, and in the vesture of buried Denmark, a ghost by death, speaking his own words to his own son's name (had Hamnet Shakespeare lived he would have been prince Hamlet's twin) is it possible, I want to know, or probable that he did not draw or foresee the logical conclusion of those premises: you are the dispossessed son: I am the murdered father: your mother is the guilty queen, Ann Shakespeare, born Hathaway?

— But this prying into the family life of a great man, Russell began impatiently.

Art thou there, truepenny?

— Interesting only to the parish clerk. I mean, we have

the plays. I mean when we read the poetry of *King Lear* what is it to us how the poet lived? As for living, our servants can do that for us, Villiers de l'Isle has said. Peeping and prying into greenroom gossip of the day, the poet's drinking the poet's debts. We have *King Lear:* and it is immortal.

Mr Best's face appealed to, agreed.

BORIS PASTERNAK

Boris Leonidovich Pasternak (1890-1960). Russian poet and author of Dr. Zhivago, *where this poem appears; translator of* Hamlet, Othello, Macbeth, Romeo and Juliet, Antony and Cleopatra, Henry IV *and* King Lear *(1953).*

Hamlet: A New Soliloquy*

The murmurs ebb; on to the stage I enter.
I am trying, standing in the door,
To discover in the distant echoes
What the coming years may hold in store.

The nocturnal darkness with a thousand
Binoculars is focussed on to me.
Take away this cup, O Abba, Father,
Everything is possible to thee.

I am fond of this thy stubborn project,
And to play my part I am content.
But another drama is in progress,
And, this once, O let me be exempt.

But the plan of action is determined,
And the end irrevocably sealed.

* Translation of Lydia Slater Pasternak.

I am alone; all round me drowns in falsehood:
Life is not a walk across a field! [1]

S. T. COLERIDGE

On Hamlet*

We will now pass to "Hamlet," in order to obviate some of the general prejudices against the author, in reference to the character of the hero. Much has been objected to, which ought to have been praised, and many beauties of the highest kind have been neglected, because they are somewhat hidden.

The first question we should ask ourselves is—What did Shakespeare mean when he drew the character of Hamlet? He never wrote any thing without design, and what was his design when he sat down to produce this tragedy? My belief is, that he always regarded his story, before he began to write, much in the same light as a painter regards his canvas, before he begins to paint—as a mere vehicle for his thoughts—as the ground upon which he was to work. What then was the point to which Shakespeare directed himself in Hamlet? He intended to portray a person, in whose view the external world, and all its incidents and objects, were comparatively dim, and of no interest in themselves, and which began to interest only, when they were reflected in the mirror of his mind. Hamlet beheld external things in the same way that a man of vivid imagination, who shuts his eyes, sees what has previously made an impression on his organs.

The poet places him in the most stimulating circumstances that a human being can be placed in. He is the heir apparent of a throne; his father dies suspiciously; his mother excludes her son from his throne by marrying his uncle. This is not enough; but the Ghost of the murdered father

[1] This is a Russian proverb.
* From a series of lectures on Shakespeare and Milton given in London in the winter 1811-1812.

is introduced, to assure the son that he was put to death by his own brother. What is the effect upon the son?—instant action and pursuit of revenge? No: endless reasoning and hesitating—constant urging and solicitation of the mind to act, and as constant an escape from action; ceaseless reproaches of himself for sloth and negligence, while the whole energy of his resolution evaporates in these reproaches. This, too, not from cowardice, for he is drawn as one of the bravest of his time—not from want of forethought or slowness of apprehension, for he sees through the very souls of all who surround him, but merely from that aversion to action, which prevails among such as have a world in themselves.

How admirable, too, is the judgment of the poet! Hamlet's own disordered fancy has not conjured up the spirit of his father; it has been seen by others: he is prepared by them to witness its re-appearance, and when he does see it, Hamlet is not brought forward as having long brooded on the subject. The moment before the Ghost enters, Hamlet speaks of other matters: he mentions the coldness of the night, and observes that he has not heard the clock strike, adding, in reference to the custom of drinking, that it is

"More honour'd in the breach than the observance."
                                        Act I., Scene 4.

Owing to the tranquil state of his mind, he indulges in some moral reflections. Afterwards, the Ghost suddenly enters.

"Hor.   Look, my lord! it comes.
Ham. Angels and ministers of grace defend us!"

The same thing occurs in "Macbeth": in the dagger-scene, the moment before the hero sees it, he has his mind applied to some indifferent matters; "Go, tell thy mistress," &c. Thus, in both cases, the preternatural appearance has all the effect of abruptness, and the reader is totally divested of the notion, that the figure is a vision of a highly wrought imagination.

Here Shakespeare adapts himself so admirably to the situation—in other words, so puts himself into it—that, though poetry, his language is the very language of nature.

No terms, associated with such feelings, can occur to us so proper as those which he has employed, especially on the highest, the most august, and the most awful subjects that can interest a human being in this sentient world. That this is no mere fancy, I can undertake to establish from hundreds, I might say thousands, of passages. No character he has drawn, in the whole list of his plays, could so well and fitly express himself, as in the language Shakespeare has put into his mouth.

There is no indecision about Hamlet, as far as his own sense of duty is concerned; he knows well what he ought to do, and over and over again he makes up his mind to do it. The moment the players, and the two spies set upon him, have withdrawn, of whom he takes leave with a line so expressive of his contempt,

"Ay so; good bye you.—Now I am alone,"

he breaks out into a delirium of rage against himself for neglecting to perform the solemn duty he had undertaken, and contrasts the factitious and artificial display of feeling by the player with his own apparent indifference;

"What's Hecuba to him, or he to Hecuba,
That he should weep for her?"

Yet the player did weep for her, and was in an agony of grief at her sufferings, while Hamlet is unable to rouse himself to action, in order that he may perform the command of his father, who had come from the grave to incite him to revenge:—

"This is most brave!
That I, the son of a dear father murder'd,
Prompted to my revenge by heaven and hell,
Must, like a whore, unpack my heart with words,
And fall a cursing like a very drab,
A scullion."

Act II., Scene 2.

It is the same feeling, the same conviction of what is his duty, that makes Hamlet exclaim in a subsequent part of the tragedy:

"How all occasions do inform against me,
And spur my dull revenge! What is a man,
If his chief good, and market of his time,
Be but to sleep and feed? A beast, no more. . . .
. . . . I do not know
Why yet I live to say—'this thing's to do,'
Sith I have cause and will and strength and means
To do't."

Act IV., Scene 4.

Yet with all this strong conviction of duty, and with all this resolution arising out of strong conviction, nothing is done. This admirable and consistent character, deeply acquainted with his own feelings, painting them with such wonderful power and accuracy, and firmly persuaded that a moment ought not to be lost in executing the solemn charge committed to him, still yields to the same retiring from reality, which is the result of having, what we express by the terms, a world within himself.

Such a mind as Hamlet's is near akin to madness. Dryden has somewhere said,[1]

"Great wit to madness nearly is allied,"

and he was right; for he means by "wit" that greatness of genius, which led Hamlet to a perfect knowledge of his own character, which, with all strength of motive, was so weak as to be unable to carry into act his own most obvious duty.

With all this he has a sense of imperfectness, which becomes apparent when he is moralising on the skull in the churchyard. Something is wanting to his completeness— something is deficient which remains to be supplied, and he is therefore described as attached to Ophelia. His madness is assumed, when he finds that witnesses have been placed behind the arras to listen to what passes, and when the heroine has been thrown in his way as a decoy.

Another objection has been taken by Dr. Johnson, and Shakespeare has been taxed very severely. I refer to the scene where Hamlet enters and finds his uncle praying, and

[1] "Great wits are sure to madness near allied."
Absalom and Achitophel, 163.

refuses to take his life, excepting when he is in the height of his iniquity. To assail him at such a moment of confession and repentance, Hamlet declares,

> "Why, this is hire and salary, not revenge."
> *Act III., Scene* 3.

He therefore forbears, and postpones his uncle's death, until he can catch him in some act

> "That has no relish of salvation in't."

This conduct, and this sentiment, Dr. Johnson has pronounced to be so atrocious and horrible, as to be unfit to be put into the mouth of a human being. The fact, however, is that Dr. Johnson did not understand the character of Hamlet, and censured accordingly: the determination to allow the guilty King to escape at such a moment is only part of the indecision and irresoluteness of the hero. Hamlet seizes hold of a pretext for not acting, when he might have acted so instantly and effectually: therefore, he again defers the revenge he was bound to seek, and declares his determination to accomplish it at some time,

> "When he is drunk, asleep, or in his rage,
> Or in th' incestuous pleasures of his bed."

This, allow me to impress upon you most emphatically, was merely the excuse Hamlet made to himself for not taking advantage of this particular and favourable moment for doing justice upon his guilty uncle, at the urgent instance of the spirit of his father.

Dr. Johnson further states, that in the voyage to England, Shakespeare merely follows the novel as he found it, as if the poet had no other reason for adhering to his original; but Shakespeare never followed a novel, because he found such and such an incident in it, but because he saw that the story, as he read it, contributed to enforce, or to explain some great truth inherent in human nature. He never could lack invention to alter or improve a popular narrative; but he did not wantonly vary from it, when he knew that, as it was related, it would so well apply to his own great purpose.

He saw at once how consistent it was with the character of Hamlet, that after still resolving, and still deferring, still determining to execute, and still postponing execution, he should finally, in the infirmity of his disposition, give himself up to his destiny, and hopelessly place himself in the power, and at the mercy of his enemies.

Even after the scene with Osrick, we see Hamlet still indulging in reflection, and hardly thinking of the task he has just undertaken: he is all dispatch and resolution, as far as words and present intentions are concerned, but all hesitation and irresolution, when called upon to carry his words and intentions into effect; so that, resolving to do everything, he does nothing. He is full of purpose, but void of that quality of mind which accomplishes purpose.

Anything finer than this conception, and working out of a great character, is merely impossible. Shakespeare wished to impress upon us the truth, that action is the chief end of existence—that no faculties of intellect, however brilliant, can be considered valuable, or indeed otherwise than as misfortunes, if they withdraw us from, or render us repugnant to action, and lead us to think and think of doing, until the time has elapsed when we can do anything effectually. In enforcing this moral truth, Shakespeare has shown the fulness and force of his powers: all that is amiable and excellent in nature is combined in Hamlet, with the exception of one quality. He is a man living in meditation, called upon to act by every motive human and divine, but the great object of his life is defeated by continually resolving to do, yet doing nothing but resolve.

ERNEST JONES

Ernest Jones (1879-1958). Friend, apostle and biographer of Freud, President of the International Psycho-Analytical Association, Jones did for Shakespeare what Freud did for Leonardo da Vinci.

HAMLET DIAGNOSED*

That Hamlet is suffering from an internal conflict the essential nature of which is inaccessible to his introspection is evidenced by the following considerations. Throughout the play we have the clearest picture of a man who sees his duty plain before him, but who shirks it at every opportunity and suffers in consequence the most intense remorse. To paraphrase Sir James Paget's well-known description of hysterical paralysis: Hamlet's advocates say he cannot do his duty, his detractors say he will not, whereas the truth is that he cannot will. Further than this, the deficient will-power is localized to the one question of killing his uncle; it is what may be termed a *specific aboulia*. Now instances of such specific aboulias in real life invariably prove, when analysed, to be due to an unconscious repulsion against the act that cannot be performed (or else against something closely associated with the act, so that the idea of the act becomes also involved in the repulsion). In other words, whenever a person cannot bring himself to do something that every conscious consideration tells him he should do— and which he may have the strongest conscious desire to do —it is always because there is some hidden reason why a part of him doesn't want to do it; this reason he will not own to himself and is only dimly if at all aware of. That is exactly the case with Hamlet. Time and again he works himself up, points out to himself his obvious duty, with the cruellest self-reproaches lashes himself to agonies of remorse—and once more falls away into inaction. He eagerly seizes at every excuse for occupying himself with any other matter than the performance of his duty—even in the last scene of the last act entering on the distraction of a quite irrelevant fencing-match with a man who he must know wants to kill him, an eventuality that would put an end to all hope of fulfilling his task: just as on a lesser plane a person faced with a distasteful task, e.g. writing a difficult letter, will whittle away his time in arranging, tidying, and fidgeting with any little occupation that may serve as a

* Extracted from *Hamlet and Oedipus*.

pretext for procrastination. Bradley[1] even goes as far as to make out a case for the view that Hamlet's self-accusation of "bestial oblivion" is to be taken in a literal sense, his unconscious detestation of his task being so intense as to enable him actually to forget it for periods.

Highly significant is the fact that the grounds Hamlet gives for his hesitancy are grounds none of which will stand any serious consideration, and which continually change from one time to another. One moment he pretends he is too cowardly to perform the deed, at another he questions the truthfulness of the ghost, at another—when the opportunity presents itself in its naked form—he thinks the time is unsuited, it would be better to wait till the King was at some evil act and then to kill him, and so on. They have each of them, it is true, a certain plausibility—so much so that some writers have accepted them at face value; but surely no pretext would be of any use if it were not plausible. As Madariaga[2] truly says: "The argument that the reasons given by Hamlet not to kill the king at prayers are cogent is irrelevant. For the man who wants to procrastinate cogent arguments are more valuable than mere pretexts." Take, for instance, the matter of the credibility of the ghost. There exists an extensive and very interesting literature concerning Elizabethan beliefs in supernatural visitation. It was doubtless a burning topic, a focal point of the controversies about the conflicting theologies of the age, and moreover, affecting the practical question of how to treat witches. But there is no evidence of Hamlet (or Shakespeare!) being specially interested in theology, and from the moment when the ghost confirms the slumbering suspicion in his mind ("O, my prophetic soul! My uncle!") his intuition must indubitably have convinced him of the ghost's veridical nature. He never really doubted the villainy of his uncle.

When a man gives at different times a different reason for his conduct it is safe to infer that, whether consciously or not, he is concealing the true reason. Wetz,[3] discussing a similar problem in reference to Iago, truly observes: "Noth-

[1] Bradley: Shakespearean Tragedy, 2nd Ed., 1905, pp. 125, 126, 410, 411.
[2] S. de Madariaga: on Hamlet, 1948, p. 98.
[3] Wetz: Shakespeare vom Standpunkt der vergleichenden Litteraturgeschichte, 1890, Ed. I, S. 186.

ing proves so well how false are the motives with which
Iago tries to persuade himself as *the constant change in
these motives.*" We can therefore safely dismiss all the
alleged motives that Hamlet propounds, as being more or
less successful attempts on his part to blind himself with
self-deception. Loening's[1] summing-up of them is not too
emphatic when he says: "They are all mutually contradictory; *they are one and all false pretexts.*" The alleged motives excellently illustrate the psychological mechanisms of
evasion and rationalization I have elsewhere described.[2] It
is not necessary, however, to discuss them here individually,
for Loening has with the greatest perspicacity done this in
full detail and has effectually demonstrated how utterly un-
tenable they all are.[3]

Still, in his moments of self-reproach Hamlet sees clearly
enough the recalcitrancy of his conduct and renews his
efforts to achieve action. It is noticeable how his outbursts
of remorse are evoked by external happenings which bring
back to his mind that which he would so gladly forget, and
which, according to Bradley, he does at times forget: particularly effective in this respect are incidents that contrast
with his own conduct, as when the player is so moved over
the fate of Hecuba (Act II, Sc. 2), or when Fortinbras takes
the field and "finds quarrel in a straw when honour's at the
stake" (Act IV, Sc. 4). On the former occasion, stung by
the monstrous way in which the player pours out his feeling
at the thought of Hecuba, he arraigns himself in words
which surely should effectually dispose of the view that he
has any doubt where his duty lies.

> What's Hecuba to him, or he to Hecuba,
> That he should weep for her? What would he do,
> Had he the motive and the cue for passion
> That I have? He would drown the stage with tears
> And cleave the general ear with horrid speech,
> Make mad the guilty and appal the free,
> Confound the ignorant, and amaze indeed

[1] Loening: Die Hamlet-Tragödie Shakespeares, 1893, S. 245.
[2] Op. cit. p. 161.
[3] See especially his analysis of Hamlet's pretext for non-action in the
prayer scene: op. cit., S. 240-2.

The very faculties of eyes and ears; yet I,
A dull and muddy-mettled rascal, peak
Like John-a-dreams, unpregnant of my cause,[1]
And can say nothing; no, not for a king,
Upon whose property and most dear life
A damn'd defeat was made: Am I a coward?
Who calls me villain, breaks my pate across,
Plucks off my beard and blows it in my face,
Tweaks me by the nose, gives me the lie i' the throat
As deep as to the lungs? Who does me this?
Ha, 'swounds, I should take it: for it cannot be
But I am pigeon-liver'd, and lack gall
To make oppression bitter, or ere this
I should ha' fatted all the region kites
With this slave's offal. Bloody, bawdy villain!
Remorseless, treacherous, lecherous, kindless villain!
O, vengeance!
Why, what an ass am I! This is most brave,
That I, the son of a dear father murder'd,
Prompted to my revenge by heaven and hell,
Must like a whore unpack my heart with words,
And fall a-cursing like a very drab;
A scullion!

The readiness with which his guilty conscience is stirred
into activity is again evidenced on the second appearance of
the Ghost, when Hamlet cries,

Do you not come your tardy son to chide,
That lapsed in time and passion lets go by
Th'important acting of your dread command?
O, say!

The Ghost at once confirms this misgiving by answering,

Do not forget! this visitation
Is but to whet thy almost blunted purpose.

In short, the whole picture presented by Hamlet, his deep
depression, the hopeless note in his attitude towards the

[1] How the essence of the situation is conveyed in these four words.

world and towards the value of life, his dread of death,[1] his repeated reference to bad dreams, his self-accusations, his desperate efforts to get away from the thoughts of his duty, and his vain attempts to find an excuse for his pro- crastination: all this unequivocally points to a *tortured con- science,* to some hidden ground for shirking his task, a ground which he dare not or cannot avow to himself. We have, therefore, to take up the argument again at this point, and to seek for some new evidence that may serve to bring to light the hidden counter-motive.

The extensive experience of the psycho-analytic re- searches carried out by Freud and his school during the past half-century has amply demonstrated that certain kinds of mental process show a greater tendency to be inacces- sible to consciousness (put technically, to be "repressed") than others. In other words, it is harder for a person to realize the existence in his mind of some mental trends than it is of others. In order therefore to gain a proper perspec- tive it is necessary briefly to inquire into the relative fre- quency with which various sets of mental processes are "repressed." Experience shows that this can be correlated with the degree of compatibility of these various sets with the ideals and standards accepted by the conscious ego; the less compatible they are with these the more likely are they to be "repressed." As the standards acceptable to conscious- ness are in considerable measure derived from the immedi- ate environment, one may formulate the following general- ization: those processes are most likely to be "repressed" by the individual which are most disapproved of by the par- ticular circle of society to whose influence he has chiefly been subjected during the period when his character was being formed. Biologically stated, this law would run: "That which is unacceptable to the herd becomes unacceptable to the individual member," it being understood that the term herd is intended here in the sense of the particular circle

---

[1] Tieck (Dramaturgische Blätter, II, 1826) saw in Hamlet's cowardly fear of death a chief reason for his hesitancy in executing his venge- ance. How well Shakespeare understood what this fear was like may be inferred from Claudio's words in "Measure for Measure:"

> The weariest and most loathed worldly life
> That age, ache, penury and imprisonment
> Can lay on nature is a paradise
> To what we fear of death.

defined above, which is by no means necessarily the community at large. It is for this reason that moral, social, ethical, or religious tendencies are seldom "repressed," for, since the individual originally received them from his herd, they can hardly ever come into conflict with the dicta of the latter. This merely says that a man cannot be ashamed of that which he respects; the apparent exceptions to this rule need not be here explained.

The language used in the previous paragraph will have indicated that by the term "repression" we denote an active dynamic process. Thoughts that are "repressed" are actively kept from consciousness by a definite force and with the expenditure of more or less mental effort, though the person concerned is rarely aware of this. Further, what is thus kept from consciousness typically possesses an energy of its own; hence our frequent use of such expressions as "trend," "tendency," etc. A little consideration of the genetic aspects of the matter will make it comprehensible that the trends most likely to be "repressed" are those belonging to what are called the innate impulses, as contrasted with secondarily acquired ones. Loening[1] seems very discerningly to have grasped this, for, in commenting on a remark of Kohler's to the effect that "where a feeling impels us to action or to omission, it is replete with a hundred reasons—with reasons that are as light as soap-bubbles, but which through self-deception appear to us as highly respectable and compelling motives, because they are hugely magnified in the (concave) mirror of our own feeling," he writes: "But this does not hold good, as Kohler and others believe, when we are impelled by *moral* feelings of which reason *approves* (for these we admit to ourselves, they need no excuse), only for feelings that arise from our *natural man,* those the gratification of which is *opposed by our reason.*" It only remains to add the obvious corollary that, as the herd unquestionably selects from the "natural" instincts the sexual one on which to lay its heaviest ban, so it is the various psycho-sexual trends that are most often "repressed" by the individual. We have here the explanation of the clinical experience that the more intense and the more obscure is a given case of deep mental conflict the more certainly will it be found on adequate analysis to centre about

[1] Loening: op. cit., S. 245, 246.

a sexual problem. On the surface, of course, this does not appear so, for, by means of various psychological defensive mechanisms, the depression, doubt, despair, and other manifestations of the conflict are transferred on to more tolerable and permissible topics, such as anxiety about worldly success or failure, about immortality and the salvation of the soul, philosophical considerations about the value of life, the future of the world, and so on.

Bearing these considerations in mind, let us return to Hamlet. It should now be evident that the conflict hypotheses discussed above, which see Hamlet's conscious impulse towards revenge inhibited by an unconscious misgiving of a highly ethical kind, are based on ignorance of what actually happens in real life, since misgivings of this order belong in fact to the more conscious layers of the mind rather than to the deeper, unconscious ones. Hamlet's intense self-study would speedily have made him aware of any such misgivings and, although he might subsequently have ignored them, it would almost certainly have been by the aid of some process of rationalization which would have enabled him to deceive himself into believing that they were ill-founded; he would in any case have remained conscious of the nature of them. We have therefore to invert these hypotheses and realize—as his words so often indicate— that the positive striving for vengeance, the pious task laid on him by his father, was to him the moral and social one, the one approved of by his consciousness, and that the "repressed" inhibiting striving against the act of vengeance arose in some hidden source connected with his more personal, natural instincts. The former striving has already been considered, and indeed is manifest in every speech in which Hamlet debates the matter: the second is, from its nature, more obscure and has next to be investigated.

This is perhaps most easily done by inquiring more intently into Hamlet's precise attitude towards the object of his vengeance, Claudius, and towards the crimes that have to be avenged. These are two: Claudius' incest with the Queen,[1] and his murder of his brother. Now it is of great importance to note the profound difference in Hamlet's at-

---

[1] Had this relationship not counted as incestuous, then Queen Elizabeth would have had no right to the throne; she would have been a bastard, Katherine of Aragon being still alive at her birth.

titude towards these two crimes. Intellectually of course he abhors both, but there can be no question as to which arouses in him the deeper loathing. Whereas the murder of his father evokes in him indignation and a plain recognition of his obvious duty to avenge it, his mother's guilty conduct awakes in him the intensest horror. Furnivall[1] remarks, in speaking of the Queen, "Her disgraceful adultery and incest, and treason to his noble father's memory, Hamlet has felt in his inmost soul. Compared to their ingrain die, Claudius' murder of his father—notwithstanding all his protestations —is only a skin-deep stain."

Now, in trying to define Hamlet's attitude towards his uncle we have to guard against assuming off-hand that this is a simple one of mere execration, for there is a possibility of complexity arising in the following way: The uncle has not merely committed *each* crime, he has committed *both* crimes, a distinction of considerable importance, since the *combination* of crimes allows the admittance of a new factor, produced by the possible inter-relation of the two, which may prevent the result from being simply one of summation. In addition, it has to be borne in mind that the perpetrator of the crimes is a relative, and an exceedingly near relative. The possible inter-relationship of the crimes, and the fact that the author of them is an actual member of the family, give scope for a confusion in their influence on Hamlet's mind which may be the cause of the very obscurity we are seeking to clarify.

Let us first pursue further the effect on Hamlet of his mother's misconduct. Before he even knows with any certitude, however much he may suspect it, that his father has been murdered he is in the deepest depression, and evidently on account of this misconduct. The connection between the two is unmistakable in the monologue in Act I, Sc. 2, in reference to which Furnivall[2] writes: "One must insist on this, that before any revelation of his father's murder is made to Hamlet, before any burden of revenging that murder is laid upon him, he thinks of suicide as a welcome means of escape from this fair world of God's, made abominable to his diseased and weak imagination

[1] Furnivall: Introduction to the "Leopold" Shakespeare, p. 72.
[2] Furnivall: op. cit., p. 70.

by his mother's lust, and the dishonour done by her to his father's memory."

> O that this too too solid[1] flesh would melt,
> Thaw and resolve itself into a dew,
> Or that the Everlasting had not fix'd
> His canon 'gainst self-slaughter, O God, God,
> How weary, stale, flat, and unprofitable
> Seem to me all the uses of this world!
> Fie on 't, O fie, 'tis an unweeded garden
> That grows to seed, things rank and gross in nature
> Possess it merely, that it should come to this,
> But two months dead, nay, not so much, not two,
> So excellent a king; that was to this
> Hyperion to a satyr, so loving to my mother,
> That he might not beteem the winds of heaven
> Visit her face too roughly—heaven and earth
> Must I remember? why, she would hang on him
> As if increase of appetite had grown
> By what it fed on, and yet within a month,
> Let me not think on 't; frailty thy name is woman!
> A little month or ere those shoes were old
> With which she follow'd my poor father's body
> Like Niobe all tears, why she, even she—
> O God, a beast that wants discourse of reason
> Would have mourn'd longer—married with my uncle,
> My father's brother, but no more like my father
> Than I to Hercules, within a month,
> Ere yet the salt of most unrighteous tears
> Had left the flushing in her galled eyes,
> She married. O most wicked speed . . . to post
> With such dexterity to incestuous sheets!
> It is not, nor it cannot come to good,
> But break my heart, for I must hold my tongue.

According to Bradley,[2] Hamlet's melancholic disgust at life was the cause of his aversion from "any kind of decided action." His explanation of the whole problem of Hamlet

[1] Dover Wilson (*Times Literary Supplement*, May 16, 1918) brings forward excellent reasons for thinking that this word is a misprint for "sullied." I use the Shakespearean punctuation he has restored.
[2] Bradley: op. cit., p. 122.

is "the moral shock of the sudden ghastly disclosure of his mother's true nature," [1] and he regards the effect of this shock, as depicted in the play, as fully comprehensible. He says: [2] "Is it possible to conceive an experience more desolating to a man such as we have seen Hamlet to be; and is its result anything but perfectly natural? It brings bewildered horror, then loathing, then despair of human nature. His whole mind is poisoned . . . A nature morally blunter would have felt even so dreadful a revelation less keenly. A slower and more limited and positive mind might not have extended so widely through the world the disgust and disbelief that have entered it."

But we can rest satisfied with this seemingly adequate explanation of Hamlet's weariness of life only if we accept unquestioningly the conventional standards of the causes of deep emotion. Many years ago Connolly,[3] a well-known psychiatrist, pointed out the disproportion here existing between cause and effect, and gave as his opinion that Hamlet's reaction to his mother's marriage indicated in itself a mental instability, "a predisposition to actual unsoundness"; he writes: "The circumstances are not such as would at once turn a healthy mind to the contemplation of suicide, the last resource of those whose reason has been overwhelmed by calamity and despair." In T. S. Eliot's [4] opinion, also, Hamlet's emotion is in excess of the facts as they appear, and he specially contrasts it with Gertrude's negative and insignificant personality. Wihan[5] attributes the exaggerated effect of his misfortunes to Hamlet's "Masslösigkeit" (lack of moderation), which is displayed in every direction. We have unveiled only the exciting cause, not the predisposing cause. The very fact that Hamlet is apparently content with the explanation arouses our misgiving, for, as will presently be expounded, from the very nature of the emotion he cannot be aware of the true cause of it. If we ask, not what ought to produce such soul-paralysing grief and distaste for life, but what in actual fact does produce it, we are compelled to go beyond this explanation and seek for

[1] Idem: op. cit., p. 117.
[2] Idem: op. cit., p. 119.
[3] Connolly: A Study of Hamlet, 1863, pp. 22, 23.
[4] T. S. Eliot: loc. cit.
[5] J. Wihan: "Die Hamletfrage," in Leipziger Beiträge zur englischen Philologie, 1921, S. 89.

some deeper cause. In real life speedy second marriages occur commonly enough without leading to any such result as is here depicted, and when we see them followed by this result we invariably find, if the opportunity for an analysis of the subject's mind presents itself, that there is some other and more hidden reason why the event is followed by this inordinately great effect. The reason always is that the event has awakened to increased activity mental processes that have been "repressed" from the subject's consciousness. His mind has been specially prepared for the catastrophe by previous mental processes with which those directly resulting from the event have entered into association. This is perhaps what Furnivall means when he speaks of the world being made abominable to Hamlet's "diseased imagination." In short, the special nature of the reaction presupposes some special feature in the mental predisposition. Bradley himself has to qualify his hypothesis by inserting the words "to a man such as we have seen Hamlet to be."

We come at this point to the vexed question of Hamlet's sanity, about which so many controversies have raged. Dover Wilson [1] authoritatively writes: "I agree with Loening, Bradley and others that Shakespeare meant us to imagine Hamlet as suffering from some kind of mental disorder throughout the play." The question is what kind of mental disorder and what is its significance dramatically and psychologically. The matter is complicated by Hamlet's frequently displaying simulation (the Antic Disposition),[2] and it has been asked whether this is to conceal his real mental disturbance or cunningly to conceal his purposes in coping with the practical problems of this task? This is a topic that presently will be considered at some length, but there can be few who regard it as a comprehensive statement of Hamlet's mental state. As T. S. Eliot[3] has neatly expressed it, "Hamlet's 'madness' is less than madness and more than feigned."

But what of the mental disorder itself? In the past this little problem in clinical diagnosis seems to have greatly

[1] Dover Wilson: *What Happens in Hamlet* (Cambridge U.P., 1934) p. 217.
[2] Cp. R. Alexander: "Hamlet, the Classical Malingerer," *Medical Journal and Record*, Sept. 4, 1929, p. 287.
[3] T. S. Eliot: Selected Essays, 1932, p. 146.

exercised psychiatrists. Some of them, e.g. Thierisch,[1] Sigismund,[2] Stenger,[3] and many others, have simply held that Hamlet was insane, without particularizing the form of insanity. Rosner[4] labelled Hamlet as a hystero-neurasthenic, an opinion contradicted by Rubinstein[5] and Landmann.[6] Most, however, including Kellog,[7] de Boismon,[8] Heuse,[9] Nicholson,[10] and others, have committed themselves to the view that Hamlet was suffering from melancholia, though there are not failing psychiatrists, e.g. Ominus,[11] who reject this. Schücking[12] attributes the delay in his action to Hamlet's being paralysed by melancholia. Laehr[13] has a particularly ingenious hypothesis which maintains that Shakespeare, having taken over the Ghost episode from the earlier play, was obliged to depict Hamlet as a melancholiac because this was theatrically the most presentable form of insanity in which hallucinations occur. Long ago Dowden made it seem probable that Shakespeare had made use of an important study of melancholia by Timothe Bright,[14] but, although he may have adapted a few phrases to his own use, the clinical picture of Hamlet differs notably from that delineated by Bright.

More to the point is the actual account given in the play by the King, the Queen, Ophelia, and above all, Polonius.[15] In his description, for example, we note—if the Elizabethan

[1] Thierisch: *Nord und Süd*, 1878, Bd. VI.
[2] Sigismund: *Jahrbuch der Deutschen Shakespeare-Gesellschaft*, 1879, Jahrg. XVI.
[3] E. Stenger: Der Hamlet Charakter. Eine psychiatrische Shakespeare-Studie, 1883.
[4] Rosner: Shakespeare's Hamlet im Lichte der Neuropathologie, 1895.
[5] Rubinstein: op. cit.
[6] Landmann: *Zeitschrift für Psychologie*, 1896, Bd. XI.
[7] Kellog: Shakespeare's Delineation of Insanity, 1868.
[8] De Boismon: *Annales médico-psychologiques*, 1868, 4e série, 12e fasc.
[9] Heuse: *Jahrbuch der deutschen Shakespeare-Gesellschaft*, 1876, Jahrg. XIII.
[10] Nicholson: *Transactions of the New Shakespeare Society*, 1880-5, Part II.
[11] Ominus: *Revue des Deux Mondes*, 1876, 3e sér., 14e fasc.
[12] Schücking: Character Problems in Shakespeare's Plays, 1922, p. 162.
[13] Laehr: Die Darstellung krankhafter Geisteszustände in Shakespeares Dramas, 1898, S. 179, etc.
[14] Timothe Bright: A Treatise of Melancholia, 1586.
[15] Act 2, Sc. 2. "Fell into a sadness," etc.

language is translated into modern English—the symptoms of dejection, refusal of food, insomnia, crazy behaviour, fits of delirium, and finally of raving madness; Hamlet's poignant parting words to Polonius ("except my life," etc.) cannot mean other than a craving for death. These are undoubtedly suggestive of certain forms of melancholia, and the likeness to manic-depressive insanity, of which melancholia is now known to be but a part, is completed by the occurrence of attacks of great excitement that would nowadays be called "hypomanic," of which Dover Wilson[1] counts no fewer than eight. This modern diagnosis has indeed been suggested, e.g. by Brock,[2] Somerville,[3] and others. Nevertheless, the rapid and startling oscillations between intense excitement and profound depression do not accord with the accepted picture of this disorder, and if I had to describe such a condition as Hamlet's in clinical terms—which I am not particularly inclined to—it would have to be as a severe case of hysteria on a cyclothymic basis.

All this, however, is of academic interest only. What we are essentially concerned with is the psychological understanding of the dramatic effect produced by Hamlet's personality and behaviour. That effect would be quite other were the central figure in the play to represent merely a "case of insanity." When that happens, as with Ophelia, such a person passes beyond our ken, is in a sense no more human, whereas Hamlet successfully claims our interest and sympathy to the very end. Shakespeare certainly never intended us to regard Hamlet as insane, so that the "mind o'erthrown" must have some other meaning than its literal one. Robert Bridges[4] has described the matter with exquisite delicacy:

> Hamlet himself would never have been aught to us, or we
> To Hamlet, wer't not for the artful balance whereby
> Shakespeare so gingerly put his sanity in doubt
> Without the while confounding his Reason.

I would suggest that in this Shakespeare's extraordinary

[1] Dover Wilson: op. cit., p. 213.
[2] J. H. E. Brock: The Dramatic Purpose of Hamlet, 1935.
[3] H. Somerville: Madness in Shakespearean Tragedy, 1929.
[4] Robert Bridges: The Testament of Beauty, I, 577.

powers of observation and penetration granted him a degree of insight that it has taken the world three subsequent centuries to reach. Until our generation (and even now in the juristic sphere) a dividing line separated the sane and responsible from the irresponsible insane. It is now becoming more and more widely recognized that much of mankind lives in an intermediate and unhappy state charged with what Dover Wilson[1] well calls "that sense of frustration, futility and human inadequacy which is the burden of the whole symphony" and of which Hamlet is the supreme example in literature. This intermediate plight, in the toils of which perhaps the greater part of mankind struggles and suffers, is given the name of psychoneurosis, and long ago the genius of Shakespeare depicted it for us with faultless insight.

Extensive studies of the past half century, inspired by Freud, have taught us that a psychoneurosis means a state of mind where the person is unduly, and often painfully, driven or thwarted by the "unconscious" part of his mind, that buried part that was once the infant's mind and still lives on side by side with the adult mentality that has developed out of it and should have taken its place. It signifies *internal* mental conflict. We have here the reason why it is impossible to discuss intelligently the state of mind of anyone suffering from a psychoneurosis, whether the description is of a living person or an imagined one, without correlating the manifestations with what must have operated in his infancy and is *still operating*. That is what I propose to attempt here.

For some deep-seated reason, which is to him unacceptable, Hamlet is plunged into anguish at the thought of his father being replaced in his mother's affections by someone else. It is as if his devotion to his mother had made him so jealous for her affection that he had found it hard enough to share this even with his father and could not endure to share it with still another man. Against this thought, however, suggestive as it is, may be urged three objections. First, if it were in itself a full statement of the matter, Hamlet would have been aware of the jealousy, whereas we have concluded that the mental process we are seeking is hidden from him. Secondly, we see in it no evidence of the arousing

[1] Dover Wilson: op. cit., p. 261.

of an old and forgotten memory. And, thirdly, Hamlet is being deprived by Claudius of no greater share in the Queen's affection than he had been by his own father, for the two brothers made exactly similar claims in this respect —namely, those of a loved husband. The last-named objection, however, leads us to the heart of the situation. How if, in fact, Hamlet had in years gone by, as a child, bitterly resented having had to share his mother's affection even with his own father, had regarded him as a rival, and had secretly wished him out of the way so that he might enjoy undisputed and undisturbed the monopoly of that affection? If such thoughts had been present in his mind in childhood days they evidently would have been "repressed," and all traces of them obliterated, by filial piety and other educative influences. The actual realization of his early wish in the death of his father at the hands of a jealous rival would then have stimulated into activity these "repressed" memories, which would have produced, in the form of depression and other suffering, an obscure aftermath of his childhood's conflict. This is at all events the mechanism that is actually found in the real Hamlets who are investigated psychologically.[1]

The explanation, therefore, of the delay and self-frustration exhibited in the endeavour to fulfil his father's demand for vengeance is that to Hamlet the thought of incest and parricide combined is too intolerable to be borne. One part of him tries to carry out the task, the other flinches inexorably from the thought of it. How fain would he blot it out in that "bestial oblivion" which unfortunately for him his conscience contemns. He is torn and tortured in an insoluble inner conflict.

G. D. F. KITTO

G. D. F. Kitto (1897-   ). Professor of Greek at the University of Bristol; author of Greek Tragedy *(1939),* The Greeks *(1951),* Form and Meaning in Drama *(1956) etc.*

[1] See, for instance, Wulf Sachs: Black Hamlet, 1937.

HAMLET AS RELIGIOUS DRAMA*

. . . The first thing that strikes us, or should strike us, when we contemplate the play is that it ends in the complete destruction of the two houses that are concerned. The character of Hamlet and the inner experience that he undergoes are indeed drawn at length and with great subtlety, and we must not overlook the fact; nevertheless, the architectonic pattern . . . is so vast as to suggest at once that what we are dealing with is no individual tragedy of character, however profound, but something more like religious drama; and this means that unless we are ready, at every step, to relate the dramatic situation to its religious or philosophical background—in other words, to look at the play from a point of view to which more recent drama has not accustomed us—then we may not see either the structure or the meaning of the play as Shakespeare thought them.

Why do Rosencrantz and Guildenstern die, and Ophelia, and Laertes? Are these disasters casual by-products of 'the tragedy of a man who could not make up his mind'? Or are they necessary parts of a firm structure? Each of these disasters we can refer to something that Hamlet has done or failed to do, and we can say that each reveals something more of Hamlet's character; but if we see no more than this we are short-sighted, and are neglecting Shakespeare's plain directions in favour of our own. We are told much more than this when we hear Horatio, and then Laertes, cry 'Why, what a King is this!', 'The King, the King's to blame'; also when Guildenstern says, with a deep and unconscious irony 'We here give up ourselves . . . ', and when Laertes talks of 'contagious blastments'. Shakespeare puts before us a group of young people, friends or lovers, none of them wicked, one of them at least entirely virtuous, all surrounded by the poisonous air of Denmark (which also Shakespeare brings frequently and vividly before our minds), all of them brought to death because of its evil influences. Time after time, either in some significant patterning or with some phrase pregnant with irony, he makes us

* Extracted from *Form and Meaning in Drama*.

see that these people are partners in disaster, all of them borne down on the 'massy wheel' to 'boisterous ruin'.

In this, the natural working-out of sin, there is nothing mechanical. That is the philosophic reason why character and situation must be drawn vividly. Neither here nor in Greek drama have we anything to do with characters who are puppets in the hands of Fate. In both, we see something of the power of the gods, or the designs of Providence; but these no more override or reduce to unimportance the natural working of individual character than the existence, in the physical world, of universal laws overrides the natural behaviour of natural bodies. It is indeed precisely in the natural behaviour of men, and its natural results, in given circumstances, that the operation of the divine laws can be discerned. In *Hamlet*, Shakespeare draws a complete character, not for the comparatively barren purpose of 'creating' a Hamlet for our admiration, but in order to show how he, like the others, is inevitably engulfed by the evil that has been set in motion, and how he himself becomes the cause of further ruin. The conception which unites these eight persons in one coherent catastrophe may be said to be this: evil, once started on its course, will so work as to attack and overthrow impartially the good and the bad; and if the dramatist makes us feel, as he does, that a Providence is ordinant in all this, that, as with the Greeks, is his way of universalising the particular event.

Claudius, the arch-villain, driven by crime into further crime, meets at last what is manifestly divine justice. 'If his fitness speaks . . .' says Hamlet; the 'fitness' of Claudius has been speaking for a long time. At the opposite pole stands Ophelia, exposed to corruption though uncorrupted, but pitifully destroyed as the chain of evil uncoils itself. Then Gertrude, one of Shakespeare's most tragic characters: she is the first, as Laertes is the last, to be tainted by Claudius; but while he dies in forgiveness and reconciliation, no such gentle influence alleviates her end. In the bedchamber scene Hamlet had pointed out to her the hard road to amendment; has she tried to follow it? On this, Shakespeare is silent; but her last grim experience of life is to find that 'O my dear Hamlet, the drink, the drink! I am poisoned' —poisoned, as she must realise, by the cup that her new husband had prepared for the son whom she loved so tenderly. After her own sin, and as a direct consequence of it, everything that she holds dear is blasted. Her part in this tragedy is indeed a frightening one. She is no Claudius, recklessly given to crime, devoid of any pure or disinterested motive. Her love for her son shines through every line she speaks; this, and her affection for Ophelia, show us the Gertrude that might have been, if a mad passion had not swept her into the arms of Claudius. By this one sin she condemned herself to endure, and, still worse, to understand, all its devastating consequences: her son driven 'mad', killing Polonius, denouncing herself and her crime in cruel terms that she cannot rebut, Ophelia driven out of her senses and into her grave—nearly a criminal's grave; all her hopes irretrievably ruined. One tragic little detail, just before the end, shows how deeply Shakespeare must have pondered on his Gertrude. We know that she has seen the wild struggle in the graveyard between Laertes and Hamlet. When the Lord enters, to invite Hamlet to the fencing-match, he says: 'The Queen desires you to use some gentle entertainment to Laertes before you fall to play.' 'She well instructs me', says Hamlet. What can this mean, except that she has vague fears of Laertes' anger, and a pathetic hope that Hamlet might appease it, by talk more courteous than he had used in the graveyard? It recalls her equally pathetic wish that Ophelia's beauty and virtue might 'bring him to his wonted ways again'. The mischief is always much greater than her worst fears. We soon see how Hamlet's gentle entertainment is received by Laertes; and she, in the blinding flash in which she dies, learns how great a treachery had been prepared against her Hamlet.

We cannot think of Gertrude's death, and the manner of it, without recalling what the Ghost had said: Leave her to Heaven. But if we are to see the hand of Providence—whatever that may signify—in her death, can we do other with the death of Polonius? A 'casual slaughter'? A 'rash and bloody deed'? Certainly; and let us by all means blame Hamlet for it, as also for the callousness with which he sends Rosencrantz and Guildenstern to their doom; but if we suppose that Shakespeare contrived these things only to show us what Hamlet was like, we shall be treating as secular drama what Shakespeare designed as something bigger. In fact, Hamlet was *not* like this, any more than he was, by nature, hesitant or dilatory; any more than Ophelia was habitually mad. This is what he has become. The dramatist does indeed direct us to regard the killing of Polonius in two aspects at once: it is a sudden, unpremeditated attack made by Hamlet, 'mad', on one who he hopes will prove to be Claudius; and at the same time it is the will of Heaven:

> *For this same lord*
> *I do repent; but Heaven hath pleased it so*
> *To punish me with this and this with me,*
> *That I must be their scourge and minister.*

Surely this is exactly the same dramaturgy that we meet in Sophocles' *Electra*. When Orestes comes out from killing his mother, Electra asks him how things are. 'In the *palace*',[1] he says, 'all is well—if Apollo's oracle was well.' Perhaps it was a 'rash and bloody deed'; it seems to bring Orestes little joy. We may think of it what we like; Sophocles does not invite us to approve, and if we suppose that he does, we have not understood his play, or his gods. Apollo approves, and Orestes, though he acts for his own reasons, is the gods' 'scourge and minister'. Polonius, no unworthy Counsellor of this King, a mean and crafty man whose soul is mirrored in his language no less than in his acts, meets a violent death while spying; and that such a man should so be killed is, in a large sense, right. Hamlet may 'repent'; Orestes may feel remorse at a dreadful act, but in each case Heaven was ordinant.

The death of Laertes too is a coherent part of this same pattern. To this friend of Hamlet's we can attribute one fault; nor are we taken by surprise when we meet it, for Shakespeare has made his preparations. Laertes is a noble and generous youth, but his sense of honour has no very secure foundations—and Polonius' farewell speech to him makes the fact easy to understand. His natural and unguarded virtue, assailed at once by his anger, his incomplete understanding of the facts, and the evil suggestions

---

[1] I italicise this word in order to represent Sophocles' untranslatable μέν, which suggests a coming antithesis that in fact is not expressed.

of Claudius, gives way; he falls into treachery, and through it, as he comes to see, he is 'most justly killed'.

Of Rosencrantz and Guildenstern, two agreeable though undistinguished young men, flattered and suborned and cruelly destroyed, there is no more to be said; but there remains Hamlet, last and greatest of the eight. Why must he be destroyed? It would be true to say that he is destroyed simply because he has failed to destroy Claudius first; but this is 'truth' as it is understood between police-inspectors, on duty. The dramatic truth must be something which, taking this in its stride, goes much deeper; and we are justified in saying 'must be' since this catastrophe too is presented as being directed by Providence, and therefore inevitable and 'right'. If 'there is a special providence in the fall of a sparrow', there surely is in the fall of a Hamlet.

Of the eight victims, we have placed Claudius at one pole and Ophelia at the other; Hamlet, plainly, stands near Ophelia. In both Hamlet and Ophelia we can no doubt detect faults: she ought to have been able to see through Polonius, and he should not have hesitated. But to think like this is to behave like a judge, one who must stand outside the drama and sum up from a neutral point of view; the critic who tries to do this would be better employed in a police-court than in criticism. We must remain within the play, not try to peer at the characters through a window of our own constructing. If we do remain within the play, we observe that what Shakespeare puts before us, all the time, is not faults that we can attribute to Ophelia and Hamlet, but their virtues; and when he does make Hamlet do things deserving of blame, he also makes it evident on whom the blame should be laid. The impression with which he leaves us is not the tragedy that one so fine as Hamlet should be ruined by one fault; it is the tragedy that one so fine should be drawn down into the gulf; and, beyond this, that the poison let loose in Denmark should destroy indiscriminately the good, the bad and the indifferent. Good and bad, Hamlet and Claudius, are coupled in the one sentence 'If his fitness speaks, mine is ready'. That Claudius is 'fit and seasoned for his passage' is plain enough; is it not just as plain that Hamlet is equally 'ready'? What has he been telling us, throughout the play, but that life can henceforth have no meaning or value to him? Confronted by what he sees in Denmark, he, the man of action, has been reduced to impotence; the man of reason has gone 'mad'; the man of religion has been dragged down to 'knavery', and has felt the contagions of Hell. There is room, though not very much, for subtle and judicious appraisal of his character and conduct; the core of his tragedy is not here, but in the fact that such surpassing excellence is, like the beauty and virtue of Ophelia, brought to nothing by evil. Through all the members of these two doomed houses the evil goes on working, in a concatenation

> *Of carnal, bloody and unnatural acts,*
> *Of accidental judgments, casual slaughters,*
> *Of deaths put on by cunning and forced cause,*

until none are left, and the slate is wiped clean.

The structure of *Hamlet,* then, suggests that we should treat it as religious drama, and when we do, it certainly does not lose either in significance or in artistic integrity. As we have seen more than once, it has fundamental things in common with Greek religious drama—yet in other respects it is very different, being so complex in form and texture. It may be worth while to enquire, briefly, why this should be so.

One naturally compares it with the two Greek revenge-tragedies, the *Choephori* and Sophocles' *Electra,* but whether we do this, or extend the comparison to other Greek religious tragedies like the *Agamemnon* or *Oedipus Tyrannus* or *Antigone,* we find one difference which is obviously pertinent to our enquiry: in the Greek plays the sin, crime or error which is the mainspring of the action is specific, while in Hamlet it is something more general, a quality rather than a single act. Thus, although there are crimes enough in the *Oresteia,* what we are really concerned with, throughout the trilogy, is the problem of avenging or punishing crime. The *Agamemnon* is full of hybris, blind folly, blood-lust, adultery, treachery; but what humanity is suffering from, in the play, is not these sins in themselves, but a primitive conception of Justice, one which uses, and can be made to justify, these crimes, and leads to chaos; and the trilogy ends not in any form of reconciliation or forgiveness among those who have injured each other, nor in any purging of sin, or acceptance of punishment, but in the resolution of the dilemma.

Hamlet resembles the *Choephori* in this, that the murder of a King, and adultery, or something like it, are the crimes which have to be avenged; also that these can be avenged only through another crime, though perhaps a sinless one; but the differences are deep and far-reaching. They are not merely that Orestes kills, and Hamlet shrinks from killing. We may say that both in the Greek trilogy and in Shakespeare's play the Tragic Hero, ultimately, is humanity itself; and what humanity is suffering from, in *Hamlet* is not a specific evil, but Evil itself. The murder is only the chief of many manifestations of it, the particular case which is the mainspring of the tragic action.

This seems to be typical. In the *Antigone* a whole house is brought down in ruin, and, again, the cause is quite a specific one. It is nothing like the comprehensive wickedness of Iago, or the devouring ambition of Macbeth, or the consuming and all-excluding love of Antony and Cleopatra. It is, quite precisely, that Creon makes, and repeats, a certain error of judgment, ἁμαρτία; and I use the phrase 'error of judgment' meaning not that it is venial, nor that it is purely intellectual, but that it is specific. It is not a trivial nor a purely intellectual mistake if a man, in certain circumstances, rejects the promptings of humanity, and thinks that the gods will approve; but this is what Creon does, and the tragedy springs from this and from nothing else. He is not a wicked man—not lecherous or envious or ambitious or vindictive. All this is irrelevant. He is simply the man to make and maintain this one specific and disastrous error.

This contrast between the specific and the general obviously has a close connexion with the contrast between the singleness of the normal Greek tragic structure and the complexity of *Hamlet*. In the first place, since Shakespeare's real theme is not the moral or theological or social problem of crime and vengeance, still less its effect on a single mind and soul, but the corroding power of sin, he will present it not as a single 'error of judgment' but as a hydra with many heads. We have shown, let us hope, how this explains, or helps to explain, such features of the play as, so to speak, the simultaneous presentation of three Creons: Claudius, Gertrude and Polonius, each of them, in his own degree, an embodiment of the general evil. Hence too the richer character-drawing. Claudius is a drunkard, and the fact makes its own contribution to the complete structure; if Sophocles had made Creon a drunkard, it would have been an excrescence on the play. Hence too the frequent changes of scene in the first part of the play; also the style of speech invented for Polonius and Osric. The general enemy is the rottenness that pervades Denmark; therefore it is shown in many persons and many guises.

Then, not only are the sources of the corruption diverse, but so are its ramifications too. We are to see how it spreads, whether from Claudius or from Gertrude or from Polonius, and how it involves one after another, destroying as it goes. To be sure, Greek tragedy shows us something similar— but it is not the same. For example, the condemnation of Antigone leads to the death of Haemon, and that to the death of Eurydice; in the *Oresteia* too there is a long succession of crime. In fact, we remarked above that Claudius recalls the *Agamemnon* and its πρώταρχος ἄτη, the crime that sets crime in motion. So he does; but there is a big difference. Both in *Hamlet* and in the Greek plays crime leads to crime, or disaster to disaster, in this linear fashion, but in *Hamlet* it spreads in another way too, one which is not Greek: it spreads from soul to soul, as a contagion, as when Laertes is tempted by Claudius, or, most notably, when, by his mother's example and Polonius' basely inspired interference, Hamlet's love is corrupted into lewdness, or when he turns against his two compromised friends and pitilessly sends them to death.

Extension of evil in this fashion is, I think, foreign to Greek tragedy. Clearly, it involves a dramatic form which is complexive, not linear and single, like the Greek. Of his successive victims, Sophocles does not even mention Haemon until the middle of the play, and Eurydice not until the end; and the effect is most dramatic. In *Hamlet* there are eight victims, all of whom we have to watch, from time to time, as they become more and more deeply involved. Further, not only are more people involved at the same time in this more generalised Tragic Flaw, but they are involved more intimately, which again makes for a richer dramatic texture. We may compare Hamlet with Orestes. Externally, they are in a similar position. But when Aeschylus has shown us that Orestes is an avenger pure in heart, and that his dilemma is from every point of view an intolerable one, it is not far wrong to say that his interest in Orestes, as a character, is exhausted; anything more would be unnecessary. Hamlet exists in a different kind of tragedy, one which requires that we should see how the contagion gradually spreads over his whole spirit and all his conduct.

The same contrast exists between Hamlet and Sophocles' Orestes and Electra. She, one might say, is drawn much more intimately than the Orestes of Aeschylus. True; but still she is drawn, so to speak, all at once: There is the situation, here is Electra, and this is the way in which it makes her act. It is not Sophocles' conception to show how her mother's continuing crime gradually warps her mind, by a stealthy growth of evil. If she is warped, it has all happened already. His dramatic interest in the characters of the avengers is focussed on this, that they, being what they are, and being affected by Clytemnestra's crime in this way, will naturally act as they do.

It is, in short, a general statement which I think will bear examination, that Greek tragedy presents sudden and complete disaster, or one disaster linked to another in linear fashion, while Shakespearean tragedy presents the complexive, menacing spread of ruin; and that at least one explanation of this is that the Greek poets thought of the tragic error as the breaking of a divine law (or sometimes, in Aeschylus, as the breaking down of a temporary divine law), while Shakespeare saw it as an evil quality which, once it has broken loose, will feed on itself and on anything else that it can find until it reaches its natural end. So, for example in *Macbeth*: in 'noble Macbeth', ambition is stimulated, and is not controlled by reason or religion; it meets with a stronger response from Lady Macbeth, and it grows insanely into a monstrous passion that threatens a whole kingdom. It is a tragic conception which is essentially dynamic, and demands the very unhellenic fluidity and expansiveness of expression which the Elizabethan theatre afforded.

Whether this is a reflection of some profound difference between Greek and Christian thought is a question which I am
not competent to discuss.

THOMAS RYMER

*Thomas Rymer (1643?-1713). Lawyer and critic. He studied
French criticism and applied its rules to the English
drama in his* Tragedies of the Last Age *(1677) and* A
Short View of Tragedy *(1692). This latter book contains,
in its analysis of* Othello, *the most famous attack ever
made on Shakespeare. Rowe began the replies to it; on
the basis of it Macaulay said that Rymer was the worst
critic who ever lived; and in the present century Mr.
T. S. Eliot remarked that he had never seen 'a cogent
refutation' of Rymer's objections. The case against Shakespeare is still largely the one put by Rymer, supported
in their different fashions by Voltaire, Tolstoy and George
III ('such stuff, only we must not say so').*

AGAINST OTHELLO*

From all the Tragedies acted on our English Stage,
Othello is said to bear the Bell away. The *Subject* is more
of a piece, and there is indeed something like, there is, as it
were, some phantom of a *Fable*. The *Fable* is always
accounted the *Soul* of Tragedy. And it is the *Fable* which is
properly the *Poets* part. Because the other three parts of
Tragedy, to wit the *Characters* are taken from the Moral
Philosopher; the *thoughts* or sence, from them that teach
Rhetorick: And the past part, which is the *expression*, we
learn from the Grammarians.

This Fable is drawn from a Novel, compos'd in Italian
by *Giraldi Cinthio*, who also was a Writer of Tragedies.
And to that use employ'd such of his Tales, as he judged

* From *A Short View of Tragedy* (1692) Cap. VII.

proper for the Stage. But with this of the *Moor,* he meddl'd
no farther. . . .

What ever rubs or difficulties may stick on the Bark,
The Moral, sure, of this Fable is very instructive.
First, This may be a caution to all Maidens
of Quality bow, without their Parents consent,
they run away with Blackamoors . . .

Secondly, This may be a warning to all good
Wives, that they look well to their Linnen.

Thirdly, This may be a lesson to
Husbands, that before their Jealousie be
Tragical, the proofs may be Mathematical . . .

. . . *Shakespear* in this Play calls 'em the *supersubtle venetians.* Yet examine throughout the Tragedy there is nothing in the noble *Desdemona,* that is not below any Countrey
Chamber-maid with us.

And the account he gives of their Noblemen and Senate,
can only be calculated for the latitude of *Gotham.*

The Character of that State is to employ strangers in
their Wars; But shall a Poet thence fancy that they will set
a Negro to be their General; or trust a *Moor* to defend
them against the *Turk?* With us a Black-amoor might rise
to be a Trumpeter; but *Shakespear* would not have him less
than a Lieutenant-General. With us a *Moor* might marry
some little drab, or Small-coal Wench: *Shake-spear,* would
provide him the Daughter and Heir of some great Lord,
or Privy-Councellor: And all the Town should reckon it a
very suitable match: Yet the English are not bred up with
that hatred and aversion to the *Moors,* as are the Venetians,
who suffer by a perpetual Hostility from them,

*Littora littoribus contraria—**

Nothing is more odious in Nature than an improbable
lye; And, certainly, never was any Play fraught, like this
of *Othello,* with improbabilities.

* 'Shores opposed to shores'—i.e. a natural hostility between the two
nations.

The *Characters* or Manners, which are the second part in a Tragedy, are not less unnatural and improper, than the Fable was improbable and absurd.

Othello is made a Venetian General. We see nothing done by him, nor related concerning him, that comports with the condition of a General, or, indeed, of a Man, unless the killing himself, to avoid a death the Law was about to inflict upon him. When his Jealousy had wrought him up to a resolution of's taking revenge for the suppos'd injury, He sets *Jago* to the fighting part, to kill *Cassio;* And chuses himself to murder the silly Woman his Wife, that was like to make no resistance.

His Love and his Jealousie are no part of a Souldiers Character, unless for Comedy.

But what is most intolerable is *Jago*. He is no Black-amoor Souldier, so we may be sure he should be like other Souldiers of our acquaintance; yet never in Tragedy, nor in Comedy, nor in Nature was a Souldier with his Character; take it in the Authors own words;

> Em.   ——*some Eternal Villain,*
> *Some busie, and insinuating Rogue,*
> *Some cogging, couzening Slave, to get some office.*
> (IV, ii, 131–3)

Horace Describes a Souldier otherwise:

> *Impiger, iracundus, inexorabilis, acer.**

Shakespear knew his Character of *Jago* was inconsistent. In this very Play he pronounces,

> *If thou dost deliver more or less than Truth,*
> *Thou are no Souldier.*——   (II, iii, 211–12)

This he knew, but to entertain the Audience with something new and surprising, against common sense, and Nature, he would pass upon us a close, dissembling, false, insinuating rascal, instead of an open-hearted, frank, plain-dealing Souldier, a character constantly worn by them for some thousands of years in the World.

* 'Action, wrathful, unyielding, fierce.'

Tiberius Cæsar had a Poet Arraign'd for his Life: because *Agamemnon* was brought on the Stage by him, with a character unbecoming a Souldier.

Our *Ensigns* and Subalterns, when disgusted by the Captain, throw up their Commissions, bluster, and are barefac'd. *Jago*, I hope, is not brought on the Stage, in a Red Coat. I know not what Livery the Venetians wear: but am sure they hold not these conditions to be *alla soldatesca.*†

Non sia egli per fare la vendetta con insidie, ma con la spada in mano. Cinthio.‡

Nor is our Poet more discreet in his *Desdemona*. He had chosen a Souldier for his Knave: And a Venetian Lady is to be the Fool.

This Senators Daughter runs away to (a Carriers Inn) the *Sagittary*, with a Black-amoor: is no sooner wedded to him, but the very night she Beds him, is importuning and teizing him for a young smock-fac'd Lieutenant, *Cassio*. And tho' she perceives the *Moor* Jealous of *Cassio*, yet will she not forbear, but still rings *Cassio*, *Cassio* in both his Ears. . . .

. . . One might think the General should not glory much in this action, but make an hasty work on't, and have turn'd his Eyes away from so unsouldierly an Execution: yet is he all pause and deliberation; handles her as calmly: and is as careful of her Souls health, as it had been her *Father Confessor. Have you prayed to Night,* Desdemona? But the suspence is necessary, that he might have a convenient while so to *roul his Eyes,* and so to *gnaw* his *nether lip* to the spectators. Besides the greater cruelty—*sub tam lentis maxillis.*

But hark, a most tragical thing laid to her charge.

Oth. *That Handkerchief, that I so lov'd, and gave thee, Thou gav'st to* Cassio.
Desd. *No by my Life and Soul; Send for the man and ask him.*
Oth.——*By Heaven, I saw my Handkerchief in his hand ——I saw the Handkerchief.*   (V, ii, 51–3, 65, 69)

* *Sueton* in Tib.
† 'In soldier's fashion.'
‡ 'He would not wish to pursue his vendetta by underhand means, but with sword in hand.'

So much ado, so much stress, so much passion and repetition about an Handkerchief! Why was not this call'd the
Tragedy of the Handkerchief? What can be more absurd
than (as *Quintilian* expresses it) *in parvis litibus has
Tragœdias movere?** We have heard of *Fortunatus his
Purse,* and of the *Invisible Cloak,* long ago worn thread
bare, and stow'd up in the Wardrobe of obsolete Romances:
one might think, that were a fitter place for this Handkerchief, than that it, at this time of day, be worn on the Stage,
to raise every where all this clutter and turmoil. Had it been
Desdemona's Garter, the Sagacious Moor might have smelt
a Rat: but the Handkerchief is so remote a trifle, no Booby,
on this side *Mauritania,* cou'd make any consequence
from it.

We may learn here, that a Woman never loses her
Tongue, even tho' after she is stifl'd.

> Desd. *O falsly, falsly murder'd.*
> Em. *Sweet* Desdemona, *O sweet Mistress, speak.*
> Desd. *A guiltless death I dye.*
> Em. *O who has done the deed?*
> Desd. *No body, I my self, farewel.*
> *Commend me to my kind Lord, O farewel.*
> (V, ii, 120, 124–8)

This *Desdemona* is a black swan; or an old Black-amoor
is a bewitching Bed-fellow. If this be Nature, it is a
laschet醇 below what the English Language can express.

For *Lardella,* to *make love, like an Humble Bee,* was, in
the Rehearsal, thought a fancy odd enough.

But hark what follows:

> Oth.   ——*O heavy hour!*
> *Methinks it shou'd be now a huge Eclipse*
> *Of Sun and Moon, and that the affrighted globe*
> *Shou'd yawn at Alteration.*   (V, ii, 101–4)

This is wonderful. Here is Poetry to *elevate* and *amuse.*
Here is sound All-sufficient. It would be uncivil to ask

---
* 'To enact tragedies in terms of petty quarrels.'
† 'Baseness'.

Flamstead, if the Sun and Moon can both together be so hugely eclipsed, in any *heavy hour* whatsoever. Nor must the Spectators consult *Gresham* Colledge, whether a body is naturally *frighted* till he *Yawn* agen. The Fortune of *Greece* is not concern'd with these Matters. These are Physical circumstances a Poet may be ignorant in, without any harm to the publick. These slips have no influence on our Manners and good Life; which are the Poets Province.

Rather may we ask here what unnatural crime *Desdemona,* or her Parents had committed, to bring this Judgment down upon her; to Wed a Black-amoor, and innocent to be thus cruelly murder'd by him. What instruction can we make out of this Catastrophe? Or whither must our reflection lead us? Is not this to envenome and sour our spirits, to make us repine and grumble at Providence; and the government of the World? If this be our end, what boots it to be Vertuous?

Desdemona dropt the Handkerchief, and missed it that very day after her Marriage; it might have been rumpl'd up with her Wedding sheets: And this Night that she lay in her wedding sheets, the *Fairey* Napkin (whilst *Othello* was stifling her) might have started up to disarm his fury and stop his ungracious mouth. Then might she (in a Traunce for fear) have lain as dead. Then might he, believing her dead, touch'd with remorse, have honestly cut his own Throat, by the good leave, and with the applause of all the Spectators. Who might thereupon have gone home with a quiet mind, admiring the beauty of Providence; fairly and truly represented on the Theatre.

> Oth.——*Why, how shou'd she be murdered?*
> Em. *Alas, who knows?*
> Oth. *You heard her say her self it was not I.*
> Em. *She did so, I must needs report a truth.*
> Oth. *She's like a liar gone to burn in Hell.*
> *'Twas I that did it.*
> Em. *O, the more Angel she!*
> *And you the blacker Devil.*
> Oth. *She turn'd to folly, and she was an Whore.*
> Em. *Thou dost belye her, and thou art a Devil.*
> Oth. *She was false as Water.*

Em. *Thou art rash as Fire,*
To say that she was false: O she was heavenly true.
                            (V. ii, 129–38)

In this kind of Dialogue they continue for forty lines farther, before she bethinks her self, to cry Murder.

Em.   *——Help, help, O help,*
The Moor has kill'd my Mistress, murder, Murder.
                             (V, ii, 169–70)

But from this Scene to the end of the Play we meet with nothing but blood and butchery, described much-what to the style of *the last Speeches and Confessions of the persons executed at Tyburn:* with this difference, that there we have the *fact,* and the due course of Justice, whereas our Poet against all Justice and Reason, against all Law, Humanity and Nature, in a barbarous arbitrary way, executes and makes havock of his subjects, *Hab-nab,* as they come to hand. *Desdemona* dropt her Handkerchief; therefore she must be stifl'd. *Othello,* by law to be broken on the Wheel, by the Poets cunning escapes with cutting his own Throat. *Cassio,* for I know not what, comes off with a broken shin. *Jago* murders his Benefactor *Roderigo,* as this were poetical gratitude. *Jago* is not yet kill'd, because there never yet was such a villain alive. The Devil, if once he brings a man to be dipt in a deadly sin, lets him alone, to take his course: and now when the *Foul Fiend* has done with him, our wise Authors take the sinner into their poetical service; there to accomplish him, and do the Devils drudgery.

Philosophy tells us it is a principle in the Nature of Man *to be grateful.*

History may tell us that *John an Oaks, John a Stiles,* or *Jago* were ungrateful; *Poetry* is to follow Nature; Philosophy must be his guide: history and *fact* in particular cases of *John an Oaks,* or *John of Styles,* are no warrant or direction for a Poet. Therefore *Aristotle* is always telling us that Poetry is σπουδαιότερον καὶ φιλοσοφώτερον, is more general and abstracted, is led more by the Philosophy, the reason and nature of things, than History: which only records things higlety, piglety, right or wrong as they happen.

History might without any preamble or difficulty, say that *Jago* was ungrateful. Philosophy then calls him unnatural; But the Poet is not, without huge labour and preparation to expose the Monster; and after shew the Divine Vengeance executed upon him. The Poet is not to add wilful Murder to his ingratitude: he has not antidote enough for the Poison: his Hell and Furies are not punishment sufficient for one single crime, of that bulk and aggravation.

> Em. *O thou dull Moor, that Handkerchief thou speak-*
>   *est on,*
> *I found by Fortune, and did give my Husband:*
> *For often with a solemn earnestness,*
> *(More than indeed belong'd to such a trifle)*
> *He beg'd of me to steal it.*   (V, ii, 228–32)

Here we see the meanest woman in the Play takes this *Handkerchief* for a *trifle* below her Husband to trouble his head about it. Yet we find, it entered into our Poets head, to make a Tragedy of this *Trifle*.

Then for the *unraveling of the Plot*, as they call it, never was old deputy Recorder in a Country Town, with his spectacles in summoning up the evidence, at such a puzzle: so blunder'd, and bedoultefied: as is our Poet, to have a good riddance: And get the *Catastrophe* off his hands.

What can remain with the Audience to carry home with them from this sort of Poetry, for their use and edification? how can it work, unless (instead of settling the mind, and purging our passions) to delude our senses, disorder our thoughts, addle our brain, pervert our affections, hair our imaginations, corrupt our appetite, and fill our head with vanity, confusion, *Tintamarre*, and Jingle-jangle, beyond what all the Parish Clarks of *London*, with their *old Testament* farces, and interludes, in *Richard* the seconds time cou'd ever pretend to? Our only hopes, for the good of their Souls, can be, that these people go to the Playhouse, as they do to Church, to sit still, look on one another, make no reflection, nor mind the Play, more than they would a Sermon.

There is in this Play, some burlesk, some humour, and ramble of Comical Wit, some shew, and some *Mimickry* to divert the spectators: but the tragical part is, plainly none other, than a Bloody Farce, without salt or savour.

THE EARL OF SHAFTESBURY

The third Earl of Shaftsbury (Anthony Ashley Cooper) (1671-1713). An important figure in eighteenth-century history of ideas; a Platonist and student of the arts and ethics. His main works are collected in Characteristicks of Men, Manners, Opinions and Times *(1711).*

OTHELLO, A WOEFUL TALE*

This Humour† our old Tragick Poet feèms to have dif-cover'd. He hit our *Tafte* in giving us a *Moorifh* Hero, full fraught with Prodigy: a wondrous *Storyteller!* But for the attentive Part, the Poet chofe to give it to Woman-kind. What paffionate Reader of *Travels,* or Student in the prodi-gious Sciences, can refufe to pity that fair Lady, who fell in Love with the *miraculous* Moor; efpecially confidering with what futable grace fuch a Lover cou'd relate the moft monftrous Adventures, and fatisfy the wondring Appetite with the moft wondrous Tales; *Wherein* (fays the Hero-Traveller)

> *Of Antars vaft, and Defarts idle,*
> *It was my Hint to fpeak:*
> *And of the* Cannibals *that each other eat!*
> *The* Anthropophagie! *and Men whofe Heads*
> *Do grow beneath their Shoulders. Thefe to hear*
> *Wou'd* Desdemona *ferioufly incline.*

Seriously, 'twas a woful Tale! unfit, one wou'd think, to win a tender Fair-one. It's true, the Poet fufficiently con-

* From *Characteristicks* (1711), I. pp. 347-8.
† I.e., our taste for 'unnatural' and 'monstrous' tales.

demns her *Fancy;* and makes her (poor Lady!) pay dearly for it, in the end. But why, amongſt his *Greek* Names, he ſhou'd have choſen one which denoted the Lady *Superſtitious,* I can't imagine: unleſs as Poets are ſometimes Prophets too, he ſhou'd figuratively, under this dark *Type,* have repreſented to us, That about a hundred Years after this Time, the Fair Sex of this Iſland ſhou'd, by other monſtrous *Tales,* be ſo ſeduc'd, as to turn their Favour chiefly on the Perſons of the *Tale-tellers;* and change their natural Inclination for fair, candid, and courteous Knights, into a Paſſion for a myſterious Race of black Enchanters: ſuch as of old were ſaid to *creep into Houſes,* and *lead captive ſilly Women.*

WILLIAM HAZLITT

MR. KEAN'S OTHELLO*

The Times.   *Drury Lane, October 27, 1817.*

Othello was played here on Saturday to a crowded house. There were two new appearances—Mr. Maywood as Iago, and a young lady as Desdemona. The name of this young *débutante* is not announced; but her reception was exceedingly flattering. Her face is handsome, her person elegant, her voice sweet, and her general deportment graceful and easy. There was also a considerable portion of tenderness and delicacy of feeling in several of the passages; but perhaps less than the character would bear. The only faults which we think it necessary to mention in her performance were, a too continual movement of the hands up and down, and sometimes a monotonous cadence in the recitation of the blank verse. Mr. Maywood's Iago had some of the faults which we have noticed in his former characters; but in the most trying scenes in the third act with Othello, we thought

---

* This is a routine newspaper notice; Hazlitt wrote up several of Kean's performances in *Othello.*

him exceedingly happy and successful. His conception was just, and his execution effective. There was a cold stillness in his manner which was more frightful than the expression of the most inveterate malignity. He seemed to crawl and watch for his prey like the spider, instead of darting upon it like the serpent. In the commencement of the part his timidity appeared to prevent him from doing justice to his intention, and once or twice his voice grew loud and unmanageable, so as to excite some marks of disapprobation. Mr. Kean's Othello is, we suppose, the finest piece of acting in the world. It is impossible either to describe or praise it adequately. We have never seen any actor so wrought upon, so 'perplexed in the extreme.' The energy of passion, as it expresses itself in action, is not the most terrific part; it is the agony of his soul, showing itself in looks and tones of voice. In one part, where he listens in dumb despair to the fiend-like insinuations of Iago, he presented the very face, the marble aspect of Dante's Count Ugolino. On his fixed eyelids 'Horror sat plumed.' In another part, where a gleam of hope or of tenderness returns to subdue the tumult of his passions, his voice broke in faltering accents from his overcharged breast. His lips might be said less to utter words, than to bleed drops of blood gushing from his heart. An instance of this was in his pronunciation of the line 'Of one that loved not wisely but too well.' The whole of this last speech was indeed given with exquisite force and beauty. We only object to the virulence with which he delivers the last line, and with which he stabs himself—a virulence which Othello would neither feel against himself at that moment, nor against the turbaned Turk (whom he had slain) at such a distance of time. His exclamation on seeing his wife, 'I cannot think but Desdemona's honest,' was 'the glorious triumph of exceeding love;' a thought flashing conviction on his mind, and irradiating his countenance with joy, like sudden sunshine. In fact, almost every scene or sentence in this extraordinary exhibition is a masterpiece of natural passion. The convulsed motion of the hands, and the involuntary swellings of the veins of the forehead in some of the most painful situations, should not only suggest topics of critical panegyric, but might furnish studies to the painter or anatomist.

RONALD BRYDEN

Ronald Bryden, (1927-   ). Dramatic critic of The New Statesman.

OLIVIER'S MOOR

All posterity will want to know is how he played. John Dexter's National Theatre *Othello* is efficient and clear, if slow, and contains some intelligent minor novelties. But in the long run all that matters is that it left the stage as bare as possible for its athlete. What requires record is how he, tackling Burbage's role for the first time at 57, created the Moor.

He came on smelling a rose, laughing softly with a private delight; barefooted, ankleted, black. He had chosen to play a Negro. The story fits a true Moor better: one of those striding hawks, fierce in a narrow range of medieval passions, whose women still veil themselves like Henry Moore sleepers against the blowing sand of Nouakchott's surrealistically modern streets. But Shakespeare muddled, giving him the excuse to turn himself into a coastal African from below the Senegal: dark, thick-lipped, open, laughing.

He sauntered downstage, with a loose, bare-heeled roll of the buttocks; came to rest feet splayed apart, hip lounging outward. For him, the great *Richard III* of his day, the part was too simple. He had made it difficult and interesting for himself by studying, as scrupulously as he studied the flat vowels, dead grin and hunched time-steps of Archie Rice, how an African looks, moves, sounds. The make-up, exact in pigment, covered his body almost wholly: an hour's job at least. The hands hung big and graceful. The whole voice was characterised, the o's and a's deepened, the consonants thickened with faint, guttural deliberation. 'Put up your bright swords, or de dew will rus' dem': not quite so crude, but in that direction.

It could have been caricature, an embarrassment. Instead, after the second performance, a well-known Negro actor rose in the stalls bravoing. For obviously it was done with love; with the main purpose of substituting for the dead grandeur of the Moorish empire one modern audiences could respond to: the grandeur of Africa. He was the continent, like a figure of Rubens allegory. In Cyprus, he strode ashore in a cloak and spiked helmet which brought to mind the medieval emirates of Ethiopia and Niger. Facing Doge and senators, he hooded his eyes in a pouting ebony mask: an old chief listening watchfully in tribal conclave. When he named them 'my masters' it was proudly edged: he had been a slave, their inquisition recalled his slavery, he reminded them in turn of his service and generalship.

He described Desdemona's encouragement smiling down at them, easy with sexual confidence. This was the other key to the choice of a Negro: Finley's Iago, bony, crop-haired, staring with the fanatic mule-grin of a Mississippi redneck, was to be goaded by a small white man's sexual jealousy of the black, a jealousy sliding into ambiguous fascination. Like Yeats's crowd staring, sweating, at Don Juan's mighty thigh, this Iago gazed, licking his dry lips, on a black one. All he need do is teach his own disease.

Mannerisms established, they were lifted into the older, broader imagery of the part. Leading Desdemona to bed, he pretended to snap at her with playful teeth. At Iago's first hints, he made a chuckling mock of twisting truth out of him by the ear. Then, during the temptation, he began to pace, turning his head sharply like a lion listening. The climax was his farewell to his occupation: bellowing the words as pure, wounded outcry, he hurled back his head until the ululating tongue showed pink against the roof of his mouth like a trumpeting elephant's. As he grew into a great beast, Finlay shrunk beside him, clinging to his shoulder like an ape, hugging his heels like a jackal.

He used every clue in the part, its most strenuous difficulties. Reassured by Desdemona's innocence, he bent to kiss her—and paused looking, sickened, at her lips. Long before his raging return, you knew he had found Cassio's kisses there. Faced with the lung-torturing hurdle of 'Like to the Pontic sea', he found a brilliant device for breaking the period: at 'Shall ne'er look back', he let the memories he was forswearing rush in and stop him, gasping with pain until he caught breath. Then, at 'By yond marble heaven', he tore the crucifix from his neck (Iago, you recall, says casually Othello'd renounce his baptism for Desdemona) and, crouching forehead to ground, made his 'sacred vow' in the religion which caked Benin's altars with blood.

Possibly it was too early a climax, built to make a curtain of Iago's 'I am your own for ever.' In Act Four he could only repeat himself with increased volume, adding a humming animal moan as he fell into his fit, a strangler's look to the dangling hands, a sharper danger to the turns of his head as he questioned Emilia. But it gave him time to wind down to superb returned dignity and tenderness for the murder. This became an act of love—at 'I would not have thee linger in thy pain' he threw aside the pillow and, stopping her lips with a kiss, strangled her. The last speech was spoken kneeling on the bed, her body clutched upright to him as a shield for the dagger he turns on himself.

As he slumped beside her in the sheets, the current stopped. A couple of wigged actors stood awkwardly about. You could only pity them: we had seen history, and it was over. Perhaps it's as well to have seen the performance while still unripe, constructed in fragments, still knitting itself. Now you can see how it's done; later, it will be a torrent. But before it exhausts him, a film should be made. It couldn't save the whole truth, but it might save something the unborn should know.

WILLIAM EMPSON

William Empson (1906-   ). Poet and author of Seven Types of Ambiguity *(1930),* Some Versions of Pastoral *(1936),* The Structure of Complex Words *(1951),* Milton's God *(1961) and several important uncollected essays on Shakespeare.*

HONEST IN OTHELLO*

The fifty-two uses of *honest* and *honesty* in *Othello* are a very queer business; there is no other play in which Shakespeare worries a word like that. *King Lear* uses *fool* nearly as often but does not treat it as a puzzle, only as a source of profound metaphors. In *Othello* divergent uses of the key word are found for all the main characters; even the attenuated clown plays on it; the unchaste Bianca, for instance, snatches a moment to claim that she is more honest than Emilia the thief of the handkerchief; and with all the variety of use the ironies on the word mount up steadily to the end. Such is the general power of the writing that this is not obtrusive, but if all but the phrases involving *honest* were in the style of Ibsen the effect would be a symbolical charade. Everybody calls Iago honest once or twice, but with Othello it becomes an obsession; at the crucial moment just before Emilia exposes Iago he keeps howling the word out. The general effect has been fully recognised by critics, but it looks as if there is something to be found about the word itself.

What Shakespeare hated in the word, I believe, was a peculiar use, at once hearty and individualist, which was then common among raffish low people but did not become upper-class till the Restoration; here as in Iago's heroic couplets the play has a curious effect of prophecy. But to put it like this is no doubt to over-simplify; the Restoration use, easy to feel though hard to define, seems really different from its earlier parallels, and in any case does not apply well to Iago. I want here to approach the play without taking for granted the previous analysis. But I hope it has become obvious that the word was in the middle of a rather complicated process of change, and that what emerged from it was a sort of jovial cult of independence. At some stage of the development (whether by the date of *Othello* or not) the word came to have in it a covert assertion that the man who accepts the natural desires, who does not live by principle, will be fit for such warm uses of *honest* as imply

* Reprinted from *The Structure of Complex Words.*

"generous" and "faithful to friends", and to believe this is to disbelieve the Fall of Man. Thus the word, apart from being complicated, also came to raise large issues, and it is not I think a wild fancy to suppose that Shakespeare could feel the way it was going.

Four columns of *honest* in the Shakespeare Concordance show that he never once allows the word a simple hearty use between equals. Some low characters get near it, but they are made to throw in contempt. 'An honest fellow enough, and one that loves quails' is said by Thersites in contempt for Ajax; 'honest good fellows' is said by the Nurse in Romeo, but of minstrels that she is turning away; 'as honest a true fellow as any in Bohemia' is from Prince Cloten and to a shepherd; 'I am with thee here and the goats, as the most capricious poet, honest Ovid, was mong the Goths' gets its joke from making the clown patronise Ovid. The nearest case is from Desdemona:

> EMIL.: *I warrant it grieves my husband*
> *As if the case were his.*
> DES.: *Oh, that's an honest fellow.*

But Emilia is butting into the talk with Cassio, and Desdemona, in this careless reply to silence her, has a feeling that Iago though reliable and faithful is her social inferior. This indeed is a sufficient reason why Iago talks with irony about the admitted fact that he is "honest"; the patronising use carried an obscure social insult as well as a hint of stupidity. Critics have discussed what the social status of Iago and Emilia would actually be, and have succeeded in making clear that the posts of ancient and gentlewoman-in-waiting might be held by people of very varying status; the audience must use its own judgement. The hints seem to place Iago and his wife definitely enough well below Desdemona but well above Ancient Pistol, say. Now at the same date as the refusal by Shakespeare to employ a flat hearty use of the word, there are uses by Dekker (for example) which only differ from the Restoration ones by coming from people of lower rank or bad reputation. One need not say that Shakespeare always had a conscious policy about the word (more likely the flat hearty use bored him; it was a blank space where one might have had a bit of word play) but his uses of it in *Othello,* when his imagination began to work on the loathsome possibilities of this familiar bit of nonsense, are consistent with his normal practice.

Most people would agree with what Bradley, for example, implied, that the way everybody calls Iago honest amounts to a criticism of the word itself; that is, Shakespeare means "a bluff forthright manner, and amusing talk, which get a man called honest, may go with extreme dishonesty". Or indeed that this is treated as normal, and the satire is on our nature not on language. But they would probably maintain that Iago is not honest and does not think himself so, and only calls himself so as a lie or an irony. It seems to me, if you leave the matter there, that there is much to be said for what the despised Rymer decided, when the implications of the hearty use of *honest* had become simpler and more clear-cut. He said that the play is ridiculous, because that sort of villain (silly-clever, full of secret schemes, miscalculating about people) does not get mistaken for that sort of honest man. This if true is of course a plain fault, whatever you think about "character-analysis". It is no use taking short cuts in these things, and I should fancy that what Rymer said had a large truth when he said it, and also that Iago was a plausible enough figure in his own time. The only main road into this baffling subject is to find how the characters actually use the term and thereby think about themselves.

I must not gloss over the fact that Iago once uses the word to say that he proposes to tell Othello lies:

> The Moor is of a free and open nature,
> And thinks men honest that but seem to be so.

This is at the end of the first act. And indeed, the first use of the word in the play seems also to mean that Iago does not think himself honest. In his introductory scene with Roderigo, he says of the subservient type of men "whip me such honest knaves"; they are opposed to the independent men like himself—"these fellows have some soul". Later there is a trivial use of the word by Brabantio, but the next important ones do not come till near the end of the act. Then

Othello twice calls Iago honest; Iago immediately (to insist on the irony) has a second meeting for plots with Roderigo, and then in soliloquy tells the audience he will cheat Roderigo too. Next he brings out the two lines just quoted; he is enumerating the conditions of his problem, and the dramatic purpose, one may say, is to make certain that nobody in the audience has missed the broad point. The act then closes with "I have it" and the triumphant claim that he has invented the plot. Even here, I think, there is room for an ironical tone in Iago's use of *honest*; he can imply that Othello's notion of honesty is crude as well as his judgements about which people exemplify it. For that matter, Iago may simply be speaking about Cassio, not about himself. He has just said that Cassio is framed to make women false, and he certainly regards the virtues of Cassio as part of his superficial and over-rewarded charm of manner. But I think that, even so, Iago has himself somewhere in view; to claim that he did not would be overstraining my argument. The introductory phrase "honest knaves" is of course a direct irony (made clear by contradiction); it can only mean that Iago has a different idea of honesty from the one that these knaves have. To be sure, you may be meant to think that he is lying by implication, but even so, this is the lie that he must be supposed to tell. However, I do not see that the uses at either end of the act put forward definite alternative meanings for the word; they lay the foundations by making it prominent. It is then, so to speak, "in play" and is used with increasing frequency. The first act has five uses; the second eleven; the third twenty-three; and the last two only six and seven. One might argue that the character of Iago is established in the first act before the verbal ironies are applied to it, since "honest knaves" is only a sort of blank cheque; but even so we learn a good deal more about him later.

Both Iago and Othello oppose honesty to mere truth-telling:

> OTH.: *I know, Iago,*
> *Thy honesty and love doth mince this matter,*
> *Making it light to Cassio. . . .*
> IAGO: *It were not for your quiet, nor your good,*

Nor for my manhood, honesty, or wisdom
To let you know my thoughts.

No doubt the noun tends to be more old-fashioned than the adjective, but anyway the old "honourable" sense is as broad and vague as the new slang one; it was easy enough to be puzzled by the word. Iago means partly 'faithful to friends', which would go with the Restoration use, but partly I think 'chaste', the version normally used of women; what he has to say is improper. Certainly one cannot simply treat his version of *honest* as the Restoration one—indeed, the part of the snarling critic involves a rather puritanical view, at any rate towards other people. It is the two notions of being ready to blow the gaff on other people and frank to yourself about your own desires that seem to me crucial about Iago; they grow on their own, independently of the hearty feeling that would normally humanize them; though he can be a good companion as well.

One need not look for a clear sense when he toys with the word about Cassio; the question is how it came to be so mystifying. But I think a queer kind of honesty is maintained in Iago through all the puzzles he contrives; his emotions are always expressed directly, and it is only because they are clearly genuine ("These stops of thine", Othello tells him, "are close delations, working from the heart") that he can mislead Othello as to their cause.

OTH.: *Is he not honest?* (Faithful, etc.)
IAGO: *Honest, my lord?* (Not stealing, etc. Shocked)
OTH.: *Ay, honest.* ("Why repeat? The word is clear enough.")
IAGO: *My lord, for aught I know. . . .* ("In some sense.")
IAGO: *For Michael Cassio*
I dare be sworn I think that he is honest.
OTH.: *I think so too.*
IAGO: *Men should be what they seem,*
Or, those that be not, would they might seem none.
OTH.: *Certain, men should be what they seem.*
IAGO: *Why then, I think that Cassio's an honest man.*

Othello has just said that Cassio "went between them very oft", so Iago now learns that Cassio lied to him in front of

Brabantio's house when he pretended to know nothing about the marriage. Iago feels he has been snubbed,[1] as too coarse to be trusted in such a matter, and he takes immediate advantage of his discomposure. The point of his riddles is to get "not hypocritical"—"frank about his own nature" accepted as the relevant sense; Iago will readily call him honest on that basis, and Othello cannot be reassured. 'Chaste' (the sense normally used of women) Cassio is not, but he is 'not a hypocrite' about Bianca. Iago indeed, despises him for letting her make a fool of him in public; for that and for other reasons (Cassio is young and without experience) Iago can put a contemptuous tone into the word; the feeling is genuine, but not the sense it may imply. This gives room for a hint that Cassio has been 'frank' to Iago in private about more things than may honestly be told. I fancy too, that the idea of 'not being men' gives an extra twist. Iago does not think Cassio manly nor that it is specially manly to be chaste; this allows him to agree that Cassio may be honest in the female sense about Desdemona and still keep a tone which seems to deny it—if he is, after so much encouragement, he must be 'effeminate' (there is a strong idea of 'manly' in *honest*, and an irony on that gives its opposite). Anyway, Iago can hide what reservations he makes but show that he makes reservations; this suggests an embarrassed defence—"Taking a broad view, with the world as it is, and Cassio my friend, I can decently call him honest." This forces home the Restoration idea—"an honest dog of a fellow, straightforward about women", and completes the suspicion. It is a bad piece of writing unless you are keyed up for the shifts of the word.

The play with the feminine version is doubtful here, but he certainly does it the other way round about Desdemona, where it had more point; in the best case it is for his own amusement when alone.

[1] Cassio does not call Iago *honest* till he can use the word warmly (ii.3.108); till then he calls him "good Iago" (ii.1.97, ii.3.34)—apparently a less obtrusive form of the same trick of patronage. Possibly as they have been rivals for his present job he feels it more civil to keep his distance. However the social contempt which he holds in check is hinted jovially to Desdemona (ii.1.165) and comes out plainly when he is drunk; Iago returns the "good" to him and is firmly snubbed for it as not a "man of quality" (ii.3.108).

And what's he then that says I play the villain?
When this advice is free I give and honest,
Probal to thinking, and indeed the course
To win the Moor again? For 'tis most easy
The inclining Desdemona to subdue
In any honest suit. She's framed as fruitful
As the free elements.

Easy, inclining, fruitful, free all push the word the same way, from 'chaste' to 'flat, frank, and natural'; all turn the ironical admission of her virtue into a positive insult against her. The delight in juggling with the word here is close to the Machiavellian interest in plots for their own sake, which Iago could not resist and allowed to destroy him. But a good deal of the 'motive-hunting' of the soliloquies must, I think, be seen as part of Iago's 'honesty'; he is quite open to his own motives or preferences and interested to find out what they are.

The clear cases where Iago thinks himself honest are at a good distance from the Restoration use; they bring him into line with the series of sharp unromantic critics like Jacques and Hamlet:

For I am nothing if not critical

he tells Desdemona to amuse her; his faults, he tells Othello, are due to an excess of this truthful virtue—

I confess, it is my nature's plague
To spy into abuses, and oft my jealousy

... in the soliloquies. Now this ... at he believes this and thinks it ... policy made him say it here: indeed we ... unlike the Restoration 'honest fellow', and for ... d it hard to combine them in one feeling about ... ord. But in a great deal of Iago's talk to Roderigo— ... own thyself! drown cats and blind puppies ... why, thou silly gentleman, I will never love thee after'—he is a wise uncle, obviously honest in the cheerful sense, and for some time this is our main impression of him.[1] It is still strong during the business of making Cassio drunk; there is no reason why he should praise the English for their powers of drinking except to make sure that the groundlings are still on his side.

Perhaps the main connection between the two sorts of honest men is not being indulgent towards romantic love:

> OTH.: *I cannot speak enough of this content,*
> *It stops me here; it is too much of joy.*
> *And this, and this, the greatest discords be*
> *That e'er our hearts shall make. (Kissing her).*
> IAGO: *Oh you are well tun'd now;*
> *But I'll set down the peggs that make this Musick,*
> *As honest as I am.*

The grammar may read 'because I am so honest' as well as 'though I am so honest' and the irony may deny any resultant sense. He is ironical about the suggestions in the patronizing use, which he thinks are applied to him—'low-class, and stupid, but good-natured'. But he feels himself really 'honest' as the kind of man who can see through nonsense; Othello's affair is a passing lust which has become a nuisance, and Iago can get it out of the way.

It may well be objected that this is far too mild a picture of Iago's plot, and indeed he himself is clearly impressed by its wickedness; at the end of the first act he calls it a "monstrous birth" and invokes Hell to assist it. But after this handsome theatrical effect the second act begins placidly, in a long scene which includes the "As honest as I am" passage, and at the end of this scene we find that Iago still

imagines he will only

Make the Moor thank

For making him egregiously ...ward me

—to be sure, the next lines say he ...

"even to madness", but even this ...

picture of the clown who makes "fool...

certainly does not envisage the holocaust ...

[1] It is a very bold and strange irony to make Othell... "love thee after" just before he kills Desdemona.

play. Thinking in terms of character, it is clear that Iago
has not yet decided how far he will go.

The suggestion of "stupid" in a patronizing use of *honest*
(still clear in 'honest Thompson, my gardener', a Victorian
if not a present-day use) brings it near to *fool;* there is a
chance for these two rich words to overlap. There is an
aspect of Iago in which he is the Restoration "honest fellow", who is good company because he blows the gaff; but
much the clearest example of it is in the beginning of the
second act, when he is making sport for his betters. While
Desdemona is waiting for Othello's ship, which may have
been lost in the tempest, he puts on an elaborate piece of
clowning to distract her; and she takes his real opinion of
love and women for a piece of hearty and good-natured
fun. Iago's kind of honesty, he feels, is not valued as it
should be; there is much in Iago of the Clown in Revolt,
and the inevitable clown is almost washed out in this play
to give him a free field. It is not, I think, dangerously far-
fetched to take almost all Shakespeare's uses of *fool* as
metaphors from the clown, whose symbolism certainly rode
his imagination and was explained to the audience in most
of his early plays. Now Iago's defence when Othello at
last turns on him, among the rich ironies of its claim to
honesty, brings in both *Fool* and the Vice used in *Hamlet* as
an old name for the clown.

> IAGO: *O wretched fool,*
> *Thou lov'st to make thine Honesty, a Vice![1]*
> *Oh monstrous world! Take note, take note*
> *(O World)*
> *To be direct and honest is not safe.*
> *I thank you for this profit, and from hence*
> *I'll love no Friend, sith Love breeds such offence.*
> OTH.: *Nay stay; thou should'st be honest.*
> IAGO: *I should be wise; for Honesty's a Fool,*
> *And loses that it works for.*
> OTH.: *By the world,*
> *I think my wife be honest, and think she is not.*

What comes out here is Iago's unwillingness to be the Fool
he thinks he is taken for; but it is dramatic irony as well,

[1] And make thyself a motley to the view. Sonnet CX.

and that comes back to his notion of *honest*; he is fooled by the way his plans run away with him; he fails in knowledge of others and perhaps even of his own desires.

Othello swears *by the world* because what Iago has said about being honest in the world, suggesting what worldly people think, is what has made him doubtful; yet the senses of *honest* are quite different—chastity and truth-telling. Desdemona is called a supersubtle Venetian, and he may suspect she would agree with what Iago treats as worldly wisdom; whereas it was her simplicity that made her helpless; though again, the fatal step was her lie about the handkerchief. *Lov'st* in the second line (Folios) seems to me better than *liv'st*. (Quarto), as making the frightened Iago bring in his main claim at once; the comma after *Honesty* perhaps makes the sense 'loves with the effect of making' rather than 'delights in making'; in any case *love* appears a few lines down. *Breeds* could suggest sexual love, as if Iago's contempt for that has spread to his notions of friendship; Othello's marriage is what has spoilt their relations (Cassio 'came a-wooing with' Othello, as a social figure, and then got the lieutenantship). In the same way Othello's two uses of *honest* here jump from 'loving towards friends, which breeds honour' to (of women) 'chaste'. It is important I think that the feminine sense, which a later time felt to be quite distinct, is so deeply confused here with the other ones.

It is not safe to be *direct* either way, to be *honest* in Othello's sense or Iago's. The sanctimonious metaphor *profit* might carry satire from Iago on Puritans or show Iago to be like them. Iago is still telling a good deal of truth; the reasons he gives have always made him despise those who are faithful to their masters, if not to their friends. It is not clear that he would think himself a bad friend to his real friends. He believes there is a gaff to blow about the ideal love affair, though his evidence has had to be forced. Of course he is using *honest* less in his own way than to impose on Othello, yet there is a real element of self-pity in his complaint. It is no white-washing of Iago—you may hate him the more for it—but he feels he is now in danger because he has gone the 'direct' way to work, exposed false pretensions, and tried to be 'frank' to himself about the whole situation. I do not think this is an oversubtle treatment of his words; behind his fear he is gloating over his cleverness, and seems to delight in the audience provided by the stage.

In the nightmare scene where Othello clings to the word to justify himself he comes near accepting Iago's use of it.

> EMIL.: *My husband!*
> OTH.:   *Ay, twas he that told me first:*
>   *An honest man he is, and hates the slime*
>   *That sticks on filthy deeds . . .* (Sexual)
> EMIL.: *My husband say that she was false?*
> OTH.:   *He, woman;*
>   *I say thy husband: dost understand the word?*
>   *My friend, thy husband, honest, honest Iago.*

From the sound of the last line it seems as bitter and concentrated as the previous question; to the audience it is. Yet Othello means no irony against Iago, and it is hard to invent a reason for his repetition of *honest*. He may feel it painful that the coarse Iago, not Desdemona or Cassio, should be the only honest creature, or Iago's honesty may suggest the truth he told; or indeed you may call it a trick on the audience, to wind up the irony to its highest before Iago is exposed. Yet Iago would agree that one reason why he was honest was that he hated the slime. The same slime would be produced, by Desdemona as well as by Othello one would hope, if the act of love were of the most rigidly faithful character; the disgust in the metaphor is disgust at all sexuality. Iago playing "honest" as prude is the rat who stands up for the ideal; as soon as Othello agrees he is finely cheated, Iago is left with his pleasures and Othello's happiness is destroyed. Iago has always despised his pleasures, always treated sex without fuss, like the lavatory; it is by this that he manages to combine the "honest dog" tone with honesty as Puritanism. The twist of the irony here is that Othello now feels humbled before such clarity. It is a purity he has failed to attain, and he accepts it as a form of honour. The hearty use and the horror of it are united in this appalling line.

Soon after there is a final use of *fool*, by Emilia, which sums up the clown aspect of Iago, but I ought to recognise that it may refer to Othello as well:

EMIL.: *He begged of me to steal it.*
IAGO: *Villainous whore!*
EMIL.: *She give it Cassio! no, alas; I found it,*
         And I did give't my husband.
IAGO: *Filth, thou liest!*
EMIL.: *By heaven, I do not, I do not, gentlemen.*
         O murderous coxcomb, what should such a fool
         Do with so good a wife?
                (Iago stabs Emilia and escapes).

[handwritten marginalia: Iago thinks it's directed at him]

On the face of it she praises herself to rebut his insults,
which are given because she is not a "good wife" in the
sense of loyal to his interests. But her previous speech takes
for granted that "she" means Desdemona, and we go
straight on to Emilia's death-scene, which is entirely selfless
and praises Desdemona only. I think she is meant to turn
and upbraid Othello, so that she praises Desdemona in this
sentence: it would be a convenience in acting, as it explains
why she does not notice Iago's sword. *Coxcomb* in any case
insists on the full meaning of "fool", which would make
a startling insult for Othello; the idea becomes not that he
was stupid to be deceived (a reasonable complaint) but that
he was vain of his clownish authority, that is, self-important
about his position as a husband and his suspicions, murderous merely because he wanted to show what he could do,
like a child. She is the mouthpiece of all the feelings in us
which are simply angry with Othello, but this judgement of
him is not meant to keep its prominence for long. Indeed
as her death-scene goes on the interpretation which the
producer should reject is I think meant to come back into
our minds; the real murderous coxcomb, the clown who did
kill merely out of vanity, was Iago. The cynic had always
hated to be treated as a harmless joker, and what finally
roused him into stabbing her was perhaps that he thought
she had called him a clown. The Lion and the Fox are thus
united in the word, but as so many things happen in the play
by a misunderstanding. It is perhaps an unnecessarily elaborate interpretation (the reference to Iago is much the more
important one) but I think it is needed for our feelings
about Emilia that she should not deliberately give herself
the praise which we none the less come to feel she deserves.
Some other words which combine the ideas of truth-

telling and generosity are affected by the same process as *honest*, though without becoming so important. Desdemona while giggling at the jokes of Iago in the second Act says, "Is he not a most profane and liberal counsellor?", and Othello echoes this *liberal* when he catches from Iago the trick of sneering at the generosity of Desdemona.

OTH.:   ... *here's a young and sweating devil here*
      That commonly rebels. Tis a good hand,
      A *frank one.*
DES.:   *You may indeed say so,*
      For twas that hand that gave away my heart.
OTH.:   *A liberal hand . . . .*
EMILIA: *No, I will speak as* liberal *as the air*
      Let heaven and men, and devils, let them all
      All, all, cry shame against me, yet I'll speak ...
      So, speaking as I think, *I die, I die.*

Indeed the whole power of Emilia's death-scene is that she ties up a variety of sacrificial virtues into a bundle labelled "mere coarse frankness". *Honest* itself seems to have rather minor connections with truth-telling, but the play as a whole is far from indifferent to that virtue, and Emilia has to steal the limelight from Iago in the eyes of those who preferred a character who could blow the gaff.

The only later use of *honest* comes when Othello's sword is taken from him by the State officer; a mark of disgrace, a symbol of cuckoldry; two possible negations of honour and honesty.

OTH.:   *I am not valiant neither,*
      But every puny whipster gets my sword.
      But why should honour outlive honesty?
      Let it go all.

The straightforward meaning, I take it (though commentators have disagreed a good deal), is something like "I have lost my civilian reputation, because the killing of my wife has turned out unjust; why then should I care about my military reputation, which depends on keeping my sword?" But the poetic or dramatic effect clearly means a great deal more. The question indeed so sums up the play that it involves nearly all of both words; it seems finally to shatter the concept of honesty whose connecting links the play has patiently removed. There are thirteen other uses of *honour* (and *honourable*); four of them by Othello about himself and five by others about Othello.[1] The effect has been to make Othello the personification of honour; if honour does not survive some test of the idea nor could Othello. And to him *honest* is 'honourable', from which it was derived; a test of one is a test of the other. Outlive Desdemona's chastity, which he now admits, outlive Desdemona herself, the personification of chastity (lying again, as he insisted, with her last breath), outlive decent behaviour in, public respect for, self-respect in, Othello—all these are honour, not honesty; there is no question whether Othello outlives them. But they are not tests of an idea; what has been tested is a special sense of *honest*. Iago has been the personification of honesty, not merely to Othello but to his world; why should honour, the father of the word, live on and talk about itself; honesty, that obscure bundle of assumptions, the play has destroyed. I can see no other way to explain the force of the question here.

There is very little for anybody to add to A. C. Bradley's magnificent analysis, but one can maintain that Shakespeare, and the audience he had, and the audience he wanted, saw the thing in rather different proportions. Many of the audience were old soldiers disbanded without pension; they would dislike Cassio as the new type of officer,

---

[1] The remaining four can all I think be connected to Othello. His wife's honour concerns him directly—the comparison of it to the handkerchief even implies that he has given it to her (iv.1.14); Cassio, we hear, is to have an honourable position—because he is to take Othello's place (iv.3.240); the state officer is "your honour" because he represents the source of that position. The only difficult case is

> Three lads of Cyprus—noble swelling spirits
> That hold their honours in a wary distance . . .
> Have I this night flustered with flowing cups. (ii.3.53.)

It will be hard for Cassio not to get drunk with them because they are "tough"; their boastful virility is likely to make them dangerous customers unless they are handled on their own footing. I think they act as a faint parody of Othello's Honour, which is a much idealised version of the same kind of thing. And on the other hand Iago does not use the word at all when he is making contradictory speeches in favour of "good name" and against "reputation", because that would make it less specific.

the boy who can displace men of experience merely because he knows enough mathematics to work the new guns. The tragedy plays into their hands by making Cassio a young fool who can't keep his mistress from causing scandals and can't drink. I don't know why Shakespeare wanted to tell us that Iago was exactly twenty-eight, but anyway he is experienced and Cassio seems about six years younger. Iago gets a long start at the beginning of the play, where he is enchantingly amusing and may be in the right. I am not trying to deny that by the end of the first Act he is obviously the villain, and that by the end of the play we are meant to feel the mystery of his life as Othello did:

> *Will you, I pray, demand that semi-devil*
> *Why he hath thus ensnared my soul and body?*

Shakespeare can now speak his mind about Iago through the convention of the final speech by the highest in rank:

> *O Spartan dog,*
> *More fell than anguish, hunger, or the sea!*

Verbal analysis is not going to weaken the main shape of the thing. But even in this last resounding condemnation the dog is not simple. Dogs come in six times. Roderigo when dying also calls his murderer Iago a dog, and Othello does it conditionally, if Iago prove false. Roderigo says that he himself "is not like a hound that hunts but one that fills up the cry"—Iago is the dog that hunts, we are to reflect.[1] Iago says that Cassio when drunk will be "as full of quarrel and offence as my young mistress's dog"; now Iago himself clearly knows what it feels like to be ready to take offence, and one might think that this phrase helps to define the sort of dog he is, the spoiled favourite of his betters. He has also a trivial reference to dogs when encouraging Cassio and saying that Othello only pretends to be angry with him "as one would beat his offenceless dog, to affright an imperious lion". It seems rather dragged in,

---

[1] Mr. Granville-Barker indeed said that Iago was "like a hound on the trail, sensitive and alert, nose to the ground, searching and sampling, appetite and instinct combining to guide him past error after error to his quarry."

as if Iago was to mention dogs as much as possible. The typical Shakespearean dog-men are Apemantus and Thersites (called "dog" by Homer), malign underdogs, snarling critics, who yet are satisfactory as clowns and carry something of the claim of the disappointed idealist; on the other hand, if there is an obscure prophecy in the treatment of *honest,* surely the "honest *dog*" of the Restoration may cast something of his shadow before. Wyndham Lewis' interesting treatment of Iago as "fox" (in *The Lion and the Fox*) leaves out both these dogs, though the dog is more relevant than the fox on his analogy of tragedy to bull-baiting; indeed the clash of the two dogs goes to the root of Iago. But the dog symbolism is a mere incident, like that of *fool;* the thought is carried on *honest,* and I throw in the others only not to oversimplify the thing. Nor are they used to keep Iago from being a straightforward villain; the point is that more force was needed to make Shakespeare's audience hate Iago than to make them accept the obviously intolerable Macbeth as a tragic hero.

There seems a linguistic difference between what Shakespeare meant by Iago and what the nineteenth-century critics saw in him. They took him as an abstract term 'Evil'; he is a critique on an unconscious pun. . . .

SAMUEL JOHNSON

On King Lear*

The Tragedy of *Lear* is deservedly celebrated among the dramas of *Shakespeare*. There is perhaps no play which keeps the attention so strongly fixed; which so much agitates our passions and interests our curiosity. The artful involutions of distinct interests, the striking opposition of contrary characters, the sudden changes of fortune, and the quick succession of events, fill the mind with a perpetual tumult of indignation, pity, and hope. There is no scene

* From the edition of 1765.

which does not contribute to the aggravation of the distress or conduct of the action, and scarce a line which does not conduce to the progress of the scene. So powerful is the current of the poet's imagination, that the mind, which once ventures within it, is hurried irresistibly along.

On the seeming improbability of *Lear's* conduct it may be observed, that he is represented according to histories at that time vulgarly received as true. And perhaps if we turn our thoughts upon the barbarity and ignorance of the age to which this story is referred, it will appear not so unlikely as while we estimate *Lear's* manners by our own. Such preference of one daughter to another, or resignation of dominion on such conditions, would be yet credible, if told of a petty prince of *Guinea* or *Madagascar*. *Shakespeare,* indeed, by the mention of his Earls and Dukes, has given us the idea of times more civilised, and of life regulated by softer manners; and the truth is, that though he so nicely discriminates, and so minutely describes the characters of men, he commonly neglects and confounds the characters of ages, by mingling customs ancient and modern, *English* and foreign.

My learned friend Mr. *Warton,* who has in the *Adventurer* very minutely criticised this play, remarks, that the instances of cruelty are too savage and shocking, and that the intervention of *Edmund* destroys the simplicity of the story. These objections may, I think, be answered, by repeating, that the cruelty of the daughters is an historical fact, to which the poet has added little, having only drawn it into a series by dialogue and action. But I am not able to apologise with equal plausibility for the extrusion of *Gloucester's* eyes, which seems an act too horrid to be endured in dramatick exhibition, and such as must always compel the mind to relieve its distress by incredulity. Yet let it be remembered that our authour well knew what would please the audience for which he wrote.

The injury done by *Edmund* to the simplicity of the action is abundantly recompensed by the addition of variety, by the art with which he is made to co-operate with the chief design, and the opportunity which he gives the poet of combining perfidy with perfidy, and connecting the wicked son with the wicked daughters, to impress this important moral, that villainy is never at a stop, that crimes lead to crimes, and at last terminate in ruin.

But though this moral be incidentally enforced, *Shakespeare* has suffered the virtue of *Cordelia* to perish in a just cause, contrary to the natural ideas of justice, to the hope of the reader, and, what is yet more strange, to the faith of chronicles. Yet this conduct is justified by the Spectator, who blames *Tate* for giving *Cordelia* success and happiness in his alteration, and declares, that, in his opinion, *the tragedy has lost half its beauty. Dennis* has remarked, whether justly or not, that, to secure the favourable reception of *Cato, the town was poisoned with much false and abominable criticism,* and that endeavours had been used to discredit and decry poetical justice. A play in which the wicked prosper, and the virtuous miscarry, may doubtless be good, because it is a just representation of the common events of human life: but since all reasonable beings naturally love justice, I cannot easily be persuaded, that the observation of justice makes a play worse; or, that if other excellencies are equal, the audience will not always rise better pleased from the final triumph of persecuted virtue.

In the present case the publick has decided. *Cordelia,* from the time of *Tate,* has always retired with victory and felicity. And, if my sensations could add any thing to the general suffrage, I might relate, that I was many years ago so shocked by *Cordelia*'s death, that I know not whether I ever endured to read again the last scenes of the play till I undertook to revise them as an editor.

There is another controversy among the criticks concerning this play. It is disputed whether the predominant image in *Lear*'s disordered mind be the loss of his kingdom or the cruelty of his daughters. Mr. *Murphy,* a very judicious critick, has evinced by induction of particular passages, that the cruelty of his daughters is the primary source of his distress, and that the loss of royalty affects him only as a secondary and subordinate evil; He observes with great justness, that *Lear* would move our compassion but little, did we not rather consider the injured father than the degraded king.

The story of this play, except the episode of *Edmund,* which is derived, I think, from *Sidney,* is taken originally from *Geoffry* of *Monmouth,* whom *Hollingshead* generally copied; but perhaps immediately from an old historical ballad. My reason for believing that the play was posteriour to the ballad rather than the ballad to the play, is, that the ballad has nothing of *Shakespeare's* nocturnal tempest, which is too striking to have been omitted, and that it follows the chronicle; it has the rudiments of the play, but none of its amplifications: it first hinted *Lear's* madness, but did not array it in circumstances. The writer of the ballad added something to the history, which is a proof that he would have added more, if more had occurred to his mind, and more must have occurred if he had seen *Shakespeare.*

A. W. SCHLEGEL

ON MACBETH AND KING LEAR*

Of *Macbeth* I have already spoken once in passing, and who could exhaust the praises of this sublime work? Since *The Eumenides* of Æschylus, nothing so grand and terrible has ever been written. The witches are not, it is true, divine Eumenides, and are not intended to be; they are ignoble and vulgar instruments of hell. A German poet, therefore, very ill understood their meaning, when he transformed them into mongrel beings, a mixture of fates, furies, and enchantresses, and clothed them with tragic dignity. Let no man venture to lay hand on Shakspeare's works thinking to improve anything essential: he will be sure to punish himself. The bad is radically odious, and to endeavour in any manner to ennoble it, is to violate the laws of propriety. Hence, in my opinion, Dante, and even Tasso, have been much more successful in their portraiture of dæmons than Milton. Whether the age of Shakspeare still believed in ghosts and witches, is a matter of perfect indifference for the justification of the use which in *Hamlet* and *Macbeth* he has made of pre-existing traditions. No superstition can

* From *Lectures on Dramatic Art and Literature* (1811).

be widely diffused without having a foundation in human nature: on this the poet builds; he calls up from their hidden abysses that dread of the unknown, that presage of a dark side of nature, and a world of spirits, which philosophy now imagines it has altogether exploded. In this manner he is in some degree both the portrayer and the philosopher of superstition; that is, not the philosopher who denies and turns it into ridicule, but, what is still more difficult, who distinctly exhibits its origin in apparently irrational and yet natural opinions. But when he ventures to make arbitrary changes in these popular traditions, he altogether forfeits his right to them, and merely holds up his own idle fancies to our ridicule. Shakspeare's picture of the witches is truly magical: in the short scenes where they enter, he has created for them a peculiar language, which, although composed of the usual elements, still seems to be a collection of formulæ of incantation. The sound of the words, the accumulation of rhymes, and the rhythmus of the verse, form, as it were, the hollow music of a dreary witch-dance. He has been abused for using the names of disgusting objects; but he who fancies the kettle of the witches can be made effective with agreeable aromatics, is as wise as those who desire that hell should sincerely and honestly give good advice. These repulsive things, from which the imagination shrinks, are here emblems of the hostile powers which operate in nature; and the repugnance of our senses is outweighed by the mental horror. With one another the witches discourse like women of the very lowest class; for this was the class to which witches were ordinarily supposed to belong: when, however, they address Macbeth they assume a loftier tone: their predictions, which they either themselves pronounce, or allow their apparitions to deliver, have all the obscure brevity, the majestic solemnity of oracles.

We here see that the witches are merely instruments; they are governed by an invisible spirit, or the operation of such great and dreadful events would be above their sphere. With what intent did Shakspeare assign the same place to them in his play, which they occupy in the history of Macbeth as related in the old chronicles? A monstrous crime is committed: Duncan, a venerable old man, and the best of kings, is, in defenceless sleep, under the hospitable roof, murdered by his subject, whom he has loaded with honours and rewards. Natural motives alone seem inadequate, or the perpetrator must have been portrayed as a hardened villain. Shakspeare wished to exhibit a more sublime picture: an ambitious but noble hero, yielding to a deep-laid hellish temptation; and in whom all the crimes to which, in order to secure the fruits of his first crime, he is impelled by necessity, cannot altogether eradicate the stamp of native heroism. He has, therefore, given a threefold division to the guilt of that crime. The first idea comes from that being whose whole activity is guided by a lust of wickedness. The weird sisters surprise Macbeth in the moment of intoxication of victory, when his love of glory has been gratified; they cheat his eyes by exhibiting to him as the work of fate what in reality can only be accomplished by his own deed, and gain credence for all their words by the immediate fulfilment of the first prediction. The opportunity of murdering the King immediately offers; the wife of Macbeth conjures him not to let it slip; she urges him on with a fiery eloquence, which has at command all those sophisms that serve to throw a false splendour over crime. Little more than the mere execution falls to the share of Macbeth; he is driven into it, as it were, in a tumult of fascination. Repentance immediately follows, nay, even precedes the deed, and the stings of conscience leave him rest neither night nor day. But he is now fairly entangled in the snares of hell; truly frightful is it to behold that same Macbeth, who once as a warrior could spurn at death, now that he dreads the prospect of the life to come,[1] clinging with growing anxiety to his earthly existence the more miserable it becomes, and pitilessly removing out of the way whatever to his dark and suspicious mind seems to threaten danger. However much we may abhor his actions, we cannot altogether refuse to compassionate the state of his mind; we lament the ruin of so many noble qualities, and even in his last defence we are compelled to admire the struggle of a brave will with a cowardly conscience. We might believe that we witness in this tragedy the over-ruling destiny of the ancients represented in perfect accordance with their ideas: the whole originates in a supernatural influence, to which the subsequent events seem inevitably linked. Moreover, we even

[1] We'd jump the life to come.

find here the same ambiguous oracles which, by their literal fulfilment, deceive those who confide in them. Yet it may be easily shown that the poet has, in his work, displayed more enlightened views. He wishes to show that the conflict of good and evil in this world can only take place by the permission of Providence, which converts the curse that individual mortals draw down on their heads into a blessing to others. An accurate scale is followed in the retaliation. Lady Macbeth, who of all the human participators in the king's murder is the most guilty, is thrown by the terrors of her conscience into a state of incurable bodily and mental disease; she dies, unlamented by her husband, with all the symptoms of reprobation. Macbeth is still found worthy to die the death of a hero on the field of battle. The noble Macduff is allowed the satisfaction of saving his country by punishing with his own hand the tyrant who had murdered his wife and children. Banquo, by an early death, atones for the ambitious curiosity which prompted the wish to know his glorious descendants, as he thereby has roused Macbeth's jealousy; but he preserved his mind pure from the evil suggestions of the witches: his name is blessed in his race, destined to enjoy for a long succession of ages that royal dignity which Macbeth could only hold for his own life. In the progress of the action, this piece is altogether the reverse of *Hamlet*: it strides forward with amazing rapidity, from the first catastrophe (for Duncan's murder may be called a catastrophe) to the last. "Thought, and done!" is the general motto; for as Macbeth says,

> The flighty purpose never is o'ertook,
> Unless the deed go with it.

In every feature we see an energetic heroic age, in the hardy North which steels every nerve. The precise duration of the action cannot be ascertained,—years perhaps, according to the story; but we know that to the imagination the most crowded time appears always the shortest. Here we can hardly conceive how so very much could ever have been compressed into so narrow a space; not merely external events,—the very inmost recesses in the minds of the dramatic personages are laid open to us. It is as if the drags were taken from the wheels of time, and they rolled along without interruption in their descent. Nothing can equal this picture in its power to excite terror. We need only allude to the circumstances attending the murder of Duncan, the dagger that hovers before the eyes of Macbeth, the vision of Banquo at the feast, the madness of Lady Macbeth; what can possibly be said on the subject that will not rather weaken the impression they naturally leave? Such scenes stand alone, and are to be found only in this poet; otherwise the tragic muse might exchange her mask for the *head of Medusa.*

I wish merely to point out as a secondary circumstance the prudent dexterity of Shakspeare, who could still contrive to flatter a king by a work in every part of whose plan nevertheless the poetical views are evident. James the First drew his lineage from Banquo; he was the first who united the threefold sceptre of England, Scotland, and Ireland: this is foreshown in the magical vision, when a long series of glorious successors is promised to Banquo. Even the gift of the English kings to heal certain maladies by the touch, which James pretended to have inherited from Edward [1] the Confessor, and on which he set a great value, is brought in very naturally.—With such occasional matters we may well allow ourselves to be pleased without fearing from them any danger to poetry: by similar allusions Æschylus endeavoured to recommend the Areopagus to his fellow-citizens, and Sophocles to celebrate the glory of Athens.

As in *Macbeth* terror reaches its utmost height, in *King Lear* the science of compassion is exhausted. The principal characters here are not those who act, but those who suffer. We have not in this, as in most tragedies, the picture of a calamity in which the sudden blows of fate seem still to honour the head which they strike, and where the loss is always accompanied by some flattering consolation in the memory of the former possession; but a fall from the highest elevation into the deepest abyss of misery, where human-

[1] The naming of Edward the Confessor gives us at the same time the epoch in which these historically accredited transactions are made to take place. The ruins of Macbeth's palace are yet standing at Inverness; the present Earls of Fife are the descendants of the valiant Macduff, and down to the union of Scotland with England they were in the enjoyment of peculiar privileges for their services to the crown.

ity is stripped of all external and internal advantages, and given up a prey to naked helplessness. The threefold dignity of a king, an old man, and a father, is dishonoured by the cruel ingratitude of his unnatural daughters; the old Lear, who out of a foolish tenderness has given away every thing, is driven out to the world a wandering beggar; the childish imbecility to which he was fast advancing changes into the wildest insanity, and when he is rescued from the disgraceful destitution to which he was abandoned, it is too late: the kind consolations of filial care and attention and of true friendship are now lost to him; his bodily and mental powers are destroyed beyond all hope of recovery, and all that now remains to him of life is the capability of loving and suffering beyond measure. What a picture we have in the meeting of Lear and Edgar in a tempestuous night and in a wretched hovel! The youthful Edgar has, by the wicked arts of his brother, and through his father's blindness, fallen, as the old Lear, from the rank to which his birth entitled him; and, as the only means of escaping further persecution, is reduced to assume the disguise of a beggar tormented by evil spirits. The King's fool, notwithstanding the voluntary degradation which is implied in his situation, is, after Kent, Lear's most faithful associate, his wisest counsellor. This good-hearted fool clothes reason with the livery of his motley garb; the high-born beggar acts the part of insanity; and both, were they even in reality what they seem, would still be enviable in comparison with the King, who feels that the violence of his grief threatens to overpower his reason. The meeting of Edgar with the blinded Gloster is equally heart-rending; nothing can be more affecting than to see the ejected son become the father's guide, and the good angel, who under the disguise of insanity, saves him by an ingenious and pious fraud from the horror and despair of self-murder. But who can possibly enumerate all the different combinations and situations by which our minds are here as it were stormed by the poet? Respecting the structure of the whole I will only make one observation. The story of Lear and his daughters was left by Shakspeare exactly as he found it in a fabulous tradition, with all the features characteristical of the simplicity of old times. But in that tradition there is not the slightest trace of the story of Gloster and his sons, which was derived by Shakspeare from another source. The incorporation of the two stories has been censured as destructive of the unity of action. But whatever contributes to the intrigue or the *dénouement* must always possess unity. And with what ingenuity and skill are the two main parts of the composition dovetailed into one another! The pity felt by Gloster for the fate of Lear becomes the means which enables his son Edmund to effect his complete destruction, and affords the outcast Edgar an opportunity of being the saviour of his father. On the other hand, Edmund is active in the cause of Regan and Goneril; and the criminal passion which they both entertain for him induces them to execute justice on each other and on themselves. The laws of the drama have therefore been sufficiently complied with; but that is the least: it is the very combination which constitutes the sublime beauty of the work. The two cases resemble each other in the main: an infatuated father is blind towards his well-disposed child, and the unnatural children, whom he prefers, requite him by the ruin of all his happiness. But all the circumstances are so different, that these stories, while they each make a correspondent impression on the heart, form a complete contrast for the imagination. Were Lear alone to suffer from his daughters, the impression would be limited to the powerful compassion felt by us for his private misfortune. But two such unheard-of examples taking place at the same time have the appearance of a great commotion in the moral world: the picture becomes gigantic, and fills us with such alarm as we should entertain at the idea that the heavenly bodies might one day fall from their appointed orbits. To save in some degree the honour of human nature, Shakspeare never wishes his spectators to forget that the story takes place in a dreary and barbarous age: he lays particular stress on the circumstance that the Britons of that day were still heathens, although he has not made all the remaining circumstances to coincide learnedly with the time which he has chosen. From this point of view we must judge of many coarsenesses in expression and manners; for instance, the immodest manner in which Gloster acknowledges his bastard, Kent's quarrel with the Steward, and more especially the cruelty personally inflicted on Gloster by the Duke of Cornwall. Even the virtue of the honest Kent bears the stamp of an iron age, in which the good and the bad display the same uncontrollable energy. Great qualities have not been superfluously assigned to the King; the poet could command our sympathy for his situation, without concealing what he had done to bring himself into it. Lear is choleric, overbearing, and almost childish from age, when he drives out his youngest daughter because she will not join in the hypocritical exaggerations of her sisters. But he has a warm and affectionate heart, which is susceptible of the most fervent gratitude; and even rays of a high and kingly disposition burst forth from the eclipse of his understanding. Of Cordelia's heavenly beauty of soul, painted in so few words, I will not venture to speak; she can only be named in the same breath with Antigone. Her death has been thought too cruel; and in England the piece is in acting so far altered that she remains victorious and happy. I must own, I cannot conceive what ideas of art and dramatic connexion those persons have who suppose that we can at pleasure tack a double conclusion to a tragedy; a melancholy one for hard-hearted spectators, and a happy one for souls of a softer mould. After surviving so many sufferings, Lear can only die; and what more truly tragic end for him than to die from grief for the death of Cordelia? and if he is also to be saved and to pass the remainder of his days in happiness, the whole loses its signification. According to Shakspeare's plan the guilty, it is true, are all punished, for wickedness destroys itself; but the virtues that would bring help and succour are everywhere too late, or overmatched by the cunning activity of malice. The persons of this drama have only such a faint belief in Providence as heathens may be supposed to have; and the poet here wishes to show us that this belief requires a wider range than the dark pilgrimage on earth to be established in full extent.

ENID WELSFORD

Enid Welsford. Author of The Court Masque *(1927) and* The Fool *(1935).*

THE FOOL IN KING LEAR*

Like others of his profession he is very ready to proffer his coxcomb to his betters, but in doing so he does not merely raise a laugh or score a point, he sets a problem. 'What am I? What is madness?' he seems to ask, 'the world being what it is, do I necessarily insult a man by investing him with motley?'

With this apparently comic question the Fool strikes the keynote of the tragedy of Lear. It is a critical, a crucial question which effects a startling division among the dramatis personae—it being for instance obvious that Goneril, Regan and Edmund are not candidates for the cap and bells. It is also a central question which at once resolves itself into a question about the nature of the universe. For the full understanding of its import it is necessary to leave for awhile our meditation on the meaning of the words of the Fool, and to consider instead their reverberation in the play as a whole: examining firstly the disposition of the characters, and secondly the movement of events.

It is a critical commonplace that in *King Lear* Shakespeare deals with the tragic aspect of human life in its most universal form. The conflict of good with evil, of wisdom with folly, the hopeless cry to the deaf Heavens for justice, are presented with something of the simplicity of a morality play. For just as in that type of drama the central figure was the soul of man competed for by the conflicting forces of good and ill; so in *King Lear* the two heroes are erring men, warm-hearted but self-willed, whose ruin or salvation depends on the issue of a conflict between two sharply opposed groups of people painted far more uncompromisingly in black and white than is customary in Shakespearian tragedy. But if *Lear* has something of the structural simplicity of the morality play it has none of its moral triteness. Where the medieval playwright furnishes answers, Shakespeare provokes questions and reveals ambiguities. Whether he ever suggests a solution is disputable; but there can be little doubt as to the urgency with which he sets the problem of the nature and destiny of goodness.

* Extracted from *The Fool*.

In *King Lear* all the 'good' characters have one striking quality in common, they have the capacity for 'fellow-feeling' highly developed. At first, it is true, the imperfect heroes demand rather than give sympathy, but the disinterestedness of their adherents is unlimited. The banished Kent

> 'Followed his enemy King, and did him service
> Improper for a slave.'

Perfect and imperfect alike take it for granted that the capacity for sympathetic love is a very valuable but quite normal attribute of human nature. This attribute makes the good characters peculiarly vulnerable and sometimes almost stupidly helpless. In the first place they instinctively trust their fellows, and this trustfulness does not sharpen their powers of discrimination. The imperfect who crave for affection are particularly liable to make silly mistakes, and their suffering and anger when they think themselves deceived make them still more unable to distinguish friend from foe. The perfectly sympathetic are foolish in a different way. They are blind to their own interests. They save others but themselves they cannot save.

The 'bad' characters are the exact opposite of the good in that they are abnormally devoid of 'fellow-feeling'. They may be hardly more egoistic than some of their opponents, but they differ from them in that they are no more anxious to receive sympathy than they are to give it. They seek only to gratify their physical lust and their will-to-power. A slight personal inconvenience seems to them more important than the agony of their closest kinsman, simply because the sense of sympathy and of human relatedness lies wholly outside their experience. For Goneril, Regan and Edmund the world is the world of Hobbes, a world where every man's hand is against every man's, and the only human ties are contracts which reason and self-interest prompt people to make as the only alternative to mutual annihilation, and which no moral scruple need hinder them from breaking when by doing so they defend their own interests. Up to a point the evil are invulnerable. Their activities are never hampered by a distaste for other people's sufferings, trustfulness never dims their powers of observation, and above all they never put themselves into anyone else's power by a desire for his affection.

The distinction between the good and the bad is clear, there is little ambiguity about the word *knave*. It is the meaning of the word *fool* which is obscure, and its obscurity increases with increasing knowledge of the attitude of the good and evil to one another.

On the whole, and this is true of other plays besides *King Lear*, Shakespeare tends to give more intellectual ability to his sinners than to his saints. Edmund, for instance, is so shrewd and witty that he almost wins our sympathy for his unabashed cruelty. To such an one goodness is simply stupidity:

> 'A credulous father! and a brother noble,
> Whose nature is so far from doing harms,
> That he suspects none: on whose foolish honesty
> My practices ride easy!'

But this is trite; Shakespeare penetrates more profoundly than this into the nature of evil. Sympathy and trustfulness make men easily gullible, and consistently egoistic utilitarians ought to value gulls. But strangely enough they find them most distasteful. 'Well you may fear too far', says Albany, when Goneril suggests that it would be prudent to dismiss her father's train. 'Safer than trust too far', is his wife's characteristic reply. This difference of outlook soon ripens into a real antipathy:

> 'GONERIL.   My most dear Gloster!   (*Exit* EDMUND.
> O, the difference of man and man! To thee
> A woman's services are due: *my fool*
> Usurps my body.
> OSWALD.   Madam, here comes my lord.   (*Exit.
> Enter* ALBANY.
> GONERIL.   I have been worth the whistle.
> ALBANY.   O Goneril!
> You are not worth the dust which the rude wind
> Blows in your face . . .
> She that herself will sliver and disbranch
> From her material sap, perforce must wither,
> And come to deadly use.

> GONERIL.   No more; the text is *foolish*.
>
> ALBANY.   Wisdom and goodness to the vile seem vile:
> Filths savour but themselves. What have you done? . . .
>
> GONERIL.   Milk-liver'd man!
> That bear'st a cheek for blows, a head for wrongs . . .
> With plumed helm thy slayer begins threats;
> Whiles thou, *a moral fool,* sitt'st still, and criest
> "Alack, why does he so?"
>
> ALBANY.   See thyself, devil!
> Proper deformity seems not in the fiend
> So horrid as in woman.
>
> GONERIL.   O vain *fool*!
>
> ALBANY.   Thou changed and self-cover'd thing, for shame,
> Be-monster not thy feature.'

Goneril's attitude reminds us of the wise advice which the Fool ironically offered to Kent. To Goneril it is the only conceivable kind of wisdom, to Albany it is just plain knavery, to the Fool it is either wisdom or folly according to your point of view. For the puzzle about evil is not that men do not live up to their principles; it is that men can reverse values and say: 'Evil, be thou my good', and that by reason alone it is not possible to prove them wrong. The bad characters in *Lear* have no fellow-feeling, and therefore act consistently from motives of self-interest. The analytic intellect cannot prove that 'fellow-feeling' is a possibility, still less that it is a duty. Respectable philosophers have founded their systems (though not their practice) on the notion that altruism can always be resolved into egoism. Are not Edmund and Goneril, then, justified in seeing the world as they do see it and acting in accordance with their insight? What have the good to say on this subject? Well, they have no intellectual arguments to offer, but two intuitions or convictions, on which they are prepared to act even at the cost of their own lives. Firstly, if love is lunacy so much the worse for sanity: the good will merely in their turn reverse values and say, 'Folly, be thou my wisdom'. Secondly, love or 'fellow-feeling' is a normal attribute of humanity, and as such it does not need proof, for it is its absence, not its presence, that requires explanation. 'Let them anatomize Regan, see what breeds about her heart. Is there any cause in nature that makes these hard hearts?' Recurrent throughout the play is the sense that the breaking of human ties, especially ties of close blood or plighted loyalty, is so abnormal and unnatural that it must be a symptom of some dread convulsion in the frame of things that must bring about the end of the world unless some Divine Power intervenes to redress the balance before it is too late. And more than that, it is so fundamentally abnormal and inhuman that the mere contemplation of it upsets the mental balance of a normal man. As Lear looks into Goneril's heart his wits begin to turn. To Edmund, on the other hand, it is the most natural thing in the world that he should pursue his own interests, whatever the expense to other people.

Which of these parties sees the truth, or rather, to speak more accurately, which point of view does Shakespeare mean us to adopt as we experience his tragedy? Or is this an instance of his notorious impartiality? Is he giving us a tragic illustration of moral relativity? Do Goneril and Cordelia separate good from evil, wisdom from folly, with very different results, only because they have different but equally valid frames of reference for their measurements? If we join the good characters in the play in asking Heaven to decide, that would seem to be the inescapable conclusion, for both Cordelia and Goneril die prematurely. And if it is a fact that some of the good survive, whereas the evil are shown to be by their nature mutually destructive; yet we may set against this the fact that the good suffer more than the evil, that love and suffering, in this play, are almost interchangeable terms and the driving force of the action is derived from the power of the evil to inflict mental agony upon the good. This is particularly important, because the physical death of the hero is not really the tragic climax of this play. Lear, after all, is an old man, and the poignant question about him is not: 'Will he survive?' but rather 'What will happen to his mind?' The real horror lies not in the fact that Goneril and Regan can cause the death of their father, but that they can apparently destroy his human integrity. I say 'apparently', because the whirling ambiguities of the Fool are reflected in the sequence of events as well as in the opinions of the dramatis personae, and it is only after a study of the arrangement of the action that we can rightly decide whether the Heavens are shown as just or wanton, deaf and dumb or most ironically vocal. For, as Aristotle taught us long ago, plot is the soul of tragedy.

It has often been pointed out that Lear has a more passive rôle than most of Shakespeare's tragic characters. Nevertheless he is involved in an event, and his relationship with the Fool is no mere static pictorial contrast, but part of the tragic movement of the play; the movement downwards towards that ultimate exposure and defeat when the King is degraded to the status of the meanest of his servants. We watch the royal sufferer being progressively stripped, first of extraordinary worldly power, then of ordinary human dignity, then of the very necessities of life, deprived of which he is more helpless and abject than any animal. But there is a more dreadful consummation than this reduction to physical nakedness. Lear hardly feels the storm because he is struggling to retain his mental integrity, his 'knowledge and reason', which are not only, as he himself calls them, 'marks of sovereignty', but the essential marks of humanity itself:

> 'O, let me not be mad, not mad, sweet heaven!
> Keep me in temper, I would not be mad!"
> 'O fool, I shall go mad!'

Lear's dread is justified, 'sweet heaven' rejects his prayer, and the central scenes on the heath are peopled by a blind, half-crazy nobleman, guided by a naked beggar supposed to be mad, and by an actually mad King served by a half-witted court-jester—an amazingly daring version of the culminating moment of the sottie: the great reversal when the highest dignitaries appear as fools, and the World or even Holy Church herself is revealed in cap and bells.

Do we then find at the heart of this greatest of tragedies the satire of the sottie transmuted into despair? That depends on what happens when we test the quality of Lear's unreason, and on how we answer the question already suggested by his brother in folly: 'Do I insult a man by investing him with motley?'

From the time when Lear's agony begins and he feels his sanity threatened he becomes gradually aware of the sufferings of other people:

> 'My wits begin to turn. . . .
> Poor fool and knave, I've one part in my heart
> That's sorry yet for thee.'

And not only are Lear's sympathies aroused, they are broadened. Goneril and Regan break the closest, most fundamental of human ties, they cannot feel even that kind of parental-filial relationship that the animals feel; whereas in his agony, Lear, who had himself been unnatural to Cordelia, suddenly realizes that all men are one in pain:

> '. . . Take physic, pomp:
> Expose thyself to feel what wretches feel,
> That thou may'st shake the superflux to them,
> And show the heavens more just.'

As Lear's brain reels, his agony increases and his sympathies expand. The same thing happens to Gloucester, whose blindness parallels Lear's madness:

> '. . . heavens, deal so still!
> Let the superfluous and lust-dieted man
> That slaves your ordinance, that will not see
> Because he doth not feel, feel your power quickly;
> So distribution should undo excess,
> And each man have enough.'

In several passages *seeing* and *feeling* are compared and contrasted with one another. It is feeling that gives the true sight. 'I stumbled when I saw.' Again we are confronted with the paradoxical reversal of wisdom and folly. At the beginning of the play both Lear and Gloucester are blind fools:

'O, Lear, Lear, Lear!
Beat at the gate that let thy folly in
And thy dear judgment out.'

Both the good and the evil would agree that Lear had
reason for self-reproach, but they would disagree as to
the nature of the folly he deplores. To the bad his folly
was the folly of trustfulness and affection, to the good it
was the folly of distrustfulness and unkindness. But now
that the worst has happened, now that Lear has lost his
sanity, he has enlarged his vision. As his wits begin to leave
him, he begins to see the truth about himself; when they are
wholly gone he begins to have spasmodic flashes of insight
in which, during momentary lulls in the storm of vengeful
personal resentment, he sees the inner truth about the world.
'Thou wouldst make a good fool', said the Fool to his
master at the beginning of his misfortunes, and he spoke as
a prophet. In his amazing encounter with the *blind* Gloucester, the *mad* Lear has something of the wit, the penetration,
the quick repartee of the court-jester. From the realistic
point of view it is no doubt a dramatic flaw that Shakespeare
does not account more clearly for the fate of the real man
in motley; but his disappearance was a poetic necessity, for
the King having lost everything, including his wits, has now
himself become the Fool. He has touched bottom, he is an
outcast from society, he has no longer any private axe to
grind, so he now sees and speaks the truth.

And what is the truth? What does the mad Lear see in
his flashes of lucidity? Does he see that Goneril was more
sensible than Cordelia? Is Mr Wyndham Lewis right in
suggesting that it is only the swelling blank verse that differentiates his voice from the disgusted snarling of Thersites?
Certainly his vision is a grim one. He sees not one particular event but the whole of human life as a vast sottie:

'LEAR. What, art mad? A man may see how this world
goes, with no eyes. Look with thine ears: see how yond
justice rails upon yond simple thief. Hark, in thine ear:
change places; and, handy-dandy, which is the justice,
which is the thief? Thou hast seen a farmer's dog bark
at a beggar?
GLOUCESTER. Ay, sir.

LEAR. And the creature run from the cur? There thou
mightest behold the great image of authority: a dog's
obeyed in office. . . .
         . . . Plate sin with gold,
And the strong lance of justice hurtless breaks;
Arm it in rags, a pigmy's straw does pierce it.
None does offend, none,—I say, none; I'll able 'em:
Take that of me, my friend, who have the power
To seal th' accuser's lips. Get thee glass eyes;
And, like a scurvy politician, seem
To see the things thou dost not.'

Already we have watched king and noblemen turned into
fools and beggars, now the great reversal of the Saturnalia
is transferred from the action of the tragedy into the mind
of the tragic hero, who discovers in his dotage, what the
evil have known from their cradles, that *in this world there
is no poetic justice*:

'When we are born, we cry that we are come
   To this great stage of fools.'

This is the favourite common-place of the Enfants-sans-
souci transposed into the minor key and made matter not
for laughter but for tears.

But it is the falling of these tears (which of course can
only be heard through the blank verse or prose rhythm)
which differentiates Lear the fool from Thersites the cynic.
Thersites gloats over the universality of evil; he never, like
Lear, recoils from his vision of sin with a passionate horror
which breaks out into broken cries reeling between verse
and prose, he never begs for 'civet to sweeten his imagination', still less does he include all under sin that he may
have mercy upon all:

'None does offend, none,—I say, none; I'll able 'em:
   Take that of me, my friend, who have the power
   To seal th' accuser's lips.'

The statement that Shakespeare tends to give more intellectual ability to the evil than to the good needs modification. In this play, at least, the loving characters when they

are perfectly disinterested or when they have lost everything
see equally clearly and more profoundly than do the cold-
hearted. But the good and evil react very differently to the
same facts seen with equal clearness, and it must not be
forgotten that the blind Gloucester and mad Lear have
come to know that to see truly 'how the world goes' is to
'see it feelingly'. And when the world is seen feelingly, what
then? Why then we must be patient. That is all.

'Patience', like 'wisdom', 'folly', 'knavery', 'nature', is
one of the key words of this tragedy. As soon as Lear begins to realize the nature of his misfortune, he begins to
make pathetic attempts to acquire it, and when his mental
overthrow is complete he recommends it as the appropriate
response to the misery of life:

> 'If thou wilt weep my fortunes, take my eyes.
> I know thee well enough; thy name is Gloucester:
> Thou must be patient; we came crying hither:
> Thou know'st, the first time that we smell the air,
> We wawl and cry.'

Edgar takes the same point of view:

> 'What! In ill-thoughts again? Men must endure
> Their going hence, even as their coming hither:
> Ripeness is all.'

What is meant? Something different from tame submissive-
ness or cold stoicism, but completely opposed to that restless activity in pursuit of our own ends which Edmund
thinks so preferable to passive obedience to fortune or
custom. Patience, here, seems to imply an unflinching, clear-
sighted recognition of the fact of pain, and the complete
abandonment of any claim to justice or gratitude either
from Gods or men; it is the power to choose love when
love is synonymous with suffering, and to abide by the
choice knowing there will be no Divine Salvation from its
consequences.

And here, I think, is the solution of the problem set by
the Fool; the problem of apparent moral relativity, 'Wisdom and goodness to the vile seem vile, filths savour but
themselves', so that Albany and Goneril have not even suffi-

cient common ground to make a real argument possible. Nevertheless, Shakespeare does not allow us to remain neutral spectators of their debate, he insists that although Goneril's case is as complete and consistent as that of Albany it is *not* equally valid, *not* equally true. In the first place Shakespeare's poetry persuades and compels us to accept the values of the friends rather than of the enemies of Lear. Secondly, Shakespeare makes the fullest possible use of the accepted convention that it is the Fool who speaks the truth, which he knows not by ratiocination but by inspired intuition. The mere appearance of the familiar figure in cap and bells would at once indicate to the audience where the 'punctum indifferens', the impartial critic, the mouthpiece of real sanity, was to be found.

Now the Fool sees that when the match between the good and the evil is played by the intellect alone it must end in a stalemate, but when the heart joins in the game then the decision is immediate and final. 'I will tarry, the Fool will stay—And let the wise man fly.' That is the unambiguous wisdom of the madman who sees the truth. That is decisive. It is decisive because, so far from being an abnormal freakish judgment, it is the instinctive judgment of normal humanity raised to heroic stature; and therefore no amount of intellectual argument can prevent normal human beings from receiving and accepting it, just as, when all the psychologists and philosophers have said their say, normal human beings continue to receive and accept the external world as given to them through sense perception. 'They that seek a reason for all things do destroy reason', notes the judicious Hooker; our data, our premises, we must simply receive, and receive not only through our heads but also through our senses and our hearts. To see truly is to 'see feelingly'.

It would seem, then, that there is nothing contemptible in a motley coat. The Fool is justified, but we have not yet a complete answer to his original query: 'What is folly?' Which is the wise man, which is the fool? To be foolish is to mistake the nature of things, or to mistake the proper method of attaining to our desires, or to do both at once. Even Edmund and Edgar, even Goneril and Albany, could agree to that proposition. But have the perfectly disinterested made either of these mistakes and have not the self-interested made them both? The evil desire pleasure and power, and they lose both, for the evil are mutually destructive. The good desire to sympathize and to save, and their desires are partially fulfilled, although as a result they have to die. Nor have the good mistaken the nature or 'mystery of things' which, after all, unlike Edmund, they have never professed either to dismiss or to understand. It is, indeed, as we have seen, the good who are normal. Lear, in his folly, is not reduced, as he fears, to the level of the beasts, but to essential naked humanity, 'unaccommodated man', 'the thing itself'. It is the evil who 'be-monster' themselves, it is the sight of Goneril which makes Albany fear that

> 'It will come,
> Humanity must perforce prey on itself,
> Like monsters of the deep.'

In this connection it is not without interest that the Elizabethan playwrights made conventional use of the inherited belief in thunder as the voice of the Divine Judge, and that the Divine inspiration of madmen has always been a widespread and deeply rooted popular superstition.

Not that I would suggest that this great tragedy should be regarded as a morality play full of naïve spiritual consolation. That Shakespeare's ethics were the ethics of the New Testament, that in this play his mightiest poetry is dedicated to the reiteration of the wilder paradoxes of the Gospels and of St Paul, that seems to me quite certain. But it is no less certain that the metaphysical comfort of the Scriptures is deliberately omitted, though not therefore necessarily denied. The perfectly disinterested choose lovingkindness because they know it to be intrinsically desirable and worth the cost, not because they hope that the full price will not be exacted. It is Kent's readiness to be unendingly patient which makes him other than a shrewder and more far-calculating Edmund. If the thunder had ceased at Lear's bidding, then Lear would not have become a sage-fool. What the thunder says remains enigmatic, but it is this Divine ambiguity which gives such force to the testimony of the human heart. Had the speech of the gods been clearer, the apparently simple utterances of the Fool would have been less profound:

> 'FOOL. He that has a little tiny wit,
> With hey, ho, the wind and the rain,
> Must make content with his fortune's fit,
> For the rain it raineth every day.
> LEAR. True, my good boy.'

And so we reach the final reversal of values. 'Ay every inch a king', says Lear in his madness, and we do not wholly disagree with him. The medieval clergy inaugurated the Saturnalia by parodying the Magnificat: Shakespeare reverses the process. Lear's tragedy is the investing of the King with motley: it is also the crowning and apotheosis of the Fool.

GEORGE ORWELL

George Orwell (pseudonym of Eric Hugh Blair) (1903-1950). Author of several novels, including Animal Farm *(1945) and* 1984 *(1949); a brilliant political, social and literary critic, whose direct prose style has had much influence on recent English writing. Wounded in Spain with the anti-Franco P.O.U.M. in 1937. His critical essays include classic studies of Swift and Henry Miller. See under Tolstoy.*

Leo Tolstoy (1828-1910). Towards the end of his life Tolstoy attacked 'Decadent' art as both obscure and immoral. At 75 he re-read Shakespeare in English and attacked him as unnatural, sycophantic, lacking in art, in an essay called Shakespeare and the Drama. *His particular contempt for* King Lear *afforded George Orwell his starting point in the present essay.*

LEAR, TOLSTOY AND THE FOOL*

Tolstoy's pamphlets are the least-known part of his work, and his attack on Shakespeare [1] is not even an easy document to get hold of, at any rate in an English translation. Perhaps, therefore, it will be useful if I give a summary of the pamphlet before trying to discuss it.

Tolstoy begins by saying that throughout life Shakespeare has aroused in him "an irresistible repulsion and tedium". Conscious that the opinion of the civilized world is against him, he has made one attempt after another on Shakespeare's works, reading and re-reading them in Russian, English and German; but "I invariably underwent the same feelings; repulsion, weariness and bewilderment". Now, at the age of seventy-five, he has once again re-read the entire works of Shakespeare, including the historical plays, and

"I have felt with an even greater force, the same feelings —this time, however, not of bewilderment, but of firm, indubitable conviction that the unquestionable glory of a great genius which Shakespeare enjoys, and which compels writers of our time to imitate him and readers and spectators to discover in him non-existent merits—thereby distorting their aesthetic and ethical understanding—is a great evil, as is every untruth."

Shakespeare, Tolstoy adds, is not merely no genius, but is not even "an average author", and in order to demonstrate this fact he will examine *King Lear*, which, as he is able to show by quotations from Hazlitt, Brandes and others, has been extravagantly praised and can be taken as an example of Shakespeare's best work.

Tolstoy then makes a sort of exposition of the plot of *King Lear*, finding it at every step to be stupid, verbose, unnatural, unintelligible, bombastic, vulgar, tedious and full of incredible events, "wild ravings", "mirthless jokes", anach-

* Reprinted from *Shooting an Elephant and Other Essays*.
[1] Shakespeare and the Drama. *Written about 1903 as an introduction to another pamphlet,* Shakespeare and the Working Classes, *by Ernest Crosby.*

ronisms, irrelevances, obscenities, worn-out stage conventions and other faults both moral and aesthetic. *Lear* is, in
any case, a plagiarism of an earlier and much better play,
King Leir, by an unknown author, which Shakespeare stole
and then ruined. It is worth quoting a specimen paragraph
to illustrate the manner in which Tolstoy goes to work.
Act III, Scene 2 (in which Lear, Kent and the Fool are
together in the storm) is summarized thus:

"Lear walks about the heath and says words which are
meant to express his despair: he desires that the winds
should blow so hard that they (the winds) should crack
their cheeks and that the rain should flood everything, that
lightning should singe his white head, and the thunder
flatten the world and destroy all germs 'that make ungrateful man'! The fool keeps uttering still more senseless words.
Enter Kent: Lear says that for some reason during this
storm all criminals shall be found out and convicted. Kent,
still unrecognized by Lear, endeavours to persuade him to
take refuge in a hovel. At this point the fool utters a
prophecy in no wise related to the situation and they all
depart."

Tolstoy's final verdict on *Lear* is that no unhypnotized
observer, if such an observer existed, could read it to the
end with any feeling except "aversion and weariness". And
exactly the same is true of "all the other extolled dramas of
Shakespeare, not to mention the senseless dramatized tales,
*Pericles, Twelfth Night, The Tempest, Cymbeline, Troilus
and Cressida*".

Having dealt with *Lear* Tolstoy draws up a more general
indictment against Shakespeare. He finds that Shakespeare
has a certain technical skill which is partly traceable to his
having been an actor, but otherwise no merits whatever.
He has no power of delineating character or of making
words and actions spring naturally out of situations, his
language is uniformly exaggerated and ridiculous, he constantly thrusts his own random thoughts into the mouth of
any character who happens to be handy, he displays a "complete absence of aesthetic feeling", and his words have
"nothing whatever in common with art and poetry".

"Shakespeare might have been whatever you like,"

Tolstoy concludes, "but he was not an artist." Moreover, his opinions are not original or interesting, and his tendency is "of the lowest and most immoral". Curiously enough, Tolstoy does not base this last judgment on Shakespeare's own utterances, but on the statements of two critics, Gervinus and Brandes. According to Gervinus (or at any rate Tolstoy's reading of Gervinus) "Shakespeare taught . . . that one *may be too good*," while according to Brandes: "Shakespeare's fundamental principle . . . is that *the end justifies the means*." Tolstoy adds on his own account that Shakespeare was a jingo patriot of the worst type, but apart from this he considers that Gervinus and Brandes have given a true and adequate description of Shakespeare's view of life.

Tolstoy then recapitulates in a few paragraphs the theory of art which he had expressed at greater length elsewhere. Put still more shortly, it amounts to a demand for dignity of subject matter, sincerity, and good craftsmanship. A great work of art must deal with some subject which is "important to the life of mankind", it must express something which the author genuinely feels, and it must use such technical methods as will produce the desired effect. As Shakespeare is debased in outlook, slipshod in execution and incapable of being sincere even for a moment, he obviously stands condemned.

But here there arises a difficult question. If Shakespeare is all that Tolstoy has shown him to be, how did he ever come to be so generally admired? Evidently the answer can only lie in a sort of mass hypnosis, or "epidemic suggestion". The whole civilized world has somehow been deluded into thinking Shakespeare a good writer, and even the plainest demonstration to the contrary makes no impression, because one is not dealing with a reasoned opinion but with something akin to religious faith. Throughout history, says Tolstoy, there has been an endless series of the "epidemic suggestions"—for example, the Crusades, the search for the Philosopher's Stone, the craze for tulip growing which once swept over Holland, and so on and so forth. As a contemporary instance he cites rather significantly, the Dreyfus case, over which the whole world grew violently excited for no sufficient reason. There are also sudden short-lived crazes for new political and philosophical theories, or for this or that writer, artist or scientist—for example, Darwin who (in 1903) is "beginning to be forgotten". And in some cases a quite worthless popular idol may remain in favour for centuries, for "it also happens that such crazes, having arisen in consequence of special reasons accidentally favouring their establishment correspond in such a degree to the views of life spread in society, and especially in literary circles, that they are maintained for a long time". Shakespeare's plays have continued to be admired over a long period because "they corresponded to the irreligious and immoral frame of mind of the upper classes of his time and ours".

As to the manner in which Shakespeare's fame *started*, Tolstoy explains it as having been "got up" by German professors towards the end of the eighteenth century. His reputation "originated in Germany, and thence was transferred to England". The Germans chose to elevate Shakespeare because, at a time when there was no German drama worth speaking about and French classical literature was beginning to seem frigid and artificial, they were captivated by Shakespeare's "clever development of scenes" and also found in him a good expression of their own attitude towards life. Goethe pronounced Shakespeare a great poet, whereupon all the other critics flocked after him like a troop of parrots, and the general infatuation has lasted ever since. The result has been a further debasement of the drama — Tolstoy is careful to include his own plays when condemning the contemporary stage—and a further corruption of the prevailing moral outlook. It follows that "the false glorification of Shakespeare" is an important evil which Tolstoy feels it his duty to combat.

This, then, is the substance of Tolstoy's pamphlet. One's first feeling is that in describing Shakespeare as a bad writer he is saying something demonstrably untrue. But this is not the case. In reality there is no kind of evidence or argument by which one can show that Shakespeare, or any other writer, is "good". Nor is there any way of definitely proving that—for instance—Warwick Deeping is "bad". Ultimately there is no test of literary merit except survival, which is itself an index to majority opinion. Artistic theories such as Tolstoy's are quite worthless, because they not only start out with arbitrary assumptions, but depend on vague terms ("sincere", "important" and so forth) which can be interpreted in any way one chooses. Properly speaking one cannot *answer* Tolstoy's attack. The interesting question is: why did he make it? But it should be noticed in passing that he uses many weak or dishonest arguments. Some of these are worth pointing out, not because they invalidate his main charge but because they are, so to speak, evidence of malice.

To begin with, his examination of *King Lear* is not "impartial", as he twice claims. On the contrary, it is a prolonged exercise in misrepresentation. It is obvious that when you are summarizing *King Lear* for the benefit of someone who has not read it, you are not really being impartial if you introduce an important speech (Lear's speech when Cordelia is dead in his arms) in this manner: "Again begin Lear's awful ravings, at which one feels ashamed, as at unsuccessful jokes." And in a long series of instances Tolstoy slightly alters or colours the passages he is criticizing, always in such a way as to make the plot appear a little more complicated and improbable, or the language a little more exaggerated. For example, we are told that Lear "has no necessity or motive for his abdication", although his reason for abdicating (that he is old and wishes to retire from the cares of state) has been clearly indicated in the first scene. It will be seen that even in the passage which I quoted earlier, Tolstoy has wilfully misunderstood one phrase and slightly changed the meaning of another, making nonsense of a remark which is reasonable enough in its context. None of these misreadings is very gross in itself, but their cumulative effect is to exaggerate the psychological incoherence of the play. Again, Tolstoy is not able to explain why Shakespeare's plays were still in print, and still on the stage, two hundred years after his death (*before* the "epidemic suggestion" started, that is); and his whole account of Shakespeare's rise to fame is guesswork punctuated by outright mis-statements. And again, various of his accusations contradict one another: for example, Shakespeare is a mere entertainer and "not in earnest", but on the other hand he is constantly putting his own thoughts into the mouths of his characters. On the whole it is difficult to feel that Tolstoy's criticisms are uttered in good faith. In any case it is impossible that he should fully have believed in his main thesis—believed, that is to say, that for a century or more the entire civilized world had been taken in by a huge and palpable lie which he alone was able to see through. Certainly his dislike of Shakespeare is real enough, but the reasons for it may be different, or partly different, from what he avows; and therein lies the interest of his pamphlet.

At this point one is obliged to start guessing. However, there is one possible clue, or at least there is a question which may point the way to a clue. It is: why did Tolstoy, with thirty or more plays to choose from, pick out *King Lear* as his especial target? True *Lear* is so well known and has been so much praised that it could justly be taken as representative of Shakespeare's best work; still, for the purpose of a hostile analysis Tolstoy would probably choose the play he disliked most. Is it not possible that he bore an especial enmity towards this particular play because he was aware, consciously or unconsciously, of the resemblance between Lear's story and his own? But it is better to approach this clue from the opposite direction—that is, by examining *Lear* itself, and the qualities in it that Tolstoy fails to mention.

One of the first things an English reader would notice in Tolstoy's pamphlet is that it hardly deals with Shakespeare as a poet. Shakespeare is treated as a dramatist, and in so far as his popularity is not spurious, it is held to be due to tricks of stagecraft which give good opportunities to clever actors. Now, so far as the English-speaking countries go, this is not true. Several of the plays which are most valued by lovers of Shakespeare (for instance, *Timon of Athens*) are seldom or never acted, while some of the most actable such as *A Midsummer Night's Dream,* are the least admired. Those who care most for Shakespeare value him in the first place for his use of language, the "verbal music" which even Bernard Shaw, another hostile critic, admits to be "irresistible". Tolstoy ignores this, and does not seem to realize that a poem may have a special value for those who speak the language in which it was written. However, even if one puts oneself in Tolstoy's place and tries to think of Shakespeare as a foreign poet it is still clear that there is something that Tolstoy has left out. Poetry, it seems, is *not* solely a matter of sound and association, and valueless outside its own language-group: otherwise how is it that some poems, including poems written in dead languages, succeed in crossing frontiers? Clearly a lyric like "To-morrow is Saint Valentine's Day" could not be satisfactorily translated, but in Shakespeare's major work there is something describable as poetry that can be separated from the words. Tolstoy is right in saying that *Lear is* not a very good play, as a play. It is too drawn-out and has too many characters and sub-plots. One wicked daughter would have been quite enough, and Edgar is a superfluous character: indeed it would probably be a better play if Gloucester and both his sons were eliminated. Nevertheless, something, a kind of pattern, or perhaps only an atmosphere, survives the complications and the *longueurs*. *Lear* can be imagined as a puppet show, a mime, a ballet, a series of pictures. Part of its poetry, perhaps the most essential part, is inherent in the story and is dependent neither on any particular set of words, nor on flesh-and-blood presentation.

Shut your eyes and think of *King Lear*, if possible without calling to mind any of the dialogue. What do you see? Here at any rate is what I see; a majestic old man in a long black robe, with flowing white hair and beard, a figure out of Blakes drawings (but also, curiously enough, rather like Tolstoy), wandering through a storm and cursing the heavens, in company with a Fool and a lunatic. Presently the scene shifts and the old man, still cursing, still understanding nothing, is holding a dead girl in his arms while the Fool dangles on a gallows somewhere in the background. This is the bare skeleton of the play, and even here Tolstoy wants to cut out most of what is essential. He objects to the storm, as being unnecessary, to the Fool, who in his eyes is simply a tedious nuisance and an excuse for making bad jokes, and to the death of Cordelia, which, as he sees it, robs the play of its moral. According to Tolstoy, the earlier play, *King Leir*, which Shakespeare adapted

"terminates more naturally and more in accordance with the moral demands of the spectator than does Shakespeare's: namely, by the King of the Gauls conquering the husbands of the elder sisters, and by Cordelia, instead of being killed, restoring Leir to his former position."

In other words the tragedy ought to have been a comedy, or perhaps a melodrama. It is doubtful whether the sense of tragedy is compatible with belief in God: at any rate, it is not compatible with disbelief in human dignity and with the kind of "moral demand" which feels cheated when virtue fails to triumph. A tragic situation exists precisely when virtue does *not* triumph but when it is still felt that man is nobler than the forces which destroy him. It is perhaps more significant that Tolstoy sees no justification for the presence of the Fool. The Fool is integral to the play. He acts not only as a sort of chorus, making the central situation clearer by commenting on it more intelligently than the other characters, but as a foil to Lear's frenzies. His jokes, riddles and scraps of rhyme, and his endless digs at Lear's high-minded folly, ranging from mere derision to a sort of melancholy poetry ("All thy other titles thou has given away; that thou wast born with"), are like a trickle of sanity running through the play, a reminder that somewhere or other in spite of the injustices, cruelties, intrigues, deceptions and misunderstandings that are being enacted here, life is going on much as usual. In Tolstoy's impatience with the Fool one gets a glimpse of his deeper quarrel with Shakespeare. He objects, with some justification, to the raggedness of Shakespeare's plays, the irrelevancies, the incredible plots, the exaggerated language: but what at bottom he probably most dislikes is a sort of exuberance, a tendency to take—not so much a pleasure as simply an interest in the actual process of life. It is a mistake to write Tolstoy off as a moralist attacking an artist. He never said that art, as such, is wicked or meaningless, nor did he even say that technical virtuosity is unimportant. But his main aim, in his later years, was to narrow the range of human consciousness. One's interest, one's points of attachment to the physical world and the day-to-day struggle, must be as few and not as many as possible. Literature must consist of parables, stripped of detail and almost independent of language. The parables—this is where Tolstoy differs from the average vulgar puritan—must themselves be works of art, but pleasure and curiosity must be excluded from them. Science, also, must be divorced from curiosity. The business of science, he says, is not to discover what happens but to teach men how they ought to live. So also with history and politics. Many problems (for example, the Dreyfus case) are simply not worth solving, and he is willing to leave them as loose ends. Indeed his whole theory of "crazes" or "epidemic suggestions", in which he lumps together such things as the Crusades and the Dutch passion of tulip growing, shows a willingness to regard many human activities as mere ant-like rushings to and fro, inexplicable and uninteresting. Clearly he could have no patience with a chaotic, detailed, discursive writer like Shakespeare. His reaction is that of an irritable old man who is being pestered by a noisy child. "Why do you keep jumping up and down like that? Why can't you sit still like I do?" In a way the old man is in the right, but the trouble is that the child has a feeling in its limbs which the old man has lost. And if the old man knows of the existence of this feeling, the effect is merely to increase his irritation: he would make children senile, if he could. Tolstoy does not know, perhaps, just *what* he misses in Shakespeare, but he is aware that he misses something, and he is determined that others shall be deprived of it as well. By nature he was imperious as well as egotistical. Well after he was grown up he would still occasionally strike his servant in moments of anger, and somewhat later, according to his English biographer, Derrick Leon, he felt "a frequent desire upon the slenderest provocation to slap the faces of those with whom he disagreed". One does not necessarily get rid of that kind of temperament by undergoing religious conversion, and indeed it is obvious that the illusion of having been reborn may allow one's native vices to flourish more freely than ever, though perhaps in subtler forms. Tolstoy was capable of abjuring physical violence and of seeing what this implies, but he was not capable of tolerance or humility, and even if one knew nothing of his other writings, one could deduce his tendency towards spiritual bullying from this single pamphlet.

However, Tolstoy is not simply trying to rob others of a pleasure he does not share. He is doing that, but his quarrel with Shakespeare goes further. It is the quarrel between the religious and the humanist attitudes towards life. Here one comes back to the central theme of *King Lear*, which Tolstoy does not mention, although he sets forth the plot in some detail.

Lear is one of the minority of Shakespeare's plays that

are unmistakably *about* something. As Tolstoy justly complains, much rubbish has been written about Shakespeare as a philosopher, as a psychologist, as a "great moral teacher", and whatnot. Shakespeare was not a systematic thinker, his most serious thoughts are uttered irreverently or indirectly, and we do not know to what extent he wrote with a "purpose" or even how much of the work attributed to him was actually written by him. In the sonnets he never even refers to the plays as part of his achievement, though he does make what seems to be a half-ashamed allusion to his career as an actor. It is perfectly possible that he looked on at least half of his plays as mere potboilers and hardly bothered about purpose or probability so long as he could patch up something, usually from stolen material, which would more or less hang together on the stage. However, that is not the whole story. To begin with, as Tolstoy himself points out, Shakespeare has a habit of thrusting uncalled-for general reflections into the mouths of his characters. This is a serious fault in a dramatist, but it does not fit in with Tolstoy's picture of Shakespeare as a vulgar hack who has no opinions of his own and merely wishes to produce the greatest effect with the least trouble. And more than this, about a dozen of his plays, written for the most part later than 1600, do unquestionably have a meaning and even a moral. They revolve round a central subject which in some cases can be reduced to a single word. For example, *Macbeth* is about ambition, *Othello* is about jealousy, and *Timon of Athens* is about money. The subject of *Lear* is renunciation, and it is only by being wilfully blind that one can fail to understand what Shakespeare is saying.

Lear renounces his throne but expects everyone to continue treating him as a king. He does not see that if he surrenders power, other people will take advantage of his weakness: also that those who flatter him the most grossly, *i.e.* Regan and Goneril, are exactly the ones who will turn against him. The moment he finds that he can no longer make people obey him as he did before, he falls into a rage which Tolstoy describes as "strange and unnatural", but which in fact is perfectly in character. In his madness and despair, he passes through two moods which again are natural enough in his circumstances, though in one of them it is probable that he is being used partly as a mouthpiece for Shakespeare's own opinions. One is the mood of disgust in which Lear repents, as it were, for having been a king, and grasps for the first time the rottenness of formal justice and vulgar morality. The other is a mood of impotent fury in which he wreaks imaginary revenges upon those who have wronged him. "To have a thousand with red burning spits come hissing upon 'em!", and:

> "It were a delicate stratagem to shoe
> A troop of horse with felt: I'll put't in proof;
> And when I have stol'n upon these sons-in-law,
> Then kill, kill, kill, kill, kill!"

Only at the end does he realize, as a sane man, that power, revenge and victory are not worth while:

> "No, no, no, no! Come, let's away to prison . . .
> . . . . and we'll wear out
> In a wall'd prison, packs and sects of great ones
> That ebb and flow by the moon."

But by the time he makes this discovery it is too late, for his death and Cordelia's are already decided on. That is the story, and, allowing for some clumsiness in the telling, it is a very good story.

But is it not also curiously similar to the history of Tolstoy himself? There is a general resemblance which one can hardly avoid seeing, because the most impressive event in Tolstoy's life, as in Lear's, was a huge and gratuitous act of renunciation. In his old age he renounced his estate, his title and his copyrights, and made an attempt—a sincere attempt, though it was not successful—to escape from his privileged position and live the life of a peasant. But the deeper resemblance lies in the fact that Tolstoy, like Lear, acted on mistaken motives and failed to get the results he had hoped for. According to Tolstoy, the aim of every human being is happiness, and happiness can only be attained by doing the will of God. But doing the will of God means casting off all earthly pleasures and ambitions, and living only for others. Ultimately, therefore, Tolstoy renounced the world under the expectation that this would make him happier. But if there is one thing certain about his later years, it is that he was *not* happy. On the contrary, he was driven almost to the edge of madness by the behaviour of the people about him, who persecuted him precisely *because* of his renunciation. Like Lear, Tolstoy was not humble and not a good judge of character. He was inclined at moments to revert to the attitudes of an aristocrat, in spite of his peasant's blouse, and he even had two children whom he had believed in and who ultimately turned against him—though, of course, in a less sensational manner than Regan and Goneril. His exaggerated revulsion from sexuality was also distinctly similar to Lear's. Tolstoy's remark that marriage is "slavery, satiety, repulsion" and means putting up with the proximity of "ugliness, dirtiness, smell, sores", is matched by Lear's well-known outburst:

> "But to the girdle do the gods inherit,
> Beneath is all the fiends';
> There's hell, there's darkness, there's the
>   sulphurous pit,
> Burning, scalding, stench, consumption," etc., etc.

And though Tolstoy could not foresee it when he wrote his essay on Shakespeare, even the ending of his life—the sudden unplanned flight across country, accompanied only by a faithful daughter, the death in a cottage in a strange village—seems to have in it a sort of phantom reminiscence of *Lear*.

Of course, one cannot assume that Tolstoy was aware of this resemblance, or would have admitted it if it had been pointed out to him. But his attitude towards the play must have been influenced by its theme. Renouncing power, giving away your lands, was a subject on which he had reason to feel deeply. Probably, therefore, he would be more angered and disturbed by the moral that Shakespeare draws than he would be in the case of some other play—*Macbeth,* for example—which did not touch so closely on his own life. But what exactly *is* the moral of *Lear*? Evidently there are two morals, one explicit, the other implied in the story.

Shakespeare starts by assuming that to make yourself powerless is to invite an attack. This does not mean that *everyone* will turn against you (Kent and the Fool stand by

Lear from first to last), but in all probability *someone* will. If you throw away your weapons, some less scrupulous person will pick them up. If you turn the other cheek, you will get a harder blow on it than you got on the first one. This does not always happen, but it is to be expected, and you ought not to complain if it does happen. The second blow is, so to speak, part of the act of turning the other cheek. First of all, therefore, there is the vulgar, common-sense moral drawn by the Fool: "Don't relinquish power, don't give away your lands." But there is also another moral. Shakespeare never utters it in so many words, and it does not very much matter whether he was fully aware of it. It is contained in the story, which, after all, he made up, or altered to suit his purposes. It is: "Give away your lands if you want to, but don't expect to gain happiness by doing so. Probably you won't gain happiness. If you live for others, you must live *for others*, and not as a round-about way of getting an advantage for yourself."

Obviously neither of these conclusions could have been pleasing to Tolstoy. The first of them expresses the ordinary, belly-to-earth selfishness from which he was genuinely trying to escape. The other conflicts with his desire to eat his cake and have it—that is, to destroy his own egoism and by so doing to gain eternal life. Of course, *Lear* is not a sermon in favour of altruism. It merely points out the results of practising self-denial for selfish reasons. Shakespeare had a considerable streak of worldliness in him, and if he had been forced to take sides in his own play, his sympathies would probably have lain with the Fool. But at least he could see the whole issue and treat it at the level of tragedy. Vice is punished, but virtue is not rewarded. The morality of Shakespeare's later tragedies is not religious in the ordinary sense, and certainly is not Christian. Only two of them, *Hamlet* and *Othello,* are supposedly occurring inside the Christian era, and even in those, apart from the antics of the ghost in *Hamlet,* there is no indication of a "next world" where everything is to be put right. All of these tragedies start out with the humanist assumption that life, although full of sorrow, is worth living, and that Man is a noble animal—a belief which Tolstoy in his old age did not share.

Tolstoy was not a saint, but he tried very hard to make

himself into a saint, and the standards he applied to literature were other-worldly ones. It is important to realize that
the difference between a saint and an ordinary human being
is a difference of kind and not of degree. That is, the one
is not to be regarded as an imperfect form of the other.
The saint, at any rate Tolstoy's kind of saint, is not trying
to work an improvement in earthly life: he is trying to bring
it to an end and put something different in its place. One
obvious expression of this is the claim that celibacy is
"higher" than marriage. If only, Tolstoy says in effect, we
would stop breeding, fighting, struggling and enjoying, if we
could get rid not only of our sins but of everything else
that binds us to the surface of the earth—including love,
then the whole painful process would be over and the Kingdom of Heaven would arrive. But a normal human being
does not want the Kingdom of Heaven: he wants life on
earth to continue. This is not solely because he is "weak",
"sinful" and anxious for a "good time". Most people get a
fair amount of fun out of their lives, but on balance
life is suffering, and only the very young or the very foolish
imagine otherwise. Ultimately it is the Christian attitude
which is self-interested and hedonistic, since the aim is
always to get away from the painful struggle of earthly
life and find eternal peace in some kind of Heaven or
Nirvana. The humanist attitude is that the struggle must
continue and that death is the price of life. "Men must
endure their going hence, even as their coming hither:
Ripeness is all"—which is an un-Christian sentiment. Often
there is a seeming truce between the humanist and the
religious believer, but in fact their attitudes cannot be
reconciled: one must choose between this world and the
next. And the enormous majority of human beings, if they
understood the issue, would choose this world. They do
make that choice when they continue working, breeding
and dying instead of crippling their faculties in the hope of
obtaining a new lease of existence elsewhere.

We do not know a great deal about Shakespeare's
religious beliefs, and from the evidence of his writings it
would be difficult to prove that he had any. But at any rate
he was not a saint or a would-be saint: he was a human
being, and in some ways not a very good one. It is clear,
for instance, that he liked to stand well with the rich and

powerful, and was capable of flattering them in the most servile way. He is also noticeably cautious, not to say cowardly, in his manner of uttering unpopular opinions. Almost never does he put a subversive or sceptical remark into the mouth of a character likely to be identified with himself. Throughout his plays the acute social critics, the people who are not taken in by accepted fallacies, are buffoons, villains, lunatics or persons who are shamming insanity or are in a state of violent hysteria. *Lear* is a play in which this tendency is particularly well marked. It contains a great deal of veiled social criticism—a point Tolstoy misses—but it is all uttered either by the Fool, by Edgar when he is pretending to be mad, or by Lear during his bouts of madness. In his sane moments Lear hardly ever makes an intelligent remark. And yet the very fact that Shakespeare had to use these subterfuges shows how widely his thoughts ranged. He could not restrain himself from commenting on almost everything, although he put on a series of masks in order to do so. If one has once read Shakespeare with attention, it is not easy to go a day without quoting him, because there are not many subjects of major importance that he does not discuss or at least mention somewhere or other, in his unsystematic but illuminating way. Even the irrelevancies that litter every one of his plays—the puns and riddles, the lists of names, the scraps of *reportage* like the conversation of the carriers in *Henry IV*, the bawdy jokes, the rescued fragments of forgotten ballads—are merely the products of excessive vitality. Shakespeare was not a philosopher or a scientist, but he did have curiosity, he loved the surface of the earth and the process of life—which, it should be repeated, is *not* the same thing as wanting to have a good time and stay alive as long as possible. Of course, it is not because of the quality of his thought that Shakespeare has survived, and he might not even be remembered as a dramatist if he had not also been a poet. His main hold on us is through language. How deeply Shakespeare himself was fascinated by the music of words can probably be inferred from the speeches of Pistol. What Pistol says is largely meaningless, but if one considers his lines singly they are magnificent rhetorical verse. Evidently, pieces of resounding nonsense ("Let floods o'erswell, and fiends for food howl on", etc.)

were constantly appearing in Shakespeare's mind of their own accord, and a half-lunatic character had to be invented to use them up.

Tolstoy's native tongue was not English, and one cannot blame him for being unmoved by Shakespeare's verse, nor even, perhaps, for refusing to believe that Shakespeare's skill with words was something out of the ordinary. But he would also have rejected the whole notion of valuing poetry for its texture—valuing it, that is to say, as a kind of music. If it could somehow have been proved to him that his whole explanation of Shakespeare's rise to fame is mistaken, that inside the English-speaking world, at any rate, Shakespeare's popularity is genuine, that his mere skill in placing some syllable beside another has given acute pleasure to generation after generation of English-speaking people—all this would not have been counted as a merit to Shakespeare, but rather the contrary. It would simply have been one more proof of the irreligious, earthbound nature of Shakespeare and his admirers. Tolstoy would have said that poetry is to be judged by its meaning, and that seductive sounds merely cause false meanings to go unnoticed. At every level it is the same issue—this world against the next: and certainly the music of words is something that belongs to this world.

A sort of doubt has always hung around the character of Tolstoy, as round the character of Gandhi. He was not a vulgar hypocrite, as some people declared him to be, and he would probably have imposed even greater sacrifices on himself than he did, if he had not been interfered with at every step by the people surrounding him, especially his wife. But on the other hand it is dangerous to take such men as Tolstoy at their disciples' valuation. There is always the possibility—the probability, indeed—that they have done no more than exchange one form of egoism for another. Tolstoy renounced wealth, fame and privilege; he abjured violence in all its forms and was ready to suffer for doing so; but it is not easy to believe that he abjured the principle of coercion, or at least the *desire* to coerce others. There are families in which the father will say to his child, "You'll get a thick ear if you do that again", while the mother, her eyes brimming over with tears, will take the child in her arms and murmur lovingly, "Now, darling, *is* it kind to Mummy to do that?" And who would maintain that the second method is less tyrannous than the first? The distinction that really matters is not between violence and non-violence, but between having and not having the appetite for power. There are people who are convinced of the wickedness both of armies and of police forces, but who are nevertheless much more intolerant and inquisitorial in outlook than the normal person who believes that it is necessary to use violence in certain circumstances. They will not say to somebody else, "Do this, that and the other or you will go to prison", but they will, if they can, get inside his brain and dictate his thoughts for him in the minutest particulars. Creeds like pacifism and anarchism, which seem on the surface to imply a complete renunciation of power, rather encourage this habit of mind. For if you have embraced a creed which appears to be free from the ordinary dirtiness of politics—a creed from which you yourself cannot expect to draw any material advantage—surely that proves that you are in the right? And the more you are in the right, the more natural that everyone else should be bullied into thinking likewise.

If we are to believe what he says in his pamphlet, Tolstoy has never been able to see any merit in Shakespeare, and was always astonished to find that his fellow-writers, Turgenev, Fet and others thought differently. We may be sure that in his unregenerate days Tolstoy's conclusion would have been: "You like Shakespeare—I don't. Let's leave it at that." Later, when his perception that it takes all sorts to make a world had deserted him, he came to think of Shakespeare's writings as something dangerous to himself. The more pleasure people took in Shakespeare, the less they would listen to Tolstoy. Therefore nobody must be *allowed* to enjoy Shakespeare, just as nobody must be allowed to drink alcohol or smoke tobacco. True, Tolstoy would not prevent them by force. He is not demanding that the police shall impound every copy of Shakespeare's work. But he will do dirt on Shakespeare, if he can. He will try to get inside the mind of every lover of Shakespeare and kill his enjoyment by every trick he can think of, including—as I have shown in my summary of his pamphlet—arguments which are self-contradictory or even doubtfully honest.

But finally the most striking thing is how little difference it all makes. As I said earlier, one cannot *answer* Tolstoy's pamphlet, at least on its main counts. There is no argument by which one can defend a poem. It defends itself by surviving, or it is indefensible. And if this test is valid, I think the verdict in Shakespeare's case must be "not guilty". Like every other writer, Shakespeare will be forgotten sooner or later, but it is unlikely that a heavier indictment will ever be brought against him. Tolstoy was perhaps the most admired literary man of his age, and he was certainly not its least able pamphleteer. He turned all his powers of denunciation against Shakespeare, like all the guns of a battleship roaring simultaneously. And with what result? Forty years later Shakespeare is still there completely unaffected, and of the attempt to demolish him nothing remains except the yellowing pages of a pamphlet which hardly anyone has read, and which would be forgotten altogether if Tolstoy had not also been the author of *War and Peace* and *Anna Karenina.*

JOHN HOLLOWAY

John Holloway (1920-   ). Fellow of Queens' College, Cambridge; poet and author of Language and Intelligence *(1951),* The Victorian Sage *(1953),* The Charted Mirror *(1960) and* The Story of the Night *(1961).*

THE RESOLUTION OF KING LEAR*

. . . One must try to record the note upon which *King Lear* is resolved. It is not easy to do so, and it is less easy than more than one distinguished critic has allowed. One interpretation, certainly, has attracted many readers. We may frame it, with Professor Chambers, as 'the victory of Cordelia and of Love'; or with Professor Knights, as the 'complete endorsement of love as a quality of being', or with Professor Wilson Knight, as 'the primary persons, good

* Extracted from *The Story of the Night.*

and bad, die into love'. It is better to see the play thus, than to regard its close as the embodiment only of cynicism, chaos and despair. But one should remind oneself at this point of what, surely, is familiar knowledge: that love (unless that word is taken, as I fear it is often taken, to mean every good thing) is a value with a great but finite place in human life; and that if it is a full description of the affirmation on which the play closes, that affirmation is a limited one; is indeed, curiously inadequate, curiously out of scale with the range, power and variety of the issues of life on which this incomparable work has touched. Those for whom the word 'love' is a talisman will find this suggestion objectionable. That may be an argument in its favour.

With these considerations in mind, one may incline to see the close of *Lear* in another light. The survivors of Cleopatra, say, and of Brutus and Coriolanus, indeed speak as though these characters enjoyed a kind of victory or triumph even in death. When, at the close of *Lear,* Shakespeare characteristically gives those who survive the protagonist lines which suggest what the audience is to see in his end, it is not to any victory or triumph, through love or anything else, that he makes them direct our attention. He causes them to agree that there has never been such a case of a man stretched out on the rack of the world, and released at last. At the close of *Macbeth* there is much emphasis on a movement of regeneration, a restoration of good at the level of the body politic. Lear ends more sombrely. 'Our present business . . . is general woe', says Albany, appealing to Kent and Edgar for nothing more optimistic than to help him rule and 'the *gor'd* state *sustain*'—the modest ambition of that last word should not be missed. The last speech of all, that of Edgar, seems peculiarly significant, for all its bald rhyming:

> The weight of this sad time we must obey:
> *Speak what we feel, not what we ought to say,*
> The oldest hath borne most; *we that are young*
> *Shall never see so much nor live so long.*

The ordeal has been unique in its protraction of torment, and the note is surely one of refusal to hide that from oneself, refusal to allow the terrible potentialities of life which the action has revealed to be concealed once more behind the veil of orthodoxy and the order of Nature. If there is such an order, it is an order which can accommodate seemingly limitless chaos and evil. The play is a confrontation of that, a refusal to avert one's gaze from that. Its affirmation is as exalted, humane and life-affirming as affirmation can be, for it lies in a noble and unflinching steadiness, where flinching seems inevitable, in the insight of its creator.

To turn to a more intimate awareness of the personal bonds on which the play closes is to extend and amplify this, and still to see something other than what deserves the name of 'love' *tout court*. Perhaps there is a clue in the fact that it is Edmund ('Yet Edmund was beloved', V. iii. 239) and only Edmund, who speaks of love by itself. We are meant, of course, to see it as embodied always in what Cordelia does; but in her sole reference to this in the later scenes of the play, what she at once goes on to speak of is not her love but, in effect, her duty:

> No blown ambition does both our arms incite,
> But love, dear love, *and our ag'd father's right*.
> > (IV. iv. 26)

This stress, not on loving alone, but on doing and being what it falls to one to do and be, is so insistent that its having been left unregarded is surprising. Cordelia's first speech of any substance to the re-awakened Lear confirms its relevance for both her and him:

> O look upon me, sir,
> And hold your hands in benediction o'er me.
> No, sir, you must not kneel.
> > (IV. vii. 57)

What she wants is for him to do what it is a father's duty to do: not what it is *her* duty to do in return. The same kind of thought is prominent in Lear's first speech after capture:

> When thou dost ask me blessing, I'll kneel down,
> And ask of thee forgiveness.
> > (V. iii. 10)

Each of them is to do what (paradoxically, in Lear's case) it is appropriate for them to do: the idea is of service and duteousness, not love in any simple or emotional sense. In just this light, too, are we invited to see Edgar's bond with his father:

> *Albany:* How have you known the miseries of your father?
> *Edgar:* By nursing them, my Lord . . .
> . . . became his guide,
> Led him, begg'd him, sav'd him from despair;
> Never—O fault!—reveal'd myself unto him
> Until some half-hour past, when I was arm'd;
> Not sure, though hoping, of this good success,
> I asked his blessing, and from first to last
> Told him my pilgrimage.
>
> (V. iii. 180–96)

Kent's devotion to Lear is of course one in which feeling means service:

> I am the very man . . .
> That from your first of difference and decay
> Have followed your sad steps.
>
> (V. iii. 285)

> I have a journey, sir, shortly to go.
> My master calls me; I must not say no.
>
> (V. iii. 321)

The bond which remains, at the play's close, among the other (or perhaps only) survivors, is of the same kind:

> *Albany:*   . . . Friends of my soul, you twain
> Rule in this realm, and the gor'd state sustain.
>
> (V. vii. 319)

With these many pointers in mind, perhaps the final import of the reconciliation of Lear to Cordelia, or Gloucester to Edgar, may also be seen as meaning more than the word 'love' can easily mean, at least in our own time; and as being, in the end, one with the whole of what happens at the close

of the drama. That the closing phase is one in which the evil
in the play proves self-destructive, is well known. Evil has
come, it has taken possession of the world of the play, it
has brought men below the level of the beasts, it has destroyed itself, and it has passed. Good (I have argued) is
far from enjoying a triumphant restoration: we are left
with the spectacle of how suffering can renew itself un-
remittingly until the very moment of death.

If, at the close, some note less despairing than this may
be heard, it comes through our apprehending that in an
austere and minimal sense, Edmund's words 'the wheel has
come full circle' extend, despite everything, beyond himself.
Below the spectacle of suffering everywhere in possession,
is another, inconspicuous but genuine: that the forces of
life have been persistently terrible and cruel, but have also
brought men back to do the things it is their part to do.
Union with Cordelia barely proves Lear's salvation: his
salvation is what Kent says, release from a life of torment.
But that union is the thing to which he rightly belongs. He
deviated from it, and life itself brought him back. So with
Gloucester. To follow the master, to sustain the state, to
bless one's child, to succour the aged and one's parents—
this idea of being brought back to rectitude is what the play
ends with. These are the things which it falls to living men
to do; and if the play advances a 'positive', I think it is that
when men turn away from how they should live, there are
forces in life which constrain them to return. In this play,
love is not a 'victory'; it is not that which stands at 'the
centre of the action', and without which 'life is meaningless';
it does not rule creation. If anything rules creation, it is
(though only, as it were, by a hairsbreadth) simply rule
itself. What order restores, is order. Men tangle their lives;
life, at a price, is self-untangling at last.

In view of these things, how fantastic it would be to call
King Lear a play of intrigue! Yet this idea, immediate
though its rejection must be, does indeed suggest the many
things going on, and being intricately fitted together, which
mark the closing scenes of the play. This very fact is what
leads back from the attitudes of the play to what is more
intimate with its substance, and with the experience which
it offers to us in its sequence. The war with France, the in-

trigue between Edmund and the sisters, the emergence of Albany, Edmund's plot with the captain and his duel with Edgar, dense into a medium of something like quotidian life, through which and beyond which Lear's own situation stands out in isolation. It is the very variety in the strands of life which brings out how, at the end, life as it were stands back from Lear; and affords him a remoteness, a separation from his fellows, in which his ordeal is completed.

This is the culmination, moreover, of how he begins. As in the tragedies which have been discussed already, at the outset the protagonist is at the focal point of all men's regard. But Lear's progressive isolation does not steal upon him, or his audience, unawares. Relinquishing the kingdom, repudiating Cordelia, banishing Kent, cursing Goneril (I. iv. 275–289), departing wrathfully from Regan:

> He calls to horse, and will I know not whither . . .
> (II. iv. 296)

—all these actions set Lear, of his own free will, apart from his fellows; and are the prelude to how he sets himself apart, first from human contact of any kind whatsoever:

> No, rather I abjure all roofs, and choose
> To wage against the enmity o' th' air . . .
> (II. iv. 207)

S. T. COLERIDGE

On Macbeth*

. . . Mr. Coleridge began by commenting on the vulgar stage error which transformed the Weird Sisters into witches with broomsticks. They were awful beings, and blended in themselves the Fates and Furies of the ancients with the sor-

* From a report of a lecture given in Bristol in 1813.

ceresses of Gothic and popular superstition. They were mysterious natures: fatherless, motherless, sexless: they come and disappear: they lead evil minds from evil to evil, and have the power of tempting those who have been the tempters of themselves. The exquisite judgment of Shakespeare is shown in nothing more than in the different language of the Witches with each other, and with those whom they address: the former displays a certain fierce familiarity, grotesqueness mingled with terror; the latter is always solemn, dark, and mysterious. Mr. Coleridge proceeded to show how Macbeth became early a tempter to himself; and contrasted the talkative curiosity of the innocent-minded and open-dispositioned Banquo, in the scene with the Witches, with the silent, absent, and brooding melancholy of his partner. A striking instance of this self-temptation was pointed out in the disturbance of Macbeth at the election of the Prince of Cumberland; but the alarm of his conscience appears, even while meditating to remove this bar to his own advancement, as he exclaims, "Stars! hide your fires!" The ingenuity with which a man evades the promptings of conscience before the commission of a crime, was compared with his total imbecility and helplessness when the crime had been committed, and when conscience can be no longer dallied with or eluded. Macbeth in the first instance enumerates the different worldly impediments to his scheme of murder: could he put them by, he would "jump the life to come." Yet no sooner is the murder perpetrated, than all the concerns of this mortal life are absorbed and swallowed up in the avenging feeling within him: he hears a voice cry, "Macbeth has murder'd sleep: and therefore, Glamis shall sleep no more."

The lecturer alluded to the prejudiced idea of Lady Macbeth as a monster, as a being out of nature and without conscience: on the contrary, her constant effort throughout the play was, if the expression may be forgiven, to *bully* conscience. She was a woman of a visionary and day-dreaming turn of mind; her eye fixed on the shadows of her solitary ambition; and her feelings abstracted, through the deep musings of her absorbing passion, from the common-life sympathies of flesh and blood. But her conscience, so far from being seared, was continually smarting within her; and she endeavours to stifle its voice, and keep down its struggles, by inflated and soaring fancies, and appeals to spiritual agency.

So far is the woman from being dead within her, that her sex occasionally betrays itself in the very moment of dark and bloody imagination. A passage where she alludes to "plucking her nipple from the boneless gums of her infant,"[1] though usually thought to prove a merciless and unwomanly nature, proves the direct opposite: she brings it as the most solemn enforcement to Macbeth of the solemnity of his promise to undertake the plot against Duncan. Had *she* so sworn, she would have done that which was most horrible to her feelings, rather than break the oath; and as the most horrible act which it was possible for imagination to conceive, as that which was most revolting to her own feelings, she alludes to the destruction of her infant, while in the act of sucking at her breast. Had she regarded this with savage indifference, there would have been no force in the appeal; but her very allusion to it, and her purpose in this allusion, shows that she considered no tie so tender as that which connected her with her babe. Another exquisite trait was the faltering of her resolution, while standing over Duncan in his slumbers: *"Had he not resembled my father as he slept,* I had done it."[2]

THOMAS DE QUINCEY

Thomas De Quincey (1785-1859). Author of The Confessions of an English Opium Eater *(1822), voluminous literary journalist, and friend of the Lake Poets.*

[1] *I would, while it was smiling in my face,*
Have pluck'd my nipple from his boneless gums,
And dash'd the brains out, had I so sworn as you.

I. vii. 56-68.

[2]   *"Had he not resembled*
My father as he slept, I had done't."

II. ii. 12-13.

ON THE KNOCKING AT THE GATE
IN MACBETH*

> "Whence is that knocking?
> How is 't with me, when every noise appals me?
> What hands are here? ha! they pluck out mine eyes.
> Will all great Neptune's ocean wash this blood
> Clean from my hand? No, this my hand will rather
> The multitudinous seas incarnadine,
> Making the green one red."
>
> MACBETH, *Act II. Scene* 2.

From my boyish days I had always felt a great perplexity on one point in Macbeth. It was this: the knocking at the gate, which succeeds to the murder of Duncan, produced to my feelings an effect for which I never could account. The effect was, that it reflected back upon the murder a peculiar awfulness and a depth of solemnity; yet, however obstinately I endeavored with my understanding to comprehend this, for many years I never could see *why* it should produce such an effect.

Here I pause for one moment to exhort the reader never to pay any attention to his understanding, when it stands in opposition to any other faculty of his mind. The mere understanding, however useful and indispensable, is the meanest faculty in the human mind, and the most to be distrusted; and yet the great majority of people trust to nothing else; which may do for ordinary life, but not for philosophical purposes. Of this out of ten thousand instances that I might produce, I will cite one. Ask of any person whatsoever, who is not previously prepared for the demand by a knowledge of perspective, to draw in the rudest way the commonest appearance which depends upon the laws of that science; as, for instance, to represent the effect of two walls standing at right angles to each other, or the appearance of the houses on each side of a street, as seen by a person looking down the street from one extremity. Now, in all cases, unless the person has happened to observe in pictures how it is that artists produce these effects, he will be utterly

* Published in 1823.

unable to make the smallest approximation to it. Yet why? For he has actually seen the effect every day of his life. The reason is—that he allows his understanding to over-rule his eyes. His understanding, which includes no intuitive knowledge of the laws of vision, can furnish him with no reason why a line which is known and can be proved to be a horizontal line, should not *appear* a horizontal line; a line that made any angle with the perpendicular, less than a right angle, would seem to him to indicate that his houses were all tumbling down together. Accordingly, he makes the line of his houses a horizontal line, and fails, of course, to pro-duce the effect demanded. Here, then, is one instance out of many, in which not only the understanding is allowed to overrule the eyes, but where the understanding is positively allowed to obliterate the eyes, as it were, for not only does the man believe the evidence of his understanding, in op-position to that of his eyes, but, (what is monstrous!) the idiot is not aware that his eyes ever gave such evidence. He does not know that he has seen (and therefore *quoad* his consciousness has *not* seen) that which he *has* seen every day of his life.

But to return from this digression, my understanding could furnish no reason why the knocking at the gate in Macbeth should produce any effect direct or reflected. In fact, my understanding said positively that it could *not* produce any effect. But I knew better; I felt that it did; and I waited and clung to the problem until further knowledge should enable me to solve it. At length, in 1812, Mr. Williams made his *début* on the stage of Ratcliffe Highway, and executed those unparalleled murders which have procured for him such a brilliant and undying reputation. On which murders, by the way, I must observe, that in one respect they have had an ill effect, by making the connoisseur in murder very fastidi-ous in his taste, and dissatisfied by anything that has since been done in that line. All other murders look pale by the deep crimson of his; and, as an amateur once said to me in a querulous tone, 'There has been absolutely nothing *doing* since his time, or nothing that's worth speaking of.' But this is wrong; for it is unreasonable to expect all men to be great artists, and born with the genius of Mr. Williams. Now it will be remembered, that in the first of these murders, (that of the Marrs,) the same incident (of a knocking at the door, soon after the work of extermination was complete) did actually occur, which the genius of Shakespeare has invented; and all good judges, and the most eminent dilettanti, acknowledged the felicity of Shakespeare's suggestion, as soon as it was actually realized. Here, then, was a fresh proof that I was right in relying on my own feeling, in opposition to my understanding; and I again set myself to study the problem; at length I solved it to my own satisfaction; and my solution is this. Murder, in ordinary cases, where the sympathy is wholly directed to the case of the murdered person, is an incident of coarse and vulgar horror; and for this reason, that it flings the interest exclusively upon the natural but ignoble instinct by which we cleave to life; an instinct, which, as being indispensable to the primal law of self-preservation, is the same in kind, (though different in degree,) amongst all living creatures; this instinct, therefore, because it annihilates all distinctions, and degrades the greatest of men to the level of 'the poor beetle that we tread on,' exhibits human nature in its most abject and humiliating attitude. Such an attitude would little suit the purposes of the poet. What then must he do? He must throw the interest on the murderer. Our sympathy must be with *him;* (of course I mean a sympathy of comprehension, a sympathy by which we enter into his feelings, and are made to understand them,—not a sympathy [1] of pity or approbation.) In the murdered person, all strife of thought, all flux and reflux of passion and of purpose, are crushed by one overwhelming panic; the fear of instant death smites him 'with its petrific mace.' But in the murderer, such a murderer as a poet will condescend to, there must be raging some great storm of passion,—jealousy, ambition, vengeance, hatred,—which will create a hell within him; and into this hell we are to look.

In Macbeth, for the sake of gratifying his own enor-

---

[1] It seems almost ludicrous to guard and explain my use of a word, in a situation where it would naturally explain itself. But it has become necessary to do so, in consequence of the unscholarlike use of the word sympathy, at present so general, by which, instead of taking it in its proper sense, as the act of reproducing in our minds the feelings of another, whether for hatred, indignation, love, pity, or approbation, it is made a mere synonyme of the word *pity;* and hence, instead of saying 'sympathy *with* another,' many writers adopt the monstrous barbarism of 'sympathy *for* another.'

mous and teeming faculty of creation, Shakespeare has introduced two murderers; and, as usual in his hands, they are remarkably discriminated: but, though in Macbeth the strife of mind is greater than in his wife, the tiger spirit not so awake, and his feelings caught chiefly by contagion from her,—yet, as both were finally involved in the guilt of murder, the murderous mind of necessity is finally to be presumed in both. This was to be expressed; and on its own account, as well as to make it a more proportionable antagonist to the unoffending nature of their victim, 'the gracious Duncan,' and adequately to expound 'the deep damnation of his taking off,' this was to be expressed with peculiar energy. We were to be made to feel that the human nature, *i. e.,* the divine nature of love and mercy, spread through the hearts of all creatures, and seldom utterly withdrawn from man,—was gone, vanished, extinct; and that the fiendish nature had taken its place. And, as this effect is marvellously accomplished in the *dialogues* and *soliloquies* themselves, so it is finally consummated by the expedient under consideration; and it is to this that I now solicit the reader's attention. If the reader has ever witnessed a wife, daughter, or sister, in a fainting fit, he may chance to have observed that the most affecting moment in such a spectacle, is *that* in which a sigh and a stirring announce the recommencement of suspended life. Or, if the reader has ever been present in a vast metropolis, on the day when some great national idol was carried in funeral pomp to his grave, and chancing to walk near the course through which it passed, has felt powerfully, in the silence and desertion of the streets, and in the stagnation of ordinary business, the deep interest which at that moment was possessing the heart of man,— if all at once he should hear the death-like stillness broken up by the sound of wheels rattling away from the scene, and making known that the transitory vision was dissolved, he will be aware that at no moment was his sense of the complete suspension and pause in ordinary human concerns so full and affecting, as at that moment when the suspension ceases, and the goings-on of human life are suddenly resumed. All action in any direction is best expounded, measured, and made apprehensible, by reaction. Now apply this to the case in Macbeth. Here, as I have said, the retiring of the human heart, and the entrance of the fiendish heart, was to be expressed and made sensible. Another world has stept in; and the murderers are taken out of the region of human things, human purposes, human desires. They are transfigured: Lady Macbeth is 'unsexed;' Macbeth has forgot that he was born of woman; both are conformed to the image of devils; and the world of devils is suddenly revealed. But how shall this be conveyed and made palpable? In order that a new world may step in, this world must for a time disappear. The murderers, and the murder, must be insulated—cut off by an immeasurable gulph from the ordinary tide and succession of human affairs—locked up and sequestered in some deep recess; we must be made sensible that the world of ordinary life is suddenly arrested—laid asleep—tranced—racked into a dread armistice; time must be annihilated; relation to things without abolished; and all must pass self-withdrawn into a deep syncope and suspension of earthly passion. Hence it is, that when the deed is done, when the work of darkness is perfect, then the world of darkness passes away like a pageantry in the clouds; the knocking at the gate is heard; and it makes known audibly that the reaction has commenced: the human has made its reflux upon the fiendish; the pulses of life are beginning to beat again; and the re-establishment of the goings-on of the world in which we live, first makes us profoundly sensible of the awful parenthesis that had suspended them.

O, mighty poet! Thy works are not as those of other men, simply and merely great works of art; but are also like the phenomena of nature, like the sun and the sea, the stars and the flowers,—like frost and snow, rain and dew, hailstorm and thunder, which are to be studied with entire submission of our own faculties, and in the perfect faith that in them there can be no too much or too little, nothing useless or inert,—but that, the further we press in our discoveries, the more we shall see proofs of design and self-supporting arrangement where the careless eye had seen nothing but accident!

G. WILSON KNIGHT

THE PILGRIMAGE OF HATE: AN ESSAY ON TIMON OF ATHENS*

In this essay I outline the nature of a tragic movement more precipitous and unimpeded than any other in Shakespeare; one which is conceived on a scale even more tremendous than that of *Macbeth* and *King Lear*; and whose universal tragic significance is of all most clearly apparent. My purpose will be to concentrate on whatever is of positive power and significance, regarding the imaginative impact as all-important however it may appear to contradict the logic of human life. My analysis will first characterize the imaginative atmosphere of the early acts and indicate its significance as a setting for the personality of Timon; next, it will show how the subsidiary persons and choric speeches are so presented that our sympathy is directed into certain definite channels; and, finally, I shall point the nature of the second half of the play, contrasting it strongly with the earlier acts and indicating the reversal of symbolic suggestion. Such an analysis will inevitably reveal important facts as to the implicit philosophy, exposing its peculiar universality, and the stark contrast of the partial and imperfect nature of humanity and the world of the senses with the strong aspiration toward infinity and perfection and the ultimate darkness of the unknown embodied in the two parts of the play.

The first acts convey the impression of riches, ease, sensuous appeal, and brilliant display. The curtain rises on a blaze of magnificence and the first persons are the Poet, Painter, Jeweller, and Merchant. In no play of Shakespeare is the opening more significant. Art, wealth, trade are represented, things which stand for human intercourse, progress, civilization, worldly success and happiness. Here poet and

* Extracted from *The Wheel of Fire*.

painter enjoy leisure to hold forth on their art, and jeweller and merchant await high payment for their wares. In the early acts we are continually reminded of wealth. Ventidius is left 'rich' by his father (I. ii. 4); Lucullus dreams of 'a silver basin and ewer' (III. i. 6); talents are thrown about like pence. Many other coins and fine articles are mentioned: we hear of solidares, crowns, 'money, plate, jewels and such like trifles' (III. ii. 23); of 'jewels' and 'rich jewels'; a 'casket', diamonds, and silver goblets. Timon appears boundlessly rich:

> If I want gold, steal but a beggar's dog,
> And give it Timon, why, the dog coins gold.   (II. i. 5)

We hear that

> Plutus, the god of gold,
> Is but his steward.   (I. i. 287)

Metaphors from metal occur:

> Let molten coin be thy damnation,   (III. i. 56)

and

> They have all been touched and found base metal.
>   (III. iii. 6)

Silver dishes are hurled by Timon at his flatterers:

> Stay, I will lend thee money, borrow none. (III. vi. 112)

These acts scintillate with the flash of gold coins and rich metals and stones. They delight the imagination's eye and touch, as the glittering proper names delight the ear. These, however, are but elements in a single effect of wealth, ease, refined luxury, and, in the earliest scenes especially, sensuous joy. Feasting in continual and elaborate:

> A banqueting-room in Timon's House. Hautboys playing loud music. A great banquet served in; Flavius and others attending . . . (I. ii)

Visitors are announced by the sound of trumpets. Besides feasting and music, we have images of visual delight meticulously described. The poet looks at the painting:

> Admirable: how this grace
> Speaks his own standing! what a mental power
> This eye shoots forth! how big imagination
> Moves in this lip! to the dumbness of the gesture
> One might interpret. (I. i. 31)

Timon later praises the same picture. We have a vivid and lengthy description of the poet's symbolical work (I. i. 43–94), and the painter outlines its visual possibilities in his 'condition' of plastic art. Beautiful animals are mentioned, such as 'greyhounds' (I. ii. 198), a 'bay courser' (I. ii. 220), and 'four milk-white horses trapped in silver' (I. ii. 192). All these things, gifts of Fortune to those she wafts to her with her 'ivory hand' (I. i. 71), build up an atmosphere of visual delight. All the senses are catered for: hence, after the feasting and music, there is a mask introduced by a boy-Cupid:

> *Cupid.* Hail to thee, worthy Timon, and to all
> That of his bounties taste! The five best senses
> Acknowledge thee their patron; and come freely
> To gratulate thy plenteous bosom; th' ear,
> Taste, touch, smell, pleased from thy table rise:
> They only now come but to feast thine eyes.
> (I. ii. 130)

The emphasis on the 'senses' is apparent. Timon bids his 'music' welcome the maskers. Then (I. ii.):

> Music. Re-enter Cupid, with a mask of Ladies as Amazons, with lutes in their hands, dancing and playing.

And,

> The Lords rise from table, with much adoring of Timon; and to show their loves, each singles out an

Amazon, and all dance, men with women, a lofty strain
or two to the hautboys, and cease.

Timon thanks the maskers and invites them to an 'idle banquet'. We are lost in a riot of display, a gold-mist of romance
and pleasures of the senses. The setting is brilliant, the
wealth apparently inexhaustible, the pleasures free. We can
imagine the rich food and wine, the blare and clash of music,
embraces, laughter, and passages of glancing love; the
coursing of blood, the flushed cheek, the mask of fair
dancers and Cupid.

Timon's world is sensuous and erotic, yet not vicious or
ignoble. Even in Flavius' denunciation of Timon's way of
life, a grand profusion, an aristocratic brilliance and richness of entertainment yet pleasures us:

> So the gods bless me,
> When all our offices have been oppress'd
> With riotous feeders, when our vaults have wept
> With drunken spilth of wine, when every room
> Hath blazed with lights and bray'd with minstrelsy,
> I have retired me to a wasteful cock,
> And set mine eyes at flow.   (II. ii. 167)

And that is the voice of reproof, when the bright day of
thoughtless expenditure is done. Whilst it is in act, we are
carried away by the magnificence of the effects, and our
imaginations are kindled by the vivid pulse of entertainment, feast, friendship, and music. The poetry of the senses
is lived before our eyes, yet withal there is refinement,
courtesy, aesthetic taste, for this world is lorded by the rich
heart of Timon. The early atmosphere of *Timon of Athens*
is thus as the poetic atmosphere of *Antony and Cleopatra*.
In both there is the same kind of atmospheric technique that
focuses our vision to the unique differing worlds of gloom
of *Macbeth* and *King Lear*; and in both this sensuous blaze
is conceived as a setting for a transcendent love. Only by
subduing our more independent faculties in abeyance to the
imaginative quality of these early scenes shall we receive
the play as poetry and know its meaning. A true interpretative faculty in the reader must be the bride of the poet's
imagination, since only so can it give birth to understanding.

So, by dwelling inwardly on the points I have adduced to indicate the imaginative quality of Timon's setting, our consciousness will be, as it were, tuned to respond to and appreciate the true erotic richness of Timon's soul.

The world of Timon and the soul of Timon are thus interdependent, and our consideration of the total imaginative impact illuminates his personality. Though at first sight there may seem something barbaric and oriental in Timon's generosity and sense of display, yet we are confronted in reality not with barbarism, but humanism. The impressions I have noted do not indicate relics of the past—though the best of a romantic Hellenism and of an Elizabethan aristocracy have contributed something—but an idealized perfected civilization. Timon himself is the flower of human aspiration. His generosity lacks wisdom, but is itself noble; his riches reflect the inborn aristocracy of his heart; his pleasures, like his love of friends, are in themselves excellent, the consummations of natural desire and in harmony with the very spirit of man's upward endeavour towards the reality of art, the joys of civilization, and love universal. Timon's world is poetry made real, lived rather than imagined. He would break down with conviviality, music, art, the barriers that sever consciousness from consciousness. He would build a paradise of love on earth. Now just as Timon's love of sweet things, though not gluttonous nor vicious, is yet eminently a thing of the senses and unrestrained; so, too, his affection for his friends, to which the rest is a setting and a direction of our sympathies, is no pale and sainted benevolence, no skeleton philanthropy nor ice-cold charity. His love, too, is the love not of the saint, but the lover; a rich erotic perception welling up from his soul, warm-blooded, instinctive, romantic and passionate. It is the love of Othello for Desdemona, of Antony for Cleopatra, of Shakespeare for the fair boy of the Sonnets. These we understand; so, too, we form some contact with the self-renouncing, ascetic, all-embracing love of the saint. But Timon's is the passionate, somewhat selfish, love of one lover for another, physical and spiritual, of the senses as of the soul; yet directed not toward one creature or one purpose but expanding its emotion among all men.

Timon is a universal lover, not by principle but by nature. His charity is never cold, self-conscious, or dutiful. He

withholds nothing of himself. His praise to the painter
(I. i. 161) is sincere appreciation; his jests with the jeweller
(I. i. 167) kind and not condescending; his chance of doing
good to his servant whose lack of wealth forbids his desired marriage is one of those god-sent adventures in kindness that make the life of Timon a perpetual romance. His
heaven is to see the young man's eyes brimming with joy.
He hates the least suggestion of insincerity and scorns
ceremony:

> Nay, my lords,
> Ceremony was but devised at first
> To set a gloss on faint deeds, hollow welcomes,
> Recanting goodness, sorry ere 'tis shown;
> But where there is true friendship, there needs none.
> Pray, sit; more welcome are ye to my fortunes
> Than my fortunes to me.   (I. ii. 15)

He does not doubt that his friends would, if occasion called,
reciprocate his generosity, and an excess of emotion at the
thought brings tears to his eyes:

> . . . Why, I have often wished myself poorer, that I
> might come nearer to you. We are born to do benefits:
> and what better or properer can we call our own than
> the riches of our friends? what a precious comfort 'tis,
> to have so many, like brothers, commanding one an-
> other's fortunes! O joy, e'en made away ere't can be
> born! Mine eyes cannot hold out water, methinks: to
> forget their faults, I drink to you.
>
> (I. ii. 105)

There is no shame in this confession of tears: he lives in a
world of the soul where emotion is the only manliness, and
love the only courage. If, as Shakespeare's imagery sometimes suggests, the lover sees his own soul symbolized in
his love, then we can say that Timon projects himself into
the world around him; mankind is his own soul; a resplendent and infinite love builds an earthly paradise where it may
find complete satisfaction in the inter-communion of heart
with heart, and gift with gift. If this transcendent love can
be bodied into shapes and forms which are finite; if the

world of actuality and sense does not play Timon false—
then humanism can thrive without religion, and an earthly
paradise is no deceiving dream.

The poet has shown us a supreme lover. Love is presented,
for purposes of the play, alone, unmixed with judgement.
Timon's generosity is extreme, and his faith child-like. But
we are not left free to criticize his acts. Even though we were
to remain insensible to the imaginative atmosphere and the
hero's lovable personality, the subsidiary characters are so
drawn as to heighten, not lessen, our respect for Timon; and
as the first gold-haze of romance and sensuous appeal thins
with the progress of the first three acts, and shapes of personification stand out clear and solid, this element of technique becomes increasingly important. The most striking
subsidiary figure is Apemantus. Contrasted with Timon's
faith and love, we have a churlish cynicism and disgust.
Timon is a universal lover, Apemantus a universal cynic.
His mind functions in terms of the foul, bestial, and stupid
attributes of man (I. i. 178–249). He makes lascivious jests.
He loathes the shape of man powerfully as Timon loves it:

> The strain of man's bred out
> Into baboon and monkey.   (I. i. 260)

And,

> What a coil's here!
> Serving of becks and jutting out of bums! (I. ii. 239)

His cynicism is a compound of ridicule, foul suggestion, and
ascetic philosophy. Timon shows him a picture:

> *Timon.* Wrought he not well that painted it?
> *Apemantus.* He wrought better that made the painter;
> and yet he's but a filthy piece of work.   (I. i. 201)

Thus swiftly are condemned God, man, and man's aspiration and endeavour. The pregnancy of this answer is amazing in its compactness and the poignance of its sting. As he
watches the observances of respect, the greetings and smiles
attendant on Alcibiades' entry, he comments:

> So, so, there!
> Aches contract and starve your supple joints!
> That there should be small love 'mongst these sweet
>   knaves,
> And all this courtesy!   (I. i. 257)

Entertainment is a mockery to him, for his thoughts are centred on the transience of shows, the brittleness of the armour of manners with which civilized man protects the foulness within from the poisoned dart of truth. Therefore he sits apart during the feast, refusing the food of Timon, gnawing roots, drinking water. Masquers enter, and he comments:

> Hoy-day, what a sweep of vanity comes this way!
> They dance! They are mad women.
> Like madness is the glory of this life,
> As this pomp shows to a little oil and root. (I. ii. 139)

He is anxious to warn Timon, feeling that he is too noble for the company that wastes his means:

> . . . It grieves me to see so many dip their meat in one
> man's blood; and all the madness is, he cheers them
> up too.   (I. ii. 42)

His respect for Timon is, however, clearly noted:

>   Even he drops down
> The knee before him and returns in peace
> Most rich in Timon's nod.   (I. i. 61)

Therefore the presence of Apemantus serves many purposes. It points us to the insincerity of Timon's friends and the probable course of events; it shows us that even the cynic cannot help but honour and respect Timon; and it makes us feel how repellent is this very cynicism, which is the opposite of Timon's faith and love. Apemantus thus enlists our respect for Timon, and even at their final meeting, when Timon has left Athens, we are again shown that Timon's hate is not as Apemantus'.

But we are repelled not alone by the churlish philosopher: we are even more repelled by the false friends of

Timon. The incident of Lucullus' refusal is exquisitely comic, yet bitterly satiric. Nothing more meanly unpleasant could well be imagined, and yet its truth to human nature cannot be denied. His greed, flattery, hypocrisy, and finally open confession of baseness, are drawn in swift, masterly strokes, culminating in:

> 'Here's three solidares for thee; good boy, wink at me, and say thou saw'st me not,' and 'Ha! now I see thou art a fool and fit for thy master.'
>
> (III. i. 47, 53)

Lucius comes off little better (III. ii). Ventidius, whom Timon has generously redeemed from prison, is found 'base metal' (III. iii. 6). And Sempronius, hearing of the failure of other friends of Timon, whom he himself had suggested were more indebted than he, refuses at last angrily on the score of his hurt feelings at being the last to whom Timon sends. Flavius' description of his failure to raise a loan is powerful enough (II. ii. 214–23). All these incidents are clearly presented to indicate the meanness inherent in these specimens of humanity. The dice are heavily loaded. Our judgements have no choice. Neither the friends of Timon nor Apemantus can usurp our sympathy. The poet and painter—whatever they may be as artists—are also depicted as time-servers: towards the end of the play, when they come to Timon to gain his favour, their dialogue with each other exposes their clear hypocrisy. In addition, the short scene between Alcibiades and the Senate (III. v) tends further to enlist our dislike of the community in which Timon lives. It suggests that Athens is suffering from an ingrateful and effete generation, greedy and mean. Says Alcibiades:

> I have kept back their foes,
> While they have told their money and let out
> Their coin upon large interest, I myself
> Rich only in large hurts.   (III. v. 108)

This reference to the state's greed and the usury 'that makes the senate ugly' (III. v. 101) serves to link the theme of Alcibiades with that of Timon's friends. We know, too, that Timon has put his fortune at the Senate's disposal. He tells Flavius to go

> to the senators—
> Of whom, even to the state's best health, I have
> Deserved this hearing—bid 'em send o' the instant
> A thousand talents to me.   (II. ii. 206)

Later, when they need his help, they confess 'forgetfulness too general, gross' (v. i. 149); and Alcibiades, speaking to Timon, talks of

> . . . cursed Athens, mindless of thy worth,
> Forgetting thy great deeds, when neighbour states,
> But for thy sword and fortune, trod upon them . . .
>   (IV. iii. 93)

The theme of Alcibiades is close-woven with that of Timon, and both endure ingratitude from the Senate, symbol of the state of Athens. We feel, in fact, that Timon's personality alone is responsible for any pleasure we have received in this Athens. It is a state of greed and ingratitude. The fine flower of civilization to which I have referred is evidently not in itself existent here, but purely a projection of Timon's mind. There are, however, certain persons who appear both good and rational: all these emphasize Timon's nobility.

It is noticeable, indeed, that references to Timon's nobility are continual throughout. We hear that he has 'a noble spirit' (I. ii. 14); he is

> A most incomparable man, breathed, as it were,
> To an untirable and continuate goodness.   (I. i. 10)

We hear of his 'good and gracious nature' (I. i. 57); his 'noble nature' (II. ii. 218); his 'right noble mind' (III. ii. 88); that 'he outgoes the very heart of kindness' (I. i. 286) and that

> the noblest mind he carries
> That ever governed man.   (I. i. 292)

Timon's words 'unwisely, not ignobly have I given' (II. ii. 184) hold finality. Such references are scattered through-

out the play and their effect on us is powerful, even though
they be sometimes spoken by insincerity. But the next group
of persons to be noticed are evidently sincere: they are (i)
the 'Strangers' who play a purely choric part, and (ii)
Timon's Servants. It is to be observed that these, who alone
express a balanced and rational view, all love and honour
Timon, and remark on this instance of his betrayal as significant of a universal and fundamental human truth. I have
noted that Timon is a universal lover: again we are directed
to the universality of the theme here presented. Three
Strangers, who have heard Lucius' refusal, comment there-
on:

> *First Stranger.* Do you observe this, Hostilius?
> *Second Stranger.*   Ay, too well.
> *First Stranger.* Why this is the world's soul; and just of
>   the same piece
> Is every flatterer's spirit. Who can call him
> His friend that dips in the same dish? for, in
> My knowing, Timon has been this lord's father,
> And kept his credit with his purse,
> Supported his estate; nay, Timon's money
> Has paid his men their wages: he ne'er drinks,
> But Timon's silver treads upon his lip;
> And yet—O, see the monstrousness of man
> When he looks out in an ungrateful shape!—
> He does deny him, in respect of his,
> What charitable men afford to beggars.
> *Third Stranger.* Religion groans at it.   (III. ii. 71)

The purpose and effect of this as expressing the meaning of
the play's movement need no comment. It is the same with
Timon's servants. Flaminius has discovered Lucullus' baseness, and thrown back the offered bribe. Lucullus leaves
him and he soliloquizes:

> May these add to the number that may scald thee!
> Let molten coin be thy damnation,
> Thou disease of a friend, and not himself!
> Has friendship such a faint and milky heart,
> It turns in less than two nights? O you gods,
> I feel my master's passion! this slave,
> Unto his honour, has my lord's meat in him:

> Why should it thrive and turn to nutriment,
> When he is turn'd to poison?
> O, may disease only work upon't!
> And, when he 's sick to death, let not that part of
>   nature
> Which my lord paid for, be of any power
> To expel sickness, but prolong his hour!   (III. i. 55)

This speech occurs when the action is working up to its tremendous climax, and embodies the tremor heralding eruption. Here civilization is beginning to assume a hideous guise, and man's form to appear as the painted outside to an inward filth. We feel the damming up of some mighty current, the impetuous and curbless love which is in Timon —and we are more than half aware of its awful impending release. This speech, and the similar one of the Servant at III. iii. 27-42, serve to direct our minds in sympathy toward the future hate of Timon. One only of his servants dares to criticize the master they all love: Flavius. His dialogue with Timon in Act II is supremely beautiful in the large-hearted simplicity and faith of master and servant:

> *Flavius.* Heavens, have I said, the bounty of this lord!
>   How many prodigal bits have slaves and peasants
>   This night englutted! Who is not Timon's?
>   What heart, head, sword, force, means, but is Lord
>   Timon's?
>   Great Timon, noble, worthy, royal Timon!
>   Ah, when the means are gone that buy this praise,
>   The breath is gone whereof this praise is made:
>   Feast-won, fast-lost; one cloud of winter showers,
>   These flies are couch'd.
> *Timon.*   Come, sermon me no further:
>   No villainous bounty yet hath pass'd my heart;
>   Unwisely, not ignobly, have I given.
>   Why dost thou weep? Canst thou the conscience
>   lack,
>   To think I shall lack friends? Secure thy heart;
>   If I would broach the vessels of my love,
>   And try the argument of hearts by borrowing,
>   Men and men's fortunes could I frankly use
>   As I can bid thee speak.   (II. ii. 174)

Flavius, in his great love for Timon, throughout the play draws us too in faith to his master, even when his words most clearly limn his faults. And in soliloquy after Timon's retirement from Athens, his love wells up in a noble eulogy of his lord:

> Poor honest lord, brought low by his own heart,
> Undone by goodness! Strange, unusual blood,
> When man's worst sin is, he does too much good!
> Who, then, dares to be half so kind again?
> For bounty, that makes gods, does still mar men.
> My dearest lord, bless'd, to be most accursed,
> Rich, only to be wretched, thy great fortunes
> Are made thy chief afflictions.   (IV. ii. 37)

The intrinsic and absolute blamelessness of Timon's generosity is emphasized. Timon's 'fault' is essential love, essential nobility, unmixed with any restraining faculty of criticism. He is spontaneous in trust and generosity. 'Every man has his fault', says Lucullus, 'and honesty is his' (III. i. 30). The heart's-gold of Timon is alloyed with no baser metal of intellect.

The faithfulness of Timon's Servants is indeed a major theme in the drama. After the final failure, and Timon's retirement to the woods, they meet, not as servants to the same lord, but rather as disciples to a loved and world-crucified master. It is significant that, though cast adrift in poverty, it is the loss of their lord, and the iniquity of his friends, that grieve them most:

> *First Servant.*   Such a house broke!
>   So noble a master fall'n! All gone! and not
>   One friend to take his fortune by the arm,
>   And go along with him!
> *Second Servant.*   As we do turn our backs
>   From our companion thrown into his grave,
>   So his familiars to his buried fortunes
>   Slink all away, leave their false vows with him,
>   Like empty purses pick'd; and his poor self,
>   A dedicated beggar to the air,
>   With his disease of all-shunn'd poverty,
>   Walks, like contempt, alone.   (IV. ii. 5)

It is as though the spirit of Timon's former love and generosity has settled among them as an everlasting bond of love. We begin to know that we have been watching something more than the downfall of a noble gentleman:

> *Third Servant.* Yet do our hearts wear Timon's livery;
>   That see I by our faces; we are fellows still,
>   Serving alike in sorrow: leak'd is our bark,
>   And we, poor mates, stand on the dying deck,
>   Hearing the surges threat: we must all part
>   Into this sea of air.
> *Flavius.*   Good fellows all,
>   The latest of my wealth I'll share amongst you.
>   Wherever we shall meet, for Timon's sake,
>   Let's yet be fellows; let's shake our heads, and say,
>   As 'twere a knell unto our master's fortunes,
>   'We have seen better days'. Let each take some;
>   Nay, put out all your hands. Not one word more:
>   Thus part we rich in sorrow, parting poor.
>
>   (IV. ii. 17)

'Nay, put out all your hands'. . . . The still poetry of deepest emotion, the grandest simplicity of the human soul, indeed do not sound their noblest notes in this play till the pages thereof are become 'rich in sorrow': and then they touch a music, as in this speech, of a more wondrous simplicity and a more mighty and heart-quelling beauty than anything in *King Lear* or *Othello*. This, however, is to forestall. This scene occurs after the shadow of eternity has overcast the drama.

Enough has been said to indicate the nature of the technique that loads and all but overcharges the first part of this play with a clear honour and love of Timon's generosity and free-hearted soul; that indicts an overplus of humanity with the uttermost degree of despisal; that leaves us in the naked knowledge of the inevitable ignition and the dynamite of passion that thunders, reverberates, and dies into silence through the latter acts. The poet unfalteringly directs our vision: to ignore the effect of these massed speeches condemning Timon's friends and all but deifying Timon is to blur our understanding, to refuse the positive and single statement of this the most masterfully deliberate of Shake-

speare's sombre tragedies. Then shall we fail before the deep
music of the two final acts. But if yet more definite indication be needed, it is to be found in the Poet's early speech, a
unique Shakespearian introduction to his own play:

> I have, in this rough work, shaped out a man,
> Whom this beneath world doth embrace and hug
> With amplest entertainment . . .   (I. i. 44)

It is all there, a clear description of the play's theme. Even
the peculiar universality is clearly noted, especially in the
next lines:

> . . . my free drift
> Halts not particularly, but moves itself
> In a wide sea of wax: no levell'd malice
> Infects one comma in the course I hold;
> But flies an eagle flight, bold and forth on,
> Leaving no tract behind.   (I. i. 46)

This is manifestly not true of Shakespeare's Poet, who has
composed his poem for Timon alone, but profoundly true
of Shakespeare himself. Again:

> Sir, I have upon a high and pleasant hill
> Feign'd Fortune to be throned: the base o' the mount
> Is rank'd with all deserts, all kind of natures,
> That labour on the bosom of this sphere
> To propagate their states: amongst them all,
> Whose eyes are on this sovereign lady fix'd,
> One do I personate of Lord Timon's frame,
> Whom Fortune with her ivory hand wafts to her;
> Whose present grace to present slaves and servants
> Translates his rivals.   (I. i. 64)

The sequel is as the action of *Timon of Athens*. Thus *Timon
of Athens* is a parable, or allegory; its rush of power, its
clean-limned and massive simplicity, its crystal and pur-
posive technique—all these are blurred and distorted if we
search for exact verisimilitude with the appearances of
human life. It is sublimely unrealistic. But if we recognize its
universal philosophic meaning, it is then apparent in all its
profundity and masterly construction. We are here judging

the chances of the spirit of perfected man to embrace Fortune and find love truly interfused in this 'beneath world':
to build his soul's paradise on 'the bosom of this sphere'.
Thus Timon is the archetype and norm of all tragedy. . . .

. . . He has one more banquet; invites his friends to it;
withholds his rage till he has made one speech of withering
scorn—then volleys the titanic fury of his kingly nature in
hate sovran as tremendous as his sovran love. There is no
tragic movement so swift, so clean-cut, so daring and so
terrible in all Shakespeare as this of Timon. We pity Lear,
we dread for Macbeth: but the awfulness of Timon, dwarf-
ing pity and out-topping sympathy, is as the grandeur and
menace of the naked rock of a sky-lifted mountain, whither
we look and tremble. Deserting Athens, he steps from time
into eternity. The world of humanity tilts over, and is reversed. We see now, not with the vision of man, but henceforth with that of the aspiring Spirit of Love that has scorned
mankind for ever. Timon will tolerate no disorder, within
and without his mind, like Lear, torn betwixt love and
loathing, division which is madness. The chaos which his
imprecations are to call on man will be as a concord within
the soul of him whose love is reversed, and who is no longer
of this world. Thus Timon preserves the grander harmony
of loneliness and universal loathing, and fronts his destiny,
emperor still in mind and soul, wearing the imperial nakedness of Hate. This unswerving majesty is a grander thing
than the barbaric fury of Othello, or the faltering ire of
Lear. The heart's-gold in Timon has seen the ingrateful and
miserly greed that would coin for use the infinity of a great
soul's love. So Timon leaves Athens.

His long curses are epics of hatred, unrestrained, limitless, wild. The whole race of man is his theme. His love was
ever universal, now his hate is universal, its theme embraces
every grade, age, sex, and profession. He hates the very
shape, the 'semblable' of man (IV. iii. 22). Timon's love,
itself an infinity of emotion, was first bodied into finite
things; finite humanity, the sense-world of entertainment
and art—and those symbols and sacraments of love: gifts.
Of all these he was patron, friend, lover. Then he too,
though gigantic in his love, was yet a confined, individualized, and lovable personality, like Othello. One knew him,
a friend. But his love, itself infinite, has proved itself 'a slave

to limit': [1] generosity was dependent on the limits of wealth, his faith in man on the limitations of human gratitude. Unwise, no doubt—supreme love is unwise: an element of judgement would borrow something of its rich worth. The poet has shown us a supreme love, dissociated from other qualities, and this love, trusting finite symbols of itself, has failed disastrously. It now appears as a naked force, undirected towards any outward manifestations, diffused and bodiless, no longer fitted to the finite, a thing inhuman, unnatural, and infinite. Timon, naked and fierce-eyed, is no longer personal, no longer one of mankind. He is pure passion, a naked rhythmic force, a rush and whirl of torrential energy loosed from any contact or harmony with temporal and confining things, a passion which

> . . . like the current flies
> Each bound it chafes. (I. i. 24)

There is thus less imaginative unity in *Timon of Athens*: rather a strongly marked duality. The latter part of the play is contrasted with and related logically to the beginning. In *Hamlet* we see the tragic superman incongruously set in a normal social unit and working chaos therein; in *Macbeth* and *Lear,* he is given a world of the same nature as himself, a single visionary universe woven in the pattern of imagination's truth. Here there is a curious time-sequence. The hero is first a resplendent man among men, superhuman, perhaps, but not inhuman: now he becomes inhuman. We need not question Timon's Athens: save for Timon himself, prince-hearted and lord of love, it is the world we know, first sensuous, and attractive, then trivial, poor-spirited, dishonest. Timon alone, with his shadow Apemantus, is in his latter hate of the anti-social and wayward nature of Ham-

---

[1] 'This is the monstruosity in love, lady, that the will is infinite and the execution confined, that the desire is boundless and the act a slave to limit.' *Troilus and Cressida,* III. ii. 87-90. The typical Shakespearian thought that the infinity of love is in conflict with actuality, or the reflection of actuality in the mind, intellect. Hence the thought, a little further on, expressed by Cressida:

> . . . to be wise and love
> Exceeds man's might; that dwells with gods above. (163-4)

With which we might compare *Timon,* IV. ii. 41: '. . . bounty, that makes gods, does still mar men'. Troilus tries unsuccessfully to enclose love's mystery in his mind, Timon to embody it in acts.

let and Lear. Thus in *Timon* we have a logical exposition of
the significance of the single tragic impact of earlier plays.
The hero's passion is clearly juxtaposed and related logically
to a normal human society. The play is in two firmly contrasted parts. During the second our universe changes with
the change in Timon, and after the brilliance of Athens the
shadow of an infinite gloom broods over the desert solitudes
where Timon communes with his hate. Mankind are then
dim spectres only, and Timon's passion alone reality. The
nature of that passion demands further attention.

The contrast between the first and second parts is clearly
a contrast between the sense-world and the finite with the
spiritual and infinite. Thus Timon's hate expresses itself
in aversion from all kinds of moral wholeness and physical
health—that is, with all finite forms. They have been proved
false coin. Hence he declaims disease, vice, confusion on
men.

> Son of sixteen,
> Pluck the lined crutch from thy old limping sire,
> With it beat out his brains! Piety, and fear,
> Religion to the gods, peace, justice, truth,
> Domestic awe, night-rest, and neighbourhood,
> Instruction, manners, mysteries, and trades,
> Degrees, observances, customs, and laws,
> Decline to your confounding contraries,
> And let confusion live! Plagues, incident to men,
> Your potent and infectious fevers heap
> On Athens, ripe for stroke!   (IV. i. 13)

So, too, he repeatedly prays Phrynia and Timandra to
spread disgusting disease among men, and Alcibiades to
paint the ground with man's blood (IV. iii). There is no
hideous crime or ghoulish dishonour or ravaging disease
that Timon would not imprecate passionately on his race.
His former world of health and pleasure has been destroyed
by one thing: the exposure of the rottenness of its love.
That love-dream killed, his eyes are opened to all forms of
human frailty, moral, physical, social. Which movement
suggests that the loss of love alone is responsible for all the
ills that flesh endures: mankind without love he would wish
to disintegrate, to rot. Any form of human organism or

political or social order incites his hate, and he calls down wholesale distintegration on mankind. Only by remembering his former pleasures taken in finite and sensible symbols of love, can we see the unity of his curses: he is violently antagonized by human health—bodily, or social. No finite thing in humanity escapes his hate. Hence his curses against the moral order: since morality is a spiritual essence satisfactorily bodied into finitude and actuality. The infinity of his passion can now tolerate no such cramping or channelling of itself, and all finite forms are anathema. But there is more than negative logic in his philosophy. Timon's original force of soul is ultimate. First infused into love of man, thence driven, it expresses itself, first in a positive and passionate aversion from all finite forms—that is, he must love or hate. Second, we have clear signs of the reality toward which this primary energy is directing him: the infinite and ineffable to which he is bound. There is a swift movement toward infinity. From the gold-haze of the mystic dream of a universal love on earth have emerged stark contours of base ingratitude: then the outward world of man and its shapes swiftly vanishes, and the inward world of infinite spirit takes its place, first expressing its nature by aversion from the other mode of life, then turning towards all that is vast, inhuman, illimitable, void. The course is direct. There is no tragic conflict, and therefore no dramatic tempest-symbolism occurs to heighten our imagination of storm and stress: Timon's curses will not ring weak—nor is there any divagation from his inhuman quest. Thus in the latter scenes we are aware of two modes in the utterance of Timon: passionate hate, and a solitary contemplation of the infinite, the two interfused or alternate. . . .

. . . He lives in a cave 'near the sea-shore'. He is now a naked son of earth, and speaks a solemn knowledge of nature's kinship with man's wants:

> Why should you want? Behold, the earth hath roots;
> Within this mile break forth a hundred springs;
> The oaks bear mast, the briers scarlet hips;
> The bounteous housewife, nature, on each bush
> Lays her full mess before you. Want! Why want?
>
> (IV. iii. 420)

He, who aspires only to the infinite, chafes at the limitations of the physical, and yet again finds solace in thought of the earth's vastness, in one of those grand undertones of harmony that characterize the tremendous orchestration of this play:

> That nature, being sick of man's unkindness
> Should yet be hungry! Common mother, thou
> Whose womb unmeasurable and infinite breast
> Teems, and feeds all; whose self-same mettle,
> Whereof thy proud child, arrogant man, is puff'd,
> Engenders the black toad and adder blue,
> The gilded newt and eyeless venom'd worm,
> With all the abhorred births below crisp heaven
> Whereon Hyperion's quickening fire doth shine;
> Yield him, who all thy human sons doth hate,
> From forth thy plenteous bosom, one poor root!
> (iv. iii. 176)

His thoughts are already set beyond the world of man; in the silence of eternity: yet he is not himself beyond the world of nature, he is, incongruously, hungry. As in this speech, Timon's utterance is often addressed with a deep recognition and intimacy toward the vast forces, the stillness, the immensities of nature, clear springs which the intellect of man has muddied. These are innocent, they wake responses in him. He addresses sun and earth as his co-equals, peers of his unsatiated and universal soul:

> O blessed breeding sun, draw from the earth
> Rotten humidity; below thy sister's orb
> Infect the air!   (iv. iii. 1)

'Thou sun, that comfort'st, burn!' he cries (v. i. 134); and, at the end, 'Sun, hide thy beams! Timon hath done his reign' (v. ii. 226). But we are also reminded that these vast forces are yet not friends of Timon: not with them will he find any but a temporary purge and solace to his pain. Says Apemantus:

> What, think'st
> That the bleak air, thy boisterous chamberlain,
> Will put thy shirt on warm? will these moss'd trees,

> That have outlived the eagle, page thy heels,
> And skip where thou point'st out? will the cold brook,
> Candied with ice, caudle thy morning taste,
> To cure thy o'er-night's surfeit? Call the creatures
> Whose naked natures live in all the spite
> Of wreakful heaven, whose bare unhoused trunks,
> To the conflicting elements exposed,
> Answer mere nature; bid them flatter thee . . .
>
> > (IV. iii. 221)

Timon also voices the thought that the animal-kingdom is no better than man's civilization—as ruthless as human nature, as devouring and cruel. He catalogues the beasts in the speech commencing:

> . . . If thou wert the lion, the fox would beguile
> thee: if thou wert the lamb, the fox would eat thee . . .
>
> > (IV. iii. 330)

He knows that sun and moon and sea and earth live, like men, by perpetual interaction, thieving, and absorption: that if he attributes personality to nature, his curses must be levelled against earth and sky, his indictment must include the whole cosmic mechanism. . . . This sweep of the fanciful imagination is profound: it involves the knowledge that the meanest of man's vices owes its viciousness to man's moral ascension. Timon cannot impose the laws of his generous soul on the unthinking mechanism of the universal scheme. Not on the breast of nature, nor in contemplation of the solar fire mated to earth or sea, can he find that to which he moves. He ranges the planetary spaces of the night and finds no home: nowhere but within the spaceless silence of the deeper night of death will he be at peace. He is thus retrogressing swiftly through the modes of being. They are, in order: chaos, or the primal night; the stellar, mundane, natural and human worlds; culminating in man's civilization. Here, starting in the first scene with the four symbolic figures of civilization, we fall back swiftly on nature, earth, sun and the ultimate void of that infinity, undisciplined to form, whose only symbol can be some suggestion of formlessness, immensity, chaos; whose favourite symbol in Shakespeare is always the sea. Timon knows the

end to which he aspires. It is so clear—so implicit in the
whole allegorical movement—that no cause of death is
given or needed:

> Then, Timon, presently prepare thy grave;
> Lie where the light foam of the sea may beat
> Thy grave-stone daily.   (IV. iii. 378)

And:

> Come not to me again: but say to Athens,
> Timon hath made his everlasting mansion
> Upon the beached verge of the salt flood;
> Who once a day with his embossed froth
> The turbulent surge shall cover: thither come,
> And let my grave-stone be your oracle.
>   (v. i. 217)

The void of Death, darkness—the Shakespearian 'nothing'
which brings Timon 'all things' (v. ii. 191). The dark sea
which is infinite formlessness, infinite depth, the surge and
swell within the soul of man, the deeps beyond intellect,
or sight, or sound. It is this surge that has throbbed within
the poetry of tremendous symbols, this tide of emotion that
breaks and sobs in Timon's passion when, his active hate
subdued, he speaks the language of a soul beyond the world
of manifestation and tuned to its own solitary music; the
psalmody of earth and sun and the wide sea of eternal
darkness beating on the rocks of creation.

We are given no chance to sentimentalize Timon's hate.
Its nobility derives solely from its utter reversal of love. It
is thus not a spiritual atrophy, a negation, a cold vacuum of
the soul, like the pain of Hamlet, but a dynamic and positive
thing, possessing purpose and direction. Therefore, though
impelled to its inevitable death-climax, the tragic movement of this play leaves us with no sense of the termination
of the essential Timon: its impact on the imagination is
rather that of a continuation, circling within and beyond
the mysterious nothing of dissolution, in a new dimension
congruous with the power and the passion which have
forced him toward death. The especial reality of Timon is

this of powerful, torrential movement to freedom: which freedom from all that we call 'life' is so necessary and excellent a consummation to the power and the direction of Timon's passion, that it can in no sense be imaged as a barrier or stoppage. It is rather as though the rushing torrent, so long chafed by the limits of its channel, breaks out into the wide smoothness of the living sea. The death-theme in *Timon* is thus of the greatest importance, the crowning majesty of the play's movement. Timon speaks to the Senators:

> Why, I was writing of my epitaph;
> It will be seen to-morrow: my long sickness
> Of health and living now begins to mend,
> And nothing brings me all things.   (v. ii. 188)

The nothingness of death becomes 'all things' to Timon who passionately desires that 'nothing'. No conceivable symbol of desire will now serve that love, therefore in desiring death it desires nothing but its own unsatiable love: there it will, as it were, turn back within its own richness. Timon, embracing this ineffable darkness with joy, is already outside himself, viewing his own tragedy, as we do, with objective delight. He thus looks toward death, and imagines his end, and sees it, as we do, to be good—to hold the gift of 'all things'. Consciousness that thus derives joy from the death of consciousness is already, as we who watch, outside the dying and the death. It is but another aspect of the living force of Timon, the vivid, dynamic, swift thing of passion which is in him: the heat of it unsatiated by the mode called 'life' has been excruciating, an expanding, explosive essence prisoned, and in death it will burn the enhampering body to fling backward its invisible brilliance in the illumination of 'all things'. 'Health and living' has been to Timon as 'a long sickness'. In so far as we have been aware of this reversal of significance during the action, we shall know that we have long walked with Timon in death. Life and death have interchanged their meaning for him, and he now voices that paradox which is at the heart of all tragedy. Therefore the grand death speeches at the close come not as a super-added adornment, a palliative, but rather as necessary and expected continuation, consummation, satisfaction. They are not to be analysed as solitary units of philosophic utterance, but as living thought precipitated by the momentum of the tragic theme as a whole, gaining their impact from the force that has driven Timon from ease and luxury to nakedness among the naked beasts and trees and planets of the night, and beyond these to the unbodied and immortal nakedness of death. We have watched a swift unwrapping of fold on fold of life's significances—civilized man, beasts, the earth, the objective universe itself, till we reach the core of pure and naked Significance, undistorted by any symbol, in the nothingness of Death. Yet at every step in Timon's history, we have been aware, not of a lessening, but of an increase of his grandeur; that is, at every stripping of the soul of Timon we have known that what was taken is but another rag, what remains, the essence, the reality. For Timon, at the end, is pure essence of significance, beyond the temporal, in touch with a conquering knowledge of his furthest destiny. Nothing will be proved the largesse of all things. Therefore he cries:

> Graves only be men's works and death their gain!
> Sun, hide thy beam! Timon hath done his reign.
> (v. ii. 225)

Again is emphasized the completeness with which Timon's love is reversed. It is not alone a turning away from mankind: rather a passionate turning inward from all forms and shapes of actuality, all manifestation, from the cosmic scheme. He would wish the race die out, the sun blackened, the glass of time exhausted. Only the rhythm of the tireless beat of waves, the crash and the whispering retraction, these alone signify some fore-echoing of the thing which is to receive Timon. This is only the last step, into the cold night of death, of the movement we have been watching all along. It is truly spoken that

> Timon is dead, who hath outstretch'd his span.
> (v. iii. 3)

His hate of man was ever but one aspect, or expression, of the turning inward of his soul toward death, and since he flung back Titanic curse on Athens, his being has been centered not in time but throughout the otherness of eternity.

Yet there is one symbol that persists throughout both parts of the play and this has important meaning: gold. Gold-symbolism is throughout percurrent, and the thought of gold and riches is woven close within the texture of thought and emotion. Timon's nature is essentially a thing of 'richness'. Mankind is amazed, from the start, at the richness of Timon's nature and the generosity and wealth in which it manifests itself. Instances of this are frequent: I have quoted some. Men are 'rich in Timon's nod' (I. i. 62); 'Plutus, the god of gold, is but his steward' (I. i. 287). Throughout the play richness of heart and actual gold are associated or contrasted. A jewel is made more valuable by Timon's wearing it (I. i. 172). In wasting Timon's riches, his flatterers 'dip their meat' in his 'blood' (I. ii. 41). At the pivotal moment of the play (III. iv.), Timon cries, 'Tell out my blood!' They 'cut his heart in sums'. 'Five thousand drops' of his heart's blood will pay his debt of five thousand crowns. The contrast is ever between gold and the heart's blood of passionate love of which it is a sacrament: the association, of the metaphoric value of gold and the value of love; or conversely, of hardness and the callousness of ingratitude—mankind is 'flinty', of an 'iron heart', to Timon, since these are metals possessing hardness without value. His flatterers prove 'base metal'. So, too, the 'hearts' of Timon's servants yet 'wear his livery' (IV. ii. 17), though payment and outward shows are at an end. And Flavius, 'whilst he has gold', will serve Timon's 'mind' (IV. ii. 50). These ideas are deeply embedded throughout. Now the gold-symbolism continued into the last two acts serves a double purpose. First, it remains to Timon a symbol of mankind's greed:

> Earth, yield me roots!
> Who seeks for better of thee, sauce his palate
> With thy most operant poison! What is here?
> Gold? yellow, glittering, precious gold? No, gods,
> I am no idle votarist: roots, you clear heavens!
> Thus much of this will make black white, foul fair,
> Wrong right, base noble, old young, coward valiant.
> Ha, you gods! why this? what this, you gods? Why, this

> Will lug your priests and servants from your sides,
> Pluck stout men's pillows from below their heads:
> This yellow slave
> Will knit and break religions, bless the accursed,
> Make the hoar leprosy adored, place thieves
> And give them title, knee and approbation
> With senators on the bench . . .   (IV. iii. 23)

Second, it draws men to him as of old, and suggests the continued richness and nobility of his nature, the native aristocracy of his heart. Even in hate he reacts on man for good, not ill. Says the Bandit:

> Has almost charmed me from my profession, by per-
> suading me to it.   (IV. iii. 454)

He is still a prince among men, the desired of men, a fate he cannot escape. The 'yellow, glittering, precious gold' which he finds endues him still with a superiority and power, and enables him to aid the army levied against Athens, thus constituting an important link between the hate of Timon and the avenging ardour of Alcibiades.

Timon, in love or hate, bears truly a heart of gold. He is a thing apart, a choice soul crucified. He has a mind 'unmatched' (IV. iii. 523). He is one

> Whose star-like nobleness gave life and influence
>   (V. i. 66)

to the world that has driven him without its walls. Sun-like he used to 'shine' on men (III. iv. 10). And the issues for which a Timon contends are the issues not of Athens but humanity. He is a principle of the human soul, a possibility, a symbol of mankind's aspiration. His servants know that his loss is as the loss of a golden age. A bright spirit has been on earth, spirit of infinite and rich love and bounty, and its wings have been soiled by mortality. Timon, who 'flashed a phoenix' (II. i. 32), is left a 'naked gull'. The elected of the heavens has been scorned of man. So the poetry of this play is large and deep, immeasurably grand, and pregnant of human fate. When Timon lifts his voice to heaven proclaiming 'one honest man' (IV. iii. 504), his words hold an echo no less universal than Abraham's prayer to Jehovah to spare the iniquitous city, if ten just men be found therein: when Timon's servants part to wander abroad separated, they are as disciples of the Christ meeting after the Crucifixion.[1] Of these thoughts the poetry is indeed most worthy. It is loaded with a massive, compulsive emotion, in comparison with which the words of Hamlet, Troilus, Othello, and even Lear, are as the plaintive accents of children. A mighty rhythm of a race's longing, of human destiny unalterable and uncomplained, sounds through the whole play, and wakes an unearthly majesty of words in the symphonic harmonies of the final acts. There is no turning aside, no regret in all the passion of Timon, but it

> holds an eagle's course, bold and forth on,
> Leaving no tract behind—

until, in the poetry of the latter half of the play, the mind is a-voyage on unfathomed and uncharted seas, whose solid deeps of passion but wanly and waveringly reflect the vastest images that man can dream. In this recurrent solemnity of utterance more grand for its massive and fathomless simplicity, we joy in that we listen not to the accents of mortality but to those of the spirit of a race. Therefore, though Flavius saves mankind from utter condemnation by one act of faith, we know that the organ notes of implacable hatred cannot so be stilled, since by them alone the soul of Timon pursues its course: he is no 'idle votarist' (IV. iii. 27):

> Hate all, curse all, show charity to none. (IV. iii. 534)

The profoundest problems of racial destiny are here symbolized and fought out. In no other play is a more forceful,

---

[1] The analogy is obvious and suggested by other passages. We have:

> There's much example for 't; the fellow that sits next him now, parts bread with him, pledges the breath of him in a divided draught, is the readiest man to kill him: 't has been proved. (I. ii. 45)

and

> Who can call him
> His friend that dips in the same dish? (III. ii. 72)

Another New Testament reference occurs at IV. iii. 472-3.

a more irresistible, mastery of technique—almost crude in its massive, architectural effects—employed. But then no play is so massive, so rough-hewn into Atlantean shapes from the mountain rock of the poet's mind or soul, as this of Timon. 'I have in this rough work shap'd out a man . . .' It is true. No technical scaffolding in Shakespeare has to stand so weighty and shattering a stress. For this play is *Hamlet, Troilus, Othello, Lear,* become self-conscious and universal; it includes and transcends them all; it is the recurrent and tormenting Hate-theme of Shakespeare, developed, raised to an infinite power, presented in all its tyrannic strength and profundity, and—killed. Three acts form the prologue. Our vision thus with infinite care and every possible device focused, we await the onrush of a passion which sums in its torrential energy all the lesser passions of those protagonists foregone. Timon is the totality of all, his love more rich and oceanic than all of theirs—all lift their lonely voices in his universal curse; Christ-like, he suffers that their pain may cease, and leaves the Shakespearian universe redeemed that Cleopatra may win her Antony in death, and Thaisa be restored to Pericles. . . .

 **BARD BOOKS**

the classics, poetry, drama and
distinguished modern fiction

FICTION

ACT OF DARKNESS	John Peale Bishop	10827	1.25
ALL HALLOW'S EVE	Charles Williams	11213	1.45
AMERICAN VOICES, AMERICAN WOMEN			
Lee R. Edwards and Arlyn Diamond, Eds.		17871	1.95
AUTO-DA-FE	Elias Canetti	11197	1.45
THE AWAKENING	Kate Chopin	07419	.95
BEETLECREEK	William Demby	07997	.95
THE BENEFACTOR	Susan Sontag	11221	1.45
BETRAYED BY RITA HAYWORTH			
Manuel Puig		15206	1.65
CALL IT SLEEP	Henry Roth	10777	1.25
THE CASE HISTORY OF COMRADE V.			
James Park Sloan		15362	1.65
A COOL MILLION and **THE DREAM LIFE OF**			
BALSO SNELL	Nathanael West	15115	1.65
THE DOLLMAKER	Harriette Arnow	11676	1.50
THE ENCOUNTER	Crawford Power	10785	1.25
FACES IN THE WATER	Janet Frame	08037	.95
THE FAMILY OF PASCUAL DUARTE			
Camilo José Cela		11247	1.45
GABRIELA, CLOVE AND CINNAMON			
Jorge Amado		18275	1.95
A GENEROUS MAN	Reynolds Price	15123	1.65
GOING NOWHERE	Alvin Greenberg	15081	1.65
THE GREATER TRUMPS	Charles Williams	11205	1.45
THE GREEN HOUSE	Mario Vargas Llosa	15099	1.65
HOUSE OF ALL NATIONS	Christina Stead	18895	2.45
I THOUGHT OF DAISY	Edmund Wilson	05256	.95
JEWS WITHOUT MONEY	Michael Gold	13953	.95
THE LANGUAGE OF CATS AND OTHER STORIES			
Spencer Holst		14381	1.65